The European Union after Lisbon

Hermann-Josef Blanke • Stelio Mangiameli
Editors

The European Union after Lisbon

Constitutional Basis, Economic Order and External Action

With Contributions by
P. Adriaanse, A. D'Atena, F. Balaguer Callejón,
Herm.-J. Blanke, P. Cherubini, E. Denza, E. Gianfrancesco,
L. Jimena Quesada, U. Häde, M. Horspool, R. Hrbek,
S. Graf von Kielmansegg, S. Mangiameli, P.-Y. Marro,
J. Meyer-Ladewig, J. Přibáň, A. Sari, G. Sautter, D. Thürer,
D. Thym, A. Weber, R.A. Wessel, A. Wyrozumska

Springer

Editors
Professor Dr. Hermann-Josef Blanke
University of Erfurt
Faculty for Economics,
Law and Social Science
Nordhäuser Straße 63
99089 Erfurt
Germany
LS_Staatsrecht@uni-erfurt.de

Professor Dr. Stelio Mangiameli
National Research Council -
Institute for the Study of Regionalism,
Federalism and Self-Government
Via dei Taurini 19
00185 Rome
Italy
direttore@issirfa.cnr.it

ISBN 978-3-642-19506-8 e-ISBN 978-3-642-19507-5
DOI 10.1007/978-3-642-19507-5
Springer Heidelberg Dordrecht London New York

Library of Congress Control Number: 2011938812

Printed on acid-free paper

Springer is part of Springer Science+Business Media (www.springer.com)

Foreword

This volume aims to analyse the constitutional basis of the European Union and the normative orientation of the Common Foreign and Security Policy (TEU) as well as the central economic and monetary provisions (TFEU) after the Reform Treaty of Lisbon. Its development was accompanied by two Conferences in Erfurt (2008) and Rome (2010) which the editors have organised in preparation for the project of a European Commentary on the Treaty of Lisbon. As an outcome of a European research compound, which is composed of authors from eight Member States, the publication underlines the aspiration of the editors to thoroughly analyse the constitutional law of the European Union currently in force.

The editors are grateful to all the authors for their contributions. A special word of thanks is due to the Fritz Thyssen Foundation for its funding of both international Conferences. For her constant patience and editorial support our thanks and appreciation also go to Dr. Brigitte Reschke from Springer Publishing. Special thanks are due to Robert Böttner, assistant at the Chair for Public Law, International Public Law and European Integration, who has put a lot of effort into the careful editing, the revision of the manuscripts and the translation of some of the contributions.

Erfurt and Rome in September 2011

Herm.-J. Blanke
Stelio Mangiameli

Contents

List of Authors

Dr. Paul Adriaanse, Leiden University, Institute for Public Law, Department of Constitutional and Administrative Law, Steenschuur 25, 2311 ES Leiden, The Netherlands

Dr. Antonio D'Atena, Professor of Constitutional Law at the University of Rome "Tor Vergata", Fellow of the Institute for the Study of Regionalism, Federalism and Self-Government, Rome, Italy

Dr. Francisco Balaguer Callejón, Professor of Constitutional Law, "Jean Monnet" Chair of European Constitutional Law, University of Granada, Spain

Dr. Hermann-Josef Blanke, Professor of Public Law and International Public Law, University of Erfurt, Germany

Dr. Piergiorgio Cherubini, Minister Plenipotentiary, CFSP/CSDP Coordinator, Ministry of Foreign Affairs of Italy, Rome, Italy

Eileen Denza, MA, LL. M, CMG, formerly Counsel to UK House of Lords and Visiting Professor of International Law University College London, UK

Dr. Eduardo Gianfrancesco, Full Professor of Public Law, University LUMSA (Rome and Palermo), Italy

Dr. Luis Jimena Quesada, Professor of Constitutional Law, University of València, Spain

Dr. Ulrich Häde, Professor of Public Law, Administrative, Financial and Monetary Law, European University Viadrina, Frankfurt (Oder), Germany

Margot Horspool, Emeritus Professor of European and Comparative law, University of Surrey, visiting professor at Queen Mary University, London and Notre Dame University London Programme

Dr. Rudolf Hrbek, Professor (Emeritus) of Political Science, University of Tübingen; Speaker of the Board of the European Center for Research on Federalism, Tübingen, Germany

Dr. Sebastian Graf von Kielmansegg, Assistant Professor of Public Law, University of Mannheim, Germany

Dr. Stelio Mangiameli, Professor of Constitutional Law and European Public Law, Universiy of Teramo, Director of the Institute for the Study of Regionalism, Federalism and Self-Government, Italy

Dr. Pierre-Yves Marro, LL. M, former assistant at the Chair for Public International, European, Swiss and Comparative Law, University of Zurich, Switzerland

Dr. Jens Meyer-Ladewig, former Head of Department in the Federal Ministry for Justice, Germany

Dr. Jiří Přibáň, LLD, Professor of Law at Cardiff Law School, Cardiff University, UK

Dr. Aurel Sari, LL.M., Lecturer in Law, University of Exeter, UK

Dr. Günter Sautter, Permanent Representation of the Federal Republic of Germany to the EU

Dr. Dr. h.c. Daniel Thürer, Professor of Public International, European, Swiss and Comparative Constitutional Law and Director of the Institute for Public International and Comparative Constitutional Law, University of Zurich, Switzerland

Dr. Daniel Thym, LL.M., Professor of Public Law, European Law and International Public Law, University of Konstanz, Germany

Dr. Albrecht Weber, Professor (Emeritus) of Public Law, Member of the Institute for Migration Research and Intercultural Studies (IMIS), University of Osnabrück, Germany

Dr. Ramses A. Wessel, Professor of the Law of the European Union and other International Organizations, University of Twente, The Netherlands

Dr. Anna Wyrozumska, Professor of European Constitutional Law and Public International Law, University of Lodz, Poland

Abbreviations

AC	Appeal Court (Court of Appeal)
AFSJ	Area of Freedom, Security and Justice Block Exemption Regulation
AJIL	American Journal of International Law
All ER	All England Law Reports
AöR	Archiv für Öffentliches Recht
Art.	Article(s)
BGBl.	Bundesgesetzblatt
Br.-Drs.	Bundesratsdrucksache
Bt.-Drs.	Bundestagsdrucksache
BVerfG	Bundesverfassungsgericht (German Federal Constitutional Court)
BVerfGE	Entscheidung des Bundesverfassungsgerichts (Decision of the German Federal Constitutional Court)
CAP	Common Agricultural Policy
cf.	confer
CFI	Court of First Instance
CFR	Council on Foreign Relations
CFSP	Common Foreign and Security Policy
cit.	cited
CJEL	The Columbia Journal of European Law
CJEU	Court of Justice of the European Union
CMLR (CMLRev.)	Common Market Law Review
CoE	Council of Europe
COR	Committee of the Regions
COREPER	Committee of Permanent Representatives
CSDP	Common Security and Defence Policy
DDA	Disability Discrimination Act
Dem. e dir.	Democrazia e Diritto
Der. const.	Derecho constitucional

DG	Directorate-General
Dir. intern.	Diritto internazionale
Dir. Lav. Rel. Ind.	Diritto del lavoro e delle Relazioni industriali
Dir. pubbl.	Diritto pubblico
Dir. soc.	Diritto e società
Dir. Un. Eur.	Diritto dell'Unione Europea
DÖV	Die Öffentliche Verwaltung
DPCE	Diritto pubblico comparato ed europeo
DVBl.	Deutsches Verwaltungsblatt
e.g.	exempli gratia (for example)
EAT	Employment Appeal Tribunal
EC	Treaty establishing the European Community/European Community/European Communities
ECB	European Central Bank
ECHR	European Convention on Human Rights and Fundamental Freedoms
ECJ	European Court of Justice (Luxembourg Court – meanwhile the acronym CJEU is recognised)
ECR	European Court Reports
ECSC	European Coal and Steel Community
ECtHR	European Court of Human Rights ("Strasbourg Court")
ed.	editor
EDA	European Defence Agency
EDC	European Defence Community
edn.	edition
eds.	editors
edt. by	edited by
EEA	European Economic Area European Electoral Act
EEAS	European External Action Service
EEC	European Economic Community
EFA Rev.	European Foreign Affairs Review
EHRR	European Human Rights Reports
EIB	European Investment Bank
ELJ	European Law Journal
ELRev.	European Law Review
EMI	European Monetary Institute
EMS	European Monetary System
EMU	Economic and Monetary union
Enc. dir.	Enciclopedia del diritto
EO	European Ombudsman
EP	European Parliament
EPL	European Public Law
EPU	European Parliamentary Union
ERDF	European Regional Development Fund

ESC	Economic and Social Committee
ESCB	European System of Central Banks
ESCB	European System of Central Banks
ESDP	European/Common Security and Defence Policy
ESF	European Social Fund
Est. Pol.	Estudios Políticos
et al.	et alii (and others)
et seq(q)	et sequential, et sequentes
EU	European Union
EUCFR	European Union Charter of Fundamental Rights
EuGRZ	Europäische Grundrechte Zeitschrift
EuR	Europarecht
EURATOM	European Atomic Energy Community
EUROPOL	European Police Office
EUSR	EU Special Representative
EuZW	Europäische Zeitschrift für Wirtschaftsrecht
ex p.	ex parte
FAZ	Frankfurter Allgemeine Zeitung
FCC	Federal Constitutional Court
Fil.	Il Filangieri
fn.	Footnote
Foro it.	Foro italiano
GC	General Court (as a body of the Court of Justice of the EU)
GEDP	General Economic Policy Guidelines
GG	Grundgesetz
Giur. cost.	Giurisprudenza costituzionale
GNI	Gross National Income
GNP	Gross National Product
GVBl.	Gesetz- und Verordnungsblatt
HL	House of Lords
HQ	Head Quarters
HRA	Human Rights Act
i.d.	idem
i.e.	id est
ibid.	ibidem
IC	Constitution of the Italian Republic
ICJ	International Court of Justice
ICR	International Court Reports
IGC	Intergovernmental Conference
INAP	Instituto Nacional de Administración Pública
Integration	Jahrbuch der europäischen Integration
JöR	Jahrbuch des Öffentlichen Rechts
JZ	Juristen Zeitung
KB	King's Bench (for older cases pre-1953)

loc. cit.	locus citatus
MEP	Member of the European Parliament
MP	Member of Parliament
NATO	North Atlantic Treaty Organisation
NJW	Neue Juristische Wochenschrift
No.	Number
NVwZ	Neue Zeitschrift für Verwaltungsrecht
nyr	Not yet reported
OJ	Official Journal
OJC	Official Journal (Communications)
OJL	Official Journal (Legislation)
op.cit.	opere citato
OSCE	Organisation for Security and Cooperation in Europe
OUP	Oxford University Press
ÖZöR	Österreichische Zeitschrift für öffentliches Recht und Völkerrecht (Austrian journal of public and international law)
p.	Page
para.	Paragraph
passim	Frequently mentioned
PJCC	Police and judicial cooperation in criminal matters
Pol. Dir.	Politica del diritto
pp.	Pages
PSC	Permanent structured cooperation
QB	Queen's Bench
QC	Queen's Counsel
QMV	Qualified majority voting
Quad. cost.	Quaderni costituzionali
Quad. fior.	Quaderni fiorentini
Quad. rass. sind.	Quaderni Rassegna Sindacale
Racc.	Raccolta della giurisprudenza della Corte di giustizia e del Tribunale di primo grado
Rass. parl.	Rassegna parlamentare
RDCE	Revista de Derecho Constitucional Europeo
RDE	Rivista di diritto europeo
RDILC	Revue de droit international et de législation comparée
RDPE	Rassegna di diritto pubblico europeo
RDSS	Rivista del Diritto della Sicurezza sociale
RDUE	Revue de droit de l'Union européenne
REDC	Revista Española de Derecho Constitucional
REP	Revista de Estudios Políticos
Riv. dir. intern.	Rivista di diritto internazionale
Riv. it. dir. pubbl. com.	Rivista italiana di diritto pubblico comunitario
Riv. stor. it.	Rivista storica italiana

Riv. trim. dir. pubbl.	Rivista trimestrale di diritto pubblico
RMC	Revue du Marché Commun
RRA	Race Relations Act
RTDeur/RTDE	Revue trimestrielle de Droit européen
RV	Reichsverfassung
s	Section
S&P	Scienza & Politica
scil.	scilicet
SDA	Sex Discrimination Act
SEA	Single European Act
ser.	Series
SIS	Schengen Information System
SpC	Spanish Constitution
SSTC	Judgments of the Spanish Constitutional Tribunal
STC	Sentencia del Tribunal Constitucional (judgment of the Spanish Constitutional Tribunal)
TCE	Treaty establishing a Constitution for Europe
TDS	Teoria del diritto e dello Stato
TEU	Treaty on European Union as amended by the Lisbon Treaty
TEU-Amsterdam	Treaty on European Union as amended by the Amsterdam Treaty
TEU-Maastricht	Treaty on European Union as amended by the Maastricht Treaty
TEU-Nice	Treaty on European Union as amended by the Nice Treaty
TFEU	Treaty on the Functioning of the European Union
ThürVerwBl.	Thüringer Verwaltungsblätter
UEF	Union Européenne des Féderalistes
UK	United Kingdom
US	United States
USA	United States of America
v/v.	versus
VAT	Value Added Tax
VCLT	Vienna Convention on the Law of Treaties
VerwArch	Verwaltungsarchiv
Vol.	Volume
VVDStRL	Veröffentlichungen der Vereinigung der Deutschen Staatsrechtslehrer
WD	Working Document
WRV	Weimarer Reichsverfassung
WTO	World Trade Organisation
ZaöRV	Zeitschrift für ausländisches öffentliches Recht und Völkerrecht
ZevKR	Zeitschrift für evangelisches Kirchenrecht

ZfV	Zeitschrift für Verwaltung
ZG	Zeitschrift für Gesetzgebung
ZÖR	Zeitschrift für öffentliches Recht (Austrian journal of Public and International Law)
ZRP	Zeitschrift für Rechtspolitik
ZSR	Zeitschrift für Schweizerisches Recht

Selected National and International Courts

National

Austria	http://www.vfgh.gv.at/
Czech Republic	http://www.concourt.cz/
France	http://www.conseil-constitutionnel.fr/
	http://www.conseil-etat.fr/
Germany	http://www.bundesverfassungsgericht.de/
Greece	http://www.ste.gr/
Hungary	http://www.mkab.hu/
Italy	http://www.cortecostituzionale.it/
Poland	http://www.trybunal.gov.pl/
Portugal	http://www.tribunalconstitucional.pt/tc/home.html
Spain	http://www.tribunalconstitucional.es/
United Kingdom	http://www.parliament.uk/business/lords/
	http://www.supremecourt.gov.uk/
United States of America	http://www.supremecourt.gov

International

Court of Justice of the European Union	http://curia.europa.eu/
European Court of Human Rights	http://www.echr.coe.int/
International Court of Justice	http://www.icj-cij.org/

Part I
Constitutional Basis

The European Constitution's Prospects

Antonio D'Atena

1 Two Apparently Contradictory Statements

I would like to begin my paper by making two apparently contradictory statements.

The first is that the Lisbon Treaty clearly reverses the trend reflected in the Rome Treaty of 2004 and resolutely shelves any prospect of a European Constitution. Indeed, in line with both the German Presidency's report dated June 2007[1] and the conclusions reached by the European Council in Brussels shortly afterwards,[2] the Treaty deliberately abandons the term "constitution". This therefore marks a sharp U-turn after the Rome Treaty, since the latter had constructed all its institutional and presentational strategy around that term.

The second statement is that the U-turn is nevertheless more apparent than real.

English translation by Catharine Rose de Rienzo (née Everett-Heath).

[1]Report from the Presidency to the European Council pursuing the Treaty reform process (14 June 2007): "A certain number of Member States underlined the importance of avoiding the impression which might be given by the symbolism and the title 'Constitution' that the nature of the Union is undergoing radical change. For them this also implies a return to the traditional method of treaty change through an amending treaty, as well as a number of changes of terminology, not least the dropping of the title 'Constitution'". From the Treaty of Rome onwards, legal scholars had expressed a similar point of view; see Caruso (2005).

[2]Presidency Conclusions – Brussels 21/22 June 2007 (11177/1/07), pp. 15 et seq.: "The IGC is asked to draw up a Treaty (hereinafter called the 'Reform Treaty') amending the existing Treaties with a view to enhancing the efficiency and democratic legitimacy of the enlarged Union, as well as the coherence of its external action. *The constitutional concept, which consisted in repealing all existing Treaties and replacing them by a single text called 'Constitution', is abandoned*" (my italics).

A. D'Atena (✉)
Via Orazio Raimondo, 18, 00173, Roma, Italy
e-mail: datena@juris.uniroma2.it

H.-J. Blanke and S. Mangiameli (eds.), *The European Union after Lisbon*,
DOI 10.1007/978-3-642-19507-5_1, © Springer-Verlag Berlin Heidelberg 2012

2 A Treaty, Not a Constitution

The U-turn is more apparent than real because, despite its title "Treaty establishing a Constitution for Europe", the Rome Treaty could not be considered a genuine constitution.[3]

From a formal point of view, first of all, it was not a constitution. In saying this, I am referring to the process followed for its creation. Such a process was the one typical of international treaties, not constitutions. As is well known, treaties obey the logic of contracts. Like contracts, they become legally binding only if all the parties involved agree on the treaty's text.[4] This has the consequence that, should a state dissent, there is no treaty. The impact on the Rome Treaty of the "No" resulting from the referenda in France and the Netherlands demonstrates this quite clearly.

The logic inspiring constitutions is totally different. It is not the logic of unanimity but rather that of the majority.[5] In order to create or change a constitution, a majority vote is required. Usually this is a qualified majority: often a two thirds majority is necessary.

In order to appreciate the significance of this fact, we can recall the constituent processes presenting the greatest number of similarities with the one developed in Europe, namely, those processes occurring in federal states. What happens in such a process is that several sovereign states decide to become one single state, ceding their sovereignty but maintaining their individual identity. This process culminates in the federal constitution's entry into force. The constitution must be approved by the Member States but it is not necessary that they do so unanimously. If the number of approving states reaches the critical mass required by the constitution, the latter normally binds those states that voted against it.[6]

---

[3]See Schmitz (2007), for the contrary opinion that the Treaty did possess the basic prerequisites of a Constitution.

[4]This is the general rule, as is well known. Derogations from it must be agreed by the parties (see Art. 24 VCLT 1969). Under Romano Prodi's presidency, a solution derogating from the general rule was studied for the Rome Treaty of 2004 but it did not meet with the Member States' favour. Known as the Penelope project and inspired by the federal techniques that will be considered below, it proposed subordinating the treaty's entry into force to ratification by a qualified majority of the Member States. See Prodi (2004) and Ziller (2003), p. 191, on this subject.

[5]On such a difference and its significance, see, for example, Ipsen (1987), pp. 203 et seq. and Grimm (1995), p. 586. Of the most recent publications in Italian, Carnevale (2005), pp. 1101 et seq. and Gabriele (2008), pp. 135 et seq., should also be noted.

[6]This is what happened both in the case of the Swiss Federal Constitution of 1848 and in that of the German Basic Law of 1949. Indeed, although neither was approved unanimously, they both also became legally binding upon the sub-national entities that had voted against them. A different solution, on the other hand, was adopted under Art. VII of the Constitution of the United States of America, which provides as follows: "The Ratification of the Conventions of nine States shall be sufficient for the Establishment of this Constitution between the States so ratifying the Same."

The reason for the difference between the process provided for the European Treaties and the one provided for federal constitutions is clear. Indeed, the federative processes give birth to a state: *e pluribus unum* (according to the motto which appears on the Great Seal of the United States). The body that emerges from the process of European integration, on the other hand, is not a state. In this latter case, the EU Member States not only maintain their individual identity (as in the case of a federation) but they also (unlike the case of a federation) preserve a good part of their sovereignty.

The point is precisely that: sovereignty. I would like to state that the issue is an extremely complex one and would therefore require an ad hoc meeting. For our purposes, it is sufficient to note that, up until now, the states have, to a large extent, preserved their sovereignty. Hence the preservation of the international treaty mechanism (and the unanimity rule tied to it).

3 The "Convention" Method

Without prejudice to the premise that what we are talking about is an international treaty, it must be stressed that the manner in which the text was achieved was not the one typical of treaties, namely, the method of intergovernmental negotiation.

A different method was followed: the "Convention" method.[7] This is not to say that intergovernmental negotiations were eliminated. On the contrary, the final text was adopted by an Intergovernmental Conference. Nevertheless, it was a Convention that was appointed to draw up the text, i.e. a body composed of national parliamentarians, national government representatives, European Parliamentarians and representatives from the European Union's (EU) Commission.[8]

The importance of this fact cannot escape us. It is indeed true that the Convention did not have to take any decisions but simply carried out work of a preparatory nature. Its composition nevertheless presented characteristics of great interest from a constitutional point of view, since it had the effect of introducing the

[7] As regards the "Convention" method, see Atripaldi (2003), pp. 213 et seq., writing with reference to the Nice Charter but in terms that lend themselves to wider contexts.

[8] The Convention provided for by the Laeken Declaration of 15 December 2001 was composed of a Chairman and two Vice-Chairmen (appointed directly by the European Council), 15 representatives of the Heads of State or Government of the Member States (one from each Member State), 13 government representatives from the accession candidate countries, 30 members of the national parliaments (two from each Member State), 26 representatives from the national parliaments of the candidate countries (two for each State), 16 members of the European Parliament and two Commission representatives. In addition, observers representing the Economic and Social Committee, the Committee of the Regions and the European Ombudsman, respectively, also participated without voting rights.

parliamentary element (i.e. both the European Parliament and national parliaments) into the decision-making process.[9]

As we know, a specific precedent in this field may be found in the Nice Charter. The Charter's text had been prepared by a Convention convened by the European Council of Tampere in October 1999.[10] However (and this is of greater interest to us here), there existed an older precedent, one tied to the history of constitutionalism and a real milestone. I am referring, of course, to the Constitutional Convention of 1787 that drew up the Constitution of the United States of America in Philadelphia. It was composed of delegates from the United States such as George Washington, Benjamin Franklin, Alexander Hamilton and James Madison, whose names remain permanently linked to the history of constitutionalism.[11]

It is true that, unlike the Philadelphia Convention, the European Convention did not have the task of drawing up the text to submit for ratification by the States. Its task was, rather, to draw up a preparatory document to submit to the Intergovernmental Conference.[12] Two not unimportant aspects should be considered, however.

First of all, there is a symbolic aspect. Indeed, it is not without significance that, during the process of creating a document entitled "Constitution for Europe", there was agreement about introducing a body named after the historic Convention that drew up the oldest federal constitution in the world.

The second aspect is institutional. As I have said, it was through this choice that the democratic/representational element was introduced into the decision-making process (and, with it, an element of democratic legitimation). It may be added, incidentally, that the method followed ought to have contributed to this same function, being as it was a method that was open to the contributions made by civil society. One can think of the hearings and the great public debate made possible by the Internet *forum*.[13]

---

[9]The importance of this aspect is emphasised by Napolitano (2004), p. 139.

[10]On the basis of the Annex to the Presidency Conclusions of the Tampere European Council (15 and 16 October 1999), its composition was as follows: 15 representatives of the Heads of State or Government of the Member States, a representative of the President of the European Commission, 16 members of the European Parliament designated by the latter and 30 members of the national parliaments (two from each national parliament).

[11]The Convention's work lasted from 25 May to 17 September 1787. As is known, it was composed of 55 delegates from all the ex-colonies except Rhode Island, the latter preferring not to be represented.

[12]As regards the mandate given to the Convention tasked with drawing up the draft Constitutional Treaty, see for example: Ferrara (2002), pp. 177 et seq. As regards the "constitutional" problems the Convention was called to face, the account given by the Vice-Chairman is significant: see Amato (2003). As regards the work's organisation, discussions and progress, see Floridia and Sciannella (2003); Ziller (2003), pp. 91 et seq. and Gabriele (2008), pp. 35 et seq. As regards the tension, in that particular case, between the Convention method and intergovernmental negotiations, see Amato (2004).

[13]The significance of this procedure is considered in Cerulli Irelli (2006), pp. 60 et seq.

But that is not all. It is true that the Treaty provided that it could only be amended by way of a new international treaty. However, this was not to be a normal international treaty (to be worked out according to the method of diplomatic negotiation). Indeed, Art. IV-443 TCE provided that the text had to be drafted by a Convention representing Parliaments, Governments and the Commission.[14]

On this occasion I shall not dwell on the simplified revision procedures, even though the Treaty provides for them (under Art. IV-444 and 445 TCE). What I am interested in emphasising is that, in this way, a dose of constitutionalism (or a principle containing constitutional DNA, if you like) was introduced into an international procedure.

Well then, as is known, the Lisbon Treaty did not follow the road paved by the Rome Treaty as regards the creation process. Indeed, it was a normal intergovernmental conference that had the task of reviving the process of reforming the Treaties and was appointed to draft the text for ratification by the Member States.[15]

Such a fact has not meant, however, that the constitutional DNA to which I have just referred was lost. Indeed, in confirming the principle introduced by Art. IV-443 TCE, Art. 48 TEU has revived the Convention method for Treaty amendment.

If one considers the formal aspects (i.e. those governing the creation and amendment process), one may conclude that the transition from Rome to Lisbon has not had particularly important consequences. In both cases, the product is an international treaty and not a constitution (as we have seen).

In both cases, nevertheless, the amendment procedure contains a constitutional type of contamination (through application of the Convention method).

4 Content

We now come to the substantive aspects or, in other words, the content of the Treaty documents.[16] From this point of view, too, it was difficult to maintain that the so-called constitutional treaty had the characteristics of a constitution.

The first factor for consideration is an extrinsic one, namely, length. It is well known that contemporary constitutions are not as straightforward as the constitution of the United States of America. Contemporary constitutions are, generally speaking, long constitutions. The Italian Constitution, for example, had 139 articles and 18 transitional and final provisions. I use the past tense because the number of articles has decreased, following the constitutional reform of 2001, even though the number of words has increased. Such a fact is not necessarily a sign of good

[14]As regards such procedure and other procedures for amending the Treaty, see Gabriele (2008), pp. 181 et seq. and Busia (2003), pp. 65 et seq.

[15]Brussels European Council, 21/22 June 2007, Presidency Conclusions, paragraph No. 10.

[16]As regards the need to go beyond a strictly formal perspective, see Walker (1996), pp. 270 et seq.

drafting. There are, moreover, constitutions that are particularly long. The Portuguese Constitution of 1976 is an emblematic example of this, with its 295 articles.

Well, the so-called European Constitution beats all the records. It actually comprised 448 articles, to which the 36 protocols were to be annexed.[17] The anomaly was not limited to such an extrinsic fact, however. It was also manifest at the level of content in the strict sense and by this I mean the kind of rules the treaty expressed.

To borrow an untranslatable German word, it may be said that, if considered in terms of the rules it contained, the Treaty was a *Sammelsurium*: that is, a collection of heterogeneous rules very many of which were totally out of place in a constitutional document.[18]

It was possible to identify a body of substantively constitutional rules within this *corpus*, nonetheless – a sort of constitution within the Constitution, as it were. These were rules that could be traced to the two basic ingredients of constitutional documents: those governing fundamental rights and those governing the organisation of the Union's institutions, their competences and the relations between them. To these two parts common to most constitutions, a third was added. This third part was common only to the constitutions of federal and regional states. It was the law governing the division of competences between the EU and the Member States.

As regards the law governing fundamental rights, the Treaty's incorporation of the Nice Charter (i.e. the European Union Charter of Fundamental Right (EUCFR), thereby conferring on such a document the formal value it had formerly lacked and still lacks[19]) should be remembered.

On this level, too, the Lisbon Treaty does not mark a retreat, however. On the contrary, it may be said that it presents a more marked "constitutional" character than the constitutional Treaty of Rome.

Such a fact is a consequence of abandoning the *Sammelsurium* model. Indeed, whilst maintaining the existing systemic structure, the Lisbon Treaty distinguishes the Treaty on European Union (TEU) from the Treaty on the Functioning of the European Union (TFEU) (which replaces the Treaty establishing the European Community) and introduces a great part of the substantively constitutional rules into the former.

---

[17]As regards this aspect see, for example, Draetta (2004), p. 528 and Gabriele (2008), pp. 139 et seq.

[18]This view is very widely held [see, from amongst the many who share it, Tizzano (2004), p. 19]. As regards the incompatibility of this content with the essence of a constitution, see Anzon (2003), pp. 330 et seq.

[19]Publications on the Charter's legal enforceability are endless. From amongst the most significant contributions, see Weber (2000); Pace (2001); Diez Picazo (2001); Bifulco et al. (2001); Braibant (2001); Ruggeri (2001); Carrillo Salcedo (2001); Weber (2002); Matia Portilla (2002); Rubio Llorente (2002); Jacqué (2002); Tomuschat (2002); Dutheil de la Rochère (2002); Toniatti (2002); Pagano (2003); Siclari (2003); Balduzzi (2003); Villani (2004); Skouris (2004); Stern (2006) and Pollicino and Sciarabba (2008).

In this respect, some specific details really should be noted. The first is with regard to the law governing fundamental rights. Indeed, unlike the Rome Treaty, the Lisbon Treaty does not incorporate the Nice Charter but provides that it shall have "the same legal value as the Treaties" (Art. 6 TEU). It therefore distributes its "constitutional" content between various documents and thus does not present the "one-document" format that is normally characteristic of constitutions.

Similar considerations may also apply to the distribution of content between the TEU and the TFEU. Indeed, the second contains a great number of rules of a substantively constitutional character. One may think, in particular, of Part I, containing principles, and Title I of Part VI, containing the institutional provisions.

Simplifying to a certain extent, it may therefore be said that the constitutional Treaty of Rome, albeit presenting the characteristics of a *Sammelsurium*, contained the "constitution". The Lisbon version of the TEU, on the other hand, contains only a part of the "constitution", whilst the remaining parts need to be sought in separate documents, i.e. the EUCFR (enjoying the same legal value as the Treaties, as we have seen) and some parts of the TFEU. To complete the framework, one may add that, on the level of contents, the innovations of the Lisbon Treaty cannot be considered insignificant.

5 In What Sense Could the Existence of a European Constitution Affirm Itself Even Before Lisbon

Despite the entry into force of the Lisbon Treaty on 1 December 2009 a question becomes unavoidable. In what sense may it be said that Europe had a constitution even before the Lisbon Treaty? I shall seek to answer this question through a series of increasingly precise observations.

The first observation I would like to make is that the act of asserting the existence of a European Constitution is not limited to observing that the European legal order (like every complex legal order) is based on a body of rules that regulates its basic structure.[20] For example, the term "constitution" (linked to the advent of the modern state) is used in this sense with reference to legal orders to which the historical and ideological concept of constitution was and is alien. One may think, for example, of Francesco De Martino's study on the constitution under the Roman legal order[21] or the works by Alfred Verdross and Piero Ziccardi on the

[20]For example, the existence of a European Constitution in this very general sense is recognised in Cassese (1991), p. 447. For a critical approach, however, see Anzon (2003), pp. 303 et seq., emphasising that it is not to such a concept of "constitution" that reference should be made when attempting to answer the question as to whether, today, Europe has a Constitution. See, also Walker (1996), p. 269.

[21]De Martino (1951, 1954, 1955).

constitution of the international legal order .[22] It is well known that the concept of a constitution in the substantive sense is applied in these cases.

When speaking of a European Constitution, something more is meant. What is meant, in particular, is that whilst the formal characteristics normally present in state constitutions are missing, there nevertheless existed and exists within the European legal order a body of rules presenting marked similarities with many of the rules contained in such state constitutions.

To what am I referring? To the rules outlining the Union's basic organisation, first of all – those rules that identify its bodies (including the institutions), establish their spheres of competence and govern decision-making.

In order to avoid misunderstanding, it should be noted that such rules do not correspond in every respect to those to be found in state constitutions. Indeed, the EU is not a state and this fact is reflected in the characteristics of its constitutional organisation (and, therefore, in those of the rules governing it).[23] Suffice it to think of the importance of the intergovernmental component in the European order, the fact that such an order does not apply the principle of the separation of powers,[24] the lack of a system of sources of law structured according to form[25] and the absence of any decentralised administration and so on. The list could continue.

In my opinion, however, one cannot deduce from such facts that the Union does not have "constitutional" rules. One should be inferring something different, namely, that the said rules differ at a substantive level (i.e. in content) from the corresponding rules to be found in the majority of national constitutions.

The differences are not radical, however.[26] One may think, for example, of the influence that the intergovernmental component enjoys in the German federal order. Here, I am referring to the *Bundesrat*, which presents not negligible similarities with the Council.[27]

One may also think of the widespread model of *Vollzugsföderalismus* (i.e. executive federalism) commonly applied in the Middle European federal systems,

---

[22]Verdross (1926) and Ziccardi (1943).

[23]A different reasoning would apply were it to be held that the term "constitution" is only appropriate in the context of a state (as does Grimm (1995), p. 590). This perspective is increasingly contested, however, since the tendency nowadays is to recognise that constitutions may exist beyond the state. Indeed, see Weiler (1999); Pernice (1999); Walker (2004) and Poiares Maduro (2004). See, also, Luciani (2001); Pinelli (2002); pp. 183 et seq. and Ruggeri (2008), on this issue.

[24]Walker (1996), pp. 269 et seq., emphasises that, as a consequence of the specific characteristics both of the EU legal order and of the role of its executive (which cannot be compared to that of national executives), the principle of the separation of powers as we know it would not be indispensable at a European level.

[25]As regards this characteristic which distinguishes European sources from national sources on structural grounds, see D'Atena (2001).

[26]Violini (1998), pp. 1251 et seq., highlights the substantive similarities between the European Constitution (in the sense it is given here) and the Member States' Constitutions.

[27]For this opinion see Fromont (1998), p. 132.

a model that, not by chance, some legal scholars also use with reference to the European legal order.[28]

Similar considerations apply to the rules governing fundamental rights. In the past many authors have inferred the inexistence of a European Constitution from the absence of such rules.[29] Those following this line of reasoning take as their model the paradigm offered by Art. 16 of the "Declaration of the Rights of Man and of the Citizen" of 1789. It is well known that this places the rules governing fundamental rights amongst the indispensable characteristics of a constitution: amongst those characteristics without which a state "does not have a constitution".

Well, it must not be forgotten that, were this the model to be applied, one would have to say that history's first great constitution (i.e. the 1787 Constitution of the United States of America) was not a constitution. Indeed, in its original version, that document did not make provision for fundamental rights. The latter were added a few years later, with the first ten amendments.[30] Significantly, these are known as the "Bill of Rights". Nor, by virtue of the same absence, could the first French Constitution (1791) be considered an authentic constitution, since its rules governing fundamental rights were very partial and fragmentary. As we know, the latter found their expression in another document of a *recognitive* rather than *constitutive* nature (in line with the natural law ideology inspiring its authors). Such a document was the "Declaration of the Rights of Man and of the Citizen" to which I have already referred.

With specific reference to the "European Constitution", this absence of rules concerning fundamental rights (which the Treaty of Lisbon redresses by recognising the Nice Charter as enjoying the same legal value as the Treaties) could be traced to motives similar to the ones inspiring the US Founding Fathers and the authors of the first federal constitutions in Europe, namely, the Swiss Constitution of 1848 and the German Constitution of 1871. I am referring here to the federal structure. Those three constitutions did not feel the need for rules governing fundamental rights. This was because such rights were (or could be) governed by the Member States' constitutions that, together with the federal constitution, contributed to the creation of an integrated constitutional system.[31]

It must be emphasised, however, that a law governing fundamental rights was not totally absent at a European level. Here, I am obviously referring to Art. 6.2

---

[28]See, Guzzetta and Marini (2006), pp. 405 et seq.

[29]This opinion is very widely held. Of the many sharing it, see Anzon (2003) and De Marco (2008), pp. 50 et seq.

[30]As regards the absence of a bill of rights in the federal Constitution, see Hamilton et al. (1787/1788).

[31]An extremely clear description of such structure may be found in Nawiasky (1920), p. 144: "The federal constitution [...] is, of its essence, incomplete. It does not give birth to a self-contained legal order, but to a partial order, which may be considered an order insofar as it refers, for its missing part, to the constitutions of the Member States, which complete it." Albeit from a different angle, Caruso (2005), p. XVI, emphasises the role of the Constitutions of the EU Member States for the purposes of guaranteeing the fundamental rights of European citizens.

TEU-Nice by virtue of which *The Union shall respect fundamental rights, as guaranteed by the European Convention for the Protection of Human Rights and Fundamental Freedoms signed in Rome on 4 November 1950 and as they result from the constitutional traditions common to the Member States, as general principles of Community law.*

Before concluding on this point, I would like to add that the rules dividing competences between the EU and the Member States should also be remembered. Such rules are incontestably constitutional in nature and in large part mirror the analogous rules present in federal constitutions.[32]

These are the reasons for which, in my opinion, it may be asserted that the existence of a "constitution" in Europe was (and is) undeniable, despite the absence of a constitutional Charter. There is a constitution scattered within the Founding Treaties[33] and its contents partly resemble those to be found in state constitutions currently or formerly in force (particularly federal ones). There obviously remain areas where the constitution differs from state constitutions. Such differences are caused by the novelty of the phenomenon to be governed. As I said earlier, the EU is not a state, but rather a new kind of legal order.[34] It is an order without precedent in the history of legal institutions. Its "constitution" therefore cannot fail to be affected by this structural implication.

6 European Constitution and National Constitutions: A Pluralistic Approach

Before ending, I would like to emphasise that the "thing" we have called a "European Constitution" does not "intervene" (if one may put it like that) in a constitutional vacuum, but rather in a space that is broadly occupied by the constitutions of the Member States.[35]

It therefore comes as no surprise that fortune has smiled on the expression "multilevel constitutionalism".[36] This term was coined to convey the phenomenon

[32]See, on this point, D'Atena (2005).

[33]An analogous line of thinking is expressed in Venizelos (2004), who speaks of a "fragmentary and in part unwritten European Constitution".

[34]For this reason, the claim to read the European constitutional phenomenon by rigidly applying models obtainable from national constitutions or, more precisely, from a part of them, may be criticised [see, taking this line, De Siervo (2001)]. This without considering that to proceed in such a manner runs the risk of denying the "constitutional" character of national constitutions that incontestably enjoy such a character [this point is most opportunely emphasised, with reference to the German Basic Law, by Mangiameli (2008), p. 394].

[35]As regards the ensuing problems, see Häberle (2005), pp. 221 et seq.

[36]In this context, reference to Ingolf Pernice is *de rigueur*. Of his works, see, in particular, Pernice (1999) and Pernice (2002), as well as, most recently, Pernice (2009).

characterised by the simultaneous presence of various integrated constitutional levels in the same legal space.

It is, however, well known that multilevel constitutionalism did not come into being with the EU. Indeed, it has accompanied federal experiences right from their historical beginnings in an era when the concept of "multilevel constitutionalism" had yet to come into existence.

In federal states (from the United States archetype onwards), the Federation's constitution exists alongside the constitutions of the Member States. Together with it, the latter contribute to creating a *complex* constitutional system: a sort of multilayered constitution.

Historically, the overall systemic connection between such levels was very evident from the outset, when the federal constitution assumed the form of a *partial constitution* (or *Teilverfassung*, to borrow German terminology).[37] Such a partial constitution was responsible for the Federation's organisation and the division of competences between the latter and the Member States. As I said earlier, it did not concern itself with the fundamental rights of citizens, as the latter were governed by the Member States' constitutional charters. The relationship between the federal constitution and the Member States' constitutions was therefore a complementary one.

The systemic connection between the two levels was not eroded even subsequently when, as a result of the nationalisation of fundamental rights following their inclusion in federal constitutions, the rules laid down by the latter on the subject *stood alongside* the corresponding rules contained in the sub-statal constitutions. Indeed, it should not be forgotten that, according to current formulations, the central rules do not *repeal* the local rules and take their place. On the contrary, the local rules – if more favourable – are to be accorded precedence.[38] Both the one set and the other therefore *make up the system* (i.e. they continue to make up the system, albeit along lines that differ from the original ones).

It is for this reason that, despite the novelty of the European legal order which is not a federal one, the experiences and considerations that have developed layer by layer in the history of federations can offer useful keys for interpreting the European context. One may think of the rules governing the division of competences between the European Community and the Member States. In some respects, these can be considered to mirror the corresponding rules present in federal constitutions. For example, there is a fairly widespread opinion that community regulations are

---

[37]It is not without significance that the concept of *Teilverfassung* is also used in relation to the European legal order, for the purposes of emphasising the latter's effect on the Member States' Constitutions. See, in this respect, Häberle (2005), pp. 221 et seq.

[38]On this subject see, for example, Tarr (1989), p. 55; Starck (1995); and Graf Vitzthum (1988), pp. 22 et seq., p. 32, fn. 91.

the expression of a competence with notable points of similarity with the German *konkurrierende Gesetzgebung*.[39]

Again, one can think of the rule contained in the EUCFR (namely Art. 53) according to which *Nothing in this Charter shall be interpreted as restricting or adversely affecting human rights and fundamental freedoms as recognised [. . .] by the Member States' constitutions*. Indeed, such a rule follows the already cited principle developed by judicial decisions in federal legal orders according to which the federal law on rights does not prevail over the law dictated by the Member States' constitutions if the latter is more favourable.

Having said that, I should also make clear that European multilevel constitutionalism has a particular characteristic that distinguishes it from the multilevel constitutionalism to be found in federal orders. There, the federal constitution is the legal order's supreme source. It therefore constitutes the yardstick by which the legitimacy of the Member States' constitutions is measured. Such a fact is most clearly expressed in the homogeneity clauses through which federal constitutions guide and delimit those of their Member States. In this context, Art. 28 of the German Basic Law and Art. 51 of the current Swiss Constitution may be remembered by way of example. The German rule provides that *the constitutional order in the Länder must conform to the principles of republican, democratic and social state governed by the rule of law*. The Swiss rule, for its part, provides as follows: *Each Canton shall adopt a democratic constitution. This requires the approval of the People and must be capable of being revised if the majority of those eligible to vote so request.*

The situation in the European order is different, however. This is not because there is no homogeneity clause in some way comparable to the corresponding clauses present in federal constitutions. In fact, it may be said, in the wake of an opinion advanced before the Lisbon Treaty, that Art. 2 TEU (former Art. 6.1 TEU) has such an effect.[40] They emphasise, in particular, that the reference to the principles of freedom, democracy and respect for human rights and the rule of law is not descriptive but prescriptive, thereby requiring states (and therefore also their constitutions) to comply with such values.[41] On such a basis, the similarity between the European Constitution and the constitutions of federal states is undeniable in this respect, too. Such an analogy cannot be taken to its extreme consequences, however. Indeed, in my opinion, one cannot deduce from the presence of a homogeneity clause in the European "Constitution" that such a constitution is superordinate to the constitutions of the Member States. Or, in

[39]From amongst the first to consider them in this sense, see Wohlfahrt et al. (1960), p. 513. For the opposite view, see Ophüls (1963), subsequently criticised by D'Atena (1981), p. 96, fn. 22.

[40]The likening of Art. 6 TEU to a homogeneity clause is to be found in Mangiameli (2008), pp. 93 et seq. and p. 389.

[41]As is known, the Commission can, pursuant to Art. 7 TEU, apply sanctions against Member States that fail to respect the principles listed under Art. 2. Moreover, it can prevent third-party countries from becoming members of the Union (Art. 49 TEU).

other words, that in the multilevel constitutional system currently in force in Europe, the Union's constitutional law enjoys supremacy.

The obstacle standing in the way of such supremacy is the continuing sovereignty of the Member States or, in other words, the fact that they have maintained areas of sovereignty. These circumstances justify a pluralistic approach.[42] By this I mean the theoretical perspective of the plurality of legal orders and its correlated principle of the relativity of legal values.[43] According to such a principle, the legal qualification of facts is not unique (and always the same) but varies according to the legal order that is chosen as the point of reference. A certain form of behaviour may be illegal under the European legal order but perfectly legal under the legal order of one or the other Member States. This means that if one chooses the perspective of the European legal order, the Treaties (and, therefore, the "constitution" they contain) must be identified as the supreme law. It also means, however, that if one chooses the perspective of the legal order of the individual Member States, then it is the national constitution that must be considered the supreme law for each one of them.[44] This is, moreover, the perspective occasionally adopted by national constitutional courts. Here, I am referring in particular to the very well known *Maastricht* and *Lisbon* judgments delivered by the German Court and the line adopted by the Italian Court.[45] Indeed, it is well known that these constitutional courts have reserved for themselves the right to check the Treaties' conformity with their national constitutions so as to avoid the possibility of the supreme principles expressed by the latter being undermined.[46]

---

[42]As regards the application of this theoretical perspective in the context of the relations between the European legal order and the national legal orders, see, in particular, Mac Cormick (1995).

[43]In this context, the classic theorisation developed in S. Romano, L'ordinamento giuridico (1918), reprint, Firenze, 1962, should be recalled, as well as the manner in which it was developed by the Italian school of public law. In particular, with specific reference to the principle of the relativity of legal values, see Gueli (1949) and Crisafulli (1970), p. 43.

[44]As regards the persistence of the two perspectives, see Barbera (2000), p. 80. According to Barbera, jurists today find themselves facing two alternatives: "either to choose the viewpoint favouring the national legal order or to choose the viewpoint favouring the Community legal order. If they choose the first viewpoint [. . .], they cannot renounce the waning sovereign legitimacy of their own constitution; if they choose the second viewpoint [. . .], they cannot renounce asserting the emerging sovereignty of the European constitution. Only were a federal constitution to be reached could the two viewpoints be united." As regards the current transitional phase, see Häberle (2005), pp. 210 et seq. and Hofmann (2004), pp. 170 et seq.

[45]The literature on both the Maastricht-Urteil and the line adopted by the Italian Court is very extensive. For a highly informative outline, see Anzon (1999) (to which the reader is referred for other references). In addition, of the most recent publications, see Vaquero Cruz (2007). On the German Lisbon Judgment: Häberle (2010); and the studies in Zeitschrift für europarechtliche Studien (ZEuS): Dingemann (2009); Bergmann and Karpenstein (2009); Bröhmer (2009); Calliess (2009); Hahn (2009); Hector (2009).

[46]The interventions by national constitutional courts before treaty ratification are inspired by analogous requirements. For example, in November 2008, the Czech Court established the compatibility of some of the Lisbon Treaty provisions with the Czech Republic's Constitution. In general, see Blanke and Mangiameli (2006), pp. LV et seq., on the significance of the

It is true that the hypotheses of the national constitutions' supremacy entertained by national constitutional courts are purely theoretical.[47] Thus the possibility of the national constitutions' supremacy being concretely asserted also remains purely theoretical. It nevertheless seems incontrovertible that, in the present situation, the existence of such (albeit potential) *controlimiti* (counterchecks) excludes the possibility of considering the relations between the European Constitution and the constitutions of the Member States in a monistic light. That is to say, it does not permit the two constitutional levels to be placed within a single hierarchical structure. Nor does it permit the European Constitution to be attributed with that status of supreme law that is usually enjoyed by contemporary written constitutions.

References

Amato G (2003) Verso la Costituzione europea. Riv It Dir Pubbl Com:291–300
Amato G (2004) Riflessioni conclusive. In: Bassanini F, Tiberi G (eds) La Costituzione europea: Un primo comment. Il Mulino, Bologna, p 285 et seqq
Anzon A (1999) I Tribunali costituzionali nell'era di Maastricht. In: Studi in onore di Leopoldo Elia, I. Giuffrè, Milano, pp 80 et seqq
Anzon A (2003) La Costituzione europea come problema. In: D'Atena A, Lanzillotta E (eds) Da Omero alla Costituzione europea. Tored, Tivoli
Atripaldi M (2003) Il "metodo" della *Convenzione* e i "valori" della Carta dei diritti: una cronaca dei lavori preparatory. In: Atripaldi V, Miccù R (eds) L'omogeneità costituzionale nell'Unione europea. Cedam, Padova
Balduzzi R (2003) La Carta dei diritti fondamentali dell'Unione europea: un esempio di *constitutional drafting*? Quaderni Regionali:381 et seqq
Barbera A (2000) Esiste una "costituzione europea"? Quad Cost:77 et seqq
Bergmann J, Karpenstein U (2009) Identitäts- und Ultra-vires-Kontrolle durch das Bundesverfassungsgericht – Zur Notwendigkeit einer Gesetzlichen Vorlageverpflichtung. ZEuS 12(4):529 et seqq
Bifulco R, Cartabia M, Celotto A (2001) Introduzione. In: Bifulco R, Cartabia M, Celotto A (eds) L'Europa dei diritti. Il Mulino, Bologna, p 25 et seqq
Blanke H-J, Mangiameli St (2006) Introduction. In: Blanke H-J, Mangiameli St (eds) Governing Europe under a constitution. Springer, Heidelberg, pp XXV et seqq

ratification procedures provided for under the domestic legislation in the individual Member States.

[47]See, on this point, Sorrentino (2008), pp. 59 et seq., who highlights the significance that European law's progressive appropriation of the Member States' common constitutional values is assuming in this respect. As regards the debt Europe owes to national constitutional values, see Häberle (1999), pp. 3 et seq. On the other hand and as is known, the process of constitutional osmosis works in both directions, as European law's growing influence on the legal orders of the Member States would confirm. On this subject, see, in general, Häberle (2005), pp. 229 et seq. and Sorrentino (2008), and, in analytical terms, Schwarze (2001) (where the issue is considered with reference to the legal orders in France, Germany, the United Kingdom, Spain, Austria and Sweden) as well as Tizzano (2008) (taking a census of the influences in the areas of European citizenship, the Euro and banks, the single market for banking and financial services, the professions and pluralism for the press, the audiovisual media and telecommunications).

Braibant G (2001) La Charte des droits fondammentaux de l'Union européenne. Seuil, Paris
Bröhmer J (2009) Containment eines Leviathans" – Anmerkungen zur Entscheidung des Bundesverfassungsgerichts zum Vertrag von Lissabon. ZEuS 4:543 et seqq
Busia G (2003) Il ruolo della Convenzione europea in vista della sottoscrizione di nuovi trattati. In: Caruso MP, Tufarelli F (eds) Quale Europa, tra Convenzione. Conferenza intergovernativa e allargamento. Rubbettino, Soveria Mannelli, pp 59–70
Calliess Ch (2009) Das Ringen des zweiten Senats mit der Europäischen Union: Über das Ziel hinausgeschossen .... ZEuS 4:559 et seqq
Carnevale P (2005) La Costituzione europea come costituzione. Giur It:1101 et seqq
Carrillo Salcedo JA (2001) Notas sobre el significado político y jurídico de la Carta de Derechos Fundamentales de la Unión Europea. Revista de Derecho Comunitario Europeo:7 et seqq
Caruso F (2005) L'integrazione europea dopo i *referendum* in Francia ed Olanda. Diritto Pubblico Comparato Ed Europeo:XV et seq
Cassese S (1991) La Costituzione europea. Quad Cost 3:487 et seqq
Cerulli Irelli V (2006) The issue of the legal nature of the constitutional treaty and the system of sources. In: Blanke H-J, Mangiameli S (eds) Governing Europe under a constitution. Springer, Heidelberg, pp 59–64
Crisafulli V (1970) Lezioni di diritto costituzionale, I Introduzione al diritto costituzionale italiano. Padova, p 43
D'Atena A (1981) Le Regioni italiane e la Comunità economica europea. Giuffré, Milano
D'Atena A (2001) L'anomalo assetto delle fonti comunitarie. Dir Un Eur:591 et seqq
D'Atena A (2005) Modelli federali e sussidiarietà nel riparto delle competenze normative tra l'Unione europea e gli Stati membri. Dir Un Eur:59 et seqq
De Marco E (2008) Riflessioni preliminari sul processo costituente europeo. In: De Marco E (ed) Percorsi del "nuovo costituzionalismo", 2nd edn. Giuffrè, Milano
De Martino F (1951, 1954, 1955) Storia della Costituzione romana, vol. 1 (1951), vol 2, part I (1954) and vol 2, part II (1995). Jovene, Napoli
De Siervo U (2001) La difficile costituzione europea. In: De Siervo U (ed) La difficile costituzione europea. Il Mulino, Bologna, p 116 et seqq
Diez Picazo LM (2001) Glosas a la nueva Carta de Derechos Fundamentales de la Unión Europea. Tribunales de Justicia, No. 5/01
Dingemann K (2009) Zwischen Integrationsverantwortung und Identitätskontrolle: Das Lissabon-Urteil des Bundesverfassungsgerichts. ZEuS 4:491 et seqq
Draetta U (2004) La Costituzione europea e il nodo della sovranità nazionale. Dir Un Eur:519–535
Dutheil de la Rochère J (2002) Les droits fondamentaux reconnus par la Charte et leurs applications. Eur Rev Public Law:227 et seqq
Ferrara G (2002) Verso la Costituzione europea? Dir Pubbl:161 et seqq
Floridia G, Sciannella LG (2003) Il cantiere della nuova Europa. Tecnica e politica nei lavori della Convenzione europea. Il Mulino, Bologna
Fromont (1998) VVDStRL 58:132
Gabriele F (2008) Europa: la "Costituzione" abbandonata. Cacucci, Bari
Graf Vitzthum W (1988) Die Bedeutung gliedstaatlichen Verfassungsrechts in der Gegenwart. In: VVDStRL 46. de Gruyter, Berlin, pp 7–56
Grimm D (1995) Braucht Europa eine Verfassung? Juristenzeitung:581 et seqq
Gueli V (1949) Pluralità degli ordinamenti giuridici e condizioni della loro coesistenza. Giuffrè, Milano
Guzzetta G, Marini FS (2006) Diritto pubblico italiano ed europeo. Giappichelli, Torino
Häberle P (1999) Per una dottrina della costituzione europea. Quad Cost:3 et seqq
Häberle P (2005) Europäische Verfassungslehre, 3rd edn. Nomos, Baden-Baden
Häberle P (2010) Das retrospektive Lissabon-Urteil als versteinernde Maastricht II-Entscheidung. JöR:317–336

Hahn M (2009) Mehr Demokratie wagen: "Lissabon" – Entscheidung und Volkssouveränität. ZEuS 4:583 et seqq
Hamilton A, Jay J, Madison J (1787/1788) Classic reflections in Federalist No. 84. Federalist Papers
Hector P (2009) Zur Integrationsverantwortung des Bundesverfassungsgerichts. ZEuS 4:599 et seqq
Hofmann H (2004) Zur Entstehung, Entwicklung und Krise des Verfassungsbegriffs. In: Blankenagel A, Pernice I, Schulze-Fielitz H (eds) Verfassung im Diskurs der Welt. Liber Amicorum für Peter Häberle. Mohr Siebeck, Tübingen, p 170 et seqq
Ipsen HP (1987) Europäische Verfassung – Nationale Verfassung. EuR:195 et seqq
Jacqué J-P (2002) La Charte des droits fondamentaux de l'Union européenne – aspects juridiques généraux. Eur Rev Public Law:107 et seqq
Luciani M (2001) Legalità e legittimità nel processo d'integrazione europea. In: Bonacchi G (ed) Una Costituzione senza Stato. Il Mulino, Bologna, p 71 et seqq
Mac Cormick N (1995) The Maastricht-Urteil: sovereignty now. Eur Law J:259 et seq
Mangiameli S (2008) L'esperienza costituzionale europea. Aracne, Rome
Matia Portilla FJ (2002) La efficacia de la Carta de Niza. In: Matia Portilla FJ (ed) La protección de los derechos fundamentales en la Unión Europea. Civitas, Madrid, p 124 et seqq
Napolitano G (2004) Overcoming the democratic deficit? New steps forward and still open problems. A supranational perspective. In: Dimitrakopoulos G, Kremlis G (eds) A new constitutional settlement for the European people. Bruylant, Athens-Bruselles
Nawiasky H (1920) Der Bundesstaat als Rechtsbegriff, p 144
Ophüls CF (1963). Quellen und Aufbau des Europäischen Gemeinschaftsrechts. NJW:1700 et seqq
Pace A (2001) A che serve la Carta dei diritti fondamentali dell'Unione europea? Appunti preliminary. Giur Cost:193 et seqq
Pagano E (2003) Il valore giuridico della Carta dei diritti fondamentali e le competenze dell'Unione. DPCE:1723 et seqq
Pernice I (1999) Multilevel constitutionalism and the treaty of Amsterdam: European constitution-making revisited? CML Rev:708 et seqq
Pernice I (2002) Multilevel constitutionalism in the European Union. Eur Law Rev:511 et seqq
Pernice I (2009) The Treaty of Lisbon: Multilevel Constitutionalism in Action. 15. Columbia J Eur Law 3:349–407
Pinelli C (2002) Il momento della scrittura. Contributo al dibattito sulla Costituzione europea. Il Mulino, Bologna
Poiares Maduro M (2004) Europe and the constitution; what if this is as good as it gets. In: Weiler JHH, Wind M (eds) European constitutionalism beyond the state. Cambridge University Press, Cambridge, p 74 et seqq
Pollicino O, Sciarabba V (2008) La Carta di Nizza oggi, tra "sdoganamento giurisprudenziale" e Trattato di Lisbona. DPCE:101 et seqq
Prodi R (2004) Il destino di un popolo. La Repubblica, 28 October 2004
Rubio Llorente F (2002) Mostrar los derechos sin destruir la Unión (Consideraciones sobre la Carta de Derechos Fundamentales de la Unión Europea). REDC:13 et seqq
Ruggeri A (2001) La "forza" della Carta europea dei diritti. DPCE:182 et seqq
Ruggeri A (2008) Una Costituzione e un diritto costituzionale per l'Europa unita. In: Costanzo P, Mezzetti L, Ruggeri A (eds) Lineamenti di diritto costituzionale dell'Unione Europea. Giappichelli, Torino, p 7 et seqq
Schmitz Th (2007) Der Vertrag über eine Verfassung über Europa als Verfassung. In: Die Ordnung der Freiheit – Festschrift für Christian Starck zum siebzigsten Geburtstag. Mohr Siebeck, Tübingen, pp 623–644
Schwarze J (ed) (2001) The birth of a European constitutional order. The interaction of national and European constitutional law. Nomos, Baden-Baden
Siclari M (ed) (2003) Contributi allo studio della Carta di diritti fondamentali dell'Unione europea. Giappichelli, Torino

Skouris V (2004) Introducing a binding bill of rights in protection of fundamental rights in the European Union. Can three parallel systems coexist harmoniously? In: Blankenagel A, Pernice I, Schulze-Fielitz H (eds) Verfassung im Diskurs der Welt. Liber Amicorum für Peter Häberle. Mohr Siebeck, Tübingen, p 261 et seqq

Sorrentino F (2008) L'incidenza del diritto comunitario sulle caratteristiche del diritto pubblico. In: Tizzano A (ed) Il processo d'integrazione europea: un bilancio 50 anni dopo i Trattati di Roma. Giappichelli, Torino, p 59 et seqq

Starck Ch (1995) The constitutions of the new German *Länder* and their origin: a comparative study. In: Stiftung KA (ed) Occasional papers. Johannesburg, June 1995

Stern K (2006) From the European convention on human rights to the European charter of fundamental rights: the prospects for the protection of human rights. In: Blanke H-J, Mangiameli S (eds) Governing Europe under a constitution. Springer, Heidelberg, p 176 et seqq

Tarr A (1989) The states and civil liberties. In: United States Advisory Commission on Intergovernmental Relations (ed) State constitutions in the federal system: selected issues and opportunities for state initiatives

Tizzano A (2004) Prime note sul progetto di Costituzione europea. In: Tizzano A (ed) Una Costituzione per l'Europa. Testi e documenti relativi alla Convenzione europea. Milano, Giuffrè

Tizzano A (ed) (2008) Il processo d'integrazione europea: un bilancio 50 anni dopo i Trattati di Roma. Giappichelli, Torino

Tomuschat Ch (2002) Common values and the place of the charter in Europe. Eur Rev Public Law:159 et seqq

Toniatti R (ed) (2002) La Carta dei diritti fondamentali dell'Unione europea. Cedam, Padova

Vaquero Cruz J (2007) The legacy of the Maastricht-Urteil and the pluralist movement. EUI Working Papers RSCAS 2007/13

Venizelos E (2004) The European constitution as an "intergovernmental" constitution and the political deficits of the European Union. In: Dimitrakopoulos G, Kremlis G (eds) A new constitutional settlement for the European people. Bruylant, Athens-Bruselles, p 35 et seqq

Verdross A (1926) Die Verfassung der Völkerrechtsgemeinschaft. Springer, Wien-Berlin

Villani U (2004) Diritti fondamentali tra Carta di Nizza, Convenzione europea dei diritti dell'uomo e progetto di Costituzione europea. Dir Un Eur:73 et seqq

Violini L (1998) Prime considerazioni sul concetto di "costituzione europea" alla luce dei contenuti delle vigenti carte costituzionali. Riv It Dir Pubbl Com:1225 et seqq

Walker N (1996) European constitutionalism and European integration. Public Law:266–290

Walker N (2004) Postnational constitutionalism and the problem of translation. In: Weiler JHH, Wind M (eds) European constitutionalism beyond the state. Cambridge University Press, Cambridge, p 27 et seqq

Weber A (2000) Die Europäische Grundrechtscharta – auf dem Weg zu einer Europäischen Verfassung. NJW:537 et seqq

Weber A (2002) Il futuro della Carta dei diritti fondamentali dell'Unione europea. Riv It Dir Pubbl Com:31 et seqq

Weiler JHH (1999) The constitution of Europe. Cambridge University Press, Cambridge

Wohlfahrt E, Everling U, Gläsner HJ, Sprung R (1960) Die Europäische Wirtschaftsgemeinschaft: Kommentar. Vahlen, Berlin-Frankfurt a.M

Ziccardi P (1953) La costituzione dell'ordinamento internazionale. Giuffrè, Milano

Ziller J (2003) La nuova Costituzione europea (translated by L. Segni), 2nd edn. Mulino, Bologna

The Union's Homogeneity and Its Common Values in the Treaty on European Union

Stelio Mangiameli

1 The Homogeneity Principle and Its Apparent Diversity of Content Within the Treaty on European Union and the Treaty of Lisbon

If you read Art. 6.1 of the Treaty on European Union (TEU)-Nice and Art. 2 of the same Treaty, as it results from the amendments introduced by the Treaty of Lisbon,[1] you will immediately realise that both provisions are different in their content and phraseology, beyond the context and their symbolic value. The first is built only with legal instruments and it is not that the beginning of the text recalls the "principles" as the basis of the Union.[2] On the contrary, the second provision leads one to think of the inclusion into the Constitution of a meta-legal content: in this sense the Union's basis makes reference to some "values".[3]

[1]For a deeper exam of the events that have led to the abandon of the Constitutional Treaty, see *La Costituzione europea*, in Mangiameli (2008), pp. 385 et seqq. However, it is necessary to specify that Art. 2 TEU-L recovers the contents of Art. I-2 TCE.

[2]Corollaries to the homogeneity principle are, on the one hand, the other paragraphs of Art. 6, and on the other hand, the provisions of Art. 7, Art. 46 lit. e and Art. 49 TEU, concerning the possibility to sanction a Member State when there is a clear risk of a serious breach of principles mentioned in Art. 6.1, the possibility to apply the purely procedural stipulations in Art. 7 before the Court, and, finally, the adhesion to the Union of new European States which respects the principles set out in Art. 6.1.

[3]Cf. Art. I-2 TCE. In the text of the Constitutional Treaty the same principles are present provided by paragraphs 2, 3 and 4 of Art. 6 and by connected provisions (Art. 46 and Art. 49) of TEU, but in a different context, i.e. with reference to the rights, see the Title II, and especially Art. I-7; in reference to the identity of the Member States, the principle is recognised within the rules governing the relationships between the Union and the Member States, see Art. I-5.1, but we must also add the provision that the Union "shall respect its rich cultural and linguistic diversity,

S. Mangiameli (✉)
ISSiRFA-CNR, Via dei Taurini 19, 00185 Rome, Italy
e-mail: stelio.mangiameli@cnr.it

H.-J. Blanke and S. Mangiameli (eds.), *The European Union after Lisbon*,
DOI 10.1007/978-3-642-19507-5_2, © Springer-Verlag Berlin Heidelberg 2012

However, this is a difference more apparent than real as behind every provision is hidden a choice of axiological type and a typical aspect of law that consists in just covering the juridical character of some elements belonging to the social reality, among which we can also find certain values.

On the other hand, while a regression from principles to values[4] is not possible, the inclusion of "values" into a legislative or constitutional act produces the effect to make them legal. So, once inserted in a legal text, these values become "principles" that can be interpreted and help create a system.[5]

The difference between both versions concerns another aspect. In the text of the TEU-Nice, the homogeneity principle is set out in a recognitive way; on the contrary, in the Lisbon Treaty – together with the aspects of recognition of previous experiences – are introduced new programmatic aspects aiming to regulate the Union's and the Member States' future behaviour.

In fact, the provision in question not only states that "[t]he Union is founded on the values of respect for human dignity, freedom, democracy, equality, the rule of law and respect for human rights, including the rights of persons belonging to minorities" – declaring that "these values are common to the Member States" – but it updates the homogeneity principle of the TEU, talking about a "a society in which pluralism, non-discrimination, tolerance, justice, solidarity and equality between

and shall ensure that Europe's cultural heritage is safeguarded and enhanced" (Art. I-3.3, last subparagraph); with regard to the financial autonomy, see Art. I-53.1 on the Union's own resources.

The sanctionatory system of the homogeneity clause (Art. I-59) is regulated in the context of Title IX, concerning the Union membership, together with the provision on the conditions of eligibility and on the procedure for accession to the Union (Art. I-58), while the specific competence of the Court of Justice was introduced in the group of the powers of this institution in Part III of the Constitution (Art. III-371). Moreover, we must consider that the characters of the homogeneity principles inserted in the text of the Constitution have a full regulation, sometimes expressed, similarly to the democratic principle that have founded its location in the Title VI of Part I, also absorbing in it the proximity principle (*Every citizen shall have the right to participate in the democratic life of the Union. Decisions shall be taken as openly and as closely as possible to the citizen*). In this context, the provision that "The functioning of the Union shall be founded on representative democracy" is rather significant, with the *direct* representation of citizens entrusted to the European Parliament and that of the States entrusted to the European Council, through the presence of the respective Heads of State or Government, or to the Council through the respective governments, "themselves democratically accountable either to their national Parliaments, or to their citizens" (Art. I-45). In other cases, the realisation of the characters of the homogeneity principle is gathered from the systematic interpretation, as in the case of the principle of the rule of law that receives force in the Union's order essentially from the provisions regulating the European justice [(see Constitution, Part III, Title VI, Chapter I, section 1, subsection 5, and, in particular, Art. III-365 (on the review of legality) and Art. III-369 (on the jurisdiction to give preliminary ruling)].

[4]This point is decisive for the legal interpretation, especially the constitutional one, as the techniques that allow a regression from the provisions (principles) to the values (see Alexy (1986), pp. 125 et seqq.), overruling the effects of the process of juridification, substitute the bind of the law with the will of the occasional decision maker.

[5]With this regard see D'Atena (2001), pp. 1 et seqq.

women and men prevail". So, it seems that TEU institutions and Member States' activities are oriented towards a certain direction.[6]

This second part of the provision can be properly considered a body of objectives to be reached jointly in the European order and in the Member States' orders. It could well be written also in Art. 3 TEU, which recalls – among the objectives that the treaty should ensure – the promotion of the Union's "values", both inside (paragraph 1) and outside (paragraph 5).

However, this dynamic part of the new homogeneity principle does not modify its structure and the typically legal character that it assumes in the European constitutional order, especially in the relationships between EU institutions and Member States. In fact, the objectives set out in the provision on the Union's "values" are a significant contribution in order to remove the internal differentiations that are considered not compatible with the whole system's structure.[7]

2 The Exclusively Legal Nature of Homogeneity and the Social-Economic Character of the Prerequisites

On the basis of this introduction, in which I would like to simply underline the continuity of the presence of a "principle of homogeneity" in the European constitutional order, with reference to the same principle we must face the questions about its capacity, character, meaning and function.

In this sense, the first question to be solved concerns the field of belonging of the homogeneity. In fact, it is controversial whether this could be considered a legal category or a general clause (*Ventilbegriffe*) that – in the area of the interpretation – opens to the evaluation of material and social conditions.[8] This matter – closely

[6]On the homogeneity principle see Ipsen (1990), pp. 159 et seqq.; Schorkopf (2000); Constantinesco (2001), pp. 299 et seqq.; Atripaldi and Miccù (2003). On the provisions concerning homogeneity in the EU Constitution Project see also Würmeling (2003), pp. 7 et seq., who underlines that "the values and aims reflect the Christian conception of mankind as well as the principle of democracy, the rule of law, and solidarity" (our translation); Pinelli (2004), pp. 33 et seqq.

[7]Something similar to what the Italian Constitution had provided in Art. 3(2), giving to the Republic the duty to remove the obstacles of economic or social nature.

[8]The author identifies homogeneity with these real and social elements in Schmitt (2008), p. 376, according to whom homogeneity of the members of the federation was given by "the *homogeneity of all federation members*, in particular on a substantial similarity that justifies a concrete, existential agreement of member states" and "[a]s with democratic homogeneity [...], substance in this context can also be part of different areas of human life", as there could exist "a national, religious, cultural, social, class, or another type of homogeneity". The author especially underlines the prevalence "in a national similarity of the population. Nevertheless, the similarity of the political principle (monarchy, aristocracy, or democracy) is still added to the homogeneity of the population as a further element of homogeneity". Also Smend (1968), pp. 119–276 (p. 223 et seqq. and pp. 268 et seqq.), who considers the federal state as an integration system in which "sich die Einzelstaaten als Gegenstand, aber vor allem auch als Mittel seiner gesamtstaalichen

related to the issue of the Union's and Member States' identity – always brings along the question of the order in which homogeneity (and identity) assumes significance: i.e. the *deontic* sphere (*Sollen*) or the *ontological* (existential) sphere (*Sein*). In fact, it is generally known how the compatibility of rules and legal acts, in which homogeneity flows, is possible – either in a unit state order or in a system characterised by different levels combining to set a composite order – only if the legal dimension is fostered by a plurality of pre- and meta-legal factors that allow the unambiguous comprehension and the uniform implementation of the rules.

The science of constitutional law knows that the existence of a charter prescribing democracy and fundamental rights is not enough in order to realise the first position in the decision-making process and to ensure the second in front of public authorities; similarly, in the case of complex orders, provisions recognising regional and local self-government are not enough in order to carry out a real devolution of functions brought about to take decisions "as openly as possible and as closely as possible to the citizen" (Art. 1.2 TEU). Indeed, both a social and economic reality and a spiritual dimension must always be present. They must coincide with the legal texts and be able to express the prerequisites of the order that allow a citizen to enjoy a certain level of effectiveness that is an essential condition of its being a "legal order".[9]

From this point of view, the expressions used in the preamble of the Treaty assume meaning, maybe even more sothe declarations of the preamble of the Charter, especially when this shall have the same legal value as the Treaties.[10]

The same "values" of the homogeneity principle resound in these expressions,[11] as also the reference to "the cultural, religious and humanist inheritance of Europe, from which have developed the universal values of the inviolable and inalienable rights of the human person, freedom, democracy, equality and the rule of law", highlighting the close link between reality and European inheritance.[12]

However, we cannot consider homogeneity in accordance with a sociological canon. The concept must not be confused with the typical elements of a social and economic homogeneity. The TEU establishes the values of homogeneity in European law, in accordance with a legal evaluation concerning both the Union and the Member States, both their organization and the exercise of the respective functions,

---

Integrationsaufgabe einordnet" (269), with the warning that "[s]taatliche Lebenswirklichkeit ist Integration, und als nächstliegenden Sinn der bundesstaatlichen Integration hat man zunächst stets mit einem gewissen Recht die dauernde Einordnung des Lebens der Einzelstaaten in das Ganze angesehen" (225), moves from the abandon of all purely legal theories of the federal State and states: "Hier handelt es sich um die Frage, wie dieser besondere Staatstypus mit seinen zwei politischen Polen, dem gesamtstaatlichen und dem einzelstaatlichen, als Wirklichkeit verständlich wird" (224).

[9]In this regard see Heller (1971), pp. 421 et seqq.

[10]See Art. 6.1, first sentence, TEU-L.

[11]In this regard the second recital of the Preamble is significant.

[12]Second recital of the Preamble of the TEU inserted with the Lisbon Treaty.

and not in order to make a real evaluation based on a correspondence between legal provision and social behaviours (as in the case of the general clauses).

Homogeneity is not a real product, linked to the actions and to the material behaviours of people living in a particular context, but it is a legal principle that gives to the central order and to the partial orders a certain way of being and makes them compatible within a general order.

Only by proceeding from a legal base of homogeneity is it possible to understand how the existential reality of some countries that are part of the enlargement – not yet in line with the principles that allow to define homogeneity – was not an obstacle to their admission in the Union; moreover, this perspective should explain the presence of a program part in the homogeneity principle, as the statement whereby "the Union shall have an institutional framework which shall aim to promote its values" (Art. 13.1 TEU).

3 Homogeneity and Constitution: Features of the Principle and Limitations to the Treaties Revision

The wording and the legal system of the homogeneity principle clearly demonstrate both its constitutional quality and its nature of fundamental principle in the Constitution. The expression used in both texts is always *The Union is founded...*, giving to the principles and to the values specified therein a different position compared with the other principles that may be possible to find in the text of the Constitution. This characteristic position comes from the fact that the elements of the homogeneity principle play a particular role in the field of the constitutional interpretation of EU law, acting in two directions: first of all, they become the hermeneutical canons to solve antinomies and to fill the gaps rising in the implementation of law; second, these elements mean for the European legislator the execution of a duty as he or she is obliged to regulate institutions and to adopt laws. Briefly, we can say that homogeneity is the body of principles that allows to identify the "identity"[13] or "the State form" of the Union, as they describe the essential principles concerning the relationships of the organisation with other elements of the order.[14] In this sense, "the values of

[13]The "identity" refers to the Preamble of the TEU which – in order to establish the common foreign and security policy, "including the progressive framing of a common defence policy, which might lead to a common defence" – states: "thereby reinforcing the European identity and its independence in order to promote peace, security and progress in Europe and in the world" [on the matter of identity of Europe see Chabod (2001); Mikkeli (2002); for a social approach of the European identity see Walkenhorst (1999); according to a more tightly constitutional point of view see Manzella (1999), pp. 923 et seqq.].

[14]Thereby, with regard to the four principles (democratic, personalistic, labouristic, pluralistic) of the Italian Constitution identified by Mortati (1975), pp. 148 et seqq.; the elements of the homogeneity principle – according to the language of the German doctrine – can be considered as the building principles of the constitution (*Bauprinzipien der Verfassung*) [see Merkl (1968),

respect for human dignity, freedom, democracy, equality, the rule of law and respect for human rights" are material regulations of the Constitution and have either institutional or organisational content or are able to create a material order. So they must be closely connected with the Union's objectives, with the internal decision-making process and, finally, with the distribution of the competences.

We must now evaluate two aspects: the first concerns the bond that homogeneity creates in the European constitutional law; the second refers to the relationship between the homogeneity principle and the matter of sovereignty.

The principle in question is expressed in a provision that is included in a Treaty of international law and not in a real constitutional text with bonds on the revision matter.[15] In fact, the Treaty does not provide the exclusion of the revision procedure for any provision or principle. We can say that limitations to the Treaties' revision do not exist formally.

However, beginning from the Maastricht Treaty, a similar perspective was not enough to explain the bind created by the Member States who decide to initiate a growing integration process. In fact, the European Treaties are significantly different from other types of international treaties as they regulate the relationships between states and constitute a supranational entity. This entity did have in the past a *functional* character as it was simply oriented to the institution of a common market. On the contrary, as the homogeneity principle shows, it has now gained a *structural* character and is characterised by the unlimited length of the same Treaty (Art. 53).[16]

Once the Union was created, the constitutive role of the Member States was complete. Now, the Union works on the provisions of the Treaties that must be implemented by the institutions and by the same Member States. But in this case their actions will be the expression of the competences recognised by the European Treaties and not the exercise of the powers of international law by the Member States. The same implementation of EU law is not submitted to the implementation of general rules of international law but to those belonging to the European order,[17] even in the case where decisions are taken by the Council by unanimity and not by a majority. This explains why the Member States – which have not lost their

pp. 77 et seqq.] or the structural principles of a state (*Strukturprinzipien eines Staates*) [see Stern (1984), pp. 551 et seqq.] that are *the constitutional framework of government* (552).

[15]See, e.g., the bind created to the constitutional revision by Art. 139 of the Italian Constitution, for the republican form; or Art. 79.III, GG, according to which "Amendments to this Basic Law affecting the division of the Federation into Länder, their participation on principle in the legislative process, or the principles laid down in Art. 1 and Art. 20 shall be inadmissible"; or Art. 89, last paragraph of the French Constitution that states: "The republican form of government shall not be the object of any amendment."

[16]It is important not to underestimate the meaning of the provision that states that "[t]his Treaty is concluded for an unlimited period" (Art. 53 TEU): this is an essential characteristic of the Union and it indicates the permanent character of the European order, different from any temporary legislation, and it gives to the Treaty – beyond the legal form of the treaty of international law – a constitutional importance and, more specifically, it configures an act of the constituent power.

[17]See Edward (2002), pp. 215 et seqq.

subjectivity of international law – cannot react against the European acts according to the principles of international law but only according to the conditions provided by the same Treaties.[18]

This circumstance has many consequences: let us consider, for example, the matter concerning the right of the Member States to withdraw from the Union. The matter has been debated for a long time and should now be solved in accordance with Art. 50 TEU. The doctrine had highlighted that – in the case of European Treaties – Member States did not have a real right to withdraw in accordance with the general rules of international law, as this mode of action could mean a violation of the obligations specifically made. The same Art. 50 states that withdrawal is not given through a unilateral act but on the basis of an agreement negotiated between the Union and the Member State concerned. This agreement sets out "the arrangements for its withdrawal, taking account of the framework for its future relationship with the Union".[19] Moreover, the Treaties shall cease to apply to the state in question, not with the notification of its intention to withdraw but from the date of entry into force of the withdrawal agreement or, failing that, 2 years after the notification of the intention to withdraw, unless the European Council, in agreement with the Member State concerned, unanimously decides to extend this period.[20]

---

[18]See, in this regard, Art. III-375.2 and Art. 3.

[19]A provision on the withdrawal of the Member States is quite rare in the federal constitutions (an example, however devoid of meaning, is given by the USSR constitution in which the clause did not have any value due to the lack of implementation legislation), but it seems that the provision of the TCE has in the background the Canadian event of the Quebec secession following the referendum of 30 October 1995, the opinion of the Supreme Court of 20 August 1998 and the federal legislation (*Clarity Act*) and provincial legislation (*Quebec Act*) of 2000. In particular, the opinion of the Supreme Court (*Renvoi Relatif à la Sécession du Quebec* [1998] 2 R.C.S., 217–297) had highlighted that a possible unilateral secession act should be unjustified from a constitutional point of view, even if founded on a referendary success, as the democratic principle did not represent the only bastion of the Canadian system and the unilateral act would have represented a breach of other principles that are equally important, "namely, the rule of law, federalism and minority rights"; similarly it should be unacceptable from the point of view of international law, as, apart from the existence in the international context of a "Quebec people", the principle of peoples' self-determination can be invoked only in the presence of a "people suffering oppressive colonial subjugation", a condition – according to the Court – "manifestly inapplicable in Quebec under existing circumstances". However, the Court states that, in the case in which the will of secession of the province was expressed with a referendum, the other members of the federation would have negotiated with Quebec and this duty should be located among the principles of the Canadian constitution [see Dawson (1999–2000), pp. 5 et seqq.; Newman (2001–2002), pp. 117 et seqq.; Russell (2004), pp. 228 et seqq.]. Apart from the fact that the Court did not lead its interpretation to the extremes, so that the opinion leaves unsolved a complicated set of constitutional problems, we must highlight the fact that, in the systems with a federative structure, the matter of withdrawal of a Member State is considered, not as an act of unilateral force, but a form of revision of the federal Constitution. This appears to be the assumption that is codified by Art. I-60 TCE.

[20]This provision has relevant characteristics for the interpretation of the European Constitution and for the definition of both the Union's position and that of the Member States, directly connected to the above-mentioned provision on the unlimited period of the Union. In fact, if it has, for express declaration, permanent character, with their accession the Member States put

In this context, the configuration of the relationships between the Union and the Member States shall produce effects comparable with the provisions of the TEU. In particular, if the Member States can act only within the legal framework of EU law, the same could be considered the basis and the content of their participation. According to this view, the same revision power of the Treaties gains a different value from the negotiation and the stipulation of a simple international agreement. In fact, the ordinary revision procedure referred to in Art. 48 is only the instrument to adjust in time the content of the Treaties and is binding on the legislation in force.

From this point of view, we can finally state that the enunciation of the homogeneity principle, showing the typical elements of the Union form, presents a certain level of rigidity as it commits itself to the relationships between the Union and the Member States even during the Treaties revision. In fact, the modification of the principles expressing homogeneity could affect the same Union identity and could cause a real constitutional breakdown.

4 The Homogeneity and the Matter on Sovereignty: A Clear Distinction Between the Two Problems

The matter concerning sovereignty is not directly connected to the homogeneity principle.[21] Those who maintain the contrary move from the premise that homogeneity – which is intended to be a national affinity of people or affinity of the political principle: the democracy – prevents from making uncontainable in the federation the antinomy caused by the "general existence of the federation and the single existence of the members of the federation"; so, thanks to homogeneity, the so-called "dualism of political existence" coming from the plot between federal cohesion and political unity, in the presence of a multiplicity of states, can live with a balance that allows the federation to continue to exist.[22] According to Carl Schmitt, until a federation exists close to the Member States, it is typical of the essence of the federation that the matter on sovereignty is always open between the federation and the same Member States; in fact, neither the federation nor the Member State plays a sovereign role against the other.[23]

themselves in the context of a constitutional law that does not provide any right to unilateral withdrawal; and the statement that the Union is still the result of an agreement between the States involved in the European order means that they keep their effective political effectiveness, which also includes the possibility for the Member States to decide on their participation and permanence in the Union.

[21]Differently Schmitt (2008) (fn. 8), pp. 370 et seqq. (378 et seq).

[22]See Schmitt (2008) (fn. 8), p. 373.

[23]Schmitt (2008) (fn. 8), pp. 373 and 379. We must observe that the meaning in which *Schmitt* uses the term "federation" surpasses the idea of the distinction between Confederation of States and federal State (see p. 477) and, with this regard, the teaching is very significant, as it allows to give a

On this basis, the more reliable position in order to explain the evolution of the European order would be the theory according to which it is possible to renounce to answer the matter on sovereignty, which is unquestionable in the context of Communitarisation *(Vergemeinschaftung)*.[24] But this is not the session to examine the ways in which the sovereign powers are shared between the EU and the Member States.

With the signing of the Lisbon Treaty, the study on this matter, in order to clarify the legal nature of the Union and of its order, shall raise a very interesting debate, as the ways in which the same intergovernmental policies play were modified compared with the previous wording of the Treaties (Maastricht, Amsterdam, Nice).

Moreover, we must consider that the matter on sovereignty cannot be explained in the presence of the homogeneity principle, which is a different concept compared with the "homogeneity" that justifies the existence of sovereignty limitations for the Member States coming from the European integration process. In fact, the homogeneity principle does not confine itself to verifying the affinities existing between the different areas of the Union but has a normative content, imposing either on the Union or on the Member States to characterise their respective orders according to certain elements, expressed in a positive way by the same principle.

So, homogeneity is not an essential requirement (existential) that leaves open the matter on sovereignty, but is an aspect of the way of being of the European order. It is a legal product of the European law, acting positively and requiring a continuous activity of implementation by EU institutions and by the Member States.

From this point of view, the ability of the homogeneity principle to bind the Member States comes from the European order and lies on the same basis, i.e. on the commitment taken by the signing of the Treaties and on the consequent submission to the EU law and to the jurisdiction of the European Court of Justice (ECJ).

5 Homogeneity as Submission to the Same Order Whose Principles Are Shared by Partial Orders: The Dangers Coming from the Unification and the Member States' Identity

The constitutional provision laying down the homogeneity principle, after listing the fundamental values of the Union, states that "these values are common to the Member States".[25]

---

right location also to the expression "association of sovereign national states" *(Staatenverbund)*, used by the German Federal Constitutional Court in the *Maastricht* case (German Federal Constitutional Court, 2 BvR 2134, 2159/92 (12 October 1993) paragraph 90 (in: BVerfGE 89, 155 [181]).

[24] Ipsen, *Europäisches Gemeinschaftsrecht*, cited, pp. 227 et seqq., that continues that this would be a contribution of the Community law to critique on sovereignty (p. 233).

[25] "in a society in which pluralism, non-discrimination, tolerance, justice, solidarity and equality between women and men prevail".

The interpretation of this provision is quite complicated. The expression is also in Art. 6.1 TEU ("principles which are common to the Member States") and comes historically from the codification of the objectives reached by the European order thanks to the jurisprudence of the ECJ. Moreover, in the actual system of the TEU, the provision has recognised the legal elements of the constitutional orders of the Member States so that it includes only a horizontal homogeneity.

On the contrary, in the provision of the Lisbon Treaty the literal interpretation is different. In fact, the provision not only embodies the common elements of the Member States but prescribes them (so-called vertical homogeneity) in the sense that the constitutions of the partial orders must ensure *respect for human dignity, freedom, democracy, equality, the rule of law and respect for human rights, including the rights of persons belonging to minorities.*

We are probably in the presence of a federal trend that gives a public nature to the relationships between the Union and the Member States, allowing the former to supervise the orders of the Member States.[26] In this sense, EU law becomes the general order in which the partial orders can move and interact, when their comparison should be given by the elements composing the homogeneity principle. But the system can lead to new evolutions thanks to the contribution of the homogeneity principle. It is known that "homogeneity" is different from *uniformity*, and that the specific element of a general order built on more levels is given by the ability to make a multiplicity live within a single context ("united in diversity").

However, in a certain way, the homogenisation processes are processes of unification that threaten the federal substance, so that some decisions are taken at the EU level and others at the Member State level. Indeed, the dynamic, not static, nature of the homogeneity principle is clear; it requires daily actions in conformity with the elements that the EU has put as the basis of its definition. This situation can raise a conflict between the multiplicity and the body of the Member States, on one side, and the unit to which the elements of homogeneity would refer on the other. In particular, if in the case of rights and protections, the science of constitutional law has found for some time a possibility of regulation in the combination of powers with the implementation of the most extended protection principle, it is not so with reference to other elements. In fact, in the case of "democracy", there is a competition with the "federal principle", so that the latest one should give in.

It is not a new matter. *Carl Schmitt* already highlighted that "both democracy or federation are founded on the essential requirement of an homogeneity" and "if a federation of democratic states rises, the necessary consequence is that the democratic homogeneity meets with the federal homogeneity", but in this fact he realises the danger of arriving at "a particular and autonomous type of state organisation": *the federal State without a federative basis.*[27] The statement that "with the

---

[26]On this point see the following paragraph.

[27]Schmitt (2008) (fn. 8), p. 388, this expression, to which *Schmitt* reconnected the United States of America and the German *Reich* of the *Weimar* Constitution, excluding that it was a federation, means a new form of state in which are recovered elements of a previous federal organisation, but

democratic concept of the constituent power of the whole people the federative basis is abrogated and with this the same federal nature"[28] should come from the circumstance of the development of the democratic decision-making process – represented by a single people within a gradually homogeneous system – leads to consider as irrelevant the *place* in which the same decision is taken.

The reason for this particular unifying evolution, coming from the mix between the democratic principle and the federal one, has been proved for a long time by the history of the federal states[29] and the same European experience is already showing its signs. In the federal States, as the democracy increased, the autonomy of the Member States decreased.[30] The clearest sign of this process, but not the only one, was the concentration of the competences in favour of the federations that has led to an impoverishment of the local legislations.[31] In Europe the strong increase of the Community competences and the intrusiveness of the powers of the European institutions were seen as a threat for the political autonomy of the Member States. However, the statement of the democratic deficit of Europe, for a long time denounced, could not reveal a good argument in order to justify the prerogatives of the Member States.[32] So, with the Maastricht Treaty, just before the wording of the homogeneity principle, the matter concerned a different aspect: i.e. the respect of the national identity of the Member States.[33]

Afterwards, in the frame of the homogeneity principle, a comparison took place between the European identity and those of the Member States, with continuous postponements, on the matter of sovereignty.[34] In this context the circumstance that the principles (and the values) of homogeneity correspond, either for the European identity or for those of the Member States, was not important, as their identity was called to play quite a different role compared with the homogeneity principle. In

---

indeed it should be a unitary state, with only people and with the abolition of the state character of the Member States, in which the matter of sovereignty is solved in the only sovereignty of the central State (p. 508).

[28]Schmitt (2008) (fn. 8), p. 389.

[29]With this regard the analysis carried out by Hesse (1962) is emblematic.

[30]See Dahl (2003).

[31]In the German case, this process is just compensated with the participation of *Länder* to the federal legislative procedure, through the *Bundesrat*.

[32]On this point see Kaufmann (1997).

[33]See Art. F, paragraph 1: "The Union shall respect the national identities of its Member States, whose systems of government are founded on the principles of democracy." The version that this principle assumes in the wording of *Amsterdam*, with the introduction of the homogeneity principle (Art. 6.1) is appreciably different, as the democratic element is inserted in the homogeneity and Art. 6.3 TEU-A limits itself to state that "[t]he Union shall respect the national identities of its Member States".

[34]The matter of identity was especially raised by the Federal Republic of Germany, with reference to the incidence that the integration process exercised on the internal federalism, with the progressive loss of "statuality" by *Länder*.

fact, notwithstanding that the identity of the Member States is founded on the same elements of the Union identity; the first aims to define the action of the second.

The matter is clearer in the wording of the identity principle in the Lisbon Treaty, precisely in the part where the relationships between the Union and the Member States are regulated (Art. 4.2 TEU). In fact, here it is stated that *the Union shall respect the equality of Member States before the Treaties as well as their national identities, inherent in their fundamental structures, political and constitutional, inclusive of regional and local self-government; it shall respect their essential State functions, including ensuring the territorial integrity of the State, maintaining law and order and safeguarding national security. In particular, national security remains the sole responsibility of each Member State.*

Together with the principle of federal equality, according to which any Member State can have a different position, except for the cases provided by the EU law, it is clear that the reference to the "national identity" is not of a material or sociological nature, i.e. it is not a reference to the culture, language or religion but it has a strong legal value.[35] This explanation is based on two different aspects.

First, the diversity of culture, language or religion is specifically protected in the Treaties. In fact, they state the development of the elements of national diversification.[36] In the TFEU, culture is a competence of the Member States; in its sphere the Union can only decide to carry out a support, coordination and complement action and in this form the flowering of "the national and regional diversity" is already present.[37]

Second, in favour of a legal meaning of the identity principle the same provision of the Treaty is placed that recalls it, as it refers to the *fundamental structure, political and constitutional, inclusive of regional and local self-government*, and specifies the "respect of the essential State function". This perspective was already included in the preamble of the Charter of Fundamental Rights where the common values are protected and developed "while respecting the diversity of the cultures and traditions of the peoples of Europe as well as the national identities of the Member States and the organisation of their public authorities at national".[38]

The identity stated in Art. 4 TEU is the identity of the Member States as an *institution*, i.e. their state form. If we look at the wording used in the Treaty we can clearly understand that protection of identity does not concern the existence of the Member States but more properly the organising elements of their legislative,

---

[35]For the concept of *Nation* referring to its constitutive elements of material type and to its interferences with the *State* and with the *people*, see Crisafulli and Nocilla (1977); see also Hobsbawm (1991); Gelner (1992); Wehler (2002); Grilli di Cortona (2003).

[36]See, Art. 3.3 last sentence, TEU and Art. 22 EUCFR.

[37]See Art. 167.1, Art. 4 and Art. 5.

[38]See EUCFR, preamble, third recital.

administrative and judicial autonomy; however, identity must not be confused with the body of the state competences.[39]

The theory that considers identity as an *integrated* expression of the state form is more acceptable, even by the light of the European process[40]; it allows the problems arising from the issue of the European sovereignty to be overcome. However, the point of arrival of this perspective is not shareable. Admitting that the duty of the respect of identity can become a simple consideration (of identity) – but not in its intangibility – means to allow the Union to gradually draw on the identity of the Member States, through the exercise of its competences.

Indeed, if the state identity is given by the elements characterising its state form, the respect of identity by the Union implies its obligation to leave the choices concerning their way of being to the full willingness of the Member States. This explains the reference, in the new wording of the Treaty, to the *fundamental structure, political and constitutional, inclusive of regional and local self-government* that concerns – of course – the same elements considered by the homogeneity principle.

Once defined, the identity principle is completed by the duty of the Union to respect the "essential State functions, including ensuring the territorial integrity of the State, maintaining law and order and safeguarding national security". In particular, we must give to this further duty a substantial and dynamical meaning, as it aims to assure the vitality of the Member States' identity. All the provisions included in the text of the Treaties that optimise the contributions given by the bodies of the Member States[41] and even by their citizens[42,43] refer to this value.

---

[39]In this regard, see the statement included in the *Maastricht* case (German Federal Constitutional Court, 2 BvR 2134, 2159/92 (12 October 1993) paragraph 161 et seq. (in: BVerfGE 89, 155 [211–212]: "The principle of subsidiarity [. . .] is intended to protect the national identity of the Member States and to preserve their powers" and the proportionality principle "may also serve to limit [. . .] the intensity of Community measures within the meaning of Art. F, paragraph 1, of the Maastricht Treaty, and thereby protect the national identity of the Member States and the responsibilities and powers of their parliaments against excessive European regulation" (translation S.M.).

[40]Hilf (1995), pp. 157 et seqq.

[41]The provision on the respect of the essential state functions must be correlated to the participation of the national parliaments, especially in the matter of security policy and justice, see Art. 12 TEU; above all the other provisions that exist in matter of competences, as Art. 5.3, second sentence TEU and Art. 352.2 TFEU; finally, we must point out the participation of the national parliaments in some procedures, as in the case of new applications for accession to the Union (Art. 49 TEU) and of the revision procedures of the treaties (Art. 48 TEU).

[42]In this context, the new wording of the proximity principle introduced in the article on the principle of the representative democracy cannot be forgotten (Art. 10.3 TEU, "Every citizen shall have the right to participate in the democratic life of the Union. Decisions shall be taken as openly and as closely as possible to the citizen").

[43]In matter of rights, in this context, the common constitutional traditions also deserve a particular mention. For them, beyond the maintenance of the present version of Art. 6.3 TEU-L: "Fundamental rights, as guaranteed by the European Convention for the Protection of Human Rights and Fundamental Freedoms and as they result from the constitutional traditions common to the Member States, shall constitute general principles of the Union's law", Art. 52 EUCFR

6 Homogeneity and Complex Order: European Constitution and Constitution of the Member States

A body of relationships comes from the homogeneity principle, between the Union and the Member States, their respective identities, their organisations, their functions and their actions. Homogeneity requires that the Union and the Member States organise their own legal form of being. The act determining this consequence is the *constitution*. In the light of the consideration we must now evaluate the range and the function, for the Member States, of the homogeneity principle provided by the TEU.

From this point of view, the situation must first be observed as such an issue cannot be put forward: the Treaties are not a constitution, the same Union presents a problematic profile, the European Community did still feel the effects of its origin as an aiming association. Moreover, it was stated that the Union is not and must not become a state; a European people capable of leading a constitution do not exist; one cannot imagine a constitution without a state. In other words, the formal possibility was denied on the one hand and the substantial capacity of the Union to act in a constitutional way on the other.

But even apart from the text of a formal constitution and from the preclusion for a recognition of constitutional value to the Treaties, we must go over the issue concerning the existence or not of a Constitution for the EU, as its presence should come from the nature of the order that the Union holds compared with the Member States and the citizens. The debate raised by the doctrine on the constitutional capacity of the Union cannot be considered more appropriate when we look at the recent development characterised by the Lisbon Treaty that highlights some historical matters on common foreign and security policies and defence policy differently.

So, in such a framework, homogeneity cannot any more be considered a simple summary of the structure principles common to the Member States and gathered from their constitutions, but only as an element of European order. In fact, homogeneity assumes a vertical character: it not only summarises but also prescribes the necessity to affirm the characterising elements, in accordance with the provision of the Treaty.

This point of arrival implies some consequences on the function of the homogeneity principle. First, if it is prescriptive of a certain content, this principle is also a source of guarantee as it requires that the Member State – and not the Union – must assure the "respect for human dignity, freedom, democracy, equality, the rule of law and respect for human rights". In this sense, homogeneity indicates a reserved

concerning *Scope and interpretation of rights and principles*, provides that "In so far as this Charter recognises fundamental rights as they result from the constitutional traditions common to the Member States, those rights shall be interpreted in harmony with those traditions" (paragraph 4) and that "Full account shall be taken of national laws and practices as specified in this Charter" (paragraph 6).

sphere, inviolable by the European order, in which the behaviour of the Member State is prescribed and consists in acquiring the structure principles and in developing them consistently in the order and in the general rule of life of the state.

Here, obviously, beyond the relationship between the European order and that of the Member State, the relationship between the European Constitution and the constitution of the Member States, who together realise a "constitutional bipolar order", is immediately discussed.[44] Homogeneity, assuring the effective possibility of an autonomous order of the Member States, represents the centre of this bipolarity and it is able to give a sense to the whole European system, contributing to its stabilisation from a constitutional point of view.[45]

If we look at the content of this guarantee for the constitutions of the Member States, we can state that it turns into the freedom to organise the state, i.e. the *fundamental structure, political and constitutional, inclusive of regional and local self-government*, in accordance with Art. 4.2 TEU. In other words, any Member State, through its own constitution, builds its own democracy and its own rule of law and does not follow a predetermined type of democracy and rule of law.

Moreover, it is possible to give the same speech with the programmatic part that is written in every constitution, concerning the future developments of the state functions. To these regulations of the constitutions of the Member States was linked the success of the Welfare State in Western Europe, in contrast to the systems of a planned economy. To these regulations the social specificity of every Member State is linked, either of those that were already in the EU or of those that have just joined it or shall come in. In this context, compared with the availability reserved for the Member States, the homogeneity principle places itself as an "instrument of protection of the highest purposes of Union",[46] which are indicated "in a society in which pluralism, non-discrimination, tolerance, justice, solidarity and equality between women and men prevail" and in the objectives set out in Art. 3 TEU.[47]

---

[44]Scharpf (1994), pp. 94 et seqq., according to whom "a European Union cannot develop according to the scheme of a nation-state – not even a federal one. If it wants to survive it has to respect and protect the vitality and autonomy of its constitutive components in their institutional and cultural diversity in a way that is even more intense as it usually is in federal states" (our translation).

[45]In this regard see Pernice (2001), pp. 148 et seqq., in particular pp. 184 et seqq.

[46]So Tripel (1917), pp. 441 and 444, but see also his *incipit* at p. 1 ("the distribution of material and formal competences among the two institutions [*Bundesstaat* and *Bundesglieder*], appointed to joint effort for the purpose of the state constitutes the most elegant part of the 'master plan' that rules the relationship between Federal State and its Member States"; our translation).

[47]Sorrentino (1999), II, pp. 1635 et seqq., dreads a danger for the principles of the social State characterizing the Italian Constitution, where the European order provides for the principle of a market economy. However, we must underline that in reality it is about a tension that can be solved without a *transformation* "of the social utility in the freedom of competition", as there is "a problem of balance between different values", to which the different ways for their realisation that are indicated by EU law are not extraneous (1653–1655).

However, the most important aspect concerns the relationships between the Union and its citizens that are *pro parte qua* the citizens of the Member States, too. In fact, through the homogeneity, the principle of the double level of protection of fundamental rights is accepted in the European system. In this respect, as well as with reference to the respect for human dignity, freedom, democracy, equality, the rule of law and to the respect for human rights, considered as elements of the principle, we must recall Art. 6 TEU which states that the "Union recognises the rights, freedoms and principles set out in the Charter of Fundamental Rights of the European Union of 7 December 2000, as adapted at Strasbourg, on 12 December 2007, which shall have the same legal value as the Treaties" (paragraph 1). This article prescribes the accession to the European Convention on Human Rights (ECHR) (paragraph 2) and recalls the provision, already in force in the Treaty, on fundamental rights, as they result from the constitutional traditions common to the Member States (paragraph 3).[48]

From this point of view, the same meaning given to this last provision seems to be different compared with the one that the ECJ had given in its jurisprudence, as the reference to the common constitutional traditions no more plays a role of temporary post compared with the gaps of EU law, but – even in the light of the interpretative canon of rights *in harmony with those traditions* (Art. 52.4 EUCFR) – a role of balance, also towards the principle of primacy of European law (in accordance with the Declaration No. 17[49]), on the basis of the competition of the (Union and Member States') protection systems and of the widest guarantee rule.[50]

[48]That "shall constitute general principles of the Union's law", as those guaranteed by the ECHR.

[49]The Note of the Secretary General of the Council to Delegations titled "IGC 2007 Mandate" council of the European Union, 26 June 2007, n. 11218/07 has provided that "Concerning the primacy of EU law, the IGC will adopt a Declaration recalling the existing case law of the EU Court of Justice" (the n. 17: "The conference recalls that, in accordance with well settled case-law of the EU Court of Justice, the Treaties and the law adopted by the Union on the basis of the Treaties have primacy over the law of Member States, under the conditions laid down by the said case-law." In addition, the conference has decided to annex to the Final Act the opinion of the Legal Service of the Council on the primacy, dated 22 June 2007 (document 11197/07 – JUR 260): "It results from the case-law of the Court of Justice that primacy of EU law is a cornerstone principle of Community law. According to the Court, this principle is inherent to the specific nature of the European Community. At the time of the first judgment of this established case-law (Costa/ENEL, 15 July 1964, Case 6/641) there was no mention of primacy in the treaty. It is still the case today. *The fact that the principle of primacy will not be included in the future treaty shall not in any way change the existence of the principle and the existing case-law of the Court of Justice*" (our italics).

[50]On this basis we can state that the need of a check of the European order, in the name of the fundamental rights, that the Italian Constitutional Court and the German Federal Constitutional Court reserved to their jurisdiction, has also been peacefully surpassed.

7 The Breach of the Homogeneity Principle

The Union states that "any European State which respects the values referred to in Art. 2 and is committed to promoting them may apply to become a member of the Union" (Art. 49 TEU): so, respect of the values is the condition for admission to the Union.[51] But, what would happen if a Member State does not respect the values referred to in Art. 2 of the Treaty?[52]

The matter directly concerns the effectiveness of the homogeneity principle in the European constitutional order and the powers that the Union can use towards the Member States, that are obviously powers of interference in their affairs and that are justified by the task of the Union to protect their own order and so to act for the preservation, protection and security of the same Union.[53]

The introduction of the homogeneity principle (in the Amsterdam Treaty) historically also brought the prevision of a sanctionatory procedure, according to which the Council, in a meeting composed of the Heads of State or Government, acting in unanimity, must determine "the existence of a serious and persistent breach by a Member State of principles mentioned in Article 6.1". One third of the Member States or the Commission would have presented the proposal of deliberation, with which the proceeding begins, and this one would have been discussed and deliberated "after inviting the government of the Member State in question to submit its observations" (Art. 7.1 TEU-Amsterdam).[54] After the determination phase, the Council, acting by a qualified majority, could decide to suspend certain rights deriving from the application of the Treaty, "including the voting rights of the representative of the government of that Member State in the Council" (Art. 7.2 TEU-Amsterdam). Obviously, the Council, always acting by a qualified majority, will be able to decide subsequently to vary or revoke measures taken "in response to changes in the situation which led to their being imposed" (Art. 7.3 TEU-Amsterdam). The obligations of the sanctioned Member State under the Treaty would have to "in any case continue to be binding on that State".

---

[51]On the accession procedure, see Art. 49 TEU.

[52]Another question concerns the way to intend the missed respect of values, whether in a purely formal sense (i.e. with the adoption of legislative acts modifying the Member State's order, making it more homogeneous to EU law) or in a substantial sense (as change of the institutional life of the Member State, which, beyond the legislative modifications of the same order, evolves in a different way compared to the characters of the homogeneity principle). The answer seems to go in the second direction, as the homogeneity principle is closely linked to the *constitutional reality* of a state.

[53]Cf. Schmitt (2008) (fn. 8), p. 378, who states also that "[i]nterventions of the federation in the affairs of its members are not a foreign interference, and they are politically and legally possible and bearable because the federation rests on an existentially substantial similarity of the members".

[54]According to Art. 7.5 TEU-A the decision of the European Parliament would have had to be "by a two-thirds majority of the votes cast. Representing a majority of its members."

This procedural framework, constitutive of a European "federal coercion" form (*Bundeszwang*), passed through a crisis in consequence of the Austrian event in 2000, leading the 14 Member States of the Union to adopt a position different from the one provided by Art. 7 TEU to a legally (and politically) unjustified isolation of Austria.[55]

On this basis, the Nice Treaty (2001) introduced in the beginning of Art. 7 TEU a new paragraph, ruling the case to determine – before initiating the determination procedure concerning the existence of a breach of the homogeneity principle – that there is *a clear risk of a serious breach by a Member State of principles mentioned in Article 6.1, and address appropriate recommendations to that State*. Even in this phase, the obligation to hear the Member State in question is provided and the possibility – Austria *docet* – "to call on independent persons to submit within a reasonable time limit a report on the situation in the Member State in question".[56]

Second, an addition to Art. 46 TEU was introduced. According to the letter (e), the ECJ was given the jurisdiction for "the purely procedural stipulations in Article 7, with the Court acting at the request of the Member State concerned within one month from the date of the determination by the Council provided for in that Article".

In this manner, we can state that we have passed from a prevision of "federal coercion" (*Bundeszwang*) to a prevision of federal execution (*Bundesexekution*).[57] The Lisbon Treaty has revised this *federal execution* model, providing three different phases in which the following competences are exercised in order to: (a) *determine* that there is *a clear risk* of a serious breach by a Member State of the values referred to in Art. 2 (competence of the Council)[58]; (b) *determine* the existence *of a serious and persistent breach* by a Member State of the values referred to in Art. 2 (competence of the European Council)[59]; (c) decide to suspend certain of the rights deriving from the application of the Treaties to the Member State in question, including the voting rights of the representative of the government of that Member State in the Council (competence of the Council).[60]

---

[55]V. *Rapporto sullo stato della democrazia in Austria*, Italian translation, in Atripaldi and Miccù (2003), pp. 209–210.

[56]It is also provided that "[t]he Council shall regularly verify that the grounds on which such a determination was made continue to apply" (Art. 7.1 (2) TEU).

[57]For a close examination of the categories cited see Kelsen (1927), pp. 127–187.

[58]See Art. 7.1 TEU, which recognises a proposal power to one third of the Member States, to the European Parliament or to the European Commission. The Council acts by a majority of four fifths of its members after obtaining the consent of the European Parliament.

[59]See Art. 7.2 TEU, which recognises a proposal power to one third of the Member States or to the Commission. The European Council acts by unanimity after obtaining the consent of the European Parliament.

[60]See Art. 7.3 TEU, where on the basis of the determination under paragraph 2, the Council, acting by a qualified majority, may decide to suspend certain rights: "The Council shall take into account the possible consequences of such a suspension on the rights and obligations of natural and legal persons."

This provision of Art. 7 TEU provides that in the course of procedures the Member State in question must always be heard[61] and gives the Council the task to regularly verify the situation that was created in the relationships between the Union and the same Member State.[62]

The whole procedure does not free the Member State from obligations under the Treaty[63] and it allows the Member State to apply to the ECJ, which "shall have jurisdiction to decide on the legality of an act adopted by the European Council or by the Council pursuant to Article 7". In this event, the object of the case should be the "determination of the European Council or of the Council" and the criteria should refer to the "respect solely of the procedural stipulations contained in that Article" (Art. 269 TFEU).[64]

We can now conclude that – even with reference to the sanction coming from the breach of the homogeneity principle – in the European order a trend to the federalisation is increasing. In fact, this trend is brought out in the preservation of the point of arrival of the Nice Treaty, which had transformed the provision of Art. 7 TEU from an expression of the *Bundeszwang* to an expression of the *Bundesexekution*, not only for the statement that "the obligations of the Member State in question under this Treaty shall in any case continue to be binding on that State" (paragraph 3 (2)), but especially for introducing a judicial procedure of control on the action of the European Council. This last prevision is absolutely necessary in order to consider the whole institution within the federal execution and not to represent a coercion form towards the Member State in question.[65]

[61]See Art. 7.1: "Before making such a determination, the Council shall hear the Member State in question and may address recommendations to it, acting in accordance with the same procedure"; and Art. 7.2: "after inviting the Member State in question to submit its observations."

[62]See Art. 7.1: "The Council shall regularly verify that the grounds on which such a determination was made continue to apply"; and Art. 7.4: "The Council, acting by a qualified majority, may decide subsequently to vary or revoke measures taken under paragraph 3 in response to changes in the situation which led to their being imposed".

[63]Naturally, the Member State in question cannot take part in the decision on the breach of the homogeneity principle as well as the suspension of its rights and will thus "not be counted in the calculation of the one third or four fifths of Member States" referred to in Art. 7.1 and 2 TEU-L (Art. 354 TFEU).

[64]"Such a request must be made within one month from the date of such determination. The Court shall rule within one month from the date of the request."

[65]Cf. Kelsen (1927) (fn. 57), pp. 160 et seqq.; ID., (1923), pp. 173 et seqq.

8 Homogeneity and the Primacy of the European Law

Homogeneity aims to regulate the relationships between the Union and the Member States. First of all, between the European Treaties and the constitutions of the Member States, it expresses *supremacy* of the European constitutional order over those of the Member States. The concept of "supremacy" is used in the relationships within complex orders, which involves more constitutional and legislative level work, as it is not an expression of a hierarchisation of the relationships between the Union and the Member States but a further strengthening of the supranational bond as an obligation to respect EU law. So, the issue of *supremacy* becomes a relationship between orders regulated by law, which means it also directly concerns the sources of European law and the legal sources of the Member States: Treaties and European legislative sources, on the one hand, and constitutions and state laws, on the other.

In this context the homogeneity principle expresses a part of the European supremacy but is not exhaustive. In fact, together with the homogeneity, the principle of primacy of European law, whose wording is due to the jurisprudence of the ECJ, beginning from the *Costa/ENEL* case,[66] stands in a complementary way.

As the primacy of European law does not involve the cancellation of the Member State's order and its sources, we can state that this principle simply represents a rule aiming to assure a wider homogeneity of the orders in the framework of the European orders. It should work only in the case of conflicts between European and State rules in order to solve the antinomies.

This circumstance shows that many links exist between the homogeneity principle and the principle of primacy. We can clarify that the relationships that fix both principles are different from those coming from the distribution of the competences expressly regulated by the TFEU.

Now, if the provision on the homogeneity prescribes the structure principles that must be observed by the Member States' orders in order that the whole European system (Union and Member States) is able to realise the Union objectives (provided by Art. 3), and if the principle of primacy prescribes that EU law prevails over the Member States' law, it should conclude that the (constitutional) autonomy, assured by the homogeneity principle to the Member States, in the definition of their "form", in any case must not lead to legal rules (constitutional or legislative) that

[66]The principle was expressed in Art. I-6 TCE, according to which "*The Constitution and law adopted by the institutions of the Union in exercising competences conferred on it shall have primacy over the law of the Member States*". In the Lisbon Treaty Art. I-6 TCE is not formally recovered, but the substance of this article lies in the *Declaration n. 17 on the primacy*, not directly annexed to the treaty but to the IGC Final Act O.J.C 306/02 (2008). This does not diminish at all the strength of the principle that is established in the case law and is considered one of the fundamental cornerstones of the European order.

can be an obstacle to the implementation of the rules belonging to the European order.[67]

Moreover, the principle of primacy implies that not only do the Treaties' provisions prevail on the Member States' law but also on *the law adopted by the Union institutions in the exercise of the competences*; this means that Member States have a further obligation, i.e. not to prevent the implementation of European law with regulations, also constitutional, of the internal order.[68] The only condition for this second obligation is that the European normative act complies with the rules of competence provided by the treaties.

In the light of the aforementioned considerations, the core of the principle of primacy seems to lie in the following aspect: the principle establishes the direct effectiveness and validity of the European law in the field of action of the Member States, without the necessity of an implementation act, in a binding manner for the Member States' authorities, judges and administrations.

We could observe that such a principle has already existed for a long time in EU law, thanks to the jurisprudence of the ECJ,[69] and that Declaration No. 17 annexed to the final declaration of the Lisbon Treaty does not introduce anything new, as the primacy of the European law should lie on the same basis on which up to now the European order has founded its roots, i.e. the will of Member States to create a supranational order. This order is formally based on the execution orders of the Treaties, under the aegis of constitutional provisions covering the respective ordinary law (in origin, for example: Art. 11 of the Italian Constitution, Art. 24 GG).

On the contrary, it should be a reconstruction that can be likely considered comprehensive of all the aspects present in this case; in particular, the effort to explain the primacy of the European law as a consequence of international law – historically justified by the work of the European judge – has always contradicted the circumstance that the direct effectiveness of the European law makes substantial

[67]Think about the fact that the contents of the constitutions of the Member States do not depend on the point of view of the matters treated by the distribution of competences, so some rules belonging to the sphere of the European competences cannot be included in them while they can include repetitions of rules of EU law.

[68]From this point of view, for example, the constitution of a Member State can repeat a rule providing the "protection of competition" (so Art. 117.2 lit. e, Italian Constitution), but cannot contradict, in the evolution of its legislation, the EU competition law.

[69]When you consider Case 26/62 *Van Gend & Loos* (ECJ 5 February 1963) in *Racc*. 1963, pp. 3 et seqq.; see also Case 6/64 *Costa v E.N.E.L* (ECJ 15 July 1964), in *Racc*. 1964, I, pp. 1131 et seqq.; Case 106/77 *Simmenthal* (ECJ 9 March 1978), in *Racc*. 1978, I, pp. 629 et seqq. This case law has led, after a long period of settlement between the European judge and the Italian and German constitutional judges, to a *modus vivendi*, in which the primacy of EU law has given rise to a mere *disapplication* of the contrasting rules of internal law, without the need of their formal elimination or declaration of illegitimacy, in function of the reconstruction of the system on the basis of the pattern of two autonomous and coordinated orders.

the power of direct intervention by the Union towards the Member States, which is an expression of the power of public law.[70]

In the system emerging after the Lisbon Treaty, the homogeneity of the Member States' order with the Union values and the implementation of the European law without obstacles represent complementary elements of the integration. All that is not covered by the homogeneity principle falls de facto within the implementation of the principle of supremacy.[71]

9 Homogeneity and the Rules of the Competence

The elements forming the homogeneity principle require to be specified through the organisation and the coherent execution of the state functions. The respect for human dignity, freedom, democracy, equality, the rule of law and respect for human rights, including the rights of persons belonging to minorities, run the risk to remain empty words if the state legislation, administration and jurisdiction do not contribute to their realisation in an efficient manner.[72]

On the other hand, homogeneity acts as an essential requirement for the fulfilment of the Union's objectives, as these can be reached only if legally homogeneous entities (the Union and the Member States) share among themselves the tasks relating to the their attainment.

---

[70]See Schmitt (2008) (fn. 8), 378, who underlines the overtaking of the so-called *impermeability* of the internal order characterising the relations of international law and that requires to adopt some adaptation procedures.

[71]So, this innovation from the point of view of the perception of the integration process is not at all secondary and really avoids dealing with the objections of those who affirm, on the basis of the disapplication of the state law, that the legal effects of the primacy principle are too limited compared to the relation of public law, as not able to produce – in the same way as the EU law – the illegitimacy of the internal rule.

Moreover, apart from the possible future developments, it is not possible – currently – to hypothesise; it is not said at all that the disapplication of the state law, with which the antinomy between EU law and internal law is solved, does not act on the basis of the presence of a flaw that makes outlawed the same statutory law. The choice between disapplication and nullification, in fact, does not depend on the existence or not of a flaw of legitimacy of the statutory law, but simply on the fact that the jurisdiction where the legal proceeding has been instituted is, or not, qualified to declare the nullification of the statutory law. Another matter concerns the possibility of the declaration of illegitimacy due to provisions of internal law, put to protect the integration process (i.e. Art. 11, combined with Art. 117 Italian Constitution, and Art. 23 GG). On this point, we must not forget a certain ambiguity of the same Court of Justice that has demanded, at least beginning from the judgment in Case 6/64 *Costa v. E.N.E.L* (ECJ 15 July 1964), that the Member State provide for the removal of the statutory law in contrast with the EU law.

[72]The same is valid also for the objectives that the European Constitution provides that must be realised in the social organisation, for "a society in which pluralism, non-discrimination, tolerance, justice, solidarity and equality between women and men prevail".

So, the homogeneity principle interacts with the distribution of the competences, provided by the TFEU, in the sense that it becomes a condition of its effectiveness and guarantee that there are relationships between the two orders based on the distribution of the public tasks in accordance with the canon of "competence".

This circumstance seems definitely proved, on the one hand, by the universality of the Union's objectives – including peace and the well-being of its peoples (Art. 3.1 TEU)[73] – and, on the other hand, by the statement that "the Union shall pursue its objectives by appropriate means commensurate with the competences which are conferred upon it in the Treaties" (Art. 3.6 TEU).

On this point, we recall that the Treaties are characterised by a complex regulation of the competence recovering the principles already included in the previous European Treaties[74] and they present some new wordings based on the necessity to really assure a distribution of the powers between the Union and the Member States.

So, the TFEU – in accordance with the categories already used in Art. I-5 TCE but following more explicitly the rules linked to the principle of the enumeration of the Union's powers, in which the contribution of the German doctrine of the federal state is clear – first, defines the exclusive competences of the Union, in which "only the Union may legislate and adopt legally binding acts" and "the Member States being able to do so themselves only if so empowered by the Union or for the implementation of Union acts" (Art. 2.1 TFEU); second, defines the competences shared with the Member States in which the Union and the Member States may legislate and adopt legally binding acts, but where the Member States can exercise their competence to the extent that the Union has not exercised its competence or has decided to cease exercising its competence (Art. 2.2 TFEU).[75]

[73]The formulation of the objectives in Art. I-3 TCE is so wide that any part of the state life could be considered ruled out, in principle, by Union interference; it also includes an area of freedom, security and justice without internal frontiers, and an internal market where competition is free and undistorted (Art. I-3.2); the sustainable development of Europe based on balanced economic growth and price stability, a highly competitive social market economy, aiming at full employment and social progress, and a high level of protection and improvement of the quality of the environment; the promotion of scientific and technological advance; the fight against social exclusion and discrimination, and the promotion of the social justice and protection, the equality between women and men, the solidarity between generations and protection of the rights of the child; the promotion of the economic, social and territorial cohesion, and the solidarity among Member States; the respect of its rich cultural and linguistic diversity and the supervision that Europe's cultural heritage is safeguarded and enhanced (Art. I-3.3). In its relations with the wider world, the Union shall uphold and promote its values and interests. It shall contribute to peace, security, the sustainable development of the Earth, solidarity and mutual respect among peoples, free and fair trade, eradication of poverty and the protection of human rights, in particular the rights of the child, as well as the strict observance and the development of international law, including respect for the principles of the United Nations Charter (Art. I-3.4).

[74]See on this point Art. I-11 TCE (Fundamental principles).

[75]It must be noted that for all the competences the provision of Art. I-12.6 TCE is relevant, according to which "[t]he scope of and arrangements for exercising the Union's competences shall be determined by the provisions relating to each area in Part III".

However, apart from the problems that it may create and from the developments that the Common Foreign and Security Policy (CFSP) may have,[76] the same TFEU provides a further eventuality of competence as the coordination of the (economic and employment) policies assigned to the Member States within the arrangements determined by the Treaty, which the Union shall have competence to provide (Art. 2.3 TFEU); otherwise, as the definition of areas in which the competence is assigned to the Union "to carry out actions to support, coordinate or supplement the actions of the Member States, without thereby superseding their competence in these areas" with the express indication that "legally binding acts of the Union adopted on the basis of the provisions of the Treaties relating to these areas shall not entail harmonisation of Member States' laws or regulations" (Art. 2.5 TFEU). Even the same clause on the *implied powers*, included in Art. 352 TFEU, provides that the eventual enlargement of powers – enacted (unanimously) by the Council on a proposal from the Commission and after obtaining the consent of the European Parliament – cannot "entail harmonisation of Member States' laws or regulations in cases where the Treaties exclude such harmonisation" (paragraph 3).

References

Alexy R (1986) Theorie der Grundrechte. Suhrkamp, Frankfurt a.M.

Atripaldi V, Miccù R (eds) (2003) L'omogeneità costituzionale nell'Unione Europea. Cedam, Padova

Azpitarte Sánchez M (2004) La cultura constitucional de la Unión Europea. Análisis del artículo 6 TUE, in Derecho constitucional y cultura. Estudios en homenaje a Peter Häberle, a cura di F. Balaguer Callejón. Tecnos, Madrid, pp 369 et seqq

Bilancia P (ed) (2002) Il processo costituente europeo. Giuffrè, Milano

Bognetti G (2001) Lo speciale federalismo dell'Unione Europea. In: Petroni AM (ed) Modelli giuridici ed economici per la Costituzione europea. Il Mulino, Bologna, pp 245 et seqq

Chabod F (2001) Storia dell'idea d'Europa, (1961) Laterza, Roma-Bari

Constantinesco V (2001) L'intégration des principes constitutionnels nationaux dans le Traité: l'article 6 § 1 du Traité sur l'Union (ex-F § 1), tel que modifié par le Traité d'Amsterdam, in Droit constitutionnel Droit communautaire. Vers un respect réciproque mutuel? Economica – PUAM, Paris, pp 299 et seqq

Craig P (1999) The nature of the community: integration, democracy and legitimacy. In: Craig P, de Búrca G (eds) The evolution of EU law. Oxford University Press, Oxford, p 27 et seqq

Crisafulli V, Nocilla D (1977) Nazione. Giuffrè, Milano

D'Atena A (2001) I principi e i valori costituzionali, in Lezioni di diritto costituzionale. Giappichelli, Torino

[76]"including the progressive framing of a common defence policy (Art. I-12.4 TCE), which seems to surpass the rules of the pure intergovernmental politics and moves towards a stricter and bounder European policy [(see also Art. I-16 (The common foreign and security policy), Art. I-40 (Specific provisions relating to the common foreign and security policy), Art. I-41 (Specific provisions relating to the common security and defence policy), and the articles included in Part III, Title V, Charter II, of the Constitution (Art. III-294/III-313)].

D'Atena A (2004) Il principio unitario nel sistema dei rapporti tra Stato e regioni, in Scritti in memoria di Livio Paladin. Jovene, Napoli
Dahl RA (2003) Quanto è democratica la Costituzione Americana? Italian translation. Laterza, Roma-Bari
Dawson PM (1999–2000) Reflections on the opinion of the Supreme Court of Canada in the Quebec Secession Reference. Natl J Constitut Law 11:5 et seqq
Di Salvatore E (2008) L'identità costituzionale dell'Unione europea e degli Stati membri. Giappichelli, Torino
Edward D (2002) Direct effect – myth, mess or mystery. in Prinssen, Schrauw en (eds.), *Direct Effect of European Law*, (Hogendorp Papers Series), Europa Law Publishing, Groningen
Gelner E (1992) Nazioni e nazionalismo, Italian translation. Editori Riuniti, Roma
Grilli di Cortona P (2003) Stati nazioni e nazionalismi in Europa. Il Mulino, Bologna
Heller H (1971) Politische Demokratie und soziale Homogenität (1928), now in Gesammelte Schriften, 2. Bd. Leiden, ed. Martin Drath et al. pp 421 et seqq
Hesse K (1962) Der unitarische Bundesstaat. Müller, Karlsruhe
Hilf M (1995) Europäische Union und nationale Identität der Mitgliedstaaten. In: Randelzhofer A, Scholz R, Wilke D (eds) Gedächtnisschrift für Eberhard Grabitz. C.H. Beck, München, pp 157 ff
Hobsbawm EJ (1991) Nazioni e nazionalismi dal 1780. Programma, mito, realtà, Italian translation. Einaudi, Torino
Ipsen HP (1990) Über Verfassungs-Homogenität in der Europäischen Gemeinschaft, in Das akzeptierte Grundgesetz, FS für Günter Dürig. C.H. Beck, München, pp 159 et seqq
Kaufmann M (1997) Europäische integration und Demokratieprinzip. Nomos, Baden-Baden
Kelsen H (1923) Verfassungs- und Verwaltungsgerichtsbarkeit im Dienste des Bundesstaates, nach der neuen österreichischen Bundesverfassung vom 1. Oktober 1920, in Zeitschrift für schweizerisches Recht, Neue Folge, 52. Band pp 173 et seqq
Kelsen H (1927) Die Bundesexekution. Ein Beitrag zur Theorie und Praxis des Bundesstates, unter besonderer Berücksichtigung der deutschen Reichs- und der österreichischen Bundes-Verfassung, in Festschrift für Fritz Fleiner. J.C.B. Mohr (Paul Siebeck), Tübingen, pp 127–187
Kirchof P (1987) Die Identität der Verfassung in ihren unabänderlichen Inhalten. In: Isensee J, Kirchof P (eds) Handbuch des Staatsrechts, Bd. I. Müller, Heidelberg, Sect. 19
Mangiameli S (eds) (2006) L'ordinamento europeo, I, I principi dell'Unione. Giuffrè, Milano
Mangiameli S (2008) L'esperienza costituzionale europea. Aracne, Roma
Manzella A (1999) L'identità costituzionale dell'Unione europea, in Studi in onore di Leopoldo Elia. Giuffrè, Milano, pp 923 et seqq
Maunz T (1990) Verfassungshomogenität von Bund und Länder. In: Kirchof P, Isensee J (eds) Handbuch des Staatsrechts der Bundesrepublik Deutschland, Bd. IV. Müller Heidelberg, p 444
Merkl A (1968) Die Baugesetze der österreichischen Bundesverfassung. In: Klecatsky HR (ed) Die Republik Österreich. Herder, Wien
Mikkeli H (2002) Europa. Storia di un'idea e di un'identità, Italian translation. Il Mulino, Bologna
Mortati C (1975) Istituzioni di diritto pubblico, vol I, IX edn. CEDAM, Padova
Nascimbene B, Sanna C (2004) Art. 6 TUE. In: Tizzano A (ed) Trattati dell'Unione europea e della Comunità europea. Giuffrè, Milano, pp 47 et seqq
Newman WJ (2001–2002) Réflexions sur la porteé ventable des principes constitutionnels dans l'interprétation et l'application de la Constitution du Canada, in National Journal of Constitutional law, vol 13
Olivetti M (2002) Nuovi statuti e forma di governo delle regioni. Verso le Costituzioni regionali? Il Mulino, Bologna
Palermo F (2005) La forma di Stato dell'Unione europea. Per una teoria costituzionale dell'integrazione sovranazionale. CEDAM, Padova
Pedrazzi M (2001) Sub Art. 6. In: Pocar F (ed) Commentario breve ai Trattati della Comunità e dell'Unione Europea. Cedam, Padova, p 25 et seqq
Pernice I (2001) Europäisches und nationales Verfassungsrecht, in VVDStRL 60. Berlin, p 148 et seqq

Petroni AM (ed) (2001) Modelli giuridici ed economici per la Costituzione europea. Il Mulino, Bologna
Pinelli C (2004) Il preambolo, i valori, gli obiettivi. In: Bassanini F, Tiberi G (eds) Una Costituzione per l'Europa. Il Mulino, Bologna
Pizzorusso A (2002) Il patrimonio costituzionale europeo. Il Mulino, Bologna
Russell PH (2004) Constitutional Odyssey. Can Canadians become a Sovereign people? 3rd edn. University of Toronto Press, Toronto
Scharpf FW (1994) Un ordine costituzionale bipolare, in *Europa/Europe*, fasc. n.1.
Schmitt C (2008) Verfassungslehre, 1928, Translated by Jeffrey Seitzer. Duke University Press, London
Schmitt H, Sydow V (2001) Liberté, democratie, droit fondamentaux et État de droit: analyse de l'article 7 du traité EU, in RDUE, pp 285 et seqq
Schorkopf F (2000) Homogenität in der Europäischen Union – Ausgestaltung und Gewährleistung durch Art. 6 Abs. 1 und Art. 7. EUV, Berlin
Smend R (1968) Verfassung und Verfassungsrecht, 1928, now in Staatsrechtliche Abhandlungen, 2nd edn. Duncker & Humblot, Berlin, pp 119–276
Sorrentino F (1999) L'influenza del diritto comunitario sulla Costituzione italiana, in Studi in onore di Leopoldo Elia, vol II. Giuffrè, Milano, pp 1635 et seqq
Stern K (1984) Das Staatsrecht der Bundesrepublik Deutschland, vol I, 2nd edn. C.H. Beck München
Tizzano A (1998a) Profili generali del Trattato di Amsterdam. Il Dir dell'Unione Europea 2–3:288 et seqq
Tizzano A (1998b) Il Trattato di Amsterdam. Cedam, Padova
Tizzano A (2002) Il Trattato di Nizza. Giuffrè, Milano
Tripel H (1917) Die Reichsaufsicht. Untersuchungen zum Staatsrecht des Deutschen Reiches. Berlin
Walkenhorst H (1999) Europäischer Integrationsprozeß und europäische Identität. Nomos, Baden-Baden
Wehler HU (2002) Nazionalismo. Storia forme e conseguenze, Italian translation. Bollati Boringhieri, Torino
Werner P (1967) Wesensmerkmale des Homogenitätsprinzips und ihre Ausgestaltung im Bonner Grundgesetz. Frankfurt a.M.
Würmeling J (2003) Entwurf des Europäischen Verfassungsvertrages. Erster Bericht zu den Ergebnissen des EU-Verfassungskonvents, Brüssel/Bayreuth, den 13. Juni 2003, 7 f

The Union's Legal Personality: Ideas and Questions Lying Behind the Concept

Daniel Thürer and Pierre-Yves Marro

> Il existe si peu d'antinomie réelle entre le phénomène international et le phénomène national, que le phénomène international se présente tantôt comme une dégradation du phénomène étatique, et tantôt au contraire comme une intégration groupale de ce phénomène, puisqu'il aboutit à une forme sociale superétatique et s'achève en Etat fédéral.[1]

1 Introduction

Responding to a toast delivered at the Harvard Commencement in 1884, Supreme Court Judge *Oliver Wendell Holmes* stated:

> Behind every scheme to make the world over, lies the question: what kind of world do we want.[2]

In this essay, we aim to apply this perspective to the issue of the Union's legal personality. We will separately analyse the legal capacity created by the Treaty of Maastricht, the Treaties of Amsterdam and the Treaty of Nice, then the Treaty

[1]Scelle (1933), p. 345 (excerpt of *Scelle's* concept of a "monisme intersocial").

[2]The Mind and Faith of Justice Holmes – His Speeches, Essays, Letters, and Judicial Opinions, selected and edited, with a new preface and afterword by *Max Lerner*, New Brunswick (USA) and Oxford (UK) 1989, p. 20.

D. Thürer (✉)
Institut für Völkerrecht und Ausländisches Verfassungsrecht, Universität Zürich, Rämistrasse 74/36, 8001 Zürich, Switzerland
e-mail: daniel.thuerer@ivr.uzh.ch

P.-Y. Marro (✉)
Rechtswissenschaftliche Fakultät, Universität Luzern, Winkelriedstrasse 14, Postfach 7992, 6007 Luzern, Switzerland; as from 1 September 2011
and
Frohburgstrasse 3, Postfach, 4466, 6002 Luzern, Switzerland
e-mail: pierre.marro@unilu.ch

H.-J. Blanke and S. Mangiameli (eds.), *The European Union after Lisbon*, 47
DOI 10.1007/978-3-642-19507-5_3, © Springer-Verlag Berlin Heidelberg 2012

establishing a Constitution for Europe, and finally the Lisbon Treaty. This is, in Holmes's words, the scheme that we examine.

In a second step, we will address the situation of the European Communities, asking ourselves what Europe should be like, and what Europe we want to live in. In this part, we shall therefore try to reflect on the idea or purpose *behind* the concept of the legal personality of the European Community (EC)/European Union (EU). In embarking on this enquiry, we shall use reflections on the locations of foreign relations in federal systems as a starting point and as background to our considerations. Arguments in favour of centralisation or non-centralisation within the foreign relations of European integration will be considered. We will end our quest for the world we want with some reflections on the tensions between democracy at the local level and universalism at the central level of organisations.

2 Legal Personality as Established by the Various Treaties

We start with some observations of a conceptual nature before going through the various layers of the different constitutional arrangements.

2.1 Concept

The central actors among the subjects of international law are the states, which enjoy full legal personality under international law – international legal personality being the capacity of having rights and duties in this legal order. As a corollary of their sovereignty, states also have the power to create international organisations. The extent to which the latter possess legal personality in international law is a question of positive law; it depends upon their constituent treaty.[3] As a general rule, most international organisations enjoy legal personality. Such personality is either provided for expressly in the constituent charter or – as is normally the case – follows from the powers or the aims and objectives of the organisation, and the practice of its organs.[4] In its *Reparation for Injuries* Advisory Opinion, the International Court of Justice (ICJ) set out the preconditions for such legal personality: An organisation is capable of possessing international rights and duties and has the capacity to assert its rights if it has its own organs and if it could not discharge its functions without legal personality.[5] In contrast to states, which are characterized

---

[3]See Seidl-Hohenveldern (1998), pp. 3 et seq. An overview over the vast jurisdiction offers *Wolff Heintschel von Heinegg*, Casebook Völkerrecht, München 2005, in footnotes 278, 279 and 281.

[4]Bindschedler (1995), p. 1299.

[5]*Reparation for Injuries Suffered in the Service of the United Nations* (Advisory Opinion of 11 April 1949), ICJ Reports 1949, p. 180: "Whereas a State possesses the totality of international rights and duties recognized by international law, the rights and duties of an entity such as the

by unlimited legal personality, the legal personality of organisations exists only within the limits of their purpose and functions, since it is defined not by general international law but on the basis of their constituent treaty.

An organisation which possesses legal personality also has responsibility under international law.[6] The duty to make reparations for internationally wrongful acts is correlative to the right, recognised by the ICJ, to claim reparations. However, responsibility extends further than the organisation's rights, since the latter only exist within the limits laid down in the constituent treaty, whereas the organisation's responsibility encompasses cases where it has exceeded powers or acted in breach of the constituent treaty.[7]

The legal personality of an organisation clearly exists in relation to its Member States: By founding or joining such an organisation, they recognise it as a person under international law. Yet the same does not automatically hold for third states: States are generally not bound without their consent, so a constituent treaty neither confers rights nor imposes duties on non-signatories.[8] Again, the decisive factor is that an international organisation – unlike a state – is not based on general international law, but on a treaty. Therefore, recognition by third states would appear to be necessary; it would then have a constitutive effect.[9] The recognition can be granted expressly or by implication, for example by the conclusion of treaties or by the establishment of diplomatic relations.

Organisation must depend upon its purposes and functions as specified or implied in its constituent documents and developed in practice." Furthermore, with regard to the objectives and tasks of the United Nations, the ICJ stated: "The functions of the Organisation are of such a character that they could not be effectively discharged if they involved the concurrent action, on the international plane, of fifty-eight or more Foreign Offices, and the Court concludes that the Members have endowed the Organisation with capacity to bring international claims when necessitated by the discharge of its functions."

[6]For the situation of the European Community see Ginther (1994), pp. 335 et seqq. ("culpa levissima" is enough); Oppermann et al. (2009), para. 15, notes 2 et seqq.

[7]See for instance Case C-327/91 *France v Commission* (ECJ 9 August 1994); Hirsch (1995), p. 10, note 50.

[8]The so-called *pacta tertiis*-rule; cf. Art. 34 (et seqq.) VCLT. This rule represents, additionally, a general principle of international law.

[9]It is not the aim to offset, at this place, the contradiction of the so-called will theory. The contradiction lies in the fact that if, as generally held, rules of law are binding only upon those who subscribe to them ("Lotus principle"), it follows that a mere agreement between Member States of an organisation to create a legal person does not suffice to endow the organisation with personality towards non-Member States. Therefore, what is needed is acceptance of the existence of the organisation by third parties, which is often captured in the word "recognition". This leads, however, to a paradox: If the will of the founders is decisive, then recognition cannot enter the picture; if recognition is required, it follows that the will of the founders is not, as such, decisive. The obvious solution then would be to strip the element of recognition from the theory, but that leaves the "will theory" vulnerable to isolation: What happens if its founders endow an organisation with personality and yet no one wants to engage with it? In that case, the will of the founders would be all the more illusory. Cf. on this Barberis (1983), pp. 145–285, esp. p. 169.

2.2 *Legal Personality Under the Treaty of the European Community*

2.2.1 Treaty Provisions

The European Communities were international organisations in the broad sense. According to the classic definition of such an organisation, that should mean that they were based on an international treaty, were equipped with proper organs, possessed a legal personality distinct from that of their Member States and had broad public powers. There is no doubt that the European Communities did indeed possess legal personality.[10] The reason for this is that express provisions on this subject had been introduced in the respective treaty texts, even though these provisions had been worded differently in different legal instruments. In fact, in the Treaty establishing the European Community two provisions were dedicated to this subject, namely Arts. 281 and 282.

Article 281 EC read:

> The Community shall have legal personality.

Article 282 EC read:

> In each of the Member States, the Community shall enjoy the most extensive legal capacity accorded to legal persons under their laws: it may, in particular, acquire or dispose of movable and immovable property and may be a party to legal proceedings. To this end, the Community shall be represented by the Commission.

The equivalent provisions in the European Atomic Energy Community (Euratom) Treaty were Arts. 184 and 185.[11] In addition, the European Coal and Steel Community (ECSC) Treaty contained a similar provision in its Art. 6.[12]

2.2.2 Legal Personality

As far as the principle of "private law personality" embodied in Art. 282 EC was concerned, the situation was relatively clear.[13] This personality related to the

---

[10]See for example Herdegen (2008), para. 5, note 8; Craig and de Búrca (2008), p. 171; Jaag (2003a), note 1206; Streinz (2008), notes 675 and 676.

[11]Their wording is even identical. Of course, it is important to note in this context that both treaties have been signed at the same date, namely on 25 March 1957, while the ECSC Treaty dated from 18 April 1951 (see footnote 12).

[12]"(1) The Community shall have legal personality. (2) In international relations, the Community shall enjoy the legal capacity it requires to perform its functions and attain its objectives. (3) In each of the Member States, the Community shall enjoy the most extensive legal capacity accorded to legal persons constituted in that State: it may, in particular, acquire or dispose of movable and immovable property and may be a party to legal proceedings. (4) The Community shall be represented by its institutions, each within the limits of its powers."

[13]See for Art. 282 EC the commentary of Armin Hatje in von der Groeben and Schwarze (2003), especially notes 28 et seqq.

capacity for the Community to act under national law, e.g. to buy property or mandate contractors. To that end, the treaty introduced a so-called assimilation principle according to which the Community had to be able to profit from all facilities accorded to national legal persons. But what about the principle of "international legal personality" embodied in Art. 281 EC? Here, the situation was different and more complicated. What use could be made of such capacity? Or, to put it differently, what was the exact nature and scope of the obligations that the respective Community adopted? The starting point for the analysis was the "attribution principle" (*principe d'attribution*) as laid down in Art. 5.1 EC for the European Community, and in Art. 7.1 sentence 2 EC as far as the individual institutions were concerned.

Article 5.1 EC read:

> The Community shall act within the limits of the powers conferred upon it by this Treaty and of the objectives assigned to it therein.

Article 7.1 sentence 2 EC read:

> Each institution shall act within the limits of the powers conferred upon by this Treaty.

Article 5.1 EC illustrated that, in order to establish the exact scope of the potential action of the European Community, attention had to be paid to both aspects, the treaty objectives and, at the same time, the concrete powers conferred upon the Community to achieve these objectives. In the area of external relations, further indications regarding the question of the legal personality could be found in Art. 101.1 Euratom Treaty. This article read:

> The Community may, within the limits of its powers and jurisdiction, enter into obligations by concluding agreements or contracts with a third State, an international organisation or a national of a third State.

The constituent treaties attributed some competences in external relations to the Community. First of all, we think of the powers of the EC in commercial affairs, or in the field of development and cooperation.[14] In order to determine the scope of the "external" competences of the Community, the doctrine developed by the European Court of Justice (ECJ) in its *ERTA/AETR*[15] judgment was of importance.[16] In that case, the Court dealt with the interpretation of Art. 210 (later 281) EC. The Court ruled that the Community enjoyed the capacity to establish external relations with

---

[14]Cf. Arts. 131–134 and 177–181a EC.

[15]Case 22/70 *Commission v Council* (ECJ 31 March 1971); on this, see also Dashwood and Hliskoski (2000), notes 1.03 et seqq.

[16]The *ERTA/AETR* judgment has been reaffirmed by a number of other decisions of the Court, such as the judgments in joined cases 3/76, 4/76, 6/76 *Kramer et al.* (ECJ 14 July 1976) paras 19–20 as well as in the findings in Opinion 1/76, *European Laying-up fund for inland waterway vessels* (ECJ 26 April 1977) para 3, Opinion 2/91 *ILO Convention on safety in the use of chemicals at work* (ECJ 19 March 1993) para 7, Opinion 2/92 *Third Revised Decision of the OECD on National Treatment* (ECJ 24 March 1995) para 29 and Opinion 1/94 *WTO-GATS and TRIPS* (ECJ 28 March 1996) para 48.

third countries within the whole field of objectives defined in Part One of the treaty.[17] The subsequent considerations of the Court laid the basis for the so-called implied powers doctrine concerning the external competences of the Community:

> Such authority arises not only from an express conferment by the Treaty [...] but may equally flow from other provisions of the Treaty and from measures adopted, within the framework of those provisions, by the Community institutions. In particular, each time the Community, with a view to implementing a common policy envisaged by the Treaty, adopts provisions laying down common rules, whatever form these may take, the Member States no longer have the right, acting individually or even collectively, to undertake obligations with third countries which affect those rules. As and when such common rules come into being, the Community alone is in a position to assume and carry out contractual obligations towards third countries affecting the whole sphere of application of the Community legal system. With regard to the implementation of the provisions of the Treaty the system of internal Community measures may not therefore be separated from that of external relations.[18]

From this "implied power" doctrine followed that, in the context of actions of the EC in international relations, the recognition of legal personality was closely linked not only to the process of achieving the treaty objectives, but also to the execution of proper powers.[19] In fact, the necessity of an interaction between treaty objectives and powers was also illustrated by the modalities mentioned in Art. 308 EC. This provision addressed the "lacunae" that might emerge once the Community intended to act to ensure the achievement of its objectives but lacked a specific power to do so. The wording of Art. 308 seemed to imply that the Community, in order to be entitled to act, had to respect not only the scope of the treaty objectives but, at the same time, the attribution principle as well. In other words, the treaty objectives were not the only point of reference determining the scope of action to be taken by the Community.[20]

2.3 *Maastricht – Amsterdam – Nice*

2.3.1 Maastricht Treaty

The Maastricht Treaty led to the creation of the Pillar system.[21] This system mirrored the desire of many Member States to extend the European Economic Community to the areas of foreign policy, military, criminal justice, and judicial cooperation. The Pillars thus represented the ambition to extend the scope of the

---

[17]Case 22/70 *Commission v Council* (ECJ 31 March 1971) para 14.

[18]Case 22/70 *Commission v Council* (ECJ 31 March 1971) paras 16–19.

[19]Cf. Dashwood (2000), supra footnote 15, notes 8.01 et seqq.

[20]For another interesting analysis see Weiler (1981), pp. 269 et seq. Joseph H.H. Weiler compares the supranational integration to a balance between political and legal processes.

[21]See for the characteristics of the pillar structure Everling (1992), pp. 1053–1077; Wellenstein (1992), pp. 205–212; Curtin and Heukels (1994).

Community; yet at the same time, they stood for misgivings of some Member States to add areas which they considered to be too sensitive to be managed by the supranational mechanisms of the European Economic Community (EEC).[22] The compromise was that instead of renaming the European Economic Community the European Union, the treaty would establish a legally separate EU comprising, as its first Pillar, the renamed EEC as well as the Euratom and the ECSC. Separately, it would delineate intergovernmental policy areas of foreign policy, military, criminal justice and judicial cooperation. This delicate, rather complicated Maastricht arrangement reflected the political ambitions and values of the Member States and European institutions of the time. In this sense, it was a new compromise between the determination to preserve national identity and the ambitions of integration as of 1997. Under Maastricht, the European Commission, the European Parliament and the ECJ were given limited powers in the areas of new intergovernmental relations established by the Second and Third Pillars: foreign policy and military matters, and criminal justice and cooperation in civil matters.

The question whether the newly created EU possessed legal personality raised controversy,[23] because the Treaty on European Union (TEU) contained no provisions akin to Arts. 281 and 282 EC. Furthermore, when the Maastricht Treaty was signed, a number of Member States explicitly requested that the EU should *not* have legal personality.

Generally speaking, one group of observers put forward the view that the Union did not have legal personality.[24] Adherents of this school of thought pointed out that there was no equivalent to Art. 281 EC in the Maastricht Treaty. Contrary to the three European Communities, the treaty did not contain an explicit provision granting legal personality to the Union. These scholars argued that the absence of such an explicit provision corresponded to an explicit "will" of the Member States. They claimed that in Maastricht, the Member States had manifested an intention to establish a politically and not a legally determined entity. According to this argument, it was not agreed in Maastricht to confer a legal personality to the Union.[25]

A second group of observers, notably from the field of public international law, held the position that the EU did possess legal personality.[26] Here, doctrines such as

---

[22]See Hilf (1982), pp. 361 et seqq.

[23]See e.g. Hilf (1994), pp. 75 et seqq.; as well as Stumpf (2009), Art. 1 EUV, notes 4 et seqq.

[24]Everling (1992), p. 1061; Pliakos (1993), p. 213; Eaton (1994), p. 221; Heukels and de Zwaan (1994), pp. 201, 202 et seq. as well as 227.

[25]Cloos et al. (1994), p. 115. There, it is said: "L'Union, dans cette approche, est un concept politique bien plus que juridique, et elle ne dispose dès lors pas de la personnalité juridique. On n'est pas arrivé au stade où les Etats membres seraient prêts à transférer leurs compétences en matière de politique étrangère à une entité juridique distincte. Ils sont d'accord pour agir collectivement sur la scène internationale, mais non pas pour disparaître en tant qu'acteurs juridiquement distincts."

[26]See for instance von Bogdandy and Nettesheim (1986), pp. 2 et seqq.; Seidl-Hohenveldern and Loibl (2000), note 0119e; von Bogdandy (1998), pp. 165 et seqq.; Zuleeg (2003), p. 931; Kaddous (2008a), p. 299 (with further reference).

the "will" theory, the "objective" theory and, more recently, the "presumptive" theory might be mentioned.[27,28] In this line of thought, a number of "formal" arguments were to be taken into account, such as the name given to the newly established institutions, certain practices, the wording of the treaty and the practice of the Second and the Third Pillars. For example, the Council governing the European *Community* was formally named "Council of the European *Union*".[29] In addition, the Permanent Representations of the Member States, established in Brussels, were as a rule, accredited "to the European Union". Moreover, the common provisions – Title I of the Maastricht Treaty – dealt prominently and extensively with the concept of a "European Union". Also, in several provisions concerning the two new Pillars, the "Maastricht" version of the TEU referred to acts of "the Union". It should be mentioned too that, formally speaking, new Member States acceeded to the EU and not to the individual Communities,[30] as was the case before "Maastricht".[31] And finally, the Official Journal of the European Community was, as a consequence of the new terminology, given the name "Official Journal of the European Union".

As described earlier, the Union comprised the three individual forms of cooperation, i.e. it served as an overall framework for the development of cooperation based on the three pillars.[32] Yet at the same time, the Union itself had no proper role to play when it came to the concrete development of each of these three forms of cooperation. In such cases the Union operated either, in the First Pillar of cooperation, through the "European Communities" or, in the Second and Third Pillars, through the "Member States". Under Maastricht, the emphasis on the role of the Presidency represented a practical solution, but it did not have legal implications as to the capacity of the Union to act as a separate legal entity. Once again, this finding corresponded with the "will" of the (majority of) delegations participating in the Intergovernmental Conference at the same time: Clearly, it was not agreed in Maastricht to confer legal personality upon the Union – otherwise, this issue would have been clarified in an unambiguous and uncontroversial matter. That is why the EU, in view of the structures as developed under the Maastricht Treaty, could only qualify as a "political" framework, overarching the three forms of cooperation –

27 Klabbers (1998), pp. 243 et seq. (Jan Klabbers remains nevertheless sceptical; see his remarks on p. 233).

28 For a short but perspective overview of the various contending theories see Kuyper (1979), pp. 3–41, especially pp. 15–19.

29 Commission Decision No. 93/591/EC concerning the name to be given to the Council following the entry into force of the Treaty on European Union, O.J. L 281/18 (1993). Then again, the Commission and the Court of Justice were still designated as "of the European Communities". On the contrary, the official name of the European Parliament contained no reference to either the Communities or the Union.

30 In a similar context, reference can be made to the "Citizenship of the Union", a capacity for persons holding the nationality of a Member State, elaborated in Arts. 17–22 EC.

31 See the former Art. 237 EC.

32 See the brief overview of the EU framework by Zuleeg (2003) (supra footnote 26), p. 931.

economic, political and justice cooperation – to be developed within the three "Pillars". On this account, we have to come to the conclusion that the EU as such did not possess legal personality.

2.3.2 Amsterdam Treaty

The innovations introduced by the Amsterdam Treaty have led to more coherence as far as the "constitutional" structures of the EU cooperation were concerned.[33] The principle of the pillar structure as such did not been changed by the Amsterdam Treaty. Nevertheless, the First Pillar cooperation has been strengthened,[34] and a number of "Community" type procedures and working methods were introduced into the Second and Third Pillar cooperation areas. However, the Amsterdam Treaty did not changed the basic structures of the Union cooperation: The main substantive powers, as far as the Second and the Third Pillar cooperation were concerned, remained in the hands of the Member States; so, the Union continued to serve as the (political) overall framework for the cooperation. As mentioned earlier, it was sometimes argued that the Union possessed legal personality under Maastricht.[35] But again, even if one concluded that the Union might indeed be a separate subject of international law, what could the Union achieve with such a capacity? Here, the primary responsibility of the Member States as the real "actors" in the Second and Third Pillar cooperation had obviously to be taken into account. It is also worth noting that the formal attribution of legal personality to the EU had again been discussed, even extensively, during the negotiations in the framework of the Intergovernmental Conference.[36] And, although support was expressed for this idea by an important number of Member States, (again) no consensus could be reached to make the legal personality of the Union explicit through the introduction of a new treaty provision in the TEU. Apparently, a number of partners feared that explicitly conferring legal personality could give rise to the – wrong – impression that the Union possessed the powers related to the policy fields concerned.[37] Such

---

[33]See Dashwood (1998), pp. 1019–1045; Curtin and Dekker (1999), pp. 83–136.

[34]A strengthening of the Community cooperation results, for example, from the conferral of new competences to the Community, e.g. in the area of employment policy (Arts. 125–130 EC) and social policy (Arts. 136–145 EC).

[35]See for instance Schroeder (2003), pp. 382 et seqq.

[36]See the documentation of Busse (1999), pp. 46 et seqq. and the proposals of the Irish resp. Dutch Presidency, CONF/2500/96 of 5 December 1996, pp. 91 et seqq. resp. CONF/2500/9, ADD.1 of 20 March 1997, p. 47.

[37]See the relevant paragraph in the final report of the Reflection Group of December 1995: "A majority of member points to the advantage of international legal personality for the Union so that it can conclude international agreements on the subject-matter of Titles V and VI concerning the CFSP and the external dimension of justice and home affairs. For them, the fact that *the Union does not legally exist* is a source of confusion outside and diminishes its external role. Others consider that the creation of international legal personality for the Union could risk

an impression of "implied powers" would not correspond with the "internal" distribution of responsibilities between the Union and the Member States. Another, however less pressing, factor may have been that the explicit conferral of legal personality could – unjustly – have been associated with a "federal" structure of the Union cooperation.

Hence, the conclusion has to be drawn that after the entry into force of the Amsterdam Treaty, the real powers in the areas of foreign and security, as well as police and criminal cooperation, still resided with the Member States. The Union still did not acquire legal personality. This final outcome not only corresponded with the "will" of the partners, it also reflected the legal and institutional structures of the cooperation in the framework of the EU.[38]

2.3.3 Nice Treaty

The Nice Treaty was concluded in December 2000, after a notoriously divided and poorly run European Council summit. Essentially, the Nice Treaty made changes to the European Community, in particular relating to the Community's institutional and decision-making structure.[39] Yet as far as our topic is concerned, the situation under the Amsterdam Treaty was not altered.[40]

2.4 Treaty Establishing a Constitution for Europe and Lisbon Treaty

2.4.1 Treaty Establishing a Constitution for Europe

Discussions and disputations over a formal Constitutional Treaty have been going on for nearly twenty years. First attempts at developing a European Constitution, as it was somewhat imprecisely called, took place back in 1984 and 1994 respectively.[41] When the issue was taken up again in 2001, the drafting process of the Constitutional Treaty was comparatively quick. Apparently, the text was not

---

confusion with the legal prerogatives of Member States." Reflection Group Report and Other References for Documentary Purposes, 1996 Intergovernmental Conference, General Secretariat of the Council of the European Union, Brussels 1996, para 150 (on p. 76) (italics ours).

[38]For a more detailed, however different, analysis see von Bogdandy (1999), pp. 887–910.

[39]See Weidenfeld (2002); Andena and Usher (2003).

[40]See Streinz (2008), notes 53 et seqq. (with further reference); furthermore Matthias Pechstein, in: Rudolf Streinz (ed.), EUV/EGV, Munich 2003, Art. 1 EUV notes 10 et seqq.; Stumpf (2009), Art. 1 EUV notes 4 et seqq., especially the overview on the doctrine in note 9.

[41]1984: Draft Treaty founding the European Union, 14 February 1984 (Spinelli Report); Council Resolution of 28 February 1994 on the Constitution of the European Union, O.J. C 61/155; on the development in general, see Bieber et al. (2009), Sect. 1.C.

adopted within days, but it is still noteworthy that agreement was reached within a few years. On the whole, it was a transparent process[42]; nonetheless, many EU citizens have been unaware of it for very long.

Certainly, some state constitutions were equally developed in a very short time. To cite but one example, the Gaullist constitution for the French Fifth Republic was drawn up in 1958 in a few months only, under the direction of its principal author *Michel Debré*. On the other hand, older constitutions, such as the 1787 Constitution founding the American Union, were results of longer and more intensive deliberation processes and constitutional battles. In this spirit, the debate at the Constitutional Convention in Philadelphia was accompanied by the publication of the "Federalist Papers", in which the pre-eminent Founding Fathers *Alexander Hamilton*, *James Madison* and *John Jay* discussed the pros and cons of the federal structures to be introduced.[43]

On its part, the Constitutional Convention on the Future of Europe worked more quickly and calmly than most national constitutional bodies; it was not beset by a public, hungry for knowledge and news. There are most likely a number of reasons for this. First of all, the purpose of this project was not to produce a sort of symbolic monument with the powers to terminate and pacify fatal conflicts between citizens, as was the case with numerous national constitutions. The draft did indeed contain some completely new elements; but large parts of the Constitution and now of the Lisbon Treaty are an – admittedly only partially successful – attempt to codify, systemise, simplify and streamline existing legislation; in Switzerland, we would call this "fine-tuning" *(Nachführung)* the current legislation. There was another reason for the speed, and also for the maintenance of a certain remoteness and introversion of the project. Under the Presidency of *Valérie Giscard d'Estaing*, the Convention was run according to strict (not to say authoritarian) guidelines. Unlike in ordinary legislative procedures, the text was not adopted subsequent to intensive debates by voting on the individual articles and sections and finally on the complete text. Instead, a consensus procedure was applied.

We think it is important to bear in mind the political environment and political circumstances that gave rise to the text in order to correctly understand its significance and function. In particular, under the provisions of the Constitutional Treaty, the three Pillars would have been merged into one legal personality called the European Union. Moreover, the Constitutional Treaty provided for a long-term Presidency of the European Council and a Union's Minister for Foreign Affairs, elected for a term of two and a half years and limited to two terms.[44] (The Lisbon Treaty provides for corresponding provisions.)

---

[42]See Jaag (2003b), pp. 104 et seqq.

[43]The dignity attributed to the assembly of the Founding Fathers becomes apparent in the story which is told that the streets and squares of Philadelphia around the Convention venue, "Liberty Hall", were covered in sawdust so that delegates would not have their deliberations disrupted by the rattling of passing carriages.

[44]Arts. I-22 and I-28 TCE.

The Constitution received varied responses from the European public. For instance, in early July 2003, *Le Monde* applauded it as a "historical step",[45] while the *Economist*, which originally had had a positive opinion of the "constitutional reform", maintained that the present text should be chucked in the wastepaper bin.[46] The Constitutional Treaty was eventually rejected in referenda in France and the Netherlands in 2005. This failure was partly due to its great ambitions. It was based on Kantian ideas of a world order, but time was not yet ripe for the realisation of such a bold project.[47] In particular, the term "Constitution" led to false impressions among the citizens suggesting a superstructure above the nation states. The state-like symbols mentioned at the outset of the documents (hymn, "national flag", Union motto, "national day", etc.) strengthened such an impression. So, many people were afraid of a technical, functional-elitist construction far remote from day-to-day life in their traditional towns, regions and home states.[48] In addition, national politics which had nothing to do with the treaty unfortunately played an important, confusing role.

2.4.2 Lisbon Treaty (Reform Treaty)

In 2007, Member States agreed to abandon the constitutional project and to amend the existing treaties, which would remain in force. At the European Council meeting of June 2007, they agreed on a detailed mandate for a new intergovernmental conference,[49] where a new treaty containing such amendments to the existing treaties would be negotiated. These negotiations were completed by the end of the year and the Member States signed the new treaty in Lisbon on 13 December 2007.

The Treaty of Lisbon is a treaty designed to streamline the workings of the EU with amendments to the TEU and the Treaty establishing the European Community.[50] The stated aim of the treaty is *[...] to complete the process started by the Treaty of Amsterdam and by the Treaty of Nice with a view to enhancing the*

[45]Le Monde, Dossiers et Documents, July 2003: "Cette future constitution va être une grande étape dans l'histoire de la construction européenne."

[46]Economist, 5 July 2003, p. 34.

[47]For a brief analysis see Thürer (2005), p. 13; and farther "From the constitution to a new round of treaty: step-by-step" (editorial comments) (2007), pp. 1229 et seqq.

[48]With 448 articles and nine protocols, the Constitution had become too bulky. The length of the text may be explained by the fact that the Convention did not limit its work to a constitutional basic law, the general part of any constitutional treaty, but also wanted to carry out itself the required adaptations to the existing treaties – in the various policy areas of the EU. Moreover, the EUCFR was included in its entirety in the treaty; cf. Schwarze (2003), pp. 535, 536 et seqq.

[49]Council of the European Union, 11177/1/07 REV 1, Brussels, 20 July 2007.

[50]See Schwarze et al. (2009).

efficiency and democratic legitimacy of the Union and to improving the coherence of its action.[51]

Prominent changes, most of them adopted from the Constitutional Treaty, are provided for such as the elimination of the Pillar structure, the creation of a "President of the European Council" and a "High Representative of the Union for Foreign Affairs and Security Policy" to present a united position on EU policies.[52] In addition, the Lisbon version of the TEU states that *[t]he Union shall replace and succeed the European Community*[53] and furthermore that *[it] shall have legal personality.*[54]

The Treaty of Lisbon was planned to have been ratified by all Member States by the end of 2008 in order to enter into force before the 2009 European elections. However, the rejection of the treaty on 12 June 2008 by the Irish electorate meant that the ratification process was stalled. In fact, the "Irish question" created a pause for reflection and deliberation on the essence, values and goals of the EU integration process.[55] It might then have the effect of introducing a deeper and broader thinking on what Europe really is and what it should become. The Irish decision was reversed in a second referendum in 2009, and the treaty eventually entered into force on 1 December 2009.

3 Legal Personality and Beyond

Lawyers have been debating for a long time whether the EC and/or the EU is an international organisation, a federal state or a federal state "in the making", whereby reflections on federalism generally take an important place in these discussions.[56] Yet if we go beyond the legal scheme established by the treaties,

---

[51]Preamble of the Treaty.

[52]See Art. 18. In fact, the provisions concerning the CFSP of the Lisbon Treaty remain practically the same as those under the Constitutional Treaty. The change, resulting from the fact that the "Union's Minister for Foreign Affairs" is renamed "High Representative" is purely symbolic in the sense that it intends to dispel the fears related to the terms evoking the image of a "constitution" or of a "State". Apart from the change in the title of the High Representative, two new declarations on CFSP clarify that no new powers are conferred to the European institutions in that matter. Cf. on the High Representative Kaddous (2008b), pp. 205–221, especially pp. 207 et seqq.

[53]Art. 1.3 sentence 3 TEU.

[54]Art. 47 TEU.

[55]See Goldsmith (2008), pp. 929 et seqq. and in this context further Frowein (2004), pp. 421 et seqq.

[56]On this see Thürer (2006), pp. 52 et seqq. Nonetheless, reasoning of this kind is not profound enough for a federal/confederal dichotomy. Cf. on this Peters (2001); von Bogdandy (2003), with contributions by *Jürgen Bast, Armin von Bogdandy, Philipp Dann, Jürgen Drexl, Christoph Grabenwarter, Ulrich Haltern, Armin Hatje, Stefan Kadelbach, Thorsten Kingreen, Paul Kirchhof, Jürgen Kühling, Franz Christian Mayer, Christoph Möllers, Martin Nettesheim, Stefan Oeter, Alexancer Schmitt Glaeser, Werner Schroeder, Robert Uerpmann, Antje Wiener, Jan Wouters,* and *Manfred Zuleeg.*

the concept of federalism arises quite apart from the attempt of describing how the EC/EU present themselves in legal terms. Firstly, it is important to deal not only with the outward appearance of the Union, but also with the question of how its legal order relates to those of its Member States. Here, too, federalism can offer valuable hints and potential explanations.[57] And secondly, it is to be borne in mind that European law – like international law in general – is formed and executed by national agents and magistrates. Hence, these actors have a double function or, to put it in the words of *Georges Scelle*, play a double role between the legal orders.[58] Here, too, the concept of federalism may best explain the interactions between the various systems.

3.1 The EU as a Federal System

The "federal state" was "invented" by the Founding Fathers of the United States in the late eighteenth century. It was adopted by Switzerland in 1848 and, subsequently, by over twenty other countries. The central tenet of a federal state is a federal constitution; the aim of such a constitution is to harmoniously combine unity and diversity within a single, federal entity. In particular, the characteristic features of the constitution of a federal state are:

- The presence of two or more legal orders which apply directly to citizens of the state;
- A constitutional distribution of powers between the different levels of the political structure, with the subsidiarity principle applying where possible and with the constituent states enjoying a substantial sphere of autonomy;
- Involvement of the constituent states in the formulation of federal policy;
- A constitutional basis that cannot be amended without the participation of the constituent states;
- Processes and institutions to facilitate cooperation in matters falling under the shared responsibility of different players in the federalist system.

Does the EU fit that description? It seems to be a new federal system, a federal system *sui generis*. From its inception, the supranational EC has always been based

---

[57]Compare Scelle (1943), p. 23: "la technique du Droit international se modèle, le plus exactement possible, sur celle de tout autre ordre juridique. On ne saurait considérer l'Etat que comme un groupement d'intérêts éminemment respectable et puissant, mais non comme un sujet de Droit, ni comme un titulaire de droits subjectifs" and p. 19: "L'Etat se présente historiquement comme l'élément politique capital de la société internationale, car tous les individus humains et tous les groupements humains, sont rattachés à des Etats ou plutôt des ordres juridiques étatiques [. . .]. Les Etats ne dépendent pas juridiquement les uns des autres, [. . .]. Mais ils sont dans un état d'*interdépendance matérielle*, en raison de la solidarité interétatique. Ils dépendent juridiquement de l'ordre juridique international." In this regard, see also the reference supra, in footnote 1.

[58]See Scelle (1956), pp. 324 et seqq., here pp. 329 et seqq.

on international treaties. But as the ECJ already recognised in the 1980s, it also has a functional, structural and institutional base ("basic constitutional charter").[59] Albeit the "constituent power" clearly resides with the Member States, the architecture of the provisions regarding the objectives and targets, the division of responsibility between the Union and the Member States, the structure and mechanics of the Union's institutions or the fundamental rights are comparable to those in state constitutions.

The Lisbon Treaty has not changed any of this: The EU and its treaty do still not fit in the traditional scheme of either the confederation or the federal state. More likely, they continue to hover somewhere in between these two poles. It is evident that in the form of the Lisbon Treaty, the EU has outgrown the model of a confederation of States or might actually never have fitted into this model. But under the treaty, the Union also lacks essential elements of a federal State. The international basis of the EU has been retained in that the "pouvoir constituant" remains with the Member States; in fact, the concession of a right of secession to the States corroborated this international aspect.[60] It pursues a third way: Even under the Lisbon Treaty, integration law remains in a state of suspension between (loose) international law and (firmly established) national law. Overall, the "para-national" features of the Union have been reinforced, as evidenced by the abolition of the "three-pillar structure" and the conferral of legal personality on the Union. Nonetheless, the Union still possesses only a rudimentary power of enforcement. It is unable to extend diplomatic protection to citizens, and the citizens have no direct tax liability towards it. To employ the familiar expressions coined by *Alexander Hamilton*, it lacks the "power of the sword" and has no direct impact on its citizens in form of the "power of the purse".

3.2 Arguments in Favour of Centralisation or Non-centralisation of Foreign Relations Within the European Integration

3.2.1 General Remarks

It is – so we think – always worthwhile to compare different federal systems. Through comparison, we may gain insights into specific processes and impulses for institutional development.

What is the relevance of our comparison as far as external relations in federal systems are concerned? Federal constitutions generally assign questions of foreign policy to the federation, particularly to the federal government. The central state is thus given a virtual monopoly over foreign affairs, even in matters over which the federal sub-entities (Länder, Cantons, States) had jurisdiction for internal purposes.

[59]Case 294/83 *Les Verts v. Parliament* (ECJ 23 April 1986) para 23.
[60]Art. 50 TEU.

It is fundamentally a matter for the federation to represent the state as a whole in its international relations and to defend it against any threats to the body politic. This is a fundamental difference between federal states proper and the EU. Unlike most states, it grew from inside to the outside: The Communities were, at the outset, charged with the regulation of the internal market; questions of foreign policy emerged later. In contrast, as far as national federal states are concerned, the first and main function to be entrusted to the federation was to represent its Member States in external relations. *Alfred Escher*, an influential Zurich statesman of the nineteenth century, coined a maxim to describe this arrangement: *internal diversity and external unity* ("Vielfalt im Innern, Einheit nach aussen").

The EC/EU have not achieved external unity. The crisis over Georgia exposed the problems and limitations afflicting Europe when it tried to realise the dream of a strong EU playing a lead role on the world stage. The European reaction has in some ways evoked the familiar stereotypes: The EU is rich but bureaucratic, sophisticated but timid, big but profoundly divided between the aging powers of the West and impatient newcomers of the East. Its main weapon is soft power. It did not want to, and probably would not have been able to, twist some arms – so the EU mission in Georgia, consisting of some 300 observers, has a mandate to patrol regions adjacent to South Ossetia and Abkhazia in Georgia proper, not the separatist regions themselves. Rather than the EU, it was *Nicolas Sarkozy*, *Silvio Berlusconi* and other leaders with good relationships with Russia who could present themselves as alternatives to, and intermediaries for, Washington. Admittedly, the "European Union Force" (EUFOR[61]) has successfully accomplished in its past four peacekeeping missions – Macedonia 2003, Bosnia 2004, Congo 2006 and Chad since 2007.

3.2.2 Varying Conceptions of a Union's External Profile

The above conclusions lead us to the controversial question of the Union's foreign policy profile. According to the Lisbon Treaty, a President of the European Council is elected to run the business of the Council for two and a half years – with the possibility to be re-elected for another two and a half years. Inter alia, the President represents the Union at an international level.[62] Clearly, such an office strengthens the external appearance of the Union and guarantees more continuity. It does also, after many years, provide an answer to *Henry Kissinger*, who famously asked: *Who do I call if I want to call Europe?* Similarly, under the Lisbon Treaty, a High Representative of the Union for Foreign Affairs and Security Policy is responsible for the development of a Common Foreign and Security Policy (CFSP). He is also, "ex officio", one of the Vice-Presidents of the Commission.[63]

---

[61]EUFOR is a temporary military deployment, not a permanent military force, coordinated by the High Representative for the CFSP.

[62]Arts. 15.5 and 6 TEU.

[63]Arts. 18.4 TEU.

With regard to these changes, there are two aspects worth considering. On the one hand, institutions and offices such as the Presidency of the foreign minister are commonly associated with the concept of the concentration of power – if only as a result of the nomenclature used to describe them. Experience has shown that power tends to be used to serve the personal interests of the occupants of the respective positions, and tempt the office-holders to abuse their power. On the other hand, we should ask ourselves whether the institutions of European integration could achieve a unique quality by providing for the representation and interaction of diverse (political) cultures. We could thus argue that nowadays, the responsible bodies of the Union should be allocated the special and genuine task of turning away from the old nation state concept of power. They could help to embrace a modern concept of values and ideals, disseminating the achievements evolved and developed over the course of Europe's rich history from the times of antiquity, through the Renaissance and Enlightenment to the modern day.

(a) *Power scepticism as a general argument against centralisation of external power*

When reading the provisions for the Union's foreign relations in the Lisbon Treaty,[64] even observers in favour of the Treaty might be led to adopt a suspicious point of view – that of the *power sceptics*. They may ask themselves whether a full-time President and a High Representative of the Union are indeed necessary and desirable.

It is true that according to the Lisbon Treaty, the bodies responsible for an EU foreign policy carry relatively little weight. But in the longer term, the question will arise whether Europe should in the end really have only *one* foreign policy with regard to important matters, share solely *one* identical Weltanschauung. So, power sceptics might ask themselves if Europe should address the outside world with only *one* voice. This vision or concept is not self-evident, because the basic concepts, traditions and identities of Europe do rather incorporate pluralism and competition.[65] People sceptical of the Union's new foreign policy will continue to query whether a common foreign policy (which some states hope to achieve in the future) does not carry the inherent risk that it will always be determined by the smallest common denominator in each case. To give an example: A Member State wishing to distinguish itself by enforcing a progressive human rights, environmental or innovative peace policy could find its initiatives unfortunately thwarted by the EU's positions on foreign policy.

From a "power-sceptic" viewpoint, there is also the question whether an integrated foreign policy will not de facto assign the greatest importance to the biggest powers and that the smaller members will cave in under the "pressure" or even "dictates" of the larger powers. The final point mentioned by "power sceptics" is that citizens all over the world, including those in Europe, are quickly becoming

---

[64] Especially Arts. 21 et seqq. TEU.

[65] On this, see Frowein (2004), pp. 430 et seq.

tired of governmental meetings which not only advance incentives and inspirations for the promotion of high-level politics over their heads and the heads of their national representatives, but also present them with *faits accomplis*.[66] Did the destiny of Europe not rest in the hands of princes and other rulers for far too long? Did not despots deploy power and egotism like the pieces in a chess game to further their own interests? Sceptics may therefore ask whether we really want the "team photos" of the European Council that appear from time to time in the media to depict a full-time President as overall boss with long-term particular internal and external responsibilities, in contrast to the rotation system employed up to now.[67]

(b) *Cosmopolitan vision as an argument for centralising foreign policy competences*

The view of the "power sceptics" is countered by an opposed one that stresses the attractiveness of the possibilities offered by the Lisbon Treaty for developing the EU's foreign policy profile. Adherents of a stronger institutionally based presence of the EU in the field of international relations share a universalistic perspective of the EU as a promoter of human rights, democracy, environmental protection and so on. They think that the EU should shoulder some responsibility within the global community.

This view point is in essence "pro-peace". Proponents of this view are indeed aware of the aforementioned objections that may be raised against the institution of a President and a High Representative of the Union. But at the same time, they believe that the proposals put forward by the defunct Convention and now by the Lisbon Treaty will preserve the distinctive features of Europe in our modern world of increasing globalisation. This argument is particularly manifest if considered from a historical perspective, since European countries have been making their stamp on other countries and the entire world in the fields of culture, science, politics and economy for three thousand years. So, foreign policy has been characterised, from the Roman Empire to the colonial period, by an imperial nature.[68] In a similar manner, the United States has in recent years been striving

[66]In addition, experience from the area of international and supranational organisations, but also federative constructs based on the law of national states, show us that precisely small units can exert an influence as "mediators" or "brokers".

[67]Cf. Allott (2002), pp. 380 et seqq., coined the expression of "Hof-Mafia". He wrote: "There were no rules about who could participate in the international court of courts but, as at Versailles or Schönbrunn or Potsdam or St Petersburg, mere presence as part of what we may call the international Hofmafia did not confer any automatic degree of power or influence or even of prestige" (p. 384) and: "The Congress of Vienna was the last great party of the old order dancing on its own grave" (p. 382).

[68]Cf. Weil (2002), p. 55: "Rome, like every colonizing country, had morally and spiritually uprooted than conquered countries. Such is always the effect of a colonial conquest. It was not a question of giving them back their roots. It was necessary they should still be a little further uprooted." Cf. also p. 17 on the link between colonialism and mission: "Missionary zeal has not

to acquire a hegemonic status. As a conscious departure from its historical tradition of power and colonial politics and as an alternative to the hegemonial attitude of the United States, it might be an attractive proposition for Europe to attempt to promote and influence a policy of human rights, democracy, the protection of minorities, environmental protection and above all the "Rule of Law"[69] in the other continents. Proponents of "para-national" foreign policy structures for the Union argue that a consolidation of forces is necessary to balance out the changing of power structures in the world. In this context, it should be mentioned that in spite of the serious errors of judgement and excesses of power of the *Bush* administration in Washington, Europe and the United States still share common values and, to a large extent, interests. In the long term, the balance of power will therefore continue to be struck between the West and the other parts of the world. In this case, should not the West attempt to establish a common international platform to promote democracy and human rights? It would seem to us that this perspective has gained force when *Barack Obama* was elected 44th President of the United States, (temporarily) suspending the "kangoroo courts" of Guantánamo on his first day in office.

Considering the actual European power dynamics, the institutions provided for by the treaty are not powerful enough to dominate or silence the multiple other voices in the Member States. Nevertheless, according to this view, representative institutions of a European foreign policy would all the same be desirable in order to provide a genuine (military) security policy.[70] At the same time, it would be perfectly feasible to appoint a "Council" instead of a President.[71] Such a board would, in true European tradition, in turn reflect and embody the diversity of the political cultures of the continent. The important factor would be the symbolic value of the institution.

If we accept the *Schuman* declaration of 1950 as the moment in which the historical concept of a constructive, active EU foreign policy was envisaged,[72] then the realisation of this concept is now at hand. Europe, having abolished conflicts on its own territory, will disseminate its modern vision of peace as an institutionalised dialog between states, nations and people to the outside world. This does not require a powerful "President of the European Republic". Nonetheless, in view of the particular history and potential for the development of Europe, an institutionally transparent pan-European authority endowed with persuasive

---

Christianized Africa, Asia and Oceania, but has brought these territories under the cold, cruel and destructive domination of the white race, which has trodden down everything."

[69] Cf. Singer (2002), particularly pp. 106 et seqq. This principle is, by the way, formally inscribed in the EU Treaty: See the reference to it in Art. 6.1, which holds the general principles for membership of the Union. Moreover, Art. 7 contains the modalities of the procedure to look after the respect, by the Member States, of the principles of Art. 6.1. In this regard, the so-called "Copenhague criterias" of course also have to be mentioned.

[70] Cf. the critical view of Nye (2004). See further Thürer (2000), pp. 452 et seqq.

[71] See however the remarks of Kaddous (2008b), pp. 219 et seq.

[72] Cf. von Bogdandy (2004), pp. 1 et seq.

powers[73] and with the flexible tools of a peace policy[74] could still bring about an improvement in global politics.

(c) *Need of a balanced view*

Is preference to be given to one of the two opposite positions? Or is there perhaps a middle way, a synthesis?

The power-sceptic reflex, which is part of the basic ethos of constitutional experts, is counterbalanced by the understanding that the main power centres in Europe will continue to reside within the individual states, and that the image of the Union will continue to be characterised by the diversity of identities and cultures shared by the European countries and peoples. If one takes a closer look at the actual policies of the EU, then the horror visions of power excesses by the new foreign policy bodies seem exaggerated. On the other hand, idealistic hopes for peace lack substance and feasibility. As a synthesis, we may therefore come to the conclusion that it is completely inappropriate to think in terms of "out" and "in", i.e. to try to make a distinction between the "European world" and the "world out there". This signifies that we are not going to witness the formation of a new monolithic "European Union" that speaks and acts uniformly, directly copying and extrapolating the old cliché of the nation state. Rather, the Union will correspond to the spirit and tradition of the broadest definition of Europe in that it will retain the concept of inward and outward flexibility and encompass variable pluralistic embodiments. Open networks of communication and cooperation may in the long run be much more productive and, paradoxically, much more effective than large-scale national or para-national structures. The concept that successful peace policies as administered in the European interior will now be employed externally appears to us an extremely rewarding ideal and objective for the Union. In our opinion, it is desirable that a European foreign policy should above all advocate human rights, international humanitarian law, democracy, the protection of minorities and environmental protection. These objectives could be aspired by the EU, but just as well by the Council of Europe, the Organization for Security and Cooperation in Europe (OSCE), and also the Member States on their own or together.

3.3 Outlook

On our journey through the world of federal institutions we have reached a most interesting and innovative stage in federal "engineering", particularly on the

[73] A better example would be – albeit in an attenuated form – the German Federal President rather than the French President.

[74] From this perspective it is also to be regretted that Europe's commitment in the area of active peace policy, in particular in peacekeeping, has diminished.

European level. The process of European integration has lifted us above the domain of the sovereign state and has confronted us with the unprecedented phenomenon of the pooling of sovereignty. National sovereignty has been transformed through the institutions that have emerged in the supranational union of states and nations. The principle of federalism has taken on new and original forms in the area of European integration. A particularly topical aspect was, of course, the ambitious plan of establishing a European constitution. It is – perhaps regrettably – hardly imaginable that the constitutional project, important and inspiring as it may be, is a substantive perspective for a new legal order of the EU. Rather, it seems clear that the European "pouvoir constituant" will continue in the foreseeable future to consist not of a single European people but of several different nations. The EU will essentially remain a union of states and of their peoples and is not going to mutate into a European nation state. This is probably axiomatic and a specific feature of the realisation of the federalist principle in the European region.

In terms of external relations, flexible arrangements have to be found between the two poles of universal ambitions of a globalising society on the one hand and states bound by democracy on the other. As *Lord Dahrendorf* put it in an article in the Neue Zürcher Zeitung, not all roads to a strong Europe lead through Brussels.[75] A strong EU element in international policies is, of course, extremely important and decisive, and it should be developed further. However, besides a unified European dimension, the role of national parliaments in foreign and European relations should also be strengthened and complemented by international arrangements. National legislative bodies could make their own home-based and politically accountable contribution. Why should, for instance, the Union as such and not (also) single states take steps and have a strong security and humanitarian presence, for instance, in the East of Congo?

The Lisbon project was confronted with the Irish question. This gave us an opportunity to reflect further on the basics of the process of European integration. There are, after all, some significant federalist findings. Is it not a frequently overlooked, but essential and by no means self-evident, effect of European integration that, in their respective field of activity, government agencies (e.g. immigration authorities and employment offices) as well as commercial enterprises and individuals must treat the "other" – i.e. the nationals of another EU Member State – as fundamentally equal? Is it not remarkable that the legislative, executive and judicial branches at all levels of government are bound to keep constantly in mind the legal orders and traditions of which European integration is composed? In this sense, institutions shape our behaviour, and practices are internalised. We see that the saying "form follows substance" does not always apply; form can also predetermine substance. Institutions shape the conduct and even the thought processes of individuals. This everyday aspect of "federalism in action" is often overlooked.

[75] Dahrendorf (2008), p. 43.

References

Allott P (2002) The health of the nations – society and law beyond the state. Cambridge
Andena M, Usher JA (eds) (2003) The Treaty of Nice and beyond: enlargement and constitutional reform. Oxford
Barberis JA (1983) Nouvelles questions concernant la personnalité juridique internationale. Recueil des Cours 179(I):145 et seqq
Bieber R, Epiney A, Haag M (2009) Die Europäische Union: Europarecht und Politik, 8th edn. Baden-Baden
Bindschedler R (1995) International organizations: general aspects. In: Bernhard R et al (eds) Encyclopedia of public international law, vol II. Amsterdam a.o., pp 1299 et seqq
Busse C (1999) Die völkerrechtliche Einordnung der Europäischen Union. Köln
Cloos J et al (1994) Le Traité de Maastricht, genèse, analyse, commentaires, 2nd edn. Brussels
Craig P, de Búrca G (2008) EU law, 4th edn. Oxford
Curtin DM, Dekker IF (1999) The European Union as a 'layered' international organisation: institutional unity in disguise. In: Craig P, de Búrca G (eds) European law: an evolutionary perspective. Oxford, pp 83 et seqq
Curtin D, Heukels T (eds) (1994) Institutional dynamics of European integration, essays in honour of Henry G. Schermers, vol II. Dordrecht
Dahrendorf R (2008) Europa – oder die irische Frage: Plädoyer für die Rückkehr zu den Quellen und für einen Neubeginn. In: Neue Zürcher Zeitung of 2 July 2008, p 43
Dashwood A (1998) External relations provisions of the Amsterdam Treaty. CMLRev 35:1019 et seqq
Dashwood A (2000) The attribution of external relations competence. In: Dashwood A, Hillion C (eds) The general law of E.C. external relations. London, pp 115 et seqq
Dashwood A, Hliskoski J (2000) The classic authorities revisited. In: Dashwood A, Hillion C (eds) The general law of E.C. external relations. London, pp 3 et seqq
Eaton MR (1994) Common Foreign and Security Policy. In: O'Keeffe D, Twomey PM (eds) Legal issues of the Maastricht treaty. London, pp 215 et seqq
Everling U (1992) Reflections of the structure of the European Union. CMLRev 29:1053 et seqq
From the Constitution to a new round of treaty: step-by-step (editorial comments). CMLRev 44:1229 et seqq
Frowein JA (2004) Die Herausbildung europäischer Verfassungsprinzipien. in: Frowein JA (ed) Völkerrecht – Menschenrechte – Verfassungsfragen Deutschlands und Europas. Berlin, pp 421 et seqq
Ginther K (1994) Verantwortlichkeit, Haftung und Verantwortlichkeit im Völkerrecht. In: Ginther K et al (eds) Völkerrecht zwischen normativem Anspruch und politischer Realität: Festschrift für Karl Zemanek zum 65. Geburtstag, Berlin, pp 335 et seqq
Goldsmith L (2008) Direct democracy and the European Union ... is that a threat or a promise? (editorial comments). CMLRev 45:929 et seqq
Herdegen M (2008) Europarecht, 10th edn. Munich
Heukels T, de Zwaan JW (1994) The configuration of the European Union: community dimensions of institutional interaction. In: Curtin D, Heukels T (eds) Institutional dynamics of European integration, essays in honour of Henry G. Schermers, vol II. Dordrecht, pp 195 et seqq
Hilf M (1982) Die Organisationsstruktur der Europäischen Gemeinschaften. Berlin a.o.
Hilf M (1994) Die Europäische Union und die Eigenstaatlichkeit ihrer Mitgliedstaaten. In: Hommelhoff P, Kirchhoff P (eds) Der Staatenverbund der Europäischen Union. Heidelberg, pp 75 et seqq
Hirsch M (1995) The responsibility of international organizations toward third parties: some basic principles. Dordrecht
Jaag T (2003a) Europarecht. Zurich
Jaag T (2003b) verfassungsvertrag für die Europäische Union. Zeitschrift für Europarecht 5:104 et seqq

Kaddous C (2008a) Effects of international agreements in the EU legal order. In: Cremona M, de Witte B (eds) EU foreign law: constitutional fundamentals. Oxford, pp 291 et seqq
Kaddous C (2008b) Role and position of the High Representative of the Union for Foreign Affairs and security policy under the Lisbon Treaty. In: Giller S, Ziller J (eds) (2008) The Lisbon Treaty: EU constitutionalism without a constitutional treaty? Vienna, pp 205 et seqq
Klabbers J (1998) Presumptive personality: the European Union in international law. In: Koskenniemi M (ed) International law aspects of the European Union. The Hague, pp 231 et seqq
Kuyper PJ (1979) The Netherlands and international organizations. In: van Panhuys HF et al (eds) International law in the Netherlands, vol II. Alphan an den Rijn, pp 3 et seqq
Nye J Jr (2004) Soft power – the means to success in world politics. New York
Oppermann T, Classen CD, Nettesheim M (2009) Europarecht, 4th edn. Munich
Peters A (2001) Elemente einer Theorie der Verfassung Europas. Berlin
Pliakos AD (1993) La nature juridique de l'Union européenne. Revue Trimestrielle de Droit Européen 29:187 et seqq
Scelle G (1933) Règles générales du droit de la paix. Recueil des Cours 46(IV):327 et seqq
Scelle G (1943) Manuel élémentaire de droit international public: avec les textes essentiels. Paris
Scelle G (1956) Le phénomène juridique du dédoublement fonctionnel. In: Schätzel W, Schlochauer H-J (eds) Rechtsfragen der internationalen Organisation, Festschrift für Hans Wehberg. Frankfurt a.M., pp 324 et seqq
Schroeder W (2003) Verfassungsrechtliche Beziehungen zwischen Europäischer Union und Europäischen Gemeinschaft. In: von Bogdandy A (ed) Europäisches Verfassungsrecht – Theoretische und dogmatische Grundzüge. Heidelberg, pp 373 et seqq
Schwarze J (2003) Ein pragmatischer Verfassungsentwurf – Analyse und Bewertung des vom Europäischen Verfassungskonvent vorgelegten Entwurfs eines Vertrags über eine Verfassung für Europa. EuR, pp 535 et seqq
Schwarze J et al (eds) (2009) Der Reformvertrag von Lissabon. Baden-Baden
Seidl-Hohenveldern I (1998) The legal personality of international and supranational organizations. In: Seidl-Hohenveldern I (ed) Collected essays on international investments and on international organizations. The Hague, pp 3 et seqq
Seidl-Hohenveldern I, Loibl G (2000) Das Recht der internationalen Organisationen einschließlich der Supranationalen Gemeinschaften, 7th edn. Cologne a.o.
Singer P (2002) One world – the ethics of globalization. New Haven
Streinz R (2008) Europarecht, 8th edn. Heidelberg
Stumpf C (2009) In: Schwarze J (ed) EU-Kommentar, 2nd edn. Baden-Baden, Art. 1 EUV
Thürer D (2000) Soft law. In: Bernhard R et al (eds) Encyclopedia of public international law, vol IV. Amsterdam a.o., pp 452 et seqq
Thürer D (2005) Wie weiter in Europa? – Von der Denkpause zu neuem föderalistischem Denken. In: Neue Zürcher Zeitung of 16 August 2005, p 13
Thürer D (2006) Perspectives of the project for a European Constitution. In: Blanke H-J, Mangiameli S (eds) Governing Europe under a constitution. Berlin, pp 41 et seqq
von Bogdandy A (1998) Die Europäische Union als einheitlicher Verband. In: von Bogdandy A, Ehlermann C-D (eds) Konsolidierung und Kohärenz des Primärrechts nach Amsterdam. EuR Beiheft 2/1998, pp 165 et seqq
von Bogdandy A (1999) The legal case for unity: the European Union as a single organizisation with a single legal system. CMLRev 36:887 et seqq
von Bogdandy A (ed) (2003) Europäisches Verfassungsrecht – Theoretische und dogmatische Grundzüge. Heidelberg
von Bogdandy A (2004) Europäische Verfassung und europäische Identität. JZ 59:53 et seqq
von Bogdandy A, Nettesheim M (1986) Die Europäische Union: Ein einheitlicher Verband mit eigener Rechtsordnung. EuR 1996:3 et seqq
von der Groeben H, Schwarze J (eds) (2003) Kommentar zum Vertrag über die Europäische Union und zur Gründung der Europäischen Gemeinschaft, vol IV, 6th edn. Baden-Baden
Weidenfeld W (ed) (2002) Nizza in der Analyse, 3rd edn. Gütersloh

Weil S (2002) Letter to a priest (Paris 1951). London
Weiler JHH (1981) The community system – the dual character of supranationalism. Yearb Eur Law 1:267 et seqq
Wellenstein EP (1992) Unity, community, union – what's in a name? (guest editorial). CMLRev 29:205 et seqq
Zuleeg M (2003) Die Vorzüge der Europäischen Verfassung. In: von Bogdandy A (ed) Europäisches Verfassungsrecht – Theoretische und dogmatische Grundzüge. Heidelberg, pp 931 et seqq

Desiring a Democratic European Polity: The European Union Between the Constitutional Failure and the Lisbon Treaty

Jiří Přibáň

1 Introduction

The problem of democracy is general and the European Union (EU) is just one of its many specific contexts. During EU constitution-making, political constructivist notions of European democratic polity-building and federal statehood in waiting were frequently courted by European politicians and political scientists. At the beginning of the new millennium, the EU was engaged in the self-generating process of supranational form of constitutionalism which was expected to legally strengthen the principle of democratic legitimacy at EU level and thus justify the concept of an 'ever-closer Union' within the context of political and legal integration.

Reflecting on what actually happened during the EU constitution-making process and its subsequent rejection by the French and the Dutch referenda in 2005, the most remarkable phenomenon was a contrast between the official EU language of public enthusiasm and the wall of private distrust of citizens in individual Member States. Ambitious statements made by Euroenthusiastic politicians were accompanied by a dismissal of any criticisms and discontents regarding the state and future of the EU as 'anti-European', 'Eurosceptic' and even 'Europhobic'. A journey from one currency to one EU politics and one European polity governed by a constitution was considered an iron law of European integration. Echoing the Marxist logic of a political and ideological superstructure catching up with an economic substructure, advocates of evermore progressive integration assumed that the Constitutional Treaty could be enacted in the same manner as the Euro currency and even be enthusiastically welcomed by the peoples of the EU, if not by the European people in waiting.

J. Přibáň (✉)
Cardiff Law School, Cardiff University, Law Building, Museum Ave, Cardiff CF10 3AX, Wales, UK
e-mail: Priban@cardiff.ac.uk

H.-J. Blanke and S. Mangiameli (eds.), *The European Union after Lisbon*,
DOI 10.1007/978-3-642-19507-5_4,

After the failure of the constitutional experiment, the Lisbon 'Reform' Treaty was drafted and all Member States except Ireland, which was constitutionally obliged to call a referendum, avoided the process of ratification by this form of direct democracy. This choice itself weakened democratic legitimacy of the Lisbon Treaty. Despite such distrust of the popular will among national governments, the Lisbon Treaty was subsequently rejected by the Irish referendum of 2008 and, while the European Council kept a low profile regarding renegotiations of the Treaty with the Irish government,[1] the Treaty suffered further ratification complications in the Czech Republic and was reviewed by constitutional courts in Germany and other Member States. The current state of the Union, therefore, persuasively illustrates that the process of economic integration does not automatically lead to supranational political integration and a constitutional momentum of state-building. It rather shows that political problems require political solutions which, within the EU institutional settings, cannot imitate processes, legitimation expectations and institutional frameworks of the modern nation state in its federal or confederative forms.

The process of transferring evermore power to the Union without adequate political accountability and democratisation indicates a political deficit of the EU[2] which has recently been exploited by nationalist populist leaders in a number of Member States. According to those politicians, the very fact of cultural and socio-political differences among EU nations makes any project of a functioning polity impossible and dangerous from the perspective of national cohesion, integrity and sovereignty.[3] The Union's impossibility to equally recognise its political potential, tasks and limits invites adherents of the dark legacy of European ethnonationalism to represent themselves as the guardians of nation state democratic institutions and democracy itself against the supranational undemocratic Union.

The populist right and left hugely benefited from the process of European integration driven by dreams rather than political reality.[4] This current ideological battleground is a semantic reflection of the Union's intrinsic structural paradoxes, which increasingly call for political reforms of the Union and enhancement of its supranational democratic legitimacy.

In this context, several questions are of primary importance regarding the Lisbon Treaty and its incorporation of the principle of democratic legitimacy and representative democracy. Does the treaty successfully avoid the conceptual obscurantism of EU constitution-making mixing international law principles with hierarchies typical of federal or confederative statehood? Does the treaty mean both significant enhancement of the Union's democratic legitimacy and a final demise of the political dream of 'EU constitutional statehood' and 'European

---

[1] *Presidency Conclusions of the Council of the European Union*, CONCL 4, No. 14368/08, 16 October 2008.

[2] J. Přibáň (2007), p. 123.

[3] B. Benoit (1997).

[4] For this incapacity, see Dahrendorf (2004), chapter 9.

polity' without democratic legitimacy of *pouvoir constituant* of the European *demos*? In other words, can the Union democratise its institutions while abandoning the project of building the democratic European polity by legal means and administrative governance?

Following these persistent issues, the chapter opens by summarising the democratic principle commitments formulated by the Lisbon 'Reform' Treaty and their impact on the character of European governance and European polity. The most recent EU attempts at democratising its forms of governance are subsequently contextualised by outlining historical links between the EU's institutional framework and the notion of European polity. The tension between instrumental legitimation by outcomes and symbolic legitimation by democratic values shows that the evolutionary dynamics of European polity is not reducible to institutional innovations and becomes evermore challenged by the principles of democratic representations and participation. Furthermore, the problem of popular sovereignty at the EU level reveals the importance of a European political identity, which is irreducible to legal documents and involves ethical self-reflections of the Union as a political organisation promoting cosmopolitan democratic values and universal humanity. The final part of the chapter, therefore, recursively analyses the political role of those values in the Union's external politics, especially recent EU enlargements.

2 Desiring the Democratic Union? The Lisbon Treaty's Incorporation of Democratic Principles

Focusing on the most recent attempts at creating the 'ever-closer Union', the Lisbon Treaty looks like a retreat from ambitious plans of progressive integration by the process of constitution-making. The other name of the Lisbon Treaty – 'the Reform Treaty' – indicates that the process of progressive integration needed to be revised and reformed after the Constitutional Treaty's rejection by the French and Dutch citizens in 2005.

Analysing the principle of democratic legitimacy and representation, it is important to emphasise that the Lisbon Treaty is neither a constitutional document of self-determination of the democratic European nation, nor an act of a democratically representative political body. If one can use the term at all, the Union's *pouvoir constituant* lies with the peoples of the EU collectively as represented by their national parliaments and governments in their political diversity. It is an international law treaty strengthening the current state of European economic and political integration and opening new options of further integration.

This retreat from constitutional ambitions is confirmed by the abandonment of the original idea behind a constitutional treaty according to which a new treaty was intended to replace all previous legal foundations of the EU and operate as a new legal basis of the Union. Unlike this idea of a constitutional beginning, the Lisbon Treaty leaves all previous treaties in place and merely operates as their novelisation.

The Constitutional Treaty's references to European 'law' and 'framework law' have been abandoned and the existing concepts of 'regulations', 'directives' and 'decisions' have been retained by drafters of the Lisbon Treaty.[5] Any possibility of jurisprudential assumptions of legal monism constructing the constitutional supremacy of the Union's legal system over legal systems of Member States has thus been ruled out and the current system of EU law continues to recognise the horizontal plurality of legal systems as well as of its own legal acts. The incorporation of the *Charter of Fundamental Rights of the European Union* and its limitation as regards the competences of the Union as well as the Union's accession to the *European Convention for the Protection of Human Rights and Fundamental Freedoms* serve as examples of this continuing legal pluralism within the EU.

Responding to the Constitutional Treaty's ratification failure and building on the democratic legitimacy commitment already incorporated in the Treaty of Amsterdam and the Treaty of Nice,[6] the Lisbon Treaty opens by an explicit proclamation turning the EU's biggest fear, the democratic legitimacy and its deficit, into a political desire. It directly links the Union's governance and its efficiency-driven 'legitimacy by outcomes' to the legitimacy by democratic values and procedures:

> DESIRING to enhance further the democratic and efficient functioning of the institutions so as to enable them better to carry out, within a single institutional framework, the tasks entrusted to them.[7]

At the level of general proclamations and principles, the Treaty thus makes the Union considerably more committed to the discourse of democratic legitimation and/or its absence. The legalist language of the EU accommodates the need to democratise representation, political participation, openness and accountability of EU institutions.

Scrutinising democratic principles of the EU in detail, Title II is an obvious starting point of any legal analysis. It is noteworthy that Art. 9 of the Treaty opens by drafting the first principle of justice as fairness – the equal treatment of all citizens before EU laws – together with the legal construction of EU citizenship as additional and not replacing national citizenship. Drafters considered the principle

---

[5]See *The Council of the European Union Note No. 11218/07*, 'IGC 2007 Mandate', Brussels, 26 June 2007, p. 3.

[6]Kohler-Koch and Rittberger (2007).

[7]Preamble of the *Treaty of Lisbon amending the Treaty on European Union and the Treaty establishing European Community, Consolidated Version of the Treaty on European Union*, O.J. C 115/15 (9 May 2008). In the text approved at the Intergovernmental Conference in Brussels in December 2007, there is an explicit remark tracing this commitment back to the Treaty of Amsterdam and the Treaty of Nice: 'Desiring to complete the process started by the Treaty of Amsterdam and by the Treaty of Nice with a view to enhancing the efficiency and democratic legitimacy of the Union and to improving the coherence of its action …' CIG 14/07, Brussels, 3 December 2007.

of civic equality before the law as a constitutive principle of any supranational form of governance by European legality[8] and thus fully adopted what has been the most important precondition of the existence of any democratic polity.

In Art. 10 TEU, the Union is specified as an organisation 'founded on representative democracy', which means that its Member States are assumed to be democratic nation states functioning through their representative political bodies. Furthermore, the Union itself guarantees direct representation of EU citizens in the European Parliament.[9] The Parliament has only limited powers regarding the legislative process in the Union and certainly does not channel the political process in a manner comparable to parliaments of nation states. Furthermore, its members do not represent the democratic sovereign will of one European nation voting according to the principle 'one citizen, one vote' beyond their Member State constituencies. Nevertheless, while the Union does not exercise its power on the assumption of direct democratic legitimacy of its officials and legislator, EU citizens are not limited to channelling their public voice and collective will through political institutions of Member States. They equally can use the European Parliament as a forum of supranational political deliberation democratically representing citizens of the EU Member States.

The EU thus emerges as a supranational organisation guaranteeing the public voice of its citizens, yet denying their political will to be shaping EU political institutions in a system comparable to that of the democratic nation state. Compensating for this structural limitation, the Lisbon Treaty seeks to strengthen democratic controls of EU institutions by the alternative strategy of making national democratically elected parliaments part of its decision-making process and effectively turning them into agencies of the EU system of political checks and balances.

This move clearly shows that suggestions of introducing more expertise-oriented and deliberative concepts of legitimation as substitutes for democratic legitimation where representative democracy cannot be implemented at EU level have only limited validity.[10] Expert knowledge, deliberation and its outcomes cannot fully sideline and substitute for institutions of representative democracy. Article 12 TEU therefore allocates more powers to national parliaments, especially their involvement in guaranteeing the EU principle of subsidiarity.[11] Due to the non-existence of the democratically elected legislator and democratically accountable government at EU level, the Union continues to be based on the principle of conferral, which is typical of international organisations. Enhancement of its democratic legitimacy, therefore, has been directly linked to the strengthening of the principles of subsidiarity and proportionality.[12]

---

[8]*Consolidated Version of the Treaty on European Union*, O.J. C 115/20 (2008).

[9]*Consolidated Version of the Treaty on European Union*, O.J. C 115/20 (2008).

[10]Joerges and Neyer (1997), pp. 273–299.

[11]*Consolidated Version of the Treaty on European Union*, O.J. C 115/20 (2008).

[12]Article 5 TEU: '1. The limits of Union competences are governed by the principle of conferral. The use of Union competences is governed by the principles of subsidiarity and proportionality.

The process of progressive integration runs as a coeval process of power transfer to the EU and increasingly growing involvement of democratic institutions of the Member States in EU policy and decision-making. This process is illustrated by two protocols attached to the Lisbon Treaty, namely the *Protocol on the role of national parliaments in the European Union* and the *Protocol on the application of the principles of subsidiarity and proportionality*. Both protocols give more influence to national legislators to potentially challenge the EU legislation and thus make democratically elected and representative institutions of the Member States directly involved in operations of EU institutions. Indeed, this involvement recursively enhances limited democratic legitimacy of the European Parliament, the Council and the Commission.

The political system of the EU thus evolves through parallel processes of the Union's self-empowering and the continuing active involvement of sovereign Member States via their independent democratic political systems. While the Union benefits from the process of power transfer from the national level to the European level, its very existence fully depends on the Member States and the system of their political negotiations and legal agreements. The system of EU politics is not superior to those of the Member States but rather coexists and benefits from them and internalises their operations.

As regards democratic legitimation, this structural setting has significant consequences because it incorporates the system of international cooperation which commonly tends to compromise parliamentary power and control. Unable to actively participate in the creation of acts of legislation, it is evermore important that national parliaments can have monitoring powers and possibly even block acts of European legislation. Furthermore, bringing national parliaments onboard EU decision-making significantly contributes to the improvement of accountability of both EU and Member State executive powers.[13]

However, the Lisbon Treaty does not treat democratic principles merely as a problem of checks and balances within the EU political system and between EU institutions and national parliaments. It fully reflects on the importance of the European public sphere as a domain of democratic will-formation and civic deliberation. This structural precondition of further democratisation of European politics is especially formulated by Arts. 10 and 11 TEU.

---

2. Under the principle of conferral, the Union shall act only within the limits of the competences conferred upon it by the Member States in the Treaties to attain the objectives set out therein. Competences not conferred upon the Union in the Treaties remain with the Member States.
3. Under the principle of subsidiarity, in areas which do not fall within its exclusive competence, the Union shall act only if and in so far as the objectives of the proposed action cannot be sufficiently achieved by the Member States, either at central level or at regional and local level, but can rather, by reason of the scale or effects of the proposed action, be better achieved at Union level.'

[13]This problem was already discussed during the process of EU constitution-making. See, for instance, Crum (2005), pp. 452–467, at 460–465.

Article 11 TEU primarily legislates for the principle of transparency of EU bodies and their public accountability but it also includes a specific procedure of civic activism and public deliberation is formulated in its section 4 which reads:

> Not less than one million citizens who are nationals of a significant number of Member States may take the initiative of inviting the European Commission, within the framework of its powers, to submit any appropriate proposal on matters where citizens consider that a legal act of the Union is required for the purpose of implementing the Treaties.[14]

In terms of civic activism and the Treaty's profound recognition of the importance of the European public sphere and civil society, the *citizens' initiative* section of Art. 11 TEU complements the fourth section of Art. 10 TEU, which states:

> [P]olitical parties at European level contribute to forming European political awareness and to expressing the will of citizens of the Union.[15]

Despite the aspirational character of this provision, which is based on the hypothesis that EU party politics may be communicated between national parliaments and the European Parliament through national political parties and their supranational coalitions formed at EU level, the principle of democratic representation is mainly elaborated by the Treaty as a system of representation of the Member States in and through EU political institutions. The principle extends to the Member State domain of democratic accountability of government to national parliaments and citizens of the country. Such democratically accountable and elected governments and/or Heads of Member State can be represented in the European Council and/or the Council.

Apart from provisions of the Lisbon Treaty's Title II, the democratic principle mainly appears in Title V, the Union's coordination of the common foreign and security policy. Under this title, Art. 21 TEU reads as follows:

> The Union's action on the international scene shall be guided by the principles which have inspired its own creation, development and enlargement, and which it seeks to advance in the wider world: democracy, the rule of law, the universality and indivisibility of human rights and fundamental freedoms, respect for human dignity, the principles of equality and solidarity, and respect for the principles of the United Nations Charter and international law.
>
> The Union shall seek to develop relations and build partnerships with third countries, and international, regional or global organisations which share the principles referred to in the first subparagraph. It shall promote multilateral solutions to common problems, in particular in the framework of the United Nations.[16]

This article primarily reflects on the stabilising and proselytising roles of the Union. It enhances the Union's self-referentiality regarding its general commitment to a set of political and legal principles and values which determine both EU enlargement policies and the Union's international policies.

---

[14] *Consolidated Version of the Treaty on European Union*, O.J. C 115/21 (2008).

[15] *Consolidated Version of the Treaty on European Union*, O.J. C 115/20 (2008).

[16] *Consolidated Version of the Treaty on European Union*, O.J. C 115/28 (2008).

3 European Governance and Its Impact on the Emerging European Polity

After the textual analysis of the Lisbon Treaty's incorporation of representative democracy, it is necessary to ask more general historical and contextual questions related to the democratic accountability and governance of the EU. The concept of polity generally signifies a state-organised society, its form and process of government. It assumes a system of legitimately exercised political power. In modern democratic polity, power circulates between the people, party politics, administration and public opinion communicated through mass media.[17] While the principle of popular sovereignty – sovereignty 'by the people' – provides the system with democratic legitimacy, political parties struggle to win power by winning a majority of the votes 'of the people' and thus form a government administering specific policies 'for the people' which can be recursively evaluated by the public, affect political preferences and thus contribute to the future processes of political majority-building.

Modern constitutional democracy is based on social communication between the state and the people. Its legitimacy ultimately rests on two main pillars: popular sovereignty and the rule of law and civil rights–based constitutionalism. A political system is democratically legitimate if it is imposed by the sovereign people on itself, and political power can be exercised either directly by the people or through their elected representatives. The system itself needs to be constitutionally legitimate in the sense that its principles, rules and procedures are expressed in legal form, and public officials and their actions are subject to the law. Democratic practices are governed by the rule of law and, at the same time, the legal rules are open to democratic change.[18]

As a form of political power, democracy is based on the representation of the people's will either directly or through a set of political institutions. Representative democracy means that the people, divided between its governing representatives and the governed citizens, constitute a political system of separated powers which mutually control and balance each other and all of which are ultimately guaranteed legitimacy by the people's sovereignty. Representation, therefore, is a method of the transformation of the popular will of individuals with equal rights and freedoms to the will and decision-making of democratically elected and accountable political institutions. By delegating certain powers to a limited number of officials, the system of representative democracy also creates private autonomy of citizens beyond the control of public political power.[19] Furthermore, it transforms the popular government into a government with the popular consent.

[17] N. Luhmann (2002), p. 258.

[18] For one of the most illuminating exchanges of views regarding constitutional and democratic legitimacy, see Habermas (1995), pp. 109–131; Rawls (1995), pp. 132–180.

[19] Schumpeter (1976).

The political constitution, backed by the sovereign power of the people, traditionally had two important functions – limiting the exercise of sovereign power by means of a system of constitutional checks and balances and symbolically constituting the whole of society. A sovereign act of popular constitution-making is constitutive of the systems of both politics and law, as well as expressing the collective identity of a democratic polity governing itself by delegating its sovereign power to its representatives. The expressive mode of collective identity stretches beyond the domain of law and politics and establishes the ethical and cultural self-reflections of the people as a real political force and a symbolically imagined community.[20]

The EU is short of power circulation, constitutional pillars and imagined collective identity typical of state-organised polities. Instead, the EU political system circulates power by the self-referential operations of its administrative organisation. State organisation is missing but alternative forms of governing and processes of decision-making are no less powerful. The absence of two out of Lincoln's three characteristics of democratic government,[21] namely government 'of the people' and 'by the people', makes the EU's political system one which primarily operates 'for the people' or, better, 'for the peoples of the EU'.

It is impossible to characterise the Union in common terms of territoriality, government, population and (in case of democratic statehood) popular legitimacy. In the absence of EU democratic government, the complex forms and processes of the Union's political decision-making are commonly labelled as a system of *European governance*. Furthermore, governance is considered a major force integrating the emerging *European polity* despite the absence of EU statehood and democratic government.[22]

The EU operating according to the legal provisions of the Lisbon Treaty clearly shall not become a democratic polity drawing on the principles of democratic will-formation and the majority rule. Its maximum 'reform effect' can be the construction of a polity operating on the enhanced principles of democratic representation of views, interests and preferences of citizens of the Union. Instead of its radical democratisation, the system of European governance continues to be an example of *negotiated governance* which has been agreed by the national governments of the Member States. Similarly, this system can hardly lead to either the establishment of the European *demos* as a symbolically imagined political community, or the creation of the European public sphere or civil society as a precondition of democratic deliberation and solidarity among citizens of the EU.

These original structural limitations of the Union have not been removed by the Lisbon Treaty. Negotiated governance and the continuing central role of the Member States effectively rules out any chance of building supranational European

---

[20]For the concept of imagined community and nationalism, see especially Anderson (1983).

[21]Lincoln (1989).

[22]Joerges and Dehousse (2002); Lindberg and Scheingold (1970); Riekmann et al. (2005).

statehood governed under a constitution. More than three decades ago, even such a strong advocate of European federalism as Leo Tindemans already warned against the utopian nature of European statehood as potentially damaging faith in Europe.[23] Instead of drafting a constitutional formula for Europe, which would imitate institutional settings of the modern nation state, the 1975 *Tindemans Report on European Union* focused on a series of unification efforts in the areas of foreign policy, economic and social policy, fundamental civil rights and institutional governance-driven alternatives of political, momentum-based, ready-made concepts of federal unification. In this context, Tindemans commented two decades later:

> Much as I would like to see a definitive federal union materialise overnight, I do not believe that it can happen or, at least, not in one sudden, gigantic step. If we were closer to some sort of popular high tide in support for the federalist model in the 1940s and 1950s, we were undoubtedly further away in 1974-5, and we are indisputably yet further away now.[24]

After the failure of EU constitution-making, the emphasis on spontaneity in the unification of Europe and the impossibility of ignoring that democratic legitimacy is embedded in the Member States became ever more urgent. European integration has become evermore dependent on democratisation of its institutions and EU democratisation has become a subject of evolution rather than a constitutional leap of faith in the European *demos* in waiting.

These trends imply two crucial questions, namely, how far the Union's powers and jurisdiction can be extended without questioning the democratic sovereignty of the Member States and to what extent effective European governance can expand without the institutional support of democratically legitimate political government.

4 Between Legitimation by Outcomes and Values: The Lisbon Treaty and Democratisation of European Polity

In recent EU history, the 'policy-generating' Single European Act (1987) was followed by the 'polity-creating' Maastricht Treaty of European Union (1993) and the 'system consolidating' Treaty of Amsterdam (1999) and Treaty of Nice (2001).[25] The Union's subsequent constitution-making did not succeed in generating the European public sphere and democratic legitimation of a constitutional treaty implementing a monistic legal system of clear hierarchies, competences and relations between the EU and its Member States. However, the

---

[23] Tindemans (1976).

[24] Tindemans (1998), pp. 130–141, at 139.

[25] Stubb (2002), p. 25.

Lisbon Treaty could not but continue in supporting the project of a *democratized European polity*.[26]

Until the Treaty of Amsterdam, Member States were assumed to be democratically governed and the principle of representative democracy did not inform the body of EU laws and functions of EU institutions. In this respect, the Lisbon Treaty reinforces former Art. 7 TEU and its enhancement by the Treaty of Nice (the *lex Austria* clause) when it makes possible for the Council 'to suspend certain of the rights deriving from the application of the Treaties to the Member State' if actions of this state constitute 'a clear risk of a serious breach'[27] of the Union's values of 'human dignity, freedom, equality, democracy, the rule of law, and respect for human rights'.[28]

Political themes of who is actually governed by EU institutions, how, in whose name and to what end[29] turned out inescapable vis-à-vis progressive European political integration, its commitment to democratic principles and impact on democratic institutions and legitimacy of the Member States. The current EU is commonly described as a multi-level polity both independent and reflexive of the Member State political systems. It can generate authoritative decisions through its self-regulatory system of governance and make them respected by interdependent nation state polities.[30] It transgresses state-centric forms of governance by shifting political decision-making to supranational institutions while preserving or even strengthening Member State power through EU membership. Although national governments remain strong participants in the processes of European governance, Member States have lost much of 'their former authoritative control over individuals in their respective territories'.[31]

The emphasis on instrumental rationality and legitimation by expertise makes European governance a challenge to the political authority of democratically elected legislative and administrative bodies. Within the EU context, this challenge is either successfully suppressed by the Union's institutions or made part of complex relations between those institutions and the EU Member States as democratically constituted political organisations. Indeed, European governance includes national governments and their specific governance networks. However, the duality of democratic government and administrative governance,[32] which is typical of national political systems, does not exist at the European level. European

---

[26]Clarke (2005), pp. 17–37, at 28.

[27]Article 7 of the *Consolidated Version of the Treaty on European Union*, O.J. C 115/19 (2008).

[28]Article 2 of the *Consolidated Version of the Treaty on European Union*, O.J. C 115/17 (2008).

[29]Banchoff and Smith (1999).

[30]For the analysis of different functional subsystems of European governance, see Marks et al. (1996).

[31]Hooghe and Marks (2001), p. 2.

[32]For the autopoietic relationship between politics and administration, see King and Thornhill (2003), pp. 79–85.

governance without government is self-regulatory and operates beyond the constraints of the government-based political systems of the Member States.

Within the context of European governance, the tension between instrumental *legitimation by outcomes* (based on policy effectiveness) and symbolic *legitimation by values* (based on the principles of democratic representation and participation)[33] has always been articulated through the often criticised but popular 'common benefit' discourse.[34] However, in the 1990s the 'permissive consensus' between the citizens of EU countries and Eurocratic elite administrative decisions was gradually replaced by a 'constraining dissensus' regarding the future direction and legal or constitutional settlement of European integration.[35]

The question of 'who governs the Union?' has often been overshadowed by the question of 'how is the Union governed?'. However, theoretical and political reflections of ever-growing European integration cannot escape the question of 'who governs' and 'who is governed' by the EU. In other words, European governance is not just a matter of instrumentality and different techniques of supranational governance but also a matter of substantive questions of democratic principles and their adoption by European polity.

Despite the wealth of debates on supranational governance, post-sovereignty, constitutionalism and the EU as a polycentric polity,[36] the discourse of popular democracy and national or European sovereignty remains an important reference point in political debates and conflicts within the context of both the EU and its Member States. It marks important political, juridical, economic and collective identity problems emerging coevally with globalisation and Europeanisation and the impossibility of continuing to build EU legitimacy on governance-driven efficiency rather than democratic accountability.[37] The dynamics of a European polity is not reducible to institutional innovations and the linking together of multiple arenas of supranational governance.

5 Europe as an Imagined Political Community and Its Democratic Cosmopolitan Ideals

Democracy is a theory of sovereignty which does not need any transcendental source of legitimation and draws on the force of political negotiation, deliberation and representation. No wonder that the EU project of ever-closer political union and integration by constitution-making, which involves the further transfer of powers from the Member States and more EU majority decision-making

[33]Scharpf (1999).

[34]Majone (1998), p. 5.

[35]Tsakatika (2007), pp. 30–54, at 31.

[36]See, for instance, Wind (2003), pp. 103–131.

[37]For the view that EU does not need demos but efficiency, see Steffek (2004), pp. 81–101.

(thus weakening the veto power of the Member States), has turned its attention to the problem of the European constituent power – the *demos*, or, rather, its absence.

As theories of democratic sovereignty and representation claim, 'the function of the majority rule is to establish a separation of powers, not between the classical *triad* of legislative, executive, and judicial power but between the *constitutive* and the *constituted* power'.[38] The growing exercise of majority power by EU institutions raises the question of compliance and obedience by dissenting states and communities within the Union. Can such compliance and obedience be justified by reference to the political community of which the dissenting parties are members and to which they give their unconditional loyalty? Does this construction of European society rely entirely on instrumental reason and political will, or does it also have the strong communal bonds and solidarity of an 'imagined community'?

The question of popular sovereignty at the EU level is inseparable from the process of the further political and legal integration of the Union. The absence of a European *demos* cannot be easily dismissed as marginal on the basis that the EU uses specific forms of governance which are indifferent to the problem of democratic legitimacy. While it is true that nation state constitutionalism and democratic politics are just one of many contextualisations of European politics and constitutionalism today, they simply cannot be rejected as 'dated and artificial',[39] because the constitutional democratic sovereignty of the Member States still remains a constitutive part of the EU's political and constitutional domain. The 'true nature' of European constitutionalism without a constitution can hardly be just 'the balancing of diverse and often conflicting interests and fears'[40] because the European people, perceived mostly as the *telos* of European political integration, has also been its presupposition.

The question of the identity of the EU polity subsequently raises the problems of political inclusion and exclusion as well as the boundaries of the EU polity[41] and its effect on the constitutional polities of the Member States. Translating the sociological constitution of society as the unity of social plurality and multitude into the EU context, one is immediately reminded of the failed Constitutional Treaty preamble speaking of 'unity in diversity' that has subsequently been reformulated in the Treaty draft as one of the Union's objectives. Article 3.3 TEU states that the Union

> shall promote economic, social and territorial cohesion, and solidarity among Member States. It shall respect its rich cultural and linguistic diversity, and shall ensure that Europe's cultural heritage is safeguarded and enhanced.[42]

---

[38]Wintgens (2001), pp. 272–280, at 279. The concept of 'the constitutive power' has the same meaning like 'the constituent power' preferred in more recent publications in the field of constitutional theory and used in this article.

[39]Maduro (2003), at p. 74.

[40]Ibid., at p. 75.

[41]Lindahl (2000), pp. 239–256, at 253–256.

[42]*Consolidated Version of the Treaty on European Union*, O.J. C 115/17 (2008).

This text contains all the paradoxes, contingencies and potential of the EU political domain without state and popular sovereignty. Political and legal unity is to be based on profound territorial pluralism, and the imagined polity of European citizens is to be built on the re-imagined and transformed ethnic nations and communities of the EU.

The EU politics is both productive and reproductive of some form of European political identity.[43] It is circular in the sense that the very existence of political integration calls for political identity as its precondition but it also already circulates the shared political values, policies and interests of the European polity in the form of legal and political communication.

Leaving aside the disputes concerning the 'right European values' and what it means to be truly 'European', it is possible to see that the European legal system, despite the failure of a constitutional treaty, strongly affects the identity of the European polity in question. This is why even the Lisbon Treaty, especially the incorporated European Union Charter of Fundamental Right (EUCFR), can supplement the national identities and symbolic self-reflections of both the nations of Member States and the stateless nation of Europe with the values of civility and the surplus of rights without necessarily weakening pre-political ethnic bonds.

However, European legal documents are not the only means of articulating a common European political identity and other forms of identity communication, most notably the European public sphere and party politics, need to evolve to support the 'thin' identity[44] of European civil rights and liberties promulgated by the Charter. It would be wrong to presuppose that the legal system can function as the exclusive tool of identity-building and political deliberation at the EU level. There is always a surplus of identity problems facilitated by discourses of collective ethics.

Furthermore, responding to the European public discontents and the referenda rejections of the Constitutional Treaty, drafters of the Lisbon Treaty abandoned the terminology of the 'Union Minister for Foreign Affairs' and removed provisions on the symbols of the EU (the flag, the anthem and the motto) to avoid any similarity between the treaty ratification and the building of European statehood and constitutional polity. Flirtations with state-like political symbols were effectively suppressed in the Lisbon Treaty.

Legal reflections of a European political identity can subsequently only reiterate existing legal and political differences, divisions and fractions within the Union and reconstruct this particular form of identity as *divided identity*. All treatises on 'overlapping identities', 'multiple identities' or 'supplementary identities' are reflections of the EU's operative paradoxes of negotiated governance, divided sovereignty, constitutionalism without a constitution, etc. In this sense, Habermas is right when he says that the problem of legal legitimacy is a central problem in

---

[43]See, for instance, Dyzenhaus (1997), p. 54.

[44]See Přibáň (2007), supra note 2 at p. 121.

modern political societies[45] and emphasises the foundational role of European identity-building. The EU can never achieve legitimacy without the constitution of a political identity. The EU political and legal sovereignty debate, which has been exponentially growing since the Maastricht Treaty and subsequent constitution-making and post-constitutional integrative efforts, is a legitimacy debate[46] drawing on 'the legal imagination'.[47]

Calls for creating a 'cosmopolitan Europe' and the adoption of European cosmopolitan law,[48] indeed, indicate that Europe may be reflected as an 'imagined community'[49] that can be shaped in many different ways, from fantasies of Kant's world republic to the pan-European humanism of Erasmus, Althusius and Leibniz.[50] In these images of Europe, social constructivism becomes normative constructivism entirely related to the symbolic political universe, and the ethics discourse becomes fully differentiated from the systems of European law and politics. Political imagination transcends both everyday power politics and formal legality and the EU becomes a metaphor of what may be described as 'the sovereignty of good'.[51]

6 The Union's External 'Democracy Dividend': A Comment on Recent EU Enlargements

Self-reflection of the Union as an organisation embodying and promoting peace among nations of the world, multilateralism in international relations, cosmopolitan values, universal humanity and social and economic progress of humankind is strongly present in the text of the Lisbon Treaty, especially those parts addressing the Union's foreign and security policy. According to Art. 21 of Title V, *General Provisions on the Union's External Action and Specific Provisions on Common Foreign and Security Policy*, the Union's founding principles including its commitment to democracy continue to inform three parallel political processes: The Union's internal development, enlargement and building of relations between the Union and third countries in the wider world.[52]

---

[45] Habermas (2006), pp. 137–142.

[46] See, for instance, Rogowski and Turner (2006), pp. 1–22, at 7, 17.

[47] De Witte (1995), pp. 145–173, at 145.

[48] See, for instance, Eleftheriadis (2003), pp. 241–263.

[49] For the elaboration of the notorious concept of 'imagined community' in the context of Europe, see Haltern (2003), pp. 14–44, at 28ff.

[50] For the latter call for European political and communal self-reflection, see Ward (2001), pp. 24–37, at 32–37.

[51] Murdoch (2001).

[52] *Consolidated Version of the Treaty on European Union*, O.J. C 115/28 (2008).

This coeval promotion of democratic principles inside the Union, outside its borders and as preconditions of EU membership has been steadily progressing over the last two decades. There were two different reasons why the Union could no longer shy away from incorporating the protection of democratic government into its legal framework in the 1990s. The first reason of its enactment by the Treaty of Amsterdam, which came into force in 1999, was internal transformation and increasing political integration of the EU after the Maastricht Treaty. The second reason was the process of EU enlargement which dominated the Union's agenda in the 1990s and primarily involved post-communist countries undergoing fundamental social and democratic transitions at that time.[53] These coeval processes of the Union's 'deepening' and 'widening' required both codification of the principle of democratic government and possible sanctions of those Member States which might breach it.

The EU can thus demand its Member States and candidate states to be democratically governed and committed to the protection of human dignity, rights, equality and freedom. However, the Union as a supranational organisation itself is short of democratic governance despite genuine efforts to democratise its internal structures and forms of decision-making. It still mainly draws on the administrative state's legitimacy by efficiency and outcomes rather than values and democratic procedures.[54]

The Union is short of democratic legitimation, yet legitimised by democratic constitutionalism at Member State level. In European legal and political studies, this structural setting is widely discussed as the EU's 'democratic deficit'. For some, the lack of democracy at EU level merely proves how wrong all Euroenthusiasts have been in pursuing their visions of European statehood. For others, the deficit has been just a minor structural deficiency fully compensated for by common benefits of EU membership and democratic legitimacy guarantees facilitated by political institutions of the Member States. Nevertheless, both sides of this argument admit that European integration has been running as a profoundly legalistic and depoliticised project short of substantial democratic deliberation.[55]

Focusing on the Union's external stabilising role, it is clear that one of historically the most noticeable common benefits was the Union's *democratising effect* on post-communist candidate states during their accession talks between 1993 and 2004.[56]

From the perspective of the candidate states, EU membership and conditionality process were equally legitimised by 'the national benefit' and received public support. After the fall of communism, the process of Europeanisation was always closely associated with the process of democratisation. Some academics even wrote

[53]For a more detailed analysis of the following issues, see especially, Přibáň (2009), pp. 337–358.

[54]Beetham and Lord (1998), pp. 15–33, at 17.

[55]Přibáň (2007), supra note 2, pp. 116–119.

[56]Ibid, p. 119.

about the 'accession's democracy dividend'[57] when examining the force, impact and limitations of the Union's external pressure on the accession countries. EU membership was considered the best protection of emerging constitutional democracies in Central and Eastern Europe against illiberal and authoritarian politics, corruption, arbitrary use of power by civil servants, lack of public accountability and many other sorts of political failures. In other words, EU institutions were expected to promote and police exactly the same goals which defined post-communist constitutional and political transformations. Weak national political and legal institutions, which suffered from insufficient resources and experience and were prone to political cronyism and corruption, were expected to be externally supported and stabilised during the transitional period by the EU.

EU institutions 'patronised' national politics and represented another check on standards and quality of constitutional and democratic transformations. In June 1993, the European Council enacted a set of EU membership conditions which became known as the 'Copenhagen criteria' and divided the EU accession conditions to three different categories – political, economic and legal. While economic conditions specified the need to establish a functioning market economy compatible with market pressures, competition and regulations within the EU, political conditions listed the need to guarantee institutional stability of emerging democracies and their constitutional systems including the rule of law principles and human rights catalogues.[58] Political conditions even included respect for and protection of minorities for which there was no ground within the framework of European law.[59]

Until the Copenhagen Council, democratic government was automatically associated with the Member States and no formal criteria for applicant countries were defined by the Union.[60] At the beginning of the EU accession process, the Commission's overall scrutiny and evaluation classified three different groups of candidate states: those already conforming to the democracy criterion (the Czech Republic, Hungary, Poland and Estonia), those on their way to meeting the criterion (Lithuania, Latvia, Romania, Bulgaria) and Slovakia as a country failing to meet it and therefore excluded from accession talks. However, the Slovak parliamentary election of 1998 resulted at the end of the Mečiar government and the new government led by Prime Minister Dzurinda subsequently reopened accession talks in February 2000 and eventually succeeded in bringing the country to the EU in the first enlargement wave in May 2004.[61]

While the Slovak example persuasively shows the public mobilisation and democratisation potential of EU membership and the Union's stabilising role in

[57]Sadurski (2004), pp. 371–401.

[58]Novak (1999), pp. 687–698.

[59]De Witte and Toggenburg (2004), pp. 59–82, at 67–68.

[60]Sadurski (2002), pp. 340–362, at 343.

[61]Schimmelfennig et al. (2005), pp. 29–50, at 37–42.

national politics,[62] conditionality criteria also strongly affected national political and legal agendas in countries classified as already having democratic governance in 1997. Indeed, the rule of law and democratic transformation originated in internal political changes in those countries. Political demands for free elections, multi-party political systems, the independent systems of justice, freedom of expression, local government, etc. had been formulated by national democratic forces. Nevertheless, it is important to emphasise that those forces could always rely on the EU as a major point of reference and supranational organisation of democratically governed liberal states based on the rule of law. The EU represented a 'normal state of things' towards which post-communist countries in transformation were heading and which, therefore, could and actually did have a strong synergistic effect in European politics.[63]

The candidate states' 'patronised status' did not change until the Union's engagement in constitution-making process. During the Convention's work on the constitutional treaty, the candidate states were invited to contribute to its drafting but they could not block any consensus that could be established amongst Member States at the time. In other words, the post-communist states' status changed from passive recipients of EU laws to active participants in EU constitution-making and fully engaged members in the post-accession EU.

7 Conclusion

The constitution of a democratic polity is a product of the *classicist* Enlightenment period. However, the current EU is typical of *baroque* political institutional settings, which can hardly generate representative democratic politics and inspire the emergence of the European demos from upside down. New checks and balances introduced by the Lisbon Treaty certainly make the Union more democratically accountable but they are far from the democratic state's constitution of popular sovereignty and power separation.

The process of democratic self-reflection and imagination of citizens of the EU cannot be governed by European comitology and self-administration. The European civic culture and the legislated EU charter of fundamental rights should not be mistaken for democratic government. Polity-building by legal means, such as European treaties and civil rights, is unable to fully substitute for ethical self-reflections and political self-determination of EU populations. It can even have harmful effects and result in human rights consumerism rather than civic activism and democratic participation.

---

[62]Pridham (2002), pp. 953–973.

[63]See, for instance, Evans (1997), pp. 201–220.

If European identity is imaginable as a legislated catalogue of civil rights and freedoms, it is more than obvious that this juridical expression of European identity further needs to be transformed to civil bonds and culture vital for any democratic statehood, especially in its supranational forms. The Lisbon Treaty enhances democratic accountability of the Union and increasingly supports EU institutions by democratically legitimate national institutions, but it cannot fulfil the task of constructing a democratic polity which stretches far beyond legal operations and depends on the *postmodernist* architecture of the reflexive European public self-generation and political mobilisation.

References

Anderson B (1983) Imagined communities: reflections on the origin and spread of nationalism. Verso, London

Banchoff T, Smith MP (eds) (1999) Legitimacy and the European Union: the contested polity. Routledge, London

Beetham D, Lord C (1998) Legitimacy and the European Union. In: Weale A, Nentwich M (eds) Political theory and the European Union: legitimacy, constitutional choice and citizenship. Routledge, London, pp 15–33

Benoit B (1997) Social-nationalism: an anatomy of French Euroscepticism. Ashgate, Aldershot

Clarke J (2005) Reconstituting Europe: governing a European people? In: Newman J (ed) Remaking governance: peoples, politics and the public sphere. The Policy Press, Bristol, pp 17–37

Crum B (2005) Tailoring representative democracy to the European Union: does the European constitution reduce the democratic deficit? Eur Law J 11(4):452–467

Dahrendorf R (2004) Der Wiederbeginn der Geschichte. Vom Fall der Mauer zum Krieg im Irak. C.H. Beck, München

De Witte B (1995) Sovereignty and European integration: the weight of legal tradition. Maastricht J Eur Comp Law 2:145–173

De Witte B, Toggenburg GN (2004) Human rights and membership of the European Union. In: Peers S, Ward A (eds) The European Union charter of fundamental rights: politics, law and policy. Hart Publishing, Oxford, pp 59–87

Dyzenhaus D (1997) Legality and legitimacy: Carl Schmitt, Hans Kelsen and Hermann Heller in Weimar. Oxford University Press, Oxford

Eleftheriadis P (2003) Cosmopolitan law. Eur Law J 9(2):241–63

Evans A (1997) Voluntary harmonisation in integration between the European community and Eastern Europe. Eur Law Rev 22(2):201–20

Habermas J (1995) Reconciliation through the public use of reason: remarks on John Rawls's political liberalism. J Philos 92(3):109–131

Habermas J (2006) Divided west. Polity, Cambridge

Haltern U (2003) Pathos and Patina: the failure and promise of constitutionalism in the European imagination. Eur Law J 9(1):14–44

Hooghe L, Marks G (2001) Multi-level governance and European integration. Rowman & Littlefield, Oxford

Joerges C, Neyer J (1997) From intergovernmental bargaining to deliberative political processes: the constitutionalisation of comitology. Eur Law J 3(3):273–299

Joerges C, Dehousse R (eds) (2002) Good governance in Europe's integrated market. Oxford University Press, Oxford

King M, Thornhill C (2003) Niklas Luhmann's theory of politics and law. Palgrave, Houndmills

Kohler-Koch B, Rittberger B (eds) (2007) Debating the democratic legitimacy in the EU. Rowman & Littlefield, Lanham
Lincoln A (1989) Speeches and writings, vol 2: 1859–1865. Library of America, New York
Lindahl H (2000) European integration: popular sovereignty and a politics of boundaries. Eur Law J 6(3):239–256
Lindberg L, Scheingold S (1970) Europe's would-be-polity: patterns of change in the European Community. Prentice-Hall, Englewood Cliffs
Luhmann N (2002) Die Politik der Gesellschaft. Suhrkamp, Frankfurt
Maduro MP (2003) Europe and constitution: what if this is as good as it gets? In: Weiler JHH, Wind M (eds) European constitutionalism beyond the state. Cambridge University Press, Cambridge, pp 74–102
Majone G (1998) Europe's 'democratic deficit': the question of standards. Eur Law J 4(1):5–28
Marks G, Scharpf FW, Schmitter PC, Streeck W (eds) (1996) Governance in the European Union. Sage, London
Murdoch I (2001) Sovereignty of good. Routledge, London
Novak M (1999) Human rights 'conditionality' in relation to entry to, and full participation in, the EU. In: Alston P, Bustello MR, Heenan J (eds) The EU and human rights. Oxford University Press, Oxford, pp 687–698
Přibáň J (2007) Legal symbolism: on law, time and European identity. Ashgate, Aldershot
Přibáň J (2009) From "Which Rule of Law?" to "The Rule of Which Law?": postcommunist experiences of European legal integration. Hague J Rule Law 1(2):337–358
Pridham G (2002) EU enlargement and consolidating democracy in post-communit states – formality and reality. J Common Market Stud 40(5):953–973
Rawls J (1995) Political liberalism: reply to Habermas. J Philos 92(3):132–180
Riekmann SP, Mokre M, Latzer M (eds) (2005) The state of Europe: transformations of statehood from a European perspective. Cambridge University Press, Cambridge
Rogowski R, Turner C (2006) Europe: law, politics, history, culture. In: Rogowski R, Turner C (eds) The shape of the New Europe. Cambridge University Press, Cambridge, pp 1–22
Sadurski W (2002) Charter and enlagement. Eur Law J 8(3):340–362
Sadurski W (2004) Accession's democracy dividend: the impact of the EU enlargement upon democracy in the new member states of central and eastern Europe. Eur Law J 10(4):371–401
Scharpf FW (1999) Governing in Europe: effective and democratic? Oxford University Press, Oxford
Schimmelfennig F, Engert S, Knobel H (2005) The impact of EU political conditionality. In: Schimmelfennig F, Sedelmaier U (eds) The Europeanization of central and eastern Europe. Cornell University Press, Ithaca, pp 29–50
Schumpeter J (1976) Capitalism, socialism & democracy. Allen & Unwin, London
Steffek J (2004) Sources of legitimacy beyond the state: a view from international relations. In: Joerges C, Sand IJ, Teubner G (eds) Transnational governance and constitutionalism. Hart Publishing, Oxford, pp 81–101
Stubb A (2002) Negotiationg flexibility in the European Union. Palgrave, Houndmills
Tindemans L (1976) 'Letter to European Council colleagues', sent on 29 December 1975; the letter later annexed to 'European Union. Report by Mr Leo Tindemans, Prime Minister of Belgium, to the European Council'. Bull Eur Commun Supplement 1/76
Tindemans L (1998) Dreams come true, gradually: the Tindemans Report a quarter of a century on. In: Westlake M (ed) The European Union beyond Amsterdam: new concepts of European integration. London, Routledge, pp 130–141
Tsakatika M (2007) The European Union and the democratic limits of governance. In: Ruzza C, Della Sala V (eds) Governance and civil society in the European Union, vol 1: normative perspectives. Manchester University Press, Manchester, pp 30–54
Ward I (2001) Beyond constitutionalism: the search for a European political imagination. Eur Law J 7(1):24–37

Wind M (2003) The European Union as a polycentric polity. In: Weiler JHH, Wind M (eds) European constitutionalism beyond the state. Cambridge University Press, Cambridge, pp 103–131

Wintgens LJ (2001) Sovereignty and representation. Ratio Juris 14(3):272–280

Consolidated Version of the Treaty on European Union, *Official Journal of the European Union*, 9 May 2008, C 115.

The Council of the European Union Note No. 11218/07, 'IGC 2007 Mandate', Brussels, 26 June 2007.

Presidency Conclusions of the Council of the European Union, CONCL 4, No. 14368/08, 16 October 2008.

The Treaty of Lisbon amending the Treaty on European Union and the Treaty establishing European Community, CIG 14/07, Brussels, 3 December 2007.

The Institutional Design of the European Union After Lisbon

Stelio Mangiameli

1 The Categories of Constitutional Law and the Institutional Design

The institutional design of the European Union (EU) has been significantly innovated by the Lisbon Treaty. The influence of the constitutionalisation process that led up to the 2004 Treaty of Rome, which was subsequently abandoned, was felt through the technique followed to frame the revised text of the Treaties.[1]

It was not only to introduce the adjustments required to codify, in the new text of the Treaty, practices that had become established over the years between the adoption of the Nice Treaty and October 2007, but also to move into a different dimension altogether, partly due to the manner in which the Union has been unified, doing away with the EU/EC (European Community) dualism, defining competences, moving beyond the three-pillar configuration, consolidating policies such as the Common Foreign and Security Policy (CFSP) and the European Security and Defence Policy (ESDP),[2] to give the EU a stronger international dimension and attempt to narrow the gap between the institutions and the citizens of the Union, following the indications that date back to the European Governance White Paper.[3]

In the case of the EU no description of the functioning of the institutions can obviously be governed simply by treaty provisions, because – as European history

[1]The Treaties were revised by salvaging the provisions of the Constitutional Treaty with only a few exceptions, which did not refer to the organisation of the EU [see Mangiameli (2008c), pp. 385 et seqq.; as well Adam and Tizzano (2010)].

[2]On this point see Gianfrancesco (2008), pp. 1129 et seqq.; Missiroli (2009), pp. 118 et seqq.

[3]COM/2001/0428 final. *European governance – A white paper*, 5.8.2001.

S. Mangiameli (✉)
ISSiRFA - CNR, Via dei Taurini 19, 00185 Rome, Italy
e-mail: stelio.mangiameli@cnr.it

H.-J. Blanke and S. Mangiameli (eds.), *The European Union after Lisbon*,
DOI 10.1007/978-3-642-19507-5_5, © Springer-Verlag Berlin Heidelberg 2012

since 1950 has shown – the Union is now a living reality, and is demonstrating its capacity to interact and evolve beyond the provisions and constraints of Treaty Law; the recent global financial crisis, which has affected Greece (and might also contaminate other Member States in the Eurozone) already provides enough arguments to corroborate this observation.[4]

However, in this initial phase, attention has to focus on the novelties incorporated into the Treaties, while awaiting the future development of the European experience to be able to examine more thoroughly the real significance of the provisions and practices which the Institutions and the Member States are able to implement.

The institutional issue has been the subject of continuous debate in European public law scholarship; it has been addressed by highlighting the differences between its organisation and the institutional form of the state and the federal state.[5]

It has long been objected that the EU is neither a state nor a federal state, as these concepts are commonly construed in constitutional law. It is impossible to attribute to the EU the notion of the form of a state[6] and appraise its institutional system in terms of categories typically used to define statehood, such as democracy, the rule of law, respect for fundamental rights and so on. For this part of the doctrine, even in the wake of the Lisbon Treaty, these are categories that are no longer applicable to the Union.

Yet even though it is undeniable that the EU is not a state, or a federal state, because the level of unification that has been achieved so far has not done away with the sovereignty of the individual Member States, it is precisely by comparing the categories of public law and constitutional law that we can now adequately account for the legal status of the Union and its development[7] on two distinct, but concurring, grounds. First, it is obvious that the idea that the Union is just one of the many international organisations governed by public international law was ruled out from the outset, when it was decided to create a common legal order shared by

[4]Just look at the European Council conclusions of 28/29 October 2010 (CO EUR 18/CONCL 4) and those of the European Council of 16/17 December 2010 (CO EUR 21/CONCL 5).

[5]This has not, however, prevented the increasing constitutionalisation of the supranational system from leading to the frequent use of the expression "form of government" in reference to the European Union: Pinelli (1989), pp. 336 et seqq.; Strozzi (1998); Cervati (2000), pp. 73 et seqq.; Gozi (2006); Fabbrini (2002); Mangiameli (2003), pp. 213 et seqq.; Patrono (2003), pp. 1762 et seqq.; Bassan (2003), pp. 973–1036; Costanzo (2008), pp. 45–60; Draetta (2008), pp. 677–694; Draetta (2009), pp. 7–22; Daniele (2009), pp. 43–54; Ilari (2010); and Sauron (2008); Constantinesco (2008); Lenski (2009), pp. 54 et seqq.; Ruffert (2009); Schoo (2009); Haratsch et al. (2010), pp. 23 et seqq.; Bieber (2010), pp. 109 et seqq.; Herdegen (2010), pp. 99 et seqq.

On the other hand, long since some influential lawyers of the law of the EU have set up the process of European integration as a kind of permanent negotiation: Tizzano (1995); Tesauro (1995).

[6]However, see Palermo (2005), passim.

[7]For a number of interesting considerations on the process of European constitutionalisation, see Calliess (2009), pp. 54 et seqq.

all the Member States which would also have a direct effect on their citizens, while its organisational structure incorporated an evident contradiction in terms of the intergovernmental character that typifies the international organisations: namely, the presence of the Assembly, made up of representatives of the national parliaments.[8] Moreover, the long process of development of the European system makes it possible to apply to the European level – not without heated debate, even quite recently (for example, the German Constitutional Court judgment on the Lisbon Treaty[9]) – the same structural features ("values") of constitutional law that had been explicitly laid down in Art. 2 TEU (and in the previous Art. 6.1 TEU), and in the Charter of Fundamental Rights of the European Union, enshrining recognition of the legal value of the Treaties (Art. 6.1 TEU).[10]

Even though there is no real separation of powers in the EU as we have traditionally understood this concept as it applies to individual nation states, it would not be accurate to conclude that there is no differentiation of powers. As the European Court of Justice (ECJ) has pointed out on various occasions in the past, relying on its case law criterion of competence, and emphasising the distinction between the roles of the institutions, the whole supranational order is characterised by acceptance of the principle of the rule of law, such that the Union could be described as a "community based on the rule of law".[11]

2 The Democratic Principle and the Role of the Member States

Even the critique about Europe's "democratic deficit", which used to be quite widespread, now appears to be only meaningless repetition. For Europe's weak propensity to take democratic decisions stemmed from the fact that the European legislator (the Council of Ministers) was also the "enforcement body" of the law it enacted, and the Council was the expression of the national governments, while the Parliament (or rather the Assembly) was unelected, and had no law-making or budgetary control powers.

In this connection, the Italian Constitutional Court issued a landmark ruling in 1973[12] in which it pronounced that, "with particular reference to the regulations

[8]Mangiameli (2008b), pp. 491 et seqq.

[9]Cf. German Federal Constitutional Court, 2 BvE 2/08 (Judgment of 30 June 2009) – *Lisbon*; for comments on the judgment see Grimm (2009); Jestaedt (2009); Khushal Murkens (2009); Schönberger (2009); Thym (2009); Wahl (2009).

[10]See Cartabia (2010), pp. 221 et seqq.

[11]101/78, *Granaria/Hoofdproduktschap voor Akkerbouwprodukten* (ECJ 13 February 1979), and on the notion of the "*Community of law*", Case 294/83, *Les Verts/Parlamento* (ECJ 23 April 1986); Opinion 1/92 [on the reception of the "rule of law principle" into the European legal system see Gianfrancesco (2006), pp. 235 et seqq.].

[12]Italian Constitutional Court, Judgment no. 183/1973 (18 December 1973).

provided by article 189, in addition to the sectoral competence restrictions *ratione materiae* on the lawmaking powers of the Council and the Commission imposed by the provisions of the Treaty, *it should be borne in mind that these organs are also subject to scrutiny by the Assembly*, which is also made up of representatives delegated by the Member States and, when the integration process hopefully develops further, will acquire greater direct political representativity and broader powers; and *that they operate with the constant and direct participation of the Italian government, and hence under the indirect, but no less vigilant and close, scrutiny of the Italian parliament*."

Subsequently, the German Constitutional Court, ruling on the Maastricht Treaty[13] at a time when the European Parliament had already long since acquired its own specific type of democratic legitimation through the direct election of its members, and was involved in enactment and not merely in scrutiny, took up this issue once again and declared that the democratic legitimacy of the EU derived from the peoples of the Member States through the European Parliament and also through their national parliaments (the so-called dual democratic legitimacy principle).

Now that the European Parliament is no longer composed of the "representatives of the peoples of the States brought together in the Community" (Art. 189 EC) but of "representatives of the Union's citizens" (Art. 14.2 TEU), as evidenced from the democratic principles of the EU (Art. 10.2 TEU),[14] it no longer appears possible to consider the democratic deficit as a limitation of the supranational system, and the different conception of European democracy that emerges from the German Constitutional Court judgment does not weaken the significance of the European democratic principle to the organisation of the Union, and characterises the European decision-making process.

It should also be borne in mind that the Lisbon Treaty included the national parliaments as a permanent part of the organisation of Europe in order to contribute "actively to the good functioning of the Union" (Art. 12 TEU), giving them the main task of guaranteeing compliance with the principle of subsidiarity (and proportionality) in the exercise of legislative powers at the European level.[15]

This means that the institutional architecture of the EU is intimately bound up with the democratic principle. Article 10 (1) TEU adopted an unusual expression: "The functioning of the Union shall be founded on representative democracy." This is a very important formulation, because it refers to features of the European legal

[13]German Federal Constitutional Court, 2 BvR 2134, 2159/92 (Judgment of 12 October 1993) (in: BVerfGE 89, 155) – *Maastricht*.

[14]An examination of the democratic principles of the Treaty to define the level of participation of Europe's citizens in the political life of the Union (Art. 10.3, sentence 1, TEU) would require a separate treatment: the principle of "open dialogue" (Art. 11.2 TEU), the principle of transparency (Art. 11.3 TEU) and the popular legislative initiative (Art. 11.4 TEU).

[15]See Bocuzzi (2008); and Casalena (2008); and Bilancia (2009), pp. 273 et seqq.; Mangiameli and Di Salvatore (2010), pp. 230 et seqq.

system that do away, once and for all, with the original ambiguities of the supranational system. For representative democracy not only seems to clash with the view of the EU as an international organisation, but above all it admits of a public law-type concept of European power typical of a sovereignty centre.

This is a particularly significant aspect because in any international organisation in which sovereignty is vested in its member states, the democratic principle cannot be applied, and even less the principle of representative democracy.

Consequently, the provision that "the functioning of the Union shall be founded on representative democracy" implies that the EU constitutes a centre of sovereignty distinct from the sovereignties of its Member States.[16]

In this paper we can ignore the issue of establishing the origin of this sovereignty, to see whether it stems from a process of self-legitimation or from a continuous and irreversible yielding of sovereignty by the Member States; what is necessary here, conversely, is to emphasise the fact that the European institutions are vested with real European sovereignty in their own right, with the result that the organisational rules set out in the European Treaties are nothing other than the ways in which this supranational sovereignty is exercised, and it is the task of the science of constitutional law to appraise it, linking the organs, functions and purposes of the EU.

It is obvious that, in this regard, the Member States and their governments have a huge part to play, but as parts of the institutional representation of the European system: "Member States are represented in the European Council by their Heads of State or Government and in the Council by their governments, themselves democratically accountable either to their national Parliaments, or to their citizens" (Art. 10.2 (2) TEU). For within the Union the Member States no longer act as subjects of international law but as members of an organ, the European Institution, and in order for their work to be effective, they are obliged to work together, more or less in harmony, now that the majority principle has been strengthened in the European Council system and will be increasingly strengthened to the detriment of

[16]This is an open issue for the moment, and the object of many differing approaches in the literature depending upon the various schools of thought. According to what would appear the most preferable position, the Member States do not forgo their sovereignty, and this causes a state of tension between the two different sovereignties. Traces of the concept of sovereignty transfer can also be found in the case-law of the ECJ, and also in the rulings of both the Italian and the German Constitutional Courts. They were recently joined by a ruling issued by the French *Conseil Constitutionnel* and the Spanish Constitutional Court, and more recently still by the Polish and the Czech Constitutional Courts. However, the case-law of the Member States' constitutional courts tend to place a number of "counter-limits" on the transfer of sovereignty from the Member States to moderate the transfer of sovereignty and highlight the way in which the sovereignty of the European Union is dependent upon the sovereignty of the Member States, and that it is the Member States that are the real holders of sovereignty. The recent German Constitutional Court judgment on the Lisbon Treaty, consciously playing down all the textual elements in the Treaty affirming the democratic principle, has reconstructed the European legal system in the following manner [for a critique of the theory of counter-limits, see Mangiameli (2010)].

the unanimity principle[17] in the light of Protocol No. 36 to the Treaty by reference to the transitional and final provisions and the procedures for moving towards majority voting.[18]

In the case of the bridging clauses, when passing from unanimous voting to majority voting (*passerelle*), the situation is obviously managed autonomously by the Member States with reference to European powers and competences. For individual states play a very important part in choosing the decision-making modalities in European procedures by taking part in the deliberations and resolutions on the Council, but it is these very deliberations and resolutions that reveal that it is not the states themselves which are acting, individually, but an organ, an Institution of the EU.

3 Powers and Competences in the Lisbon Treaty

The power system, as it emerges from the Treaty after a long evolutionary process, must also be considered from the point of view of its substance. It is said that the EU is a "general-purpose entity"[19] despite the division of competences and the principle of *Einzelermächtigungkompetenz*, i.e. of conferral competence. For the European competences no longer derive solely from the principle of attribution, which has characterised the European tradition since the beginning, but also from "concurrent competence" linked to the principle of subsidiarity which, since Maastricht, has made it legally possible to enact legislation for matters falling to the competence of individual states.[20]

With the adoption of the Lisbon Treaty, this approach was confirmed by Art. 5 TEU. But the new Treaty also introduced further innovations into the organisational structure and powers, doing away with the three pillar–based system and consequently superseding the distinction between the intergovernmental and the Community methods. All the European powers are therefore incorporated into a unitary system which has made it possible to define competences more specifically in the present Treaties than was the case in the earlier ones.[21]

---

[17]The unanimity principle is a spurious international law element and has already been weakened in reality, because the decisions taken on a unanimous basis culminate in acts which do not need ratification or internal implementation because they are always acts of the EU, whose only specific feature is the fact that they require a unanimous vote.

[18]It should be recalled that the Treaty contains numerous bridging clauses on the basis of which the Member States on the Council unanimously resolve that a particular matter can be adopted by a majority voting.

[19]See Mangiameli (2008a), p. 90.

[20]On the distribution of powers see Mangiameli (2006); Moscarini (2006a, b); Scaccia (2006).

[21]See Caruso (2008).

Policies previously ascribed to the intergovernmental pillar are now of a different nature as a result of these changes. In the CFSP and the ESDP, especially in the part relating to justice and police powers, there are a number of acts which, on closer examination, have the nature of legislative acts in the sense given to this term in the Treaty.[22] For example, unanimous decisions taken by the Foreign Affairs Council provided in the part relating to Art. 23 et seqq. TEU can, from the point of view of sources of European law, be described without difficulty as legislative sources or non-legislative normative sources.

The sources under Art. 336 et seqq. TFEU, the acts and the cases for which the ordinary procedure is prescribed, or the special legislative procedure followed by the Parliament, or by the Council, etc. all confirm that there is a complex nomenclature of procedures in the Treaties, all of which are at the service of a single system of competences empowering the Union to act legally in every direction.

The structure of European power and its system of competences, with the application of the subsidiarity principle, affects the whole institutional set-up of the EU, because it is not a matter of the distribution of power between the institutions, limited as had originally been the case, to only a few economic issues, but wide-ranging powers relating de facto to every area, including institutional relations between the players in the European legal system and in general the life of all Europe's citizens, without any sectors being effectively excluded.

4 The Institutional System of the European Union: The Institutions

The first benchmark to which we must refer is Art. 13 TEU. For Art. 13 TEU is the one which sets out the European institutional system. The Union is endowed with an institutional framework designed to promote its values (Art. 2 TEU), pursue its objectives (Art. 3 TEU), serve the interests of both the citizens and the Member States of the Union and guarantee the consistency, effectiveness and continuity of its policies and its activities.

After this introduction regarding the institutional framework, the article lists the institutions of the Union: the European Parliament, the European Council, the Council, the European Commission (hereafter the Commission), the Court of Justice of the European Union, the European Central Bank and the Court of Auditors.

According to this article, each institution acts within the bounds of its powers under the Treaties consistently with the procedures, conditions and purposes enshrined in them.

---

[22]See Cannizzaro and Bartolini (2007); Condinanzi (2007); Paladini (2010).

The institutions have traditionally implemented the principle of sincere cooperation in their relations with the Member States (now in Art. 4.3 TEU) but this principle now applies to their mutual relations as well. Article 13.2 TEU provides that "[e]ach institution shall act within the limits of the powers conferred on it in the Treaties, and in conformity with the procedures, conditions and objectives set out in them. The institutions shall practise mutual sincere cooperation".[23]

The provisions relating to the European Central Bank and Court of Auditors appear together, with detailed provisions regarding the other institutions, in the *Treaty on the Functioning of the European Union*. This fragment was rendered necessary because many of the provisions governing institutions other than the two mentioned above fall within the scope of the Treaty on European Union (TEU).

The article ends with the following provisions: "The European Parliament, the Council and the Commission shall be assisted by an Economic and Social Committee and a Committee of the Regions acting in an advisory capacity."

The European institutional framework laid down in Art. 13 TEU, however, is neither precise nor exhaustive. First, it must be pointed out that the Committee of the Regions cannot be seen as a purely consultative body in view of the powers vested in it by the Protocol on the Principle of Subsidiarity and on the Principle of Proportionality.[24] Second, the institutional design of the EU can only be deemed complete if account is taken not only of the "national parliaments", whose participation in the European system is summarised in Art. 12 TEU to which reference was briefly made above, but also of the European political parties to which the Treaty only devotes a very short provision (Art. 10.4 TEU), but whose specific role has grown somewhat in the brief experience of the past two years, in which the President of the European Commission, the President of the European Union and the High Representative of the Union for Foreign Affairs and Security Policy have been appointed.[25]

5 The Representation of the European Union Between Institutions and Individual Organs: External Representation

European representation is a particularly complex issue to address. In order to put some order into the different positions taken regarding representation one may draw a distinction between internal representation and external representation, but as we shall see immediately, this distinction is far from being able to define a clear separation between these two spheres.

[23]See Pizzetti (2006).

[24]Regarding the particular powers vested in the Committee of the Regions, with reference to controlling subsidiarity, this body has been defined as "semi-institution".

[25]See Bonvicini et al. (2009).

The EU's external representation system was formally linked to the system of the revolving Presidency, and the role of the European Commission and in particular of its President. With the Lisbon Treaty, external representation has become more complex, because it is now entrusted to the President of the European Council (Art. 15.5 and 6 TEU), the High Representative of the Union for Foreign Affairs and Security Policy (Art. 18 TEU) and the European Commission (Art. 17.1 TEU) with only vaguely defined remits. The President of the European Council ensures the external representation of the Union on issues concerning its CFSP, "without prejudice to the powers of the High Representative of the Union for Foreign Affairs and Security Policy"; the latter conducts the Union's common foreign and security policy (and also the common security and defence policy), contributing by making proposals for the development of that policy, acting on a Council mandate; the Commission (and primarily its President), with the exception of the CFSP, and other cases provided in the Treaties, ensures the Union's external representation.

This new model of external representation would therefore seem to hinge around two specific officers, and one Institution: the President of the European Council, the High Representative[26] and the Commission. The President remains in office for two years and six months, and may be re-elected once only, and may not hold a national office, and while not heading the Council, the powers vested by the Treaty (Art. 15.6 TEU) ensure that he will inevitably be the guarantor of the work of the Council and of the prerogatives of the Member States in relation to the European system, as well as being the external representative of the Council.

It must be clearly understood that in order for the President of the Council to perform his/her mandate properly, de facto overcoming the fact that the Head of State of Government of the revolving Presidency operates by his/her side, he/she must be an outstanding European personality of the calibre of the most authoritative members of the European Council. If the Member States do not follow this rationale when choosing the President of the European Council they will weaken the unity of European representation and ensure the continuity of the institutional (and political) fragmentation that so often characterises the stances adopted by the EU.

The High Representative, elected by the parliament acting on a proposal submitted by the European Council,[27] formally retains all the powers vested by *Maastricht* and *Amsterdam*, but his/her role is reduced by the presence of the President of the European Council and, as the Vice President of the Commission, is subject to the procedures governing the functioning of the Commission which might erode his/her capacity for external representation, particularly when the High

[26]See Santini (2010).

[27]As provided by Art. 214.2 EC-Nice.

Representative has little political status at the European level, despite the fact that the provisions of the Treaty vest the High Representative with the function.[28]

For the High Representative, his/her important institutional position, which makes it possible to sustain the external representation role, derives from the fact of presiding over the Foreign Affairs Council (Art. 18.3 TEU). For there, being the (sole) President of the Council makes it possible to frame the Union's foreign policy agreed by the representatives of the governments of the Member States which can also be imposed in relations with the other Institutions in the event of a dispute. For it is obvious that there is a certain antagonism against the President of European Council, as now, in comparison with the past, the policy of driving and steering the Council in the matter of foreign policy is also the responsibility of that organ as well as of the High Representative.

Another element strengthening the position of the High Representative stems from the fact that in the event of the European Parliament vote through a motion of no confidence in the Commission would affect the High Representative in his/her capacity as the Vice President of the Commission, but not in respect of the role performed in foreign policy.

The external representation function of the Commission was not explicitly spelt out in the past, but no one ever doubted that this function was vested in the Commission, because recognition of this function derived from the Commission's place in the institutional design of the Community – that is to say, as the high authority of an international organisation, acting as its representative. Even though this function was not explicitly provided for, it was taken for granted on the basis of Art. 300 EC, which provided that the Commission had competence for negotiating agreements between the Community and one or more states or with an international organisation.[29]

By laying down an arrangement that is closer to that of a federation of states, the changed institutional architecture resulting from the Lisbon Treaty makes it necessary to expressly prescribe the Commission's external representation capacity, also because the legal character of the European Commission, even with the Treaty of Lisbon, remains problematic. For – as will be seen shortly – the Commission does not resemble an institution that can be compared wholly with the government of a federal State, even though there is a fiduciary relationship with the Parliament.

---

[28]On the one hand, Art. 15.6, sentence 2, TEU limits the role of the President of the European Council to ensuring "the external representation of the Union on issues concerning its common foreign and security policy, without prejudice to the powers of the High Representative of the Union for Foreign Affairs and Security", meaning that the latter prevail; on the other hand, however, Art. 18.4 TEU provides not only that the High Representative is one of the Vice Presidents of the Commission, but also gives him/her a particular role on the Commission. For the High Representative is responsible for ensuring "the consistency of the Union's external action", and on the Commission is vested with "the responsibilities incumbent on it in external relations and for coordinating other aspects of the Union's external action".

[29]On this point see Caliguri (2004), pp. 1336–1337.

6 Internal Representation: The European Council and the Council

The question of internal representation is even more complex; the individual officers (the President of the European Council, the President of the Commission and the High Representative) are required to perform external representation functions, and are therefore vested with their own powers to do so. However, from the internal point of view, they do not have a representation role, but only to drive and link the institutions: the President of the European Council in respect of the European Council ("shall chair it and drive forward its work", "ensure the preparation and continuity of the work of the European Council", "facilitate cohesion and consensus within the European Council") presents a report to the European Parliament after each of the meetings of the European Council, and chairs the General Affairs Council, in cooperation with the President of the Commission (Art. 15.6 TEU).

The President of the Commission lays down guidelines with which the Commission is required to work, decides on the internal organisation of the Commission, ensuring that it acts consistently, efficiently and collegially; the President of the Commission is also responsible for appointing the Vice Presidents, except the High Representative of the Union for Foreign Affairs and Security Policy. The President of the Commission may request the resignation of a member of the Commission (including the High Representative), who is obliged to resign if requested (for the High Representative there is a special procedure to be followed).

The High Representative within the European institutional system appears to have a liaison function: appointed by the European Council (with the agreement of the President of the Commission), the High Representative chairs the Foreign Affairs Council, and is one of the Vice Presidents of the Commission, subject to a vote of confidence by the European Parliament. "In fulfilling his mandate, the High Representative shall be assisted by a European External Action Service", and handles relations with all the institutions, performing his/her functions by liaising with them. The person selected for this office must be a politically prominent personality on the European stage, because the office of the High Representative entails strengthening the policies which best guarantee federal unity as the Union evolves: foreign policy, security policy and the common defence policy.

Having dealt with the three main officers, the issue of internal representation clearly involves all the institutions: the European Council, the Council and the European Parliament, to which we may add the Commission, which, because of the fiduciary relationship it enjoys with the Parliament and the appointment procedure, also takes part in the representation process. The question of representation within the overall institutional architecture of the EU makes it possible to appraise relations between the "institutions", and in particular to show which of these institutions is the actual body of "government" in the constitutional sense of that term, namely, the organ which can guarantee the functionality of the decision-making process and the continuity of the European system.

The representation for which all the various institutions are responsible differs in each case as one can immediately see. The European Council still retains an international law-related character, despite the fact that it now forms part of the regular organisation of the new Union (Art. 13.1 TEU),[30] an arrangement which is evidenced from three elements: first, the fact that the Council does not legislate;[31] second, the frequency of its sessions meetings – only twice a year, save when convened in extraordinary session; and third, the voting system, because the European Council, unless otherwise provided by the Treaties, resolves by consensus.

It should be noted that the European Council has undergone a twofold change. Originally its formation and its dynamic were external to the Community, governed by public international law because of its positioning within the international community. But with the Maastricht Treaty the European Council already lost its international law character because it was then placed within the particular legal form of the EU until the Lisbon Treaty. With this status it was polyhedral in character because through the revolving Presidency system it performed the external representation function, and as a collegial body it guaranteed the strategic direction of the Union.

Now that the Lisbon Treaty has made provision for a President of the European Council with external representation functions, tasked with coordinating the European Council and the Council, it seems to be more projected into an internal representation role, with a central position in a federal dimension.[32] The European Council has the political function of laying down strategic guidelines ("The European Council shall provide the Union with the necessary impetus for its development and shall define the general political directions and priorities thereof" (Art. 15.1 TEU). Furthermore, in addition to electing its President it also has the task of appointing the High Representative (with the consent of the President of the Commission), submitting nominations to the European Parliament of candidates to serve as President of the Commission, stipulating the number of Commissioners (Art. 17.5 TEU) and deciding on the rotation system (Art. 244.1 TFEU). Lastly,

---

[30]It should not be forgotten that the European Council is made up of the Heads of State or Government of the Member States, its President and by the President of the Commission, and that the High Representative of the Union for Foreign Affairs and Security Policy also takes part in its deliberations (Art. 15.2 TEU); moreover, each member of the European Council may decide to be assisted by a minister, and the President of the Commission by a member of the Commission (Art. 15.3 TEU). And this differs from the previous situation: under Art. 4 TEU-Amsterdam, the members of the European Council could be assisted by the foreign ministers of the Member States and by a member of the Commission.

[31]Leaving aside what emerges from the final considerations of sessions of the European Council, for the law-making activities of the Council and the European Parliament, it must be admitted that in some areas (judicial cooperation in matters of criminal law and security) it makes its influence felt more strongly (cf. Art. 82.3, 83.3, 86.4, 87.3 TFEU).

[32]This perspective is strengthened by the primary law provisions according to which an act of the European Council which produces legal effects on third parties may be submitted to the ECJ for a ruling on its legitimacy (Art. 263 TFEU), and permit the Member States to take the European Council to Court in the event that it fails to pronounce (Art. 265 TFEU).

there is the competence of the European Council with regard to the composition of the European Parliament, resolving jointly with the Parliament itself, and deciding on the list of Council formations (Art. 236 TFEU) and its role in the procedures for revising the Treaties (Art. 48.3 and 7 TEU).

Yet judging from the aspects addressed above, important as it is, the European Council's driving function cannot be considered to be continuous, and its paramount role can therefore only be fully appreciated when the Union is in crisis.

The Council, linked to the European Council, at least in its "General Affairs" configuration, through the President of the European Council, is in a somewhat different position. The Council has always been a sort of federal institution in the European tradition, both as the main, albeit not the sole, legislative body, and subsequently, when its law-making powers were shared with the European Parliament and when it came to resemble a chamber (of governments) of the Member States, which is its present status under the Lisbon Treaty (Art. 10.2, sentence 2, TEU). Its federal character has been heightened with the abolition of unanimous voting and the acceptance of majority voting,[33] which now prevails (Art. 16.3 TEU).[34]

Furthermore, the Council has always played a very important part in the application of European law; one novelty to be noted in the Lisbon Treaty is that its executive function is clearly recessive. For Art. 16.1 TEU states that "[t]he Council shall, jointly with the European Parliament, exercise legislative and budgetary functions". The fact that different tasks still lie with the Council also has repercussions on the rules governing its public sessions, which only apply when it deliberates in a legislative capacity (Art. 16.8 TEU).

In this connection, it must also be recalled that the Council is also responsible for all European policies, which is why its configuration changes according to the policy under deliberation. The Treaty only makes express provision for two configurations: the "General Affairs" Council chaired by the President of the European Council, and the "Foreign Affairs" Council chaired by the High Representative, separating what the Constitutional Treaty had merged (the "General Affairs and External Relations Council"). All the other configurations of the Council are decided by the European Council which, under Art. 236 TFEU, lays

[33]On majority voting on the Council see the earlier comments by Götz (1995), pp. 339 et seqq., cf. also Buccino Grimaldi and Gazzoletti (2001), and now in Tizzano (2002), pp. 93 et seqq.

[34]The general provisions of paragraph 3 are followed by those of paragraph 5 ("The transitional provisions relating to the definition of the qualified majority which shall be applicable until 31 October 2014 and those which shall be applicable from 1 November 2014 to 31 March 2017 are laid down in the Protocol on transitional provisions") laying down the timing of the various majority voting rules, and have now been joined by Art. 238 TFEU and Protocol No 36 "On transitional provisions". In essence, one can identify three periods: (a) from the entry into force of the Treaty until 2014, (b) from 2014 to 2017, (c) 2017 and beyond [see Ponzano (2009), pp. 77 et seqq.].

down the list and the revolving Presidencies from among the representatives of the Member States' governments (Art. 16.6 and 9 TEU).[35]

One must infer from Art. 16.2 TEU, which provides that "[t]he Council shall consist of a representative of each Member State at ministerial level, who may commit the government of the Member State in question and cast its vote", that the different configurations depend on the policies on which the Council is deliberating and voting, although the Treaty says nothing about this. On the subject of the two configurations for which express provision is made, namely, the "General Affairs" Council and the "Foreign Affairs" Council, the Treaty merely specifies their remit,[36] but without detailing their composition. This has made it possible to find room for the national formation in this regard, which, for particular policies and thanks to the Constitutional procedures of the Member States, has also enabled the representatives of the Regional governments of the Member States to take part in the deliberations of the Council. Suffice it to refer to the provisions of Art. 23 GG and Art. 117 of the Italian Constitution in this connection.[37]

In conclusion, the Council is an institution which is highly representative in character, working in every direction within the Union, although no longer prevalently so, and no longer more or less alone as had been the case in the past. For it now operates in close cooperation with the other Institutions, particularly the Commission and the European Parliament. Furthermore, one can also apply to the Council what has already been said about the European Council, namely, that from the point of view of European constitutional law this is a kind of "intermittent" institution, where the permanent organs of the (bureaucratic) structure of the EU are the "Committee of Permanent Representatives of the Governments of the Member States" (Art. 16.7 TEU), which is "responsible for preparing the work of the Council", and the "Political and Security Committee" to "monitor the international situation in the areas covered by the common foreign and security policy and contribute to the definition of policies by delivering opinions to the Council" (Art. 38 TEU). It therefore follows that the Council does not have the function of guaranteeing the functioning and the development of the European legal system.

[35]Particularly significant for the implementation of this provision is Declaration 9 annexed to the Treaty containing a "Draft decision of the European Council on the exercise of the Presidency of the Council".

[36]Art. 16.6, sentence 2, TEU provides that "[t]he General Affairs Council shall ensure consistency in the work of the different Council configurations. It shall prepare and ensure the follow-up to meetings of the European Council, in liaison with the President of the European Council and the Commission", and Art. 16.6, sentence 3, TEU provides that "[t]he Foreign Affairs Council shall elaborate the Union's external action on the basis of strategic guidelines laid down by the European Council and ensure that the Union's action is consistent".

[37]On these procedures, see Di Salvatore (2008), pp. 100 et seqq.; Di Salvatore (2007).

7 Internal Representation: The European Parliament

At this point we have to address the question of the value of the statement, among the democratic principles enshrined in the Treaty, that the functioning of the Union is based on representative democracy. This principle is expressed in particularly forthright terms ("The functioning of the Union shall be *founded on...*"), but in the dynamic of Title II of the Treaty this wording has to be construed in legal terms, linked to the provisions describing a participatory system not linked solely to representative democracy but to which the Treaty attributes indisputable value in the decision-making process. It is no coincidence that the expressions "representative associations", "by appropriate means", "transparent and regular dialogue" and "consultations with parties concerned" are used. Provision is also made for a form of citizens' initiative.

If this were not sufficient, Art. 12 TEU also provides that the "National Parliaments contribute actively to the good functioning of the Union", exercising various powers and functions, according to the rationale of "circular democracy".

It is a simple matter to incorporate the function of the internal representation of the European Parliament into this context, noting that as an institution it has been playing an increasingly important role across the years, until Title III TEU placed it at the top of the list of the institutions (Art. 13) and in the Treaty rules on the Functioning of the EU.

For Art. 14 sets the European Parliament in the European institutional system in relation to its legislative, budgetary and scrutiny functions and its power to elect the President of the Commission, describing it as the organ representing the citizens of the Union.

This is a framework that has emerged from the evolutionary process through which the supranational system has emerged and become widely consolidated, like all the other powers and functions envisaged in the other provisions of the TEU and the Treaty on the Functioning of the European Union (TFEU): beginning with the collective vote of approval to which the President, the High Representative of the Union for Foreign Affairs and Security Policy and the other members of the Commission (Art. 17.7 TEU) are subject, the possibility of passing a censure motion against the Commission (Art. 234 TFEU), the quasi-power of legislative initiative by requesting the Commission to submit a legislative proposal (Art. 225 TFEU), establishing the status and general conditions for the exercise of the functions of members of the European Parliament (Art. 223.2 TFEU), the possibility of setting up temporary Parliamentary Committees of Enquiry (Art. 226 TFEU), the right of citizens to submit petitions to the European Parliament (Art. 227 TFEU) and the election of European ombudsmen (Art. 228 TFEU).

It is in this context that the provision has been retained which enables the European Parliament and the Council to use the ordinary legislative procedure (Art. 294 TFEU, ex Art. 251 EC) to lay down the regulations governing political parties at the European level, and in particular the rules regarding their financing

(Art. 224 TFEU) and the question of electoral provisions. In the latter case, the Treaty of Lisbon seems to provide different rules from those of the EC: the European Council (Art. 190.4 EC) provided that the draft produced by the European Parliament to permit elections by direct universal suffrage following a uniform procedure in all the Member States or according to the principles common to all the Member States would be purely indicative, because ultimately it was the task of the Council, resolving with a unanimous vote, *after the European Parliament had issued a concurring opinion*, to decide on which provisions to recommend for adoption by the Member States according to their respective internal constitutional procedures; now, conversely, the Lisbon Treaty provides that the Council, acting unanimously in accordance with a special legislative procedure and after *obtaining the consent of the European Parliament*, lays down the "necessary provisions", and that "these provisions shall enter into force following their approval by the Member States in accordance with their respective constitutional requirements" (Art. 223.1 TFEU).

Regardless of what further changes may be possible, to fully equate the European Parliament with a Chamber representing the people in a Federation, overcoming the organisational constraints (such as the principle of regressive proportionality) which still afflict the institution and on which the German Constitutional Court focused in particular in its judgment on the Treaty of Lisbon,[38] it must be noted that the role and the functioning of the European Parliament today is

[38]In its ruling on the Lisbon Treaty, the German Federal Constitutional Court found that the European system still seriously infringes the democratic principle and the system of internal representation precisely because of the criteria adopted by the Treaty regarding the composition of the European Parliament; cf. German Federal Constitutional Court, 2 BvE 2, 5/08, 2 BvR 1010, 1022, 1259/08, 182/09 (Judgment of 30 June 2009) – *Lisbon* (English translation available online): "Even in the new wording of Art. 14.2 TEU Lisbon, and contrary to the claim that Art. 10.1 TEU Lisbon seems to make according to its wording, the European Parliament is not a representative body of a sovereign European people. This is reflected in the fact that it is designed as a representation of peoples in the respective national contingents of Members, not as a representation of Union citizens in unity without differentiation, according to the principle of electoral equality" (para 280); "as seats are allocated to the Member States, the European Parliaments factually remains a representation of the peoples of the Member States" (para 284); "In federal states, such marked imbalances are, as a general rule, only tolerated for the second chamber existing beside Parliament [. . .]They are, however, not accepted in the representative body of the people" (para 286); – "This consideration at the same time clarifies why representation in the European Parliament does not take as its nexus the equality of the citizens of the Union (Art. 9 TEU Lisbon) but nationality" (para 287); "As regards electoral equality and the mechanism of direct parliamentary representation, the democratic legitimisation of political rule is also in party democracies based on the category of the individual's act of voting and not assessed according to the quantity of those affected" (para 292); "Also the institutional recognition of the Member States' Parliaments by the Treaty of Lisbon cannot compensate for the deficit in the direct track of legitimisation of the European public authority that is based on the election of the Members of the European Parliament" (para 293); "Mere participation of the citizens in political rule which would take the place of the representative self-government of the people cannot be a substitute for the legitimising connection of elections and other votes and of a government that relies on it: The Treaty of Lisbon does not lead to a new level of development of democracy" (para 295).

very similar to that of the fully fledged modern Parliament[39] and that the anomalies recorded in no way detract from the importance that this European Institution has now acquired. Even the German Constitutional Court, which has been so critical of its democratic character, has had to admit that its role is decisive in the decision-making process, and that "the democracy of the European Union is approximated to federalised state concepts".[40]

At this point it has to be noted that the role that has been attributed to the European Parliament in the institutional structure of the EU as it stands today marks a considerable change in the European institutional design. For the unification of the EU and the European Council into the Union, and the merger of the pillars, have created a supranational unity of system and action which, on account of its founding values (article 2 TEU), and the part played by the democratic principle, make the European Parliament the centrepiece of the functioning of Europe's institutions, leading to the parliamentarisation of institutional relations. For despite the fact that there is a clear-cut division of competences limiting the role of all the Institutions, it is precisely the way the Parliament operates and its close cooperation with the Commission that make it one of the players constantly acting in the process of European unification. In addition to its legislative function, which the Treaty has now made particularly broad, this is evidenced from the way the European Parliament acts in practice in areas that are – formally – the exclusive preserve of the governments and the Council, such as the CFSP, over which the Treaty only gives the Parliament the right to be consultated, acting on the advice of the High Representative, and the power to table questions or make recommendations, not only to the Council but also to the High Representative in debates to be staged twice a year (Art. 36 TEU).[41] For submitting recommendations to the Council of Ministers and the European Council in the form of *resolutions* has proven to be a formidable instrument of political guidance through which the Parliament has tried to make up for the limited powers it enjoys within the CFSP, and has even managed to acquire *a role in the decision-making process itself.*[42]

Like any other modern Parliament, the European Parliament can therefore be considered to be a permanent body in the European system, because its work is ongoing and helps to guarantee the functional unity of the Union. In view of this distinguishing feature of the EU, which differentiates it from the European Council and from the Council, we can no longer be content with the European democracy, because in the form of European government we can already see a degree of political collaboration that supersedes national spheres and considers European policies as the unitary and common dimension.

---

[39]See Mangiameli (2008b), pp. 491 et seqq.

[40]German Federal Constitutional Court, 2 BvE 2, 5/08, 2 BvR 1010, 1022, 1259/08, 182/09 (Judgment of 30 June 2009) para 288 – *Lisbon*

[41]This article also provides that the High Representative must "ensure that the views of the European Parliament are duly taken into consideration" [see Mangiameli (2009a)].

[42]For examples and common practice see Novi 2005, p. 141.

8 Internal Representation: The Commission

Within the institutional design of the Union, the Commission occupies a place it has earned through the long European Community experience. This is not to say that its role has not changed over the years. Indeed, its status would appear to be quite problematic precisely because all the functions that are now vested in it place it in a similar situation to that of a high authority in an international organisation and, at the same time, that of the government of a federation. The former is a reference to its task of fostering the general interests of the Union, adopting appropriate initiatives to that end, monitoring the application and enforcement of the Treaties and measures adopted by the Institutions under the Treaties and the application of EU law under the oversight of the ECJ. The latter would seem to include the implementation of the budget and the management of programmes; exercising coordinating, implementation and management functions; initiating the process of annual and multi-year Union planning and programming, to conclude inter-institutional agreements; and the external representation of the Union (with the exception of the CFSP) (Art. 17.1 TEU).

The Commission's power of legislative initiative falls halfway between the two roles; formerly, the Commission's initiative was addressed to the Council, but it is now addressed to the legislative organs, i.e. the Council and the European Parliament (Art. 17.2 TEU). This competence, which the Lisbon Treaty subjects to a possible right to request the Council and the European Parliament to take the initiative, is typical of the law of the origin of the supranational system, which was the international public law, but also of an *ancient regime* government in which the legislative initiative used to be vested in the King, as the person holding the executive branch of government.

Taken as a whole, one might say that the Commission has a central position in the whole institutional design, as a stable organ guaranteeing the Union's functional continuity together with the European Parliament. Its positioning is also consequent upon the procedure for its formation. Accordingly, on the one hand, the Commission cannot be considered to be a political organ because it should be characterised by its *neutrality* in respect of the political interests of the individual Member States ("The Commission shall be completely independent", and the Member States "shall refrain from any action incompatible with their duties or the performance of their tasks" Art. 17.3 TEU). In view of this, the members of the Commission are "chosen on the ground of their general competence and European commitment from persons whose independence is beyond doubt". It is therefore particularly significant that its membership comprising individuals with a particular political, but also technical, weight is determined by the governments, and that the Presidency of the Commission is to be held by eminent personalities belonging to a Member State, who are able to ensure the governments – in view of the functions they have previously performed and the previous relationships established in their earlier political roles – that their prerogatives will be respected.

For a long time the Commission has been collectively subject to a vote of approval by the European Parliament of the President and its members (Art. 17.7 TEU), and is answerable to it because the latter can express a vote of no-confidence in it and require the Commissioners to resign (this is reiterated in Art. 17.8 TEU).

The Lisbon Treaty has reinforced these profiles by requiring that following "appropriate consultations, the European Council, acting by a qualified majority, shall propose to the European Parliament a candidate for President of the Commission", which was further developed in Declaration no. 11, which states that "in accordance with the provisions of the Treaties, the European Parliament and the European Council are jointly responsible for the smooth running of the process leading to the election of the President of the European Commission". By virtue of this, "prior to the decision of the European Council, representatives of the European Parliament and of the European Council will thus conduct the necessary consultations in the framework deemed the most appropriate".[43]

This circumstance pays a great service to enhancing European political life and to strengthening the role of the Parliamentary groups within the European Parliament, but at the same time it gives the Commission an unprecedented political closeness to the Parliamentary majority which gives its "vote of consent".

It will be the responsibility of the European Parliament to use these provisions to characterise its role in relations with the Commission and the President of the Commission which, in view of the changes that have been introduced by the Lisbon Treaty, makes it possible to view the Presidency as nothing short of a political post.

The President of the Commission, moreover, even before the Lisbon Treaty, had been viewed as an organ endowed with a certain *vis*, empowering him to head the Commission, take part in the sessions of the institutions and lay down political guidelines. The revised Treaties have given the President full control over the "internal organisation of the Commission, ensuring that it acts consistently, efficiently and as a collegiate body" (Art. 17.6 lit. b TEU); the President decides on the configuration of the Commission because, once elected, he must consent with the Council to the adoption of the list of the other candidates proposed by the governments for appointment to membership of the Commission. The President may also request the resignation of a member of the Commission, and their resignation is mandatory; this applies equally to the High Representative of the Union for Foreign Affairs and Security Policy, who is obliged to resign following the procedure given in Art. 18.1 TEU, because despite being the de jure Vice President, with the specific powers of the President of the "Foreign Affairs" Council, the High Representative

[43]"In accordance with the first subparagraph of Art. 17(7)", Declaration no. 11 went on to say that "these consultations will focus on the backgrounds of the candidates for President of the Commission, taking account of the elections to the European Parliament. The arrangements for such consultations may be determined, in due course, by common accord between the European Parliament and the European Council."

owes his/her position to the consent of the President of the Commission with the European Council (Art. 18.1 TEU).

There is one final profile which deserves attention to show the developments affecting the institutional positioning of the Commission, namely, "The Commission appointed between the date of entry into force of the Treaty of Lisbon and 31 October 2014, shall consist of one national of each Member State, including its President and the High Representative of the Union for Foreign Affairs and Security Policy who shall be one of its Vice-Presidents" (Art. 17.4 TEU), whereas "As from 1 November 2014, the Commission shall consist of a number of members, including its President and the High Representative of the Union for Foreign Affairs and Security Policy, corresponding to two thirds of the number of Member States, unless the European Council, acting unanimously, decides to alter this number" (Art. 17.5 TEU).[44]

The composition of the Commission has passed through several phases: the earlier rules drew a distinction between the large Member States with two Commissioners, and the small Member States with only one Commissioner. With enlargement, it has now reached the present composition, which already appeared not to be functional at the Laeken Convention, where the idea was broached to cut back on the number of Commissioners to a level below the number of the Member States. However, the two thirds of the number of Member States rule, however much tempered by the principles of rotation and territorial combination, which has been defined as "squaring the circle",[45] leads to a fairly broad lack of representation on the Commission, which can raise the problem of the acceptance of the Institution, for which any gains in terms of efficiency are of scant importance. Indeed, the Treaty itself has provided a possible way out by enabling the European Council to vote (unanimously) to change this number.

What appears to emerge from these developments is that the role and work of the Commission, in a configuration which does not include the presence of a Commissioner from each Member State, can only be acceptable if it acts in a truly European dimension in which the Member States' interests are taken up in a unitary and supranational dimension.

[44]This article continues as follows: "The members of the Commission shall be chosen from among the nationals of the Member States on the basis of a system of strictly equal rotation between the Member States, reflecting the demographic and geographical range of all the Member States. This system shall be established unanimously by the European Council in accordance with Art. 244 of the Treaty on the Functioning of the European Union" while Art. 244 TFEU lays down two principles: (a) Member States shall be treated on a strictly equal footing as regards determination of the sequence of, and the time spent by, their nationals as members of the Commission; consequently, the difference between the total number of terms of office held by nationals of any given pair of Member States may never be more than one; and (b) subject to point (a), each successive Commission shall be so composed as to satisfactorily reflect the demographic and geographical range of all the Member States.

[45]Schoo (2009), p. 66.

9 The Functional Profile of the European Institutional Design: Inter-Institutional Dialogue

It would be meaningless to examine the institutional design without taking account, albeit briefly, of the functional aspect of the form of European governance, founded on the values of the Union (Art. 2 TEU) and designed to pursue the objectives of the Union (Art. 3 TEU). Also in this perspective there are two elements to be considered as forming part of the post–Lisbon Treaty system: the individual personal posts (the President of the European Council, the President of the Commission and the High Representative for Foreign Policy) and the Institutions.

Obviously, the appraisal made in this paper does not consider the procedures established by the Treaties, such as the legislative procedure (Art. 194 TFEU), the budgetary procedure (Art. 310 and 313 et seqq. TFEU) or those for negotiating international agreements (Art. 218 TFEU), because it refers to the way the Union functions in the absence of any specific provisions defining the operations of the Institutions.

From this point of view, all European relations, and not only those between the Member States and the Union (which was previously governed by Art. 10 TEC), presuppose compliance with the principle of sincere cooperation which, following the case law of the ECJ,[46] has been codified in Art. 13.2 TEU,[47] and which is the most effective in the relationship between the individual officials and the Institutions, and between the Institutions, i.e. in the inter-institutional relations which are not fully codified in the Treaty but on which the effectiveness of the European legal system depends.

Some of the rules of conduct are found in the Declarations annexed to the Treaties relating to the personal official posts: Declaration no. 6, for example, provides that when these officers are appointed, "due account is to be taken of the need to respect the geographical and demographic diversity of the Union and its Member States"; conversely, Declaration no. 11, which gives the European Parliament and the European Council joint responsibility "for the smooth running of the process leading to the election of the President of the European Commission" refers not to the geographic and demographic spheres but to the necessary consultations between the representatives of the European Parliament and of the European

[46] Case C-65/93, Parliament v Council (ECJ 30 March 1995), which stated that "the Court has held that inter-institutional dialogue, on which the consultation procedure in particular is based, is subject to the same mutual duties of sincere cooperation as those which govern relations between Member States and the Community institutions".

[47] Article 13.2 TEU: "Each institution shall act within the limits of the powers conferred on it in the Treaties, and in conformity with the procedures, conditions and objectives set out in them. The institutions shall practise mutual sincere cooperation." It should be noted that in the codified procedures, in addition to sincere cooperation, relations between the Institutions require the procedural phases to be implemented with each Institution respecting the competences of the other institutions involved, a principle that is only partially derivable from sincere cooperation.

Council which "focus on the backgrounds of the candidates for President of the Commission, taking account of the elections to the European Parliament". Something similar is also found in Declaration no. 12, referring to the appointment/ election of the High Representative of the Union for Foreign Affairs and Security Policy, which requires "appropriate contacts [to be] made with the European Parliament".

Naturally, the political value of these decisions will essentially depend on the role of the European Parliament as an Institution, but above all on the conduct of the European political parties with their groups present in the Parliament. It will be easier to gain a better appreciation of this dimension, even though various signals point to the increasing politicisation of the European public area, by examining the decisions that will be taken in 2014 when the first experience of personal office-holders will have been completed.

However, as far as relations between the Institutions are concerned, the Treaties only provide that in addition to the formal procedures, "[t]he European Parliament, the Council and the Commission shall consult each other and by common agreement make arrangements for their cooperation. To that end, they may, in compliance with the Treaties, conclude inter-institutional agreements which may be of a binding nature" (Art. 295 TFEU).

This new provision, based on previous experience,[48] is particularly important from many different points of view: first, it formalises "inter-institutional dialogue" as the basis for the practical functioning of the EU and, to that end, it places the three Institutions just mentioned on an equivalent footing; second, it provides that any jointly decided agreements are binding in character, even though these agreements, which govern cooperation in writing and in detail, retain their contractual character and do not acquire the rank of sources of law in the full sense of the term.

However, the provision which seems to complete the arrangement for "inter-institutional dialogue" and which gives Art. 295 TFEU its dynamic character is the one which vests the Commission with the task of initiating "the Union's annual and multiannual programming with a view to achieving inter-institutional agreements" (Art. 17.1, sentence 7, TEU).

To conclude, one must assume that the guarantee of the "good" functioning of the supranational system has been entrusted to the Commission, and the value that its ability to conclude agreements and make it possible to move forward in the integration process, and the fact that this process today still seems to be linked to mediation between the Member States, mainly on the Council, make it likely that as the European experience proceeds, the integration process will increasingly take on a more political character, considering the increasing closeness between the Commission and the European Parliament, and the gradual political colouring of the Commission itself. These are all aspects which will become more visible as the

[48]For which we would refer to our article, Mangiameli (2009b).

"one Commissioner per Member State" rule increasingly goes out of currency, and the principle that account must be taken of the results of the European Parliamentary elections will be fully able to play its linkage function.

10 The Particular Position of the European Court of Justice and the Principle of the Primacy of European Law

No examination of the European institutional design can ignore the role of the ECJ. For this institution, which does not seem to be particularly affected by the provisions of the Treaties[49] and whose composition retains the principle of "one judge from each Member State" (Art. 19.2 TEU) cannot really be considered in terms of the neutrality of the judicial function, recalling the provisions of ex Art. 220 EC, according to which the Court ensures "that in the interpretation and application of the Treaties the law is observed" (Art. 19.1 TEU).[50]

In reality, throughout the European experience the ECJ has never restricted its work to exercising its power to interpret the Treaty alone, but has used interpretation to spread European law, particularly in dialogue with the national courts, through the preliminary ruling procedure; it has also been thanks to the Court, through its early case law rulings,[51] that European law has been strengthened by establishing the principle of the primacy of European law over domestic law, to the point of requesting national lawmakers to repeal laws which are inconsistent with European law. In this way, the Court of Justice has been a benchmark for the integration of our legal systems, playing a creative part in European law by identifying the general principles of the Community legal system and exploiting the value of the Member States' shared constitutional traditions. It has been able to

[49]The only innovation, which had originally been raised at the Convention, is to filter the Member States' nomination proposals along the lines of the system used for appointing judges to the higher courts of the Member States, which was ultimately included in Art. 255 TFEU ("A panel shall be set up in order to give an opinion on candidates' suitability to perform the duties of Judge and Advocate-General of the Court of Justice and the General Court before the governments of the Member States make the appointments referred to in Arts. 253 and 254." "The panel shall comprise seven persons chosen from among former members of the Court of Justice and the General Court, members of national supreme courts and lawyers of recognised competence, one of whom shall be proposed by the European Parliament. The Council shall adopt a decision establishing the panel's operating rules and a decision appointing its members. It shall act on the initiative of the President of the Court of Justice").

[50]In this connection, see the excellent essay by Monaco (1972), pp. 417 et seqq.

[51]Case 26/62, *Van Gend & Loos v. Amministrazione olandese delle imposte* ECJ 5 February 1963); Case 6/64, *Flaminio Costa v. E.N.E.L.* (ECJ 15 July 1964); Case 106/77, *Amministrazione delle finanze dello Stato v. SpA Simmenthal* (ECJ 9 March 1978).

introduce the protection of fundamental rights at the European level.[52] To a great extent, this has been a constitutional operation that must be acknowledged.[53]

The Court's constitutional role does not, obviously, refer to setting political guidelines or to the functioning of the form of government, but to establishing the European system as a whole. It is one of the features of the supranational system that when the European integration process is flagging, the Court can use the best weapons in its armoury to guarantee the effectiveness of European law in relations with the Member States.

In this regard, recent ECJ case law appears to be particularly significant: seizing on the difficulties of European law in this phase, it has given a powerful fresh boost to the "principle of the primacy of European law" which has played a particularly important role in the consolidation of the European system.[54]

This principle had previously been incorporated into the 2004 Constitutional Treaty (Art. 1–6 TCE: "The Constitution and law adopted by the Union institutions in exercising competence conferred upon it by the Constitution shall have primacy over the law of the member states") but its federal symbology, expressing the supremacy of the Union, gave rise to a number of issues, with the result that in the Lisbon Treaty it was expressly removed from the Note of the General Secretariat of the Council to the delegations,[55] which had stated that "[c]oncerning the primacy of EU law, the IGC will adopt a Declaration recalling the existing case law of the EU Court of Justice".[56] Furthermore, the Conference decided to annex to the Final Act the opinion of the Council Legal Service on primacy, issued on 22 June 2007 and set out in the document 11197/07 (JUR 260).[57]

The ruling by the German Constitutional Court also took this into account, and it was recently taken up again in the *Mangold* judgment.[58] In its case law regarding

---

[52]By extracting them from constitutional traditions and placing them among the general principles of the European legal system. Cf. among the many rulings, Case 29/69, *Internationale Handelsgesellschaft* (ECJ 12 November 1969); Case 4/73, *Nold* (ECJ 14 May 1974); Case 222/84, *Johnston* (ECJ 15 May 1986).

[53]See Calvano (2001, 2004).

[54]See Di Salvatore (2006), pp. 477 et seqq.

[55]See IGC 26 June 2007, no. 11218/07.

[56]No. 17: "The Conference recalls that, in accordance with well settled case law of the Court of Justice of the European Union, the Treaties and the law adopted by the Union on the basis of the Treaties have primacy over the law of Member States, under the conditions laid down by the said case law."

[57]"It results from the case law of the Court of Justice that primacy of EC law is a cornerstone principle of Community law. According to the Court, this principle is inherent to the specific nature of the European Community. At the time of the first judgment of this established case law [Case 6/64, *Costa/ENEL* (ECJ 15 July 1964)], there was no mention of primacy in the treaty. It is still the case today. *The fact that the principle of primacy will not be included in the future treaty shall not in any way change the existence of the principle and the existing case law of the Court of Justice*" (emphasis added).

[58]German Federal Constitutional Court, 2 BvR 2661/06 (Order of 6 July 2010) para 55–71 – *Honeywell*.

the Lisbon Treaty, the German Constitutional Court admitted that it could rule on European law in the light of the division of competences and the constitutional identity of the Federal Republic of Germany, and concluded that it could decide not to apply European law, even setting aside the case law of the ECJ.[59]

This situation can obviously create tension in relations between the Constitutional Courts and the ECJ,[60] even though it was precisely the *Mangold* case that should have provided reassurance, because the German Constitutional Court in its judgment of 2010, on a direct constitutional appeal, submitted, after the corresponding decision of the Court of Justice,[61] by the losing party in the European case, not merely to refrain from judging the judgment of the European Court, suffering – according to the applicant – by an excess of jurisdiction (ultra vires), as it could be considered according to the *Lisbon* judgment, but said the coordinating role of the European Court, in the interpretation and application of European law, in order to ensure the unity and consistency of supranational law, thus closing the loophole earlier judgment on the Treaty of Lisbon,[62] and by reducing their harshness, and

[59]German Federal Constitutional Court, 2 BvE 2/08 (Judgment of 30 June 2009) – *Lisbon* : "The primacy of application of European law remains, even with the entry into force of the Treaty of Lisbon, an institution conferred under an international agreement, i.e. a derived institution which will have legal effect in Germany only with the order to apply the law given by the Act Approving the Treaty of Lisbon" (para 330); "–The Basic Law aims to integrate Germany into the legal community of peaceful and free states, but does not waive the sovereignty contained in the last instance in the German constitution. There is therefore no contradiction to the aim of openness to international law if the legislature, exceptionally, does not comply with the law of international agreements – accepting, however, corresponding consequences in international relations – provided this is the only way in which a violation of fundamental principles of the constitution can be averted. (...) Factually at any rate, it is no contradiction to the objective of openness towards European law, i.e. to the participation of the Federal Republic of Germany in the realisation of a united Europe (Preamble, Art. 23.1 sentence 1 of the Basic Law), if exceptionally, and under special and narrow conditions, the Federal Constitutional Court declares European Union law inapplicable in Germany" (para 340).

[60]See Donnarumma (2010), pp. 407 et seqq.

[61]Case 144/04 *Mangold v Helm* (ECJ 22 November 2005), by reference to the German law regarding fixed-term labour contracts, was attacked quite strongly in the German literature (Buer–Arnold, in NJW 2006; Dashwood, in CYELS 2007; Reic, in EuZW 2006, 20), because it had declared German law to be in violation of the principle of non-discrimination on the grounds of age, on the basis of various international instruments and constitutional traditions shared by the Member States. However, the German Constitutional Court, in its 2010 judgment brought in the wake of the decision of the ECJ by the company which had concluded these fixed-term contracts, actually abstained from ruling on the ECJ judgment in which, according to the plaintiff, the court had acted *ultra vires*, despite the fact that in the *Lisbon* judgment the German Constitutional Court had admitted that type of control.

[62]How would the statement *Das Lissabon-Urteil des Bundesverfassungsgerichts: Auswege aus dem drohenden Justizkonflikt* signed by German eminent scholars and politicians (e.g. Armin von Bogdandy, Christian Calliess, Christian Koenig, Ingolf Pernice, Christian Tomuschat), who underlined the absence in the judgment on the Lisbon Treaty the principle of cooperation between the Constitutional Court and the ECJ, which had characterised the writing of the judgment of the Constitutional Court on the Maastricht Treaty.

ensures that the tensions are balanced cooperatively, in coherence with the idea of European integration and through the principle of mutual attention, for which the control ultra vires may be exercised only *Europarechtsfreundlich* (openness towards European law).[63] The German Constitutional Court comes to recognise that, in principle, it must comply with the judgments of the Court of Justice as binding interpretation of Union law.[64]

It remains a fact that, pending the rethinking of the German Constitutional Court, the ECJ has reactivated, in the logic of supranational law, its stabilisation role, which it had previously performed through the principle of the primacy of European law. In this regard refer the recent case law of the Court of Justice: in its judgment in the *Filipiak* case[65] it pointed out that the principle of *the primacy of European law* could not be subjected to particular domestic procedures, even if constitutional in nature,[66] and that regardless of any domestic ruling by the national Constitutional Court (which found it to be unconstitutional, but delayed the date of effectiveness of its ruling exercising the power conferred on it by the Polish Constitution), "*pursuant to the principle of the primacy of Community law* a conflict between a provision of national law and a directly applicable provision of the Treaty is to be resolved by a national court applying Community law, if necessary by refusing to apply the conflicting national provision, and not by a declaration that the national provision is invalid, the powers of authorities, courts and tribunals in that regard being a matter to be determined by each Member State".

Consequently, "[i]n those circumstances, the primacy of Community law obliges the national court to apply Community law and to refuse to apply conflicting provisions of national law, irrespective of the judgment of the national constitutional court which has deferred the date on which those provisions, held to be unconstitutional, are to lose their binding force".[67]

In a later ruling,[68] dealing once again with the principle of age-based non-discrimination, the ECJ reiterated "the need to ensure the full effectiveness of the principle of non-discrimination on grounds of age, as given expression in Directive

[63]German Federal Constitutional Court, 2 BvR 2661/06 (Order of 6 July 2010) para 57, 58 – *Honeywell*.

[64]German Federal Constitutional Court, 2 BvR 2661/06 (Order of 6 July 2010) para 60 – *Honeywell*, where a new *Solange* ("As long as") is declared ("As long as the Court of Justice did not have an opportunity to rule on the questions of Union law which have arisen, the Federal Constitutional Court may not find any inapplicability of Union law for Germany").

[65]Case 314/08, *Filipiak* (ECJ 19 November 2009). The Polish administrative court had referred a case to the ECJ for a preliminary ruling on the extension of the principle of primacy, and in particular on whether this could also extend to a ruling by the Polish Constitutional Court, which delayed the effect of one of its rulings on a provision that violated the right of establishment guaranteed by Art. 43 EC.

[66]A principle dating back to Case 106/77, *Simmenthal* (ECJ 9 March 1978), para 24.

[67]Case 314/08, *Filipiak* (ECJ 19 November 2009) para 85.

[68]Case C-555/07, *Seda Kücükdeveci / Swedex GmbH & Co. KG* (ECJ 19 January 2010), para 53 et seqq.

2000/78, means that the national court, faced with a national provision falling within the scope of European Union law which it considers to be incompatible with that principle, and which cannot be interpreted in conformity with that principle, must decline to apply that provision, without being either compelled to make or prevented from making a reference to the Court for a preliminary ruling before doing so".

In this case the question was quite complex because the referring court had requested the ECJ for a preliminary ruling on the interpretation of European law before disappplying a domestic provision deemed to be in conflict with that law, on the grounds that "pursuant to national law the referring court cannot disapply a current provision of domestic law if this has not been previously declared to be unconstitutional by the Federal Constitutional Court".

The response of the ECJ, once again drawing on its recent case law, insisted on the primacy of European law, stating that "the possibility thus given to the national court by the second paragraph of Art. 267 TFEU of asking the Court for a preliminary ruling before disapplying the national provision that is contrary to European Union law cannot, however, be transformed into an obligation because national law does not allow that court to disapply a provision it considers to be contrary to the constitution unless the provision has first been declared unconstitutional by the Constitutional Court. By reason of the principle of *the primacy of European Union law*, which extends also to the principle of non-discrimination on grounds of age, contrary national legislation which falls within the scope of European Union law must be disapplied (para 54)."

Similar opinions were issued in various judgments in 2010, all as a result of cases referred to the ECJ by the German courts,[69] so that one may conclude that in the matter of the primacy of Union law, and the obligation to directly apply European law, and to apply it uniformly, necessarily disapplying any domestic provisions in conflict with it, and the principle of sincere cooperation on the part of

[69]See Case C-14/09, *Hava Genc v Land Berlin* (ECJ 4 February 2010) para 36 (According to well-established case law, it follows both from the primacy of European Union law over Member States' domestic law and from the direct effect of a provision such as Art. 6 of Decision No 1/80 that a Member State is not permitted to modify unilaterally the scope of the system of gradually integrating Turkish workers into the host Member State's labour force); Case C-409/06, *Winner Wetten GmbH v Bürgermeisterin der Stadt Bergheim* (ECJ 8 September 2010) para 53 et seqq. ("according to settled case-law, in accordance with the principle of the precedence of Union law, provisions of the Treaty and directly applicable measures of the institutions have the effect, in their relations with the internal law of the Member States, merely by entering into force, of rendering automatically inapplicable any conflicting provision of national law"); Case C-429/09, *Günter Fuss v Stadt Halle* (ECJ 25 November 2010) para 7 ("the Court has already held that the exercise of rights conferred on private persons by directly applicable provisions of EU law would be rendered impossible or excessively difficult if their claims for compensation based on the infringement of EU law were rejected or reduced solely because the persons concerned did not apply for grant of the right which was conferred by EU law provisions, and which national law denied them, with a view to challenging the refusal of the Member State by means of the legal remedies provided for that purpose, invoking the *primacy and direct effect of EU law*").

the Member States' authorities, "any provision of a national legal system and any legislative, administrative or judicial practice which might impair the effectiveness of Union law by withholding from the national court having jurisdiction to apply such law the power to do everything necessary at the moment of its application to set aside national legislative provisions which might prevent directly applicable Union rules from having full force and effect are incompatible with the requirements which are the very essence of Union law".[70] It concluded by ruling that, "rules of national law, even of a constitutional order, cannot be allowed to undermine the unity and effectiveness of Union law".[71]

11 The Construction of the European Political System

Any institutional model needs to be grounded on an underlying political system. This applies to the form of governance of a State, but it is no less true of the EU. What makes it necessary to refer to the political system in the case of the EU has nothing to do with its legal nature but derives directly from the nature of the power exercised by the Union. This power is not an expression of international public law, but has constitutional law significance, because the Union, with its own values and its own aims and purposes, is the expression of the European *res publica* and refers directly to the individual players in the European legal system (Member States, corporations and European citizens).

The existence of the European political system, moreover, is also made manifest in the provisions of the Treaties. Under the Maastricht Treaty, *Political parties at European level are important as a factor for integration within the Union. They contribute to forming a European awareness and to expressing the political will of the citizens of the Union* (Art. 191 (1) TEC), and the Nice Treaty later added that *The Council, acting in accordance with the procedure referred to in Article 251, shall lay down the regulations governing political parties at European level and in particular the rules regarding their funding* (Art. 191.2 EC), while the financing of European political parties was governed specifically by Regulation 2004/2003 of

[70] Case C-409/06, *Winner Wetten GmbH v Bürgermeisterin der Stadt Bergheim* (ECJ 8 September 2010) para 56, "It is to be noted, moreover, that, according to settled case-law, the principle of effective judicial protection is a general principle of Union law stemming from the constitutional traditions common to the Member States, which has been enshrined in Arts. 6 and 13 of the European Convention for the Protection of Human Rights and Fundamental Freedoms, signed in Rome on 4 November 1950, and which has also been reaffirmed by Art. 47 of the Charter of fundamental rights of the European Union, and that, under the principle of cooperation laid down in Art. 10 EC, it is for the Member States to ensure judicial protection of an individual's rights under Union law" (para 58).

[71] Case C-409/06, *Winner Wetten GmbH v Bürgermeisterin der Stadt Bergheim* (ECJ 8 September 2010) para 61; see, formerly, Case C-11/70, *Internationale Handelsgesellschaft* (ECJ 17 December 1970) para 3.

the European Parliament and of the Council of 4 November 2003.[72] Subsequently, the political parties Regulation was amended by a Decision of the European Parliamentary Bureau on 29 March 2004 and by Regulation 1524/2007 of the European Parliament and of the Council of 18 December 2007, which gave political parties the possibility of establishing *Europewide political foundations*.[73]

The Lisbon Treaty placed Europe's political parties among the democratic principles: Art. 10.4 TEU (*Political parties at European level contribute to forming European political awareness and to expressing the will of citizens of the Union*), while the Charter of Fundamental Rights of the Union, which must now be viewed as having the same legal status as the Treaties themselves (Art. 6.1 TEU), provides, in Art. 12.2 EUCFR, that "[p]olitical parties at Union level contribute to expressing the political will of the citizens of the Union", and includes this provision within the area of freedom (Title II), and of freedom of association, in particular. The rules governing political parties, mainly in relation to their financing, are placed among the rules governing the institutional operation of the European Parliament (Art. 224 TFEU).

As this shows, the provisions of the Treaties and the Charter are quite similar to what one finds in a national liberal democratic Constitution which considers political parties to be a way in which citizens exercise their freedom, and as an element of democratic integration, transferring the popular will into representative institutions, and as a factor of the functioning of the very institutions of which they form part.

At the European level, this issue refers directly to the degree of political maturity reached by the European Parliament, in which Europe's political parties are present in the form of the Parliamentary groups.[74] The European political parties were originally established as a sort of federation of national parties with varying degrees of kinship in terms of their ideological concerns, but mainly to manage the financial contributions provided at the European level.[75]

---

[72]This Regulation provides that to qualify for financing, the following are the constituent elements of the European political party: (a) the party must have a legal personality in the Member State in which it is established; (b) it must have been represented in at least one fourth of the Member States by members of the European Parliament or by members of the national or regional parliaments, or regional assemblies; (c) they must observe the principle of freedom, democracy, respect for human rights and fundamental freedoms, and the role the rule of law; (d) they must have participated in the elections to the European Parliament or expressed the intention to take part.

[73]These foundations are organisations affiliated to a European political party, with a legal personality distinct from the party which it supports, and whose objectives it pursues. The European political foundation observes, analyses and provides input further debate on European public policy, and also performs practical activities such as organising workshops, conferences and studies.

[74]See Gianfrancesco (2002), pp. 278 et seqq.

[75]Regarding the political parties, the European Federation and the Parliamentary groups on what has been called the three-sided polygon, see Bardi (1989); Bardi and Ignazi (2004); Grasso (2008), pp. 609 et seqq.; Ciancio (2009).

Their political importance would appear to be somewhat weakened by the fact that what counts most is not so much the ideological stances of the Members of the European Parliament as their national origins. This is partly due to the lack of a European electoral law conferring a unitary character on the parties at election time, with the result that this remains in the hands of the national parties which select the candidates, run the election campaign and decide on what commitments to enter into with regard to the European policies that will be debated and adopted by the European Parliament. From an ideological point of view, it has also been noted that the national nature of the parties operating within the European Parliament is also the result of the absence of a European "people" as such, of a *demos* in its own right, such that European politics is thereby a fragmentation of the reality of Europe.

One further critical note regarding the political value of the European party system is the fact that unlike what occurs in national political systems, where the political competition culminates in the formation of a majority and an opposition, and is designed for the governance and management of the State itself, at the European level, even with the formation of the various Parliamentary groups it would not be possible to envisage a competition between a majority and an opposition, and there could not be any real fight on "European government" because of the many anomalies that would exist in a European governmental system, but which are absent from a nation state.[76]

It cannot be denied that these are serious critiques. For even though European legislation on the political parties appears to be more advanced than they are themselves, and despite the progress that has been made across the years, Europe's political level still does not have political parties comparable with the national parties.

Nevertheless, none of these considerations appear to fully express the reality of the European dimension, not only because of the political growth of Europe, but above all because of the new direction that the European political system now seems to have reached.

It therefore appears highly debatable whether the European political parties are only accidental federations, for several reasons: first, they have been created on the basis of the international or transnational structuring of political parties linked by powerful ideological stances (such as the Socialist, Christian Democrat or Liberal Internationals), and this feature emerges most clearly in the groups that have always been present in the European Parliament; second, the rules of procedure of the European Parliament have made it impossible to talk in terms of technical or occasional groups, without any real ideological basis, as evidenced among other things from the disputes that have been referred to the European Court;[77] third, the

[76]See Rizzoni (2009); Saitta (2007), pp. 114 et seqq.

[77]See Joined Cases T-222/99, T-327/99 and T-329/99, *Martinez – De Grulle – Front National – Bonino et al. v Parlamento europeo* (CFI 2 October 2001); Case C-486/01 P, *Front National/ European Parliament* (ECJ 29 June 2004).

fact that the European political parties have emerged from Parliamentary groups, in the sense that they are therefore specifically Parliamentary in character, does nothing to rob them of their effectiveness and their ability to proceed politically;[78] and lastly, the projection of the national parties has shown that this does not prevent an autonomous political and party experience within the European system, but on the contrary, the European dimension of the political parties has created a physiognomy of its own, both institutional and political, differing from their national characters.

The lack of a European election law, which has been the subject of criticism for a long time, cannot be an argument opposed wholly to the political role of the European parties because their formation and establishment do not take place in the area of representation, but in the European public space which, under the Lisbon Treaty, has been defined as the "society of Europe's citizens". As noted elsewhere,[79] within the system of treaties, this is not an expression of sociological or ethnographic and cultural significance, but refers to the citizens as active players in the integration process, and has produced a form of unification that ranges beyond even the issue of the presence of *demoi* and the absence of one *demos*.

Neither can it be said that there is no distinction between a majority and an opposition in the Parliament, even though consensus is the main procedure, particularly when performing the legislative function, with cooperation between the three largest and more firmly established Parliamentary groups. For it is the case that since the Maastricht Treaty, political division within the European Parliament has been felt more strongly with regard to Parliamentary investiture of the President of the Commission, as was the case with President *Prodi*[80] and with President *Barroso* in 2004,[81] as both had been identified taking account of the election results (anticipating the provisions of the Lisbon Treaty) on the basis of the declarations by the European People's Party (EPP), which would not have accepted a candidate from outside its own ranks,[82] but also in its later experience because, since the President represents the Conservative majority in the European Parliament, he has to constantly measure up to the opposition of the Socialist and other Left-wing groups in the European Parliament.[83]

We cannot be silent then at the time of the election of President *Barroso*, beginning his second term, when on the eve of the entry into force of the new Treaty, political negotiations between the Council and the Parliamentary groups of the European Parliament played a very important part.

---

[78]Guidi (1983), p. 37; Ciancio (2008), pp. 80 et seqq.

[79]Mangiameli (2010), p. 333.

[80]For a more detailed examination of this case, see Mangiameli (2003), p. 206.

[81]See Schillaci (2004).

[82]See Bonvicini et al. (2009), p. 183.

[83]See Helms (2009), pp. 200 et seqq.

12 Who Heads the Union?

These statements, having reached the end of this overview of the institutional design of the post-Lisbon Union, pose us the question: *Who heads the Union?*

This question will perhaps not be answered, because Europe is still and more than ever before in the quicksands as far as its identity and functioning are concerned, and it is precisely the way in which the President of the Commission is reconfirmed in office (as well as the choice of the President of the European Council and the High Representative, in whose designation the EPP and ESP parliamentary groups played a major part in the negotiations between the governments of the Member States) that suggests that the answer is still a long way off.

However, it would not be mistaken to approach this question with a medium-term perspective. The answer to the question "who heads the Union?" has always been based not so much on the power to lay down political guidelines for establishing policy, but on the power over the functioning of the supranational system, and according to this approach, the answer has always invariably been "the Member States", or rather their governments, with the power to appoint the European Commission, the President and the Commissioners. A contribution to this approach has been made by an expression, used in a somewhat distorted way as the *Lisbon* judgment did, coined by *Hans Peter Ipsen*, who described the Member States as the "Lords of the Treaties" (*die Herren der Verträge*).[84]

It is evident from the reconstruction of the institutional design of the Union set out in this paper that the amendments that have been gradually introduced into the Treaties in an attempt to give continuity and representativity to the European legal system have gradually staked out the part played by the Member States, confining them to specific Institutions and following specific procedures. The Member States and the Institutions they drive (the European Council and the Council) do not play a permanent role, and already they can no longer guarantee the functioning of the Union on an exclusive basis. Their function is intermittent, and emerges particularly forceful at times of crisis or tension.

The Commission must certainly be seen as the Institution which guarantees the functioning of the supranational system, but it is above all the representative political role that the European Parliament and the political parties operating within it play which weighs most heavily on the appointment of the Commission members.[85]

---

[84]See Mangiameli (2010).

[85]The Commission and the European Parliament are very closely linked: the Commission is collectively answerable to the European Parliament alone. The Parliament, with its vote of approval, legitimises the mandate of the Commission; the candidate for the Presidency of the Commission is nominated by the European Council, *taking account of the European Parliamentary elections,* and after appropriate consultations the election is made by the Parliament, which may vote on a censure motion at any time, which, if carried out, requires the members of the Commission to resign.

It is no coincidence that these institutions have developed much closer working relations that have already enabled the political parties to make their political weight felt, and so the answer to the question *who heads the union?* should now be different from the traditional reply, namely, the Member States and the European Parliament (and through it the European political parties, on the basis of the consensus support of Europe's citizens) head it.

In the near future, beginning in 2014, when the membership of the Commission will be equivalent to two thirds of the number of the Member States, it is likely that its composition will have a heightened political value, which will not be dependent on the political thinking of the governments of the Member States, despite the expected squaring of the circle, but on the results of the European Parliamentary elections.

In this case, the proposal that has also been made in the literature, and only taken on board so far by the ESP, to democratise European political life by nominating a candidate to the Presidency of the Commission before the forthcoming European elections[86] takes on a special relevance.[87] For coming from the European political parties, supported by the vote of Europe's citizens, it would necessarily place a clear binding constraint on the European Council proposal. In that case, the question *who heads the Union?* would call for a completely different answer altogether.[88]

References

Adam R, Tizzano A (2010) Lineamenti Di Diritto dell'Unione europea. Giappichelli, Torino

Aldecoa Luzárraga F, Guinea Llorente M (2010) La Europa que viene: el Tratado de Lisboa. Buenos Aires, Marcial Pons, Madrid

Bardi L (1989) Il Parlamento della Comunità europea. Il Mulino, Bologna

Bardi L, Ignazi P (2004) Il Parlamento europeo. Il Mulino, Bologna

Bassan F (2003) Regolazione ed equilibrio istituzionale nell'Unione europea. Rivista Italiana di Diritto Pubblico Comunitario, pp. 973 et seqq

Bieber R (2010) Institutionelles system. In: Bieber R, Epiney A, Haag M (eds) Die Europäische Union. Europarecht und Politik, 8th edn. Nomos, Baden-Baden, pp 109 et seqq

Bilancia P (2009) The role and power of European and National Parliaments in the dynamics of integration. DPCE, pp 273 et seqq

[86]See Bonvicini et al. (2009), pp. 182 et seqq.

[87]See Bonvicini et al. (2009), pp. 182 et seqq.

[88]But the European political parties could play a very important part in appointing the High Representative for Foreign Affairs and Security Policy, not only because the appointment must be made by agreement with the President of the Commission, but also because the High Representative is also required to pass the scrutiny of the European Parliament as a member of the Commission and its Vice President. The parties could also influence the appointment of the President of the European Council, whose election is exclusive responsibility of the European Council, by adopting a position in favour of one or other candidate.

Bocuzzi I (2008) The National Parliaments in their control over the Governments. Teoria del Diritto e dello Stato, pp 331 et seqq

Bonvicini G, Tosato GL, Matarazzo R (2009). I partiti politici europei e la candidatura del Presidente della Commissione. Il Diritto dell'Unione Europea, pp 179 et seqq

Buccino Grimaldi G, Gazzoletti F (2001) La riponderazione del voto in seno al Consiglio. Dir Un Eur (also in Tizzano A (ed) Il Trattato di Nizza. Milano, pp. 93 et seqq)

Caligiuri A (2004) Art. 300, in Trattati dell'Unione europea e della Comunità europea, a cura di A. Tizzano, Milano, Giuffré

Calliess Chr (2009) Mitverantwortung der Rechtswissenschaft für die Verwendung des Verfassungstopos – Die Europäische Verfassung als Opfer der symbolischen Tragweite des Begriffes? In: Pernice I (ed) Der Vertrag von Lissabon: Reform der EU ohne Verfassung? Nomos, Baden-Baden, pp. 54 et seqq

Calvano R (2001) Verso un sistema di garanzie costituzionali dell'UE? La giustizia costituzionale comunitaria dopo il trattato di Nizza. Giur Cost:209 et seqq

Calvano R (2004) La Corte di Giustizia e la Costituzione europea. CEDAM, Padova

Cannizzaro E, Bartolini ME (2007) La "costituzionalizzazione" del terzo pilastro dell'Unione europea. Il Diritto dell'Unione Europea, pp 471 et seqq

Cartabia M (2010) I diritti fondamentali in Europa dopo Lisbona: verso nuovi equilibri? Giorn Dir Amm:221 et seqq

Caruso F (2008) Le competenze di Stati membri ed Unione nel Trattato di Lisbona, in Studi in onore di U. Leanza, Editoriali Scientifica, Napoli

Casalena PG (2008) The role of national Parliaments in the Lisbon Treaty. Teoria del Diritto e dello Stato, pp 348 et seqq

Cervati AA (2000) Elementi di indeterminatezza e di conflittualità nella forma di governo europea, in *La Costituzione europea*, Atti XIV Convegno AIC, Perugia 7-8-9- ottobre 1999. CEDAM, Padova, pp. 73 et seqq

Ciancio A (2008) I gruppi parlamentari. Studi intorno ad una manifestazione del pluralismo politico, Milano Giuffré

Ciancio A (2009) I partiti europei e il processo di democratizzazione dell'Unione. In: *Federalismi. it*, no. 9

Condinanzi M (2007) Fonti del "terzo pilastro" dell'Unione europea e ruolo della Corte costituzionale. Il diritto dell'Unione Europea, pp 513 et seqq

Constantinesco V (2008) Le processus de décision: vers une nouvelle gouvernance? Europe. Actualité du Droit Communautaire, pp 51 et seqq

Costanzo P (2008) Oscillazioni della "forma di governo" dell'Unione europea nel "Traité simplifié compliqué". *Diritto Pubblico Comparato ed Europeo*, pp 45 et seqq

Craig P (2010) The Lisbon treaty. Law, politics, and treaty reform. Oxford University Press, Oxford

Daniele L (2009) Le istituzione politiche dell'Unione europea dopo il Trattato di Lisbona: verso un nuovo equilibrio? Studi Sull'integrazione Europea, pp 43 et seqq

Di Salvatore E (2006) La prevalenza del diritto europeo nel Trattato costituzionale alla luce dell'esperienza comunitaria. In: Mangiameli S (ed) L'ordinamento europeo, II, L'esercizio delle competenze. Giuffrè, Milano, pp 477 et seqq

Di Salvatore E (2007) Le relazioni delle regioni italiane con l'Unione europea: fondamento costituzionale, normativa statale e disciplina statutaria. Rass Parl:641 et seqq

Di Salvatore E (2008) L'identità costituzionale dell'Unione europea e degli stati membri. Il decentramento politico istituzionale nel processo di integrazione. Giappichelli, Torino

Donnarumma MR (2010) Il processo di "costituzionalizzazione" dell'Unione europea e la tensione dialettica tra la giurisprudenza della Corte di Giustizia e le giurisprudenze delle Corti costituzionali. Riv Ital Dir Pubbl Comunitario:407 et seqq

Draetta U (2008) La funzione legislativa ed esecutiva dell'Unione europea nel Trattato di Lisbona. Diritto Comunitario e Degli Scambi Internazionali, pp 677 et seqq

Draetta U (2009) Composizione e funzionamento di Consiglio e Consiglio europeo del Trattato di Lisbona. Studi Sull'integrazione Europea, pp 7 et seqq

Fabbrini S (ed) (2002) L'Unione europea. Le Istituzioni e gli attori di un sistema sopranazionale. Laterza, Roma Bari
Gianfrancesco E (2002) I limiti alla costituzione di gruppi politici all'interno del Parlamento europeo. Dir Pubbl Comp Eur:278 et seqq
Gianfrancesco E (2006) Il principio dello Stato di diritto e l'ordinamento europeo. In: Mangiameli S (ed) L'Ordinamento europeo, I, I principi dell'Unione. Giuffrè, Milano, pp 235 et seqq
Gianfrancesco E (2008) La politica estera e di sicurezza. In: Mangiameli S (ed) L'ordinamento europeo, vol III. Giuffrè, Milano, pp 1129 et seqq
Götz V (1995) Mehrheitsbeschlüsse des Rates der Europäischen Union. In: FS für U. Everling. Nomos, Baden-Baden, pp 339 et seqq
Gozi S (2006) Il governo dell'Europa, 3rd edn. Il Mulino, Bologna
Grasso G (2008) Partiti politici europei. Dig Disc Pubbl, III, agg II, Torino, pp 609 et seqq
Grimm D (2009) Das Grundgesetz als Riegel vor einer Verstaatlichung der Europäischen Union. Zum Lissabon-Urteil des Bundesverfassungsgerichts. Der Staat 48/4:475 et seqq
Guidi G (1983) I gruppi parlamentari del Parlamento europeo, Rimini Maggioli
Gutiérrez Espada C, Cervell Hortal MJ (2010). La adaptación al tratado de Lisboa (2007) del sistema institutional decisorio de la Unión, su acción exterior y personalidad juridíca. Granada
Haratsch A, Pechstein M, Koenig Chr (2010) Die Europäische Union, 7th edn. Mohr Siebeck Tübingen
Helms L (2009) Parliamentary opposition and its alternatives in a transnational regime: the European Union in perspective. In: Parliamentary opposition in old and new democracies. Routledge, London, pp 200 et seq
Herdegen M (2010) Europarecht, 12th edn. C.H.Beck, München
Ilari S (2010) Sulla nozione di forma di governo e l'ordinamento dell'Unione Europea. Aspetti problematici del difficile cammino verso un nuovo ordine politico. In Studi in onore di V. Atripaldi, Jovene Editore, Napoli
Jacqué JP (2010) Droit institutionnel de l'Union européenne, 6th edn. Dalloz, Paris
Jestaedt M (2009) Warum in die Ferne schweifen, wenn der Maßstab liegt so nah? Verfassungshandwerkliche Anfragen an das Lissabon-Urteil des BVerfG. Der Staat 48/4:497 et seqq
Khushal Murkens JE (2009) Identity trumps integration. The Lisbon Treaty in the German Federal Constitutional Court. Der Staat 48/4:517 et seqq
Lenski E (2009) Rat und Europäischer Rat nach dem Vertrag von Lissabon (Reformvertrag). In: Pernice I (ed) Der Vertrag von Lissabon: Reform der EU ohne Verfassung? Nomos, Baden-Baden, pp 54 et seqq
Mangiameli S (2003) La forma di governo europea. Teoria del diritto e dello Stato, pp 213 et seqq
Mangiameli S (2006) La competenza europea, il suo esercizio e l'impatto sugli ordinamenti degli Stati membri. In: Mangiameli S (ed) L'ordinamento Europeo, II, L'esercizio delle competenze dell'Unione. Giuffrè, Milano, pp 1 et seqq
Mangiameli S (2008a) Diritto costituzionale e Integrazione europea. In: L'esperienza costituzionale europea. Aracne, Roma, pp 90 et seqq
Mangiameli S (2008b) Il ruolo del Parlamento europeo e il principio della democrazia rappresentativa. Teoria del diritto e dello Stato, pp 491 et seqq
Mangiameli S (2008c) La Costituzione europea. L'esperienza costituzionale europea. Aracne, Roma, pp 385 et seqq
Mangiameli S (2009a) Il ruolo del Parlamento europeo nella PESC, alla luce delle innovazioni apportate dal Trattato di Lisbona. In: Decaro C, Lupo N (eds) Il "dialogo" tra parlamenti: obiettivi e risultati. LUISS University Press, Roma, p 417 et seqq
Mangiameli S (2009b) L'Europa sopranazionale. In: La società europea. Identità, simboli, politiche. Giappichelli, Torino, pp 333 et seqq
Mangiameli S (2010) Unchangeable core elements of national constitutions and the process of European integration. For a criticism to the theory of the "controlimiti" (counter-limits / Schranken-Schranken). Teoria del Diritto e dello Stato, pp 1 et seqq
Mangiameli S, Di Salvatore E (2010) Il nuovo assetto dell'Unione europea e l'impatto sulla forma di governo italiana. www.issirfa.it

Mangiameli St, Di Salvatore E (2010) La democrazia italiana: forme, limiti, garanzie, Italianieuropei, Solaris, Rome
Missiroli A (2009) L'impatto del trattato di Lisbona sulla PESC e la PESD: opportunità e incognite. In: Bilancia P, D'Amico M (eds) La nuova Europa dopo il trattato di Lisbona. Giuffrè, Milano, pp 118 et seqq
Monaco R (1972) Scritti di diritto europeo. Giuffrè, Milano
Moscarini A (2006a) Il principio della competenza concorrente nell'ordinamento dell'Unione europea. In: Mangiameli S (ed) L'ordinamento Europeo, II, L'esercizio delle competenze dell'Unione. Giuffrè, Milano, pp 125 et seqq
Moscarini A (2006b) Il principio di sussidiarietà. In: Mangiameli S (ed) L'ordinamento Europeo, II, L'esercizio delle competenze dell'Unione. Giuffrè, Milano, pp 153 et seqq
Paladini L (2010) I conflitti fra i pilastri dell'Unione europea e le prospettive del Trattato di Lisbona. Il diritto dell'Unione europea, pp 87 et seqq
Palermo F (2005) La forma di Stato dell'Unione europea. Per una teoria costituzionale dell'integrazione sovranazionale. Cedam, Padova
Patrono M (2003) La forma di governo dell'Unione europea: una breve storia. Diritto pubblico comparato ed europeo, pp 1762 et seqq
Pinelli C (1989) Ipotesi sulla forma di governo europea. Riv Trim Dir Pubbl:336 et seqq
Piris J-C (2010) The Lisbon treaty. A legal and political analysis. Cambridge University Press, Cambridge
Pizzetti FG (2006) Il principio di leale cooperazione dell'ordinamento europeo. In: Mangiameli S (ed) L'ordinamento europeo, I, I principi dell'Unione. Giuffrè, Milano, pp 331 et seqq
Ponzano P (2009) Il voto nel Consiglio: il compromesso di Ioannina alla luce del Trattato di Lisbona. Il Diritto dell'Unione europea, pp 77 et seqq
Rideau J (2010) Droit institutionnel de l'Union européenne, 6th edn. LGDJ, Paris
Rizzoni G (2009) Il problema dell'opposizione politica nella forma di governo dell'Unione europea. Rass Parl:905 et seqq
Ruffert M (2009) Institutionen, Organe und Kompetenzen – der Abschluss eines Reformprozesses als Gegenstand der Europarechtswissenschaft. Europarecht Beiheft 1:31 et seqq
Saitta A (2007) Il rapporto maggioranza opposizione nel parlamento europeo. In: Castorina E (ed) Profili attuali e prospettive di diritto costituzionale. Giappichelli, Torino, pp 114 et seqq
Santini A (2010) Le nuove figure di vertice dell'Unione europea: potenzialità e limiti. Dir UE:909 et seqq
Sauron JL (2008) Les institutions: la victoire de la complexité? Europe. Actualité du droit communautaire, pp 47 et seqq
Scaccia G (2006) Il principio di proporzionalità. In: L'ordinamento Europeo, II, L'esercizio delle competenze dell'Unione. Giuffrè, Milano, pp 225 et seqq
Schillaci A (2004) Il difficile avvio della Commissione Barroso. www.associazionedeicostituzionalisti.it. Accessed 24 Nov 2004
Schönberger Chr (2009) Die Europäische Union zwischen "Demokratiedefizit" und Bundesstaatsverbot. Anmerkungen zum Lissabon-Urteil des Bundesverfassungsgerichts. Der Staat 48/4:535–558
Schoo J (2009) Das neue institutionelle Gefüge der EU. Europarecht Beiheft 1:51 et seqq
Strozzi G (1998) Diritto istituzionale dell'Unione europea. Dal trattato di Roma al Trattato di Amsterdam. Giappichelli, Torino
Tesauro G (1995) Diritto comunitario. CEDAM, Padova
Thym D (2009) Europäische Integration im Schatten souveräner Staatlichkeit. Anmerkungen zum Lissabon-Urteil des Bundesverfassungsgerichts. Der Staat 48/4:559 et seqq
Tizzano A (1995) Introduzione al Codice UE. CEDAM, Padova
Tizzano A (2002) Il trattato di Nizza, Milano Giuffré
Tizzano A, Adam R (1995) Lineamenti Di Diritto dell'Unione europea. Giappichelli, Torino
Wahl R (2009) Die Schwebelage in Verhältnis von Europäischer Union und Mitgliedstaaten. Zum Lissabon-Urteil des Bundesverfassungsgerichts. *Der Staat* 48/4:587 et seqq

The Role of National Parliaments in the EU

Rudolf Hrbek

1 Introduction

Since the 1980s the role of national parliaments related to issues of European integration and politics in the European Community/European Union (EC/EU) has been given greater attention.[1] First, there were efforts within national parliaments of EC/EU Member States to introduce provisions for new institutional and procedural rules designed to give (and strengthen) the respective parliament a role in EC/EU-related decision-making, focusing on the national level. As a consequence, one could observe concrete activities of national parliaments in dealing with EC/EU matters. Second, there were statements made at the European level – in the context of treaty revisions starting with the Treaty of Maastricht – not only mentioning the role of national parliaments in the institutional architecture of the EU, but demanding that their role be strengthened. These efforts culminated in considerations within the European Convention on the role of national parliaments and, as a result, in new provisions included into the Constitutional Treaty. Following the failure of this treaty project, the respective provisions are now included in the Treaty of Lisbon.

For the first time national parliaments are mentioned in the main text of the Treaty and not only in Protocols and Declarations attached to previous treaties:

- Article 10.2 TEU reads: "Citizens are directly represented at Union level in the European Parliament. Member States are represented in the European Council by their Heads of State or Government and in the Council by their governments,

[1] It was, however, not before the early/mid-1990s that larger academic analyses were published: Weber-Panariello (1995); and Norton (1996b).

R. Hrbek (✉)
Universität Tübingen, Institut für Politikwissenschaft, Melanchthonstr. 36, 72074 Tübingen, Germany
e-mail: rudolf.hrbek@uni-tuebingen.de

H.-J. Blanke and S. Mangiameli (eds.), *The European Union after Lisbon*,
DOI 10.1007/978-3-642-19507-5_6, © Springer-Verlag Berlin Heidelberg 2012

themselves democratically accountable either to their national Parliaments or to their citizens."

- Article 12 TEU reads: "National Parliaments contribute actively to the good functioning of the Union", followed by a list of six points – (a) to (f) – with more detailed provisions referring to two Protocols annexed to the treaty (Protocol No. 1 on the role of national parliaments, Protocol No. 2 on the application of the principles of subsidiarity and proportionality) and to articles in this treaty and in the Treaty on the Functioning of the EU.
- Article 5.3 (2) TEU stipulates: "The institutions of the Union shall apply the principle of subsidiarity as laid down in the Protocol on the application of the principles of subsidiarity and proportionality. National Parliaments ensure compliance with the principle of subsidiarity in accordance with the procedure set out in that Protocol." This procedure, called "early warning system", has been perceived as the main novelty of the new treaty related to the role of national parliaments.

Thus the Treaty of Lisbon, which entered into force on 1 December 2009, confirmed that national parliaments are an integral part of the institutional architecture of the EU, attributing to them a role in its decision-making system. There are expectations linked to these new provisions as to a more active role of national parliaments in the future. At the beginning of 2010, however, it is an open question how national parliaments will use the new treaty provisions, in how far they will meet the expectations and become an important institutional actor in the decision-making system of the EU. Considering this question, one should take into account previous experiences with activities of national parliaments in EU matters and be aware of problems which have arisen and been identified.[2]

This article[3] will, therefore, be structured as follows: the first section will give an overview on the functions which are attributed to national parliaments in democracies with a system of parliamentary government and make brief remarks on the basic organisational structures of parliamentary assemblies (2). The article will then remind us of the role of national parliaments in the early years of European integration and give a brief overview on later developments, namely initiatives taken by national parliaments in Member States of the EC/EU and those taken in connection with subsequent treaty reforms (3). The next section will explain the provisions laid down in the Treaty of Lisbon (4). The article will then deal with various aspects and problems which have arisen in the past and which should be taken into account related to the future role of national parliaments in the EU; this

[2]Very good and concise overviews have recently been given by Raunio (2009) and Benz and Broschek (2010). Much more detailed contributions are, amongst others, the following volumes: Maurer and Wessels (2001); Maurer (2002); Janowski (2005); O'Brennan and Raunio (2007).

[3]This article is based on and will follow in parts a contribution by the author, see Hrbek (2010).

will include drawing the attention to changes in the framework conditions of the EU system and of governance in this system (5). Finally, the article will have a look at parliaments at regional ("sub-national") level, since there are Member States with a federal or regionalised structure that have regional parliaments with legislative powers, which means that provisions on the role of national parliaments may apply to them as well (6).

2 Functions and Organisational Features of Parliaments in Democratic Political Systems

Reflections on the role of national parliaments have to be related to specific functions which are attributed to parliaments. There is wide consensus on the following list of functions[4]:

- Representing the citizens (with their beliefs, interests and demands) of the respective polity and performing particular tasks and functions on their behalf. Closely connected with representation are the functions of interest aggregation and interest articulation and, not to forget, the communication function vis-à-vis the citizens/the electorate.
- Legislation in various policy fields, which implies taking initiatives and submitting draft legislative acts, discussing them publicly and finally deciding on them according to the formal rules given in the respective Constitution.
- Electing the executive/government (in most cases: the head of government).
- Controlling the executive and making it accountable to the citizens. This may include a vote of censure against the government forcing it to resign or removing it from office.
- Generating democratic legitimacy or rather contributing to legitimacy of the political system and the decision-making process by fulfilling the above-mentioned tasks and functions properly.

National parliaments are assemblies composed of deputies belonging to political parties competing with each other; they form party groups in the parliament. The party-political division within a parliament is the major factor for the dynamics of the intra-parliamentary political process; the relations between the party groups oscillate between cooperation and competition. The intensity of competition depends primarily on the political-ideological distance of the party groups.

[4]As early as in 1867 Walter Bagehot published his book "The English Constitution", listing five functions of the House of Commons on pp. 115–120 (edition of 1958 by Oxford University Press, London). Various authors have drawn on this list, sometimes using different terms.

All EU Member States have a parliamentary system of government, which means that in general the government is supported by the majority in the parliament; in most cases this majority is formed by a coalition of party groups. The minority in the parliament is the opposition. The behaviour of these two groupings will vary with respect to the performance of parliamentary functions. This applies particularly to the control function, which is the major domain of the opposition, whereas the parliamentary majority will refrain from (publicly) criticising the government and instead will give support to the government and its legislative projects.

Party groups form one major component of the parliament's organisational structure; the others are specialised committees for the whole range of policy fields. Committee meetings – most of them held behind closed doors – are, first, the framework for intense discussions on legislative business; the participants are deputies and members of the executive (ministers or higher civil servants from the ministries); the division between parliamentary majority – which includes the government – and opposition will determine the pattern of communication. Second, committees are the framework for exercising parliamentary scrutiny vis-à-vis the executive: their representatives usually attend these meetings and they are obliged to attend on demand (of a qualified minority) of the committee.

Plenary sessions, held publicly, are the framework for primarily exercising the functions of representation, interest articulation and communication. As far as legislation is concerned, legislative acts require formal ratification by a majority in the plenary; plenary sessions serve primarily the purpose of publicly explaining the respective project and the (in many cases: competing and adverse) attitudes of the majority and the opposition. The latter will, in this context, use plenary sessions as another occasion for exercising political control.

In the next sections we shall repeatedly come back to these general remarks on functions of parliaments and major aspects of their organisational structure, with a focus on committees and party groups, related to the performance of functions.

This article will not deal with Second Chambers, since these differ in composition, organisational structure and functions from national parliaments in the sense of First Chambers, always elected directly by the citizens and equipped with a list of functions which have developed in the course of emerging systems of parliamentary government. Second Chambers have primarily developed in the framework of federal structures of a polity, such as in Austria, Belgium and Germany, but also in regionalising/regionalised countries such as Italy and Spain. Their role related to decision-making in EU matters has generally been dealt with in consideration of the effects of the European integration process on sub-national entities ("regions") and their attempts to respond to this challenge via adapting institutions and procedures, and via developing new activities and strategies.[5]

[5]For the German case see Hrbek (1999).

3 Development of the Role of National Parliaments in the EC/EU

3.1 The Early Years of European Integration

Until the early 1980s, European integration issues were – as far as the Member States of the three Communities were concerned – a domain of national governments and their administrations: they had negotiated and agreed on the founding treaties; steps towards further development of the Communities (the EC) and going on with the integration process were – in many cases on the initiative of the European Commission – decided via intergovernmental bargaining; and the legislative activities of the EC – very technical in substance and character – were dominated by the Council of Ministers, an institution formed by members of the executive (ministers or civil servants) of the Member States, which had to decide by unanimity without the obligation to share power with the European Parliament (EP), which, at that time, was restricted to a mere advisory role.

In this period the role of national parliaments was marginal and weak.[6]

- They were – according to the constitutional provisions of the respective country – involved in ratifying the founding treaties (and later each treaty amendment). Since the governments which had negotiated the treaties could rely on the support of their respective parliamentary majorities, ratification was – with one exception[7] – a formal act. This was even more the case, since the European integration project could enjoy the support of the vast majority of political forces in the founding countries of the Community.
- National parliaments were not involved in day-to-day decision-making on EC matters directly, but only indirectly in the context of the respective system of parliamentary government which makes the executive accountable to the parliament in general. In practice, the government (with the prime minister as chairperson) has been taking the lead and could rely on the support of "its" majority in parliament. And since in the early years of the EC issues on the legislative agenda were very technical in nature, they did not cause partisan conflicts; criticism was voiced, if at all, by the parliamentary opposition. And since the government did always claim to be concerned about national interests, opposition parties were more than reluctant to challenge the government publicly.
- EC directives, a special form of European legislative acts giving a more or less wide framework, need to be transformed into national legislation, leaving the

[6] See Schweitzer (1978).

[7] In August 1954, a majority in the French Parliament stopped the project of establishing a European Defence Community, as another supranational organisation following the example of the European Coal and Steel Community, by refusing to put the issue on the agenda; parties of the coalition government were divided on this project.

Member States the possibility to fill this framework. Here, national parliaments play a (formal) role, but experience shows that the domestic implementation of such directives has been dominated by the administration of the government with its expert knowledge.

- Until 1979, national parliaments of the EC Member States have sent deputies into the EP; these European deputies, therefore, had a dual mandate. They had to make a choice individually regarding which mandate they should give priority to, because they could not engage efficiently in both parliamentary assemblies. And in practice there was no regular and intense communication and feedback between the two bodies and their members.

3.2 New Developments in Connection with the First Enlargement of the EC

When Denmark became a member of the EC in 1973, a very special coordination system for dealing with EC matters was established which gave the Danish parliament considerable influence over Danish policy in EC matters.[8] This system has been referred to and perceived outside Denmark as a model for the role of national parliaments in the EC/EU. One has, however, to be aware of two basic factors which explain the introduction of that system in Denmark:

- There is a tradition to have minority governments, lacking continuous and stable support of a majority of deputies in parliament. Parties do not give office-seeking (by entering in a coalition government) priority; they follow another logic: to offer the (minority) government support on a case-by-case basis in exchange for gains and rewards in particular cases to which they give political priority. Since the government needs support, it has to communicate regularly with all party groups and try to find consensual decisions.
- Membership in the EC was a controversial issue in the Danish society. There had to be a referendum in 1972 and the carriers in the campaign were not only political parties but a specially established "People's Movement against the EC" with activists and followers from various parties. The referendum resulted in the approval of membership, but the issue did remain on the domestic agenda and continued to divide the society. The People's Movement was not dissolved but continued its anti-membership activities, amongst them the participation of the Movement in European Parliament elections, with remarkable electoral success at the expense especially of the Social Democratic Party, over decades the strongest political force. The saliency of the issue and the divide amongst the citizens explain why (minority) governments had a strong interest to find

[8]See Arter (1996); Laursen (2001).

approval for their policies in the EC. The coordination system, introduced in 1973, was designed to serve this goal.

The key feature of this coordination system is the institutionalisation of parliamentary control over the executive expressed in political mandates prior to Council meetings. The system should "ensure that the Danish government did not agree to decisions in Brussels that could not subsequently be passed in the Danish parliament."[9] A European Affairs Committee was established, consisting of 17 deputies according to party group strength. Article 6(2) of the Danish Law of Accession of 1972 can be regarded as the legal basis, in that it stipulates in a very general way the following: "The government notifies a parliamentary committee about proposals for Council decisions which will have direct effect in Denmark or for the fulfilment of which the participation of the parliament is necessary."[10]

The working of this system has been described as follows[11]: "The Committee meets with the government ministers on a regular basis, normally the Friday before a Tuesday meeting in the Council of Ministers. At these meetings, the minister in question presents the Danish standpoint on the matters on the agenda before the Committee. The Committee members are entitled to pose questions and discuss the cases with the minister. The voting rules in the Committee are such that as long as the government does not have a majority against it, it can proceed to the meetings in Brussels with the consent of the Danish parliament. If there is a majority against the minister, he or she is forced to come up with a new solution to which the Committee can agree."

It was the Committee itself which in special reports did define details of the coordination system. The first report of 1973 "clarified that the objective is to 'secure the Folketing the greatest possible influence in European affairs' and that the government should consult the Committee in European policy questions of 'substantial significance'".

Although this system has been understood as a model for the role of national parliaments in the EC/EU – and new EU Member States from Central and Eastern Europe which joined the EU in 2004 and 2007 respectively are said to have followed this model – there are observations and experiences which cast doubts as to the model quality of the system. These deserve to be taken into account in considerations on the future role of national parliaments in the EU.

- One observation has to do with the information given to the Committee by the government. This "has been continuously improved [...] so that it now includes an assessment of the proposal's consequences for Danish legislation [...], an evaluation on the keeping of the principle of subsidiarity and, when possible, information about the political standpoints of other countries and the preliminary

[9]Sousa (2008), p. 432.

[10]Quoted in Sousa (2008), p. 433.

[11]The following quotes are from Sousa (2008), pp. 432–435.

views of the Danish government." The growing quantity of information, given on a weekly basis, has had, in the eyes of analysts and observers, a boomerang effect: "the number of documents and cases, together with the limited time between meetings, make the conditions for control and oversight rather difficult."

- Another point has to do with the relationship between this Committee and the standing specialised committees. Whereas the latter dispose of expert knowledge needed for technical and highly specialised matters, the former's concern is primarily about securing "a coherent European policy." But the specialised standing committees have not been involved in European matters properly, with negative results.
- Focusing on government's positions at Council meetings is another point of concern for critical observers and analysts, which will be considered more systematically in another section.

A lesson to be learned from the Danish case is that considerations on the role of national governments should take into account the constitutional and political patterns of the respective EU Member State. This factor can be illustrated by briefly looking at the British case.[12] The European Communities Act of 1972 stipulated that all European legal acts would automatically become part of the British legal order without explicit approval of the British parliament. Since this meant the annulment of the principle of parliamentary sovereignty – a cornerstone of Britain's democratic system – there were demands for introducing new forms of controlling Britain's European policy.

In May 1974 the House of Commons established a "Committee on European Secondary Legislation", which has to be comprehensively informed by the government on all European legislative projects. The Committee, then, has to decide how the parliament as a whole should react: it can recommend merely taking notice of a project; it can submit a report; it can recommend a plenary debate which applies to a very small number of projects of high saliency. The whole clearing process proved to be too time-consuming: the House of Commons, belonging to the category of a "debating" (not: "working") parliament, established in 1980 two "European Standing Committees" which should debate the projects in place of the plenary. Debates, however, are no formal mandates; the scrutinising role of the British parliament in European matters has been, in comparison to the Danish pattern, much weaker.

3.3 Strengthening the Role of National Parliaments Since the 1980s (1): Initiatives of National Parliaments

The early 1980s marked a turning point for the role of national parliaments in EC decision-making in all Member States. At that time, national parliaments identified

[12]See Norton (1996a, b); Carter (2001); Janowski (2005), pp. 133–139.

an interest and a need to get better involved and participate more effectively in decision-making on EC matters. There were two main reasons for this new situation:

- First, the EC had entered into the phase of "positive" (or policy) integration. In other words, the functional scope of the EC had started to extend considerably and this trend was going to continue and intensify. A large variety of issues appeared on the European agenda which were of supreme interest and concern for national political actors, such as political parties and interest associations, and therefore for national parliaments as well. The latter found themselves marginalised as institutional actors, since European policy was almost exclusively in the hands of the executive (government and the bureaucracy); national parliaments were concerned that they might become "losers".[13]
- Second, and closely connected to the first point, the legitimacy of the EC (its political system, its decision-making process and its policies) became an issue; the slogan of a "democracy deficit"[14] appeared on the political (and the academic) agenda and was discussed.[15] One strategy to respond to this challenge focused on the EP which had been strengthened by direct elections in 1979. A second strategy was to give national parliaments a more influential role in EC decision-making. Such efforts were launched by national parliaments themselves, resulting in institutional and procedural adaptations and arrangements. There can be no doubt that the Danish "model" was taken as incentive and encouragement.

The German example shall illustrate the arduous task of giving national parliaments a (stronger) role in EC decision-making.[16] In October 1983 the German Bundestag established the *Europa-Kommission*,[17] not as an ordinary parliamentary committee, but as an institution according to the rules for special committees for enquiry. The new body, therefore, was not entitled to take decisions, but could only produce reports and submit recommendations. The reason for this reduced legal status was widespread resistance within the Bundestag to set up another ordinary committee as a rival to specialised committees which have been dealing with EC matters falling in their respective portfolio. The major feature of the new institution was its composition, with the same number of members coming from the Bundestag and from the EP; the new body should primarily serve as an institution for inter-parliamentary cooperation.

---

[13]See title of the volume by Maurer and Wessels (2001).

[14]One of the first comprehensive contributions to this topic was Naßmacher (1972).

[15]See Hrbek (1980, 1995).

[16]The following is based on and taken from Hrbek (2010), pp. 141–144.

[17]The monograph of Peter Mehl: Die Europa-Kommission des Deutschen Bundestages. Eine neue Einrichtung interparlamentarischer Zusammenarbeit, Kehl and Strasbourg, 1987, informs on all aspects of this new institution.

The spectrum of functions of the new body included: support for the EP in its efforts to widen and strengthen its competences; input for debates on EC matters in the Bundestag and a step towards giving the Bundestag a more influential role in participating in debates and decisions on EC matters at national level; and, finally, to strengthen the links between the two parliamentary assemblies. The new body met twice a month and 35 times within four years (election period 1983–1987). It produced 13 reports which were discussed in the Bundestag plenary. Performance and efficiency of the new body, however, were poor. Its impact on the role of the Bundestag in dealing with EC matters was modest; its reports and recommendations were not given much attention. This was primarily due to the resistance of the other specialised committees, amongst them the Foreign Affairs Committee, to sharing competences. And concerning the function of the new body as crystal point for linking the two parliamentary assemblies, the members of the EP gave preference to the already existing forms of cooperation on party group level: German EP members used to attend party group meetings in the Bundestag. The new institution, therefore, was not re-established in the following election period of the Bundestag.

The next step was the establishment of another type of institution: in June 1987 the Bundestag decided to set up a Sub-Committee of the Foreign Affairs Committee for EC matters, consisting only of Bundestag members. The efficiency of this new body was, again, poor. Since EC matters go far beyond the functional scope of the Foreign Affairs Committee, the Sub-Committee, obliged to observe this limit, was not entitled to deal with specialised EC policies and played only a very marginal role.

In June 1991 the Bundestag took a next step and established an "EC Committee". This, however, was not yet the breakthrough for the institutionalisation of parliamentary (the Bundestag's) participation in EC matters; once more, there was a dispute on functional scope and competences of the new body. The result was that it was not authorised to deal with the Treaty of Maastricht, at that time on the political agenda. Instead, the Bundestag in October 1992 set up an additional specialised committee ("European Union"), which should prepare, as lead committee (and with only a minor role for the EC Committee), the ratification of the Maastricht Treaty.

This treaty, which has been perceived as a landmark in the integration process and in deepening the EC – giving it a new name ("European Union") and structure (with three "pillars" under the roof of the EU), extending the functional scope of the EU substantially and introducing far-going institutional and procedural reforms – was at the same time a catalyst for giving the Bundestag, and national parliaments in general, a strengthened permanent role in the decision-making system of the EU. In connection with the discussion on the new treaty, an amendment to the German constitution was decided. Two new articles dealt with the role of the national parliament:

- Article 23 GG (on the participation in developing the EU) introduced provisions on the participation of the Bundestag (and, through the Bundesrat, the Länder) in matters concerning the EU. Paragraph 2 stipulates: "The Federal Government shall keep the Bundestag and Bundesrat informed, comprehensively and at the earliest possible time." Paragraph 3 stipulates: "Before participating in legislative acts of the EU, the Federal Government shall provide the Bundestag with an opportunity to state its position. The Federal Government shall take the position of the Bundestag into account during the negotiations. Details shall be regulated by a law."[18]

- Article 45 GG introduced provisions on a special Committee on EU matters: the Bundestag shall appoint this committee and "may authorize it to exercise the rights of Bundestag under Art. 23 vis-à-vis the Federal Government."[19]

With these constitutional provisions the Bundestag has acquired, under a legal point of view, a strong position in the decision-making process on EU matters at domestic level.

3.4 *Strengthening the Role of National Parliaments Since the 1980s (2): Incentives in the Context of Treaty Reforms*[20]

Not only were efforts taken by national parliaments themselves to strengthen their role in the EC/EU, but beginning with the Treaty of Maastricht, there were initiatives and incentives in connection with the series of treaty reforms, as well. This shows that from a European point of view and in the perception of actors at Community/Union level national parliaments should become an integral part of the decision-making system of the EC/EU. The respective initiatives have been based on concerns about democratic legitimacy of the integration project.

- Declaration No. 13 of the Treaty of Maastricht (1993) "on the role of the national parliaments in the EU", obviously taking up what has already been introduced and experienced in several Member States, stressed "that it is important to encourage greater involvement of national parliaments in the activities of the European Union." It then specified that "[to] this end, the exchange of information between national parliaments and the European Parliament should be stepped up. In this context, the governments of the Member States will ensure that national parliaments receive Commission proposals for legislation in good

[18]Law on the Cooperation of the Federal Government and the German Bundestag in European Union Affairs of 12 March 1993 (BGBl I 1993, p. 311). The law was amended on 17 November 2005 (BGBl I, p. 3178); in addition to and related to the law, Bundestag and Federal Government concluded on 28 September 2006 an Agreement on the Cooperation in EU Affairs (BGBl I 2006, pp. 2177–2180), dealing with all details of their cooperation. The Law was, as a consequence of the decision of the Federal Constitutional Court on the Treaty of Lisbon of 30 June 2009, again amended (draft of 21 August 2009, Deutscher Bundestag Drucksache 16/13925).

[19]This latter clause has in practice been used only rarely.

[20]The following is based on and taken from Hrbek (2010), pp. 144–147.

time for information or possible examination" and "that it is important for contacts between the national parliaments and the European Parliament to be stepped up, in particular through the granting of appropriate reciprocal facilities and regular meetings between members of Parliament interested in the same issues."

- Declaration No. 14 of the same treaty "on the Conference of the Parliaments (Assizes)" recommended meetings of such a new institution and specified: "The Conference of the Parliaments will be consulted on the main features of the European Union, without prejudice to the powers of the European Parliament and the rights of the national parliaments. The President of the European Council and the President of the Commission will report to each session of the Conference of the Parliaments on the state of the Union." The background for this proposal was a reunion in June 1990 in Rome, bringing together 173 members of national parliaments and 85 members of the EP. This conference, expected to give an input to the preparation of treaty reforms, had adopted a resolution on the two intergovernmental conferences (on the Economic and Monetary Union and on the Political Union). "But since the overall majority of national parliaments did not want to repeat the 'Rome exercise', Declaration No. 14 has never been activated."[21]
- The Treaty of Amsterdam (1999) went on with a "Protocol on the role of the national parliaments in the EU". The aim was to enhance the ability of national parliaments "to express their views on matters which may be of particular interest to them." The Protocol did focus on two points. First, on the improvement of information flow for national parliaments by stipulating that "all Commission consultation documents (green and white papers and communications) shall be promptly forwarded to national parliaments"; furthermore, "Commission proposals for legislation [. . .] shall be made available in good time" and that a six-week period shall elapse before the respective issue is put on the agenda of the Council. Second, on institutionalised links between national parliaments and the EP, by referring to the Conference of European Affairs Committees (COSAC), which was established in November 1989. It meets twice a year in the EU Member State which holds the EU's six-month Presidency. Each national parliament sends six members,[22] and the EP is represented by six members of its Institutional Committee. COSAC has its own secretariat in the EP. The Protocol has tried to specify the functions of COSAC, by stipulating that it "may address to the European Parliament, the Council and the Commission any contribution which it deems appropriate on the legislative activities of the Union, notably in relation to the application of the principle of subsidiarity, the area of freedom, security and justice as well as questions regarding fundamental rights." The Protocol, however, underlines that COSAC contributions "shall in no way bind

[21]Krekelberg (2001), p. 477.

[22]Parliaments of applicant countries were invited to send six members each as observers.

national parliaments or prejudge their position." COSAC has given itself Rules of Procedure, adopted in November 1989 in Paris; they have been amended several times: in October 1999 in Helsinki, in May 2003 in Athens.[23]

- Although the Treaty of Nice (2001) was disappointing since the member governments could not reach agreement on substantial treaty reforms, the member governments committed themselves to continue the reform process towards deepening the EU. In the "Declaration on the Future of the EU", attached as Declaration No. 23 to the Treaty, they listed four issues which should primarily be given attention in the next Governmental Conference (scheduled for 2004) on treaty reforms, amongst them "the role of national parliaments in the European architecture." The governments were obviously determined to formally institutionalise national parliaments in the decision-making system of the EU.
- In order to realise the goal formulated in the above-mentioned declaration, the Member States' governments went further than only amending the Treaties. They convened a "Convention" which from February 2002 to July 2003 elaborated a Constitutional Treaty that included provisions on the role of national parliaments. Ratification of this Treaty, however, failed: following two negative referendums in France and the Netherlands in May/June 2005, the ratification process was stopped. The Member States agreed on a comprehensive treaty reform as an alternative approach: in December 2007 they signed the Treaty of Lisbon, which is in large parts identical with the Constitutional Treaty. This applies also to provisions on the role of national parliaments.

4 Provisions on the Role of National Parliaments in the Treaty of Lisbon

As already mentioned in the introductory section of this article, the Treaty of Lisbon makes national parliaments an integral part of the institutional architecture of the EU. For the first time, there are provisions on the role of national parliaments in the main text of the treaty. Article 12 TEU stipulates generally that "national parliaments contribute actively to the good functioning of the Union"; it gives more detailed provisions in a list of six points – (a) to (f) – some of them explicitly referring to two Protocols annexed to the Treaty. Article 5.3 TEU attributes national parliaments a special role in ensuring compliance with the principle of subsidiarity, again referring to the respective Protocol.

---

[23]European Parliament, *Rules of Procedure of the Conference of Community and European Affairs Committees of Parliaments of the European Union*, O.J. C 27/6 (2008).

4.1 Protocol (No. 1) on the Role of National Parliaments in the European Union

The Protocol starts by "recalling that the way in which national Parliaments scrutinise their governments in relation to the activities of the Union is a matter for the particular constitutional organisation and practice of each Member State". This statement considers that national parliaments have already been engaged in performing a control function according to the rules given and developed in the respective Member State. It will be up to each Member State to decide on how to amend such rules in the light of the Treaty of Lisbon provisions. The Protocol continues with a second statement which, in accordance with statements and provisions in previous treaties, explains its major goal and intention, namely "to encourage greater involvement of national Parliaments in the activities of the European Union and to enhance their ability to express their views on draft legislative acts of the Union as well as on other matters which may be of particular interest to them." The provisions of the Protocol appear under two titles: "Information for national Parliaments" (with eight articles) and "Interparliamentary Cooperation" (with two articles).

Under the first title ("Information for national Parliaments") the Protocol stipulates the following:

- The Commission shall forward to national parliaments (at the same time as to the EP and the Council) its consultation documents, its annual legislative programme "as well as any other instrument of legislative planning or policy"; and to the Court of Auditors, its annual report.
- Draft legislative acts, originating from whatever institution or a group of Member States, shall be forwarded to national parliaments directly from the respective institution or the Council.
- "National Parliaments may send [...] a reasoned opinion on whether a draft legislative act complies with the principle of subsidiarity" (referring to the procedure laid down in Protocol No. 2) to the institution or body concerned.
- "An eight-week period shall elapse between a draft legislative act being made available to national Parliaments in the official languages of the Union and the date when it is placed on a provisional agenda for the Council for its adoption or for adoption of a position under a legislative procedure", with exceptions "in cases of urgency".
- The Council is obliged to forward directly to national parliaments the agendas for and the outcome of its meetings, "including the minutes of meetings where the Council is deliberating on draft legislative acts."
- In cases of treaty amendments via the "simplified revision procedure" as laid down in Art. 48.7 TEU, "national Parliaments shall be informed of the initiative of the European Council at least six months before any decision is adopted."

Additionally Art. 48.7 TEU gives each single national parliament the right to veto such European Council initiatives.[24]

- Finally, Art. 8 of the Protocol specifies that "[w]here the national Parliamentary system is not unicameral, Arts. 1 to 7 shall apply to the component chambers."

On the basis of these provisions, national parliaments shall posses a comprehensive set of information, enabling them to get better and deeper involved in decision-making on EU matters: vis-à-vis their respective national governments when decisions are prepared and taken at domestic level, and vis-à-vis the institutions of the EU in Brussels.

Under the second title ("Interparliamentary Cooperation") the Protocol stipulates that "the European Parliament and national Parliaments shall together determine the organisation and promotion of effective and regular interparliamentary cooperation within the Union." It mentions COSAC explicitly and specifies that this institution "shall promote the exchange of information and best practice between national Parliaments and the European Parliament, including their specialised committees and that it may also organise interparliamentary conferences on specific topics, in particular to debate matters of common foreign and security policy, including common security and defence policy." It is remarkable that these latter issues – sensitive in character and traditionally reserved more or less exclusively for the executive – are now included as matters for discussion at parliamentary level. In accordance with statements in previous treaties, the Protocol underlines that "contributions from the conference shall not bind national Parliaments and shall not prejudge their positions."

4.2 *Protocol (No. 2) on the Application of the Principles of Subsidiarity and Proportionality*

Since the entry into force of the Treaty of Maastricht with a new article on the principles of subsidiarity and proportionality, there have continuously been disputes on the proper application of these two principles.[25] As a response, the Protocol has been designed "to ensure that decisions are taken as closely as possible to the citizens of the Union" and "to establish the conditions for the application of the principles of subsidiarity and proportionality [. . .] and to establish a system for monitoring the application of those principles". The focus of the Protocol (with nine articles) is on procedural aspects of how to ensure compliance with the principles.

---

[24]This is the so-called Passerelle Clause.

[25]Hrbek (2000).

- All draft legislative acts and amended drafts, originating from whatever institution or a group of Member States, shall be forwarded to national parliaments; the same applies to legislative resolutions of the EP and positions of the Council in the course of the legislative process.
- The introduction of a so-called early-warning system represents a genuine innovation in that it gives national parliaments specific rights in the monitoring of the principles' application: "Any national Parliament or any chamber of a national Parliament may, within eight weeks from the date of transmission of a draft legislative act, in the official languages of the Union, send to the Presidents of the European Parliament, the Council and the Commission a reasoned opinion stating why it considers that the draft in question does not comply with the principle of subsidiarity." In addition, Art. 6 of the Protocol stipulates: "It will be for each national Parliament or each chamber of a national Parliament to consult, where appropriate, regional parliaments with legislative powers." This clause, thus, increases the number of actors involved in the monitoring process; there are Member States having regional parliaments with legislative powers.[26]
- The institutions "shall take account of the reasoned opinions." In case that these represent at least one third of all the votes allocated to the national Parliaments (Art. 7 rules: "Each national Parliament shall have two votes, shared out on the basis of the national Parliamentary system. In the case of a bicameral Parliamentary system, each of the two chambers shall have one vote"), "the draft must be reviewed." In special cases – "a draft legislative act submitted on the basis of Article 76 [TFEU] on the area of freedom, security and justice" – the threshold will be even lower, namely one quarter. As a result of such a review, the institutions "may decide to maintain, amend or withdraw the draft" and they must give reasons for their decision.
- In addition, the Protocol adds for cases "under the ordinary legislative procedure" the following rule: "where reasoned opinions on the non-compliance of a proposal for a legislative act with the principle of subsidiarity represent at least a simple majority of the votes allocated to the national Parliaments [...], the proposal must be reviewed." If the Commission would, having reviewed the proposal, decide to maintain it, the whole issue would have to be submitted to the Union legislator (EP and Council) for final decision. For such cases the Protocol stipulates: "If, by a majority of 55 % of the members of the Council or a majority of the votes cast in the European Parliament, the legislator is of the opinion that the proposal is not compatible with the principle of subsidiarity, the legislative proposal shall not be given further consideration."
- Once a legislative act had passed the legislative process and a national parliament continued to argue that the act does not comply with the principle of subsidiarity, this national parliament or a chamber thereof could bring the

[26] See point 6 below, dealing with Regional Parliaments.

issue before the European Court of Justice, via notification by the respective Member State's government.

- Last but not least, the Commission is obliged to submit a report on the application of Art. 5 TEU not only to the other institutions, but also to national parliaments.

This set of provisions laid down in the two Protocols aims towards strengthening considerably the role of national parliaments in the EU. They have become upgraded as institutional actors in the decision-making system of the EU, which comprises, as a multi-level system, the national, the regional and the supranational levels. Strengthening the role of national parliaments has been expected to improve and strengthen the democratic legitimacy of the EU which shall be provided by two sources: EP and national parliaments.

4.3 The Special Case of Germany Pursuant to the Ruling of the Federal Constitutional Court on the Treaty of Lisbon[27]

In its ruling, the German Federal Constitutional Court "rejected every objection that had challenged the compatibility of the Treaty of Lisbon with the Basic Law. [...] The Court's only criticism was directed at the national law of implementation (which defines the participatory powers of the German legislative bodies), and found that these powers had not been sufficiently strengthened."[28] The conclusion, therefore, was "that Germany can continue with the ratification of the treaty only after introducing a new implementation law."[29] In its decision (147 pages long, with 421 paragraphs), based on its decision on the Treaty of Maastricht of 1993,[30] the Court has, now in a very detailed way, given "concrete instructions to the German legislature: whenever the EU institutions wish to apply certain strategic decisions under the Treaty of Lisbon, the German government may agree to them only after the two national legislative chambers [...] have given their prior approval. [...] The strategic decisions in question mainly concern what the Court considers to be, or at least potentially to be, *de facto* treaty amendment procedures by which EU institutions may dynamically expand their competences or change decision-making rules without having to resort to the regular ratification procedure for new treaties."[31]

---

[27]German Federal Constitutional Court, 2BvE 2/08 (30 June 2009) (in: BverfGE 123, 267) – *Lisbon*.

[28]Tomuschat (2009), p. 1259.

[29]Schorkopf (2009), p. 1219.

[30]German Federal Constitutional Court, 2 BvR 2134, 2159/92 (12 October 1993) (in: BVerfGE 89, 155) – *Maastricht*.

[31]Kiiver (2009), p. 1287.

These instructions focus on the following points[32]:

- Passerelle (or bridge) clauses, "which allow the Council to move from unanimity to qualified majority voting or from the special to the ordinary legislative procedure" (Art. 48.7 TEU, the general bridge clause, furthermore various specific – subject matter–related – bridge clauses scattered in both the Treaty on European Union (TEU) and the Treaty on the Functioning of the European Union (TFEU)). Whereas the Treaty of Lisbon gives national parliaments six months to veto such a change, the Court goes much further "by holding that Germany's representative in the Council must in no case agree to a change in procedure unless and until the legislature has voted on the matter. 'Silence on the part of the Bundestag and Bundesrat', the Court explains, 'is [...] not sufficient for exercising this responsibility.' Moreover, with regard to the general [...] bridge clauses; a vote by the legislature is not enough. Here the Court requires the German legislature to make the extra step and pass a law to ratify what the Court describes as a change in primary treaty law within the meaning of Basic Law Article 23(1)."
- The "emergency brake" system which, with respect to legislative proposals in the fields of criminal law (Art. 82.3 and 83.3 TFEU) and social security (Art. 48.2 TFEU), stipulates that "a Council member may raise an objection that suspends consideration of the measure and refers the matter to the European Council." Here, "the Court subjects these emergency brakes [...] to an affirmative instruction on the part of the Bundestag and, where appropriate, the Bundesrat."
- The flexibility clause of Art. 352 TFEU (the former Art. 308 EC), reminding us of the "implied powers" doctrine in the USA, or the French doctrine of "effet utile in international treaty law". Here the Court "subjects any Council decision to resort to the general implied powers provision of Article 352 TFEU to a ratification law pursuant to Basic Law Article 23(1)." Whereas the former Art. 308 EC demanded (and justified) that the use of this clause serve the goals of the internal market, Art. 352 TFEU allows "the invocation of implied powers in the service of all 'policies defined in the Treaties'. In the Court's view, this new generality leaves the scope of the flexibility clause ill-defined and, thus, tantamount to an invitation to substantive, fundamental treaty changes." The Court has been concerned about not giving the Union plenary powers or the power to determine its own competences.

The Ruling of the Court has been received in Germany with much criticism from political actors and academics.[33] The major arguments of this criticism are oriented against basic assumptions and premises on which the Court has built its decision.

[32] The following (including quotes) is based on Halberstam and Möllers (2009), pp. 1243–1246.

[33] See, for example, the contributions in the Special Section of German Law Journal, quoted above.

- "The first premise is that of electoral democracy as a classical form of legitimization for the self-determination of citizens under the condition of equality."[34] It is the citizen, equipped with human dignity and personal freedom, "who stands in the centre of things." The state is perceived "as a necessary organizational form of the political community of individuals – a historically grown and identity-forming community."[35] "For the Court, democracy is a concept that is limited to a state with a people and its territory."[36] The EU, with a legal order derived from that of the Member States, is different and of minor quality, which relates to its democratic legitimacy. The EP, since there is no European people, cannot claim democratic representation of a real parliament; moreover, the Court underlines "that the voting mechanisms to the European Parliament do not function according to a strict rule of democratic equality, one (wo)man, one vote."[37] In conclusion, "the main democratic roots of the European Union lie in the democratic processes of the twenty-seven member countries"[38] with their national parliaments as the key institutions.
- The second premise is that of the identity of the constitution, in the German case: the Basic Law. This does relate to principles laid down in Art. 20 in conjunction with Art. 79.3 GG, amongst them the democratic principle. If this principle "is neither amenable to balancing nor violable, then the constituent parliament, maybe not even the *pouvoir constituant*, can dispose of this facet of the identity of the free constitutional order."[39] With this reasoning, the Court guarantees German statehood. In addition, the Court listed the areas – public tasks – to be regulated nationally which belong to this constitutional identity as well. The major importance of the Court's ruling, in this context, lies in the perception of the German constitution, according to which the European integration process must not touch on these essentials of German statehood.[40] "The Court constructs a line of defence against any possible infringement of German sovereignty, stating that certain fields [...] must forever remain under German control."[41] These fields are identical with the list of public tasks, forming an integral part of the constitutional identity.

These premises have to be understood as guidelines and criteria in all cases submitted to the Constitutional Court, which claims to be the supreme authority in defining direction and substance of the integration process. It remains, however, an open question, how the Court in the future will perform and fulfil this role. As far as

[34]Schorkopf (2009), p. 1221.
[35]Schorkopf (2009), p. 1222.
[36]Halberstam and Möllers (2009), p. 1247.
[37]Halberstam and Möllers (2009), p. 1247.
[38]Tomuschat (2009), p. 1261.
[39]Schorkopf (2009), p. 1223.
[40]Nettesheim (2009), p. 2868.
[41]Tomuschat (2009), p. 1260.

the Court's ruling in the Lisbon Case is concerned, most observers noted an obvious lack of judicial self-restraint.

The instructions given by the Court on the basis of the above-mentioned premises to the German legislature define the content of what has to be observed carefully by all institutional actors under the Basic Law committed to what has been called "integration responsibility". This applies primarily to the national parliament. The instructions of the Court have been transformed in the *Integrationsverantwortungsgesetz*, the law on integration responsibility, of 22 September 2009,[42] strengthening the competences of the Bundestag and Bundesrat in EU matters, as described above. It remains an open question as to how the legislative bodies will use these competences; moreover, how EU bodies will use the new (bridge and flexibility) clauses.

5 Aspects and Problems Related to the Future Role of National Parliaments in the EU

Reflecting on the future role of national parliaments in the EU requires taking into account, first, functions attributed to parliamentary assemblies in democratic political systems in general, which has been done under point 2 of this article. And it is our premise that the EU has to be conceived as a political system.[43] Position, role and performance of national parliaments, however, vary from Member State to Member State, since they are embedded in the respective system of parliamentary government, in a specific political culture (competitive or cooperative/consensual) and in customs and conventions.[44] Second, the role of national parliaments have to be seen in relation to features of the decision-making system of the EU which have undergone substantial changes and which will most probably continue to change under the new provisions of the Treaty of Lisbon. And, third, experiences with the role of national parliaments during the past decades, especially since the early 1990s with the provisions of the Treaty of Maastricht, should be observed carefully.

[42]IntVG of 22 September 2009, BGBl. 1, pp. 3022 et seqq.

[43]The EU, which is neither a state nor an international organisation, has been conceived as a compound with nation states as component parts. From a political science point of view, the concept of a "political system", applied primarily to nation states, has been applied to the EU as well. See Hix (2005).

[44]Norton (1996a, b), pp. 1–2, distinguishes between different types of legislatures: the "policy-making legislature" (it "can modify or reject policy brought forward by the executive, and can formulate and substitute policy of its own"), which can be found in the Nordic countries and in Austria; the "policy-influencing legislature" ("it can modify policy brought forward by the executive, but cannot formulate and substitute policy of its own"), to be found in France, Germany, the Netherlands and the United Kingdom; and the "legislature with little or no policy effect" (it "can neither modify or reject policy brought forward by the executive, nor formulate and substitute policy of its own"), to be found primarily in Southern Europe.

Many of these experiences are linked with organisational and institutional innovations built up with respect to the role of national parliaments in EU decision-making. At present, all national parliaments possess European Affairs Committees (EACs); their legal status and their political quality and performance, however, vary. Furthermore, we can observe that specialised committees – in charge of special policy fields – have become involved, besides the EACs, in dealing with EU matters. And there can be no doubt that members of national parliaments in the meantime pay more attention to EU affairs and perceive the EU system as a framework offering them career perspectives. With treaty articles on the role of political parties (beginning with the Treaty of Maastricht)[45] and especially with a special Statute (2003, already amended in 2007),[46] "parties at European level" have been entering the EU arena as political actors, offering party groups in the EP and in national parliaments a point of political orientation. As far as the collective role of national parliaments is concerned, interparliamentary cooperation and communication have become consolidated and – especially with COSAC – institutionalised. It is worth being aware of the fact that all these aspects apply to the new EU Member States and their parliaments as well.

5.1 *Features and Recent Changes in the Decision-Making System of the EU*[47]

Especially during the past two decades, the decision-making system of the EU has developed a much more complex structure, with a growing number of actors involved and with a plethora of institutional and procedural innovations. A second major change lies in the emergence of informal means and channels in the decision-making system of the EU, complementing the formalised ones as laid down in legal rules and provisions. Both complexity and informality are a challenge for national parliaments as actors and participants in the decision-making system and require a proper response.

- The introduction of the co-decision procedure and its extension to a larger number of policy issues (with the Treaty of Lisbon adding some more to this

[45]Article 138a EC (Maastricht) = Art. 191 EC (Amsterdam) stipulates: "Political Parties at European level are important as a factor for integration within the Union. They contribute to forming a European awareness and to expressing the political will of the citizens of the Union." The wording of the provision has been slightly modified in the Treaty of Lisbon; Art. 10(4) TEU reads: "Political Parties at European level contribute to forming European political awareness and to expressing the will of citizens of the Union."

[46]European Parliament/Council Regulation No. 2004/2003 *on the regulations governing political parties at European level and the rules regarding their funding*, O.J. L 297/1 (2003); amendment: Regulation No. 1524/2207, O.J. L 343/5 (2007).

[47]See for example Sousa (2008), pp. 435–438; or Benz and Broschek (2010), pp. 2–3.

list) has had two effects: first, since co-decision is linked with qualified majority voting in the Council, the national veto by one single Member State does not any longer exist in these cases. Instead, national governments have to form alliances via negotiations and bargaining, which requires flexibility in the Council or in Council formations. A (narrowly defined) mandate for a national government from its national parliament can, therefore, be counterproductive. Second, the EP – now co-legislator – has been strengthened. National parliaments, eager to influence decision-making in EU matters, cannot continue to focus on the Council via scrutinising national governments; they have to deal with the EP as the "target" of their activities and efforts as well.

- Comitology committees with various categories of civil servants as members play a greater role in issuing (draft) directives on behalf of the Commission, which modifies the traditional pattern of decision-making and, especially, decision preparation. National parliaments are challenged by the need to become involved in decision-making processes as early as possible, since otherwise they would see themselves marginalised.
- A larger number of issues have been dealt with in working groups of the Council; here national civil servants, with the active participation of Commission civil servants, try to reconcile national interests. When they succeed, the respective issues need not become subject to the strictly formalised Community method; again, national parliaments may become marginalised or even excluded.
- Another type of preparatory and informal meetings is the trialogue with civil servants from the Commission and the Council Presidency and members of the EP, introduced with respect to the co-decision procedure. The meetings, held weekly, seem to play an important role in the decision-making process. All these informal arenas (such as trialogues, working groups and committees) shall help to reach decisions earlier. National parliaments have no access to these bargaining processes and when an issue appears on the formal agenda of the Council, it will most probably be too late to intervene. Focusing on the Council, therefore, will not be the appropriate strategy for national parliaments.
- Intergovernmental coordination, as a second mode of governance in the EU, has become especially important in Common Foreign and Security (and Defence) Policy, and for "third pillar" issues and activities towards establishing an Area of Freedom, Security and Justice. And the new Open Method of Coordination (OMC), intergovernmental in character, has been perceived as representing executive federalism without participation of parliaments.[48]

---

[48]See Duina and Raunio (2007). The authors argue that "with regard to participation . . . OMC risks further marginalizing national parliaments. On the other hand, when we consider its output, the OMC provides national legislators with opportunities that the traditional Community method of legislation cannot offer. First, the OMC gives national legislators access to insights and tools for producing successful laws. Second, the OMC gives those legislators grounds for criticizing the policies of government officials" (p. 489).

If national parliaments intend to really influence EU decision-making, they must be aware of these more recent developments in EU governance, and try to respond to the challenge by adapting their strategies, which requires not to rely on formal channels and instruments only and to improve established strategies.

5.2 Activities of National Parliaments at Domestic Level: Aspects and Problems

National parliaments will continue with these activities, focusing on scrutinising the government which represents the Member State in the Council. There are, as experience shows, aspects affecting the role of national parliaments and its effectiveness, which should be taken into account.

- EACs and specialised committees coexist. The former, besides dealing with "constitutional" questions of the EU, have as primary task the coordination of the Member State's European policy. This requires cooperation with the specialised committees. The pattern of their relation, however, has often been one of rivalry and competition, although they are to a certain extent dependent on each other for the fulfilment of the control function versus the executive.
- Since committees in general meet behind closed doors, debates in the plenary are important with respect to the function to generate democratic legitimacy. In the past, however, there were only few plenary debates on EU matters in national parliaments. This has been due to the often very technical and highly specialised character of EU matters, which do not attract attention either in the public or in the media. It has further been due to the fact that the elites in most EU Member States agree on basics of the integration project and are, in general, more "pro EU" than the citizens; this may explain the reluctance of parliamentarians – at least those of the established mainstream parties – to have public debates. Furthermore, these could be used by populist or extremist political forces for arguing against the EU (e.g. making it the scapegoat for what they criticise as negative and against "national" interests). Opposition parties could hesitate to publicly criticise the government, which could, in return, accuse the opposition of violating national interests. Plenary debates, however, play an essential role in performing the "teaching" function of a parliament.[49]
- In case of a two-chamber system, both chambers have to cooperate and coordinate their EU-related activities at domestic level. This will apply particularly with respect to the early-warning system in the application of the principle of subsidiarity.

---

[49]This was one of the functions which Walter Bagehot (see fn. 4) in his frequently quoted catalogue of parliamentary functions has listed.

- The informational basis for activities of national parliaments is well developed and has been improved continuously. The growing quantity of information, however, raises the question as to how parliaments (committees and individual deputies) can manage to make a reasonable selection and decide where to focus on. Parliaments have already invested in the respective resources, but with respect to the extending EU agenda, they need to do more and better in this field. National parliaments have started to establish their own representations in Brussels, not incorporated in the Permanent Representation of the respective Member State (its executive) in the EU. Being on the spot within the Brussels arena can only support having access to all kind of information and to informal communication networks.
- As far as the scrutiny system is concerned, one can distinguish between a "document-based" model (here national parliaments process and scrutinise EU documents, with the goal of finding a consensual solution, supporting the government) and a "mandating" model (here national parliaments use to give a direct mandate to their governments before Council meetings).[50] The latter obviously does not fit with new patterns in the decision-making system as mentioned above (5.1), since it does not correspond with the needs of bargaining processes requiring flexibility.

5.3 Links Between National Parliaments and the European Parliament

Both national parliaments and the EP have been attributed the function of contributing to the emergence of democratic legitimacy for the EU. It seems, therefore, plausible that they cooperate and organise their relations in the sense of structured and institutionalised links. We may observe that various forms and patterns of such links have been established, some of them experimental in character and open to changes and further development.

The most common form of such links is for national parliaments to draw on the knowledge and experience of EP members by inviting them into the national parliament. This can be arranged either in the framework of committees, with considerable emphasis on specialised committees, or of party groups (either as a whole or with working groups for selected policy fields as organisational framework). Party group affiliation as a point of orientation seems to be superior to policy specialisation in committees. Steps towards consolidating and further developing parties at European level may contribute to confirm and further develop this pattern. One should, however, not underestimate time constraints as a factor which will reduce possibilities of the physical presence of members of the EP in committees or

[50]See Raunio (2009), pp. 5–6; and Benz and Broschek (2010), pp. 16–17.

party groups of their respective national parliament to a minimum. Furthermore, one has to take into account, that European parliamentarians in the EP with respect to the European legislative process under the co-decision procedure follow a more cooperative and consensus-seeking logic, which differs from the much more competitive approach of party groups in national parliaments.

5.4 *Horizontal Cooperation of National Parliaments*

COSAC, established in late 1989, has acquired the role of an institutionalised platform for inter-parliamentary communication. Its main function has been that EACs of national parliaments exchange information. They do not deal with specialised EU policies. COSAC has never had an impact in the field of controlling or participating in EU policy-making. An inter-parliamentary information network ("Inter-parliamentary EU Information Exchange") was established by COSAC in 2002; it has the function to collect information on how national parliaments deal with current legislative projects of the EU.

Provisions on the "early-warning system" related to the application of the principles of subsidiarity and proportionality point to a more demanding function of national parliaments' horizontal cooperation, going far beyond supplying and exchanging information as in the COSAC framework. EU institutions will be obliged to review draft legislative acts if reasoned opinions of national parliaments, stating why they consider that the draft in question does not comply with the principle of subsidiarity, represent at least one third of all the votes allocated to the national parliaments. Making proper use of this provision will require from national parliaments – primarily its specialised committees dealing with draft legislative acts under subsidiarity scrutiny – to develop new forms of communication, coordination and cooperation amongst each other, and to respond to the special challenge of the time factor (time period of only eight weeks available). Especially a group of national parliaments (one third or the majority), as a collective actor, could really have in impact on EU legislation.

Horizontal cooperation of national parliaments could have an additional function related to the "European Citizens' Initiative",[51] as laid down in Art. 11.4 TEU, which stipulates: "Not less than one million citizens who are nationals of a significant number of Member States may take the initiative of inviting the European Commission within the framework of its powers, to submit any appropriate proposal on matters where citizens consider that a legal act of the Union is required for the purpose of implementing the Treaties." Mobilising the necessary support – one

[51]See Maurer and Vogel (2009). The European Commission has submitted a *Green Paper on the Citizens' Initiative*, COM (2009) 622 final of 11 November 2009.

million citizens in at least one third of the Member States[52] – is a task requiring organisational efforts. Amongst the actors which could get involved in fulfilling this task could be – besides interest associations, NGOs, Civil Society groupings and political parties – party groups in national parliaments, experienced in the legislative "business" in general and in EU legislation in particular. Performing the task, party groups belonging to the same party family would need to build up and intensify communication relations amongst each other, another aspect of horizontal cooperation of national parliaments.

In their efforts to strengthen their role in EU decision-making, thus contributing to enhance democratic legitimacy in the EU,[53] national parliaments are not only confronted with greater complexity of the decision-making system and of governance structures in the EU, but their involvement would rather add to this complexity.

6 Parliaments at Regional ("Sub-national") Level[54]

Considerations on the role of national parliaments must not ignore parliamentary assemblies at regional level. In a number of EU Member States we can identify territorial entities at sub-national level, possessing an institutional structure with an executive and a parliamentary assembly. Since European integration has been a challenge for sub-national entities,[55] these have responded in trying to get involved in decision-making on EU matters. In these efforts, the respective executives (governments and their administrations) have been, and still are, dominant. But the respective parliaments have tried to get involved as well.[56] This relates to formalised or informal participation in decision-making on EU matters, to controlling the respective regional executives, and, last but not least, to establishing an organised network of regional parliaments in the EU. The provision in Art. 6 of the subsidiarity Protocol, stipulating that national parliaments may consult regional parliaments with legislative powers, may be an incentive for the latter to intensify their EU-related activities.

[52]The European Commission *proposal for a Regulation of the European Parliament and of the Council on the citizens' initiative*, COM (2010) 119 final of 31 March 2010, has proposed the minimum number at one third.

[53]See the volume Kohler-Koch and Rittberger (2007); especially the following chapters: Auel and Benz (2007), and Rittberger (2007).

[54]The following is based on and taken from Hrbek (2010), pp. 147–149.

[55]See Hrbek (1999).

[56]See Straub and Hrbek (1998); the volume covers the cases of Austria, Belgium, Spain, Italy, France and Germany, and it contains a documentation on practical activities of regional parliaments.

Basic structures already exist, as can be illustrated with the German example.[57] Länder parliaments have established special committees for EU affairs,[58] which have to deal with the same problem mentioned above for the national parliament's EAC: the rivalry with specialised committees and difficulties in acquiring something like a coordination role. Activities of parliaments are oriented towards the respective government. There are provisions ruling the relationship of the two institutions,[59] which include the obligation of the government to inform the parliament on EU matters as early and comprehensively as possible; the right of the parliament to formulate its opinions, which, although not binding, shall be taken into account by the government (especially in the Bundesrat); and the obligation of the government to submit an annual report on how EU policies affect the Land and what the government has done. As far as the informational basis is concerned, parliaments are dependent on the executive. Only recently, some parliaments have started to establish a modest representation (a civil servant of the parliament's administration) of their own in Brussels, placed within the Land Representation. Observers of activities and performance of EU committees conclude that the impact of parliamentary activities has been poor.[60] This is partly due to a lack of sufficient resources. If Land parliaments wish to play a more influential and more efficient role in EU decision-making, they need to overcome these deficiencies.

With regard to interparliamentary cooperation as another strategy of regional parliaments to strengthen their involvement in decision-making on EU matters, a meeting of presidents of regional parliaments with legislative powers in October 1997 in Oviedo (Asturia) agreed to establish CALRE[61] as a political network,[62] which represents 73 regions from eight EU Member States: Austria, Belgium, Germany, Spain, Italy, Portugal (the regions Azores and Madeira), the UK (Scotland and Wales) and Finland (the Aaland Islands). CALRE meetings, held annually, focus on political and "constitutional" questions; two working groups on these issues have been set up in 2006, and a third group deals with e-democracy. The major value of this network seems to lie in the field of internal communication amongst its members; there is, however, potential for strengthening the network to the benefit of this group of regional parliaments which might play a role in scrutinising the application of the principle of subsidiarity.

---

[57] See the detailed descriptive analysis by Johne (2000).

[58] See Bauer (2005).

[59] In some Länder these have been included in the respective Land constitution.

[60] Bauer (2005).

[61] CALRE = Conférence des Assemblées législatives régionales d'Europe.

[62] See Kiefer (2006).

References

Arter D (1996) The Folketing and Denmark's,European Policy': the case of an 'Authorising Assembly'. In: Norton P (ed) National parliaments and the European Union. London, pp 110–123

Auel K, Benz A (2007) Expanding national parliamentary control: does it enhance European democracy? In: Kohler-Koch B, Rittberger B (eds) Debating the democratic legitimacy of the European Union. Lanham, pp 57–74

Bauer MW (2005) Europaausschüsse – Herzstück landesparlamentarischer Beteiligung in Angelegenheiten der Europäischen Union? In: Europäisches Zentrum für Föderalismus-Forschung Tübingen (ed) Jahrbuch des Föderalismus 2005. Baden-Baden, pp 632–647

Benz A, Broschek J (2010) Nationale Parlamente in der europäischen Politik. Funktionen, Probleme und Lösungen, Friedrich-Ebert-Stiftung, Internationale Politikanalyse, März http://library.fes.de/pdf-files/id/ipa/07084.pdf (accessed 15 January 2011)

Carter CA (2001) The parliament of the United Kingdom: from scrutiny to unleashed control? In: Maurer A, Wessels W (eds) National parliaments on their ways to Europe: losers or latecomers? Baden-Baden, pp 395–423

Duina F, Raunio T (2007) The open method of co-ordination and national parliaments: further marginalization or new opportunities? J Eur Publ Pol 14(4):489–506

Halberstam D, Möllers C (2009) The German Constitutional Court says *"Ja zu Deutschland!"*. German Law J 10(8) (Special Section: The Federal Constitutional Court's *Lisbon Case*, pp 1241–1257)

Hix S (2005) The political system of the European Union, 2nd edn. Houndmills

Hrbek R (1980) Demokratiegebot und Europäische Gemeinschaft. In: Hartmann K (ed) Die Demokratie im Spektrum der Wissenschaften. Freiburg, pp 285–322

Hrbek R (1995) Der Vertrag von Maastricht und das Demokratie-Defizit der Europäischen Union – Auf dem Weg zu stärkerer demokratischer Legitimation? In: Randelzhofer A, Scholz R, Wilke D (eds) Gedächtnisschrift für Eberhard Grabitz. München, pp 171–193

Hrbek R (1999) The effects of EU integration on German federalism. In: Jeffery C (ed) Recasting German federalism. The legacies of unification. London, pp 217–233

Hrbek R (2000) Das Subsidiaritätsprinzip in der EU – Bedeutung und Wirkung nach dem Vertrag von Amsterdam, in: Europäisches Zentrum für Föderalismus-Forschung Tübingen (Hrsg.): Jahrbuch des Föderalismus 2000. Föderalismus, Subsidiarität und Regionen in Europa. Baden-Baden, pp 510–531

Hrbek R (2010) Parliaments in EU multi-level governance. In: Hrbek R (ed) Legislatures in federal systems and multi-level governance. Baden-Baden, pp 136–150

Janowski CA (2005) Die nationalen Parlamente und ihre Europa-Gremien. Legitimationsgarant der EU? Baden-Baden

Johne R (2000) Die deutschen Landtage im Entscheidungsprozess der Europäischen Union. Parlamentarische Mitwirkung im europäischen Mehrebenensystem. Baden-Baden

Kiefer A (2006) Gesetzgebende Regionalparlamente und ihr europäischer Verband: die CALRE. In: Europäisches Zentrum für Föderalismus-Forschung Tübingen (ed) Jahrbuch des Föderalismus 2006. Baden-Baden, pp 606–629

Kiiver P (2009) German participation in EU decision-making after the Lisbon case: a comparative view on domestic parliamentary clearance procedures. German Law J 10(8) (Special Section: The Federal Constitutional Court's Lisbon Case, pp 1287–1296)

Kohler-Koch B, Rittberger B (eds) (2007) Debating the democratic legitimacy of the European Union. Lanham

Krekelberg A (2001) The reticent acknowledgement of national parliaments in the European treaties: a documentation. In: Maurer, A and Wessels, W (eds.) National Parliaments on their Ways to Europe. Losers or Latecomers? Baden-Baden, pp 477–489

Laursen F (2001) The Danish folketing and its European affairs committee: strong players in the national policy cycle. In: Maurer A, Wessels W (eds) National parliaments on their ways to Europe: losers or latecomers? Baden-Baden, pp 99–115
Maurer A (2002) Parlamentarische Demokratie in der Europäischen Union. Der Beitrag des Europäischen Parlaments und der nationalen Parlamente. Baden-Baden
Maurer A, Vogel S (2009) Die Europäische Bürgerinitiative. Chancen, Grenzen und Umsetzungsempfehlungen, SWP-Studie S 28, Berlin, Oktober 2009
Maurer A, Wessels W (eds) (2001) National parliaments on their ways to Europe: losers or latecomers? Baden-Baden
Naßmacher K-H (1972) Demokratisierung der Europäischen Gemeinschaften. Bonn
Nettesheim M (2009) Ein Individualrecht auf Staatlichkeit? Die Lissabon-Entscheidung des BVerfG. NJW 39:2867–2869
Norton P (1996a) The United Kingdom: political conflict, parliamentary scrutiny. In: Norton P (ed) National parliaments and the European Union. London, pp 92–109
Norton P (ed) (1996b) National parliaments and the European Union. London
O'Brennan J, Raunio T (eds) (2007) National parliaments within the enlarged European Union. From "victims" of integration to competitive actors? Abingdon
Raunio T (2009) National parliaments and European integration. What we know and what we should know. ARENA Working Paper No 02, Oslo, January 2009
Rittberger B (2007) Constructing parliamentary democracy in the European Union: how did it happen? In: Kohler-Koch B, Rittberger B (eds) Debating the democratic legitimacy of the European Union. Lanham, pp 111–137
Schorkopf F (2009) The European Union as an association of sovereign states: Karlsruhe's ruling on the treaty of Lisbon. German Law J 10(8) (Special Section: The Federal Constitutional Court's *Lisbon Case*, pp 1219–1240)
Schweitzer C-C (1978) Die nationalen Parlamente in der Gemeinschaft – ihr schwindender Einfluss in Bonn und Westminster auf die Europagesetzgebung. Bonn
Sousa MM (2008) Learning in Denmark? The case of Danish parliamentary control over European union policy. Scand Polit Stud 31(4):428–447
Straub P, Hrbek R (eds) (1998) Die europapolitische Rolle der Landes- und Regionalparlamente in der EU. Baden-Baden
Tomuschat C (2009) The ruling of the German Constitutional Court on the treaty of Lisbon. German Law J 10(8) (Special Section: The Federal Constitutional Court's *Lisbon Case*, pp 1259–1261)
Weber-Panariello PA (1995) Nationale Parlamente in der Europäischen Union. Baden-Baden

The Protection of Fundamental Rights in Europe

Hermann-Josef Blanke

Since the entry into force of the Treaty on European Union (TEU) on 1 December 2009 the people of Europe,[1] the citizens of the European Union (EU), have taken a great leap forward in terms of their codified legal rights and liberties. For a long time they have been living mostly under judge-made law, be it as a result of the interpretation of the European Convention for the Protection of Human Rights and Fundamental Freedoms (ECHR) by the European Court of Human Rights (ECtHR) in Strasbourg or of the creation or recognition of fundamental rights by the European Court of Justice (ECJ) in Luxembourg. While the Strasbourg Court grants legal protection as measured by human rights with universal character, the ECJ in its established case law guaranteed the protection of fundamental rights which the relevant parties sought within the scope of application of the Community Treaties.[2] Now the Treaty of Lisbon recognises rights, freedoms and principles at Union level in a more comprehensive understanding – beyond the mere market-based context – setting them out in the Charter of Fundamental Rights of the European Union (EUCFR) and giving its provisions binding legal force (Art. 6.1 TEU).

The development of fundamental rights on the supranational level is mainly the result of the admonitions on the part of the national (constitutional) courts,

Translated by Robert Böttner, assistant at the Chair for Public Law, International Public Law and European Integration at the University of Erfurt. The author would like to thank Professor Eileen Denza for reviewing the translation.

[1]Cf. the first paragraph of the Preamble of the Charter of Fundamental Rights of the European Union: "The people of Europe [. . .]."

[2]Cf. Müller (2005), p. 15, 25; Skouris (2005), p. 31, compares the ECJ in its function with a "supreme specialised court".

H.-J. Blanke (✉)
Chair for Public Law and International Public Law, University of Erfurt, Postfach 90 02 21, 99105 Erfurt, Germany
e-mail: LS_Staatsrecht@uni-erfurt.de

H.-J. Blanke and S. Mangiameli (eds.), *The European Union after Lisbon*,
DOI 10.1007/978-3-642-19507-5_7,

especially of the Italian *Corte Costituzionale*[3] and the French *Conseil Constitutionnel*. Most striking, however, was the support given by the German *Bundesverfassungsgericht*, which called for a protection of such rights in the Community or even reserved for itself the right to review Community action on grounds of fundamental rights as long as the Community did not dispose of its own guarantees (*infra* Sect. 6).[4] These signals, which originated from national actors in the framework of the European protection of fundamental rights, were enhanced by initiatives by the other institutions, in particular by those of the European Parliament which introduced several proposals for recognition of fundamental rights in the European Community's (EC) legal order.[5] Thus, the call for a review of "secondary Union law and other acts of the European Union" on grounds of fundamental rights[6] and the abstention from exercising this national jurisdiction only as long as the EU guarantees an application of fundamental rights which in substance and effectiveness is essentially similar to the protection of fundamental rights required unconditionally by the German Basic Law[7] is obviously *the* paradigm

[3]Cf. for this analysis the decision of the Italian Constitutional Court, judgment 349/2007 (22 October 2007), Legal considerations sub 6.1.

[4]Cf. German Federal Constitutional Court, 2 BvL 52/71 (Order of 29 May 1974) para 44 et seqq. (in: BVerfGE 37, 271, 280 et seqq.) – *Solange I* (English translation in: Bundesverfassungsgericht (1992), pp. 270 et seqq.): "As long as the integration process [. . .]."

[5]Resolution adopting the Declaration of fundamental rights and freedoms, O.J. C 120/51 (1989); in a modified version reconsidered as Title VIII of the Draft Constitutional Treaty of 10 February 1994, O.J. C 61/155 (1994).

[6]Cf. German Federal Constitutional Court, 2 BvR 197/83 (Order of 22 October 1986) para 104 (in: BVerfGE 73, 339, 376) – *Solange II* (English translation in: Bundesverfassungsgericht (1992), pp. 613 et seqq.): "In so far as sovereign power is accorded to an international institution within the meaning of Article 24 (1) which is in a position within the sovereign sphere of the Federal Republic to encroach on the essential content of the fundamental rights recognized by the Basic Law, it is necessary, if that entails the removal of legal protection existing under the terms of the Basic Law, that instead, there should be a guarantee of the application of fundamental rights which in substance and effectiveness is essentially similar to the protection of fundamental rights required unconditionally by the Basic Law [. . .]."; in the same way the German Federal Constitutional Court, 2 BvL 1/97 (Order of 7 June 2000) para 61 (in: BVerfGE 102, 147, 164) – *Banana Market* (English translation available online).

[7]German Federal Constitutional Court, 2 BvR 197/83 (Order of 22 October 1986) (in: BVerfGE 73, 339) – *Solange II* – Headnote 2: "As long as the European Communities, in particular European Court case law, generally ensure effective protection of fundamental rights as against the sovereign powers of the Communities which is to be regarded as substantially similar to the protection of fundamental rights required unconditionally by the Constitution, and in so far as they generally safeguard essential content of fundamental rights, the Federal Constitutional Court will no longer exercise its jurisdiction to decide on the applicability of secondary Community legislation cited as the legal basis for any acts of German courts or authorities within the sovereign jurisdiction of the Federal Republic of Germany, and it will no longer review such legislation by the standard of the fundamental rights contained in the Basic Law; references to the Court under Article 100 (1) Basic Law for those purposes are therefore inadmissible."

of a dialogue between the Luxembourg Court and the German Federal Constitutional Court.[8]

Both systems, that of the Council of Europe and, in some degree, that of the EU, exhibit several similarities to national systems of constitutional protection. Thus, the superior European courts and the superior domestic courts are dealing with similar matters, applying similar provisions of substantive law and following similar procedural rules. As a result, the standards of European fundamental rights, especially those of the Union, are "constitutionalised" by the guarantees enshrined in the various national bills of rights. Simultaneously, there is "a kind of bilateral interplay between the EU and Convention law, thereby producing a twofold process of 'conventionalisation' of Union law and 'unionisation' of Convention law, though with different timings and intensity."[9] Therefore, it is possible to draw a triangle that has, at its three vertices, the various supreme or constitutional courts, the ECJ and the ECtHR. As the legal systems concerned do not only coexist but also overlap each other,[10] it is within this triangle that cooperation in the field of human rights develops and provokes collisions at the same time.[11]

1 The Protection of Fundamental Rights Under the EC and the EU Treaty of Maastricht in the Case Law of the European Court of Justice

Although the 1957 Treaty of Rome did not contain specific provisions on the protection of fundamental rights, the ECJ has nonetheless upheld the need for respect for fundamental rights in the context of action at EC/EU level since the Community's early days.[12] In the *Stauder* judgment on occasion of its review of a disposition of secondary Community law about the purchase of butter at a reduced price for reasons of social assistance the Court concluded its analysis: "Interpreted in this way the provision at issue contains nothing capable of prejudicing the

[8]For the term "judicial dialogue" cf. Advocate General *Poiares Maduro* in his Opinion submitted to the Court (ECJ, Case C-127/07, Opinion of Advocate General Poiares Maduro, 21 May 2008, para 15–17): "On the contrary, it is inherent in the very nature of the constitutional values of the Union as constitutional values common to the Member States that they must be refined and developed by the Court in a process of ongoing dialogue with the national courts, in particular those responsible for determining the authentic interpretation of the national constitutions. The appropriate instrument of that dialogue is the reference for a preliminary ruling and it is in that context that the question raised here must be understood" (para 17). Cf. further the contributions by Oeter (2007) and Merli (2007).

[9]Callewaert (2008).

[10]Wildhaber (2005b), p. 43.

[11]Garlicki (2008), pp. 511 et seq.

[12]Cf. Rodriguez Iglesias (1995), pp. 1271 et seqq.; Blanke (2006), pp. 267 et seq.

fundamental human rights enshrined in the general principles of Community law and protected by the Court."[13] In *Internationale Handelsgesellschaft*, the ECJ concluded that "[i]n fact, respect for fundamental rights forms an integral part of the general principles of law protected by the ECJ. The protection of such rights, whilst inspired by the constitutional traditions common to Member States, must be ensured within the framework of the structure and objectives of the Community."[14] General legal principles which are common to the legal systems of Member States form an element of unwritten primary Community law.

Following the cases of *Stauder* and *Internationale Handelsgesellschaft*, the ECJ, both in the opinions of its Advocates General and in its judgments, has regularly referred to its duty to ensure observance of the general principles of law, of which fundamental rights form an integral part. This recourse to the general principles of law reflects the French approach to fundamental rights, according to which they are understood rather as principles, attributing to them the character of objective rights.[15] In identifying particular rights and interpreting their content, the Court in *Internationale Handelsgesellschaft* draws inspiration also from the constitutional traditions common to the Member States and thus reaffirms and specifies the general principles of law as sources for recognition of fundamental rights within the legal order of the Community. Finally in the case of *Nold* the Court referred to guidelines supplied by international treaties for the protection of human rights on which the Member States have collaborated or to which they are signatories, including in particular the ECHR,[16] thus underpinning the Community's protection of fundamental rights in a twofold concept: "As the Court has already stated, fundamental rights form an integral part of the general principles of law, the observance of which it ensures. In safeguarding these rights, the Court is bound to draw inspiration from constitutional traditions common to the Member States, and it cannot therefore uphold measures which are incompatible with fundamental rights recognized and protected by the Constitutions of those States. Similarly, international treaties for the protection of human rights on which the Member States have collaborated or of which they are signatories can supply guidelines which should be followed within the framework of Community law."[17]

These international instruments are not directly applied as legally binding provisions under international law but rather used as sources for establishing

[13]Cf. Case 29/69 *Erich Stauder v City of Ulm* (ECJ 12 November 1969) para 7; see also Case 44/79 *Hauer v Land Rheinland-Pfalz* (ECJ 13 December 1979) para 15: "[...] that fundamental rights form an integral part of the general principles of the law, the observance of which [the Court] ensures [...]".

[14]Case 11/70 *Internationale Handelsgesellschaft mbH v Einfuhr- und Vorratsstelle für Getreide und Futtermittel* (ECJ 17 December 1970) para 4.

[15]Cf. Mayer (2009), p. 89; see also Rodriguez Iglesias (1998).

[16]For the first time the ECJ explicitly referred to the ECHR in Case 36/75 *Roland Rutili v Ministre de l'intérieur* (ECJ 28 October 1975) para 32.

[17]Cf. Case 4/73 *Nold KG v Commission* (ECJ 14 May 1974) para 13.

general principles common to the legal orders of the Member States. At the same time, examination of the extensive case law in which reference is made to the ECHR (beginning with *Rutili* to *Hoechst* and *Orkem* up to *Defrenne* and *Wachauf*) shows that the Court has indeed applied the provisions of the Human Rights Convention as part of Community law independent of the theoretical explanation of their legal significance as an element for the identification of general principles of law. Thus one can say that even before the forthcoming accession of the Union the ECHR has had a function equivalent to that of a formally recognised catalogue of fundamental rights.[18]

This interplay between both sources, the general principles of law, especially the constitutional traditions common to the Member States, and the ECHR was already enshrined in the Treaty of Maastricht in 1992 (Art. 6 TEU) as a cornerstone of the protection of fundamental rights at the level of the Union. Since the beginning of the 1990s, though, the fundamental rights arguments of the ECJ have focused unequivocally on the ECHR rights. Although general principles are still mentioned, they are not developed on a comparative legal basis in the case law of the ECJ. Successive Treaties from Maastricht onwards have strengthened the position of fundamental rights in the EU. But it is the Charter of Fundamental Rights which is supposed to be a "huge step forward for the European citizen" (*A. Duff*) for it provides for visibility and publicity of fundamental rights guarantees and thus leads to increased legal certainty. It facilitates the Europe-wide discourse on, and enhances the legitimating power of, fundamental rights.[19]

2 The Protection of Fundamental Rights in the Union According to Art. 6 TEU

2.1 An Interwoven System of Protection

The Treaty of Lisbon, which is a reform treaty, substantially revises Art. 6 TEU. Articles 6.1 to 3 TEU cover a tripartite interwoven system for the protection of fundamental rights in the EU[20] by:

---

[18]Cf. Rodriguez Iglesias (1995), p. 1273, 1275, 1280, with an interpretation of the references in the various cases to the ECHR.

[19]Cf. Kühling (2003), p. 586.

[20]See also Pernice (2008), p. 240: "three pillars"; contrary to this systematisation, German Federal Constitutional Court, 2 BvE 2, 5/08, 2 BvR 1010, 1022, 1259/08, 182/09 (Judgment of 30 June 2009) para 35 (in: BVerfGE 123, 267, 283) – *Lisbon* (English translation available online), considers the protection of fundamental rights in the TEU as based on *two* foundations, the Charter of Fundamental Rights of the European Union and the Union's unwritten fundamental rights, both complemented by the authorisation and obligation of the Union to accede to the European Convention for the Protection of Human Rights and Fundamental Freedoms.

1. Recognising the rights, freedoms and principles set out in the EUCFR in its revised version of 12 December 2007[21] in a legally binding way and thus declaring them a legal source of Union law, establishing at the same time a safeguard for the competences of the Member States,
2. Setting out the authorisation and obligation of the EU to accede to the ECHR, which by this means becomes a legal source of Union law as well, and
3. Declaring the fundamental rights, as guaranteed by the ECHR and as they result from the constitutional traditions common to the Member States, constituent "general principles" of Union law which thus remain a source of legal guidance for the interpretation especially of the Charter of Fundamental Rights as a legal source of the Union.[22] Thereby, the Treaty of Lisbon – with slight adaptions – takes up the case law of the ECJ and its codification by the Treaty of Maastricht (*supra* Sect. 1). The source for the interpretation of the law – as opposed to an actual source of law – is not directly binding but rather has an effect similar to that of a norm by serving as a means of orientation for the interpretation of the source of law.[23]

The juxtaposition of the codified (Art. 6.1 (1) TEU) and uncodified (Art. 6.3 TEU) catalogue of fundamental rights has been criticised as "unusual" and in need of reform. For a dynamic development of the fundamental rights with regard to further development of the ECHR and the national constitutions to be possible,[24] Art. 6.3 TEU would not have been required since Art. 52.3 and 4 EUCFR bind the ECJ in this respect anyway.[25] On the other hand, with regard to the codification of European fundamental rights, emphasis has been put on the "interaction of the fundamental rights culture at Member State and European level" as well as the significance of the "diversity of the human rights culture in the current and future Member States" that has proven to be an "impetus for the steady improvement of the protection of human rights".[26] This solution, which is based on the competition of different systems of fundamental rights by means of constitutional comparison, however, misjudges the fact that for a long time the ECJ has derived fundamental rights essentially from the ECHR which it applies as part of Community law (*infra* Sect. 2.3). In the future it will see its task to be the decision of cases with fundamental rights implication submitted to it by applying the Charter of Fundamental Rights, whose guarantees – in the light of the authentic interpretation

[21]*Charter of Fundamental Rights of the European Union*, O.J. C 303/1 (2007).

[22]Hilf and Schorkopf, in Grabitz and Hilf (2002), Art. 6 EUV para 46; also – regarding the common constitutional traditions of the Member States – Ladenburger, in Tettinger and Stern (2006), Art. 52 GrCh para 65 et seqq.

[23]For the concept of a source for the interpretation of the law (*Rechtserkenntnisquelle*) cf. Kühling (2003), p. 589.

[24]See the Considerations of Working Group II of the Constitutional Convention, CONV 354/02 of 22 October 2002, p. 9.

[25]Cf. Kingreen, in Calliess and Ruffert (2011), Art. 6 EUV para 16 et seqq.

[26]Cf. Kirchhof (2003), p. 902; cf. also p. 928 (our translation).

of the rights of the Convention by the ECtHR – it has to lead to a high level of protection.

2.2 Fundamental Rights as Principles (Art. 6.3 TEU)

The Union Treaty restates the differentiation already found in the Preamble of the Charter of Fundamental Rights (6th recital) and Art. 52 EUCFR between "rights" and "freedoms" on the one hand and "principles" on the other (Art. 6.1 TEU). The Explanations of the Praesidium of the Convention[27] classify individual Articles of the Charter of Fundamental Rights as principles (e.g. Art. 25, 26 and 27, but also Art. 34.1 and 3 and Art. 35, 36, 38). The distinction is another confusing and unsatisfactory peculiarity of the Charter which is further consolidated by the wording of Art. 6.1 TEU and 51 EUCFR. The United Kingdom has been most reluctant to talk about economic and social *rights*,[28] but preferred instead to use the word "principles". "Principles" have no definite, but a *prima facie* validity and are thus rather imperatives for optimisation. Their implementation is only feasible within the framework of a balancing with other objectives of primary law.[29] As such, they are "factors to be taken into account by courts when interpreting legislation, but which do not in and of themselves create enforceable rights".[30] "Principles" are binding, but justiciable only in so far as Member States have adopted laws or taken administrative actions (i.e. have adopted "acts") when "implementing" Union law (Art. 52.5 EUCFR).[31] Subjectively enforceable fundamental rights are different from the fundamental principles which may be implemented through legislation. It would be decisive for the distinction, whether the relevant provision (also) relates to the *protection of rights of individuals* or this is expressly excluded.[32] However, the stumbling block for the distinction remains

---

[27]Updated under the responsibility of the Praesidium of the European Convention, in the light of the drafting adjustments made to the text of the Charter by that Convention – notably to Art. 51 and 52 EUCFR.

[28]See Cologne Presidency Conclusions 1999, Annex IV.

[29]Schmidt (2010), pp. 55 et seqq., 112 et seqq., 178 et seqq.

[30]House of Lords Constitution Committee, European Union (Amendment) Bill and the Lisbon Treaty: *Implications for the UK Constitution*, 6th Report, 2007-8, HL Paper 84, para 60–61. See also Goldsmith (2001), p. 1212.

[31]Cf. Hogan, Der Einfluß der Europäischen Grundrechte-Charta auf die irische Verfassung, in Tettinger and Stern (2006), A VI para 41; with the same result Schmidt (2010), pp. 90 et seqq., 198 et seqq., who favours a judicial review competence in so far as the observing of all guarantees of these principles within this balancing of objectives can be subject to review; Mik, The Charter of Fundamental Rights: determinants of Protective Standards, in Barcz (2009), Sect. 12 II pp. 66 et seqq.; Bodnar, The Charter of Fundamental Rights: Differentiated Legal Character of Charter's Provisions, Their Consequences for Individuals, Courts and Legislator (2009), Sect. 33 IV pp. 155 et seqq.

[32]Cf. Ladenburger, in Tettinger and Stern (2006), Art. 52 GrCh para 98 et seqq.

that the Charter does not identify which provisions contain rights and which principles.

The principles pursuant to Art. 6.1 TEU are to be distinguished from the "general principles" of Art. 6.3 TEU. By using this term – following the case law of the ECJ (*Stauder*) as well as Art. F.2 TEU-Maastricht – it summarises the fundamental rights of the ECHR and the fundamental rights as they result from the constitutional traditions common to the Member States, thereby making them a source for the interpretation of Union law.[33] The significance of the common constitutional traditions is so far regarded marginal, since the ECJ will not refrain from an autonomous interpretation of the Charter, equivalent to the interpretation of the Treaties. At the same time, comparative evaluation would affect the achievements made by the codification of fundamental rights in the Charter.[34] The interpretation of the Charter itself is bound by its general provisions in Title VII (Art. 51–54 EUCFR) on the one hand and by the "Explanations referred to in the Charter" (historical interpretation) which themselves are limited to those "that set out the sources of those provisions" (Art. 6.1 (3) TEU) on the other.

2.3 *The European Charter of Fundamental Rights*

2.3.1 Origin, Entry into Force and Relevance of the Charter

The EUCFR was prepared by the first broadly based Convention, encompassing members of the European Parliament and of national parliaments. At the summit in Nice in December 2000, the Member States were not yet unanimously ready to incorporate the Charter into the Treaty of Nice. Instead, the EUCFR, drawing on the "constitutional traditions and international obligations common to the Member States" was "solemnly proclaimed" by the European Parliament, the Commission and the Council.[35] Prior to the adoption of the draft Charter by the Convention, the Bureau of the Convention prepared Explanations for each Article of the Charter. The Explanations are intended to clarify the provisions of the Charter, indicating the sources and scope of each of the rights set out.

The second Convention incorporated the Charter as Part II into the Treaty establishing a Constitution for Europe (TCE) signed in Rome on 29 October 2004.[36] Since the Constitutional Treaty failed to be ratified by all Member States,

[33]Cf. Kingreen, in Calliess and Ruffert (2011), Art. 6 EUV para 6 et seq.

[34]Cf. Ladenburger, in Tettinger and Stern (2006), Art. 52 GrCh para 78.

[35]*Charter of Fundamental Rights of the European Union*, O.J. C 364/1 (2000).

[36]*Treaty establishing a Constitution for Europe*, O.J. C 310/1 (2004) with the *Charter of Fundamental Rights of the European Union* at p. 41 et seqq.

the Charter continued to live on as a solemn political proclamation. The Intergovernmental Conference (IGC 2007) decided, in line with its June mandate, to make the Charter legally binding but without incorporating the text into the Treaty of Lisbon.

One day before the signing of the Treaty of Lisbon, the Charter was solemnly proclaimed in Strasbourg for a second time by the European Parliament, the Council and the European Commission. The EUCFR has been published in the Official Journal of the EU with the Explanations relating to the Charter of Fundamental Rights.[37] It entered into force on 1 December 2009 along with the TEU and the Treaty on the Functioning of the European Union (TFEU) without, however, becoming a part of the Union Treaty itself. The United Kingdom and the Netherlands were afraid that the incorporation of the Charter into the Reform Treaty would create the impression of a "statehood" at Union level. In order to make it a fully adequate and equivalent document in the legal system of the Union, the second clause of Art. 6.1 TEU provides that the Charter shall have the same legal value as the TEU and the TFEU. Nevertheless, this is an impairment of the concept of unity envisaged by the Constitutional Treaty.

The Charter of Fundamental Rights "confirms the fundamental rights guaranteed by the European Convention for the Protection of Human Rights and Fundamental Freedoms and as they result from the constitutional traditions common to the Member States."[38] Their guarantees concern civil, political and economic freedoms and social rights ("rights to respect", "rights to protect" and "rights to fulfil"). Bringing together various rights which were previously enshrined preponderantly in other human rights documents, and thus making them "more visible"[39] for the citizens of the Union, the Charter is a manifestation of shared European values. The codification not only underlines and clarifies the legal status and freedoms of the Union's citizens vis-à-vis the institutions of the Union, but also satisfies the need for fundamental rights facing and limiting the enlarged powers at Union level – especially the crucial ones regarding the "area of freedom, security and justice" (Title V of the TFEU) which were brought within the "Community method".[40] The result will be the most up-to-date human rights document in the world, and it offers the citizens a basis for scrutinising EU institutions and Member States when they implement EU law.

---

[37] Cf. the *Declaration concerning the explanations relating to the Charter of Fundamental Rights (Declaration 12)* annexed to the Treaty establishing a Constitution for Europe, O.J. C 310/424 (2004), updated once more in O.J. C 303/17 (2007).

[38] See the first clause of the *Declaration (1) concerning the Charter of Fundamental Rights of the European Union* annexed to the Treaty of Lisbon, O.J. C 83/337 (2010).

[39] Cf. the Preamble of the EUCFR (3rd consideration).

[40] Pernice (2008), p. 238.

2.3.2 The Likely Effect of the Legally Binding Force of the Charter for the Protection of Fundamental Rights in the Case Law of the ECJ

The most important change relates to the legal status of the Charter: new Art. 6.1 (1) TEU provides that the Charter, which has been excluded from the Union Treaty, will have the same legal value as the Treaties ("incorporated by reference"). Declaring the Charter to be legally binding will of course be likely to encourage and probably speed up the development of the case law of the ECJ which within the framework of Union law will try to gain mastery in the protection of human rights in competition with the Strasbourg Court. So far the ECJ has rarely proved itself to be a pioneer and precursor with regard to the establishment of a high level of protection. The ECJ has only rarely declared a European legal act void for its incompatibility with European fundamental rights.[41] Nonetheless, even without the Charter of Fundamental Rights it could examine European acts for their conformity with fundamental rights more resolutely. It is true that in its *Omega* ruling the Court has shown a sense of proportion for the somehow vague guarantee of "human dignity" as a fundamental cornerstone of the German Constitution: Here the Court recognises that "the Community legal order undeniably strives to ensure respect for human dignity as a general principle of law" and "that the objective of protecting human dignity is compatible with Community law"; therefore human dignity as a principle validated in the Union's legal order[42] "justifies (within the scope of proportionality) a restriction of the obligations imposed by Community law, even under a fundamental freedom guaranteed by the Treaty such as the freedom to provide services."[43]

Nevertheless, "it is not indispensable in that respect for the restrictive measure issued by the authorities of a Member State to correspond to a conception shared by all Member States as regards the precise way in which the fundamental right or legitimate interest in question is to be protected."[44] In fact the "double test" which the ECJ applies to national restrictions of the obligations imposed by Union law allows for different standards of protection in domestic law.[45] Contrary to this filtered and differentiated method of the handling of the fundamental rights

---

[41]As one of the few cases Mayer (2009), p. 97, mentions the decision in Case C-340/00 *Commission v Cwik* (ECJ 13 December 2001).

[42]Nickel (2009), p. 334, criticises that "not all EU Member State constitutions contain a legal concept of human dignity which guarantees it *as an individual right*, and to some – such as the UK – such a concept is completely alien to the legal system. Additionally, only few Member States would interpret the protection of human dignity in a way that it could also be used *against* its bearers (in the *Omega* case, the players of Gotcha). In the end, the ECJ created a "new" common constitutional concept in the name of constitutional pluralism."

[43]Case C-36/02 *Omega Spielhallen- und Automatenaufstellungs-GmbH v Oberbürgermeisterin der Bundesstadt Bonn* (ECJ 14 October 2004) para 34, 36.

[44]Case C-36/02 *Omega Spielhallen- und Automatenaufstellungs-GmbH v Oberbürgermeisterin der Bundesstadt Bonn* (ECJ 14 October 2004) para 37.

[45]Cf. Schwarze (2005), pp. 41 et seq.

traditions of the Member States, in the *Bosphorus* decision, although the Luxembourg Court thoroughly examined the principle of proportionality, it rather blurred the question of the limits of Art. 1 of the first Protocol to the ECHR on the protection of property by merely stating that the guarantee of property can be limited by a public interest/general interest but without a detailed review as to whether the seizure of the aircraft by the Irish authorities met the requirements of "the conditions provided for by law and by the general principles of international law."[46]

Summarising the "fundamental rights rhetoric" of the ECJ, the question of the protection or the normative area (which fundamental right is affected?) and the question of the admissible restrictions (to be determined in the future according to Art. 52.1 and 52.3 EUCFR) and consequently the justification for such restriction needs to be made clearer and dealt with more extensively in its case law. In those cases in which there is no express restriction, the possibility of a de facto or indirect invasion, which may also lead to a violation of fundamental rights, should be examined.[47] Despite the codification of the principle of proportionality with regard to its second element (necessity) and third element (appropriateness: "limitations [must] meet objectives of general interest [...] or [...] the rights and freedoms of others"), a coordinated method of application is still often lacking in the ECJ's examination of fundamental rights.[48] However, after the rulings in *Kadi*[49] and *Yussuf*,[50] there is no doubt about the Court's willingness to give its case law a higher profile in matters concerning fundamental rights. The reason for a predictable evolution of the substantial standards of fundamental rights protection by the Luxembourg Court lies also in the fact that the ECJ will be increasingly asked to interpret the ECHR, given that a number of Charter rights are derived from that document. By this means, the growing caseload of the ECtHR can be alleviated in the long run.

2.3.3 The Effect of the Charter on the Interpretation and Application of Fundamental Rights

The entry into force of the Charter following the ratification of the Lisbon Treaty will not be without impact on the method of defining the scope and content of fundamental rights in the case law of the ECJ. So far its task has been in a first step

[46]Case C-84/95 *Bosphorus v Minister for Transport, Energy and Communications et al.* (ECJ 30 July 1996) para 21, 26.

[47]Blanke (2006), pp. 271 et seq.; Kühling (2003), pp. 613 et seqq.

[48]Cf. Blanke (2006), pp. 273 et seq.

[49]Case T-315/01 *Kadi v Council and Commission* (CFI 21 September 2005), appealed by Joined Cases 402/05 P and 415/05 P *Kadi et al. v Council and Commission* (ECJ 3 September 2008).

[50]Case T-306 *Yusf et al. v Council and Commission* (CFI 21 September 2005), appealed by Joined Cases 402/05 P and 415/05 P *Kadi et al. v Council and Commission* (ECJ 3 September 2008).

to identify the common European standards of fundamental rights by analysing the national legal orders as part of the general legal principles of European law and align them with the guarantees of the ECHR as they have been interpreted in the case law of the Strasbourg Court. Due to codification of the fundamental rights of dignity, freedom and equality as well as the incorporation of social ("solidarity"), civil and judicial rights into the Charter, the Luxembourg Court's task will now be to outline especially those guarantees which have no parallel provision in the ECHR,[51] as subjective rights[52] ("rights to fulfil") in contrast to the "rights to respect" and the "rights to protect",[53] and to determine their content with regard to human rights in such a way – also in the analysis of the scope of protection – that they are not reduced to mere ciphers. In so far as the guarantees recognised by the Charter are a reception of the constitutional traditions common to the Member States, the Court is obliged to interpret these rights "in harmony with those traditions" pursuant to Art. 52.4 EUCFR. Thus, the ECJ could be confronted with national essential principles on which the respective guarantees are based. However, on the one hand, the sphere of the rights included in paragraph 4 is vague, for many rights are founded on several sources. On the other hand, the explanations of the Praesidium in paragraph 4 call for "a high standard of protection" so that it is not to be expected that the ECJ will be kept by paragraph 4 from an autonomous interpretation of the Charter according to the established method of interpretation of the Treaties.[54]

Meanwhile the Court will have to be more systematic and methodically stringent in its interpretation of fundamental rights in order to ensure rationality and understanding of its decisions. On this basis the second step of defining the scope of fundamental rights will still be determined by a process that has been characteristic of the established interpretation of fundamental rights by the ECJ. The Court will have to fit the various listed fundamental rights into the structures and aims of the Union which are spelt out in Art. 3, 6 and 9 TEU and the horizontal clauses of Art. 10–13 TEU in particular. This "Union reserve competence" is now partially codified by the specification of "objectives of general interest recognised by the Union" in Art. 52.1 EUCFR. This implies that restrictions cannot be justified merely by reference to aims for which a competence is conferred upon the EU even though the Union legislator may not impose restrictions to fundamental rights for the pursuit of discretionary chosen aims or "as such". Safeguarded interests include among others the status of churches and of secular and religious

[51]According to Art. 52.3 EUCFR "the meaning and scope of those rights [i.e. Charter rights which correspond to rights guaranteed by the ECHR] shall be the same as those laid down by the said Convention."

[52]In German terminology it describes the normative obligation for the protection of individual interests, giving the beneficiary the legal power to enforce those interests in a court of law.

[53]See for the differentiation of these three categories Blanke, The Economic Constitution of the European Union, in this Volume, sub. 5.1.

[54]Cf. Ladenburger, in Tettinger and Stern (2006), Art. 52 GrCh para 68, 77 et seq.

communities, the rights of children, and consumer and animal protection.[55] Restrictions of fundamental rights are to be in accordance with the principle of proportionality, in accordance with its definition in Art. 52.1, second sentence, where EUCFR requires appropriateness for purpose as well as necessity (adequateness) and the balancing with other interests. Thus, in addition to objectives of general interest to the Union, the "need to protect the rights and freedoms of others" has to be taken into consideration. Any limitation to the exercise of a fundamental right of the Charter may in each individual case be justified not only by a specific Union interest, but also by individual interests of third parties. In return, however, these conflicting interests are themselves restricted by general limits to the restrictability or "counter limits" (i.e. the so-called *Schranken-Schranken*). In the existing case law on the review of the proportionality of a restriction the ECJ has too strongly stressed the interest of the Community, thereby neglecting the examination of the importance of conflicting interests.[56]

In recent cases the ECJ seems to be, however, more sensitive for the need to weigh and balance the interests involved on the ground of the principle of proportionality.[57] Thus, the Court argues, that any limitation to the exercise of a fundamental right "must apply only in so far as is strictly necessary".[58] The ruling also spells out the clear message to the Union's institutions to justify more intensively their measures, both, with regard to pursue the adoption of measures which might affect fundamental rights and in the context of a judicial review of such measures.[59]

If the Court more thoroughly systemises also the methodical approach of the examination of fundamental rights, expectations set in the Charter will be met: Due to its legally binding force the Charter will make it more straightforward for individuals to enforce rights which are guaranteed under international law. Although the Charter reaffirms rights and principles which already substantially exist, albeit in many cases only at an international level, the Luxembourg Court will turn the "soft" law standards in the field of international human rights on the basis of the Charter into "hard" law. A risk could be that a difference in approach to the human rights guarantees which are enshrined identically in the Charter and in the Convention may develop between the Strasbourg and Luxembourg Court. This might be remedied by the Union signing up to the ECHR.

---

[55]Cf. Ladenburger, in Tettinger and Stern (2006), Art. 52 GrCh para 37.

[56]Cf. Selmer (1998), pp. 81 et seqq.; critical Mayer (2009), p. 98; see also v. Arnauld (2008).

[57]Cf. Schroeder (2011), pp. 465 et seqq.

[58]Joined Cases C-92/09 and C-93/09 *Schecke GbR and Eifert v Land Hessen* (ECJ 9 November 2010) para 77, 86.

[59]This can be inferred from Case C-58/08 *Vodafone et al. v Secretary of State for Business Enterprise and Regulatory Reform* (ECJ 8 June 2010) para 63 et seqq., 68 et seqq.

2.3.4 Further Provisions on Interpretation

Art. 6.1 (3) TEU also stipulates that the Charter rights are to be interpreted in accordance with the "horizontal" provisions of the Charter, i.e. Art. 51 through 54 EUCFR clarifying the Charter's scope and applicability and with "due regard" to the Explanations prepared by the Bureau of the Charter Convention. The Explanations now referred to in this general provision on fundamental rights of the TEU, and retained in the Preamble to the Charter (5th recital, sentence 2) as well as in its Art. 52.7, are attached to the text of the Charter and published in the same Official Journal as the Charter itself.[60]

The Explanations do not have the value of an "agreement relating to the treaty which was made between all the parties in connection with the conclusion of the treaty" or of an "instrument which was made by one or more parties in connection with the conclusion of the treaty" in the sense of Art. 31 VCLT.[61] These Explanations are rather "supplementary means of interpretation, including the preparatory work of the treaty and the circumstances of its conclusion" in the sense of Art. 32 VCLT. In literature and comments on Art. 6 TEU this meaning of the Explanations is briefly confirmed by emphasis on their lack of any "legal value" or on their "non-binding" character.[62]

Article 51.1 EUCFR provides that the Charter provisions are addressed to EU institutions, bodies, offices and agencies of the Union and to Member States only when implementing EU law, a qualification which is absent from the terms of Art. 6.1 TEU itself. This means that the ECJ will be in a position to examine whether the Member States comply with their obligations resulting from the fundamental rights guarantees of the Charter when implementing Union law because exclusion of this control on the basis of ex-Art. 46 lit. d TEU is no longer possible since the entry into force of the Lisbon Treaty (Art. 19.3 lit. c TEU). The Charter also provides that the principle of subsidiarity is to be respected. Article 51.2 EUCFR states that the Charter does not extend the field of application of Union law beyond the powers of the Union; nor does it establish or modify any Union powers or tasks. From Art. 51.1 EUCFR it follows that it does not apply to situations involving purely domestic

---

[60]Cf. the *Declaration concerning the explanations relating to the Charter of Fundamental Rights (Declaration 12)* annexed to the Treaty establishing a Constitution for Europe, O.J. C 310/424 (2004), updated once more in O.J. C 303/17 (2007). Following Pernice (2008), p. 242, the explanations will have at least symbolically "more weight" by reason of their new position within the Treaty compared to the Constitutional Treaty where they have been situated amongst the basic principles and objectives.

[61]Cf. the Introduction to the explanations (O.J. C 303/17 (2007)): These explanations "do not as such have the status of law, they are a valuable tool of interpretation intended to clarify the provisions of the Charter".

[62]Ladenburger, in Tettinger and Stern (2006), Art. 52 GrCh para 127; Kornobis-Romanowska, Strengthening of an Individual's Status in the EU after the EU's Accession to the ECHR – Consequences for the Legislator and National Courts – Practical Results, in Barcz (2009), Sect. 65 I pp. 305 et seqq.

law; for the Charter to be directly relevant there must be a link to Union law. National courts may, however, find inspiration in EU law even when applying purely domestic law.

Article 52.3 EUCFR contains the obligation to an interpretation of the provisions of the Charter that is consistent with the ECHR ("the meaning and scope of those rights shall be the same"); this does not change the ECHR's character as a source for the interpretation of the law (Art. 6.3 TEU).[63] As a result, this leads to a synchronisation of substantive law of the Charter with the law of the Convention. Although this does not mean that the Convention becomes an integral part of Union law, the normative content of the Charter provisions is adapted to that of the corresponding provisions of the Convention by means of systematic interpretation. In principle, this inclusion refers to the scope, the definition of what is considered an interference with fundamental rights as well as the requirements of the corresponding Charter provisions to justification of interferences. Nonetheless, it also requires – depending on the respective level of the review – a differentiated and, referring to the individual case, flexible solution.[64] Article 52.4 EUCFR provides that rights resulting from constitutional traditions common to the Member States are to be interpreted in harmony with those traditions.[65] Thus, Art. 52.4 EUCFR can be understood in the sense that in addition to the general reservation of Art. 52.1 EUCFR – and also in addition to Art. 52.3 EUCFR – one can deduce further requirements for the justification of limitations.[66] In particular, the need for guidance on the distinction between "rights" and "principles" was the justification for the new Art. 52.5 EUCFR.

2.3.5 Limits of the Guarantees

Article 6.1, sentence 2, TEU makes clear that "[t]he provisions of the Charter shall not extend in any way the competences of the Union as defined in the Treaties". It also confirms that the Charter does not extend the field of application of Union law or of Union tasks. Additionally the Declaration on the Charter of Fundamental Rights (included in the Final Act under No. 1) was annexed to the Treaty of Lisbon, in which the Conference and thus all of the Member States assert that the Charter which is to have a legally binding force confirms the fundamental rights guaranteed by the ECHR and as they result from the constitutional traditions common to the Member States.

New Art. 6.3 TEU reflects ex-Art. 6.2 TEU-N, a provision which has been used extensively by the ECJ in developing its case law on fundamental rights. It provides that "[f]undamental rights, as guaranteed by the [ECHR] and as they result from the

[63]See Kingreen, in Calliess and Ruffert (2011), Art. 52 GrCh para 21, 37 et seq.

[64]See Kingreen, in Calliess and Ruffert (2011), Art. 52 GrCh para 27 et seqq.

[65]Cf. Frenz (2009), para 132 et seqq.

[66]Schneiders (2010), pp. 226 et seqq.

constitutional traditions common to the Member States, shall constitute general principles of the Union's law." Limits to a wide interpretation of the European "Bill of Rights" by the ECJ are not only set by the already mentioned Art. 6.1, first sentence, TEU and the Declaration on the Charter of Fundamental Rights, but also by Art. 52.6 EUCFR, which provides that full account is to be taken of national laws and practices as specified in the Charter, and this would appear to give some weight to the references to national law.

On the basis of Art. 6 TEU it can therefore be concluded that the application of the Charter is limited on several levels by conditions set in the Charter itself, confirmed subsequently by the Treaty of Lisbon in Art. 6.1 and given political weight by the Declaration of the Conference (i.e. the Member States).

3 The Loss of Unity and Unanimity on Human Rights Standards Among the Member States?

The somewhat awkward status of the Charter of Fundamental Rights came to an end with the ratification of the Treaty of Lisbon. However, unanimity among the Member States' governments has come at a price. The United Kingdom and subsequently Poland have insisted on a Protocol on the application of the Charter of Fundamental Rights, containing an exemption from the "operation of specific provisions of the Charter" (10th indent of Protocol No. 30) in both countries. According to the Protocol, neither "the Court of Justice of the European Union, [n]or any court or tribunal of Poland or of the United Kingdom" will be entitled "to find that the laws, regulations or administrative provisions, practices or action of Poland or of the United Kingdom are inconsistent with the fundamental rights, freedoms and principles that [the Charter] reaffirms" (Art. 1.1 of the Protocol). Title IV referring to "social rights" ("solidarity") does not create "justiciable rights applicable to Poland or the United Kingdom except insofar as Poland or the United Kingdom has provided for such rights in its national law" (Art. 1.2 of the Protocol). References in the Charter to domestic law or practice do not apply to the United Kingdom or Poland unless the rights are recognised in the law or practices of these countries (Art. 2 of the Protocol). As provided in Art. 51 TEU, the Protocol has the same legal value as the Treaties.

According to the British Foreign Minister in the European Scrutiny Committee of the UK House of Commons this is not meant to be an "opt-out" from the Charter as a whole.[67] *Alan Dashwood*, who has advised the UK government extensively on the

[67]Cf. European Scrutiny Committee, Thirty-fifth Report of Session 2006-07, European Union Intergovernmental Conference, HC 1014; cf. in this sense also: Pernice (2008), p. 245; Mayer (2009), p. 94. See also Barnard (2008), p. 258, according to whom "for Eurosceptic audiences, the UK government has been willing to let it be referred to as an opt-out. Yet for more informed audiences the UK government insists that it is not an opt-out but merely clarification."

Constitutional Treaty, also writes that the function of the Protocol is "interpretative – to state unequivocally, and with the force of primary law, what ought to be obvious from a reading of the Charter in the light of the horizontal provisions and of the official explanations."[68] This view is supported by the Preamble to the Protocol which says, as mentioned above, that the purpose of the Protocol is to "clarify certain aspects of the application of the Charter." In other words, following this view the Protocol contains clarifications, but does not change the *status quo* of the protection of fundamental rights in the EU and does not exclude the jurisdiction of the ECJ in this field in relation to Poland and the United Kingdom.

However, depending on the reading of Art. 1 of the Protocol, there might be elements of opt-out for the United Kingdom and Poland. While Art. 1.2 states that "nothing in Title IV of the Charter creates justiciable rights applicable to Poland or the United Kingdom except insofar as Poland or the United Kingdom has provided for such rights in its national law", the Protocol obviously covers some economically crucial provisions of the Charter on workers' rights under the heading of "Solidarity". The United Kingdom believed that the content of this title related to non-justiciable *principles*, not rights (*supra* Sect. 2.2), so that the question of their direct effectiveness would not arise. However, two of the provisions under the title of solidarity which caused British businesses most concern, Art. 28 EUCFR on collective bargaining and action and Art. 30 EUCFR on unjustified dismissal, appear to be drafted in terms of rights, not principles, and are thus potentially justiciable.[69] Article 1.2 of the Protocol therefore makes clear that if any of the provisions of Title IV are in fact classed as rights they are not justiciable in respect to the United Kingdom and Poland. Why are Art. 28 and Art. 30 EUCFR so sensitive to the United Kingdom and Poland, respectively?[70]

The United Kingdom, with its absence of a written constitution, has no "right to strike". Instead, trade unions enjoy only immunity from being sued in tort when certain conditions are satisfied. By contrast, in the immunity-based system, strikes are seen as unlawful and trade unions have to justify why they are going on strike. Given the structural differences in approach between common law and civil law, the UK government has been concerned about the EU introducing a "right" to strike in the United Kingdom. Beyond this, UK businesses were concerned that Art. 30 EUCFR gave individuals the right to protection against unfair dismissal. Finally,

[68]'The paper tiger that is no threat to Britain's fundamental rights' *Parliamentary Brief*, 10 March 2008 (http://www.thepolitician.org/articles/the-paper-tiger-646.html).

[69]See e.g. the UK's submissions to the Court in the *Viking* case (Case C-438/05 *International Transport Workers' Federation* v. *Viking Line ABP* [2007] ECR I-000) discussed in Bercusson, 'The Trade Union Movement and the European Union: Judgment Day' (2007) 13 *ELJ* 279, 300; see also Mik, The Charter of Fundamental Rights: determinants of Protective Standards, in Barcz (2009), Sect. 14 I p. 75.

[70]See for the following interpretation Barnard (2008), p. 269 et seqq.

there is a perplexing irony about the Polish position under Art. 1.2 of the Protocol in particular. The Polish Declaration on the Protocol stated:[71]

> Poland declares that, having regard to the tradition of social movement of 'Solidarity' and its significant contribution to the struggle for social and labour rights, it fully respects social and labour rights, as established by European Union law, and in particular those reaffirmed in Title IV of the Charter of Fundamental Rights of the European Union.

This Declaration appears to undermine significantly any potential use of Art. 1.2 of the Protocol as an "opt-out" with respect to Poland. In fact, as this Declaration shows, Poland's concerns are not with social and labour rights. Poland's real fears lie with subjects such as gay marriage and abortion, but the Protocol does not touch on these issues.[72]

Reading the Protocol, one comes to the conclusion that in "reality" it "lies somewhere in between [. . .] opt-out" and mere "clarification".[73] Federal admissibility of different levels of protection of fundamental rights – even in the application of federal law in the relation between the states and the federation – can be seen in the federal model of the Federal Republic of Germany (Art. 142 GG) with derogation from the principle that "Federal law shall take precedence over *Land* law" (Art. 31 GG). However, this provision requires "consistency" of the fundamental rights provided for by *Land* constitutions and the rights of the individual as guaranteed by the federal constitution.[74] The differences regarding fundamental rights between the relevant norms of labour and social rights in the United Kingdom (and Poland) on the one hand and the guarantees of the Charter of Fundamental Rights of the Union on the other would be substantially diminished in that, regardless of the Charter's limited scope of application in these two countries, their commitment to the fundamental rights of the ECHR – which are in most cases identical to those of the Charter – and the constitutional traditions common to the Member States (Art. 6.3 TEU) as general principles of law and thus the binding case law of the ECJ in the field of fundamental rights remain untouched. The binding case law relating to fundamental rights of the ECtHR would remain unaffected. In the field of the protection of fundamental rights the Union seems to become once

[71]*Declaration (No. 62) by the Republic of Poland concerning the Protocol on the application of the Charter of Fundamental Rights of the European Union in relation to Poland and the United Kingdom* annexed to the TEU, O.J. C 83/358 (2010).

[72]With regard to gay marriage the Charter is concerned in so far as the anti-discrimination clause (Title III: Art. 21 EUCFR) prohibits also discriminations on grounds of "sexual orientation".

[73]Convincingly Barnard (2008), p. 258.

[74]Article 28.1 GG reads: "The constitutional order in the *Länder* must conform to the principles of a republican, democratic and social state governed by the rule of law, within the meaning of this Basic Law. In each *Land*, county and municipality the people shall be represented by a body chosen in general, direct, free, equal and secret elections. In county and municipal elections, persons who possess citizenship in any member state of the European Community are also eligible to vote and to be elected in accord with European Community law [. . .]." See also Tettinger and Schwarz, in v. Mangoldt et al. (2010), Art. 28 GG para 11 et seqq. (26 et seqq.) with further reference.

more a "Europe à la carte". The unity and the common basis of values in EU law seem to be partly diminished.

4 The Relationship Between the System of Protection of Fundamental Rights by the Union and the ECHR

4.1 Coherence in the Case Law

For some time the Luxembourg Court has obviously tried to stress coherence of its case law with that of the ECtHR.[75] So far the most obvious conflict between the two European courts in the case of *Senator Lines* has been alleviated by the ECtHR's decision on dismissal of the action. This case was about provisional legal protection against the setting of a fine by the European Commission for infringement of European competition rules. The applicant company – the Senator Lines shipping company with its registered office in Bremen, Germany – regarded its economic existence as threatened due to the refusal of deferment of the required security by means of a bank guarantee. It took legal remedies against the decision of the ECJ[76] by bringing an action before the ECtHR (as *ultima ratio*) against all the Member States of the EC – a highly unusual procedure. In a later decision, which became final in the absence of an appeal, the Luxembourg Court of First Instance quashed the fine.[77] Therefore the ECtHR in accordance with the ECHR could find that there was no continuing infringement of fundamental rights and that the applicant was not a victim of a violation.[78] Hence there was no more room for a possible diverging interpretation of fundamental rights by the ECtHR and the ECJ.

4.2 Remaining Potential for Conflict

At the same time there still remains the potential for conflicts in European competition law, in particular concerning the right to refuse to provide testimony in anti-trust suits or the question whether the Court provides the same level of protection for actions within business premises as for those within private residences or whether it will – regardless of the decision by the ECtHR in the case of *Niemietz*[79] – stick to the

[75] Cf. Krüger and Polakiewicz (2001), p. 97.

[76] Case T-191/98 R *DSR-Senator Lines v Commission* (CFI 21 July 1999), appealed by Case C-364/99 P(R) *DSR-Senator Lines v Commission* (ECJ 14 December 1999).

[77] Joined Cases T-191/98, T-212/98 to T-214/98 *Atlantic Container Line et al. v Commission* (CFI 30 September 2003).

[78] Case 56672/00 *SENATOR LINES GmbH v Members of the EC* (ECtHR 10 March 2004).

[79] Case 13710/88 *Niemietz v Germany* (ECtHR 16 December 1992).

general line of the *Hoechst* decision[80] in the sense of differentiating between "private premises" and "business premises", thereby holding on to the distinction between "employed" and "self-employed". According to Advocate General *Juliane Kokott* the protection of legal professional privilege does not apply for the benefit of enrolled in-house lawyers in anti-trust proceedings of the European Commission. Internal company communications with enrolled in-house lawyers, even if he/she is a member of a Bar or Law Society, does not enjoy legal professional privilege as guaranteed by fundamental rights at Union level (Art. 8.1 ECHR in conjunction with Art. 6.1 ECHR and Art. 6.3 lit. c ECHR – right to fair trial – Art. 7 EUCFR in conjunction with Art. 47 (1), Art. 47 (2), second sentence, and Art. 48 (2) EUCFR) between a lawyer and his client.[81] It could not be concluded that the principle of equal treatment (Art. 20 and 21 EUCFR) was infringed as "with regard to their respective degrees of independence when giving legal advice or providing representation in legal proceedings, there is therefore usually a significant difference between a lawyer in private practice or employed by a law firm, on the one hand, and an enrolled in-house lawyer, on the other."[82] Hence the protection of the legal privilege with regard to documents seized during a search according to EU anti-trust law is reduced. Evidently, the ECJ is influenced by the argument that further-reaching protection of fundamental rights would interfere with the proper functioning of effective control by the authorities of compliance with anti-trust and competition rules.[83]

4.3 The Accession of the Union to the European Convention for the Protection of Human Rights and Fundamental Freedoms of 4 November 1950

In the light of the efforts for coherence, compatibility and harmony between the legal principles of the existing Treaties (Art. 6.3 TEU), the rights of the Charter of Fundamental Rights and the rights contained in the Strasbourg Convention, Art. 6.2, first sentence, TEU provides for the accession of the Union to the ECHR. By now the guarantees of the ECHR form a *European public order* with objective character, i.e. an order that is not limited to bilateral commitments among states but rather imposes objective obligations on them. The Court called the Convention

[80]Joined Cases 46/87 and 227/88 *Hoechst v Commission* (ECJ 21 September 1989) para 57 et seqq.

[81]Cf. Opinion of Advocate General J. Kokott delivered on 29 April 2010, Case C-550/07 P *Akzo Nobel Chemicals and Akcros Chemicals v Commission et al.*, para 45 et seqq. (in appeal procedures of Akzo Ltd. Against a judgment of the General Court – (former Court of First Instance), Joined Cases T-125/03 and T-253/03 *Akzo Nobel Chemicals Ltd und Akcros Chemicals Ltd v Commission* (CFI 17 September 2007).

[82]Opinion of Advocate General J. Kokott delivered on 29 April 2010, Case C-550/07 P *Akzo Nobel Chemicals and Akcros Chemicals v Commission et al.*, para 75 et seqq. (82).

[83]See Schwarze (2005), p. 43 et seq.

"a constitutional instrument of European public order (*ordre public*)", thereby stressing the states' obligation "to have regard to the special character of the Convention and the Protocols thereto as a treaty for the collective enforcement of human rights and fundamental freedoms."[84] As a consequence of the accession of the Union to the Convention the Strasbourg Court will be recognised as the final authority in the field of human rights.

At the same time the new provision meets the requirement of a treaty revision spelled out by the ECJ in its Opinion 2/94 on the accession of the EC to the ECHR.[85] Realisation of the accession is only possible by meeting the strict prerequisites set by the Lisbon Treaty. The Council must decide unanimously to accept the terms of accession. Moreover, accession requires not only the consent of the European Parliament but also of all Member States in accordance with their respective constitutional requirements (Art. 218.6 lit. a (ii), 218.8 TFEU). Additionally, there was a need to create an exception (i.e. make special provision) for the accession of the Union to the ECHR to which originally only members of the Council of Europe could accede (Art. 59 ECHR, Art. 4 of the Statute of the Council of Europe). This was done by Protocol No. 14, which entered into force on 1 June 2010. Pursuant to its Art. 17, a new paragraph has been inserted in Art. 59 ECHR providing that "[t]he European Union may accede to this Convention."

This amendment was not sufficient to allow for an immediate accession to the ECHR. The accession of the EU, which is neither a State nor a member of the Council of Europe and which has its own specific legal system, requires certain adaptions to the Convention system. These include: amendments to provisions of the Convention to ensure that it operates effectively with the participation of the EU; supplementary interpretative provisions; adaptations of the procedure before the ECtHR to take into account the characteristics of the legal order of the EU, in particular the specific relationship between an EU Member State's legal order and that of the EU itself; and other technical and administrative issues not directly pertaining to the text of the Convention, but for which a legal basis is required.

These recent amendments, defining the status of the European Union as a High Contracting Party to the Convention and the Protocols, were set out in the "Agreement on the Accession of the European Union to the European Convention on Human Rights and Fundamental Freedoms".[86] Accession to the Convention and the Protocols will impose on the European Union obligations with regard only to acts, measures or omissions of its institutions and bodies, offices or agencies, or of persons, acting on their behalf. Pursuant to Article 6.2 TEU it does not "require the European Union to perform an act or adopt a measure for which it has no competence under European Union law" (amendment to Art. 59.2 lit. c ECHR).

[84]Cf. Ress (2002), p. 3.

[85]Opinion 2/94 *Accession by the Community to the European Convention for the Protection of Human Rights and Fundamental Freedoms* (ECJ 28 March 1996).

[86]Draft legal instruments on the accession of the European Union to the European Convention on Human Rights, CDDH-UE(2011)16 final of 19 July 2011.

4.3.1 Relevance of External Control by the ECtHR

Only the accession of the Union to the ECHR will allow European citizens to bring before the ECtHR actions against the decisions of the authorities of the Union or against judgments of the Luxembourg Court which are not in accordance with the ECHR or with the case law of the Strasbourg Court. This will allow legal proceedings (now guaranteed by domestic law in similar situations) where an infringement of the fundamental rights enshrined in the Convention is asserted. Until now at Union level there has been no correlation between the subjection of EU citizens and their legal protection by an external judicial review – although this is demanded by the principle of *subiectio trahit protectionem.*

After the entry into force of the Charter of Fundamental Rights it would have appeared somewhat anachronistic that the EU should remain the only legal area in Europe not subject to external review by the ECtHR. Given the background of extended Union competences through the Treaty of Lisbon, in particular in the area of police and judicial cooperation ("area of freedom, security and justice" – Art. 82 et seqq., 87 et seqq. TFEU), the existence of the Charter implies that the ECJ will be confronted with far more questions having fundamental rights implications than before through request for preliminary rulings. Many issues will contain aspects on which there is yet no established case law of the Strasbourg Court. Therefore, the fourth consideration of the Agreement on the Accession of the EU to the ECHR expressly recognises the need to give the individual "the right to submit the acts, measures or ommissions of the European Union to the external control" of the ECtHR.

With accession, the Union, as did its Member States before it, recognises the necessity for the "sheet anchor of a human rights constitution" (*Ch Tomuschat*), a function which the Convention already performs at the level of the Member States. Due to the lack of specification the Union itself will determine the rank of the ECHR within its legal order. According to the rulings of the ECJ international agreements (as well as international customary law) take precedence over secondary Union law.[87] Secondary law of the Union thus cannot effectively derogate from international obligations of the Union within its legal order. In case of a violation of the Convention by secondary law the ECJ has to declare void the respective act of Union law.[88] The primacy of primary Union law over international agreements and hence also over the ECHR stems from the fact that the Union is not authorised to amend the European Treaties, i.e. the TEU and the TFEU (Art. 48 TEU, Art. 218.5 and 6 TFEU).[89] If, however, a norm of an international agreement, in this case some

[87]Case C-61/94 *Commission v Germany* (ECJ 10 September 1996) para 52; Case C-192/89 *Sevince v Staatssecretaris van Justitie* (ECJ 20 September 1990) para 9.

[88]Schneiders (2010), pp. 259 et seqq., who, regarding primary law, takes a view that differs from the position represented in this text.

[89]In this sense Opinion 2/94 *Accession by the Community to the European Convention for the Protection of Human Rights and Fundamental Freedoms* (ECJ 28 March 1996) para 4.

provisions within the ECHR, has the status of a provision of *ius cogens* these norms will take precedence over primary and secondary Union law. Any conflict would lead to the relevant provision of Union law being invalid (Art. 53 VCLT).[90] As a result the Strasbourg Convention thus – in parallel to its position in between constitutional and ordinary law in Germany – will take its place between secondary and primary law of the Union. This implies that even with the accession it will rank below the Charter of Fundamental Rights, which according to Art. 6.1, second clause, TEU is part of primary Union law. Nonetheless, pursuant to Art. 52.3 EUCFR, the ECHR constitutes the substantive minimum standard also for fundamental rights of the Union which will be interpreted through recourse to the ECHR and to the case law of the ECtHR. The competence of the ECtHR to asses the conformity of EU law with the provisions of the Convention will not prejudice the principle of the autonomous interpretation of EU law.[91]

4.3.2 Safeguarding of Substantive and Procedural Coherence

It has often been said that the accession to the ECHR would assist to avoid any risk of conflict between EU law and the ECHR as interpreted in Strasbourg, by placing fundamental rights on a single consistent foundation throughout the EU. At the same time it appears that in the light of the development of fundamental rights in the case law of the ECJ the argument of creating substantive cohesion between the protection of fundamental rights within the Union and the protection by the Strasbourg system is not as powerful as it was during the debate over the last decades on the accession favoured by the Council of Europe and many Member States. The decisions of the Strasbourg Court have become a "means of orientation"[92] for the ECJ which is reflected in the efforts of the Luxembourg Court to follow the interpretation of the ECHR by the Strasbourg Court in the development of general principles of European law. In the *Bosphorus* decision of 2005 the ECtHR confirmed that the Community enjoyed a level of protection of fundamental rights "equivalent" (i.e. comparable, not identical!) to that of the ECHR (*infra* Sect. 4.4). Accordingly it is to be assumed that a Contracting Party does not deviate from the requirements of the Convention if it merely complies with its obligations required by membership in an international organisation.[93] Such a (refutable)

[90]Cf. Schmalenbach, in Calliess and Ruffert (2011), Art. 216 para 50.

[91]Cf. Kingreen, in Calliess and Ruffert (2011), Art. 6 EUV para 27; see also DRAFT Explanatory report the Agreement on the Accession of the European Union to the European Convention on Human Rights, CDDH-UE (2011) 16 final of 19 July 2011, p. 11 para 5.

[92]Cf. H. Mosler, Schlussbericht, in: I. Meier, Europäischer Rechtsschutz, Schranken und Wirkungen, 1982, p. 355, cited in Ress (2002), p. 4.

[93]Case 45036/98 *Bosphorus Hava Yollar Turizm ve Ticaret Anonim Şirketi v Ireland* (ECtHR 30 June 2005) para 152 et seq.: While the Convention "does not prohibit Contracting Parties from transferring sovereign power to an international (including a supranational) organization [each]

"presumption of compliance with the Convention"[94] is given when substantive guarantees exist and judicial control mechanisms are also provided. Nonetheless, in the context of the increase in ECJ decisions with fundamental rights implications which is to be expected (*supra* Sect. 4.3.1) and given the *Bosphorus* decision, one should recall a statement by *G. Ress* in 2002 according to which it "cannot be excluded that with a lack of an institutional link (by means of accession) the interpretation and application of the ECHR (by the ECtHR and the ECJ) will grow apart without there being any (other) remedy."[95]

At least as urgent as the aspect of ensuring substantive coherence is now the need for procedural coherence between the legal order of the Union and the Strasbourg system.[96] Despite the tendencies of substantive convergence the Union could not itself be party in proceedings before the ECtHR due to its not being a Party to the ECHR. Only accession will allow EU institutions to directly present their standpoint before the Strasbourg Court in cases related to Union law (*ius standi*). At present the Member States are solely responsible for compliance with the ECHR, and also in so far as the execution or application of Union law is concerned. How paradoxical this situation is became evident in the *Matthews* case,[97] which dealt with the issue of the inhabitants of Gibraltar being denied the right to vote in the European Parliament elections. This right was expressly excluded by the terms of Annex II to the Council Decision and the Act of 1976 concerning the European Parliament election by direct universal suffrage.[98] This Act of 1976 was not an

---

Contracting Party is responsible under Article 1 of the Convention for all acts and omissions of its organs regardless of whether the act or omission in question was a consequence of domestic law or of the necessity to comply with international legal obligations."

[94]Case 45036/98 *Bosphorus Hava Yollar Turizm ve Ticaret Anonim Şirketi v Ireland* (ECtHR 30 June 2005) para 156: "[T]he presumption will be that a State has not departed from the requirements of the Convention when it does no more than implement legal obligations flowing from its membership of the organization. However, any such presumption can be rebutted if, in the circumstances of a particular case, it is considered that the protection of the Convention rights was manifestly deficient. In such cases, the interest of international cooperation would be outweighed by the Convention's role as a constitutional instrument of European public order." Unlike the *Bundesverfassungsgericht* ("*Solange II*") the ECtHR does not a priori abstain from an evaluation of the justification and holds complaints, which claim an insufficient level of protection of fundamental rights of the Union, inadmissible pursuant to Art. 35 ECHR; cf. Haratsch (2006), p. 935.

[95]Ress (2002), p. 5 (our translation); Kingreeen, in Calliess and Ruffert (2011), Art. 6 EUV para 23 holds that divergences in case law are "not very likely anymore."

[96]See the third consideration of the Draft Agreement on the Accession of the European Union to the European Convention on Human Rights, CDDH-UE(2011)16 final of 19 July 2011, p. 2.: "Considering that the accession of the European Union to the Convention will enhance coherence in human rights protection in Europe." Cf. also Kornobis-Romanowska, in Barcz (2009), Sect. 65 I pp. 305 et seqq.

[97]Case 24833/94 *Matthews v United Kingdom* (ECtHR 18 February 1999).

[98]Council Decision 76/787/ECSC, EEC, Euratom *relating to the Act concerning the election of the representatives of the Assembly by direct universal suffrage*, O.J. L 278/1 (1976), corr. O.J. L 326/32 (1976).

ordinary legislative act of the ECs but an international agreement supplementing the primary law of the EC and thus part of Community law. Hence, it could not be challenged before the ECJ.

The ECtHR affirmed the applicability of Art. 3 of Protocol No. 1 to the ECHR and thus a violation of the European *status activus* (i.e. the human right to free expression in the choice of the legislature). By that the Strasbourg Court assumed a continuing collective responsibility of the Member States to ensure an interpretation of transferred sovereign powers in a way that is in conformity with the Convention. However, the changes to Union law necessary in such a case could not be made solely by the State found in breach by the Court in Strasbourg. In the *Matthews* case, proceedings had been taken only against the United Kingdom, and not against all of the then Member States of the Union. Hence, the accession of the Union to the ECHR is a logical and useful supplement to the codification of the Charter of Fundamental Rights, not only for reasons of *substantive* coherence between the law of the Union and of the Convention but also to establish legal clarity and certainty.

4.4 Jurisdictional Competition and Coherence: Normative Precautions of the Charter of Fundamental Rights

Article 6.2 TEU contains an authorisation for the accession of the Union to the ECHR as well as a commitment of the Member States to ensure this very accession, which requires an amendment of the Convention according to the Protocol (No. 8) on the accession of the Union to the ECHR (Art. 1). In the long run the accession will contribute to a decrease of potential divergences in the case law of the Strasbourg and the Luxembourg Court. Competition among the courts has been recognised as an element with structural effects on the law in Europe.[99] It results from overlapping functions of lègal protection in the European "compound of constitutions" (*Verfassungsverbund*) and leads to potential areas of conflict.[100]

Such areas of overlap are of special interest in federal and confederal (EU) multilevel governance systems. However, the relationship between the ECJ and the ECtHR is not free from conflict either. This is especially true in cases in which the ECJ established a certain interpretation of the guarantees before the ECtHR and then found itself subject to correction due to subsequent decisions by the Strasbourg Court (*Hoechst* decision). Despite the expectation that the Luxembourg Court would "revise its case law in the sense of an approach towards the Strasbourg

[99]Cf. Merli (2007); Ch. Menè, Judicial review of the relationship between the European courts and the national constitutional courts (Germany, Italy and Spain), PhD thesis 2008.

[100]Cf. Krüger and Polakiewicz (2001), p. 98; Oeter (2007).

Court" the accession of the Union to the ECHR resembles a strategy for conflict prevention. Additionally, with the Treaty of Lisbon this is all the more necessary since the inclusion of the area of freedom, security and justice in the Community method (Art. 67 TFEU) implies an increase of Union competences in areas with sensitive human rights implications (such as asylum, immigration policy and police and judicial cooperation in criminal matters) as a result of which divergences in the case law of the two courts will be more likely.

The situation of a *horizontal* competition between the Strasbourg and the Luxembourg jurisdictions regarding the protection of human rights is the *ratio legis* of Art. 52.3 EUCFR which attempts to ensure the coherence of the European protection of fundamental rights intended by Art. 6.3 TEU in the relation between the ECHR and the EUCFR. Through the transfer clause of sentence 1 of Art. 52.3 EUCFR, which also includes the case law of the ECtHR and of the ECJ, the "meaning and scope" of the rights granted by the ECHR is adopted where these rights are reflected in the Charter. In this context the judgments of the ECtHR have a prejudicial effect for the ECJ in the way of interpretation.[101] Exceptions in the scope are transferred from the law of the Convention if it cannot be inferred from the Charter that a more comprehensive protection than in the Convention is intended.[102] The guarantees of these rights and their possible restrictions are determined in the legal order of the Union by the established principles of the application of the ECHR. It also results from Art. 52.3 EUCFR that the law of the Convention covers all the sovereign action which – directly or indirectly – has a negative effect on the fundamental rights of the individual. In addition to limitations of fundamental rights this may also include a violation of a duty to protect as being in need of justification.[103] The restrictions on the limitations as they result from the ECHR influence the general provision on the restriction of limitations of Art. 52.1 EUCFR but does not replace it.[104]

Upon request the Praesidium of the Convention on Fundamental Rights in its Explanations compiled a list of those provisions of the Charter that correspond to rights of the ECHR as well as a summary of Charter provisions whose scope is wider than that of the corresponding ECHR provisions.[105] Hence, Art. 52.3 EUCFR directly binds the European institutions to the equivalent rights within the ECHR. This in effect ensures that even before the accession of the Union to the ECHR the institutions of the EU must observe the Convention.[106] In so far as Charter provisions correspond to rights granted by the ECHR they have the same meaning and scope. Sentence 2 of Art. 52.3 EUCFR ensures that the level of protection

[101]Schneiders (2010), pp. 241 et seqq.

[102]Schneiders (2010), pp. 180 et seqq.

[103]Schneiders (2010), pp. 184 et seqq.

[104]See Kingreen, in Calliess and Ruffert (2011), Art. 52 GrCh para 28, 38.

[105]Explanation on Article 52 – Scope and interpretation of rights and principles, no. 1 and 2, O.J. C 303/32 et seqq. (2007).

[106]See Callewaert (2003), p. 200; v. Danwitz, in Tettinger and Stern (2006), Art. 52 GrCh para 51.

provided by the ECHR is observed as the minimum standard. This provision also allows an independent development of protection of fundamental rights in the Union more extensive than the ECHR. This guarantees a limited but at the same time substantively continuing independence of the protection of fundamental rights in the Union from the ECHR.[107] Union law can provide further-reaching protection than the ECHR.

An important landmark judgment in the history of the relations between the two European Courts is certainly the one delivered in the *Bosphorus* case, in which the Strasbourg Court considered the protection of fundamental rights under Community law *sensu stricto* – i.e. within the former so-called first pillar – to be "equivalent" to that which the Convention provides. The Court did state that "equivalent" meant the same as "comparable", as any requirement that the organisation's protection be "identical" rather than "comparable" could run counter to the interests of international cooperation (*supra* Sect. 4.3.2).[108] This general competence of the Luxembourg Court for the review of the Union acts with regard to fundamental rights has been put under the condition of a sort of "*Solange*"-reserve competence (i.e. the reserve competence that the German Federal Constitutional Court claims for itself vis-à-vis the judiciary of the ECJ). This means that the presumption of a principally sufficient level of protection of fundamental rights within the Union may be set aside in the circumstances of a particular case if "it is considered that the protection of Convention rights was manifestly deficient."[109]

Actually there seems to be at least one essential difference between the two approaches. Whereas the German Constitutional Court requires the presumption of equivalence to be rebutted that a general or large-scale drop in the EU-standards be established, under the *Bosphorus* jurisprudence the presumption can be rebutted on a case-by-case basis.[110] Thus, the Strasbourg Court has accepted with respect to the "Convention compliance" of the national implementation of EC law mutual recognition as the rule, stricter scrutiny as the exception. In such exceptional cases it takes on a "residual competence" (*Auffangzuständigkeit*). By that the ECtHR can incidentally review the act of Union law because the Strasbourg Court, unlike the

[107]Cf. Braibant (2001), Art. 52, p. 264; v. Danwitz, in Tettinger and Stern (2006), Art. 52 GrCh para 4, 51 et seqq.

[108]Case 45036/98 *Bosphorus Hava Yollar Turizm ve Ticaret Anonim Şirketi v Ireland* (ECtHR 30 June 2005) para 155: "State action taken in compliance with legal obligations [flowing from the membership in a supranational organization] is justified as long as the relevant organization is considered to protect fundamental rights, as regards both the substantive guarantees offered and the mechanisms controlling their observance, in a manner which can be considered at least equivalent to that for which the Convention provides." Cf. with regard to the assumption of equivalence Haratsch (2006), pp. 927 et seqq. Also Garlicki (2008), p. 509, must concede that "the manifest deficiency test may not be easy to meet and that the burden of proof seems to be placed upon an applicant [. . .]".

[109]Case 45036/98 *Bosphorus Hava Yollar Turizm ve Ticaret Anonim Şirketi v Ireland* (ECtHR 30 June 2005) para 156.

[110]Cf. Wildhaber (2005b), pp. 47 et seq.

German Federal Constitutional Court, is not restricted by the principle of primacy. With the accession of the Union to the ECHR the existing residual competence of the ECtHR will become a competence for all cases in which a violation of Art. 52.3 EUCFR either by a Union act or a domestic act of implementation is asserted, i.e. it is covered by the minimum level of protection set by the ECHR. However, the Strasbourg Court – in the light of the *Bosphorus* decision – is likely to exercise this competence in the event of an individual application (Art. 34 ECHR) brought before it against any such act only if it establishes that the level of protection of fundamental rights against such an act at domestic or at Union level is "manifestly deficient"[111] and leads – in terms of the admissibility of the application – to a "significant disadvantage" (Art. 35.3 lit. b ECHR) of the applicant.

5 The Relationship Between the National (Constitutional) Courts and the Strasbourg Court Within the Judicial Dialogue in Europe

The relationship between the German Federal Constitutional Court and the ECJ – at least until the *Mangold* decision by the ECJ – was characterised by latent judicial conflict regarding the residual competence claimed by the Karlsruhe Court.[112] Differences between the courts in Karlsruhe and Strasbourg, however, are of a substantive nature.[113] Such manifest divergence in the case law of the German Federal Constitutional Court on the one hand and the ECtHR on the other became evident in the mid-1990s in the case of the secondary school teacher *Vogt* who was dismissed from German school service because of her membership in the German Communist Party (*Deutsche Kommunistische Partei, DKP*). This case, which the German Federal Constitutional Court decided not to entertain on the grounds that the constitutional complaint had insufficient "prospects of success", led the ECtHR to criticise the disproportionate interference with freedom of expression and freedom of association since the German Federal Constitutional Court had not banned this party.[114] Nonetheless the Court found it admissible to oblige every civil servant to political loyalty to the Constitution, i.e. to protect the free democratic basic order.

[111]Similarly the expectations of Kingreeen, in Calliess and Ruffert (2011), Art. 6 EUV para 23.

[112]Cf. Frenz (2009), para 146 et seqq.

[113]Limbach (2000), p. 420.

[114]Case 17851/91 *Vogt v Germany* (ECtHR 26 September 1995), EuGRZ 1995, 590 para 60 et seq. and 66 et seqq.

5.1 The Case Görgülü Before German and European Courts

The further development of the relationship between the Strasbourg Court and the national courts can be highlighted on the basis of the *Görgülü* decision of the German *Bundesverfassungsgericht*. In this case the Court had to decide on the right of access to and custody of a father to his son who was born out of wedlock and who was given up for adoption by his mother one day after he was born. In September 2003 the Naumburg Court of Appeal dismissed the application of the biological father Görgülü to award a mandatory injunction recognising such visiting rights. Following this decision *Görgülü*, a Turkish national living in Germany, submitted an application to the ECtHR pursuant to Art. 34 ECHR. The applicant alleged in particular that a court decision refusing him access to and custody of his son violated his right to respect for his family life under Art. 8 ECHR. The Strasbourg Court ruled that the reasons relied on by the Court of Appeal to suspend the applicant's access to his child were insufficient to justify such a serious interference in the applicant's family life. There had therefore been a violation of Art. 8 ECHR. The Naumburg Court of Appeal, however, in two further decisions overturned the judgment of the Federal Constitutional Court and denied the right of access and custody of *Görgülü* to his biological son.[115] In three constitutional complaints which were lodged, the Karlsruhe Court had to rule on the legal relationship between the European Convention on Human Rights and the German Constitution.

The Court stated and reaffirmed in *Görgülü I* that, in Gemany, the Convention and its Protocols have the status of a federal statute. This implies that, in Germany, as in any other country whose domestic law does not treat the Convention as the supreme law of the land, there is a theoretical possibility of conflict between the requirements of the Convention and those of domestic law.

As the German Constitutional Court had pointed out in *Görgülü I*, a problem can arise in areas where the rights of different parties may give rise to conflict, so that any extension of the right of one party will be tantamount to a restriction of the right of another or may conflict with other provisions of the domestic constitution. In such areas, an extensive interpretation by the ECtHR of one of the rights involved may result in a conflict with domestic constitutional law in so far as this protects conflicting rights of others. The *Bundesverfassungsgericht* mentions family law as one of several examples. Giving an extensive reading to the rights of a biological father under Art. 8 ECHR may theoretically result in restricting constitutionally protected rights to family life of foster parents or of the children who live with them. It is with regard to situations of this type that the reasons of the *Görgülü* decision analyse the possibility of conflict between the Convention and domestic law, and the obligations of German courts with respect to this possibility. The Court's observations sound as if "'multipolar situations' were rare birds whereas in

[115]Cited in German Federal Constitutional Court, 2 BvR 1481/04 (Order of 14 October 2004) para 17 (in: BVerfGE 111, 307, 312 et seq.) – *Görgülü I* (English translation available online).

real life such situations are daily reality". It is obvious that in a pronouncement of the Strasbourg Court the interests of third parties are duly taken into account. Hence it follows that the Karlsruhe judges should acknowledge that its emphasis on the peculiarity of "multipolar situations" "lacks solid foundations"; the relevant doctrine is suitable only for instances where general regimes are to be established by way of legislation, but not with respect to the execution of judgments in individual cases.[116]

As the Constitutional Court puts it, the German Basic Law has not "taken the greatest possible steps in opening itself to international-law connections."[117] The greatest possible step would have been to endow international agreements and other international laws with the status of constitutional law – or an even higher status – and thereby to reduce to a minimum or even exclude the possibility of conflict between national and international law. This step has not been taken in Germany – neither generally nor with respect to the Convention in particular. The Convention has only been given the status of an ordinary federal statute.[118]

Nevertheless, "the decision of the [ECtHR] must be taken into account in the domestic sphere, that is, the responsible authorities or courts must discernibly consider the decision and, if necessary, justify understandably why they [. . .] do not follow the international-law interpretation of the law" when interpreting national law – including the fundamental rights and the guarantees.[119] The very vague legal terms "to take into account" and "to consider" are to be interpreted in the sense of a duty to (understandably) justify decisions (*Begründungspflicht*) that arise when a national court in its decision intends to disregard a guarantee of the ECHR in its interpretation by the ECtHR as this would lead to an irresolvable conflict with a norm of German constitutional law. The terminology used by the *Bundesverfassungsgericht* is meant to underline that national courts are required to embed a judgment of the Strasbourg Court into the relevant differentiated and graduated system of law.[120] The Federal Constitutional Court thus signals to the Strasbourg Court once more after the case of *Caroline* that certain balancing

---

[116]Cf. Tomuschat (2010), pp. 524 et seq.

[117]German Federal Constitutional Court, 2 BvR 1481/04 (Order of 14 October 2004) para 34 (in: BVerfGE 111, 307, 318) – *Görgülü I.*

[118]Cf. Lübbe-Wolff (2006), para 8.

[119]German Federal Constitutional Court, 2 BvR 1481/04 (Order of 14 October 2004) para 50 (in: BVerfGE 111, 307, 324 et seq.) – *Görgülü I.*

[120]Cf. Papier (2005), p. 124, who (p. 123) bases the use of the term "to take into account" and "to consider" also on Art. 46.1 ECHR; this Article, Papier argues, provides that final judgments of the Strasbourg Court are only binding on the *contracting party*, and has no universal validity or bindingness (in the meaning of Sect. 31.1 Statute of the Federal Constitutional Court – BVerfGG). Tomuschat (2010), p 523, criticises this passage of the pronouncement of the Constitutional Court as "unfortunate". In his opinion the conclusion drawn at the end of the legal grounds to the effect that the relevant domestic court "is not bound regarding the actual outcome" of the further proceedings (German Federal Constitutional Court, 2 BvR 1481/04 [Order of 14 October 2004] para 69) "fails grossly in reflecting the correct legal position".

decisions not only have to be taken at domestic level but instead are exclusively matters of the national courts. At the same time, however, the Karlsruhe Court allows for national constitutional complaints in case a German court has not taken notice of an ECtHR decision or has disregarded the domestic legal force of the respective judgment. The *Bundesverfassungsgericht* had previously held that it could act in a corrective way only if the erroneous application of Convention law also conflicted with German constitutional law, especially if it was arbitrary.[121] The German Court in its *Görgülü* decision thus shows its effort to strengthen the general concept of a "commitment to international law" (*Völkerrechtsfreundlichkeit*) of the German Basic Law and its willingness to enter into an open analysis of the arguments of the ECtHR on its grounds, which is characteristic of a dialogue of legal orders.[122]

The responsible German authorities have to regularly interpret national laws in the light of the Convention and the binding effect of the judgments of the ECtHR (Art. 46 ECHR), giving primacy to the guarantees of the Convention in the case of a conflict between the Convention and national law.[123] In the case of a violation of German constitutional law caused by the binding effect of a judgment of the Strasbourg Court, the national law, however, prevails on account of its hierarchically superior position. Accordingly, there is namely the possibility of such a contradiction between the Convention and higher-ranking domestic law, and the Federal Constitutional Court has made it clear that in the case of such a conflict, it is the Basic Law – not the conflicting international agreement – that the German courts would have to apply: "The Basic Law accords particular protection to the central stock of international human rights [...]. As long as applicable methodological standards leave scope for interpretation and weighing of interests, German courts must give precedence to interpretation in accordance with the Convention. The situation is different only if observing the decision of the [ECtHR], for example, because the facts on which it is based have changed, clearly violates statute law to the contrary or German constitutional provisions [or] the fundamental

[121]German Federal Constitutional Court, 2 BvR 731/80 (Order of 17 May 1983) para 63 (in: BVerfGE 64, 135, 157) and 2 BvR 209/84 (Order of 13 January 1987) para 90 (in: BVerfGE 74, 102, 128); a limited constitutional review on the application of the Convention by the specialised courts was for the first time affirmed by the Federal Constitutional Court in the order in the case of *Pakelli*, 2 BvR 336/85 (Order of 11 November 1985) (in: NJW 1986, 1425) and then again in 2 BvR 1226/83, 101, 313/84 (Order of 12 May 1987) para 191 et seq. (in: BVerfGE 76, 1, 78) – *Family Reunification*.

[122]Cf. Schilling (2010), pp. 253 et seqq. (255).

[123]German Federal Constitutional Court, 2 BvR 1481/04 (Order of 14 October 2004) para 47 (in: BVerfGE 111, 307, 323 et seq.) – *Görgülü I*: "[T]he binding effect of decisions of the [ECtHR] depends on the area of competence of the State bodies and the relevant law. Administrative bodies and courts may not free themselves from the constitutional system of competencies and the binding effect of statute and law by relying on a decision of the [ECtHR]. Both, a failure to consider a decision of the [ECtHR] and the 'enforcement' of such a decision in a schematic way, in violation of prior-ranking law, may therefore violate fundamental rights in conjunction with the principle of the rule of law" (Art. 20.3 GG).

rights of third parties. 'Take into account' means taking notice of the Convention provision as interpreted by the [ECtHR] and applying it to the case, provided the application does not violate prior-ranking law, in particular constitutional law. In any event, the Convention provision as interpreted by the [ECtHR] must be taken into account in making a decision; the court must at least duly consider it."[124] In this context, however, the Karlsruhe Court refers only to the entirely theoretical situation in which the principal facts of a case have changed after it had already been decided by the Strasbourg Court.[125]

In the cases of *Görgülü II* and *III* the German *Bundesverfassungsgericht* held that the Naumburg Court failed in its obligation to deal with the question "how the Art. 6.2 sentence 1 of the German Basic law" [guarantee of the parents' rights] could be interpreted in a way that respects the obligations of the Federal Republic of Germany under international law."[126] In *Görgülü III* the Federal Constitutional Court reaffirmed that an applicant can by means of a constitutional complaint rely on the affected fundamental right in connection with the principle of the rule of law of the national constitution by alleging that the national authorities have disregarded or not taken into account a judgment of the ECtHR.[127]

The Italian *Corte Costituzionale* comes to a similar conclusion in its landmark decision 349/2007 in which it had to examine the compatibility of an *ordinary* domestic provision with Art. 1 of Protocol No. 1 to the ECHR on the protection of property. The Italian Court confirmed its case law according to which the ECHR ranks as an ordinary law in Italy. At the same time, however, it emphasised the obligation of the "national legislator to respect the provisions of the Convention with the consequence that an ordinary domestic norm that is incompatible with a provision of the ECHR and thus with 'international obligations' pursuant to Art. 117.1 [of the Italian Constitution][128] for those reasons violates this constitutional standard."[129] Also as regards the judges' obligation to interpret domestic law in the

[124]German Federal Constitutional Court, 2 BvR 1481/04 (Order of 14 October 2004) para 62 (in: BVerfGE 111, 307, 329) – *Görgülü I*.

[125]Following Lübbe-Wolff (2006), para 17, "this latter possibility should normally never come to be realized, because, as the Constitutional Court has stressed, courts and other state organs are obliged to do anything legally possible to interpret German law in such a way as to avoid its realization".

[126]German Federal Constitutional Court, 1 BvR 1664/04 (Order of 5 April 2005) para 25 – *Görgülü II* (English translation available online).

[127]German Federal Constitutional Court, 1 BvR 2790/04 (Order of 10 June 2005) para 35 – *Görgülü III* (English translation available online), referring to German Federal Constitutional Court, 2 BvR 1481/04 (Order of 14 October 2004) para 30, 60 et seqq. – *Görgülü I*.

[128]Article 117 of the Italian Constitution (as of 18 October 2001) states: "Legislative powers shall be vested in the State and the Regions in compliance with the Constitution and with the constraints deriving from EU legislation and international obligations [. . .]."

[129]Cf. Italian Constitutional Court, judgment 349/2007 (22 October 2007), Legal considerations sub 6.2 (our translation): "[. . .] l'obbligo del legislatore ordinario di rispettare dette norme, con la conseguenza che la norma nazionale incompatibile con la norma della CEDU e dunque con gli

light of the ECHR there is significant equivalence (even including the wording) between the German *Bundesverfassungsgericht* and the Italian *Corte Costituzionale*. The Italian Constitutional Court regards the ordinary national courts as obliged to "take into consideration Art. 117.1 of the Italian Constitution as the relevant standard for the evaluation and to determine on a systematic basis whether the (national) norm reviewed is in compliance with Art. 1 of Protocol No. 1 to the ECHR as interpreted by the ECtHR." If the ordinary judge concludes that there is no interpretation that would be in conformity with the Convention or if he even doubts this he has to submit the question to the Constitutional Court, which examines the issue in compliance with Art. 117.1 of the Italian Constitution.[130] According to the decision which had to rule on the conformity of an ordinary law with the ECHR, it is not the guarantee of the ECHR itself which has to be "taken into consideration" but rather the national implementing norm of Art. 117.1 of the Italian Constitution which requires an interpretation of domestic law consistent with the "international obligations" of Italy. This is merely a difference of method and not of substance as regards the binding nature of the ECHR. Additionally the Italian Constitutional Court establishes "in a general line" that the guarantees of the ECHR contain "interpretative value" also for the constitutional parameters.[131]

Thus, the *Görgülü* decision series dwelt on the issue of conflict at some length and underlined at the very beginning the "national sovereignty" aspect in the case of a conflict between national law and the rights in the Convention. What aroused particular criticism in this regard is that the Court used the terms "take into account" and "consider" (rather than "abide by", "obey" or "implement") to specify the national courts' duties in dealing with ECtHR judgments, that it referred to certain reserve competences of "sovereignty", and that it seemed to disapprove of applying ECtHR judgments in a "schematic" way.[132] Nevertheless, the Federal Constitutional Court stated the ordinary judge's obligation to interpret German

'obblighi internazionali' di cui all'art. 117, primo comma, viola per ciò stesso tale parametro costituzionale."

[130]Cf. Italian Constitutional Court judgment 349/2007 (22 October 2007), Legal considerations sub 6.2 (our translation): "[...] che deve essere preso in considerazione e sistematicamente interpretato l'art. 117, primo comma, Cost., in quanto parametro rispetto al quale valutare la compatibilità della norma censurata con l'art. 1 del Protocollo addizionale alla CEDU, così come interpretato dalla Corte dei diritti dell'uomo di Strasburgo [...]. Ne consegue che al giudice comune spetta interpretare la norma interna in modo conforme alla disposizione internazionale, entro i limiti nei quali ciò sia permesso dai testi delle norme. Qualora ciò non sia possibile, ovvero dubiti della compatibilità della norma interna con la disposizione convenzionale 'interposta', egli deve investire questa Corte della relativa questione di legittimità costituzionale rispetto al parametro dell'art. 117, primo comma [...]".

[131]Cf. Italian Constitutional Court judgment 349/2007 (22 October 2007), Legal considerations sub 6.1.1 (our translation): "In linea generale, è stato anche riconosciuto valore interpretativo alla CEDU, in relazione sia ai parametri costituzionali che alle norme censurate [...]". The Court thereby refers to judgment n. 505/1995 and ordinanza n. 305/2001.

[132]Lübbe-Wolff (2006), para 9 and 3 with references to Kadelbach (2005), 480, 484, and Cremer (2004), p. 688.

constitutional law (Art. 6.2 GG) in accordance with the international obligations of Germany. While the domestic courts are under an obligation to give full effect to the judgments of the ECtHR, they have to avoid situations in which implementation of an ECtHR judgment would result in violation of constitutionally protected rights of the other parties to the original dispute. If an ordinary court fails to take due account of a decision of the ECtHR, the party concerned may take this to the Constitutional Court as a violation of the relevant constitutional right.[133] Nevertheless, on the part of the ECtHR, the Polish judge admitted in a general comment that "the Court (scil: the ECtHR) must remain particularly cautious in cases concerning private relations, where – at least to some extent – the Convention applies horizontally. The ECtHR lacks full information, here, and local courts seem much better equipped to assess what solution would be best in protecting the rights and interests of all involved parties. Such caution would apply, particularly, to cases in which the lapse of time may change the situation."[134]

As shown in the reasoning outlined above, the German *Bundesverfassungsgericht* (case *Görgülü*) and the Italian *Corte Costituzionale* (decision 349/2007), both recognise the ECHR – regardless of its status in the law of the Member States[135] – as a "constitutional instrument of European public order"[136] in the sphere of protection of human rights which the supreme courts of the States Parties to the Convention cannot escape unless they want to risk "helping" the applicant to gain a claim for *restitutio in integrum* in the sense of satisfaction if he/she successfully sues the relevant State for violation of the Convention or one of its Protocols on the domestic level (Art. 41 ECHR).[137] This process of

[133]Cf. also Papier (2006), p. 2; Dörr (2006), p. 1092; Meyer-Ladewig and Petzold (2005), p. 19; Roller (2004).

[134]Garlicki (2008), p. 521.

[135]Cf. Grabenwarter (2009a), Sect. 3; Hoffmeister (2001), pp. 357 et seqq., 364 et seqq.

[136]Case 15318/89 *Loizidou v Turkey* (ECtHR 18 December 1996) para 70, 75, 93; cf. Hoffmeister (2001), p. 353: ECHR as "fundamental rights constitution [*Grundrechtsverfassung*]"; see already Frowein (1988), p. 152, who calls the ECHR a "European partial constitution [*europäische Teilverfassung*]" which has formed a "common European area of fundamental rights [*gemeineuropäischer Grundrechtsfreiraum*]".

[137]Cf. Case 71503/01 *Assanidze v Georgia* (ECtHR 8 April 2004) para 198: "[A] judgment in which it finds a breach [of the convention] imposes on the respondent State a legal obligation to put an end to the breach and to make reparation for its consequences in such a way as to restore as far as possible the situation existing before the breach." In the *Görgülu* case the ECtHR awarded the applicant 15.000 € in damages: Case 74969/01 *Görgulü v Germany* (ECtHR 26 February 2004). Lübbe-Wolff (2006), para 11 et seq., has stressed – in reference to the *Görgülü I* decision of the FCC (para 34) – that "the statement that the national constitution has precedence is a statement made *from the point of view of domestic law*. [. . .] From the point of view of international law, the matter looks very different. Obviously, a national court which, in a case of conflict between the national constitution and an international agreement, gives precedence to the constitution, will, in doing so, produce a violation of international law [. . .]. In such a case, *future* conflicts of the same type can be avoided by changing the relevant law." See also Weber (2007), p. 1759, critically distancing from the *Görgülü I* decision of the German Federal Constitutional Court.

"constitutionalisation" of international human rights systems (especially the ECHR) forms the third side of a triangle, which due to the danger of an overlapping of the judiciaries at different levels that are behind the substantive regimes of fundamental rights has even been called a "Bermuda Triangle";[138] it consists of three vertices: the various national supreme or constitutional courts, the ECJ and the ECtHR.[139]

5.2 *The Case Caroline von Hannover Before German and European Courts*

In the same line is the ruling of the German Federal Constitutional Court in the last *Caroline* judgment of 26 February 2008 – part of the famous series of landmark judgments in the *Caroline von Hannover* case which have deeply influenced the relationship between the Strasbourg Court and the German *Bundesverfassungsgericht*.[140] The Strasbourg Court had considered that the German courts had not struck a fair balance between the competing interests involved, namely the respect for her private life guaranteed by Art. 8 ECHR against the freedom of expression guaranteed by Art. 10 ECHR. Accordingly the Strasbourg Court held that there had been a violation of Art. 8 ECHR and that it was not necessary to rule on the applicant's complaint relating to the respect for her family life.[141]

The Federal Constitutional Court pointed out in its final decision that the ordinary judges have to interpret the German constitutional provisions on the limits of the freedom of press in the light of the guarantees of the ECHR as they are interpreted by the ECtHR, and that they have to balance the reluctant constitutional guarantees, i.e. the freedom of press on the one hand and the protection of the private life of *Caroline* on the other, in accordance with the relevant guarantees of the ECHR. The *Caroline von Hannover* decisions confirm the thesis of an ongoing

---

[138] See remarks of former Advocate General at the ECJ *C. O. Lenz* to the *Gibraltar* judgment of the ECtHR, EuZW 1999, pp. 311 et seq.; critical Limbach (2000), pp. 417 et seqq.; the term is also used by Garlicki (2008), p. 512, but in the sense of "collisions [within] the triangle of cooperation [that] may degenerate into a 'Bermuda triangle' in which individual rights and liberties might simply disappear".

[139] Cf. Garlicki (2008), pp. 511 et seq.

[140] *Caroline von Hannover* had on several occasions unsuccessfully applied to the German courts for an injunction preventing any further publication of a series of photographs of herself with her children on the ground in the German magazines "Bunte", "Freizeit Revue" and "Neue Post". *Caroline* claimed that they infringed her right to protection to control the use of her image. The Federal Constitutional Court granted the applicant's injunction regarding the photographs in which she appeared with her children on the ground that their need for protection of their intimacy was greater than that of adults. However, the German Constitutional Court considered that the applicant, who was undeniably a contemporary "public figure", had to tolerate the publication of photographs of herself in a public place, even if they showed her in scenes from her daily life rather than engaged in official duties. The Constitutional Court referred in that connection to the freedom of the press and to the public's legitimate interest in knowing how such a person generally behaved in public.

[141] Cf. Case 59320/00 *Hannover v Germany* (ECtHR 24 June 2004).

constitutional discourse about the scope and limits of fundamental rights. Domestic courts and constitutional courts increasingly apply the art of distinction, well-known to common law countries, in order to avoid head-on collisions with the ECHR. This "tactic of avoidance" is deemed to represent a soft answer to the potential ambitions of the ECtHR to become *the* constitutional court of Europe.[142] Nonetheless, the *Caroline* decision of the ECtHR still raises the fundamental question if the Strasbourg Court should provide a "common European [i.e. *ius publicum europaeum*] (minimum) standard for the protection of human rights" through leading – and in structural and systematic terms corrective – decisions rather than through merely "bringing individual justice in a single case" and thereby through "balancing in the individual case".[143]

5.3 Confirmation of Coherent Case Law in Relations Between the German Federal Constitutional Court and the ECtHR: The **Zaunegger** *Case and the Cases* **Schmitz v. Germany** *and* **Mork v. Germany**

Coherence in the case law of the ECtHR and the German Federal Constitutional Court can also be found in the decision of the Karlsruhe Court in the case of *Zaunegger*, which dealt with the question of whether it is in accordance with the German Basic Law that a transfer of parental custody for children born out of wedlock (whether in joint custody or in sole custody) to the father beneath the threshold of removal of custody of Section 1666 BGB (*Bürgerliches Gesetzbuch*, German Civil Code) is not possible against the mother's will, that having regard to the relevant provisions of family law is not possible. The ECtHR when first deciding the case held that the general exclusion of a judicial review of the initial attribution of sole custody to the mother with regard to the aim pursued, i.e. the protection of the well-being of a child born out of wedlock, was disproportionate. Hence, Art. 14 in conjunction with Art. 9 ECHR was violated.[144] Subsequent to and in accordance with this decision the Federal Constitutional Court found that Section 1626a para 1 no. 1 and Section 1672 para 1 BGB in the version of the Act Reforming the Law of Parent and Child (*Gesetz zur Reform des Kindschaftsrechts*) of 16 December 1997[145] are incompatible with Art. 6.2 of the Basic Law.[146]

Given the background of this development it is far from certain whether the assumption will be confirmed that further conflicts between the Federal Constitutional

[142]Nickel (2009), pp. 337 et seq.

[143]Cf. Papier (2005), p. 126 (our translation); agreed on by Müller (2005), p. 23.

[144]Case 22028/04 *Zaunegger v Germany* (ECtHR 3 December 2009).

[145]BGBl. 1997 I, p. 2942.

[146]German Federal Constitutional Court, 1 BvR 420/09 (Order of 21 July 2010) Headnote 1.

Court and the Strasbourg Court are more likely as a stronger ECHR will develop into an independent objective legal order, which like the law of the EU would have *direct* effect within the States Parties to the Convention.[147]

As long as the Council of Europe's "living instrument" keeps growing, differences between the levels of protection of the ECHR and national constitutions can, however, appear anywhere, and anytime.[148] This is particularly true after the series of judgments of the ECtHR in the cases of *M. v. Germany*,[149] *Kallweit v. Germany*,[150] *Schmitz v. Germany*[151] and *Mork v. Germany*.[152] Until 1998, in Germany the maximum duration of the first placement in preventive detention could not exceed ten years. After the relevant provision of the Criminal Code was changed and infinite preventive detention was made possible, and German courts prolonged the detention also of detainees who had been convicted *before* 1998, the ECtHR held that this retrospective application violated the Convention. All provisions on the retrospective prolongation of preventive detention and on the retrospective order of such detention were held incompatible with the Basic Law by the *Bundesverfassungsgericht* which overruled its earlier case law. The German Court held again that "the guarantees of the ECHR have constitutional significance in that they influence the interpretation of fundamental rights and of principles of the rule of law contained in the Basic Law. [Thereby] the Bundesverfassungsgericht takes into account the decisions of the [ECtHR] even if they do not concern the same subject-matter of the dispute. This is based on the de facto function of guidance and orientation which the case law of the ECtHR in interpreting the ECHR contains, even beyond the individual case."[153] With reference to the domestic fundamental rights that "have to be understood as characteristics of human rights and which have absorbed them as minimum standards" (Art. 1.2 GG), the Court explains "the openness of the Basic Law towards international law is the expression of an understanding of 'sovereignty' that not only does not hinder integration into inter- and supranational contexts as well as their further development, but even has that as a precondition. Against this background the 'last word' of the German Constitution does not oppose a European dialogue of the Courts but instead is its normative foundation."[154]

---

[147]In this sense the evaluation of Voßkuhle, in: v. Mangoldt et al. (2010), Art. 93 GG para 87 et seq.

[148]Cf. Ingrid Leijten (2011)

[149]Case 19359/04 *M. v Germany* (ECtHR 17 December 2009).

[150]Case 17792/07 *Kallweit v Germany* (ECtHR 13 January 2011).

[151]Case 30493/04 *Schmitz v Germany* (ECtHR 9 June 2011).

[152]Case 31047/04 and 43386/08 *Mork v Germany* (ECtHR 9 June 2011)

[153]German Federal Constitutional Court, 2 BvR 2365/09 et al. (Judgment of 4 May 2011) para 88, 89 (our translation).

[154]German Federal Constitutional Court, 2 BvR 2365/09 et al. (Judgment of 4 May 2011) para 89 (our translation)

This is a remarkable fact of "dialogue", as indeed, the ECtHR also seems to have noticed. The Court stresses its enthusiastic appreciation of Germany's efforts to comply with the Convention by stating that "[i]t welcomes the Federal Constitutional Court's approach for interpreting the provisions of the Basic Law also in the light of the Convention and this Court's case-law, which demonstrates that court's continuing commitment to the protection of fundamental rights not only on national, but also on European level."[155]

6 The Relationship Between the National Supreme Courts and the Luxembourg Court

6.1 *From a General Guarantee of the Unalterable Standards of Basic Rights Through Ultra Vires Review to Identity Review*

This aspect is mainly focused on the quarrel between the Luxembourg Court and the German Federal Constitutional Court caused by the *Solange I* decision (1974) where the German Court reserved the competence to review mainly secondary Union law (i.e. directives, regulations and decisions) in the light of the fundamental rights enshrined in the German Constitution as far as these legal acts have to be executed by German authorities. In 1986 the German Court determined that the legal protection by the institutions of the EC, especially of the ECJ, was equivalent to the protection of fundamental rights guaranteed by the German list of constitutional rights (*supra* before Sect. 1).[156] In its decision on the Treaty of Maastricht the Federal Constitutional Court confirmed that where necessary it is willing to procedurally guarantee protection of fundamental rights if the substance of these fundamental rights is threatened by a decrease in European standards of fundamental rights.[157]

---

[155] Case 30493/04 *Schmitz v Germany* (ECtHR 9 June 2011) para 41; Case 31047/04 and 43386/08 *Mork v Germany* (ECtHR 9 June 2011) para 54.

[156] German Federal Constitutional Court, 2 BvR 197/83 (Order of 22 October 1986) para 104, 107, 130 (in: BVerfGE 73, 339, 376, 378, 384) – *Solange II*: "There are no decisive factors to lead one to conclude that the standard of fundamental rights which has been achieved under Community law is not adequately consolidated and is only of a transitory nature [. . .]. Nor is it to be expected in the view of the state of European Court case law achieved at the present stage that a decline in the standards of fundamental rights under Community law might result through the legal connection of Community law with the constitutions of member states to an extent that makes it impossible on constitutional grounds to regard a reasonable protection of fundamental rights as being generally available." Cf. the comment of Rupp (1987), pp. 241 et seq.

[157] German Federal Constitutional Court, 2 BvR 2134, 2159/92 (Judgment of 12 October 1993) paras 106, 157 (in: BVerfGE 89, 155, 188, 210) – *Maastricht* (English translation in Oppenheimer 1994, pp. 527–575): "If, for instance, European institutions or authorities were to apply or extend the Union Treaty in some way which was no longer covered by the Treaty in the form which constituted the basis of the German law approving it, the resulting legal act would not be binding

This interrelation between the national reserve competence regarding the "general guarantee of the unalterable standards of basic rights" on the one hand and the guarantee for protection of fundamental rights by the Luxembourg Court "in each individual case for the entire territory of the European Communities" on the other was coined by the Federal Constitutional Court with the term "relationship of cooperation [*Kooperationsverhältnis*]".[158] The "how" of this review, however, remained unanswered. In its decision on the *Banana Market* Regulation the German Court, however, asserted its position on the need for protection of fundamental rights by EC law, with reference to the judgments of the ECJ in relation to the Banana Market Regulation, which, "in so far as they generally safeguard the

on German sovereign territory. The German organs of State would be prevented, on constitutional grounds, from applying those legal acts in Germany. Accordingly, the Federal Constitutional Court examines whether legal acts of the European institutions and bodies keep within or exceed the limits of the sovereign rights granted to them (cf. BVerfGE 58, 1 [30f.]; 75, 223 [235, 242]). [. . .] Hitherto a dynamic extension of the existing Treaties has been based on a liberal application of Article 235 of the EEC Treaty, along the lines of a 'competence to perfect the Treaty' [i.e. the lacuna-filling competence], on the idea of the inherent competences of the European Communities ('implied powers') and on an interpretation of the Treaty as implying the fullest possible utilisation of Community powers ('effet utile') (cf. Zuleeg, in: von der Groeben, Thiesing, Ehlermann, EWG-Vertrag, 4th edition 1991, Art. 2, para 3). In future, however, when Community institutions and bodies interpret rules conferring competence, it will have to be borne in mind that the Union Treaty draws a fundamental distinction between the exercise of a sovereign power granted on a limited basis and amendment of the Treaty. Any interpretation of that Treaty must not, therefore, amount in effect to an extension of it. Such an interpretation of rules conferring competences would not give rise to any binding effect for Germany"; in its decision on the Treaty of Lisbon (German Federal Constitutional Court, 2 BvE 2, 5/08, 2 BvR 1010, 1022, 1259/08, 182/09 (Judgment of 30 June 2009) para 338 (in: BVerfGE 123, 267, 399 et seq.) – *Lisbon*) the Federal Constitutional Court underlines that it had already found in its decision on the Treaty of Maastricht "whether legal instruments of the European institutions and bodies remain within the limits of the sovereign powers conferred on them or if the Community jurisdiction interprets the treaties in an extensive manner that is tantamount to an inadmissible autonomous Treaty amendment."

[158]Cf. German Federal Constitutional Court, 2 BvR 2134, 2159/92 (Judgment of 12 October 1993) para 70 (in: BVerfGE 89, 155, 174 et seq.) – *Maastricht*: "The Federal Constitutional Court guarantees, by virtue of its jurisdiction [. . .], that persons resident in Germany are assured in general of effective protection of basic rights, even in relation to the sovereign power of the Communities, and that this protection is essentially to be regarded as substantively equivalent to the protection of basic rights laid down as inalienable by the Basic Law, especially as the Court guarantees in general the substance of the basic rights. The Federal Constitutional Court thus also safeguards that substance vis-à-vis the sovereign power of the Community (cf. BVerfGE 37, 339 [386]). The acts of a special public authority of a supranational organization, which is separate from the State authority of the Member States, also concern those entitled to basic rights in Germany. They thus affect the guarantees contained in the Basic Law and the tasks of the Federal Constitutional Court which have as their object the protection of basic rights in Germany and, to that extent, not only in relation to German State organs [. . .]. However, the Federal Constitutional Court exercises its jurisdiction over the applicability of secondary Community law in Germany in a 'relationship of cooperation' with the European Court of Justice. The European Court of Justice guarantees the protection of basic rights in each individual case for the entire territory of the European Communities and the Federal Constitutional Court is therefore able to confine itself to providing a general guarantee of the unalterable standard of basic rights (cf. BVerfGE 73, 339 [387])."

essential content of fundamental rights", have been met, because the case law of the ECJ "generally ensure[s] effective protection of fundamental rights as against the sovereign powers of the Communities which is to be regarded as substantially similar to the protection of fundamental rights required unconditionally by the Basic Law."[159] This is considered a confirmation of the formula used by the Federal Constitutional Court in its *Solange II* decision which then was adopted in the first sentence of Art. 23.1 GG.[160] Thus, to revive domestic protection of fundamental rights vis-à-vis acts of secondary Union law would require a – hypothetical – general decline of fundamental rights in their substantive aspects.

A new stage in the relation between German constitutional jurisdiction and the ECJ, which was established to "ensure that in the interpretation and application of the Treaties the law is observed" (Art. 19.1 TEU), could be initiated by the judgment of the Federal Constitutional Court on the Union Treaty of Lisbon.

Here the Court, in an intentionally ambiguous way, claims exclusive competence within the context of an *identity review* (*Identitätskontrolle*) for an *ultra vires review* in accordance with the principle of the Basic Law's openness towards European Law (*Europarechtsfreundlichkeit*) – and in accordance with the principle of subsidiarity (sentence 2 of Art. 5.1 and 5.3 TEU) – "where Community and Union institutions transgress the boundaries of the sovereign powers accorded to them by way of conferred power", especially "if legal protection cannot be obtained at the Union level." It, however, limits this reserve competence for a review to cases of "*obvious* transgressions".[161] On the other hand and with regard to "the [...] core content of the Basic Law's constitutional identity" it claims the right to review "whether due to the action of European institutions, the principles under Article 1 and Article 20 of the Basic Law, which are declared inviolable in Article 79.3 of the Basic Law, are violated."[162] This right – previously claimed by the Federal Constitutional Court in its *Maastricht* judgment – to review (1) "whether legal acts of the European institutions and bodies keep within or exceed the limits of the

[159]German Federal Constitutional Court, 2 BvL 1/97 (Order of 7 June 2000) para 61 (in: BVerfGE 102, 147, 164) – *Banana Market*; Cf. the comment of Classen (2000), pp. 1157 et seqq.

[160]Article 23.1, first sentence, GG: "With a view to establishing a united Europe, the Federal Republic of Germany shall participate in the development of the European Union that is committed to democratic, social and federal principles, to the rule of law, and to the principle of subsidiarity, and that guarantees a level of protection of basic rights essentially comparable to that afforded by this Basic Law."

[161]German Federal Constitutional Court, 2 BvE 2, 5/08, 2 BvR 1010, 1022, 1259/08, 182/09 (Judgment of 30 June 2009) para 240 et seq. (in: BVerfGE 123, 267, 353 et seq.) – *Lisbon*; see also para 339: "[...] in any case in the *clear* absence of a constitutive order to apply the law [...]" (emphasis added).

[162]German Federal Constitutional Court, 2 BvE 2, 5/08, 2 BvR 1010, 1022, 1259/08, 182/09 (Judgment of 30 June 2009) para 240 et seq. (in: BVerfGE 123, 267, 353 et seq.) – *Lisbon*. The Court thereby refers to its judgment 2 BvR 2236/04 (18 July 2005) para 70 (in: BVerfGE 113, 273, 296) – *European Arrest Warrant*.

sovereign rights granted to them"[163] and (2) whether "a general guarantee of the unalterable standards of basic rights" is safeguarded[164] has now been supplemented by the Karlsruhe judges by a third analysis of the revival of the Federal Constitutional Courts' review power that is "rooted in constitutional law."

Referring to the German Federal Constitutional Court, the Polish Constitutional Tribunal also shares the view "that the competences, under the prohibition of conferral, manifest about a constitutional identity, and thus they reflect the values the Constitution is based on [...]. Therefore, constitutional identity is a concept which determines the scope of 'excluding – from the competence to confer competences – the matters which constitute [...] "the heart of the matter", i.e. are fundamental to the basis of the political system of a given state', the conferral of which would not be possible pursuant to Article 90[165] of the [Polish] Constitution."[166] Despite the expansion of the protection of fundamental rights at the international level, and the binding force of the Charter of Fundamental Rights as a means of creation of identity at the supranational level,[167] the national fundamental rights, given their different historical shape and judicial review, remain a key element in the catalogue of identity values of national constitutions[168] and thus vehicles to review the process of transferring "sovereign powers" to the Union.

---

[163]German Federal Constitutional Court, 2 BvR 2134, 2159/92 (Judgment of 12 October 1993) para 106 (in: BVerfGE 89, 155, 188) – *Maastricht*; previously in: German Federal Constitutional Court, 2 BvR 1107, 1124/77 and 195/79 (Order of 23 June 1981) para 91 et seq. (in: BVerfGE 58, 1, 30 et seq.) – *Eurocontrol I*; German Federal Constitutional Court, 2 BvR 687/85 (Order of 8 April 1987) para 43, 58 (in: BVerfGE 75, 223, 235, 242) – *Kloppenburg*.

[164]German Federal Constitutional Court, 2 BvR 2134, 2159/92 (Judgment of 12 October 1993) para 70 (in: BVerfGE 89, 155, 175) – *Maastricht*.

[165]Article 90.1 of the Polish Constitution provides: "The Republic of Poland may, by virtue of international agreements, delegate to an international organization or international institution the competence of organs of State authority in relation to certain matters."

[166]Polish Constitutional Tribunal, Decision Ref. No. K 32/09 (24 November 2010 English translation available online) pp. 22, 40, referring to K. Działocha, Commentary to Art. 8 of the Constitution of the Republic of Poland, in L. Garlicki (ed.), Konstytucja RP, Komentarz, Warszawa 2007, vol. 5, p. 14. The Polish Constitutional Court (p. 23) includes the following matters in the concept of the constitutional identity, thus prohibiting a conferral of "decisions specifying the fundamental principles of the Constitution and decisions concerning the rights of the individual which determine the identity of the state, including, in particular, the requirement of protection of human dignity and constitutional rights, the principle of statehood, the principle of democratic governance, the principle of a state ruled by law, the principle of social justice, the principle of subsidiarity, as well as the requirement of ensuring better implementation of constitutional values and the prohibition to confer the power to amend the Constitution and the competence to determine competences."

[167]Critical with regard to the Charter of Fundamental Rights of the EU Körner (2009), p. 359 et seqq.

[168]See Polish Constitutional Tribunal, Decision Ref. No. K 32/09 (24 November 2010) p. 23: "The constitutional identity remains in a close relation with the concept of national identity, which also includes the tradition and culture."

6.2 *Bone of Contention and Pacifying the Fronts: The Mangold Case and the Honeywell Case*

Among the ECJ decisions that have fostered suspicions of an *ultra vires* application of law is the case of *Tanja Kreil*[169] that opened up service in the German Armed Forces to women. This decision probably met "the outermost limits of acceptable legal interpretation" and would have encountered severe criticism if it had not met a political trend.[170] An example of "[ECJ] case law transgressing the limits" of the competences conferred by the Treaty is considered to be the 2005 case of *Mangold*.[171]

6.2.1 The *Mangold* Case

Mangold had had a fixed-term employment contract, the limitation of which had been deliberately based by both parties to the contract exclusively on sentence 4 of Section 14.3 of the German "Law on Part-Time Working and Fixed-Term Contracts" (*Gesetz über Teilzeitarbeit und befristete Arbeitsverträge – Teilzeit- und Befristungsgesetz* – TzBfG), thereby intentionally triggering court proceedings. This provision – valid until 31 December 2006 – permitted a fixed term to be set for the employment relationship with an employee who had reached the age of 52 without justification other than the age of the employee and without limitation regarding duration or number of renewals. The case was referred to the ECJ for preliminary ruling by the Munich Labour Court. The ECJ held that fixed-term employment contracts pursuant to sentence 4 of Section 14.3 TzBfG introduced direct discrimination on grounds of age. Unequal treatment on grounds of age could be justified by Art 6.1 of Directive 2000/78/EC[172] – which at the time of the ECJ decision had not yet been transposed into German law – only if a legitimate aim was thereby pursued. Making age the only criterion required for setting a fixed term for the employment contract – with no consideration of the particular case of the individual employee and without "proof" of the objective necessity of the amended provision for encouraging the employment of older unemployed persons – was neither appropriate nor necessary for achieving the aim pursued.[173]

The fact that Directive 2000/78/EC, in accordance with the additional period for transposition provided for by the Directive itself (Art. 18(2) of the Directive), had not yet been implemented in Germany had been regarded immaterial by the ECJ.

---

[169]Case C-285/98 *Tanja Kreil v Germany* (ECJ 11 January 2000).

[170]Tomuschat (2005), p. 872 (our translation).

[171]Herzog and Gerken (2008); Bauer and Arnold (2006); Preis (2006).

[172]Council Directive 2000/78/EC *establishing a general framework for equal treatment in employment and occupation*, O.J. L 303/16 (2000).

[173]Case C-144/04 *Werner Mangold v Rüdiger Helm* (ECJ 22 November 2005) para 60 et seqq.

On the one hand, a period for transposition that had not yet expired was without significance due to the principle of advance effect (*Vorwirkung*). This principle provides that Member States must refrain from taking any measures that are seriously liable to compromise the attainment of the objective set out in a Directive. Sentence 4 of Section 14.3 TzBfG was considered by the ECJ as such a measure.[174] On the other hand, the prohibition of discrimination on grounds of age had to be regarded as a general principle of Union law that was effective unconditional of the Directive. The ECJ thus held that the principle of non-discrimination was not laid down in Directive 2000/78/EC but was rather restated by it. The prohibition of discrimination on various grounds included in the Directive (religion, belief, disability, age, sexual orientation) already originated from several international instruments and from the constitutional traditions common to the Member States.[175]

In its decision *Kücükdeveci* of 19 January 2010 the ECJ clearly emphasised the problems raised by the core statements of the *Mangold* judicature: Section 622 BGB, according to which periods of employment completed before the age of 25 are not to be taken into account in calculating the notice period, violates the Union's fundamental rights principle of non-discrimination on grounds of age as reflected in Directive 2000/78/EC and may thus not be applied in that specific case. In contrast to the *Mangold* case, by the time of the dismissal the period for transposing the relevant anti-discrimination directive had already expired.[176]

The *Mangold* decision of the ECJ has been qualified as a "misjudgment."[177] But even those who are in favour of the result of the decision recognise significant methodical weaknesses in the reasoning of the Court. The horizontal advance effect (*Dritt-Vorwirkung*) assumed by the ECJ – in the relationship between the employer and the employee – has been regarded as a violation of Art. 288.3 TFEU and thus as a disregard of the express will of the European primary law legislator. The finding of the ECJ that there existed a general principle of Union law prohibiting discrimination on grounds of age was considered the result of an invention, a grasp into the Platonic sphere of ideals ("ein Griff in den 'platonischen Begriffshimmel'")[178] by which the Court would act as the creator of primary law – because Finland is the only Member State of the EU that now prohibits discrimination based on age (Paragraph 6.2 of the Finnish Constitution). The specific application of the principle of non-discrimination is entrusted by Art. 10 TFEU to the European legislator, not to the ECJ. Such political law-making by the Court was not envisaged by the

[174]Case C-144/04 *Werner Mangold v Rüdiger Helm* (ECJ 22 November 2005) para 67 et seqq.

[175]Case C-144/04 *Werner Mangold v Rüdiger Helm* (ECJ 22 November 2005) para 74.

[176]Case C-555/07 *Kücükdeveci v Swedex GmbH & Co. KG* (ECJ 19 January 2010) para 20, 21, 50, 51, 54.

[177]Cf. Gerken et al. (2009), p. 67.

[178]Papier (2009), p. 114 with reference to the criticism in Case C-411/05 *Palacios de la Villa v Cortefiel Servicios SA* (Opinion of Advocate General *Jàn Mazák* 15 February 2007) para 79 et seqq., 87 et seqq., 138.

transfer of German sovereign power to the EU for it violates the principles of the democratic state governed by the rule of law.[179]

6.2.2 The *Honeywell* Case: Assessing the *Mangold* Judgment

After the German Federal Labour Court, applying the *Mangold* judgment in a decision of 26 April 2006[180] regarding fixed-term employment for older persons, declared that the possibility in sentence 4 of Section 14.3 TzBfG to conclude fixed-term contracts with employees aged 52 and older without giving objective reasons was "inapplicable" for reason of discrimination on grounds of age,[181] the defeated entrepreneur raised a constitutional complaint against this judgment. Some critics of the *Mangold* decision saw the Federal Constitutional Court faced with the alternatives either "to review the excessive case law of the ECJ more strictly in the future or to give up its function as a watchdog once and for all."[182]

In its judgment of 6 July 2010 the German Federal Constitutional Court has rejected the constitutional complaint as unfounded.[183] On the ultra vires review the judges of the Karlsruhe Court have taken up a "reserved" stance[184] by pointing out again that "as long as the Court of Justice did not have an opportunity to rule on the questions of Union law which have arisen, the Federal Constitutional Court may not find any inapplicability of Union law for Germany [. . .]. Ultra vires review by the Federal Constitutional Court can moreover only be considered if it is manifest that acts of the European bodies and institutions have taken place outside the transferred competences. A breach of the principle of conferral is only manifest if the European bodies and institutions have transgressed the boundaries of their competences in a manner specifically violating the principle of conferral (Article 23.1 of the Basic Law), the breach of competences is in other words sufficiently qualified [. . .]. This means that the act of the authority of the European Union must be manifestly in violation of competences and that the impugned act is highly significant in the structure of competences between the Member States and the Union with regard to the principle of conferral and to the binding nature of the statute under the rule of law."[185]

---

[179]Cf. Gerken et al. (2009), pp. VII et seq., 17 et seqq., 67 et seqq.

[180]German Federal Labour Court (Bundesarbeitsgericht), 7 AZR 500/04 (Judgment of 26 April 2006) and press release no. 27/06 – *Honeywell.*

[181]Cf. Bauer (2006).

[182]Herzog and Gerken (2008), p. 2 (our translation).

[183]Cf. German Federal Constitutional Court, 2 BvR 2661/06 (Order of 6 July 2010) – *Honeywell. (English translation available online)*

[184]German Federal Constitutional Court, 2 BvR 2661/06 (Order of 6 July 2010) para 66 – *Honeywell.*

[185]German Federal Constitutional Court, 2 BvR 2661/06 (Order of 6 July 2010) para 60 et seq. – *Honeywell.*

At the same time the Federal Constitutional Court concedes to the ECJ in view of the "'uniqueness' of the Treaties and goals that are inherent to them" methodological autonomy in finding the law, which must be interpreted as a recognition of the Court of Justice's case law tradition, which is orientated in line with the *effet utile* principle. The Karlsruhe Court even admits to the Luxembourg Court a "right to tolerance of error" in individual cases as long as there are neither "considerable [shifts] in the structure of competences [nor] impacts on fundamental rights to arise which constitute a burden or do not oppose domestic compensation for such burdens."[186] As a result, the case law of the *Bundesverfassungsgericht* as characterised by the *Solange II* decision (*supra* Sect. 6.1) has been confirmed and the relationship of cooperation with the ECJ has not been denounced (*infra* Sect. 6.3).

Thus, the Karlsruhe Court has avoided an open conflict with the ECJ – a "clash of courts" – and proved sense of proportion. The expected clarification[187] of the requirements under which the reserve competence of the Federal Constitutional Court can be activated was achieved at least in some crucial points: When – i.e. according to which criteria – do legal instruments of the European institutions transgress the limits of the sovereign power conferred upon them? What are the content and scope of "the unalterable standard of basic rights"? Does a disregard of the limited powers of the Union in an individual case – like *Mangold* – suffice to justify an intervention by the Federal Constitutional Court or should such a course require structural defects? Does the explicit limitation of the reserve competence to the "general guarantee of the unalterable standard of basic rights" release the Federal Constitutional Court from a review of the individual case? The deciding criteria are in accordance to the *Honeywell* decision that the impugned act of the authority of the EU constitutes a "manifest" breach of the principle of conferral ("sufficiently qualified") and that it is "highly significant" in the structure of competences between the Member States and the Union.

In his dissenting opinion Justice *H. Landau* accused the Second Senate of the *Bundesverfassungsgericht* saying that "the majority one-sidedly dissolves the tension occurring here between the principle of safeguarding democratic

---

[186]German Federal Constitutional Court, 2 BvR 2661/06 (Order of 6 July 2010) para 66 – *Honeywell*: "[. . .] the task and status of the independent suprastate case-law must be safeguarded. This means, on the one hand, respect for the Union's own methods of justice to which the Court of Justice considers itself to be bound and which do justice to the 'uniqueness' of the Treaties and goals that are inherent to them [. . .]. Secondly, the Court of Justice has a right to tolerance of error. It is hence not a matter for the Federal Constitutional Court in questions of the interpretation of Union law which with a methodical interpretation of the statute can lead to different outcomes in the usual legal science discussion framework, to supplant the interpretation of the Court of Justice with an interpretation of its own. Interpretations of the bases of the Treaties are also to be tolerated which, without a considerable shift in the structure of competences, constitute a restriction to individual cases and either do not permit impacts on fundamental rights to arise which constitute a burden or do not oppose domestic compensation for such burdens."

[187]Cf. Gerken et al. (2009), p. 58.

legitimation", which itself underlines the principle of conferral, "and the functioning of the Union in favour of functionality." From the point of view of Justice *Landau* the judgment in the case of *Honeywell* "continues to pursue a problematic tendency which is already recognisable in the previous case-law of the Federal Constitutional Court, that is of only asserting on paper the democratically founded national right to hand down a final ruling on the application of sovereign power in one's own territory and the concomitant responsibility for compliance with the competences granted to the Union, and of shying away from effectively implementing them in practice." Justice *Landau* points out that, with its judgment in the case of *Mangold*, "the Court of Justice manifestly transgressed the competences granted to it to interpret Community law with the Mangold judgment and acted *ultra vires*."[188]

This decision of the Federal Constitutional Court seems to be quite contained or even a withdrawl in comparison to its ruling on the Treaty of Lisbon. After the "proclamation" of the constitutional yardsticks for the review of secondary Union law in its pronouncement of 30 June 2009 the Karlsruhe Court in Honeywell obviously relents vis-à-vis the Luxembourg judges. Meanwhile, it would have appeared questionable to turn the *Mangold* judgment of the ECJ into a "leading case" which would be decisive for the future relationship between Luxembourg and Strasbourg. Misjudgments are not unknown to domestic case law either, as can be seen in the judgment of the Higher Regional Court (*Oberlandesgericht*) of Naumburg in the case of *Görgülü* (*supra* Sect. 5.1). *Mangold* and similar decisions should not merely lead to a breach in the relationship of cooperation but rather lead to a continuous practice of that relationship in reality. For the ECJ this means that its rulings must bear in mind the limits of the competences of the EU. The Court should thus not approach individual cases without solid reasons or by means of a general construction that applies general principles of Union law to areas for which the Union or one of its institutions is not competent. On the other hand, as regards the supreme domestic courts, the relationship of cooperation requires the recognition of the ECJ's monopoly on the interpretation of the European Treaties which they should accept – while recognising the right to a lawful judge (sentence 2 of Art. 101.1 GG) and the guarantee of effective legal protection (Art. 19.4 GG)[189] – by deciding to refer relevant cases to the ECJ but no longer regarding such proceedings as implying the risk of subordination to the integration guidelines of the Luxembourg Court.[190]

---

[188]German Federal Constitutional Court, 2 BvR 2661/06 (Order of 6 July 2010) para 100, 104 et seq. – dissenting opinion of Justice Landau in the case of *Honeywell*.

[189]For this double foundation – though with regard to the obligation of the specialised courts to refer – cf. Papier (2009), p. 117.

[190]Schwarze (2005), pp. 47 et seq.; for basic remarks on the obligation to refer, see Mayer (2003), pp. 232 et seqq. The then President of the German Federal Constitutional Court, *H.-J. Papier*, considered "especially the national specialised courts [to be] called upon" to seize the opportunity for cooperation with the ECJ, which is necessary for effective legal protection. "Meanwhile it is not improbable that one day even the Bundesverfassungsgericht will refer to the Court a question concerning the validity of a Community legal act, namely when proceedings before a specialised

6.3 Towards a Practiced Relationship of Cooperation

Regardless of justified objections against the case law of the ECJ some consequences of the claim of the Karlsruhe Court to protect indispensable elements of the German constitutional order and thus of the national control monopoly for the "relationship of cooperation" between the ECJ and the *Bundesverfassungsgericht* in the field of fundamental rights protection remained uncertain until the *Honeywell* decision (*supra* Sect. 6.2.2). The Federal Constitutional Court in its *Lisbon* ruling with regard to the "fundamental rights [as] part of the core contents of the constitution that restrict the transfer of sovereign powers to the European Union" spelled out again the *Solange II* formula, under which it "no longer exercises its jurisdiction to decide on the applicability of secondary Union law and other acts of the European Union cited as the legal basis for any acts of German courts or authorities within the sovereign sphere of the Federal Republic of Germany *only for as long as*[191] the Union guarantees an application of fundamental rights which in substance and effectiveness is essentially similar to the protection of fundamental rights required unconditionally by the Basic Law".[192] Nevertheless, in one of the following paragraphs the Federal Constitutional Court pointedly underlines that "in view of the position of the Community institutions, which is derived from international treaties", it could "recognise the final character of the decisions of the Court of Justice only 'in principle'."[193] This term "in principle", which is strikingly often used throughout the entire judgment, clearly reveals that the Federal Constitutional

court have not been required or possible" (our translation) – cf. Papier (2009), p. 116 with FN 49. References for preliminary ruling pursuant to Art. 267 TFEU have already been made by the Austrian Constitutional Court (Case C-465/00 *Österreichischer Rundfunk et al.* (ECJ 20 May 2003)) as well as the Italian Constitutional Court (Sentenza No. 102 (13 December 2008) – *Tasse di Lusso Sardegna*); see also Huber (2009), p. 582.

[191]Therefore, the *Lisbon* decision could be described as the "Solange III" decision of the Federal Constitutional Court.

[192]German Federal Constitutional Court, 2 BvE 2, 5/08, 2 BvR 1010, 1022, 1259/08, 182/09 (Judgment of 30 June 2009) para 191 (in: BVerfGE 123, 267, 335) – *Lisbon*, emphasis added. This principle was repeated by the German Court in its decision: German Federal Constitutional Court, 1 BvR 256/08, 1 BvR 263/08 and 1 BvR 586/08 (Judgment of 2 March 2010) para 181 – *Data Retention*: "The Federal Constitutional Court, however, generally no longer exercises its jurisdiction to decide on the applicability of Community law or now Union law cited as the legal basis for any acts of German courts or authorities within the sovereign sphere of the Federal Republic of Germany, and no longer reviews this legislation against the standard of the fundamental rights of the Basic Law as long as the European Communities (now the European Union), especially the case law of the European Court, generally ensure effective protection of fundamental rights, which is to be regarded as substantially similar to the protection of fundamental rights required unconditionally by the Basic Law, and in so far as they generally safeguard the essential content of fundamental rights (cf. BVerfGE 73, 339, 387; 102, 147, 162 et seq.). These principles apply to domestic legal provisions as well which transpose mandatory requirements of a directive into German legislation. Constitutional Complaints that challenge the application of binding legislation of the European Union in this sense are generally inadmissible (cf. BVerfGE 118, 79, 95; 121, 1, 15)" (our translation).

[193]German Federal Constitutional Court, 2 BvE 2, 5/08, 2 BvR 1010, 1022, 1259/08, 182/09 (Judgment of 30 June 2009) para 337 (in: BVerfGE 123, 267, 399) – *Lisbon*, referring to German

Court reserves for itself the right to deviate exceptionally from decisions of the Luxembourg Court. The Court holds that such a (limited) recognition (only "in principle") is due to the fact that "the position of the Community institutions [. . .] is derived from international agreements."[194]

The Court's remarks in the *Lisbon* judgment are further obscured[195] in that in terms of constitutional procedure it considers placing an *ultra vires* review as well as an identity review within the existing procedures, e.g. in application of the "legal concept [of the concrete review of statutes] expressed in Article 100.1 of the Basic Law",[196] i.e. a procedure which the *Bundesverfassungsgericht* since its *Solange I* decision regards applicable accordingly with regard to a review of the conformity of domestic law with Community law.[197] Nevertheless, following its *Solange II* decision the Court did not consider making any further use of it.[198]

Since secondary Union law as such is not an act of German public authority (Art. 93.1 no. 4a GG) that could be directly challenged by a constitutional complaint,[199] this procedure is not appropriate for the initiation of an *ultra vires review* or an *identity review*. These procedural obstacles have led the Federal Constitutional Court to suggest to the German legislator – in a way that disregards the Luxembourg Court's monopoly of interpretation – the possibility of the "creation [. . .] of an additional type of proceedings before the Federal Constitutional Court that is especially tailored to *ultra vires* review and identity review." By doing so it challenges the foundation of the Union as a legal community, i.e. the Union-wide consistent, uniform and effective validity of Community law.[200] The

Federal Constitutional Court, 2 BvR 197/83 (Order of 22 October 1986) para 76 (in: BVerfGE 73, 339, 367) – *Solange II*.

[194]German Federal Constitutional Court, 2 BvE 2, 5/08, 2 BvR 1010, 1022, 1259/08, 182/09 (Judgment of 30 June 2009) para 337 (in: BVerfGE 123, 267, 399) – *Lisbon*.

[195]With the same result Gärditz and Hillgruber (2009), pp. 873 seq.

[196]German Federal Constitutional Court, 2 BvE 2, 5/08, 2 BvR 1010, 1022, 1259/08, 182/09 (Judgment of 30 June 2009) para 241 (in: BVerfGE 123, 267, 354 et seq.) – *Lisbon*.

[197]German Federal Constitutional Court, BvL 52/71 (Order of 29 May 1974) para 55 (BVerfGE 37, 271, 280 et seqq.) – *Solange I*; Daiber (2010), p. 29; differently Hillgruber and Goos (2006), para 598.

[198]In *Solange II* (German Federal Constitutional Court, 2 BvR 197/83 (Order of 22 October 1986) para 132 (in: BVerfGE 73, 339, 387)) the *Bundesverfassungsgericht* dissociates itself from *Solange I* (supra footnote 5) and declares that it "will no loner exercise its jurisdiction to decide on the applicability of secondary Union law cited as the legal basis for any acts of German courts or authorities within the sovereign jurisdiction of the Federal Republic of Germany, and it will no longer review such legislation by the standard of the fundamental rights contained in the Bais Law"; reference pursuant to Art. 100.1 GG it holds "inadmissible".

[199]Cf. Schlaich and Korioth (2007), para 214.

[200]Correctly Pache (2009), p. 297; also Classen (2009), p. 888: "remarkable and unnecessary" as well as "contrary to European law" (our translation); characteristic of the position of Gärditz and Hillgruber (2009), p. 874, vis-à-vis this axiom of European integration is their recommendation to the legislator (both ordinary and with the power to change the constitution) to "follow this advice [of the *Bundesverfassungsgericht*]" (our translation).

supporters of a review competence for the national constitutional courts meet these objections by arguing that the European legal order would not be fragmented by such control if the ECJ took "this decision into consideration in its judgments." Only national constitutional courts could "provide protection against uncontrolled and unauthorised law-making by judges."[201] This, however, outlines a relationship of cooperation, the standards of which are set by national constitutional courts.

If with direct textual reference to these procedural considerations the Federal Constitutional Court enumerates areas of regulation with relevance to constitutional identity, which by virtue of closeness to democratic principles (Art. 23.1, 20.1 and 2 with Art. 79.3 GG) call for a special level of protection in the light of safeguarding the state sovereignty,[202] it sets constitutional limits to the process of European integration. Meanwhile within this *domaine réservé* the judicial reserve competence regarding the application of a national standard of fundamental rights can be realised: This is particularly appropriate to the "important area for fundamental rights" of the administration of criminal law,[203] but also in all emanations of democratic self-determination that rely on the possibility "to assert oneself in one's own cultural area."[204]

The reserve competence claimed by the *Bundesverfassungsgericht* can also lead to dismissal of secondary Union law, which has been adopted in these areas, and by the *ultra vires review* as well as the *identity review* because according to the Federal Constitutional Court the provisions of a secondary legal act of the Union that affect sovereignty imply "an inadmissible autonomous Treaty amendment"[205] and *at the same time* are below the standards of the fundamental rights of the Basic Law. Such a situation does not seem unrealistic since the Court, in terms of *Solange II*, recognises the final character of even the decisions of the Court of Justice with relevance to fundamental rights "only 'in principle'."[206] Meanwhile it does not feel obliged by the principle of primacy of Union law (Declaration (No. 17) concerning primacy) "if the mandatory order to apply the law is evidently lacking" or "if *within* or outside the sovereign powers conferred, these powers are exercised [...] in such a way that a violation of the constitutional identity [...] is the consequence."[207]

---

[201]Cf. Gerken et al. (2009), p. 58, 68 (our translation).

[202]German Federal Constitutional Court, 2 BvE 2, 5/08, 2 BvR 1010, 1022, 1259/08, 182/09 (Judgment of 30 June 2009) para 244 et seqq. (in: BVerfGE 123, 267, 356) – *Lisbon*.

[203]German Federal Constitutional Court, 2 BvE 2, 5/08, 2 BvR 1010, 1022, 1259/08, 182/09 (Judgment of 30 June 2009) para 253, 364 (in: BVerfGE 123, 267, 359 et seq., 413) – *Lisbon*.

[204]German Federal Constitutional Court, 2 BvE 2, 5/08, 2 BvR 1010, 1022, 1259/08, 182/09 (Judgment of 30 June 2009) para 260 (in: BVerfGE 123, 267, 363) – *Lisbon*.

[205]German Federal Constitutional Court, 2 BvE 2, 5/08, 2 BvR 1010, 1022, 1259/08, 182/09 (Judgment of 30 June 2009) para 338 (in: BVerfGE 123, 267, 399 et seq.) – *Lisbon*, with reference to German Federal Constitutional Court, 2 BvR 2134, 2159/92 (Judgment of 12 October 1993) para 106, 157 (in: BVerfGE 89, 155, 188, 210) – *Maastricht*.

[206]German Federal Constitutional Court, 2 BvE 2, 5/08, 2 BvR 1010, 1022, 1259/08, 182/09 (Judgment of 30 June 2009) para 337 (in: BVerfGE 123, 267, 399) – *Lisbon*.

[207]German Federal Constitutional Court, 2 BvE 2, 5/08, 2 BvR 1010, 1022, 1259/08, 182/09 (Judgment of 30 June 2009) para 339 (in: BVerfGE 123, 267, 400) – *Lisbon* (emphasis added).

Evidently this is to limit a dismissal of the application of legal acts of the Union by the Federal Constitutional Court to exceptions only.[208] Nonetheless, the German Court in the *Lisbon* decision claimed for itself the right to decide on the exercise of powers even in areas in which competences have clearly been conferred upon the Union. Such a course would thwart the role of national parliaments that has been granted to them procedurally by Protocol (No. 2) on the application of the principles of subsidiarity and proportionality (Art. 6 and 7 of the Protocol) for the review of draft legislative acts by the Union by the standards of the principle of subsidiarity (sentence 2 of Art. 5.1 TEU). The Federal Constitutional Court – as had been the case ever since the judgment in *Solange I*[209] – finds it necessary to first refer the case for a preliminary ruling according to Art. 267 TFEU.[210] The Court thereby recognises the judicial power granted to the ECJ by the Treaty of Lisbon for an infringement of the principle of subsidiarity by a legislative act (Art. 8 of the Protocol). Nonetheless, only the *Honeywell* decision ensures that the formula of the "relationship of cooperation", which stems from the decision on the Maastricht Treaty, does not degenerate into an idle chatter.[211]

7 Primacy of Union Law

7.1 The Significance of Primacy for the Protection of Fundamental Rights Pursuant to the Lisbon Judgment of the Federal Constitutional Court

Protection of fundamental rights by domestic courts on the one hand and the European Court on the other is closely related to the question of primacy of Union law. In the Greek legal order, for example, "the few existing areas of difficulty [. . .] in which actual conflicts between Union law and the Greek constitution seem to exist, [can be found] in the field of fundamental rights rather than

[208] In this sense the evaluation of Voßkuhle, in: v. Mangoldt et al. (2010), Art. 93 GG para 84a to 84c; Gerken et al. (2009), p. 69.

[209] German Federal Constitutional Court, BvL 52/71 (Order of 29 May 1974) para 55 (BVerfGE 37, 271, 280 et seqq.) – *Solange I*.

[210] German Federal Constitutional Court, 2 BvE 2, 5/08, 2 BvR 1010, 1022, 1259/08, 182/09 (Judgment of 30 June 2009) para 240 (in: BVerfGE 123, 267, 353) – *Lisbon*.

[211] See also Pache (2009), pp. 297 et seq.; Broß (2008), p. 229, prefers the term "complementary relationship [*Komplementärverhältnis*]", so that "the *Bundesverfassungsericht* [. . .] does not put itself in the subordinate position of an institution with a reserve competence, but rather [. . .] actively and strategically signals that it will always consider taking actions if, from the perspective of German constitutional law, a development at Community level gives a reason to complain" (our translation).

the field of competences, sovereignty, and democracy."[212] On the occasion of the decisions of different constitutional courts of the Member States regarding the constitutional conformity of the Treaty of Lisbon, several outstanding academic contributions have dealt with this axiom of the legal order of the Union, making it the starting point of the analysis of the "architecture of the European area of fundamental rights."[213] Rightly, it has been indicated that although Union law takes precedence it does not claim to be supreme in the sense of a subordination of the national legal orders.[214]

In a problematic section of its *Lisbon* decision the German Federal Constitutional Court explained that "[t]he *ultra vires* review as well as the identity review may result in Community law or, in future, Union law being declared inapplicable in Germany" (*supra* Sects. 6.1 and 6.3). It thereby considers different procedures in which such a challenge can be brought before the Constitutional Court, all of which pursue the aim of "not to apply in individual cases in Germany legal instruments of the European Union that transgress competences or that violate constitutional identity."[215] At the same time the Federal Constitutional Court makes the primacy of application conditional upon the case that the relevant legal act of the Union does not clearly show "absence of a constitutive order to apply the law." The order to apply the law will have legal effect only if given "by the Act Approving the Treaty of Lisbon." In the clear absence of a constitutive order to apply the law the Federal Constitutional Court claims the right to establish "the inapplicability of such a legal instrument to Germany." Such determination would also have to be made if, within or outside the sovereign powers conferred, these powers were exercised with the consequent effect on Germany of a violation of its constitutional identity, which is inviolable under Art. 79.3 GG and is also respected by European treaty law, namely Art. 4.2, first sentence, TEU.[216] The Karlsruhe judges thus claim for themselves the competence to exclude legal acts of the Union or acts of implementation by the German state authority from the primacy of application of Union law and declare them inapplicable in Germany if according to their evaluation they violate Art. 1 GG – as well as the human dignity content of any other fundamental right of the Basic Law – or Art. 20 GG.

[212] Cf. Iliopoulos-Strangas (2007a), pp. 830 et seq. (our translation); Iliopoulos-Strangas (2007b), para 34 et seqq.

[213] Cf. Dederer (2006); Iliopoulos-Strangas (2007a), pp. 825 et seqq.; Mayer et al. (2008); Niedobitek (2008); Grabenwarter (2009b), pp. 123 et seqq. has comprehensively covered the relationship between Union law and national constitutional law in his contribution.

[214] Niedobitek (2008), p. 82; Dederer (2006), p. 582, on the other hand, speaks of "primacy" as a "rule of hierarchy" without any further explanation. Nonetheless, national constitutional law and Union law are not connected in a hierarchical relation, but rather both areas of law are to be distinguished with regard to the principle of their respective competences.

[215] German Federal Constitutional Court, 2 BvE 2, 5/08, 2 BvR 1010, 1022, 1259/08, 182/09 (Judgment of 30 June 2009) para 241 (in: BVerfGE 123, 267, 354 et seq.) – *Lisbon*.

[216] Cf. German Federal Constitutional Court, 2 BvE 2, 5/08, 2 BvR 1010, 1022, 1259/08, 182/09 (Judgment of 30 June 2009) para 339 (in: BVerfGE 123, 267, 400) – *Lisbon*.

An even further-reaching view was expressed in 2008 by then Federal Constitutional Court judge *S. Broß* (Second Senate) – one of the judges in the *Lisbon* decision – that the primacy of application of Union law over contradicting national law as established by the ECJ in *Flamino Costa* (1964),[217] and over national constitutional law and fundamental rights as expressly extended in *Internationale Handelsgesellschaft* (1970),[218] and the "hierarchy of norms between Community law and domestic law" connected therewith did not "at least at that time" take into account the international law structure of the Community Treaties. The Luxembourg Court thus without due "restraint" presumed to take the role of a "constitutional court of the Community." This magisterial case law he identifies as an infringement of the principle of democracy and the principle of the rule of law, which was one of the reasons for the "slowing down of the integration process" and the failure of the Constitutional Treaty.[219]

This view, however, fails to recognise that primacy of Community law and the direct effect resulting from it are essential characteristics of the supranational structure of this organisation.[220] Anticipating those objections *St. Mangiameli* has rightly emphasised that "the ECJ in the EC had to establish a system for the protection of fundamental rights in order to ensure primacy of the Community legal order."[221] The development of Community fundamental rights in the case law of the ECJ thus is a consequence of its previously *praeter legem* established principle of the primacy of Community law, which, however, is inextricably linked to supranationality itself. Its codified outcome, the European Charter of Fundamental Rights, has been understood "as counterpart to the principle of primacy of European law",[222] providing for effective protection of the individual rights and freedoms of the citizens of the EU, whilst they cannot invoke fundamental rights of the national constitutions against "the Treaties and the law adopted by the Union."[223]

In the area of fundamental rights the principle of primacy has the effect that Union law, once in force, cannot be reviewed against national standards of fundamental rights (because of this very principle). Well before the highly controversial rulings of the

[217]Case 6/64 *Flamino Costa v E.N.E.L.* (ECJ 15 July 1964).

[218]Case 11/70 *Internationale Handelsgesellschaft mbH v Einfuhr- und Vorratsstelle für Getreide und Futtermittel* (ECJ 17 December 1970).

[219]Broß (2008), pp. 230 et seq. (our translation).

[220]See Opinion 1/91 *European Economic Area* (ECJ 14 December 1991) para 21.

[221]Cf. Mangiameli, Impulse aus dem italienischen Verfassungsrecht für den europäischen Grundrechtsschutz, in Tettinger and Stern (2006), A VII para 35 (our translation); Broß (2008), p. 231 "replies" to this argument that "the ECJ has only been able to develop the protection of fundamental rights at Community level by claiming for itself a *Kompetenz-Kompetenz* [i.e. the power to set one's own competences] which it has actually not been entitled to" (our translation).

[222]Pernice (2008), p. 236, 239 et seq.

[223]Case 11/70 *Internationale Handelsgesellschaft mbH v Einfuhr- und Vorratsstelle für Getreide und Futtermittel* (ECJ 17 December 1970).

German Federal Constitutional Court, *H.P. Ipsen*, the nestor of the German European law school, acknowledged "in principle" the priority of application of Community law to national fundamental rights, and set no limits based on Art. 79.3 GG to the effects of the priority rule in terms of its application.[224] While he still considered the Communities to be "special-purpose associations [*Zweckverbände*] for functional integration", the competences of the Union have grown remarkably since the Single European Act (1986) and the Treaty of Maastricht. The EU is sometimes said to have state-like sovereign power. Does this development require establishing the national supreme courts as "counterweights" to European jurisdiction so that they can safeguard the role of the Member States as "Masters of the Treaties", which is essential for the protection of national sovereignty?[225] Are the reserved competences of the national supreme courts even essential to control the limits imposed to national sovereignty in the course of European integration in order to protect indispensible national constitutional rights from invasion by supranational sovereign power?

This is evidently the objective of the *Bundesverfassungsgericht* in particular when it recognises "the primacy of application of Union law only [. . .] by virtue and in the context of the constitutional empowerment that continues in effect."[226] The same is true for the Italian *Corte Costituzionale*, which reserves the right to define the limits of integrational power; or the *Conseil Constitutionnel*, which ranks the French Constitution at the top of the hierarchy of norms as not affected by the Union Treaties (*infra* Sect. 7.3.3). The supreme courts of the Member States thus claim the competence to review and reject Union law – even if only in case of an "emergency" – against the standard of what they consider the essential, inviolable and founding elements of their constitutional identity and the definitive competences of the relevant national constitutional order, thereby, however, undermining the monopoly of the Court of the European Union for the interpretation of the Treaties (Art. 19.3 lit. b TEU).

As a result, the unity of the legal system of the EU is at stake, especially if the supreme courts of all Member States decided to use the *domaines réservés* of their respective constitutional orders to protect their own values against a valid legal act of the Union in order to prevent its application in the domestic sphere. With reference to the *Mangold* case it is suggested that the ECJ, frankly in unilateral diktat rather than as a result of multilateral dialogue and cooperation, "no longer appl[ies] a principle of Community law established by the Court itself that has been dismissed in one of the Member States – i.e. single-handedly – for not being covered by the national act of approval." At the same time, with regard to the monopoly of interpretation of the ECJ, the due respect called for by the ECJ for such a national act of dismissal is interpreted in a philistine way as a contribution to

[224] Ipsen (1972), p. 289, 720.

[225] Cf. Gerken et al. (2009), pp. 53 et seqq. (57).

[226] German Federal Constitutional Court, 2 BvE 2, 5/08, 2 BvR 1010, 1022, 1259/08, 182/09 (Judgment of 30 June 2009) para 240 (in: BVerfGE 123, 267, 353 et seq.) – *Lisbon*.

"ensure unity of Community law."[227] Clarification of those "close and clear-cut requirements" for the breakaway of the national judiciary from the legal order of the Union is expected by its supporters to come from the Federal Constitutional Court itself.[228] Meanwhile, however, the solution for the conflict between the realisation of the aims of integration and the respect for fundamental rights at Union level can only be found through the enhanced development of the supranational protection of fundamental rights.[229]

7.2 Codification and Significance of Primacy

The principle, found at a prominent place in the failed TCE, according to which "[t]he Constitution and law adopted by the institutions of the Union in exercising competences conferred on it shall have primacy over the law of the Member States"[230] and thus determine the relationship between the Union and the Member States, has not been adopted in the Treaty of Lisbon due to especially British resistance. The concern about primacy – expressed by the UK Government (and others) in the context of the Constitution for the EU – was mainly based on the fact that as the Constitution was drafted it would have applied to the then Second Pillar and would have therefore called into question the ultimate independence of the Member States in the conduct of their foreign policy. The abolishment of the principle of primacy in the text of the TEU is in this view one of the big substantive improvements in Lisbon.[231] Pursuant to the "Declaration concerning primacy" (No. 17) the Conference recalls that "in accordance with well settled case law of the Court of Justice of the European Union, the Treaties and the law adopted by the Union on the basis of the Treaties have primacy over the law of Member States, under the conditions laid down by the said case law", making this rule on a conflict of laws nothing more than a declaration governing the future interpretation of the Union Treaties.[232] Nevertheless, this failed codification in the Treaty is not detrimental for it would have had

[227]Gerken et al. (2009), p. 58.

[228]Gerken et al. (2009), p. 58 (our translation).

[229]Correctly Kühling (2003), p. 585.

[230]Article I-6 TCE: "La Constitution et le droit adopté par les institutions de l'Union dans l'exercise des compétences qui lui sont attribués ont la primauté sur le droit des États membres".

[231]Cf. Denza (2004), pp. 267 et seqq.

[232]Grimm (1995), pp. 49 et seq., – as opposed to mere "constitutionality" – holds that the point of no return to a "nationalisation of the European Union [i.e. its becoming a state]" has been reached once "those elements have been included in the Treaties that so far they lack to actually call them a constitution in the proper meaning of the word." Then, "primacy of Community law over national law would no longer be the result of an order for the Member States to apply the principle contained in the Treaties but rather a constitutional order rooted in the constitution of the Community" (our translation).

merely declaratory, not constitutive, force.[233] This is confirmed by the Opinion of the Council Legal Service according to which "the existence of the principle and the existing case-law of the Court of Justice" is in no way to be altered.[234] With a correct interpretation of the Declaration, which does not impose limitations to the existing *acquis*, it can be assumed that the principle established by the ECJ of the primacy of European law over national constitutional law remains unaffected as well.[235]

The primacy of application of European law does not, as the *Bundesverfassungsgericht* has pointed out again in its *Lisbon*[236] and *Honeywell*[237] decisions, affect the validity of conflicting law in the Member States and only inhibits its application (not its validity) to the extent required by the Treaties. The primacy rule is different from the provision of the German Basic Law that federal law shall take precedence over conflicting *Land* law (Art. 31 GG). Law of a Member State that is contrary to Community and Union law is rendered inapplicable merely to the extent required by the conflicting regulatory content of Community and Union law. The principle of primacy of Union law nullifies the effect of conflicting national law and inhibits its going into effect within the area of application of the relevant Union law.[238] This interpretation of the primacy of Union law explains why, for instance, in the case of *Mangold* (*supra* Sect. 6.2) German labour law (sentence 1 and 4 of Section 14.3 TzBfG) remained inapplicable in Germany by reason of incompatibility with the Union principle of non-discrimination on grounds of age.

---

233 Cf. Niedobitek (2008), pp. 102 et seq.

234 Doc. 1197/07.

235 Cf. Mayer (2007), who raises the question whether this postulated primacy over the constitutional law of the Member States "is confirmed by primary law". At the same time he points out that there is no limitation by the Opinion of the Council Legal Service; cf. also Mayer (2006).

236 German Federal Constitutional Court, 2 BvE 2, 5/08, 2 BvR 1010, 1022, 1259/08, 182/09 (Judgment of 30 June 2009) para 331, 335 (in: BVerfGE 123, 267, 396 et seq. and 398) – *Lisbon*. Previously in German Federal Constitutional Court, 2 BvR 197/83 (Order of 22 October 1986) para 103 (in: BVerfGE 73, 339, 375) – *Solange II* and 2 BvR 687/85 (Order of 8 April 1987) para 61 (in: BVefGE 75, 223, 244) – *Kloppenburg*.

237 German Federal Constitutional Court, 2 BvR 2661/06 (Order of 6 July 2010) para 53 et seqq. – *Honeywell*.

238 Cf. Case 106/77 *Amministrazione delle Finanze dello Stato v Simmenthal SpA* (ECJ 9 March 1978), Joined Cases C-10/97 to C-22/97 *Ministero delle Finanze v IN.CO.GE.'90 Srl et al.* (ECJ 22 October 1998); for this see Niedobitek (2008), p. 80, who rightly holds that – counter to the majority's opinion – "in the end" the effect of "the primacy of application is the same as an absolute or unrestricted primacy without, however, directly questioning the formal validity of conflicting national law" (our translation). For an interpretation of Art. I-6 TCE with regard to national constitutional provisions ("Federal law shall take precedence over *Land* law") cf. di Salvatore (2006). As a result and taking into account the grammatical-lexical, the systematic and the teleological interpretation of the European Constitutional Treaty, he only assumes (p. 397) an inapplicability of the domestic provision. He thereby opposes the thesis of *E. Grabitz*, Gemeinschaftsrecht bricht nationales Recht, 1966, pp. 113 et seqq., according to which the conflicting relationship between national law and law of the Community leads to the voidness of the national provision.

Indirectly, the ECHR and the case law of the Strasbourg Court specifying its provisions are already part of the principle of primacy of Union law over national law. As a source for the interpretation of the fundamental rights of the Union, especially their scope and content, the ECJ uses the ECHR in its interpretation by the ECtHR. Although in a number of Member States the ECHR has only the status of an ordinary law,[239] it obtains primacy over constitutional law through the case law of the ECJ.[240] With the accession of the Union to the ECHR the law of the Convention will *directly* take part in the primacy of Union law over the law of the Member States. This also applies to the Protocols to the ECHR, such as Protocol No. 1, which have been ratified by all Member States. The binding to the law of the Convention integrated into Union law is limited to the scope of Union law.[241]

7.3 The Legal Situation in the Member States of the Union and the Interpretation of Primacy at the Highest Judicial Level

Undisputed as the primacy of Union law over ordinary national law may be today,[242] the history of its relationship to national constitutional law is controversial and complex. According to *Ch. Grabenwarter*[243] three groups of states can be distinguished: those in which Union law is attributed full primacy of application (the Netherlands and Austria); states in which Union law enjoys limited primacy (Italy, Germany, Belgium, Denmark, but also Spain, Sweden, Ireland, the United Kingdom,[244] Hungary and the Czech Republic); and those states in which national constitutional law takes precedence over Union law (France and Poland).

---

[239]In Germany the ECHR has the rank of a federal law (Art. 59.2, first sentence, GG) and in Italy that of a "legge ordinaria"; for the legal situation in Italy, where there is no respective constitutional provision, cf. Italian Constitutional Court, judgments n. 388/1999, n. 315/1990, n. 188/1980, n. 349/2007; ordinanza n. 464/2005.

[240]Dederer (2006), p. 591, speaks of a "'tectonic' movement between the international and national level" (our translation).

[241]Schneiders (2010), pp. 255 et seqq., who talks of a comprehensive primacy, irrespective of the reservations of a Member State and the lack of ratification of a Protocol.

[242]Primacy of Union law over ordinary law has been expressly provided for by a series of acceding states from central and eastern Europe in their national constitutions: Lithuania (Art. 2 of the constitutional act on the membership of the Republic of Lithuania in the European Union) as well as Slovakia (Art. 7 of the Slovak Constitution in the version of the constitutional act 90/2001). The constitutional situation in Malta (similar to Art. 117 of the Italian Constitution in the version of the amendment of 2001) is in need of interpretation. According to Art. 65 of the Maltese Constitution the Parliament makes laws in full accordance with inter alia "the international and regional obligations of Malta, especially those that result from the Treaty on the accession to the European Union signed in Athens on 16 April 2003."

[243]Grabenwarter (2009b), pp. 123 et seqq.

[244]House of Lords, *Factortame Ltd. v. Secretary of State*, (1991) 1AC 603.

With regard to the interpretation of primacy, the decisions of the national supreme courts of the states in groups two and three are most enlightening. Despite different starting points of the courts it can be said with regard to the safeguarding of indispensable constitutional standards (of fundamental rights) in their relationship to the EU that the majority of those courts through an interpretation that is in conformity with European law and through a method of balancing conflicting rights and principles ("practical concordance") – even when expressly placing the national constitution, not the Union legal order, at the top of the domestic legal order (French *Conseil Constitutionnel*, Polish Constitutional Tribunal) – endeavour to reconcile real conflicts which can arise between Community/Union law and the relevant domestic constitutional provisions. Additionally, relying on the national constitution they reserve the right to intervene in cases of exceptional, general violations of substantial rules,[245] which are, however, according to the description of those cases of conflict by the supreme national courts of a rather hypothetical nature.

The position of the *Bundesverfassungsgericht*, which places primacy of application of a supranational legal act under the condition of the existence of a "constitutive order to apply the law", is most widely shared among the highest courts of the Member States by the Italian *Corte Costituzionale* and the Spanish *Tribunal Constitucional*. In spite of the fact that the French *Conseil Constitutionnel* and the Polish Constitutional Tribunal place their national constitution at the top of the respective domestic legal order, it is unmistakable that there is considerable overlap between the decisions of the *Bundesverfassungsgericht* and the decisions of those two courts in the establishing of judicial claims to protect essential constitutional elements.

7.3.1 The Italian Corte Costituzionale

In Italy, primacy of Union law is based on Art. 11 of the Italian Constitution according to which "Italy agrees, on conditions of equality with other States, to such limitations of sovereignty as may be necessary to a world order ensuring peace and justice among the Nations" and that it "promotes and encourages international organisations furthering such ends." In the early 1970s the Italian *Corte Costituzionale* – while principally recognising primacy of Union law as well as the monopoly of the ECJ for the interpretation of Community law – has reserved the right to "[review] the act implementing the Treaty as regards compliance with basic principles [. . .] of the [Italian] Constitution and the inalienable rights of the person."[246] For this case the *Corte* has furthermore reserved the right to personally

[245]Cf. Everling (2005), pp. 70 et seq.

[246]Italian Constitutional Court, 170/1984 (8 June 1984) – *Granital*, in: Giurs. Cost. 1984, pp. 1222 et seqq., with reference to judgment 183/1973 (27 December 1973) – *Frontini*, in: Giur. Cost. 1973, pp. 2401 et seqq. (part 9 of the grounds); see for this Tizzano (2010) and Mangiameli (2008), pp. 15 et seqq., 30 et seqq.

examine the constitutionality "of the continuing compatibility of the Treaty with said principles" even at the risk that such an approach could call into question Italy's remaining in the Community.[247] Meanwhile the Italian Constitutional Court in a reasoning related to the protection of fundamental rights has emphasised that through an innovative interpretation it intends to clarify the contours of the fundamental rights of the Italian Constitution. In this context it has underlined Italy's obligation to contribute to the development of the EU.[248]

This is used in Italian academic literature as the foundation for the theory of *controlimiti* (counter limits – *supra* Sect. 2.3.3), which describes the limits of the power of integration.[249] It is essentially based on the thought that while the Italian legal order recognises and approves of limitations to sovereign power by Union law it also sets limits to them in order to safeguard fundamental values of the Italian legal order. Individual opinions in Italian writings regard Art. 117 of the Italian Constitution, which has been amended by a constitutional reform in 2001, as confirmation and codification of the case law of the *Corte Costituzionale* through which in consequence Union law would merely enjoy a limited primacy at the constitutional level by virtue of the theory of *controlimiti*.[250]

7.3.2 The Spanish Tribunal Constitucional

Following its decision on the Treaty of Maastricht of 1 July 1992 in which it expressly reserved the right to review the constitutionality of Community law,[251] the Spanish *Tribunal Constitucional* in its judgment on the Constitutional Treaty confirmed the compatibility of the primacy clause of the TCE with its own constitutional order. Despite this "existential requirement" of the legal order of the EU it regards the relationship between the national constitution and the law of the EU as unaffected. Supremacy of the Spanish Constitution, which "is not necessarily sustained on hierarchy" but, however, "[i]n principle [. . .] implies primacy", is conserved in that the principle of primacy of Union law in the sense of "preferential or prevalent

---

[247]Cf. to judgment 183/1973 (27 December 1973) – *Frontini*, Foro italiano 1974, para 9; to judgment 170/1984 (8 June 1984) – *Granital*, Foro italiano 1984 I, para 7.

[248]The *Corte* thereby referred to its judgments for giving substance to the inviolable rights of the person (Art. 2 of the Italian Constitution), the right to life (judgments no. 27/1975, no. 35/1997; 223/1996), the right to personal identity, the right of privacy (judgment no. 13/1999), the right to liberty, the right to self-determination (judgment no. 30/1962) as well as the right to information (judgments no. 84/1969 and no. 348/1990). Cf. Mangiameli (2006), p. 476, who talks about a circular process of the development of fundamental rights in the relationship between the European and the Italian legal order.

[249]Cf. Randazzo (2008) and Ruggeri (2005).

[250]Cf. the references and critical objections in Panara (2007), para 37 et seqq.

[251]Printed in *Journal des Tribunaux* 1992, p. 6670 as well as EuGRZ 1993, p. 285; see on this also Lopez Castillo and Polakiewicz (1993), p. 281; Estella de Noriega (1999), p. 279; Garcia de Enterria and Alonso Garcia (2000), p. 298.

application" is provided for in the Spanish Constitution itself (Art. 93 of the Spanish Constitution) and "it is not a primacy with a general scope."[252] Therefore, on the one hand, Art. 93 of the Spanish Constitution, which enables the transfer of competences, is understood as a "door" between the legal orders in the sense of an "opening-up of Spanish legislation."[253] On the other hand, the primacy of Union law is limited to "the scope of the exercise of the competences attributed to the European institutions." At the same time the Spanish Constitutional Tribunal postulates an – albeit hypothetical – reserve competence: "In the unlikely case where, in the ulterior dynamics of the legislation of the European Union, said law is considered irreconcilable with the Spanish Constitution, without the hypothetical excesses of the European legislation with regard to the European Constitution itself being remedied by the ordinary channels set forth therein, in a final instance, the conservation of the sovereignty of the Spanish people and the given supremacy of the Constitution could lead this Court to approach the problems which, in such a case, would arise. Under current circumstances, said problems are considered inexistent through the corresponding constitutional procedures [. . .]."[254] But even in this *ultima ratio* case of a reserve competence, the reference for a preliminary ruling before the ECJ (Art. 256.3 in conjunction with Art. 267 TFEU) is considered procedurally superior to those procedures provided for by Spanish constitutional law.

7.3.3 The French Conseil Constitutionnel

In precedent cases, the French *Conseil Constitutionnel* has held that secondary Union law is not limited by national law, neither by ordinary nor by constitutional provisions, and therefore that supranational law has primacy also over Art. 88.1 of the French Constitution which provides the legal authorisation from the French nation for participation in the ECs and in the EU. The French *Conseil Constitutionnel* intends, however, to except cases where an explicit clash with the French Constitution results from the implementation of an EC directive ("qu'ainsi, la transposition en droit interne d'une directive communautaire résulte d'une exigence constitutionnelle à laquelle il ne pourrait être fait obstacle qu'en raison

---

[252]Cf. Spanish Constitutional Tribunal, DTC No. 1/2004 (13 December 2004) fundamentos 3 and 4, in: EuR 2005, 339, 343 et seqq. (English translation available online).

[253]Cf. Spanish Constitutional Tribunal, DTC No. 1/2004 (13 December 2004) fundamento 2; Grabenwarter (2009b), pp. 126 et seq.

[254]Spanish Constitutional Tribunal, DTC No. 1/2004 (13 December 2004) fundamento 4: "En el caso difícilmente concebible de que en la ulterior dinámica del Derecho de la Unión Europea llegase a resultar inconciliable este Derecho con la Constitución española, sin que los hipotéticos excesos del Derecho europeo respecto de la propia Constitución europea fueran remediados por los ordinarios cauces previstos en ésta, en última instancia la conservación de la soberanía del pueblo español y de la supremacía de la Constitución que éste se ha dado podrían llevar a este Tribunal a abordar los problemas que en tal caso se suscitaran, que desde la perspectiva actual se consideran inexistentes, a través de los procedimientos constitucionales pertinentes [. . .]."

d'une disposition expresse contraire de la Constitution").[255] Restating this caveat explicitly in the décisions n° 2004-497 DC of 1 July 2004,[256] n° 2004-498 DC[257] and n° 2004-499 DC[258] of 29 July 2004 with regard to dispositions which affect the identity of the French Constitution, the *Conseil Constitutionnel* then endeavoured to refine bit by bit its reserve competence by adding implicitly that the constitutional disposition has to reveal not only an express connection,

---

[255]French Constitutional Council, Décision n° 2004-496 (10 June 2004) consideration 7 – *Loi pour la confiance dans l'économie numérique (E-commerce)*. In the *Arcelor* case, the French *Conseil d'Etat* decided in accordance with these decisions of the *Conseil Constitutionnel* that a legal challenge of the validity of an EC directive based on the *French constitutional* right to equality should be referred instead to the ECJ so that it could examine the question in the light of the *common European* principle of equality: French *Conseil d'Etat*, Decision No. 287110 DC (8 February 2007) – *Société Arcelor Atlantique et Lorraine et autre* (EuR 2008, pp. 57 et seqq.): "La suprématie conférée par les dispositions de l'article 55 de la Constitution aux engagements internationaux ne saurait s'imposer, dans l'ordre interne, aux principes et dispositions à valeur constitutionnelle. Eu égard aux dispositions de l'article 88-1 de la Constitution, dont découle une obligation constitutionnelle de transposition des directives, le contrôle de constitutionnalité des actes réglementaires assurant directement cette transposition est appelé à s'exercer selon des modalités particulières dans le cas où sont transposées des dispositions précises et inconditionnelles. Dans ce cas, si le contrôle des règles de compétence et de procédure ne se trouve pas affecté, il appartient au juge administratif, saisi d'un moyen tiré de la méconnaissance d'une disposition ou d'un principe de valeur constitutionnelle, de rechercher s'il existe une règle ou un principe général du droit communautaire qui, eu égard à sa nature et à sa portée, tel qu'il est interprété en l'état actuel de la jurisprudence du juge communautaire, garantit par son application l'effectivité du respect de la disposition ou du principe constitutionnel invoqué. Dans l'affirmative, il y a lieu pour le juge administratif, afin de s'assurer de la constitutionnalité du décret, de rechercher si la directive que ce décret transpose est conforme à cette règle ou à ce principe général du droit communautaire. Il lui revient, en l'absence de difficulté sérieuse, d'écarter le moyen invoqué ou, dans le cas contraire, de saisir la Cour de justice des Communautés européennes d'une question préjudicielle, dans les conditions prévues par l'article 234 du traité instituant la Communauté européenne. En revanche, s'il n'existe pas de règle ou de principe général du droit communautaire garantissant l'effectivité du respect de la disposition ou du principe constitutionnel invoqué, il revient au juge administratif d'examiner directement la constitutionnalité des dispositions réglementaires contestées." Once the case had reached the ECJ, the Advocate General *Poiares Maduro*, in his Opinion submitted to the Court (Case C-127/07, Opinion of Advocate General Poiares Maduro, 21 May 2008, para 15–17), praised the attitude of the French supreme administrative court and underlined the importance of a judicial dialogue between national supreme courts and the ECJ in matters of fundamental rights protection (*supra* footnote 7). The judgment of the ECJ itself (16 December 2008) did not dwell on the underlying judicial dialogue question and just addressed the substantive question, concluding that the EC directive did not violate the general principle of equality. Cf. de Witte (2009).

[256]French Constitutional Council, Décision n° 2004-497 DC (1 July 2004) consideration 18 – *Loi relative aux communications électroniques et aux services de communication audiovisuelle*.

[257]French Constitutional Council, Décision n° 2004-498 DC (29 July 2004) consideration 4 – *Loi relative à la bioéthique*.

[258]French Constitutional Council, Décision n° 2004-499 DC (29 July 2004) consideration 7 – *Loi relative à la protection des personnes physiques à l'égard des traitements de données à caractère personnel*.

but also a specific interrelation with the principles laid down in the law of the Union.[259]

Supplementing these criteria to an increasing extent, the caveat of the conformity of secondary Union law with the French Constitution was refined in the case law of the high court which strived to define in the best way possible the constitutional framework of the relationship between national law and secondary Union law. The opportunity to clarify this case law presented itself vey quickly on the occasion of decision n° 2006-540 DC of 27 July 2006,[260] when the *Conseil Constitutionnel* consolidated its reserve competence considering that "the transposition of a directive cannot run counter to a rule or principle inherent to the constitutional identity of France, except when the constituting power consents thereto."[261] This decision, which strongly marked a shift in and the stabilisation of the case law, was then taken up as a canon in the decisions n° 2006-543 DC[262] and n° 2008-564 DC,[263] the latter constituting actually the high point of the achievement of a case law consistent in its basic principles since 2004 and in its formulation since 2006.[264]

The conformity of the primacy of Union law as codified by the failed Constitutional Treaty has been recognised by the *Conseil Constitutionnel*. In its decision on the TCE and following its previous case law it has not judged this principle of primacy of Union law over domestic law of the Member States (Art. I-6, then Art. I-5 TCE) as a "revision" of the French Constitution. Only when international commitments assumed by France "contain a clause running counter to the Constitution, call into question constitutionally guaranteed rights and freedoms or affect the fundamental conditions of the exercising of national sovereignty" a revision of the Constitution would be required. This has been contradicted by the *Conseil Constitutionnel* with regard to the Constitutional Treaty for Europe which is in substantive respects identical with the Treaty of Lisbon.[265] The binding effect of

---

[259]See French Constitutional Council, Décision n° 2004–498 DC (29 July 2004) consideration 6, according to which the freedom of communication as set out in Art. 10 of the Declaration of 1789 is not considered specific to the national legal order since it. "estégalement protégée en tant que principe général du droit communautaire sur le fondement de l'article 10 de la Convention européenne de sauvegarder des droits de l'homme et des libertés fondamentales"

[260]French Constitutional Council· Décision n° 2006-540 DC (27 July 2006) préc. – *Loi relative au droit d'auteur et aux droits voisins dans la société de l'information (Loi DADVSI)* (English translation available online).

[261]French Constitutional Council, Décision n° 2006-540 DC (27 July 2006) consideration 19 – *Loi relative au droit d'auteur et aux droits voisins dans la société de l'information.*

[262]French Constitutional Council, Décision n° 2006-543 DC (30 November 2006) consideration 6 – *Loi relative au secteur de l'énergie* (English translation available online).

[263]French Constitutional Council, Décision n° 2008-564 DC (19 June 2008) consideration 44 – *Loi relative aux organismes génétiquement modifiés* (English translation available online).

[264]Cf. Zinamsgvarov (2008), pp. 5 et seq.

[265]Cf. French Constitutional Council, Décision n° 2004-505 DC (19 November 2004) considerations 7 and 13 – *Traité établissant une Constitution pour l'Europe (*English translation available online; German translation in EuR 2004, 911 et seqq. and in EuGRZ 2005, 45 et seqq.).

the European Charter of Fundamental Rights is not considered unconstitutional. The *Conseil* also refers to the case law of the ECtHR, e.g. to interpret the European fundamental right of freedom of religion in such a way that it does not interfere with the French principle of laïcité (secularity).[266]

In general, however, the *Conseil Constitutionnel* left no doubt that the naming of the international treaty it reviewed ("Constitutional Treaty") "has no effect upon the existence of the French Constitution and the place of the latter at the summit of the domestic legal order."[267]

7.3.4 The Polish Constitutional Tribunal

In its decisions of 11 May 2005 regarding Poland's membership in the EU[268] and of 24 November 2010 on the Treaty of Lisbon[269] the Polish Constitutional Tribunal ruled:

> The accession of Poland to the European Union did not undermine the supremacy of the Constitution over the whole legal order within the field of sovereignty of the Republic of Poland. The norms of the Constitution, being the supreme act which is an expression of the Nation's will, would not lose their binding force or change their content by the mere fact of an irreconcilable inconsistency between these norms and any Community provision. In such a situation, the autonomous decision as regards the appropriate manner of resolving that inconsistency, including the expediency of a revision of the Constitution, belongs to the Polish constitutional legislator. [...] [T]he validity and efficacy of the accession [of Poland to the EU] are dependent upon fulfilment of the constitutional elements of the integration procedure, including the procedure for delegating competences.
>
> [A] collision would occur in the event that an irreconcilable inconsistency appeared between a constitutional norm and a Community norm, such as could not be eliminated by means of applying an interpretation which respects the mutual autonomy of European law and national law. Such a collision may in no event be resolved by assuming the supremacy of a Community norm over a constitutional norm. Furthermore, it may not lead to the situation whereby a constitutional norm loses its binding force and is substituted by a Community norm, nor may it lead to an application of the constitutional norm restricted to areas beyond the scope of Community law regulation. In such an event the Nation as the sovereign, or a State authority organ authorised by the Constitution to represent the Nation, would need to decide on: amending the Constitution; or causing modifications within Community provisions; or, ultimately, on Poland's withdrawal from the European Union.

And the Polish Constitutional Tribunal adds:

> The principle of interpreting domestic law in a manner 'sympathetic to European law', as formulated within the Constitutional Tribunal's jurisprudence, has its limits. In no event

[266]Cf. French Constitutional Council' Décision n° 2004-505 DC (19 November 2004) consideration 18 – *Traité établissant une Constitution pour l'Europe*.

[267]Cf. French Constitutional Council' Décision n° 2004-505 DC (19 November 2004) consideration 10 – *Traité établissant une Constitution pour l'Europe*.

[268]Polish Constitutional Tribunal, Decision Ref. No. K 18/04 (11 May 2005 – English translation available online).

[269]Polish Constitutional Tribunal, Decision Ref. No. K 32/09 (24 November 2010 – English translation available online).

> may it lead to results contradicting the explicit wording of constitutional norms or being irreconcilable with the minimum guarantee functions realised by the Constitution. In particular, the norms of the Constitution within the field of individual rights and freedoms indicate a minimum and unsurpassable threshold which may not be lowered or questioned as a result of the introduction of Community provisions.
>
> [. . .] The Member States maintain the right to assess whether or not, in issuing particular legal provisions, the Community (Union) legislative organs acted within the delegated competences and in accordance with the principles of subsidiarity and proportionality. Should the adoption of provisions infringe these frameworks, the principle of the precedence of Community law fails to apply with respect to such provisions. [. . .]
>
> The [ECJ] is the primary, but not the sole, depositary of powers as regards application of the Treaties within the legal system of the Communities and Union. The interpretation of Community law performed by the ECJ should fall within the scope of functions and competences delegated to the Communities by its Member States. It should also remain in correlation with the principle of subsidiarity. Furthermore, this interpretation should be based upon the assumption of mutual loyalty between the [. . .] Union institutions and the Member States. This assumption generates a duty for the ECJ to be sympathetically disposed towards the national legal systems and a duty for the Member States to show the highest standard of respect for Community norms.[270]

In its judgment on the Treaty of Lisbon the Polish Constitutional Tribunal maintained its stance presented in the statement of reasons for the judgment of 11 May 2005, pursuant to which "the Constitution remains – due to its unique status – 'the supreme law of the Republic of Poland' with regard to all international agreements which are binding for the Republic of Poland. This also concerns ratified international agreements about conferral of competences 'in relation to certain matters'. Due to the primacy of the binding force of the Constitution [. . .] the Constitution enjoys precedence as to the binding force and application in the territory of the Republic of Poland."[271]

7.3.5 The Czech Constitutional Court

In its decision of *Lisbon Treaty II* the Czech Constitutional Court reserved the right to review the Treaties for the reform of the EU which had not yet entered into force against the entire national constitution. Thereby, "the Constitutional Court acquires an opportunity to evaluate to a certain extent the constitutionality of the interpretation of already existing EU law norms by the Court of Justice, without coming into direct conflict with it."[272] Unlike the right claimed by the *Bundesverfassungsgericht* to review "in individual cases [. . .] legal instruments of the European Union that transgress competences or that violate constitutional identity [scil.:

[270]Polish Constitutional Tribunal, Decision K 18/04 (11 May 2005) No. 1 and 2 as well as 13–16.

[271]Polish Constitutional Tribunal, Decision Ref. No. K 32/09 K (24 November 2010) p. 33 et seq., 35.

[272]Cf. Czech Constitutional Court, Pl. US 29/09 (3 November 2009) para 172 et seq. – *Lisbon Treaty II* (English translation available online).

secondary legal acts]" the Czech Constitutional Court refers to the examination of primary Union law not yet in force at that time, i.e. it respects the primacy of Union law with regard to secondary legal acts of the Union. In the *European Arrest Warrant* case the Czech Constitutional Court implicitly found that a "possible inconsistency" of national law and Union law can be removed "not only by priority application of European law norms, but also through constitutional amendments".[273]

In the same decision the Czech Constitutional Court adds: "Thus, if there are several interpretations of the constitutional order, which includes the Charter of Fundamental Rights and Freedoms, and only some of them lead to fulfilling the obligation that the Czech Republic assumed in connection with its membership in the EU, that interpretation must be selected which supports fulfillment of that obligation, and not an interpretation that prevents such fulfillment."[274]

Emphasising this starting point and with reference to the *Maastricht* decision of the German *Bundesverfassungsgericht* the Czech Constitutional Court in its *Lisbon Treaty I* decision had already declared that it in the future it could "function as an *ultima ratio* and may review whether any act of Union bodies exceeded the powers that the Czech Republic transferred to the EU under Art. 10a of the Constitution. However, the Constitutional Court assumes that such a situation can occur only in quite exceptional cases; these could be, in particular, abandoning the identity of values and, as already cited, exceeding the scope of conferred competences."[275] By that it has also reserved the right to an identity review and an *ultra vires* review in exceptional cases.

7.3.6 The Position of an Undecided Member State: The Legal Situation in Greece

Like the constitutions of other Member States, the Greek Constitution leaves unanswered the question of primacy of Union law over national constitutional law (Art. 28.2 and 3 and an "interpretative explanation"). In a proceeding concerning the compatibility of some provisions of Greek press and media law, according to which companies that are "associated" with Greek media companies are excluded from participating in public tender procedures (Act 3021/2002), the Fourth Chamber of the Council of State (Supreme Administrative Court) in extended composition (Grand Chamber) pronounced in favour of supremacy of the Greek Constitution. According to the opinion of the judges issuing the majority judgment of this decision

---

[273]Czech Constitutional Court, Pl. US 66/04 (3 May 2006) – *European Arrest Warrant* (English translation available online), cited in: Czech Constitutional Court, Pl. US 19/08 (26 November 2008) para 94 – *Lisbon Treaty I* (English translation available online).

[274]Czech Constitutional Court, Pl. US 66/04 (3 May 2006) – *European Arrest Warrant*, cited in: Czech Constitutional Court, Pl. US 19/08 (26 November 2008) para 114 – *Lisbon Treaty I.*

[275]Cf. Czech Constitutional Court, Pl. US 19/08 (26 November 2008) para 120 – *Lisbon Treaty I* (emphasis in the original).

the supremacy of the Constitution applies "at least in the present stage of development of Community law and as long as a European constitutional document as superior provision has not been adopted which would bind the Member States to amend their constitutions in case of conflicts with this superior provision."[276] This formula goes far beyond the respective reserve competences which the supreme and constitutional courts of other Member States claim for themselves.[277]

In a dissenting opinion to the judgment, two judges held that the primacy of application of Community law is effective also over Greek constitutional provisions with the "only self-evident" condition that the respective applicable provision of Community law respects the principles of the protection of fundamental rights and the basis of the democratic form of government. They also expressly referred to the case law of the German *Bundesverfassungsgericht* (*Solange II*) and the Italian *Corte Costituzionale* (*Granital* and others). Nonetheless, primacy of Union law over national constitutional law must be dealt with as an issue which is still open and controversial in the Greek legal order.[278] In an earlier proceeding the Plenum of the Council of State challenged the attempt of the Sixth Chamber to explicitly recognise supremacy of the constitution over Community law.[279] It seems to trust that there will be no such conflict.

7.4 The Binding Power of Fundamental Rights for the (Supranational) Codification and the (National) Implementation of Margin of Appreciation of the Member States

National fundamental rights do not – at least from the perspective of Union law – undermine the validity of the supranational Treaties as such or their effect in the Member States. On the other hand, the Charter of Fundamental Rights in its interpretation in the light of international agreements on human rights, especially the ECHR, can influence the interpretation of domestic fundamental rights; this applies to the transposition and implementation of secondary Union law into the domestic legal order as well as to national courts and administrative authorities in their interpretation and application of provisions of secondary Union law, to the interpretation of domestic law in conformity with Union law and also to the

---

[276]Greek Council of State, Decision No. 3242/2004 (16 November 2004), NoB 2005, pp. 1878 et seqq. (1893) (our translation).

[277]Cf. Iliopoulos-Strangas (2007a), pp. 835 et seqq.

[278]Expressly Iliopoulos-Strangas (2007a), p. 844: "weiterhin offen"; Iliopoulos-Strangas (2007b), para 37 et seqq.; The opinion of Grabenwarter (2009b), p. 131, is thus not shared, for he classifies Greece in one group with France regarding primacy.

[279]Cf. Greek Council of State, Decision No. 3457/1998 (25 September 1998), *ToS* 1998, pp. 961 et seqq.

cumulative application of domestic provisions in the execution of secondary law. A commitment, resulting from primary law, that could bind the Member States to fundamental rights can only be considered for situations that are not exhaustively regulated by secondary law.[280] The Charter of Fundamental Rights does not, however, restrict the fundamental rights commitment of the Member States to the execution of secondary Union law. The Union fundamental rights must be observed, especially with regard to the express (e.g. Art. 36, 51, 62 TFEU) and implicit (*Cassis de Dijon*) exemptions to the market freedoms.[281]

A further-reaching domestic guarantee of fundamental rights does not apply either, if an implementing act of a Member State infringed a national fundamental right but at the same time was necessary due to Union law which is in conformity with the Charter, i.e. if the Member State has no margin of appreciation. As early as 1992 the *Conseil Constitutionnel* ruled that the protection of fundamental rights of the individual provided by the ECJ was sufficient to guarantee fundamental rights as provided for by the national constitutions.[282] Following its own Chamber decision[283] the First Senate of the *Bundesverfassungsgericht* also clarified that national provisions that are required by Union law are not reviewed against the standards of the domestic fundamental rights catalogue if and in so far as national legislative bodies have no margin of appreciation. Hence, in these cases German specialised courts are to examine requirements made by Union law only against fundamental rights of the Union and, if necessary and with regard to the guarantee of effective legal protection (Art. 19.4 GG), make a reference for preliminary ruling according to Art. 267 TFEU. Only if the ECJ then annuls the directive in question will there be room to review the national implementing act against the standards of German fundamental rights and to refer the case pursuant to Art. 100.1 GG.[284]

This case law is in most parts identical to the requirements made by the ECJ regarding the Member States' obligations to give effect to European fundamental rights.[285] In its review of the Directive on Family Reunification[286] the Court distinguishes between two intertwined legal levels: on the one hand, provisions of a directive which impose direct and precise obligations on the Member States and,

---

[280]In this respect Spanish Constitutional Tribunal, DTC No. 1/2004 (13 December 2004) fundamentos 5 and 6.

[281]Bleckmann (2011), pp. 15 et seqq., 82 et seqq., 131 et seqq.

[282]French Constitutional Council, Decision No. 92-308 DC (9 April 1992) – *Maastricht I* (English translation available online), *RUDH* 1992, pp. 336 et seqq.; in this respect see also French *Conseil d'État*, Decision No. 287110 DC (8 February 2007); Fromont (1995), p. 132.

[283]See German Federal Constitutional Court, 2 BvG 1/89 (Judgment of 11 April 1989) (in: BVerfGE 80, 74 and NJW 1990, 974) – *Broadcasting Directive*.

[284]Cf. German Federal Constitutional Court, 1 BvF/05 (Order of 13 March 2007) para 72 (in: BVerfGE 118, 79, 95) – *Emissions Trading I* = DVBl. 2007, pp. 821 et seqq., with reference to Art. 23.1 GG.

[285]Cf. Schmal (2008), pp. 16 et seqq.

[286]Council Directive 2003/86/EC *on the right to family reunification*, O.J. L 251/12 (2003).

on the other hand, those which leave a margin of appreciation.[287] Also, those provisions of a directive, which "afford the Member States a certain margin of appreciation and allow them in certain circumstances to apply national legislation derogating from the basic rules imposed by the Directive", are to be examined against the standards of fundamental rights of the Union.[288] This is consistent in so far as those clauses guaranteeing an individual transposal of an EU directive by a Member State ("opening clauses") are not part of national law but of Union law for which the fundamental rights of the Union are the relevant standard of evaluation.[289]

This is to be distinguished from the question if and to what extent implementing acts of Member States issued under the discretion conferred by the opening clause are to be examined against the standards of the fundamental rights of the Union or of the domestic fundamental rights order. Following the position of the ECJ – which is in accordance with the view of the *Bundesverfassungsgericht*[290] – if it is an implementing act required without any margin of appreciation, only a review based on Union fundamental rights can be considered. If, on the other hand, it is an implementing act for which the Member States may use a margin of appreciation, the ECJ holds that "the requirements flowing from the protection of general principles recognised in the Community legal order, which include fundamental rights, are also binding on Member States when they implement Community rules, and that consequently they are bound, as far as possible, to apply the rules in accordance with those requirements."[291] Since Member States are obliged by the general principles of Union law when using their margin of appreciation, they are bound by the fundamental rights of the Union in this legal sphere. In contrast, the *Bundesverfassungsgericht* limits the application of Union fundamental rights to the case that "Community law leaves no room for appreciation but imposes mandatory requirements."[292] Fundamental rights of the Union are to be binding on the Member States only if they implement mandatory requirements.[293] This is

---

[287]Case C-540/03 *Parliament v Council (family reunification)* (ECJ 27 June 2006) para 60 et seq.

[288]Case C-540/03 *Parliament v Council (family reunification)* (ECJ 27 June 2006) para 22.

[289]Cf. Lindner (2007), p. 72.

[290]German Federal Constitutional Court, 1 BvR 2036/05 (Order of 14 May 2007) para 8 – *Emissions Trading II*.

[291]Case C-540/03 *Parliament v Council (family reunification)* (ECJ 27 June 2006) para 104 et seq.

[292]German Federal Constitutional Court, 1 BvR 2036/05 (Order of 14 May 2007) para 8 – *Emissions Trading II* (our translation); yet even before: German Federal Administrative Court, NVwZ 2005, 1178 (1181 et seqq., 1183 et seqq.)

[293]This position had been emphasised by the then President of the Federal Constitutional Court, *Papier*, by using the misleading term "complementarity of the protection of fundamental rights" (our translation): cf. Papier (2009), pp. 113 et seqq., 116; affirmative Calliess (2009), p. 486, with reference to the "graduated bindingness [*gestufte Verbindlichkeit*]" (H. P. Ipsen) of those directives and underlining the fact that the so-called systemic decision of a directive (*Bundesverfassungsgericht*) works as a corrective; also affirmative Bleckmann (2011), pp. 150 et seqq. (164 et seqq.); critical Blanke (2009), pp. 149 et seq.

only "complementary protection of fundamental rights" in so far as either the European or the respective domestic fundamental rights order is applied; i.e. in so far as actions of either level that are not bound by fundamental rights are thus unimaginable. The divergence between the ECJ and the German Federal Constitutional Court on that matter is, however, put into context in that the *Bundesverfassungsgericht* generally regards the fundamental and systemic decision of a directive as part of the mandatory requirements.[294] A third opinion holds that when operating under a appreciation clause the national legislator is to be obliged by Art. 53 EUCFR – besides being fully bound by domestic fundamental rights – to respect the fundamental rights of the Union. Thus, the protection of fundamental rights is doubled, with the domestic fundamental rights functioning as "enhanced protection of European fundamental rights."[295] Even if Member States have a margin of appreciation, this is to be filled by safeguarding not only the national fundamental rights but also the fundamental rights of the Union due to the Member States' commitment to mandatory purposes of the Union.[296]

8 The Role of the Courts in Multilevel Constitutional Governance

European States are embedded in multiple and overlapping layers of regional and national "constitutional governance". Courts, it seems, inevitably foster a constitutionalisation of the legal order(s) of the arising transnational global society. The results are multiple legal regimes – and multiple regime-collisions of a growing complexity[297] – with courts as "gateways and interfaces".[298] Today's intensity of European integration would have never been possible if in addition to the "competition of legal orders" – most recently manifested with the Charter of Fundamental Rights – between Union law, the ECHR and domestic law, a "competition of judiciaries" between the national constitutional courts, the ECtHR and the ECJ had not developed.[299]

The "bilateral interplay" between the EU and Convention law was described as "a twofold process of 'conventionalisation' of Union law and 'unionisation' of Convention law, though with different timings and intensities."[300] This transformation

[294]In this sense the German Federal Administrative Court, NVwZ 2005, 1178 (1181 et seq.).

[295]Calliess (2009), p. 485 (our translation).

[296]Cf. Thym (2006), p. 3250; Szczekalla (2006), p. 1021; Lindner (2007), p. 73; Calliess (2009), pp. 485 et seqq.

[297]Cf. Wildhaber (2005b), p. 45.

[298]Nickel (2009), p. 338.

[299]Merli (2007), p. 397.

[300]Cf. Callewaert (2008).

from a competition of legal orders into a competition of judiciaries, as reflected by the line of the case law of the German Federal Constitutional Court (*Solange I – Solange II – Maastricht – Banana Market*), is a decisive step towards the unity of the European legal order, which in turn forms a fundamental premise of the systemic rationality of law.[301] In the wake of the structural problems of the European multilevel governance system, the rationality and the objective adequacy of law are repeatedly put to the test.[302] For this the "critical discourse" in the exchange of thesis and antithesis, the advancing of argument and counterargument between the participating courts, but not, however, the authority of "the final say" is a substantial requirement. This competition of judiciaries, it is held, excludes efforts for convergence but ensures "protection of coherence [*Kohärenzvorsorge*]" through which a significant amount of trust between the courts involved is created.[303]

An important expression of this protection of coherence vis-à-vis the national constitutional traditions can be found in the *Open door* case of the Strasbourg Court in which the scope of protection of a fundamental right had been determined by weighing a specific guarantee of the ECHR (freedom of expression pursuant to Art. 10.2 ECHR) against a domestic fundamental right of constitutional law (right to life of the unborn child according to Art. 40.3.3 of the Irish Constitution).[304] This case shows how difficult it is to avoid contradictions in the triangle of the judiciaries in Strasbourg, Luxembourg and the Member States because the result of the careful considerations by the ECtHR contrasts with the previous case law of the ECJ which had affirmed that medical termination of pregnancy constitutes a service but denied that there had been a violation of the right to free distribution of information on such services.[305] The plea that former ECtHR President, *Luzius Wildhaber*, has directed to the national courts equally

[301]Oeter (2007); Hoffmann-Riem (2002), p. 473: "A minimum of unity of the legal order, at least its systemic consistency, is a widely accepted aim, regardless of the obvious evidence of a pluralisation of values, a fragmentation of living environments and heterogeneity of interests" (our translation).

[302]Oeter (2007).

[303]Oeter (2007), who states that "without provisions of coherence the compound of judiciaries would be doomed to failure" (our translation); previously Wildhaber (2005b), pp. 45 et seq., who considers a "coherent approach in respect of the rights which are common to most of the legal systems concerned" as "essential" while observing "a clear commitment to ensure harmony between the Luxembourg and the Strasbourg jurisprudence" in the sense of coherence and coordination are to be understood the proposals made by Krüger and Polakiewicz (2001), whereas Papier (2005), p. 117, with regard to the substantive protection of fundamental rights, talks about "a steady convergence" (not coherence) "between the requirements and expectations of national constitutional law on the one hand and the effective protection of fundamental rights by Community law on the other".

[304]Case 14234/88 *Open door and Dublin Well Woman v Ireland* (ECtHR 29 October 1992).

[305]Case 159/90 *The Society for the Protection of Unborn Children Ireland v Grogan et al.* (ECJ 4 October 1991) para 21, 32.

applies to the ECJ: In order to create legal certainty and convergence the Luxembourg Court is also required as far as possible in its deliberations to respect the ECHR and its interpretation by the Strasbourg Court.[306]

References

Barcz J (ed) (2009) Fundamental rights protection in the European Union. Beck, Warszawa

Barnard C (2008) The 'Opt-Out' for the UK and Poland from the Charter of Fundamental Rights: Triumph of Rhetoric over Reality? In: Griller St, Ziller J (eds) The Lisbon Treaty. EU Constitutionalism without a Constitutional Treaty? Wien et al: Springer, pp 257 et seqq http://www.law.cam.ac.uk/faculty-resources/summary/barnard-uk-opt-out-and-the-charter-of-fundamental-rights/7309, accessed date 15 January 2011

Bauer J-H (2006) EuGH, BVerfG, BAG – Ober schlägt Unter? NJW, pp 1 et seqq

Bauer J-H, Arnold Ch (2006) Auf "Junk" folgt "Mangold" – Europarecht verdrängt deutsches Arbeitsrecht. NJW, pp 6 et seqq

Blanke H-J (2006) Protection of Fundamental Rights afforded by the European Court of Justice in Luxembourg. In: Blanke H-J, Mangiameli St (eds) Governing Europe under a constitution. Springer, Heidelberg, pp 265 et seqq

Blanke H-J (2009) Diskussionsbeitrag. In: Stern K (ed) 60 Jahre Grundgesetz: Das Grundgesetz für die Bundesrepublik Deutschland im Europäischen Verfassungsverbund. Beck, München

Bleckmann M (2011) *Nationale Grundrechte im Anwendungsbereich des Rechts der Europäischen Union*. Tübingen: Mohr Siebeck

Braibant G (2001) La Charte des droits fondamentaux de l'Union européennne. Témoignage et commentaries. Le Seuil, Paris (coll. Points, inédit essais)

Broß S (2008) Überlegungen zur europäischen Staatswerdung. JZ, pp 227 et seqq

Bundesverfassungsgericht (ed) (1992) Decisions of the Bundesverfassungsgericht. International Law and the Law of the European Communities 1952–1989, vols. I and II. Nomos, Baden-Baden

Callewaert J (2003) Die EMRK und die EU-Grundrechtecharta, Bestandsaufnahme einer Harmonisierung auf halbem Weg. EuGRZ, pp 198 et seqq

Callewaert J (2008) "Unionisation" and "Conventionalisation" of fundamental rights in Europe. In: Wouters J, Nollkaemper A, De Wet E (eds) The status of public international law in the EU and its member states. TMC Asser Press, The Hague

Calliess Ch (2009) 60 Jahre Grundgesetz – ein Jubiläum im Lichte der Europäisierung. Anwaltsblatt, pp 478 et seqq

Calliess Ch, Ruffert M (eds) (2011) EUV/AEUV, Das Verfassungsrecht der Europäischen Union mit Europäischer Grundrechtecharta, Kommentar, 4th edn. Beck, München

Classen CD (2000) Zur Verfassungsmäßigkeit der Bananenmarktordnung. JZ pp 1155 et seqq

Classen CD (2009) Legitime Stärkung des Bundestages oder verfassungsrechtliches Prokrustesbett? Zum Urteil des BVerfG zum Vertrag von Lissabon. JZ, pp 881 et seqq

Cremer H-J (2004) Zur Bindungswirkung von EGMR-Urteilen. EuGRZ, pp 683 et seqq

Daiber B (2010) Die Umsetzung des Lissabon-Urteils des Bundesverfassungsgerichts durch Bundestag und Bundesrat. DÖV, pp 293 et seqq

de Witte B (2009) The Lisbon Treaty and National Constitutions. More or Less Europeanisation? In: Closa C (ed) The Lisbon Treaty and National Constitutions Europeanisation and Democratic Implications, pp 25–48. http://www.astrid-online.it/Riforma-de/Studi-e-ri/Archivio-25/ARENA-Report-3_2009.pdf, accessed date 15 January 2011

[306] Wildhaber (2005a), pp. 314, 316, 318.

Dederer H-G (2006) Die Architektur des europäischen Grundrechtsraums. ZaöRV 66:575–624 et seqq
Denza E (2004) Lines in the sand: between common foreign policy and single foreign policy. In: Tridimas T, Nebbia P (eds) EU law for the twenty-first century: re-thinking the new legal order, vol I. Hart Publishing, Oxford, pp 259 et seqq
di Salvatore E (2006) The Supremacy of European law in the Treaty establishing a Constitution for Europe in the light of Community experience. In: Blanke H-J, Mangiameli St (eds) Governing Europe under a constitution. Springer, Heidelberg, pp 375 et seqq
Dörr O (2006) Rechtsprechungskonkurrenz zwischen nationalen und europäischen Verfassungsgerichten. DVBl, pp 1088 et seqq
Estella de Noriega A (1999) A dissident voice: the Spanish Constitutional Court case law on European Integration. Eur Publ Law 5, pp 269 et seqq
Everling U (2005) Europäische Union, Europäische Menschenrechtskonvention und Verfassungsstaat. In: Zentrum für Europäisches Wirtschaftsrecht (ed) Die Entwicklung einer Europäischen Grundrechtsarchitektur. Symposium zu Ehren von U. Everling. Zentrum für Europ. Wirtschaftsrecht, Bonn, pp 63 et seqq
Frenz W (2009) Handbuch Europearecht, Europäische Grundrechte, vol 4. Springer, Berlin et al
Fromont M (1995) Europäische integration und nationales. Verfassungsrecht in Frankreich. In: Battis U, Tsatsos D, Stephanou D. (eds.) Europäische integration und nationales Verfassungsrecht. Nomos, Baden-Baden, pp 127 et seqq
Frowein JA (1988) Die Herausbildung europäischer Verfassungsprinzipien. In: Kaufmann A et al (eds) Rechtsstaat und Menschenwürde. FS für W. Maihofer. Vittorio Klostermann, Frankfurt, pp 149 et seqq
Garcia de Enterria E, Alonso Garcia R (2000) Spanischer Landesbericht. In: Schwarze J (ed) Die Entstehung einer europäischen Verfassungsordnung. Nomos, Baden-Baden, pp 287 et seqq
Gärditz KF, Hillgruber Ch (2009) Volkssouveränität und Demokratie ernst genommen – Zum Lissabon-Urteil des BVerfG. JZ, pp 872 et seqq
Garlicki L (2008) Cooperation of courts: the role of supranational jurisdictions in Europe. Int J Constit Law 6, pp 509 et seqq
Gerken L, Rieble V, Roth GH, Stein T, Streinz R (2009) "Mangold" als ausbrechender Rechtsakt. Sellier, München
Goldsmith L (2001) A charter of rights, freedoms and principles. CMLRev 38, pp 1201 et seqq
Grabenwarter Ch (2009a) Europäische Menschenrechtskonvention, 4th edn. Beck/Manz, München/Wien
Grabenwarter Ch (2009b) Staatliches Unionsverfassungsrecht. In: v. Bogdandy A, Bast J (eds) Europäisches Verfassungsrecht, 2nd edn. Springer, Berlin et al, pp 121 et seqq
Grabitz E, Hilf M (2002) Das Recht der Europäischen Union, Kommentar. Beck, München
Grimm D (1995) Braucht Europa eine Verfassung. Carl-Friedrich-von-Siemens-Stiftung, München
Haratsch A (2006) Die *Solange*-Rechtsprechung des Europäischen Gerichtshofs für Menschenrechte – Das Kooperationsverhältnis zwischen EGMR und EuGH. ZaöRV 66, pp 927 et seqq
Herzog R, Gerken L (2008) Stoppt den Europäischen Gerichtshof! In: Centrum für Europäische Politik (ed.) also published in FAZ of 8 September 2008. http://www.cep.eu/fileadmin/user_upload/Pressemappe/CEP_in_den_Medien/Herzog-EuGH-Webseite.pdf, accessed date 15 January 2011
Hillgruber Ch, Goos C (2006) Verfassungsprozessrecht, 2nd edn. Müller, Heidelberg
Hoffmann-Riem W (2002) Kohärenz der Anwendung europäischer und nationaler Grundrechte. EuGRZ, pp 473 et seqq
Hoffmeister F (2001) Die Europäische Menschenrechtskonvention als Grundrechtsverfassung und ihre Bedeutung in Deutschland. Der Staat 40, pp 349 et seqq
Huber PM (2009) Das europäisierte Grundgesetz. DVBl., pp 574 et seqq
Iliopoulos-Strangas J (2007a) Der Vorrang des Gemeinschafts-/Unionsrechts gegenüber der Verfassung. In: Grote R et al (eds) Die Ordnung der Freiheit. FS für Ch Starck. Mohr Siebeck, Tübingen, pp 825 et seqq

Iliopoulos-Strangas J (2007b) Offene Staatlichkeit: Griechenland. In: von Bogdandy A, Cruz Villalón P, Huber PM (eds.) Handbuch Ius Publicum Europaeum, vol II, § 16. Müller, Heidelberg, pp 71 et seqq

Ipsen HP (1972) Europäisches Gemeinschaftsrecht. Mohr, Tübingen

Kadelbach S (2005) Der Status der Europäischen Menschenrechtskonvention im deutschen Recht. JURA, pp 480 et seqq

Kirchhof P (2003) Die rechtliche Struktur der Europäischen Union als Staatenverbund. In: v. Bogdandy A, Bast J (eds) Europäisches Verfassungsrecht. Springer, Berlin et al, pp 893 et seqq

Körner K (2009) Identitätsstiftung durch den Europäischen Verfassungsvertrag. Duncker & Humblot, Berlin

Krüger HCh, Polakiewicz J (2001) Vorschläge für ein kohärentes System des Menschenrechtsschutzes in Europa. EuGRZ, pp 92 et seqq

Kühling J (2003) Grundrechte. In: v. Bogdandy A, Bast J (eds) Europäisches Verfassungsrecht. Springer, Berlin et al, pp 538 et seqq

Leijten I (2011) Schmitz v. Germany and Mork v. Germany: Applause for the German Constitutional Court – Does 'Dialogue' Solve it All?, http://strasbourgobservers.com/2011/06/22/schmitz-v-germany-and-mork-v-germany-applause-for-the-german-constitutional-court%E2%80%94does-%E2%80%98dialogue%E2%80%99-solve-it-all/ (accessed 25 June 2011)

Limbach J (2000) Die Kooperation der Gerichte in der zukünftigen europäischen Grundrechtsarchitektur, Ein Beitrag zur Neubestimmung des Verhältnisses von Bundesverfassungsgericht, Gerichtshof der Europäischen Gemeinschaften und Europäischem Gerichtshof für Menschenrechte. EuGRZ, pp 417 et seqq

Lindner JF (2007) Grundrechtsschutz gegen gemeinschaftsrechtliche Öffnungsklauseln. EuZW, pp 71 et seqq

Lopez Castillo A, Polakiewicz J (1993) Verfassung und Gemeinschaftsrecht in Spanien. EuGRZ, pp 277 et seqq

Lübbe-Wolff G (2006) ECHR and national jurisdiction – The Görgülü Case. In: Humboldt Forum Recht (HFR) December 2006, pp 138 et seqq. http://www.humboldt-forum-recht.de/media/Druckansicht/pdf/2006-12.pdf, accessed date 15 January 2011

Mangiameli St (2006) Il contributo dell'esperienza costituzionale italiana alla dommatica europea della tutela dei diritti fondamentali. In: Pace A (ed) Corte costituzionale e processo costituzionale nell'esperienza della rivista Giurisprudenza costituzionale. Giuffrè, Milano

Mangiameli St (2008) Diritto costituzionale e integrazione europea, in: Lésperienza costituzionale europea, Aracne, Rome, pp 1 et seqq

Mayer FC (2003) Europäische Verfassungsgerichtsbarkeit. In: v. Bogdandy A, Bast J (eds) Europäisches Verfassungsrecht. Springer, Berlin et al, pp 229 et seqq

Mayer FC (2006) Supremacy – lost? In: Rynkowski M, Dann Ph (eds) The Unity of the European Constitution. Springer, Berlin et al, pp 87 et seqq

Mayer FC (2007) Die Rückkehr der Europäischen Verfassung? Ein Leitfaden zum Vertrag von Lissabon. ZaöRV 67, pp 1141 et seqq

Mayer FC (2009) Der Vertrag von Lissabon und die Grundrechte. EuR Beiheft 1, pp 87 et seqq

Mayer FC, Lenski E, Wendel M (2008) Der Vorrang des Europarechts in Frankreich – zugleich Anmerkung zur Entscheidung des französischen Conseil d'Etat vom 8 February 2007 (Arcelor u.a.). EuR, pp 63 et seqq

Merli F (2007) Rechtsprechungskonkurrenz zwischen nationalen Verfassungsgerichten, Europäischem Gerichtshof und Europäischem Gerichtshof für Menschenrechte, in *VVDStRL 66*. Bundesstaat und Europäische Union zwischen Konflikt und Kooperation, pp 392 et seqq

Meyer-Ladewig J, Petzold H (2005) Die Bindung deutscher Gerichte an Urteile des EGMR – Neues aus Straßburg und Karlsruhe. NJW, pp 15 et seqq

Müller JP (2005) Einleitungsreferat. In: Juristenverein S (ed) 3rd European Jurists´ Forum. Coordination of the Protection of Fundamental Rights. Zeitschrift für Schweizerisches Recht/Revue de droit suisse, vol 124/II. Helbing & Lichtenhahn, Basel, pp 9 et seqq

Nickel R (2009) Transnational borrowing among judges towards a common core of european and global constitutional law? In: Nickel R (ed) Conflict of laws and laws of conflict in Europe and beyond. Patterns of supranational and transnational juridification, pp 309 et seqq.. ARENA Report No 1/09. http://arno.uvt.nl/show.cgi?fid=96532, accessed date 15 January 2011

Niedobitek M (2008) Der Vorrang des Unionsrechts. In: Niedobitek M, Zemánek J (eds) Continuing the European constitutional debate. Duncker & Humblot, Berlin, pp 63 et seqq

Oeter St (2007) Rechtsprechungskonkurrenz zwischen nationalen Verfassungsgerichten, Europäischem Gerichtshof und Europäischem Gerichtshof für Menschenrechte, in *VVDStRL 66*. Bundesstaat und Europäische Union zwischen Konflikt und Kooperation, pp 361 et seqq

Oppenheimer A (ed) (1994) The relationship between European Community Law and national law: the cases, vol 1. Cambridge University Press, Cambridge

Pache E (2009) Das Ende der europäischen Integration. Das Urteil des Bundesverfassungsgerichts zum Vertrag von Lissabon, zur Zukunft Europas und der Demokratie. EuGRZ, pp 285 et seqq

Panara C (2007) Offene Staatlichkeit: Italien. In: von Bogdandy A, Cruz Villalón P, Huber PM (eds) Handbuch Ius Publicum Europaeum, vol I (Sect. 18). Müller, Heidelberg, pp 143 et seqq

Papier H-J (2005) Koordination des Grundrechtsschutzes in Europa – die Sicht des Bundesverfassungsgerichts. In: Juristenverein S (ed) 3rd European Jurists' Forum. Coordination of the protection of fundamental rights. Zeitschrift für Schweizerisches Recht/Revue de droit suisse, vol 124/II. Helbing & Lichtenhahn, Basel, pp 113 et seqq

Papier H-J (2006) Execution and effects of the judgments of the European court of human rights – from the perspective of German national courts. Hum Rights Law J, pp 1 et seqq

Papier H-J (2009) Die Bedeutung des Grundgesetzes im Europäischen Staatenverbund. In: Stern K (ed) 60 Jahre Grundgesetz: Das Grundgesetz für die Bundesrepublik Deutschland im Europäischen Verfassungsverbund. Beck, München, pp 107 et seqq

Pernice I (2008) The treaty of Lisbon and fundamental rights. In: Griller St, Ziller J (eds) The Lisbon treaty. EU constitutionalism without a constitutional treaty? Springer, Wien et al, pp 235 et seqq. (also WHI-Paper 7/08, available online www.whi-berlin.de/documents/whi-paper0708.pdf), accessed date 15 January 2011

Preis U (2006) Verbot der Altersdiskriminierung als Gemeinschaftsgrundrecht. Neue Zeitschrift für Arbeitsrecht, pp 401 et seqq

Randazzo A (2008) I controlimiti al primato del diritto comunitario: un futuro non diverso dal presente? http://www.forumcostituzionale.it/site/images/stories/pdf/documenti_forum/paper/0048_randazzo.pdf, accessed date 15 January 2011

Ress G (2002) Das Europarecht vor dem Europäischen Gerichtshof für Menschenrechte in Straßburg. Paper presented at the Humboldt-Universität (Berlin) on 11 April 2002. FCE 2/02. www.whi-berlin.de/documents/ress.pdf, accessed date 15 January 2011

Rodriguez Iglesias GC (1995) Zur Stellung der Europäischen Menschenrechtskonvention im europäischen Gemeinschaftsrecht. In: Beyerlin U, Bothe M, Hofmann R, Petersmann E-U (eds) Recht zwischen Umbruch und Bewahrung. FS für R. Bernhardt. Springer, Berlin et al, pp 1269 et seqq

Rodriguez Iglesias GC (1998) Reflection on the general principles of community law. In: Centre for European Legal Studies, A. Dashwood & A. Ward (eds.) The Cambridge yearbook of European legal studies, Hart Publishing, vol I, pp 1 et seqq

Roller St (2004) Die menschenrechtskonventionsgemäße Auslegung. Deutsche Richterzeitung, pp 337 et seqq

Ruggeri A (2005) Il Trattato costituzionale e l'europeizzazione dei controlimiti e tecniche di risoluzione delle antinomie tra diritto comunitario e diritto interno (profili problematici). http://www.forumcostituzionale.it/site/index3.php?option=content&task=view&id=223, accessed date 15 January 2011

Rupp HH (1987) Zur Prüfungskompetenz des BVerfG über die Verfassungsmäßigkeit von Akten des Europäischen Gemeinschaftsrechts. JZ, pp 236 et seqq
Schilling JM (2010) Deutscher Grundrechtsschutz zwischen staatlicher Souveränität und menschenrechtlicher Europäisierung. Mohr Siebeck, Tübingen
Schlaich K, Korioth St (2007) Das Bundesverfassungsgericht, 7th edn. Beck, München
Schmal St (2008) Grundrechtsschutz im Dreieck von EU, EMRK und nationalem Verfassungsrecht. EuR Beiheft 1, pp 7 et seqq
Schmidt J (2010) Die Grundsätze im Sinne der EU-Grundrechtecharta. Mohr Siebeck, Tübingen
Schneiders B (2010) Die Grundrechte der EU und die EMRK. Nomos, Baden-Baden
Schwarze J (2005) Der Schutz der Grundrechte durch den Europäischen Gerichtshof – Eine Analyse der jüngeren Rechtsprechung. In: Zentrum für Europäisches Wirtschaftsrecht (ed) Die Entwicklung einer Europäischen Grundrechtsarchitektur, Symposium zu Ehren von U. Everling. Zentrum für Europ. Wirtschaftsrecht, Bonn, pp 35 et seqq
Schroeder W (2011) Neues zur Grundrechtskontrolle in der Europäischen Union. *EuZW*, pp 462 et seqq
Selmer P (1998) Die Gewährleistung des unabdingbaren Grundrechtsstandards durch den EuGH. Nomos, Baden-Baden
Skouris V (2005) Die Persepektiven des Gerichtshofes der Europäischen Gemeinschaften. In: Juristenverein S (ed) 3rd European Jurists' Forum. Coordination of the protection of fundamental rights. Zeitschrift für Schweizerisches Recht/Revue de droit suisse, vol 124/II. Helbing & Lichtenhahn, Basel, pp 31 et seqq
Szczekalla P (2006) Grenzenlose Grundrechte. NVwZ, pp 1019 et seqq
Tettinger PJ, Stern K (2006) Kölner Gemeinschaftskommentar zur Europäischen Grundrechte-Charta. Beck, München
Thym D (2006) Europäischer Grundrechtsschutz und Familienzusammenführung. NJW, pp 3249 et seqq
Tizzano A (2010) Der italienische Verfassungsgerichtshof (Corte Costituzionale) und der Gerichtshof der Europäischen Union. EuGRZ, pp 2 et seqq
Tomuschat Ch (2005) Das Europa der Richter. In: Bröhmer J (ed) Internationale Gemeinschaft und Menschenrechte. FS für G. Ress. Heymanns, Köln et al, pp 857 et seqq
Tomuschat Ch (2010) The Effects of the Judgments of the European Court of Human Rights According to the German Constitutional Court. German Law Journal, pp 513 et seqq
v. Arnauld A (2008) Theorie und Methode des Grundrechtsschutzes in Europa – am Beispiel des Grundsatzes der Verhältnismäßigkeit. EuR Beiheift 1, pp 41 et seqq
v. Mangoldt H, Klein F, Starck, Ch (2010) Kommentar zum Grundgesetz, 6th edn. Vahlen, München
Weber A (2007) Double ou triple protection des droits fondamentaux en Europe? In: Renouveau du droit constitutionnel, Mélanges en l'honneur de Louis Favoreu. Dalloz-Sirey, Paris, pp 1747 et seqq
Wildhaber L (2005a) Opening speech: about co-existence of three different legal systems and three jurisdictions. Zeitschrift für Öffentliches Recht = Austrian J Publ Int Law 60(3), pp 313 et seqq
Wildhaber L (2005b) The coordination of the protection of fundamental rights in Europe. In: Juristenverein S (ed) 3rd European Jurists' Forum. Coordination of the protection of fundamental rights. Zeitschrift für Schweizerisches Recht/Revue de droit suisse, vol 124/II. Helbing & Lichtenhahn, Basel, pp 43 et seqq
Zinamsgvarov N (2008) L´identité constitutionelle française: un circept. Contribution for the 7th Congress of the A.F.D.C. http://www.afdc.fr/congresParis/comC1/ZinamsgTXT.pdf, accessed date 15 January 2011

The Rule of Law in the Case Law of the Strasbourg Court*

Jens Meyer-Ladewig

1 Introduction

Our subject is the rule of law (*l'Etat de droit ou la prééminence du droit, die Rechtsstaatlichkeit*) in the case law of the European Court of Human Rights (ECtHR) in Strasbourg. But why this particular Court and not the Court of Justice of the European Union in Luxembourg? The answer is that the Strasbourg Court established by the European Convention on Human Rights and Fundamental Freedoms (ECHR) of 1950 is a European Constitutional Court, the jurisprudence of which is of importance not only for the 47 Member States of the Council of Europe but also for the European Union (EU) with 27 Member States. All EU Member States are also members of the Council of Europe and all Member States of the Council are also Contracting Parties to the Human Rights Convention. Indeed the EU was in comparison late in the field of protection of human rights, understandable because it had other aims. The Council of Europe was established earlier and the Union refers to the Convention in its basic Treaties. That was done in Art. F.2 TEU-Maastricht where the Treaty as amended declared that the Convention rights are "general principles of community law".

The EU Treaty as amended by the Lisbon Treaty goes further and stipulates in Art. 6.2 TEU that the Union shall accede to the ECHR. The EU Charter of Fundamental Rights (EUCFR), now legally binding (Art. 6.1 TEU), refers in its Preamble (recital 5) to the Human Rights Convention and the case law of the Strasbourg Court as does Art. 52.3 EUCFR. And that is why it is right to begin with the Strasbourg case law.

*This contribution deals exclusively with the case law of the ECtHR.

J. Meyer-Ladewig (✉)
Steering Committee on Human Rights, Auf dem Köllenhof 74, 53343 Wachtberg, Germany
e-mail: jens-m-ladewig@nexgo.de

H.-J. Blanke and S. Mangiameli (eds.), *The European Union after Lisbon*,
DOI 10.1007/978-3-642-19507-5_8, © Springer-Verlag Berlin Heidelberg 2012

2 The Rule of Law in International Documents

It is necessary to look at international documents which refer to the rule of law and are the basis for the jurisprudence of international courts. It would not be very helpful for our purpose to go far back into history, but it seems appropriate to make a few remarks. From the beginning of the seventeenth and eighteenth centuries the rule of law was a weapon against voluntary and arbitrary acts of sovereigns; it later became and still is important as a weapon against dictatorship. Its core remains to protect individuals against interferences by the State, to protect their liberties, their human rights. For this reason the rule of law is always mentioned together with human rights, democracy and liberty. This aim of protection was the background of the activities in the United Nations (UN) and the Council of Europe after World War II: the objective was that atrocities of the kind that happened during the time of the Nazi regime should never happen again. That was restated after the fall of the Berlin Wall with regard to the violations of human rights under the Communist regimes. Thus, the rule of law is of particular importance for States in transition on their way from dictatorship to democracy.

The Universal Declaration of Human Rights of 10 December 1948 was the first important step. The Declaration refers to the rule of law in recital 3 of the Preamble and makes clear that this principle has not only formal but also substantive aspects: the inherent aim of protecting human rights. The Declaration was a milestone: it had enormous influence on national constitutions, including the German Basic Law, but it was only a declaration and as such not legally binding. The Council of Europe on a regional basis went further in its Convention on Human Rights and created a catalogue of human rights, established the obligation of the Contracting Parties to ensure them as well as a very effective system of judicial protection. The basis of that Convention was the rule of law. The Statute of the Council of Europe of 5 May 1949 reaffirms in recital 2 of the Preamble the spiritual and moral values which are the common heritage and "the true source of individual freedom, political liberty and the rule of law, principles which form the basis of all genuine democracy." In Art. 3 the Statute obliges the Member States to "accept the principles of the rule of law" and of human rights and fundamental freedoms. The ECHR of 1950 repeats in the last recital of its Preamble the idea of the "common heritage of political traditions, ideals, freedom and the rule of law" and sets out the aim of the Convention to "take the first steps for the collective enforcement of certain rights stated in the Universal Declaration". In proceeding along these lines and the rule of law the Convention created its judicial control mechanism which was constantly improved and achieved its perfection with Protocol No. 11 of 1994. Since the entry into force of Protocol No. 11 each person may without any special declaration by the defendant State claim in an application to the Court that his or her human rights were violated. The Court then decides after a judicial procedure whether the defendant State has violated the Convention and if so awards just satisfaction (Art. 41 ECHR). The judgments are legally binding (Art. 46 ECHR).

As mentioned above, the European Community came late into this field. The ECtHR has described developments in the EU in its *Bosphorus*[1] judgment. The original Treaties did not mention the protection of human rights at all. Later, however, came the above-mentioned reference in the former EU Treaty to the rule of law and to the Convention. The EU Treaty as amended by the Lisbon Treaty now lists the rule of law in Art. 2 TEU among the fundamental values on which the Union is founded. So does the EUCFR in recital 2 of its Preamble. The relevance of the Strasbourg Convention and case law for the Union will be enhanced when the Union accedes to the Convention as Art. 6.2 TEU stipulates.

3 Legal Basis

The main source for the Strasbourg Court is the Convention on Human Rights, including its Preamble. That is of importance since the notion of the rule of law appears in the Preamble but in none of the following articles. So the Strasbourg Court in its judgments draws inspiration from the Preamble when dealing with the principle of the rule of law, and it also refers to the Statute of the Council of Europe as an organisation of which every Contracting State of the Convention is a member. It has done so on many occasions. The leading case in this respect is that of *Golder v United Kingdom* of 1975,[2] where the Court found that Art. 6 ECHR guarantees the right of access to a court. The Court quotes Art. 31.2 of the Vienna Convention on the Law of Treaties (VCLT), which makes clear that the Preamble to a treaty forms an integral part of it. The Court found it both natural and in conformity with the principle of good faith – the fundamental principle of interpretation of treaties laid down in Art. 31.1 VCLT – to bear in mind the profound belief in the rule of law when interpreting Art. 6 ECHR.

4 Aspects of the Rule of Law in the Strasbourg Case Law

4.1 The Rule of Law as Leitmotiv

It is – or it should be – a good practice of all courts to strictly limit its reasons to the specific case to be decided and to refrain from making observations *obiter*. The Strasbourg Court follows this line. The result is that the ECtHR does not give a general definition of the rule of law but decides whether – in a specific case – this principle gives guidelines for the interpretation of an Article in the Convention.

[1]Case 45036/98 *Bosphorus v Ireland* (ECtHR 30 June 2005), German translation NJW 2006, 197.

[2]Case 4451/70 *Golder v United Kingdom* (ECtHR 21 February 1975) para 34.

This can apply to all Articles of the Convention with guarantees of human rights, because, as the Court has stressed several times, the rule of law is inherent in all Articles of the Convention.[3] So we find judgments regarding all Convention provisions with human rights guarantees in which the Court refers to the rule of law. And we shall see that the Court bases its judgments on different aspects of the principle of the rule of law. The case law is founded on this principle. It is the concept inherent throughout the Convention, the basis of the protection of human rights – it is the leitmotiv.

4.2 *Rule of Law and Democracy*

Article 2 TEU and recital 2 of the Preamble of the EUCFR both mention the rule of law together with democracy. The Court has stressed the connection between these notions several times. In the above-mentioned judgment of *former King of Greece v Greece*[4] the Court speaks of "the rule of law, one of the fundamental principles of democratic society". The same words are used in the *Carbonara and Ventura* judgment.[5] In judgments against Turkey regarding the prohibition of political parties[6] the Court was more explicit and mentions that the Preamble to the Convention "establishes a very clear connection between the Convention and democracy", and "in that common heritage are to be found the underlying values of the Convention".

The second paragraphs in Arts. 8 through 11 ECHR allow for interferences in the rights guaranteed under certain conditions, one being that the interference is "necessary in a democratic society". The Court has repeatedly stressed the importance of that yardstick and made clear that "the only type of necessity capable of justifying an interference with any of those rights is, therefore, one which may claim to spring from 'democratic society'. Democracy thus appears to be the only political model contemplated by the Convention and, accordingly, the only one compatible with it."[7]

---

[3]Case 19776/92 *Amuur v France* (ECtHR 25 June 1996) para 50; Case 25701/94 *The former King of Greece et al. v Greece* (ECtHR 23 November 2000) para 79, German translation NJW 2002, 45; Case 5410/03 *Tysiac v Poland* (ECtHR 20 March 2007) para 112; Case 24638/94 *Carbonara and Ventura v Italy* (ECtHR 30 May 2000) para 63; Case 49429/99 *Capital Bank AD v Bulgaria* (ECtHR 24 November 2005) paras 133–134.

[4]Case 25701/94 *The former King of Greece et al. v Greece* (ECtHR 23 November 2000) para 79.

[5]Case 24638/94 *Carbonara and Ventura v Italy* (ECtHR 30 May 2000) para 63; see also Case 22860/02 *Wos v Poland* (ECtHR 8 June 2006) paras 92, 97.

[6]Case 133/1996/752/951 *United Communist Party of Turkey et al. v Turkey* (ECtHR 30 January 1998) para 45; in Case 41340/98 *Refah Partisi v Turkey* (ECtHR 13 February 2002) para 86, German translation NVwZ 2003, 1489, the Court quoted these reasons.

[7]Case 133/1996/752/951 *United Communist Party of Turkey et al. v Turkey* (ECtHR 30 January 1998) para 45; Case 72881/00 *Moccow branch of the Salvation Army v Russia* (ECtHR 5 October 2006) para 60.

4.3 The Principle of Legitimacy

4.3.1 Law in the Formal Sense

The principle of legitimacy means that authorities need a legal basis for measures which interfere with a right of an individual, and that the executive and the judiciary are bound by law. The Court has frequently addressed this principle as one of the aspects of the rule of law. One example is the *Carbonara and Ventura* judgment of 2000,[8] where the Court has reasoned that "the first and most important requirement of Art. 1 of Protocol No. 1 is that any interference by a public authority with the peaceful enjoyment of possessions should be lawful." Lawfulness means under the case law of the Court "the obligation to conform to the substantive and procedural rules of national law".[9] In the *McKay* judgment of 2006[10] the Court mentions with regard to Art. 5 ECHR the "repeated emphasis on the lawfulness of the detention, procedurally and substantively, requiring scrupulous adherence to the rule of law."

4.3.2 Quality Requirements for the Law

The Court does not limit itself to making sure that interference is formally in conformity with a legal provision. It requires "firstly, that the impugned measure should have some basis in domestic law" but refers also "to the quality of the law in question". The law must in particular be "compatible with the rule of law."[11] But what does that mean?

Accessibility, Foreseeability, Legal Certainty

With regard to the formalities it means that the law must be adequately accessible, and that the citizen must have the possibility to acquire knowledge of the law without difficulties. In the field of statute law this requirement is normally fulfilled when the law is published in an official gazette. The law must in addition be adequately foreseeable, it must be "formulated with sufficient precision to enable the individual – if need be with appropriate advice – to regulate his conduct" accordingly,[12] that is "to foresee, to a degree that is reasonable in the circumstances,

[8]Case 24638/94 *Carbonara and Ventura v Italy* (ECtHR 30 May 2000) para 63.

[9]Regarding Art. 5 ECHR see Case 22414/93 *Chahal v United Kingdom* (ECtHR 15 November 1996) para 118, German translation NVwZ 1997, 1093.

[10]Case 543/03 *McKay v United Kingdom* (ECtHR 3 October 2006) para 30.

[11]Case 19776/92 *Amuur v France* (ECtHR 15 June 1996) para 50.

[12]Case 30985/96 *Hasan a. Chaush v Bulgaria* (ECtHR 26 October 2000) para 84.

the consequences which a given action may entail,"[13] compatible with the rule of law.[14] Legal certainty as a special aspect of the rule of law is of particular importance in penal matters with the principle of *nulla poena sine lege* (laid down in Art. 7 ECHR). This principle is "not confined to prohibiting the retrospective application of the criminal law to an accused's disadvantage; it also embodies, more generally, the principle that only the law can define a crime and prescribe a penalty".[15] The consequence is that the criminal law must not be extensively construed to an accused's detriment, for instance by analogy. Nevertheless, the Court is aware of the fact that "however clearly drafted a legal provision may be, in any system of law, including criminal law, there is an inevitable element of judicial interpretation" and that "there will always be a need for elucidation of doubtful points and for adaptation to changing circumstances."[16] In matters other than criminal the law may also confer a discretion which is not in itself inconsistent with these requirements "provided that the scope of the discretion and the manner of its exercise are indicated with sufficient clarity, having regard to the legitimate aim in question to give the individual adequate protection against arbitrary interference."[17]

In the context of substantive requirements for a law it is worthwhile to look at a judgment concerning the killing of fugitives at the Berlin Wall by the border police of the former German Democratic Republic (GDR), the *Streletz, Kessler and Krenz* judgment.[18] The applicants had complained that Art. 7 ECHR had been violated by their conviction for killing of fugitives because the GDR state practice had allowed these measures to protect the border. The Court did not accept their arguments. It reasoned that GDR state practice had flagrantly violated human rights and above all the right to life and therefore cannot be covered by the protection of Art. 7 ECHR and cannot be described as "national law" within the meaning of the article.[19]

Legal certainty has been relevant in the Strasbourg case law in a very different context. The Court mentioned that in its *Christine Goodwin* judgment[20] when discussing the choice between sticking to its former case law and taking a dynamic and evolutionary approach. The response to changing conditions is a problem often arising in cases concerning moral convictions. In the *Goodwin* case the Court had to decide on the legal recognition of transsexuals. The Court reasoned: "While the Court is not formally bound to follow its previous judgments it is in the interest of

[13]Case 12963/87 *Margareta and Roger Andersson v Sweden* (ECtHR 25 February 1992) para 75.

[14]Case 54934/00 *Weber and Saravia v Germ*any (ECtHR 29 June 2006) para 84.

[15]Case 20166/92 *S.W. v United Kingdom* (ECtHR 22 November 1995) para 35.

[16]Case 20166/92 *S.W. v United Kingdom* (ECtHR 22 November 1995) para 36.

[17]Case 20166/92 *S.W. v United Kingdom* (ECtHR 22 November 1995) para 35.

[18]Case 34044/96 *Streletz, Kessler and Krenz v Germany* (ECtHR 22 March 2001), German translation NJW 2001, 3035.

[19]Case 20166/92 *S.W. v United Kingdom* (ECtHR 22 November 1995) para 36.

[20]Case 28957/95 *Christine Goodwin v United Kingdom* (ECtHR 11 July 2002) para 74, German translation NJW-RR 2004, 289.

legal certainty, foreseeability and equality before the law that it should not depart, without good reason, from precedents laid down in previous cases [...]."

Legitimate Aim, No Arbitrariness

The substantive requirements for a law can be found in particular in the case law in paragraphs 2 of Arts. 8 through 11 ECHR which allow for interference or restrictions only if – inter alia – the measure has one or more "legitimate aims" which are listed in the provisions. In line with that the Court has developed the general quality criterion for the law on which the measure is based that it must be in keeping with the aims of the Convention and in particular with the purpose to protect the individual from arbitrariness. This can be seen with regard to Art. 5 ECHR (right to liberty),[21] but also regarding Art. 7 ECHR (no retroactive application of criminal law).[22] In a case concerning Art. 8 ECHR (right to respect for private and family life), the *Storck* judgment, the Court explains that it is usually the responsibility of national courts to interpret national law. "However" – the Court continues – "the Court is called upon to examine whether the effects of such an interpretation are compatible with the Convention" and that the national courts are obliged to apply national law in the spirit of its rights.[23]

Proportionality

One of the most important principles is that of proportionality and – closely related to that – the search for a fair balance of the interests involved. Both are essential elements of the rule of law as the case law clearly demonstrates. The Court often reiterates and did so in the famous *Öcalan* judgment that "inherent in the whole of the Convention is a search for a fair balance between the demands of the general interest of the community and the requirements of the protection of the individual's fundamental rights".[24] In following this approach the Court underlines the obligation to respect the principle of proportionality. The Court holds interferences only justified under paragraphs 2 of Arts. 8 through 11 ECHR when there is a "pressing social need" for them; the authorities must give pertinent reasons which show that.

---

[21] See Case 19776/92 *Amuur v France* (ECtHR 15 June 1996) para 50; Case 22414/93 *Chahal v United Kingdom* (ECtHR 15 November 1996) para 118.

[22] Case 20166/92 *S.W. v United Kingdom* (ECtHR 22 November 1995) para 34.

[23] Case 61603/00 *Storck v Germany* (ECtHR 16 June 2006) para 93; in the same sense Case 69498/01 *Pla and Puncernau v Andorra* (ECtHR 13 July 2004) para 46, German translation NJW 2005, 875 – violation of Art. 8 in connection with Art. 14 ECHR by a judicial decision interpreting a testament.

[24] Case 46221/99 *Öcalan v Turkey* (ECtHR 12 May 2005) para 88, German translation NVwZ 2006, 1267.

"The Court will [then] assess whether the reasons adduced to justify such measures were relevant and sufficient and whether the aforementioned proportionality principle has been adhered to [...]",[25] which means that there must be a "reasonable relationship of proportionality between the means employed and the aim pursued."[26]

When dealing with terrorism, fair balance of interests and the principle of proportionality are also a topical problem in connection with the rule of law. Europe has had experience of terrorism and organized crime for a long time – for instance with the Northern Ireland conflict, the Mafia in Italy, the Bader-Meinhof gang in Germany, the *brigati rossi* in Italy, the Basque region in Spain, the Kurdish problems in Turkey and the Russian problems in Chechnya. So the Court has dealt often and over a very long period with terrorist crimes. In its judgments it has often stressed its understanding of the difficulty for the authorities in efficiently investigating such crimes. In the leading case of *Brogan*[27] the applicant had been arrested under suspicion of involvement of terrorism. The Court had to decide whether the fact that the applicant was brought before a judge more than four days after his arrest – which was allowed by special legislation in Ireland – was a breach of Art. 5.3 ECHR. In its judgment the Court acknowledged the difficult situation in Northern Ireland resulting from the threat posed by organized terrorism. It stressed the need to find a proper balance between the defence of institutions of democracy and the protection of individual rights. Judicial control – so the Court reasoned – is implied by the rule of law referred to in the Preamble "from which the whole Convention draws its inspiration". More than four days and six hours – so the Court concluded – is not prompt in the sense of Art. 5.3 ECHR and is therefore a violation of this judicial right.

4.4 Protection Against Violations of Human Rights

The protection of individuals against arbitrary interferences with their fundamental rights and freedoms has been a key aspect of the rule of law from the very beginning.

4.4.1 By Legislative Measures

The Contracting States can choose by which means they want to efficiently protect human rights. Such protection is required through legislative measures. For example, Art. 2 ECHR (right to life) enjoins the State to refrain from unlawful taking of

[25]Case 41604/98 *Buck v Germany* (ECtHR 28 April 2005) para 45, German translation NJW 2006, 1495.

[26]Case 19133/91 *Scollo v Italy* (ECtHR 28 September 1975) para 32; see also Case 7525/76 *Dudgeon v United Kingdom* (ECtHR 22 October 1981) para 53.

[27]Case 11209/84 *Brogan et al. v United Kingdom* (ECtHR 29 November 1988) paras 48, 58–62.

life. The Court has found that Art. 2 ECHR read in conjunction with Art. 1 ECHR obliges the States also to "take appropriate steps to safeguard the lives of those within its jurisdiction", in particular by "putting in place effective criminal law provisions to deter the commission of offences against a person, backed up by law-enforcement machinery for the prevention, suppression and punishment of breaches" of this provision. Prompt response by the authorities – according to the Court – in such investigations "may generally be regarded as essential in maintaining public confidence in their maintenance of the rule of law [...]."[28] Under certain conditions the authorities are obliged to take preventive measures to protect an individual whose life is at risk from criminal acts of others.

4.4.2 By Administrative Measures, Investigations

Protection is also required through administrative measures. As regards the duty of States to protect individuals against violations of their rights the Court accepts the need for international cooperation and has found that the arrest of a criminal as a result of an extradition arrangement does not make the arrest unlawful because it "is in the interest of all nations that offenders who flee abroad should be brought to justice."[29] But extradition or expulsion can be a violation of Convention rights, for instance of Art. 3 ECHR (prohibition of torture) when the offender runs the risk of torture in the State to which he is to be surrendered. The key judgment is that of *Soering v United Kingdom* of 1989[30] in which the Court referred to the rule of law: "It would hardly be compatible with the underlying values of the Convention, that 'common heritage of political traditions, ideals, freedom and the rule of law' to which the preamble refers, were a Contracting State knowingly to surrender a fugitive to another state where there were substantial grounds for believing that he would be in danger of being subjected to torture [...]." The judgment endorsed the argument put forward by the agent of the German Government – entitled to make submissions in a case against the United Kingdom because *Soering* is a German national.

There are other examples of the obligation to take measures regarding Art. 2 ECHR (right to life) and Art. 3 ECHR (prohibition of torture). Following the case law of the Court the obligation under Art. 1 ECHR to secure to every person the Convention rights "requires by implication that there should be some form of effective official investigation when individuals have been killed as a result of the use of force." Prompt response by the authorities – as the Court stressed – in such

[28]Case 35072/97 *Simsek et al. v Turkey* (ECtHR 26 July 2005) paras 114–116; Case 34056/02 *Gongadze v Ukraine* (ECtHR 8 November 2005) para 177, German translation NJW 2007, 895.

[29]Case 46221/99 *Öcalan v Turkey* (ECtHR 12 May 2005) para 88, German translation NVwZ 2006, 1267.

[30]Case 14038/88 *Soering v United Kingdom* (ECtHR 7 July 1989) para 88, German translation NJW 1990, 2183.

investigations "may generally be regarded as essential in maintaining public confidence in their maintenance of the rule of law [...]."[31]

The same is said in the *Gongadze* judgment[32] regarding the celebrated case of the killing of a journalist with the alleged involvement of the Ukrainian President. Again it is emphasized that this is an essential element of the rule of law – protection of the individual and guaranteeing his/her security.

Connected with that is the concern that in some cases prosecution and justice are not organized properly. There is again emphasis on the duty to take administrative measures. The main obligation in this regard flows from Art. 6 ECHR (right to a fair trial). The Court has in many judgments and so in the *Scordino* judgment found that this article "imposes on the Contracting States the duty to organize their judicial system in such a way that their courts can meet each of its requirements, including the obligation to hear cases within a reasonable time [...]."[33] The first judgment to that effect was that of *König v Germany* of 1978 (the first judgment incidentally which found a violation of the Convention by Germany and that 26 years after Germany's ratification) which concerned the length of proceedings before administrative courts. The Court reasoned in this judgment that the State whose judicial system is too complex so as to result in a procedural maze must "draw the conclusions and if need be [...] simplify the system with a view to complying with Art. 6.1 of the Convention."[34]

4.4.3 By a Court

The protection of human rights by the judiciary certainly is a core aspect of the rule of law. A State governed by the rule of law has to ensure an effective court system and a proper administration of justice. Here again the principle of separation of powers comes into play and requires that the judiciary is independent in particular from the executive. The consequence is that the Court has to deal with problems connected with judicial protection very often – in fact, in most of its judgments.

In Arts. 5.3 and 4 ECHR and above all in Art. 6 ECHR, the Convention sets out the provisions with paramount importance for assessing control by a court and that with regard both to quantum and to importance.

[31]Case 35072/97 *Simsek et al. v Turkey* (ECtHR 26 July 2005) paras 114–116.

[32]Case 340056/02 *Gongadze v Ukraine* (ECtHR 8 November 2005) para 177.

[33]Case 36813/97 *Scordino v Italy* (ECtHR 29 March 2006) para 183, German translation NJW 2007, 1259.

[34]Case 6232/73 *König v Germany* (ECtHR 28 June 1978) para 100.

(a) Right to a Court, Right of Access to Justice, Fair Trial

Article 6 ECHR guarantees the right to a hearing before an independent and impartial tribunal and to a fair trial before the court. The leading case with regard to Art. 6.1 ECHR is *Golder v United Kingdom*,[35] which is worthy of close study. Citing references to the rule of law in the Preamble to the Convention and in the Preamble and Art. 3 of the Statute of the Council of Europe the Court reasons: "And in civil matters one can scarcely conceive of the rule of law without there being a possibility of having access to the courts." The Court concluded that Art. 6 ECHR "embodies 'the right to a court', of which the right of access, that is the right to institute proceedings before courts in civil matters, constitutes one aspect only." "To this is added" – said the Court – "the guarantees laid down by Art. 6.1 as regards both the organisation and composition of the court, and the conduct of proceedings. In sum the whole makes up the right to a fair hearing." In a nutshell that means: The principle of rule of law requires that there must be courts to decide on disputes, that the individual has the right of access to them and that the courts decide after a fair trial.

The *Golder* judgment mentions civil disputes. It has to be kept in mind that the Court interprets the notion "civil rights" in Art. 6.1 ECHR in an autonomous way so that nearly all administrative and social matters are covered, but not financial matters. The right to a court is also guaranteed for criminal matters.

(b) A Court Established by Law, Independent and Impartial

As guaranteed by Art. 6 ECHR the court must be established by law, independent and impartial. That it must be established by law again reflects the rule of law. The notion of "law" comprises in particular the legislation on the establishment but also on the competence of judicial organs. The consequence for instance is that a court having no jurisdiction under domestic law to decide a specific dispute is not established by law. The same is true when the composition of the chamber does not respect domestic legislation. That means that the Strasbourg Court examines whether national law has been complied with in this respect.[36]

The Court has defined a tribunal in the sense of Art. 6.1 ECHR as "characterized [. . .] by its judicial function , that is to say determining matters within its competence on the basis of the rule of law and after proceedings conducted in a prescribed manner". The court must also satisfy other conditions as the independence of its members and the length of their term of office, impartiality and the existence of procedural safeguards.[37]

[35]Case 4451/70 *Golder v United Kingdom* (ECtHR 21 February 1975) paras 34–36.

[36]Case 74613/01 *Jorgic v Germany* (ECtHR 12 July 2007) paras 64, 65.

[37]Case 32492/96 *Coeme et al. v Belgium* (ECtHR 22 June 2000) para 99.

The court must be independent notably of the executive – that is required by the principle of separation of powers – but independent also from the parties to the case: it must be impartial. According to the Strasbourg Court a judicial body must also give the appearance of independence.[38]

The independence of courts and the confidence in their impartiality are precious *acquis Européen* which need to be protected and maintained by all means. That may be self-evident for many States but we cannot take it for granted in all European States. In some States of east and central Europe in particular one can still see problems in this respect with the consequence that in public opinion confidence in the impartiality of judges is lacking. This has again and again been a matter of concern for the Council of Europe and for the European Union. As an example one may have to cite the *Sovtransauto* judgment[39] as a really extraordinary case. During court procedures in Ukraine between a Russian and a Ukrainian company the Ukrainian company wrote a letter to the Ukrainian President asking him to ensure that Ukrainian interests were safeguarded. And – astonishing as that may seem – the Ukrainian President in a letter urged the President of the Court to defend the interests of Ukrainian nationals. Regarding this problem the Strasbourg Court in its *Öcalan* judgment[40] stated very pertinently: "What is at stake is the confidence which the courts in a democratic society must inspire in the public and above all, as far as criminal proceedings are concerned, in the accused." In the *Nikula* judgment[41] domestic courts are described as "guarantors of justice, whose role is fundamental in a State based on the rule of law" and which "must enjoy public confidence".

(c) Right of Access to a Court

The right of access to a court is – as the ECtHR has reasoned in the *Golder* judgment[42] – "an element which is inherent in the right stated by Art. 6 para. 1" and fundamental to the rule of law.

In civil matters this right means that every individual has the right to bring a dispute before a court for decision – that is to institute proceedings before a court.[43] When in administrative matters an administrative act is performed or reviewed on appeal by an administrative authority or a body which does not satisfy the requirements for a court, Art. 6 ECHR obliges the Member States to give the person concerned the possibility to bring the matter before a court which can decide on it

---

[38]Case 7819/77 *Campbell and Fell v United Kingdom* (ECtHR 28 June 1984) para 78.

[39]Case 48553/99 *Sovtransauto v Ukraine* (ECtHR 25 July 2002).

[40]Case 46221/99 *Öcalan v Turkey* (ECtHR 12 May 2005) para 88.

[41]Case 31611/96 *Nikula v Finland* (ECtHR 21 March 2002) para 45.

[42]Case 4451/70 *Golder v United Kingdom* (ECtHR 21 February 1975) para 34.

[43]Case 21987/93 *Akzoy v Turkey* (ECtHR 18 December 1996) para 92; Case 22860/02 *Wos v Poland* (ECtHR 8 June 2006) para 97.

with full jurisdiction,[44] that is on the facts and the law without being bound in any way by the administrative decision. The same is true when in minor criminal offences, for instance violation of traffic rules, the police fines a person. That creates no problem under Art. 6 ECHR so long as the person concerned can appeal to a court.

Article 13 ECHR with its right to an effective remedy is of importance in this context. It "guarantees the availability at national level of a remedy to enforce the substance of the Convention rights...", which means that there must be "a domestic remedy allowing the competent national authority both to deal with the substance of the relevant Convention complaint and to grant appropriate relief [...]."[45] Articles 6 and 13 together with Art. 35 ECHR, which requires as admissibility criterion that all domestic remedies have been exhausted, make clear that the Convention system is subsidiary – the Court has again and again underlined that it is in the first instance the responsibility of the Member States, in particular the responsibility of domestic courts, to prevent violations of the Convention or to give relief if they have happened.

As mentioned above the ECtHR interprets the notions of "civil rights" and "criminal charge" in Art. 6 ECHR in an autonomous way. Their meaning in the relevant national law is of interest but not decisive. The reason for that approach is that the concepts are understood in a different way among the Contracting Parties, and also to avoid the possibility of the State itself deciding on the extent of its obligations under the Convention. This idea is repeated often in the case law also with regard to immunity from jurisdiction. In the *Wos* judgment the Court has reasoned: "[I]t would not be consistent with the rule of law [...] if a State could, without restraint or control by the Convention enforcements bodies remove from the jurisdiction of the Courts a whole range of civil claims or confer immunities from civil liability on large groups [...] of persons."[46] The Court accepts the immunities that are given under public international law to foreign governments and diplomats (though in the case of state immunity there have been significant challenges).

(d) Influence on Court Procedures by Legislation

An interesting problem is that of influence on court procedures by legislation and this again relates to the rule of law and the separation of powers. This may be illustrated by the following situation. A citizen initiates court proceedings against a state body claiming a right based on a certain legal provision. During the court

[44]Case 12235/86 *Zumtobel v Austria* (ECtHR 21 September 1993) para 29; Case 22860/02 *Wos v Poland* (ECtHR 8 June 2006) para 92.

[45]Case 21987/93 *Akzoy v Turkey* (ECtHR 18 December 1996) para 95.

[46]Case 22860/02 *Wos v Poland* (ECtHR 8 June 2006) para 99; in the same sense Case 1398/03 *Markovic et al. v Italy* (ECtHR 14 December 2006) para 97.

proceedings parliament deletes the provision that was the basis of the citizens' claim with the consequence that the proceedings necessarily fail. An example is the judgment of *Stran Greek Refineries* of 1994[47] in which the ECtHR found a violation of the Convention. In the case of *Scordino*[48] mentioned above the Court reasoned that "although, in theory, the legislature is not prejudiced in civil matters from adopting new retrospective provisions to regulate rights arising under existing law, the principle of the rule of law and the notion of fair trial enshrined in Art. 6 of the Convention preclude any interference by the legislature – other than on compelling grounds of general interest – with the administration of justice designed to influence the judicial determination of a dispute." Budgetary considerations and the intention to implement a political programme are not such required "obvious and compelling general interests".

(e) Respect for Judgments

In the *Assanidze* judgment of 2004[49] the ECtHR stated that "the principle of legal certainty – one of the fundamental aspects of the rule of law – precludes any attempt by a non-judicial authority to call the judgment into question or to prevent its execution."[50] So the legal situation is clear: the judgment has to be respected when it is final and no administrative action or legislation can call it into question or quash it. That is particularly true when the judgment has been rendered against the State.

It seems indeed to be a compelling consequence of the rule of law and the separation of powers that a final judgment has to be respected. A very practical result is that the Court recognizes a right to execution of a judgment. The Court reasoned for instance in the *Hornsby* judgment that the right to a court as guaranteed in Art. 6 ECHR "would be illusory if [...] legislation allowed a final, binding judicial decision to remain inoperative to the detriment of one party." That would lead "to situations incompatible with the rule of law which the Contracting States undertook to respect when they ratified the Convention."[51] In recent years the Court has found a violation of Art. 6 ECHR and of Art. 1 of Protocol No. 1 in very many cases in judgments against eastern and central European States Parties because a final judgment had not been executed in due time.

A special problem is that of revision proceedings leading to reopening of proceedings and quashing the final judgment. In this case it is the judiciary itself that interferes with the final and binding judgment. The ECtHR again draws inspiration from the rule of law and the principle of legal certainty and concludes

[47]Case 13427/87 *Stran Greek Refineries v Greece* (ECtHR 9 December 1994) para 49.

[48]Case 36813/97 *Scordino v Italy* (ECtHR 29 March 2006) para 126.

[49]Case 71503/01 *Assanidze v Georgia* (ECtHR 8 April 2004), German translation NJW 2005, 2207.

[50]Case 68050/01 *Ekholm v Finland* (ECtHR 24 July 2007) para 72.

[51]Among many judgments see Case 18357/91 *Hornsby v Greece* (ECtHR 19 March 1997) para 40.

that a final judgment should also in this way in principle not be called into question. The Court underlines that "no party is entitled to seek a review of a final and binding judgment merely for the purpose of obtaining a rehearing and a fresh determination of the case [...]. A departure from this principle is" – according to the Court – "justified only when made necessary by circumstances of a substantial and compelling character."[52] Such circumstances may be the need to correct judicial errors and miscarriages of justice but not an appeal in disguise.[53] The Court has had to deal in many cases with supervision or objection procedures in new States Parties in which a final judgment was set aside on appeal by the Prosecutor or on the initiative of the President of a higher court. The leading case is that of *Brumarescu v Romania*,[54] in which on appeal of the Prosecutor-General the Supreme Court set aside a final and binding judgment which was in favour of the applicant. The ECtHR found a violation of Art. 6 ECHR and of Art. 1 of Protocol No. 1. In its judgment, following decisions on similar issues,[55] the Court reasoned that such a procedure violates the principle of legal certainty, one of the fundamental aspects of the rule of law.

(f) Right to Fair Trial

In the *Golder* judgment[56] in particular the Strasbourg Court has stressed the close connection between the rule of law and the right to a fair trial. The Court understands the notion of fair trial as very extensive and has elaborated it in many judgments. It is impossible to go into details here, so only a few aspects can be mentioned.

One of the main elements of fair trial is that of the right to adversarial proceedings. It gives a party the right to present his or her case to the court and to have the possibility to take part in the proceedings in an active manner. Part of this right is the right to be heard and to have knowledge of and be able to comment on observations filed or evidence adduced by the other party.[57] Another important aspect is the principle of equality of arms.

Of immense practical importance is the right to a court decision within a reasonable time. Article 6 ECHR speaks of a "hearing within a reasonable time" but this is understood to include the final court decision. In German cases this in principle means the decision of the Federal Constitutional Court. The violation of

---

[52]Case 560/02 *Nikolay Zhukov v Russia* (ECtHR 5 July 2007) para 36.

[53]Case 52854/99 *Ryabykh v Russia* (ECtHR 24 July 2003) paras 51–53.

[54]Case 28342/95 *Brumarescu v Romania* (ECtHR 28 October 1999).

[55]Case 52854/99 *Ryabykh v Russia* (ECtHR 24 July 2003) paras 51–53; Case 48553/99 *Sovtransauto v Ukraine* (ECtHR 25 July 2002) para 77.

[56]Case 4451/70 *Golder v United Kingdom* (ECtHR 21 February 1975); see also Case 560/02 *Nikolay Zhukov v Russia* (ECtHR 5 July 2007).

[57]Case 12952/87 *Ruiz-Mateos v Spain* (ECtHR 23 June 1993) para 63.

this right has been and still is claimed in very many applications and mostly successfully. It was mentioned above that the States Parties of the Convention have the obligation under Art. 6 ECHR to organize their judicial system in such a way that the courts can meet all the requirements of Art. 6 ECHR including that of a decision within a reasonable time. The cases show that many States fail to do so. That is true all over Europe, not only in new Member States, but elsewhere as well. Most judgments in this regard have been rendered against Italy. The time element in the judicial protection of the rule of law – proper administration of justice – is still a reason for concern. In the *Sürmeli* judgment[58] the ECtHR mentions once again the continuing accumulation of applications in which the only or principal allegation is that of a failure to ensure a hearing in reasonable time. The Court draws attention to the important danger for the rule of law in national legal orders and repeats that Art. 13 ECHR requires a national remedy in these cases. In the case of Germany there has been a finding of a violation of Art. 13 ECHR because an effective remedy is lacking. As a consequence of that, draft legislation to make a special remedy available is under discussion in Germany.

Articles 6.2 and 6.3 ECHR make special provision for particular aspects of fairness in the context of criminal matters. The presumption of innocence required by Art. 6.2 ECHR is a key element of the rule of law[59] and of a fair trial. Also of importance is the right to remain silent and not to incriminate oneself, which is not mentioned in Art. 6 ECHR but covered by the notion of a fair trial and an important aspect of the rule of law.[60]

5 Conclusions

The principle of the rule of law is a leitmotiv for the Convention as a whole. When analysing the many judgments in which the ECtHR refers to it one may have doubts whether the results would have been different if the reasoning had not been based on this principle. But it is abundantly clear that the founding fathers of the Convention had the rule of law in mind when drafting the Convention. The same may will be true of human dignity, not mentioned in the Convention (except perhaps in Art. 3), but inherent in all of its guarantees. These two principles nevertheless offer guidelines for the interpretation of the entire Convention.

The ECHR when giving the rule of law substance in its provisions did so also in the provisions regarding human rights protection by the ECtHR in Strasbourg. The international protection of human rights by the Court is certainly an element of the rule of law. We have seen that domestic courts have to come to final decisions

[58]Case 75529/01 *Sürmeli v Germany* (ECtHR 8 June 2006), German translation NJW 2006, 2389.

[59]Case 37568/97 *Böhmer v Germany* (ECtHR 3 October 2002) para 67, German translation NJW 2004, 43.

[60]Case 18731/91 *John Murray v United Kingdom* (ECtHR 8 February 1996) para 45.

within a reasonable time and the Court is severe when assessing performance in that regard. Unfortunately the Court itself increasingly cannot meet the same requirement. The Court in an analysis of January 2010 reports that 26% of the applications allocated to a chamber were pending more than three years. The Court would normally conclude that there had been a violation of Art. 6 ECHR if a national court in any one instance were to take as long. From the applications allocated to a committee or a single judge, implying that they were easy cases, 33% were pending more than two years. That means that many cases did not meet the requirements of the Court regarding the length of domestic court proceedings. And most of these cases were petty cases which were not particularly difficult.

The Court cannot be blamed for this deplorable situation. The work load of the Court is enormous and it is growing steadily. There are now 47 Contracting States to the Convention, and the number has increased sharply since the fall of the Berlin Wall. Now more than 800 million persons are living within the jurisdiction of the ECtHR in an area stretching from the Atlantic to the Pacific. The number of new applications has been multiplied by six within eight years and is now running at 57,000 per year. The current number of pending cases is about 130,000. The Court has issued warnings for years and has predicted this situation. The Member States are obliged under the Convention to deliver a proper administration of justice – that obligation is also valid at the European level. They must – also at the European level – organise the justice in such a way that the Strasbourg Court can meet all the requirements of the Convention including that of coming to final decisions within a reasonable time. The remedy is not easy, and wise and experienced people have considered the possibilities. The first step has been taken with the ratification of Protocol No. 14 which provides for amendments of the Convention streamlining the procedure, in particular by giving jurisdiction to a single judge and also to committees of three judges. There is no doubt that further steps will be necessary. The Member States have confirmed that at their high-level Conference at Interlaken on the Future of the Court in February 2010.

The Relations Between the EU Court of Justice and the Constitutional Courts of the Member States

Francisco Balaguer Callejón

1 Introduction

A discussion of the relationship between constitutional justice and the European integration process naturally leads to the challenges that this process is facing. This is so because constitutional courts develop their functions in relation to the body of law that they are called on to interpret and apply. For this reason, the relationship between European Law and the law of the Member States is essentially articulated by the relationship between the European Court of Justice (ECJ – Art. 19 TEU) and the national constitutional courts. The courts do not adopt a passive role in this respect. There is no doubt, however, that the configuration of each body of law, and the relationship between them, also influences the way in which courts act. Because of that, the relationship between courts and the integration process raises a range of issues that go beyond the exclusive sphere of judicial activity, at the same time conditioning and exceeding it.

The first of these issues is whether the EU needs a constitution and, if so, what sort of constitution is needed in order to further the integration process. The complexity and wide implications of this question are discouraging. This debate has not disappeared with the entry into force of the Lisbon Treaty on 1 December 2009 and the issue must be tackled, as the answer to this question will help disentangle the relationship between national and European Law. It is starting from this premise that we approach the argument of this contribution, i.e. the structural conditions that determine the functioning of constitutional courts, and the question of whether these conditions favour the furthering of the integration process and the solving of conflicts at all levels (based on criteria that are commonly accepted – a condition intrinsic to the principle of legal certainty).

Francisco Balaguer Callejón (✉)
Departamento de Derecho Constitucional, Facultad de Derecho, Plaza de la Universidad s/n, 18001 Granada, Spain
e-mail: balaguer@ugr.es

H.-J. Blanke and S. Mangiameli (eds.), *The European Union after Lisbon*,
DOI 10.1007/978-3-642-19507-5_9, © Springer-Verlag Berlin Heidelberg 2012

In approaching these issues, one cannot claim to offer an answer that explains the relationship between European Law and each of the different legal systems of the Member States. This would be an impossible task, given the present heterogeneity of the national legal systems. This heterogeneity affects, in several other spheres, the very existence of constitutional jurisdiction.[1] Where there is no constitutional jurisdiction, one cannot find a dialectic relationship between legal systems of the kind that emerged between some national constitutional courts (in particular, the Federal Constitutional Court (*Bundesverfassungsgericht*) in Germany and the Italian Constitutional Court (*Corte Costituzionale*)) and EU law.

For this reason, our considerations on this subject cannot be extended to all Member States, although such an enterprise would be useful, because national constitutional courts are actors directly involved (and not simply invited to participate) in the integration process, and they have acted as such, generating new impulses to, and the furthering of, the constitutionalisation process.[2] If, and under what conditions, they may continue to do so in the future is one of the questions we must reflect upon.

2 The ECJ and the National Constitutional Courts

2.1 *Constitutional Justice, the ECJ and National Constitutional Courts*

The first aspect to clarify in connection with the relationship between constitutional justice and European integration is the very meaning of the notion of 'constitutional justice'. The most obvious answer would be that we refer here to state, or national, constitutional courts. Including the ECJ in this definition would already mean making an important choice, for if we attribute to the ECJ the *status* of constitutional court, we implicitly admit that the legal order it is called to guarantee is a constitution.[3] However, as we shall see, the ECJ is something more than

[1] As Cruz Villalón (2004), p. 71, shows, considering this heterogeneity, "whatever proposal made in relation to the *role* of national constitutional courts, *in plural*, shall always have a relative value, as the proposal is made from a *national* perspective. At the same time, the fact that the proposal is voiced from the perspective of a system framed by the majoritarian EU model of national constitutional guarantee, it allows us to expect that the proposal shall be projected so as to be plausible beyond the boundaries of the legal system where it originates from" (our translation).

[2] "[...] the European Court of Justice has not been the only actor in the constitutionalisation process: its constitutional jurisprudence was elaborated within the framework of the dialogue with national judges and courts, with the other Community institutions and with the Member States" (our translation). See Rodríguez Iglesias and Baquero Cruz (2006), p. 300.

[3] Opinion of Advocate-General Poiares Maduro in Case C-402/05 P *Yassin Abdullah Kadi and Commission of the European Communities* (ECJ 16 January 2008) para 35.

a constitutional court, precisely because the legal system it is called to guarantee is not yet a constitution.

We shall not take this step, or at least, not for the moment. It is impossible not to acknowledge that the ECJ performs important functions that are analogous to those of national constitutional courts. I do not think that this can be denied. The question is, however, whether these functions are performed in a normative context that makes the ECJ something more than a national constitutional court.[4] No national constitutional court, in spite of how decisive and important its work in the interpretation of the national constitution could be, ever played or could play such a crucial role in the shaping of the national constitutional system the same way the ECJ did in the shaping of the European legal system.[5]

This crucial role derives from the non-existence of a normative constitution which would allow the complete and systematic ordering of the constitutional levels of the EU. What we have for now are principles within a fragmented system – principles that could be qualified as "norms without provisions", if we adopt the distinction between "norms" and "provisions" introduced by *Crisafulli*.[6] We are thus in the presence of a constitution "without words", or without a textual basis such as the one on which national constitutional courts work.

This fundamental difference between the ECJ and national constitutional courts derives from the fact that, in the rule of law systems where the constitutional courts operate, the constitutional order is based on the equilibrium among three essential factors – constituent, legislative power and judiciary – interacting in a pre-defined context given by constitutional provisions and norms. The national constitutional courts produce law under determined structural conditions, which favour the delimitation of their powers, and thereby their inclusion in a balanced system of public institutions. The output of the national constitutional courts lacks the plenitude that

---

[4]Balaguer Callejón (2001); text available at http://www.ugr.es/~redce/. See also: *Jahrbuch des öffentlichen Rechts der Gegenwart*, Mohr Siebeck, Tübingen, Bd. 53, 2005, at pp. 411–428 – for the German version; *Revue Française de Droit Constitutionnel*, no. 60, Presses Universitaires de France, Paris, October 2004, at pp. 675–693 – for the French version; and *Revista Seqüência, Universidade Federal de Santa Catarina*, Florianópolis (Brasil), Año XXV, no. 50, July 2005, at pp. 237–258 – for the Portuguese version.

[5]The ECJ specifies that the Community constitutes a new legal order of international law for the benefit of which the States have limited their sovereign rights and the subjects of which comprise not only Member States but also their nationals. The Court concludes from this a fundamental principle: that of the direct effect of Community law. Important judgments in the development of the Community legal order: Case 1/58 *Stork v ECSC High Authority* (ECJ 4 February 1959); Joined Cases 36/59, 37/59, 38/39, 40/59 *Ruhrkohlen-Verkaufsgesellschaft et al. v ECSC High Authority* (ECJ 15 July 1960); Case 26/62 *Van Gend en Loos*, (ECJ 5 February 1963); Case 25/62 *Plaumann v Commission EEC* (ECJ 21 December 1962); Case 6/64 *Flaminio Costa v E.N.E.L* (ECJ 15 July 1974); Case 40/64 *Sgarlata et al. V Commission EEC* (ECJ 1 April 1965); Case 29/69 *Stauder v Stadt Ulm* (ECJ 12 November 1969); Case 11/70 *Internationale Handelsgesellschaft* (ECJ 17 December 1970); Case C-415/93 *Bosman et al.* (ECJ 15 December 1995); Case C- 108/96 *Mac Quen et al.* (ECJ 1 February 2001).

[6]See Crisafulli (1959), pp. 258–260 and Crisafulli (1964), pp. 195–209.

characterises the output of the legislative power. Legislation remains the main instrument shaping the legal order in a state characterised by the rule of law, and it is the outcome of a normal functioning of law-making mechanisms. Jurisprudence has a corrective potential to be employed to solve conflicts; thus the case law of national constitutional courts is a complementary source within the legal system.

By contrast, the ECJ, in the absence of a thorough constitutional context, must perform a constitutive function in many areas, to the point that it was the ECJ itself that has introduced the principles articulating the Community legal order and its relationship with national legal system (for example, the primacy principle[7]). A paradigmatic example of this function is to be found in the area of Fundamental Rights, where the ECJ has incorporated principles derived from external elements (common constitutional traditions,[8] the European Court of Human Rights, ECtHR[9]). At the same time, this constitutive function has a legislative vocation[10] which is necessary in order to give effect to the fundamental rights in question. The ECJ thus also acts within the legislative and constituent spheres.[11]

---

[7]Case 6/64 *Flaminio Costa v E.N.E.L.* (ECJ 15 July 1964) para 8; di Salvatore (2006), p. 375.

[8]The constitutions of all Member States protect property rights, see Case 4/73 *Nold KG v Commission* (ECJ 14 May 1974) para 14 ; Case 36/75 *Rutili v Ministre de l'Interieur* (ECJ 28 October 1975) para 27–32.

[9]The ECJ explicitly recognised the protection of the rights protected in the European Convention of Human Rights: Case 44/79 *Hauer v Land Rheinland-Pfalz* (ECJ 13 December 1979) para 15: "The Court also emphasized in the judgment cited, and later in the judgment of 14 May 1974 Nold (1974) ECR 491, that fundamental rights form an integral part of the general principles of law, the observance of which it ensures; that in safeguarding those rights, the Court is bound to draw inspirations from constitutional traditions common to the Member States, so that measures which are incompatible with the fundamental rights recognized by the constitutions of those states are unacceptable in the Community; and that, similarly, international treaties for the protection of human rights on which the Member States have collaborated or of which they are signatories, can supply guidelines which should be followed within the framework of Community law. That conception was later recognized by the Joint Declaration of the European Parliament, The Council and The Commission of 5 April 1988, which, after recalling the case-law of the Court, refers on the one hand to the rights guaranteed by the constitutions of the Member States and on the other hand to the European Convention for the protection of Human Rights and Fundamental Freedoms of 4 November 1950 (Official Journal C 103, 1977, p. 1)."

[10]As Guillén López (2005), pp. 57–85, indicates, progress made in the democratisation of the system of European Law sources should also produce a progressive change in the interpretation patterns employed by the ECJ, towards admitting the presumption of constitutionality in favour of the democratic legislature.

[11]Historically, the original European Treaties did not contain any mention about the human rights protection. [See Paolo Maria Gangi, *The new European Convention: some observations*, http://www.dialettico.it/european.htm#_ftn27] The reason is that, at the beginning, the EU was only an economic Union without any competence in the protection of fundamental rights. Human beings were not protected for themselves but as they played a role in the economic integration. In other words, only the *homo oeconomicus*' rights were protected. Nevertheless, the question of the protection of human rights has begun to play an important role in European Law as a consequence of the ECJ case law.

One could say that, where the ECJ developed the constitutional order, it did not act as a real court, but it performed a constituent function. By contrast, when it acted as a real court, it did so in relation to a normative body of law that is not, strictly speaking, constitutional law. In other terms, the closer the ECJ got to constitutional law matters, the farther it went from being a court, and the more it acted as a real court, the farther it distanced itself from constitutional law. This is by no means a criticism of the ECJ, whose impressive role in the constitutional building of the European Union (EU) cannot but be acknowledged. This is precisely why it is impossible to compare the work of the ECJ with the constitutional case law of courts operating within the national legal systems, by reference to a predetermined constitution, in dialectic tension with the democratic constituent and legislative bodies, in relation to a structured political community, and within a consolidated public space.

Taking into account these fundamental differences between the ECJ and the national constitutional courts, our starting hypothesis is that the relationship between constitutional justice and the integration process is, above all, one that affects the national constitutional courts, in so far as they doubtlessly perform a constitutional justice function in the legal context that characterises a state governed by the rule of law. This definition of "constitutional justice", which may be considered restrictive, does not exclude the ECJ, which remains relevant to the second topic of this contribution: the European integration process.

The ECJ remains relevant because the relationship between national constitutional courts and European Law is, to a large extent, intermediated by it. It is well known that this function led to important advances in the area of fundamental rights, given the reserve of national constitutional courts, and the consequent fear that such reserve may affect the uniformity of European Law when conflicts with the national constitutional law arise.[12] The idea of dialogue or cooperation between national constitutional courts and the ECJ,[13] so much circulated in recent years, also

[12]See Cámara Villar (2005), pp. 9–42.

[13]German Federal Constitutional Court, 2 BVR 2134, 2159/92 (12 October 1993) para 70 (in: BVerfGE 89, 155 [174–175]): "The Federal Constitutional Court by its jurisdiction guarantees that an effective protection of basic rights for the inhabitants of Germany will also generally be maintained as against the sovereign powers of the Communities and will be accorded the same respect as the protection of basic rights required unconditionally by the Constitution, and in particular the Court provides a general safeguard of the essential content as against the sovereign powers of the Community as well (see BVerfGE 73, 339(386)). Acts done under a special power, separate from national powers of the Member States, exercised by a supranational organisation also affect the holders of basic rights in Germany. They therefore affect the guarantees of the Constitution and the duties of the Constitutional Court, the object of which is the protection of constitutional rights in Germany – in this respect not merely as against German state bodies (diverging from BVerfGE 58, 1 (27)). However, the Court exercises its jurisdiction on the applicability of secondary Community legislation in Germany in a "relationship of co-operation" with the European Court, under which that Court guarantees protection of basic rights in any particular case for the whole area of the European Communities, and the Constitutional Court can therefore restrict itself to a general guarantee of the constitutional standards that cannot be dispensed with (see BVerfGE 73, 339 [389])."

describes the need to keep the ECJ at the centre of the debate over the relationship between constitutional justice (here understood as national, or state justice) and the European integration process.[14]

This idea of dialogue structures this contribution. We begin by discussing the role of the national constitutional courts in the European integration process, and then we move on to discuss the role of the ECJ in connection with constitutional law.

2.2 The Roles of the ECJ and of National Constitutional Courts

Placing the national constitutional courts in the sphere of constitutional justice (at least as a starting point), and the ECJ in the sphere of the European integration process, may be considered arguable. Yet it is perfectly justified, considering the primary function that each of these judicial bodies are called upon to perform. Each of them is called to guarantee the effectiveness of the legal system to which it is related, under the conditions and within the limits established by the respective legal system.

Indeed, the primary function of national constitutional courts is to guarantee the constitutional order. This function, in the performance of which the national constitutional courts act as last-instance interpreters, is in principle neutral with respect to the European integration process.[15] The link between constitutional

[14]In effect, the position of the ECJ was provoked by some judgments of the Italian and German Constitutional Court: Italian Constitutional Court n. 183 (18 December 1973) (in: Gazzetta ufficiale n. 2 del 2 gennaio 1974) Case *Frontini* of the Italian Constitutional Court (1974) 2 CMLRev 372 and German Federal Constitutional Court, 2 BvL 52/71 (29 May 1974) (in: BVerfGE 37, 271) *Solange I* of the German Constitutional Court (1975) 2 CMLRev 434. The Italian and the German Constitutional Court had affirmed that if the European Law would have violated the fundamental rights contained in the constitution of those countries they would not have applied the European Law in order to protect the fundamental human rights. Coming from these positions of the Italian and German constitutional courts the ECJ feared the impossibility of affirming the supremacy of European Law over national law. It was, then, an instrumental reason, and not an ideal one, that brought the ECJ to affirm the relevancy of the protection of the human rights in European Law. In *Solange II* the German Federal Constitutional Court, 2 BvR 197/83 (22 October 1986) para 132 (in: BVerfGE 73, 339 [387]) ruled: "As long as the European Communities, in particular European Court case law, generally ensure effective protection of fundamental rights as against the sovereign powers of the Communities which is to be regarded as substantially similar to the protection of fundamental rights required unconditionally by the Constitution, and in so far as they generally safeguard the essential content of fundamental rights, the Federal Constitutional Court will no longer exercise its jurisdiction to decide on the applicability of secondary Community legislation cited as the legal basis for any acts of German courts or authorities within the sovereign jurisdiction of the Federal Republic of Germany, and it will no longer review such legislation by the standard of the fundamental rights contained in the Basic Law; references to the Court under Article 100 (1) Basic Law for those purposes are therefore inadmissible."

[15]Notwithstanding this, as La Pergola (2003), p. 255, argues, the logic of the primacy of European Law over national law turned the national constitutional courts into "potential antagonists" of the ECJ.

justice and the constitution makes the European integration process subject to the judicial control performed by national constitutional courts only within the parameters established by the national constitution, and according to the characteristics of the national constitutional system. In this sense, it is not the same, for example, if the constitution does not contain specific provisions related to the integration process other than a general mandate that allows the state integration into the EU,[16] or if, as in the case of Germany, the constitution establishes conditions for, and limits to, integration. It also makes a difference whether or not the constitution establishes limits to reform, for example through intangibility clauses (as in the case of Italy[17] and Germany[18]).

The relationship between national constitutional law and European Law, and the relationship between national constitutional courts and the ECJ, is naturally shaped by the relationship that each judicial body has its own legal system. Thus, the national constitutional courts have manifested reluctance vis-à-vis European Law because of its specificity and its (temporary) inadequacy in terms of mechanisms of constitutional guarantee, especially in relation to fundamental rights.[19]

Finally, the judicial bodies cannot modify the relationship unconditionally, be it by the ECJ or by a national constitutional court. To the contrary, the configuration of each legal order shapes the dialogue. Hereby, the dialogue between the ECJ and the national constitutional courts is bound by initial limits and/or conditions. The dialogue between the courts cannot solve problems related to the configuration of each legal order, or to the relationship between them.[20]

---

[16]As in the case of Spain. On reform proposals, see Rubio Llorente and Alvarez Junco (2006).

[17]This, to a certain extent, has been Italy's experience, for the Italian Constitutional Court has upheld the principle that the Act implementing Community law is subject to constitutional review. However, it has limited the judgment on constitutionality to cases in which there is a conflict with the fundamental principles of the Italian constitutional system and a violation of inviolable human rights, thereby equating the constitutional judgment on laws implementing European treaties to the judgment on constitutional laws and laws revising the Constitution. See Italian Constitutional Court, n. 183 (27 December 1973) (in: Giur. cost. 1973, 2401 et seq. 2420); see in this context Italian Constitutional Court, n. 98, (27 December 1965) (in: Giur. cost 1965, 1322 et seq., 1339 et seq.); on the so-called counter-limitations see, in the literature, Barile (1966), pp. 14 et seq.; or more broadly Cartabia (1995), pp. 95 et seq.

[18]See Art. 23.3, sentence 3, and Art. 79.3 Basic Law.

[19]German Federal Constitutional Court, 2 BvL 52/71 *Solange I* (29 May 1974) para 56 (in: BVerfGE 37, 271 [285]): "As long as the integration process has not progressed so far that Community law receives a catalogue of fundamental rights decided on by a parliament and of settled validity, which is adequate in comparison with the catalogue of fundamental rights contained in the Basic Law, a reference by a court of the Federal Republic of Germany to the Federal Constitutional Court in judicial review proceedings, following the obtaining of a ruling of the European Court under Article 177 of the Treaty, is admissible and necessary if the German court regards the rule of Community law which is relevant to its decision as inapplicable in the interpretation given by the European Court, because and in so far as it conflicts with one of the fundamental rights of the Basic Law."

[20]Cf. German Federal Constitutional Court, 2 BvR 197/83 *Solange II* (22 October 1986) para 132 (in: BVerfGE 73, 339[387]).

We must therefore acknowledge that the dialogue is shaped by structural conditions, or, to put it otherwise, there is a dialectic tension between the national constitutional courts and the ECJ. These structural conditions do not come from the courts' competences, but from the configuration of the legal orders in which the courts operate. For this reason, the issue of the configuration of the legal orders must be considered at the highest level, the constitutional one. This leads us to the key issue of the constitutional (or pre-constitutional) nature of the EU.

3 The (Pre-)Constitutional Nature of the European Union

3.1 Fear of the Constitution?

We inevitably must deal first with a situation that causes perplexity among constitutional law specialists and the citizens alike: lack of trust in the notion of a European "constitution".[21] The distrust towards the notion of a European constitution is surprising, if one thinks of the high prestige that the notion of constitution has acquired in the modern age, and still maintains today within the national context. Most surprising is the contradictory meaning employed within certain circles when referring to the notion of "constitution". On the one hand, its functionality in relation to the integration process is discarded on grounds that it is related to the national state, and on the other hand, new concepts of "constitution" are developed to overcome the shortcomings of the connection with the notion of nation state and render the notion more adequate to the singular nature of the European integration process. These are 'light' or minimalist concepts of "constitution", as if the notion of "constitution" were dangerous for the EU[22] (but not so for the Member States, where the notion maintains its prestige intact).

The distrust towards the notion of a "constitution" for the EU context is caused by a variety of factors, which are also related to the position adopted for a long period by the national constitutional courts towards the integration process. The first of these factors comes from an alleged weakness of the nation state, an issue that we shall tackle in what follows.

[21] As Cruz Villalón (2004), p. 22, indicates, a first challenge to the constitutional debate in the EU originates from the presentation of a European constitution as being a problem for Europe.

[22] A paradigmatic example in this sense is the statement of Weiler (2004), p. 113: "It is worthwhile to listen carefully to the rhetoric of the constitutional discourse. It sounds like a military march, including when recited by great humanists."

3.2 The Reinforcement of State Sovereignty by Supranational Institutions

At a general level, the phenomenon of "fearing the constitution" must be placed in the context of the objective conditions that have shaped the integration process so far. Contrary to what is commonly argued – namely that the European integration process was, and continues to be, a manifestation of the weakness of the nation state – I believe in the opposite hypothesis: the integration process has so far been a clear manifestation of the strength of the nation state. European integration has not weakened the state sovereignty, but to the contrary, it has allowed for a strengthening of the state, if we think about the limitations and challenges posed by globalisation and democratisation to the state political powers. If the integration process follows on the same path as it has, the nation state will continue to be for many years to come the main reference point in EU politics, and it will have succeeded to avoid many of the obstacles that have been placed in its way, by globalisation at the international level, and by democratisation and territorial tensions internally.

So far, one of the characteristics of the nation state is that it has combined the limitation of sovereignty and the application of democratic principles internally with the affirmation of sovereignty and lack of submission to democratic control in its external actions.[23]

From this perspective, it could be argued that the supranational limitation of external state sovereignty in the context of the EU has not succeeded to improve the internal democratic quality of the Member States – to the contrary, it has actually diminished it.

The Member States have succeeded, due to the integration process and through the transfer of competences to a supranational organisation, to exercise the sovereignty that previously could not be exercised because of the limitations imposed by the democratic rule of law in the domestic sphere.[24] The integration process allowed the European governments to fulfil, if only partially, the dream of many politicians: the exercise of power without responsibility. We must keep in mind that the integration process historically developed in parallel with the internal democratisation process (with legal limitations of the state power through constitutional

---

[23]In the words of Ferrajoli (1996), p. 175 "While the liberal-democratic nation-state was internally based on the subjection of all public powers to the rule of law and to popular representation, in its external relations it was not subject to any legal limits" (our translation).

[24]Case 130/75 *Prais v Council* (ECJ 27 October 1976); Case C-300/89 *Commission v Council (Titandioxid)* (ECJ 11 June 1991); Case C-376/98 *Germany v Parliament and Council (Tabakverbot)* (ECJ 5 October 2000); Joined Cases C-387/02, C-391/02,C- 403/02 *Berlusconi et al.* (ECJ 3 May 2005); Case C-144/04 *Mangold* (ECJ 22 November 2005); Case C-354/04 and C-355/04 *Segi und Gestoras pro amnistia v Council* (ECJ 27 February 2007). See Mangiameli (2006).

norms) and globalisation (the second globalisation started during the second half of the twentieth century and has accelerated its path over the last years). Both of these processes made the state lose political power internally and externally. This political power was recovered in part through the integration process. The integration process thus appears to be, in its genetic structure, an answer of the states to the processes of democratisation and globalisation.

The state has transferred competences towards a supranational organisation, governed fundamentally by international principles, and thereby subject to the decision-making procedures defined by international law[25] which are based on state sovereignty. Those transferences allowed the Member States to shift decisions that were considered problematic at the domestic level towards the European institutions, thus shifting responsibility towards institutions where the power is *hidden*.[26] This modus operandi presents unequalled advantages, especially in times of change, reconversions and interventions, which limit the social rights and the social pact that, in some European countries, gave birth to the constitutional rule of law. The Member States commonly agree through supranational mechanisms (or confederal mechanisms, if we like), thus shielding these decisions from the internal constitutional control and public debate, and commit themselves to applying these decisions by inserting them into a federal legal system that binds through the primacy principle.[27]

Are European governments ready to give up such advantages and, if so, under what conditions? This is the key question that we should seek an answer to, because the fundamental impulses that can further the integration process depend on these answers. This brings us to the great uncertainty derived from an opposition, or

[25]As Lanchester (2002), p. 76, argues: "[U]nanimity and the veto right (mitigated by the foreseen *constructive abstention* right) constitute, from a theoretical perspective, the negation of the existence of an internal public legal order, thus recalling the sphere of international public law; from a practical perspective, they are emblematic symbols of the difficulties of the integration process."

[26]I refer here to the expression employed by Pinelli (2005), p. 7: "From the constitutional perspective, what matters is the principle of correspondence between power and responsibility, which cannot be disregarded without inducing a strong regression of democracy. Thus, when the centres of power are articulated, fragmented, or perhaps hidden, as it occurs everywhere well beyond the division between the three levels, supra-national, national and regional, the constitutional specialist must look for and identify corresponding and more adequate forms of accountability in the exercise of power" (our translation).

[27]Weiler (2004), pp. 107–108, explains the situation very clearly, although not on the critical terms that we employ to analyse it from a *constitutional* perspective. As Weiler argues, in the EU there is a normative primacy (he calls it "hierarchy") of European Law over state law, which is not corresponded by a hierarchy of the competences or real power, while primacy is constructed from above (from the Union to the states), the hierarchy of competences and real power is constructed from below (from the states to the Union). At bottom-line, the real power continues to belong to the states, which is what characterises the European *sonderweg*, its particular form and identity: a "combination between a *confederal* institutional system and a *federal* legal system" (our translation).

possibly even a conflict that cannot be solved, between the constitutionalism of the Member States and the European integration process, which underlines many of the discourses seeking to separate the constitutional and European processes.

These discourses build upon maintaining conventional negotiation and decision-making mechanisms inspired from international law, and which are in clear contradiction with the consolidation of a European political community based on democratic decision-making criteria. At bottom-line, the effect of these discourses is that, in the essential confrontation between the agents on which the integration process relies, namely the states and the citizens, preference continues to be given to the states. This goes along with the incorporation of corrective mechanisms (such as the involvement of national parliaments), which cannot be considered democratic advances because they follow the same philosophy: the integration process continues to be controlled by the states.

However, the days of this apparent contradiction between constitutional law and the integration process might be counted. As integration deepens and the EU gradually enlarges, the decision-making mechanisms that were designed for a much smaller supranational organisation become insufficient. At the same time, the accelerated rhythm of globalisation obliges the European states to make an unavoidable choice: either to have a common European voice in the international context or to lose influence in the international arena – an influence that none of the European states will be able to maintain individually for more than three decades. The Member States' control of the process is ever weaker, and the need to build a constitutional decision-making space based on a political community shaped around the European citizenship becomes evermore pressing. The apparent contradiction between constitutionalism and pro-European positions based on the maintenance of the key role of the state (which are not genuine pro-European positions) must gradually dissolve in order to give way to the idea that European integration can only be of a constitutional nature: an integration process in which the European citizens are protagonists.

3.3 The Reaction of National Constitutional Courts in Defence of the Constitution

If some of our previous considerations are correct, or at least acceptable as such, then the idea that a European constitution cannot be moulded on the model of the nation state does not respond to the fear that the European constitution could be the founding act for a federal European state, as much as it does to the fear that it would be the death sentence for the nation state and for the political world as we know it in Europe. Thus, surprisingly, it is inconsistent to deny a model of constitution that seems undesirable in Europe, and, at the same time, argue that this model must be preserved in the Member States. In other words, denying the transfer of constitutional notions and control mechanisms to the European level, where state competences have previously been transferred, implies maintaining an internal constitutional state (in spite of the criticism that this model gives ground to) and, furthermore, it allows the states to exert a power in the supranational sphere that is not subject to constitutional control criteria.

This contradiction is explained by the fact that, in reality, the nation state has not lost sovereignty through the integration process, but instead has consolidated it, as we have argued before.

It strengthened its sovereignty in the sense that, through integration in a supranational organisation, it eluded some of the internal limits to sovereignty established by the constitution, and it has done so by transferring competences and decision-making powers to supranational institutions where the agreement of states is necessary in order to make decisions.[28]

In this way, the integration process has benefited the states and the national political groups. This would not be so if integration were to be taken to its full meaning, as this would thereby entail fear of the constitution, which is nothing else than a fear of Europe, of concluding the integration process (as a true pro-European position can only mean aiming for the creation of a European political community and a European constitutional space). The more evident this natural constitutional implication of the integration process becomes, the more resistance it provokes, and the more necessary it seems to "de-legitimise" or deprive it of the real meaning of "constitution" by incorporating foreign elements into it, which do no allow it to perform its functions.

The reasons for the resistance to the idea of giving a role to the national constitutional courts in the European debate become understandable from this perspective. In an integration process that has allowed avoiding internal constitutional controls by transferring responsibility to the European level, the position of the national constitutional courts was not – as it seemed to be, and it was made to believe – one of defending state prerogatives. Defending the idea of constitutionality in the exercise of public power does not mean defending the sovereignty of the state, but defending that state actions must be subject to normative limitations, which have by and large been eroded through the transfer of decision-making powers to the European level (notwithstanding the impressive effort of the ECJ to prevent it).

---

[28]For example, an argument that shows the necessity of a written constitution, and in some aspects is also related to what has been said so far, regards the problem of access of individuals to justice and the reform of Art. 230 (4) EC. Article 230 (4), however, has been interpreted by the ECJ in a strict way. In the Case C-50/00 P, *Unión de Pequegnos Agricultores v Council ("UPA")* (ECJ 25 July 2002) para 44, the ECJ stated: "According to the system for judicial review of legality established by the Treaty, a natural or legal person can bring an action challenging a regulation only if it is concerned both directly and individually. Although this last condition must be interpreted in the light of the principle of effective judicial protection. . .such an interpretation cannot have the effect of setting aside the condition in question, expressly laid down in the Treaty, without going beyond the jurisdiction conferred by the Treaty on the Community Courts."

To the extent that the acts of the national constitutional courts could only be based on the national constitution, the widespread perception at the European level was that their acts were in disagreement with the integration process. This is an erroneous perception, because being in favour of constitutional control over the exercise of public power does not mean resistance to the integration process; it is only a critique of the way in which integration was carried out.

At any rate, this resistance of the national constitutional courts generated an inaccurate image of them, and a false image of the constitution. The apparent contradiction between the "constitution" and "integration" throughout the (still short) history of the integration process is one of the factors explaining the incomprehensible devaluation of the notion of constitution in the European integration process.

In essence, the integration process evolved as an international, or *supranational*, action of the state, and not as a *constitutional* action of the state. The separation between the supranational action and the constitutional order allowed the state to exercise full sovereignty at the domestic level. The state thus managed to avoid the constitutional limits to its power and transfer responsibility to the European level, where the constitutional limits to the exercise of power and the guarantees of rights typical of the internal constitutional order did not exist.[29] This direction given to the integration process thus generated a confrontation between the supranational action of the state and the national constitution.

Given that the constitutional weakness of the European order was functionally exploited by the state, we may entertain the idea that fear of the fulfilment of the European dream through full political integration, through the set-up of a federation, is not a fear that the dream could become a nightmare through the emergence of a centralising and authoritarian super-state, but in reality it is a fear of fulfilling the actual dream, which implies an unavoidable change of the conditions in which political power is exercised not only at the European level, but also at the national level. It is not a fear of the emergence of a European super-state, but one of the disappearance of the nation state, or of its conversion in a political structure subordinated to the European institutions and to full constitutional control of the

---

[29]In Case C-303/05, *Advocaten voor de Wereld VZW* (ECJ 3 May 2007), the ECJ handed down its long-awaited judgment on the European Arrest Warrant (EAW). Expectations ran high, as the validity of the Union's pioneering instrument on extradition was at stake. The Framework Decision on the EAW (FD EAW) was the first instrument at EU level that incorporated the principle of mutual recognition into criminal matters. This principle was established at the European Council of Tampere in 1998 as the new cornerstone of judicial cooperation in both civil and criminal matters. An argument that shows the necessity of a written constitution, and in some aspects is also related to what has been said so far, regards the problem of privileges and immunities of Members of the European Parliament: Case C-168/91 *Konstantidinis* (ECJ 30 March 1993); Case C-148/02 *Gracía Avello* (ECJ 2 October 2003); Case C-353/06 *Grunkin and Paul* (ECJ 14 October 2008).

exercise of power.[30] This is so because the issue of the democratic and constitutional deficit of Europe[31] does not only relate to the exercise of a European power not subjected to constitutional limits outside of the boundaries of the state, but also (or above all) to the internal subtraction of the state from the constitutional limits and controls to which it was submitted before transferring competences to the European level, competences that it now continues to be exercised to indirectly.

4 European Law, Constitutional Law and European Constitutional Law

One of the structural conditions for facilitating dialogue between jurisdictions is the existence of a common legal language. Until now this common legal language did not exist, because the ECJ spoke essentially from the perspective of European Law (and it could not have been otherwise) whereas national constitutional courts spoke essentially from the perspective of the constitutional law. A common language would be necessary for establishing a true dialogue. The ideal would be, of course, to merge the notions of "European Law" and "constitutional law" and consolidate a genuine "European constitutional law".[32]

As long as this does not happen, it is understandable that the ECJ will continue to perform the function of guaranteeing European Law, and the national constitutional courts will continue to guarantee national constitutional law. This does not imply that European Law is not, in part, constitutional already or that internal constitutional law is not yet partly European. The two perspectives have naturally come closer,[33] because the ECJ was obliged to adopt constitutional techniques in order to deploy its functions, and the national constitutional courts had to align to the European logic. It is clear, however, that we are in the course of a process where the necessary adjustments between the different actors have not yet taken place.

As we have shown before, the tasks entrusted to each of these judicial bodies are different. While national constitutional courts are called to guarantee the internal constitutional order, the ECJ is called to guarantee European Law. As a matter of fact, from the early days, the ECJ embarked on the mission to structure, or give uniformity, to a fragmented legal order whose relationship with the internal legal

[30]As La Pergola (2003), p. 252, argues: "The attachment of all Member States (big and small) to national sovereignty currently blocks the real possibility that the integration achieved so far lead to the emergence of a super-state".

[31]See Balaguer Callejón (1997), pp. 593–612. On some aspects of this "constitutional deficit" of the integration process, see also Rodríguez (2004), pp. 357–370.

[32]Cf. Häberle (2008), pp. 273 et seqq.; Blanke and Mangiameli 2006, p. XXIX et seqq.

[33]As shown by Rodríguez Iglesias (1993), p. 1197, the national constitutional courts have reached decisions in the majority of cases that are compatible with those of the ECJ, although based on different motivations and the own constitutional law.

orders of the Member States was not clearly defined by the founding Treaties.[34] We must acknowledge that from this perspective European Law is less developed by comparison to that of the national constitutional systems – where uniformity has been one of the principles laying the foundation for the construction of a constitutional rule of law.

In a certain sense, the national constitutional courts have also played an important part in the reconstruction of the uniformity of the legal order during the transition from the legal to the constitutional rule of law. The symbol of this transition is precisely constitutional justice. Its existence has made the constitutional reconstruction of the uniformity of the legal order possible, and it has reaffirmed the principles on which the constitutional rule of law relies: political (and, generally, also territorial) pluralism, pluralist democracy, the fundamental consensus among different sectors of the society and the judiciary guarantee of this consensus. The normative character was not an inherent feature of the constitution, but the outcome of constitutional justice.

There are, however, significant differences between the work of the constitutional courts and that of the ECJ. Above all, the constitutional rule of law and constitutional evolution do not depend, either exclusively or primarily, upon constitutional justice. To the contrary, this evolution is the outcome of an interaction between the constitution, legislation and judiciary work. The interaction between the constituent, the legislative power and constitutional justice (in the wide sense of the term) does not exist at the European level, strictly speaking for the lack of a constitutional reference point, while the weakness of the constituent and the democratic legislative power has led to an intense protagonism of the judiciary.

Moreover, we must keep in mind that the ECJ operates on the basis of a fragmented legal order, which is furthermore a legal order still in evolution (on the flip-side of the coin). There is no doubt that the EU has a legal order of its own.[35] At the same time, this legal order is still evolving from the point of view of its fundamental basis, which is now widely broadened by the legal bindingness of the European Union Charter of Fundamental Rights (EUCFR). Additionally, the new *ius standi* for individuals who are affected by regulatory acts (Art. 230.4 TFEU)

[34]Case 26/62 *Van Gend & Loos* (ECJ 5 February 1963) [direct effect of Community law]; Case 35/76 *Simmenthal II* (ECJ 15 December 1976) [The Community's supremacy]; Case 80/70 *Defrenne I* (ECJ 25 May 1971) [vertical direct effect and horizontal direct effect of Treaty Articles]; See Azpitarte (2004), pp. 75–95.

[35]Case 6/64 *Flaminio Costa v E.N.E.L.* (ECJ 15 July 1964): "By creating a Community of unlimited duration, having its own institutions, its own personality, its own legal capacity and capacity of representation on the international plane and, more particularly, real powers stemming from a limitation of sovereignty or a transfer of powers from the Sates to the Community, The Member States have limited their sovereign rights, albeit within limited fields, and have thus created a body of law which binds both their nationals and themselves."

closes a gap in the system of legal protection of the EU.[36, 37] Until then, the system of fundamental rights of the EU still relies on Art. 6.2 TEU and the common constitutional traditions of the Member States. Nevertheless, the entry into force of the Lisbon Treaty – and, therefore the EUCFR – will contribute in a significant way to the development of the fundamental level, i.e. the constitutional level, of the EU.

The dynamic character of the integration process, if properly understood, should be to a large extent relevant to the case of national constitutional systems. We should assume that, in a system characterised by the spatial cohabitation of different constitutional orders, the transformations taking place in each of them affects the others. Therefore an orientation in a European sense of the national constitutions implies, inter alia, the perception of a more dynamic constitutional reform.[38] Notwithstanding, it is certain that an essential distinction between the European and the national legal systems will continue to exist for some time. In the case of the former, the dynamic character is a fundamental feature typical of founding a system. In the case of the latter, it is an external condition that, beyond natural trends of adaptation to social change, is determined by integration into the European legal system.

The right path to follow for an integration process aiming at the construction of a legal order characterised by features making legal certainty viable – namely uniformity, coherence and plenitude – is that of the convergence between the notions of "constitutional" and "European". This concerns both the European and the national legal systems. The European legal order should be more constitutional, and the national legal orders should be more European. Both objectives are difficult to attain.

The first – the constitutionalisation of the European legal system – is difficult because it encounters social, political and doctrinal resistance. At the root of this resistance lies fear of the emergence of a future European federal state – this explains why it is argued that, if a European constitution ever were to come to life, this should occur outside the frameworks of a state, even if the state is a federal one.

The second – the difficulty encountered in giving a European orientation to the national legal systems – is due to a variety of factors, including the inertia inherent

---

[36]Article 230 (4) EC has been interpreted by the ECJ in the past in a strict way. In the Case C-50/00 P *Unión de Pequeños Agricultores* v *Council* ("UPA") (ECJ 25 June 2002), the ECJ stated: "According to the system for judicial review of legality established by the Treaty, a natural or legal person can bring an action challenging a regulation only if it is concerned both directly and individually. Although this last condition must be interpreted in the light of the principle of effective judicial protection...such an interpretation cannot have the effect of setting aside the condition in question, expressly laid down in the Treaty, without going beyond the jurisdiction conferred by the Treaty on the Community Courts."

[37]Case C-340/99, *TNT Traco SpA v Poste Italiane SpA et al.* (ECJ 17 May 2001); Case C-173/99 *BECTU v Secretary of State for Trade and Industry* (ECJ 8 February 2001); Case C-353/99 P, *Council v Hautala et al.* (ECJ 6 December 2001).

[38]See Balaguer Callejón (2002); and Balaguer Callejón (2003), pp. 181–213.

to a static vision of the constitutional systems. Notwithstanding the fact that the constitutional rule of law is the reference model for the construction of the European constitutional system, the national constitutional rule-of-law model is in crisis as a paradigm of unitary configuration of the legal systems in pluralist democracies. It remains to be seen if this crisis will lead to the emergence of a new paradigm. For now, we should be aware that, in the same way that many European states underwent a transition form the legal state to the constitutional rule of law, we are nowadays assisting to a second transition, motivated by the European integration process. It is the transition from the constitutional rule of law towards a new model whose features we cannot yet see clearly, but which will be dogmatically shaped by the emerging European constitutional law.

5 The Impact of the Lisbon Treaty on the Relationship Between the ECJ and National Constitutional Courts

5.1 The Formal Rejection of the Constitutionality of the EU

From the perspective of the historical cleavage between the notions of "constitutional" and "European", the Lisbon Treaty represents an important step further in the process of material constitutionalisation of the Union, in contrasts with its express rejection of constitutional symbols. The general philosophy of the Lisbon Treaty is to dissimulate, if not to directly hide, the European constitutional law that had been incorporated into the Constitutional Treaty, and thus to minimise the constitutionality of the EU. The manoeuvre is so evident, and it was done in such a publicly open and publicised way, that it results as extraordinarily paradoxical because, usually, when something needs to be hidden, it is not done in such a blatant way.[39]

Moreover, the manoeuvre went together with the questioning of all elements that could have symbolically been associated with the idea of the EU as a state or "super-state": the Treaty could not include symbols or formulations associating the image of the EU with that of a state. In this way, the reduction of the visual impact of constitutionality was accompanied by the denial of the 'state' nature of the Union, thus unwillingly generating a connection between the notion of state and that of constitutionality, which is particularly interesting.

The denial of the notion of state was evident in the Declaration made by Chancellor *Angela Merkel* on 14 June 2007, which did not leave any room for

[39]See Balaguer Callejón (2008), Portuguese versión: O Tratado de Lisboa no diva. Uma reflexão sobre estatalidade, constitucionalidade e União Européia, *Revista Brasileira de Estudos Constitucionais*, no. 7, July–September 2008, text available at http://www.editoraforum.com.br/sist/conteudo/lista_conteudo.asp?FIDT_CONTEUDO=55215.

the doubts raised by the Euro-sceptics (doubts that were acknowledged, although not shared, by Germany and the more pro-European states). After qualifying the fear of the 'state' nature of the EU as the fear of the European citizens that the Member States will unnecessarily be weakened, Chancellor *Merkel* goes on to mention that the symbols and terminology similar to the ones used by states shall not be included in the new Treaty because some of the Member States identify them with the idea of the so-called super-state.[40]

Following this Declaration, the European Council sealed the denial of the idea of 'state' and the attempt to hide the constitutionality of the EU. Thus, in Annex I to the Conclusions of the Presidency of the European Council in Brussels of 21–22 June 2007 in Paragraph 3 of the General Observations on the Intergovernmental Conference Mandate (Section I), the following is stipulated: "The TEU and the Treaty on the Functioning of the Union will not have a constitutional character. The terminology used throughout the Treaties will reflect this change: the term 'Constitution' will not be used, the 'Union Minister for Foreign Affairs' will be called High Representative of the Union for Foreign Affairs and Security Policy and the denominations 'law' and 'framework law' will be abandoned, the existing denominations 'regulations', 'directives' and 'decisions' being retained. Likewise, there will be no article in the amended Treaties mentioning the symbols of the EU such as the flag, the anthem or the motto. Concerning the primacy of European law, the IGC will adopt a Declaration recalling the existing case law of the EU Court of Justice."

The Lisbon Treaty is proof of the persistent resistance of some Member States and of certain sectors of the public opinion to formalising the process of constitutionalisation of the EU (although this process has continued from the substantial point of view) through the adoption of a terminology specific to constitutional law, resistance that is caused by the fear that constitutional law could attribute statehood.[41] This resistance was justified through the negative outcome of the *referenda* on the Constitutional Treaty in France and the Netherlands. Nevertheless, as the only *referenda* held so far on the ratification of the Lisbon Treaty initially had a negative outcome (we refer to the first *referendum* held in Ireland on 12 June 2008,

[40]"As I am sure you will understand, I cannot anticipate the results of consultations in the Council next week. But one development is already taking shape: state-like designations and symbols will not be included in a new treaty. For too many of our partners, they stand for the so-called European super state which I mentioned earlier. I do not share this concern, but I have to respect it. After all, we know that it is not always specific content, paragraphs and competences which move people. It is often a case – in the truest sense of the word – of the self-understanding of states and their citizens." See http://www.bundesregierung.de/Content/EN/Regierungserklaerung/2007/06/2007-06-14-regierungserklaerung-eu-gipfel__en.html.

[41]German Federal Constitutional Court, 2 BvE 2/08 et al. (30 July 2009) para 351, however, rules out a statehood of the EU: "The newly established competences are – at any rate with the required interpretation – no 'elements that establish a state', which also in an overall perspective do not infringe the sovereign statehood of the Federal Republic of Germany in a constitutionally relevant manner."

not to the second one held on 2 October 2009), it seems clear that the problem was not defining the Treaty as "constitution".

Independently of whether this disguising operation was founded or not (considering the outcome of the first *referendum* in Ireland), what is certain is that the fear of constitutional law materialised in the Lisbon Treaty through the exclusion of any term which might have made reference to a state framework. It is clear, however, that the terms of "constitutional law" and "state" are not equivalent. To the contrary, many states do not have constitutional law (although they do have legal provisions denominated "constitution"), as there are areas of political power fully submitted to constitutional control although they do not amount to a "state" in the classic acceptance of the term.

The fear of a constitutional culture that – paradoxically – cannot be separated from the democratic configuration of the European space is nothing more than a "survivance", whose effects are prolonged by an outdated institutional structure and mentality that responded to the nature of the integration process during its first 50 years. If there is something positive in the Lisbon Treaty, it is the open and uninhibited manifestation of this fear, as reflected in the fundamental texts of the EU – a fear motivated ultimately (although erroneously) by the resistance to the idea of a 'state' quality for the EU. This resistance is clearly historically outdated, because it carries over a vision of the nation state that was relevant at the end of the nineteenth century and the beginning of the twentieth century, a nation state which no longer exists within the EU. Neither are the Member States any longer nation states in that acceptance, nor does the EU cease to have a state quality because it is not a nation state.[42]

In reality, what the EU already has in the way of a state quality has not always been associated with a democratic political space, efficient mechanisms for the control of the exercise of power and guarantees of the fundamental rights of constitutional law nature. The real paradox of the EU is that the incorporation of constitutional law will not render it more of a 'state' in its nature. Instead, by maintaining the 'state' attributes that it already has, this incorporation will provide it with a democratic character comparable to the one of democratic systems in the

[42]Cf. also in this regard the Lisbon decision of the German Constitutional Court which expressly underlines the role of the nation states as the "masters of the Treaties" German Federal Constitutional Court, 2 BvE 2/08 et al. (30 July 2009) para 231: "The empowerment to exercise supranational competences comes, however, from the Member States of such an institution. They therefore permanently remain the masters of the Treaties. In a functional sense, the source of Community authority, and of the European constitution that constitutes it, is the peoples of Europe with their democratic constitutions in their states. The "Constitution of Europe", the law of international agreements or primary law, remains a derived fundamental order. It establishes a supranational autonomy which is quite far-reaching in political everyday life but is always limited factually. Here, autonomy can only be understood – as is usual regarding the law of self-government – as an autonomy to rule which is independent but derived, i.e. is accorded by other legal entities. In contrast, sovereignty under international law and public law requires independence of an alien will particularly for its constitutional foundations."

Member States, a democratic character that it lacks today. The polemic is therefore absurd: constitutional elements will not make the EU more of a 'state' than it already is. In contrast, they would contribute to developing the European constitutional space, and they would render possible the constitutional control of the European political power. The EU would become a more democratic 'state'.[43]

5.2 *The Break of the Clear Dividing Line Between Internal Constitutional Systems and the EU Legal Order*

In spite of the formal rejection of constitutional symbols, the Lisbon Treaty will reformulate and develop the European constitutional law from the date of its entry into force on 1 December 2009. The new Treaty on European Union will start to be effective in "Europeanising" the *counter-limits* that, for example[44] the judges will have to start to consider the scope of the provision in Art. 52.1 of the Charter, guaranteeing the essence of fundamental rights. The constitutionality of the EU will set in place a dialectic interaction with the constitutional order of the Member States, thus contributing to the development of the European constitutional law in its broad sense – the constitutional law of the distinct European constitutional spheres (European, national, territorial).

---

[43]Cf. in contrast German Federal Constitutional Court, 2 BvE 2/08 et al. (30 June 2009) para 278: "With the present status of its integration, it is ... not required to democratically develop the system of the European institutions in analogy to that of a state." Ibid. (para 295): "Mere participation of the citizens in political rule which would take the place of the representative self-government of the people cannot be a substitute for the legitimising connection of elections and other votes and of a government that relies on it: The Treaty of Lisbon does not lead to a new level of development of democracy. The elements of participative democracy, such as the precept of providing, in a suitable manner, the citizens of the Union and "representative" associations with the possibility of making their views heard, as well as the elements of associative and direct democracy, can only have a complementary and not a central function when it comes to legitimising European public authority. Descriptions of, and calls for, a 'Citizens' Europe' or the 'strengthening of the European Parliament' can politically convey the European level and contribute to increasing acceptance of 'Europe' and to explaining its institutions and procedures. If such descriptions and calls are, however, converted into normative statements, which is partly done by the Treaty of Lisbon, without this being connected with an elaboration of the institutions that takes due account of equality, they are not suited to introduce a fundamentally new model on the level of the law."

[44]An attempt to Europeanise the counter-limits occurred previously with Art. I-5.1 TCE and now with Art. 4.2 TEU, modified by the Lisbon Treaty, which stipulates that the Union shall respect the national identity of the Member States, which is inherent to their fundamental political and constitutional frameworks, including in so far as regional and local autonomy is concerned. It follows that the Union itself recognises that there is a constitutional nucleus, composed of the fundamental political and constitutional frameworks of the Member States, which must be preserved. This opens the door for a latent conflict between the Member States and the Union in the constitutional sphere, which allows for the consideration of a possible elasticity of the primacy principle. This is not, however, an easy endeavour, as the very existence of the Union as a legal system depends on this principle. For this reason, the constitutional conflict still lacks an easy solution.

The new fundamental law of the EU will thus become part of a plural constitutional sphere, with diverse constitutional spaces. In essence, the Lisbon Treaty will contribute to doing away with the usual perception of a dividing line between the European legal system and the internal legal systems of the Member States. The high degree of interdependency between the diverse constitutional spaces in Europe will be further enhanced by the Lisbon Treaty, to the point where it will become difficult to deal with the constitutional systems of the Member States from an exclusively national perspective, and to deal with the European legal system from an exclusively European perspective, as if the two spheres were separated.

The interaction between the two types of legal systems will generate new constitutional developments at the European and national levels. As argued by *Peter Häberle*,[45] the interaction between the two legal systems will shape the real constitution of each Member State, which is partly European and partly national.

The EUCFR plays an essential role in this process of dialectic interaction. Notwithstanding the limitations of the European political space, the Charter will contribute to developing a legal space for the citizenship at the European level, a space for the public debate of the European public policies, and a powerful instrument for the open interpretation[46] of European constitutional law. The European constitutional debate will move from theory to practice, and will receive impetus from the potential conflict which comes from the exercise of citizens' rights.

Thus, it should not come as a surprise that, during the debate over the Lisbon Treaty, the Charter was the target of some of the fiercest attacks by the Euro-sceptics. Its transfer to a sort of legal "limbo", where it will eventually have acquired the same legal weight as the Treaties based on Art. 6.1 TEU and the Protocol on the application of the Charter in the United Kingdom and Poland (and shortly in the Czech Republic), stands proof of the resistance that the Charter has met. Although objections to the Charter finally did not amount to anything in terms of its effectiveness, one cannot disregard the profound symbolical implications of such objections.

The entry into force of the Charter is the seed of the final constitutionalisation of Europe. It will establish a direct link between the European institutions and the citizens, contributing to the shaping up of an articulated legal status for the European citizenship, and of a specific European constitutional identity.[47]

---

[45]See Häberle (2004a); See also, by the same author: Häberle (1999), pp. 84 et seq.; Häberle (2004b), pp. 11–24; Häberle (2008).

[46]See Häberle (1975), pp. 297–305.

[47]German Federal Constitutional Court, 2 BvE 2/08 (30 June 2009) para 35: "According to the Treaty of Lisbon, the fundamental-rights protection in the European Union is based on two foundations: the Charter of Fundamental Rights of the European Union in its revised version of 12 December 2007 (OJ no. C 303/1; Federal Law Gazette 2008 II pp. 1165 et seq.), which shall have the same legal value as the Treaties (Art. 6.1 sentence 1 TEU Lisbon) and thus becomes legally binding, and the Union's unwritten fundamental rights, which continue to apply as general principles of the Union's law (Art. 6.3 TEU Lisbon). These two foundations of European fundamental-rights protection are complemented by Art. 6.2 TEU Lisbon, which authorises and obliges the European Union to accede to the European Convention for the Protection of Human Rights and Fundamental Freedoms of 4 November 1950 (Federal Law Gazette 2002 II p. 1054)."

6 The Structural Conditions Shaping the Dialogue Between National Constitutional Courts and the ECJ

While the constitutionalisation process is on the way, the absence of a convergence between the notions of "constitutional" and "European" can raise obstacles to the dialogue or cooperation between national constitutional courts and the ECJ.[48] We argued earlier that at present these judiciary bodies speak different languages: one of constitutional law on the one hand, and one of European Law on the other. This causes problems in the relationship, because dialogue requires the use of a common (legal) language.

Even if we admit that the language of the ECJ has constitutional connotations, and that of the national constitutional courts has a European orientation, the problem still resides. It is, furthermore, a problem that cannot be solved exclusively by the courts themselves, no matter how much determination is put into it, because the solution to the problem depends to a large extent on external factors. Some of them are of a procedural nature, and can no doubt favour the dialogue. This is the case of national constitutional courts making use of the preliminary ruling procedure.[49] Yet we should not forget that the most important factors are of substantive, and not of procedural, nature. They do not relate to instruments for the dialogue, but to the very possibility of establishing it: the need for a common legal language, that of the European constitutional law.

It is precisely the deficit of European constitutional law – a deficit of constitutional nature in the European sphere and of European nature in the internal constitutional sphere of the Member States – to hinder the creation of a common legal language. The difficulty originates from conditions that cannot but be partially attributed to a lack of will on behalf of the European political leaders and institutions, including the ECJ and national constitutional courts. For the rest, the

---

[48]On the dialogue between the national constitutional courts and the ECJ, see: Azpitarte (2002); Luther (2005), pp. 159–181; and Groppi (2006), pp. 225–243.

[49]*In France*: CC Décision Nr. 74–54 (15 January 1975) (in: Rec. 19); CE *Sarran et Levacher* (30 October 1998) (in: RFDA 1998, p. 1091); Cass. *Mlle Fraisse* (2 July 2000) (in: Bulletin 2000 A.P. N. 4 p. 7); CC Décision n. 2004–496 (10 June 2004) (in: Journal officiel 22.06.2004); CC Décision n. 2004–505 *Traité établissant une Constitution pour l'Europe* (19 November 2004) (in: Journal officiel (Nr. 273) 24.11.2004, 19885–19888); CC Décision Nr. 2007–560 *Traité de Lisbonne modifiant le traité sur l'Union européenne et le traité instituant la Communauté européenne* (20 December 2007) (in: Recueil, p. 459, Journal officiel 29 December 2007). *In Italy*: Italian Constitutional Court n. 14 (7 March 1964) (in: Giur. cost. 1964); n. 98 (27 December 1965) (in: Giur. cost. 1965); n. 183 (27 December 1973) (in: Giur. cost 1973); n. 232 (30 October 1975), (in: Giur. Cost. 1975); n.163 (29 December 1977) (in: Giur. Cost. 1977); n. 170 (8 June 1984) (in: Giur. Cost. 1984); n. 113 (23 April 1985) (in: Giur. cost. 1985); n.389 (11 July 1989) (in: Giur. cost. 1989); n. 384 (10 November 1994) (in: Giur. cost. 1994); n. 94 (30 March 1995) (in: Giur. cost. 1995). *In Spain*: The Constitutional Court of Spain 1/2004 (13 December 2004) (in: BJC enero 2005, p. 7); S.T.C. n. 233/2004 (2 December 2004) (in: BJC enero 2005, p. 49). See also Azpitarte (2002) and Alonso García (2005).

difficulty originates from the incapacity of the different actors concerned with improving the integration process on the basis of constitutional principles.

The external structural conditions are well known: the absence of a consolidated European public space, the absence of a European political community and the multiple current asymmetries of the EU – asymmetries which are accentuated by the enlargement process in terms of territory, population, economic conditions, cultural values, political systems, forms of government, state frameworks, language, legal systems, etc.[50]

These structural external conditions cannot be disregarded, and represent a tremendous obstacle to the shaping up of a European political community. We should note, however, that some of them have faded over the last years, and others are questionable, depending on the national perspective from which they are contemplated. For example, the need of "a European people" to build a European political community and identity is not seen with the same eyes in Germany,[51] Spain or Italy. Societies comprising diverse national configurations have less difficulty understanding the problems currently faced by the Union, and are less prone to viewing the notions of "nation" and "state" as interchangeable. Similarly, as immigration phenomena shape a multicultural and multi-ethnic reality in many European societies, the concept of "people" becomes insufficient to guarantee a democratic articulation of the public power. If, to the contrary, we take a reformulated notion of citizenship as a starting point, voided of its national connotations, then it becomes easier to shape a European political community and identity – understood here as citizenship identity.

Depending on the orientation of the European political and judiciary actors, these divergences can be either accentuated, thus rendering the integration process more difficult, or attenuated, thus facilitating integration. This brings us to a second type of structural conditions, which are not external, but rather depend to a large extent on the will of the European and national political actors and judiciary. This is where, unfortunately, I am less optimistic. This is so not only because the current dynamic of internal political processes maintains the distance between the citizens and the integration process, but also because the political actors are evidently interested in favouring this dynamic and in keeping the internal, state control over the integration process.

[50]See Grimm (1994), pp. 339–367. See also Balaguer Callejón (2005), pp. 401–410.

[51]See German Federal Constitutional Court, 2 BvE 2/08 et al. (30 July 2009) para 280–286: "Even after the new formulation Article 14.2 TEU Lisbon, and contrary to the claim that Article 10.1 TEU Lisbon seems to make according to its wording, the European Parliament is not a body of representation of a sovereign European people. This is reflected in the fact that it, as the representation of the peoples in their respectively assigned national contingents of Members, is not laid out as a body of representation of the citizens of the Union as an undistinguished unity according to the principle of electoral equality. . . . It is not the European people that is represented within the meaning of Article 10.1 TEU Lisbon but the peoples of Europe organised in their states, with their respective distribution of power that has been brought about by democratic elections taking account of the principle of equality and which are shaped in advance by party politics."

At any rate, the structural conditions shaping the relationship between the ECJ and national constitutional courts could be improved in several ways. Although it might not yet be possible to create the common legal language of a consolidated European constitutional law, we can still look for *formulae* favouring a productive interaction between the two legal spheres. This would require intervention at the two levels, to render the internal constitutional law more European, and European Law more constitutional:

(A) At the level of national constitutional law, we would first need a change of perspective, of the general attitude that some national constitutional courts have developed towards European Law. Admittedly, the interaction between European and national law does not allow the adoption of an internal "defensive" line impeding the penetration of European Law.[52] For instance, with respect to the principle of institutional autonomy, the national constitutional courts should acknowledge that European Law has an impact on the internal distribution of competences, and that merely avoiding dealing with this problem is not a solution.[53]

Second, denying the constitutional nature of the internal application of European Law, as some of the national constitutional courts have done, is not compatible with the constitutional logic and does not favour the dialectic interaction between national constitutional law and European Law. From the perspective of a normative constitution, any infringement of European Law is an infringement of internal constitutional law. Given that the validity of European Law stems from the constitution, any infringement of European Law is also an infringement of the constitution. A different matter altogether is whether this infringement should be judicially reviewed by the national constitutional courts. A validity control by the national constitutional courts is not necessary, in so far as European Law replaces

[52]German Federal Constitutional Court, 2 BVR 2236/04 (18 July 2005) (in: BVerfGE 113, 273): "When adopting the Act implementing the Framework Decision on the European arrest warrant, the legislature was obliged to implement the objective of the Framework Decision in such a way that the restriction of the fundamental right to freedom from extradition is proportionate. In particular, the legislature, apart from respecting the essence of the fundamental right guaranteed by Art. 16.2 of the Basic Law, has to see to it that the encroachment upon the scope of protection provided by it is considerate. In doing so, the legislature has to take into account that the ban on extradition is precisely supposed to protect, inter alia, the principles of legal certainty and protection of public confidence as regards Germans who are affected by extradition." The Act to Implement the Framework Decision on the European Arrest Warrant and the Surrender Procedures between the Member States of the EU (European Arrest Warrant Act (Gesetz zur Umsetzung des Rahmenbeschlusses über den Europäischen Haftbefehl und die Übergabeverfahren zwischen den Mitgliedstaaten der Europäischen Union, Europäisches Haftbefehlsgesetz – EuHbG)) of 21 July 2004 (Federal Law Gazette (Bundesgesetzblatt – BGBl) I p. 1748) violates Art. 2 subsection 1 in conjunction with Art. 20 subsection 3, Art. 16 subsection 2 and Art. 19 subsection 4 of the Basic Law (Grundgesetz – GG) and is void.

[53]See Balaguer Callejón (2002), pp. 99–130. For Italy, see Rodríguez Iglesias (1993), footnote no. 78.

national law by virtue of the primacy principle, a principle that is concerned with the effectiveness of the norms, and not with their validity.[54]

Third, more flexibility, homogeneity and pro-European orientation at the level of the national legal systems would be beneficial. The introduction of more flexible reform procedures would improve the capacity of national legal systems to adapt to the requirements of a pluralist legal order, in which each constitutional space (European, national, territorial) responds to the changes that occur in the other – especially in the relationship between the European and national spheres, and the one between the national and regional spheres. More homogeneity – in conditions of respecting pluralism and the diversity of national legal systems – and a pro-European orientation would facilitate the work of the national constitutional courts and their relationship with the ECJ. In relation to this, it is also necessary to take into account the new methodological perspectives stemming from European constitutional law, such as comparative law as a method of legal interpretation[55] and the gradual development of texts,[56] as argued by Peter Häberle.

(B) At the level of European Law, we must first accept that a European constitution cannot be articulated in a fragmented, patchy manner, without a clear reference to the basic principles of national constitutional law. These basic constitutional principles allow us to define the common set of values on which the future European constitutional order will rely.[57] The fear of the constitution that is nowadays present among the European institutions and in certain doctrinal spheres is not compatible with the high value attributed to the constitution within the Member States. The exercise of public power that has implications for the citizens cannot at the same time be subjected to constitutional control internally and placed out of the reach of constitutional control at the European level.

[54]See Balaguer Callejón (1997), pp. 593–612.

[55]See Häberle (1989), p. 913; Sommermann (2004), para 15 et seqq. See also Ridola (2006); Sperti (2006). From the perspective of sources of law, see Pizzorusso (2005).

[56]See Häberle (1992), pp. 3–26.

[57]German Federal Constitutional Court, 2 BvE 2/08 (30 June 2009) para 36: "Title II of the new version of the Treaty on European Union contains 'provisions on democratic principles'. Accordingly, the functioning of the European Union shall be founded on representative democracy (Article 10.1 TEU Lisbon), complemented by elements of participative, associative and direct democracy, in particular by a citizens' initiative (Article 11 TEU Lisbon). The principle of representative democracy makes reference to two tracks of legitimisation: The European Parliament, which 'directly' represents the citizens of the Union, and the Heads of State or Government, represented in the European Council, and the Member States' members of government represented in the Council, 'themselves democratically accountable either to their national Parliaments, or to their citizens' (Article 10.2 TEU Lisbon)."

Second, the current constitutional needs of Europe ask for decided action in the direction of constitutionalising the integration process.[58] Yet the constitutionalisation process cannot rely exclusively on normative acts (like the Lisbon Treaty and the entry into force of the Charter); it should also involve developing a constitutional decision-making space at the European level. This requires serious action in the direction of creating a real European political space, with European political parties, political actors and European mass media. At the current stage of the integration process, these elements are necessary components of the constitutionalisation process, as they help set the material ground on which the European constitution and constitutional culture shall be planted and grown. A European political and constitutional space is also necessary for the interaction between the national and European judiciaries to be productive, for the emergence of a true European community of legal specialists.

Third, favouring the constitutional integration also means to focus on the working methods of, and the case law developed by, the national constitutional courts. The experience accumulated by the national constitutional courts, especially the constitutionality control techniques that they have developed, will be useful references in the course of articulating and consolidating the European constitutional space.[59]

References

Alonso García R (2005) Justicia Constitucional y Unión Europea. Civitas, Madrid

Azpitarte M (2002) El Tribunal Constitucional ante el control del Derecho comunitario derivado. Civitas, Madrid

Azpitarte M (2004) Las relaciones entre el Derecho de la Unión y el Derecho del Estado a la luz de la Constitución Europea. Revista de Derecho Constitucional Europeo 1:75–95. http://www.ugr.es/~redce/, accessed date 5 June 2010

[58]German Federal Constitutional Court, 2 BvE 2/08 (30 June 2009) para 55: "The Treaty of Lisbon pursues the objective of achieving more transparency concerning the division of competence between the Union and the Member States (see Laeken Declaration on the Future of the European Union of 15 December 2001, Bulletin EU 12–2001, I.27 <Annex I>), and it extends the European Union's competences."

[59]German Federal Constitutional Court, 2 BvE 2/08 (30 June 2009) para 32: "The Preamble of the Treaty of Lisbon does not make reference to the failed Constitutional Treaty but establishes a direct line between the Treaty of Lisbon and the Treaties of Amsterdam and Nice. It repeats the objective of the Intergovernmental Conference's mandate – enhancing the efficiency and democratic legitimacy of the Union, as well as the improvement of the coherence of its action – but it no longer specifically emphasises the coherence of the Union's external action. While all former amending treaties served to enhance the efficiency and the coherence of the European Communities or the European Union, the Treaty of Lisbon for the first time explicitly pursues the objective of enhancing the Union's democratic legitimacy" (see also Fischer (2008), pp. 91–92).

Balaguer Callejón F (1997) La constitucionalización de la Unión Europea y la articulación de los ordenamientos europeo y estatal. In: Herrera MAG (ed) El constitucionalismo en la crisis del Estado social. Universidad del País Vasco, Bilbao, pp 593–612

Balaguer Callejón F (2001) Livelli istituzionali e tecniche di riconoscimento dei diritti in Europa. Una prospettiva costituzionale. In: Rolla G (ed) Tecniche di garanzia dei diritti fondamentali. G. Giappichelli Editore, Torino, pp 113–130 (Spanish version in Revista de Derecho Constitucional Europeo, no. 1, January–June 2004, at pp 25–46)

Balaguer Callejón F (2002) El *status* constitucional de la reforma y la fragmentación del Poder Constituyente. In: AA.VV., La democracia constitucional. Estudios en homenaje al Profesor Rubio Llorente, vol I. Congreso de los Diputados, Tribunal Constitucional, Madrid

Balaguer Callejón F (2003) Fuentes del Derecho, espacios constitucionales y ordenamientos jurídicos. Revista Española de Derecho Constitucional 69:181–213

Balaguer Callejón F (2005) Die europäische Verfassung auf dem Weg zum Europäischen Verfassungsrecht. In: Jahrbuch des öffentlichen Rechts der Gegenwart. Mohr Siebeck, Tübingen, Bd. 53, pp 401–410

Barile P (1966) *Le libertà nella costituzione*. Lezioni. Padova: Cedam

Blanke HJ, Mangiameli S (Eds.) *Governing Europe under a Constitution. The hard Road from the European Treaties to a European Constitutional Treaty*. Heidelberg: Springer

Callejón B (2008) El Tratado de Lisboa en el Diván. Una reflexión sobre constitucionalidad, estatalidad y Unión Europea. Revista Española de Derecho Constitucional 83:57–92

Cartabia M (1995) *Principi inviolabili e integrazione europea*. Milano: Giuffré

Cámara Villar G (2005) Los Derechos Fundamentales en el proceso histórico de construcción de la Unión Europea y su valor en el Tratado Constitucional. Revista de Derecho Constitucional Europeo 4:9–42. http://www.ugr.es/~redce/, accessed date 15 June 2010

Crisafulli V (1959) Atto normativo. In: Enciclopedia del Diritto, vol IV. Milano: Giuffrè pp 258–260

Crisafulli V (1964) Disposizione (e norma). In: Enciclopedia del Diritto, vol XIII. Milano, pp 195–209

Cruz Villalón P (2004) La Constitución inédita. Estudios ante la constitucionalización de Europa. Editorial Trotta, Madrid

di Salvatore E (2006) The Supremacy of European Law in the Treaty establishing a Constitution for Europe in the light of Community experience. In: H.-J. Blanke & S. Mangiameli (Eds.). Governing Europe under a Constitution. The hard Road from the European Treaties to a European Constitutional Treaty (pp. 375–400). Heidelberg: Springer

Ferrajoli L (1996) Más allá de la soberanía y de la ciudadanía: un constitucionalismo global, originally published in Richard Bellamy (ed) (1996) Constitutionalism, democracy and sovereignity. Avebury, London, and translated to Spanish by Gerardo Pisarello, in *ISONOMÍA*, no. 9, October 1998, pp 173–184

Fischer KH (2008) *Der Vertrag von Lissabon*. Baden-Baden: Nomos

Grimm D (1994) Braucht Europa eine Verfassung? Italian version, Una costituzione per Í Europa? In: Zagrebelsky G, Portinaro PP, Luther J (eds) Il futuro della costituzione. Einaudi, Torino, pp 339–367

Groppi T (2006) La primauté del Derecho europeo sobre el derecho constitutcional nacional. Un punto de vista comparado. Revista de Derecho Constitucional Europeo 5:225–243. http://www.ugr.es/~redce/, accessed date 15 June 2010

Guillén López E (2005) El Parlamento Europeo. Revista de Derecho Constitucional Europeo 3:57–85. http://www.ugr.es/~redce/, accessed date 15 June 2010

Häberle P (1975) Die offene Gesellschaft der Verfassungsinterpreten. Juristen Zeitung:297–305

Häberle P (1989) Grundrechtsgeltung und Grundrechtsinterpretation im Verfassungsstaat – Zugleich zur Rechtsvergleichung als "fünfter" Auslegungsmethode. Juristen Zeitung:913–919

Häberle P (1992) Textstufen als Entwicklungswege des Verfassungsstates. In: Häberle P (ed) Rechtsvergleichung im Kraftfeld des Verfassungsstaates. Methoden und Inhalte, Kleinstaaten und Entwicklungsländer. Duncker & Humblot, Berlin, pp 3–26

Häberle P (1999) Europa –eine Verfassungsgemeinschaft? In: Häberle P (ed) Europäische Verfassungslehre in Einzelnstudien. Nomos, Baden-Baden

Häberle P (2004a) ¿Tienen España y Europa una Constitución? Spanish version by Miguel Azpitarte Sánchez, with a Preface by Ángel López López. Fundación El Monte, Sevilla

Häberle P (2004b) Europa como comunidad constitucional en desarrollo, Spanish version by Francisco Balaguer Callejón, Revista de Derecho Constitucional Europeo 1:11–24. http://www.ugr.es/~redce/, accessed date 15 June 2010

Häberle P (2008) Europäische Verfassungslehre, 5th edn. Nomos/Dike, Baden-Baden/Zürich/St Gallen

La Pergola A (2003) El Juez Constitucional italiano ante la primacía y el efecto directo del derecho comunitario. Notas sobre unas jornadas de estudio. In: Colneric N, Edgard D, Puissochet J-P, Colomer DR-J (eds) Une communauté de droit, Festschrift für Gil Carlos Rodríguez Iglesias. Berliner Wissenschafts Verlag, Berlin

Lanchester F (2002) La Carta europea dei diritti fondamentali tra aspirazioni e realtà. In: Carocci (ed) AA.VV., Sfera pubblica e Costituzione europea. Roma

Luther J (2005) Jueces europeos y jueces nacionales: la Constitución del diálogo. Revista de Derecho Constitucional Europeo 3:159–181. http://www.ugr.es/~redce/, accessed date 15 June 2010

Mangiameli S (2006) Ordinamento europeo, vol II. L'esercizio delle competenze, Giuffré

Pinelli C (2005) Multilevel Constitutionalism e principi fondativi degli ordinamenti sopranazionali. http://www.giuripol.unimi.it/eventi/Pinelli%20Milano, accessed date 15 June 2010

Pizzorusso A (2005) Comparazione giuridica e sistema delle fonti del Diritto. G. Giappichelli Editore, Torino

Ridola P (2006) La giurisprudenza costituzionale e la comparazione. http://www.associazionedeicostituzionalisti.it/materiali/anticipazioni/giurisprudenza_comparazione/index.html, accessed date 15 June 2010

Rodríguez A (2004) La Constitucionalización de Europa, Anuario de la Facultad de Derecho de la Universidad de Extremadura, no. 22, pp 357–370

Rodríguez Iglesias GC (1993) Tribunales Constitucionales y Derecho comunitario. In: AA.VV., Hacia un nuevo orden internacional y europeo. Estudios en homenaje al profesor Don Manuel Díez de Velasco. Tecnos, Madrid

Rodríguez Iglesias GC, Baquero Cruz J (2006) Funciones constitucionales del Tribunal de Justicia de las Comunidades Europeas. Fundamentos, nº 4, Junta General del Principado de Asturias

Rubio Llorente F, Alvarez Junco J (eds) (2006) El informe del Consejo de Estado sobre la reforma constitucional. Texto del informe y debates académicos. CEPC, Madrid

Sommermann KP (2004) Funktionen und Methoden der Grundrechtsvergleichung, in: D. Merten H.-J. Papier (Eds.). *Handbuch der Grundrechte*, Vol. 1 (pp. 631–678). Heidelberg: Möller

Sperti A (2006) Il dialogo tra le corti costituzionali ed il ricorso alla comparazione giuridica nella esperienza piu' recente. *Rivista di diritto costituzionale*, pp. 125–165

Weiler JHH (2004) El principio de tolerancia constitucional: la dimensión espiritual de la integración europea (Spanish version by Miguel Azpitarte Sánchez). In: Balaguer Callejón F (ed) Derecho constitucional y cultura. Estudios en Homenaje a Peter Häberle. Tecnos, Madrid

The Concept of Citizenship in the European Union

Margot Horspool

> The importance of the TEU citizenship provisions lies not in their content but rather in the promise they hold out for the future.[1]

1 Introduction[2]

The Lisbon Treaty contains relatively little that is new as regards the citizenship articles. I propose, therefore, to set the scene with a brief introduction, a little of the history and philosophy on citizenship, then to focus on the changes in the Lisbon Treaty and finally, discuss a number of recent cases in which the Court of Justice of the European Union (CJEU) advances its interpretation of citizenship and non-discrimination, or equality, as a general principle of European Union (EU) law (Art. 9 TEU). This paper discusses some of the legislation which was adopted by the EU, based on the Citizenship Articles in the Treaty of Nice (and originally in the Treaty of Maastricht).

The ratification of the Lisbon Treaty, in December 2009, had been in doubt because of a negative note vote in the first Irish referendum in May 2008. This was followed by an Irish "yes" vote in October 2009 after a number of concessions had been made to the Irish (a promise of an Irish Commissioner, concessions re defence matters). During the intervening period, a number of seminars in London and Oxford considered what could be achieved in the event of the non-ratification of

[1]O'Keeffe and Twomey (1994).

[2]I am much indebted for contributions throughout this article to Ms. Clare Williams, Kingston University.

M. Horspool (✉)
British Institute of International and Comparative Law, Charles Clore House, 17 Russell Square, London WC 1B 5JP, UK

H.-J. Blanke and S. Mangiameli (eds.), *The European Union after Lisbon*,
DOI 10.1007/978-3-642-19507-5_10, © Springer-Verlag Berlin Heidelberg 2012

Lisbon, and what parts of Union law could be progressed just as well under the existing Nice Treaty. It was fairly clear that some matters did need and would in fact achieve improvement through the Treaty. Equally well, there were many parts of the Treaty which it did not seem essential to change in order for Europe to progress satisfactorily.

One such is undoubtedly that of citizenship and non-discrimination. There is no doubt that the main mover in this respect has been the CJEU's expansive interpretation of the existing articles in the Nice Treaty. This contribution will deal with this development. Another document which is focussed on Citizens' rights to a greater extent than the Treaty itself is, of course, the European Union Charter of Fundamental Rights (EUCFR), which has now achieved full legal status in the Lisbon Treaty.

Additional rights can be found to those set out in the EC Treaty under the fifth subheading of the Charter, Citizens' Rights. Article 41 EUCFR provides for the *Right to Good Administration.* This appears to mirror other provisions of the Charter falling mainly under the subheading of Justice, but entails the right to have one's affairs handled *impartially, fairly and within a reasonable time by the institutions, bodies, offices and agencies of the Union.*[3] Article 42 EUCFR provides for the right of access to documents of institutions of the Union. Finally, Art. 43 EUCFR sets out the rights of freedom of movement and residence. While paragraph 1 sounds familiar, paragraph 2 of this Article is of interest. It states: *Freedom of movement and residence may be granted, in accordance with the Treaty establishing the European Union, to nationals of third countries legally resident in the territory of a Member State.*

Until the entry into force of the Lisbon Treaty the Charter (which is not included in the main text) did not have binding status. Nevertheless, its impact can already be seen in the Opinions of Advocates General and judgments of the ECJ. It remains to be seen, however, whether the Charter is a precursor to a European immigration policy and border control. Given that permanent residence status is only available to Member State nationals after (usually) 5 years' residence in the host Member State,[4] and that this status brings with it few entitlements to social aid, it is unlikely that free movement and residence of third-country nationals within the Union will gain any social welfare benefits from the acquisition of such freedoms. Whether in time such residence allowances might entail political rights, however, is entirely another matter. The attribution of political rights to Member State nationals in a host Member State, while currently being a token gesture, is likely to be expanded. At the present time, voting rights and the right to stand in elections are confined to local and European elections. With the aim of increased social cohesion across Europe

[3]Treaty Establishing a Constitution for Europe, Part II, the Charter of Fundamental Rights of the Union, Art. II-101.1 (2004).

[4]See Art. 16 et seqq. of Parliament/Council Directive 2004/38 *on the right of citizens of the Union and their family members to move and reside freely within the territory of the Member States*, O.J. L 158/77 (2004).

as one of the principal goals at the moment, arguments against full voting rights for Member State nationals in a host Member State are becoming less and less sustainable. Another step further would be to extend such rights also to third-country nationals who have acquired permanent residence status in the host country. Directive 2004/38 consolidates most of the existing rights, but creates few new ones.

2 The Concept of Citizenship

Cicero, himself a lawyer, claimed that the proudest boast of an individual in the Roman Empire was: *Civis Romanus sum*. In a European context it is an aspiration, but probably no more than that for the present, that one day the European citizen will regard the accolade of European citizenship with the same respect and pride. Advocate General *Jacobs* in *Konstantinidis v Stadt Altensteig*[5] referred to this aspiration, where a citizen would proudly claim '*Civis Europeus sum*'. A Community national, the Advocate General says in this context, is entitled, wherever he goes in the Union, to "be treated in accordance with a common code of fundamental values."[6]

Formally established by the Maastricht Treaty in 1993, citizenship of the EU is a relatively new legal attribute. However, theories of an integrated citizenry of Europe had been in circulation for many decades previously and, as such, the idea of the European Citizen is not new. Yet what is meant by "European Citizenship" is a question to which there is no clear answer. One can point to the respective rights laid down in Treaties and the case law of the CJEU, and yet still not be able to define what constitutes a unified, heterogeneous population. Indeed, the question of what is citizenship on a national, or even sub-national level, appears to raise more questions than answers. Theories of nationality, residence, cultural ties, familial bonds, political beliefs and so on have all been used to justify various notions of modern citizenship.

If, however, we consider citizenship from the viewpoint of a supranational entity such as the EU, many of these theories would require a complete rethink. The Union, first, is not a state, and second, has no identifiable *demos*.

The new status of Union citizen as established by Art. 20.1 TFEU has been defined by the CJEU in consistent case law as follows: "Union citizenship is destined to be the fundamental status of nationals of the Member States, enabling those who find themselves in the same situation to enjoy the same treatment in law irrespective of their nationality, subject to such exceptions as are expressly provided for."[7]

---

[5]Case C-168/91 *Konstantinidis v Stadt Altensteig* (ECJ 30 March 1993).

[6]Case C-168/91 *Konstantinidis v Stadt Altensteig* (Opinion of Advocate General Jacobs of 9 December 1992) para 46.

[7]Case C-184/99 *Rudy Grzelczyk v Centre public d'aide sociale d'Ottignies-Louvain-la-Neuve* (ECJ 20 September 2001), para 31.

According to Advocate General *Cosmas*[8] Art. 20.2 lit. c and Art. 21 TFEU establish "for nationals of the Member States (now designated citizens of the Union) a possibility of a substantive nature, namely a right, in the true meaning of the word, which exists with a view to the autonomous pursuit of a goal, to the benefit of the holder of that right and not to the benefit of the Community and the attainment of its objectives." The provision enshrines "a right of a different kind, a true right of movement, stemming from the status as a citizen of the Union, which is not subsidiary in relation to European unification, whether economic or not." These statements would appear to move the citizenship provisions forward to a more fundamental concept, placing the citizen at the centre of the Union with subjective rights not connected to economic parameters.

3 The Philosophy of Citizenship

Of particular interest is the dichotomy that arguably remains between nationality and citizenship. While of general importance, an examination of the two terms is vital in relation to a discussion of European citizenship, due to the post-national nature of the institutions at the heart of the debate. Some definitions of nationality and citizenship mostly tend to be in reference to the nation state, and need therefore to be reinterpreted in relation to the EU.

However, for the preliminary discussions of the current rights and duties of citizenship in law, a few definitions are hereby offered in an attempt to inform what follows.

While not always the case, in the majority of references nationality is characterised as the outward-looking aspect of one's ties to a state. By contrast, citizenship is characterised as the inward-looking aspect of rights and responsibilities one exercises and performs within the society of that state. In the renowned *Nottebohm*[9] case, the International Court of Justice (ICJ) described nationality as *a legal bond having as its basis a social fact of attachment, a genuine connection of existence, interests and sentiments, together with the existence of reciprocal rights and duties*. Nationality is the legal expression of the fact that the individual upon whom it is conferred, either directly by law or as a result of an act of the authorities, is in fact more closely connected with the population of the state conferring the nationality than with any other state. However, this definition has its problems. The absence of any clear legal or theoretical delineation separating nationality from citizenship has meant the interpretation of the concepts along some rather different lines. Where consensus has occurred, nationality has come to mean the affiliation of an individual with a state from the external point of view of international law, while

[8] Case C-378/97 *Criminal proceedings against Florus Ariël Wijsenbeek* (Opinion of Advocate General Cosmas of 16 March 1999) para 84 et seq.

[9] Case *Liechtenstein v Guatamala (Nottebohm)* (ICJ 6 April 1955) p. 23 (ICJ Reports 1955, p. 4).

citizenship implies the internal host of national rights and duties incumbent upon the individual.

While *Halsbury's Laws of England* describe nationality as a term denoting the quality of political membership of a state (in itself a term that implicitly refers to citizenship), *Closa* has defined nationality as "the external face of a complex concept which also possesses an internal face which is citizenship".[10] For *Shaw*, the area between the dichotomy that characterises the individual-collective dualism and the multi-level non-state polity sees an interaction definitive of citizenship. This latter can, however, also be characterised as an institution, a "dynamic patchwork displayed in the constantly negotiated and re-negotiated tension between identity and rights".[11] Defining citizenship, Evans has stated that *the constitutional arrangements made for participation by a defined category of individuals in the life of the State*[12] sum up the main characteristics. However, given the ideal of access to fundamental rights by all, regardless of nationality or citizenship, plus the attribution of certain rights upon residence status, plus the dependence of citizenship on nationality in some cases, yet their respective independence in others, it becomes easy to see that one rule simply cannot fit all.

Citizenship as a relational, ultimately subjective concept is one that requires much more debate. Of particular absence in current discourse on this topic is any discussion of the inherent internalisation of the public/private dichotomy within the individual, and the importance of this process in formulating notions of citizenship. As such, any definitive conclusions cannot claim to have taken into account the whole picture.

"Rights and duties" of citizenship are commonly referred to together, yet while a series of Treaty Articles are devoted to the rights conferred on citizens of the Union, relevant duties are conspicuous by their absence from the Treaty. Duties of citizenship seem to be left to the sole competence of Member States to impose and enforce, such as military service, jury service, etc. It remains to be seen whether this is dependent on direct democracy and whether enabling this in the Union, and thereby improving democratic accountability, will see the introduction of Union duties.

A document published in December 2008 by the British government entitled "Citizenship, our common Bond" commissioned by Lord Goldsmith, former Attorney General, to which my Institute contributed a lengthy report, sets out some "definitions" or descriptions of the concept of citizenship. "Citizenship has been the basic form of connection between individuals and the state. In modern terms, it is the statement of a reciprocal relationship under which the individual offers loyalty in exchange for protection." In early conceptions this relationship was drawn in narrow terms, meaning defence against an external threat. It increasingly meant protection against other citizens, but did not extend in great part to provision

[10]Quoted in Guild (1996), p. 32.

[11]Shaw (1998), p. 294.

[12]Evans (1991).

of welfare. In this conception non-citizens were not entitled to protection and they were often seen as a potential threat. For example, the 1793 Aliens Act obliged aliens to register when coming into the United Kingdom and to obtain a passport in order to travel within the country. The Home Secretary had the power to deport. Citizens could only be expelled under much more rigorous criteria, representing a total repudiation of the connection between the citizen and the State.

This concept is now, of course, outdated. Especially over the last century, citizenship has undergone massive change. The connection with the State is much closer, including much more protection in healthcare, housing, etc., and protection against discrimination. Citizenship has become also a basis for connection between individuals. Thus, citizenship has risen in importance although it has not replaced or superseded other forms.

The lines between citizenship and non-citizenship have also become blurred and one consequence is that social and economic aspects of citizenship are not closely linked to the status of a legal citizen. There is a clear distinction between the rights of citizens and those with limited leave to be in the United Kingdom. However, the distinction between the rights of citizens and permanent residents – those with unlimited leave to remain in the UK (e.g. EU nationals) – is less clear.

4 The History of European Citizenship in the Treaties

Following the rejection of the Constitution by France and the Netherlands in 2005, and a 2-year period of reflection, the Intergovernmental Conference agreed on a mandate to draw up a new Treaty on Institutional Reform by the end of 2007. This Treaty has taken the form of the Lisbon Treaty (formerly known as the 'Reform Treaty') signed in December 2007 and should have come into force in January 2009 when it was assumed that all Member States would ratify. A spanner in the works was the rejection of the Treaty by an Irish referendum in the summer of 2008, and since then concessions have been drawn up in separate texts to allow the Irish to vote again in the autumn of 2009. With an Irish "Yes" this time and the final ratification in Germany, Poland and the Czech Republic, the Lisbon Treaty finally entered into force on 1 December 2009.

Before discussing the citizenship provisions in the new Treaty, I will focus on the most important historical developments regarding European citizenship in the EU. Concrete steps were first taken towards the establishment of a European citizenship in 1974 at the Paris Summit with the establishment of a working group to study the conditions under which *citizens of the Member States could be given special rights as members of the Community*.[13] The Tindemans Report subsequently advocated the grant of certain civil and political rights to nationals of Member States, including the right to vote and stand for public office. Reports

[13]Bull EC 12-1974, point 111, as quoted in O'Keeffe (1994), p. 87.

such as the European Parliament's Scelba Report, and the Addonino Reports on "A People's Europe", discussed rights of citizens, though the terms "citizenship" was much used, but seldom defined. The importance of free movement of citizens for the enhancement of the economic development of the Union was recognised early, and the Commission's guidelines for a Community Policy on Migration suggested that freedom of movement for citizens should go beyond that extended to workers for the purposes of employment.[14] The first traceable reference to the concept of citizenship in the European context is to be found in a letter of the Prime Minister of Spain to the President in Office of the Council prior to the Dublin summit in June 1990.[15] The summit endorsed Spain's proposal, and submitted to the Council the following question for consideration: *How will the Union include and extend the notion of Community citizenship carrying with it specific rights (human, political, social, the right of complete free movement and residence, etc.) for the citizens of the Member States by virtue of these States belonging to the Union?*[16] The Spanish government further submitted a Memorandum on European Citizenship,[17] which was designed to address the problem of Member State nationals being treated as no more than "privileged foreigners". The proposals included the granting to all citizens of the Union the rights to full freedom of movement and residence including political participation in the host Member State, specific rights in the areas of health, social affairs, education, culture, the environment and consumer protection, rights to assistance and diplomatic protection by other Member States, rights to petition the European Parliament and other rights to be agreed in the future.

The Commission opinion of 21 October 1990 made clear its agreement with Spain's proposals, stating that it saw the creation of citizenship of the Union as a way of counteracting democratic deficit in the Union, and strengthening democracy. This was seconded by the Danish government's proposal of the right of Community nationals to vote in local elections in the Member State in which they were resident. The issue of the protection of citizens' rights eventually resulted in the creation of the office of the Ombudsman. While the Council did not consider human rights to be part of the provisions on citizenship, the Commission and Parliament rejected this stance, arguing for the inherent inclusion of fundamental rights within the Treaty to be invoked by citizens, and the need for the Community to accede to the European Convention on Human Rights (ECHR). The citizenship provisions that were finally approved by the personal representatives of the Heads of State and Government, at ministerial level, and at the Luxembourg European Council, and which were inserted into the TEU largely resembled the outline given

[14] Supplement 9/85. Bull EC, p. 5, in O'Keeffe (1994).

[15] *Europe* No. 5252, 11 May 1990, p. 3, in O'Keeffe (1994).

[16] Bull EC 6-1990, Annex 1, p.15, in O'Keeffe (1994).

[17] Towards a European Citizenship, *Europe Documents*, No. 1653, 2 October 1990, in O'Keeffe (1994).

at the Rome Summit. The one reference to human rights was contained in a separate provision under Art. F(2) TEU.

The preamble to the TEU set out that the High Contracting Parties *resolved to establish a citizenship common to the nationals of their countries*. This was followed up in Art. B of the Common Provisions, stating one of the objectives of the Union as *to strengthen the protection of the rights and interests of the nationals of its Member States through the introduction of a citizenship of the Union*. The fact that provisions on citizenship are contained in a separate Part of the Treaty has been interpreted by some commentators as significant, indicating the relative importance of the measures and their implementation.[18]

5 The Citizenship Directive 2004/38

Directive 2004/38, the "Citizenship" Directive, also sets out the rights of freedom of movement, both extensively in the Preamble, and in Chapter III of the body of the Directive. The separate directives described in the Introduction, relating to different categories of people, have now been replaced by the single Directive 2004/38, date of implementation May 2006. This Directive applies to all EU citizens and their families. However, the pre-existing differences between the rights of the economically active and the non-economically active have been incorporated into Directive 2004/38 and will continue to apply, but only for the first 5 years of residence. After that time a citizen and his or her family will acquire an unconditional right to live permanently in the host state on equal terms with nationals of that state.

In all cases, Member States can refuse entry or terminate the right to residence on grounds of public policy, public security and public health. The provisions of Directive 2004/388 are set out and discussed with an explanation of the changes it introduces to existing law. It replaces the previous "piecemeal" approach to rules on free movement with a single Directive applicable to all EU citizens and their families. However, due to the preservation of distinctions between economically active and non-economically active, it remains important to understand the existing case law in relation to the separate categories.

Directive 2004/38 establishes citizenship of the EU as the "fundamental status" of those exercising their right of free movement (Preamble, paragraph 3). This approach is founded on the status of citizenship (Arts. 20–21 TFEU, ex-Arts. 17–18 EC) and the principle of non-discrimination (Art. 18 TFEU, ex-Art. 12 EC).[19]

---

[18] O'Keeffe (1994), p. 90.

[19] Horspool and Humphreys (2010), pp. 450 et seq.

6 Changes in the Lisbon Treaty

6.1 The Project of "Citizen Empowerment"

The Lisbon Treaty introduces few substantive and almost no substantial changes to existing EC and EU provisions as regards the legal status. Note that no working group in the Convention for the Constitution addressed the problem. All one can look at, therefore, is what Professor *Jo Shaw*, in a Federal Trust Paper,[20] calls "the project of citizen empowerment", which results from the changes in the Treaty texts from where earlier there was mention of either "nationals" or "peoples" this has now been replaced by "citizens".

Most of the ideas come from the Treaty establishing a Constitution for Europe, which preceded the Lisbon Treaty and was rejected by referenda in France and the Netherlands in May/June 2005. The constitutional idea of that Treaty was deliberately abandoned in the Lisbon Treaty, which, although it resembles the unsuccessful Treaty in many ways, attempts to show more modest aspirations.

The reference to the "will of the citizens to build a common future" in the Constitutional Treaty has been dropped (Art. I-1 TCE). This "Madisonian ideal" is replaced by the more modest text of Lisbon, which reasserts the position of the Member States as the sole masters of the Treaties. Thus, the same criticisms that were levelled at the Amsterdam and Maastricht Treaties remain here. At the time, questions were raised as to the contribution made by citizenship articles, limited as they were by references to the exceptions in the Treaty articles concerning the free movement of persons (Arts. 39.3 and 39.4, 45, 46 and 55 now Arts. 45.3 and 45.4, 51 and 62 TFEU). These concentrated on the remodelling of the Treaty on European Union (TEU) to ensure it would fulfil many of the same functions and comprise most of the same core elements as part one of the Constitutional Treaty. Pre-Lisbon, there had been no mention of "citizenship", only of citizens, although the concept is not defined. Article I-10 TCE did refer to citizenship. The July 2007 version of Lisbon did not contain a reference to citizenship, only one to *equality* of citizens, and possibly inspired by Art. 20 EUCFR, which refers to "equality before the law" and, in its final version, Art. 9 TEU reads as follows:

> In all its activities, the Union shall observe the principle of equality of its citizens, who shall receive equal attention from its institutions, bodies, offices and agencies. Every national of a Member State shall be a citizen of the Union. Citizenship of the Union shall be additional to national citizenship and shall not replace it.

[20]Shaw (2008).

However, the status of the European Parliament as a representative body does undergo a number of changes.

The heading of the citizenship articles in Part 2 of the Treaty on the Functioning of the European Union (TFEU) now reads: Non-Discrimination and Citizenship. The most significant difference between pre-Lisbon and post-Lisbon in Arts. 20–24 TFEU concern the wording of the relationship between national citizenship and citizenship of the EU. The TEU speaks of *additionality* (*Zusätzlichkeit*) whereas previously Union citizenship was expressed as *complementary* (*ergänzend*) to national citizenship. Both texts make it clear that citizenship does not *replace* national citizenship. This was insisted upon by Member States in order to reinforce the point that EU citizenship can only *add* rights, and cannot *detract* from national citizenship. Citizenship of a Member State remains the sole decision of a Member State subject to any relevant Treaty provisions. In *Shaw's* view this is a more accurate delineation of the two statuses as it avoids the possible implication that there is somehow a duty on one to bend to the will of the other to achieve the desired "complementarity". Conceptually, it also indicates that it is not a "zero" game in which rights given at one level have to be detracted from the other. However, in practice, this is not likely to make much difference. The citizenship attributions which the CJEU has defined in cases starting with *Martinez Sala*[21] have not detracted from national citizenship, except in terms of undermining its exclusivity by extending the territorial boundaries of the welfare state.

Citizens' initiatives outlined in Art. 11.4 TEU are given a legal basis in Art. 24 TFEU and a new paragraph has been added to Art. 23 TFEU with a special legislative procedure, involving consultation of the European Parliament, for the Council to establish the coordination and cooperation measures necessary to facilitate diplomatic and consular protection.

Measures under ex-Pillar 3, Area of Freedom, Security and Justice, the special legal basis for the adoption of measures regarding passports, identity cards and residence permits (Art. 77.3 TFEU) no longer need to be excluded from Art. 21.3 TFEU (ex-Art. 18 EC).

It is a pity that citizenship definitions have not been included in the Court's interpretation in the same way as was done with fundamental rights in Art. 6.1 (ex-Art. 6.3 EC) as general principles of Union law. There are some statements by the CJEU, such as the one in *Grzelczyk*[22]and *Bidar*[23]: It should be recalled that "Union citizenship is destined to be the fundamental status of nationals of the Member States, enabling those who find themselves in the same situation to enjoy the same treatment in law irrespective of their nationality, subject to such exceptions as are expressly provided for."

[21]Case C-85/96 *Martínez Sala v Freistaat Bayern* (ECJ 12 May 1998).

[22]Case C-184/99 *Rudy Grzelczyk v Centre public d'aide sociale d'Ottignies-Louvain-la-Neuve* (ECJ 20 September 2001) paras 30 and 31.

[23]Case C-209/03 *Dany Bidar v London Borough of Ealing* (ECJ 15 March 2005) para 31.

6.2 *The Democratic Life of the Union*

In accordance with Art. 10.3 TEU "[e]very citizen shall have the right to participate in the democratic life of the Union." There does not seem to be much improvement in the participation of citizens in the exercise of their political rights within the functioning of the Union founded on representative democracy (Art. 10.1 TEU).

6.3 *The Citizenship Initiative, Introduced in the Lisbon Treaty*[24]

Under the previous Treaties, direct democracy played virtually no role in the functioning of the Union. The closest was perhaps the right to petition the European Parliament in Arts. 21 and 194 EC, in the hope that the Commission may make corresponding proposals. Popular initiatives exist in a number of Member States, including Austria, Hungary, Italy, Latvia, Lithuania, Poland, Romania, Slovakia, Slovenia and Spain. Other Member States, e.g. France and Sweden, make constitutional provision for some form of popular initiative only at regional/municipal level, some others such as Germany and the Netherlands have experimented with various national and/or local popular initiatives by subordinate legislative means.

Proposals for a popular initiative at Union level in order to deal with the democratic deficit were first made during the Constitutional Convention, included in an amended form in the proposed Constitution and have now been reproduced by the Lisbon Treaty. Article 11.4 of the revised TEU[25] provides:

> Not less than one million citizens who are nationals of a significant number of Member States may take the initiative of inviting the European Commission, within the framework of its powers, to submit any appropriate proposal on matters where citizens consider that a legal act of the Union is required for the purpose of implementing the Treaties.
>
> The procedures and conditions required for such a citizens' initiative shall be determined in accordance with the first paragraph of Article 24 the Treaty on the Functioning of the European Union.

Article 24.1 TFEU reads as follows:

> The European Parliament and the Council, acting by means of regulations in accordance with the ordinary legislative procedure, shall adopt the provisions for the procedures and conditions required for a citizens' initiative within the meaning of Article 11 of the Treaty on European Union, including the minimum number of Member States from which such citizens must come.

---

[24]From Editorial Comment CMLRev. 45, No 4 August 2008 'Direct Democracy and the European Union. . .is that a threat or a promise?

[25]See *Consolidated version of the Treaty on European Union* of 30 March 2010, O.J. C 83/13 (2010).

Many commentators considered this insertion of little importance; a report on the draft Treaty by the French Senate, for example, doesn't even mention it. The Common Market Law Review (*CMLRev*) sets outs the advantages of such initiatives,[26] although they often seem to remain theory. They enhance mass participation in the exercise of power between parliamentary elections, offer "single-issue" movements a formal channel to express themselves and can give a voice to minority groups. More generally they may contribute to reducing the voter apathy and public cynicism which often affect mature democracies by giving citizens some sense of constitutional ownership and political responsibility. How much of this is translated into reality is questionable, but it might help in giving a higher profile to, for example, European elections, in which, as we have seen yet again in June 2009, voter participation is woefully low.

However, any real effect of these articles would very much depend on how they are interpreted and how they would operate in practice. Article 11.4 TEU lays down basic but very vague parameters. Article 24 TFEU merely provides for procedures and conditions to be adopted subsequently. A number of questions emerge:

1. Union law would have to clarify the threshold conditions for the validity of Citizenship Initiatives (CIs). Who would endorse it? Rules for participation would follow those for European Parliament elections, but these are not uniform. Thus, there would be differences as regards age thresholds, disqualification criteria and residence requirements. And what about third-country nationals who *can* vote in European Parliament elections, such as is the case apparently in Austria, Hungary, Italy, Latvia, Lithuania, Poland, Romania and Slovenia, but not in others, including the United Kingdom. As the text of Art. 11.4 TEU specifically refers to nationals they could not take part in such a CI.
2. The requirement of a million signatures which have to come from "a significant number of countries". Again, this is to be defined by implementing legislation. One could have a fixed percentage but that would disadvantage bigger states, e.g. a 5% threshold would require over 4 million signatures for Germany, or even 1% would require 825,000. On the other hand, a minimum of a fixed percentage of overall signatures would disadvantage small countries.
3. According to Art. 11.4 TEU, an initiative may "invite the Commission, within the framework of its powers", to submit any appropriate proposal on matters where a Union legal act is deemed to be required for the implementation of the Treaties. Clearly this is not limited to the normal legislative proposals by the Commission, so what else would this extend to? It could include just about anything as long as it is "within the competence of the Union", including non-legislative measures or any other non-legal acts. It is even suggested that this could include proposals for actual treaty amendment, although this would seem unlikely to be regarded as a legal act required for the implementation of the treaties. What about the Common Foreign and Security Policy (CFSP) where

[26] See Editorial Comment CMLRev. 45, No 4 August 2008, p. 932.

the High Representative acts in two different capacities, exercising the powers of the Commission itself as well as those of the High Representative. The CMLRev editorial favours formal proposals to be put to the Commission according to the normal method.

4. What obligations could or should a valid CI impose on the Union institutions? Article 11.4 TEU seems to adopt a rather weak approach: it imposes no express obligations on the Commission even to consider, or respond to, let alone bring forward any formal proposals based on a valid CI. But how far could the Council and the European Parliament impose particular procedural or even substantive obligations? If no formal proposal by the Commission were to be forthcoming it might well offend, in any case, the Charter principle of good administration. But could the article really be used to compel the Commission to bring forward a proposal? This is unlikely and the Commission would presumably consider this decision to be in its own discretion. Otherwise, it would infringe the Commission's prerogative of legislative initiative and the principle of the Commission acting in complete independence.
5. What about resources? It would require a considerable amount of administrative time, energy and finance. And what about the CJEU's role in all this? If it is in an expansive mood it could of course play a crucial role, particularly when called upon to review the limits of the Union legislature's discretion to regulate the procedures and conditions applicable to a CI under Art. 24 TFEU.
6. The role of the European Parliament, the supposed representatives of the European citizens, is not addressed in Art. 11.4 TEU and is confined to laying down procedures and conditions to regulate a CI, together with the Council, in Art. 24 TFEU. The CI provisions are so vague on the one hand and so wide on the other that they may never be used or, in contrast, may take on a meaning of their own and make a real difference. As we have seen with the original citizenship provisions in the Maastricht Treaty, they too were originally considered as nothing more than window dressing, until the ECJ in *Martinez Sala* used Art. 18 EC for the first time.[27]

Whilst it is accepted that the European CI has the potential to raise an awareness in citizens of EU politics and how they can be more involved in its development, the Commission has the difficult task of striking the right balance between allowing citizens to shape the law with the wider interests of the EU. Whether the Commission strikes the right balance remains to be seen when it produces its regulation on the initiative.[28]

[27]Case C-85/96 *Martínez Sala v Freistaat Bayern* (ECJ 12 May 1998).

[28]Horspool and Humphreys (2010), p. 460.

6.4 Citizenship and the Role of the European Parliament

The Citizenship provisions in the Lisbon Treaty now refer to "citizens", where earlier they referred to "peoples" (Arts. 10.2, 10.3, 14.2 TEU). Article 10.2 TEU reads as follows:

> Citizens are directly represented at Union level in the European Parliament. Member States are represented in the European Council by their Heads of State or Government and in the Council by their governments, themselves democratically accountable either to their national Parliaments, or to their citizens.

This provision not only takes up the dual legitimation of the EU, but also lays it down as a form of organization of the citizens of Europe in the European Parliament on the one hand and of the peoples of Europe on the other. The adoption of this double model of legitimation by the Treaty of Lisbon illustrates that a reduction of the institutional and social democratic deficit can only be achieved if both chains of legitimation are put into conclusive relation.

Art. 14.2 TEU provides that "[t]he European Parliament shall be composed of representatives of the Union's citizens", which clearly shows self-conception and ambition of this institution. The text of Art. 14.3 TEU, which provides that "the European Parliament shall be elected [...] by direct universal suffrage" of European citizens "in a free and secret ballot", is restated in Art. 39 EUCFR. This status had, in any case, already been clarified in the cases of *Spain v United Kingdom*[29] (see also the European Court of Human Rights (ECtHR) case of *Matthews v United Kingdom*[30]) and *Eman and Sevinger (Aruba)*.[31] The latter case concerned a national rule which excluded Dutch nationals from voting in European Parliament elections so long as they were resident in Aruba (one of the "overseas countries and territories" (OCT) of the Netherlands), but allowed them to vote in general elections in the Netherlands under expatriate voting rules. The Court answered that those possessing the nationality of a Member State and who reside in an OCT may rely on the citizenship rights contained in the EC Treaty. Member States were free "in the current state of Community law" to define these rights on the basis of criteria of residence in the territory in which elections are held, these criteria should not result in unequal treatment of nationals in comparable situations, unless such treatment was objectively justified.[32] The *Aruba* case leads to the conclusion that citizens of the Union cannot be deprived of their right to vote in elections to the European

[29]Case C-145/04 *Kingdom of Spain v United Kingdom of Great Britain and Northern Ireland* (ECJ 12 September 2006).

[30]Case 24833/94 *Matthews v United Kingdom* (ECtHR 18 February 1999).

[31]Case C-300/04 *Eman and Sevinger v College van burgemeester en wethouders van Den Haag* (ECJ 12 September 2006).

[32]Article 19 EC and Art. 22 TFEU speak of an equal treatment right of nationals in comparable situations: nationals of Member States resident in other Member States have the right to vote for the EP under the same conditions as nationals.

Parliament as a normal incidence of EU citizenship, even if it is not explicitly stated in the Treaties. The strongest statement came from Advocate General *Tizzano*[33]:

> [I]t can be directly inferred from Community principles and legislation as a whole, thus overriding any indications to the contrary within national legislation, that there is an obligation to grant the voting rights [in European elections] to citizens of the Member States and, consequently, to citizens of the Union.

The Lisbon Treaty still does not wholly reflect the principle of equal representation as the number of MEP's is still not proportionate to the population of a country (5 members for Malta with a population of about 420,000; 99 members for Germany with a population of about 82 million). However, even the Federal Constitutional Court in Germany considered that total equality was not necessary and in any case impossible to achieve in this context.[34] Furthermore, the democratic deficit is diminished by the fact that there is still no uniform European electoral procedure. According to Art. 223.1 TFEU the codification of a uniform procedure on the elections of the Members of the European Parliament continues to be conditional on a legislative act which needs to be approved by all Member States in accordance with their respective constitutional requirements.

References

Birkinshaw P (2003) European public law. Butterworths, London

Evans AC (1991) Nationality law and European integration. Eur Law Rev 16:190–215

Guild E (1996) The legal framework of citizenship of the European Union. In: Cesari D, Fulbrook M (eds) Citizenship, nationality and migration in Europe. Routledge, London, pp 30–56

Horspool M, Humphreys M (2010) European Union law, 6th edn. Oxford University Press, Oxford

O'Keeffe D (1994) Union citizenship. In: O'Keeffe D, Twomey PM (eds) Legal issues of the Maastricht Treaty. Hart Publishing, Oxford

O'Keeffe D, Twomey PM (eds) (1994) Legal issues of the Maastricht Treaty. Hart Publishing, Oxford

Shaw J (1998) The interpretation of European Union citizenship. Modern Law Rev 61(3):293–317

Shaw J (2008) The Treaty of Lisbon and Citizenship. European Policy Brief for the Federal Trust for Education and Research. available online at http://www.fedtrust.co.uk/admin/uploads/PolicyBrief_Citizenship.pdf. Date of access: 15 August 2011

Weiler JHH (1999) The constitution of Europe. Cambridge University Press, Cambridge

---

[33]Case C-145/04 *Spain v United Kingdom* (Opinion of Advocate General Tizzano of 6 April 2006) para 67.

[34]German Federal Constitutional Court, 2 BvE 2, 5/08, 2 BvR 1010, 1022, 1259/08, 182/09 (Judgment of 30 June 2009) para 284 et seqq.

The Charter of Fundamental Rights of the Union as a Source of Law

Eduardo Gianfrancesco

1 A Concise Evaluation of the Successes and Failures of the Charter of Nice Before the Lisbon Treaty

First of all, the aim of this paper is to give a concise evaluation of the 7 years following the coming into effect of the European Charter of Fundamental Rights (EUCFR).

According to me the non-binding nature of this act was confirmed during this period, as the Charter did not become the core of a new system of fundamental rights. And, in hypothesis, the definition of this system would have been a problematic attempt, as we will see further on.

The heart of the system of the protection of rights in European law remained based on Art. 6 TEU-Maastricht – as interpreted by the European Court of Justice (ECJ) and the Court of First Instance (CFI) – and the reference to constitutional traditions common to the Member States as general principles. This does not mean of course that the EUCFR had no significance for European law. The absence of a binding nature does not imply a lack of juridical relevance: it is a (well-known) prejudice of continental (civil law) scholars to overlap these two aspects.

The EUCFR played a "confirmative role" in the above-mentioned system of rights protection based on constitutional common traditions as interpreted by European Courts. Whenever the Charter has been quoted by the ECJ, it has been mentioned *after* and not *before* the fundamental rights inferred by the Court. What is more significant is that there are no decisions based only on the EUCFR.[1] As far

[1]See, recently, Case C-47/07P *Masdar* (ECJ 16 December 2008) para 50; Case C-402/05P and C-415/05P *Kadi v Council and Commission* (ECJ 3 September 2008) para 335; Case C-450/06 *Varec* (14 February 2008) para 48; Case C-275/06 *Promusicae* (ECJ 29 January 2008) para 69; Case

E. Gianfrancesco (✉)
Facoltà di Giurisprudenza, Libera Università Maria Ss. Assunta, Via della Traspontina, 21, 00193 Roma, Italy
e-mail: e.gianfrancesco@lumsa.it

H.-J. Blanke and S. Mangiameli (eds.), *The European Union after Lisbon*,
DOI 10.1007/978-3-642-19507-5_11, © Springer-Verlag Berlin Heidelberg 2012

as the Italian experience is concerned, the Constitutional Court adopted the same solution: the Court quoted the Charter only in a few decisions.[2]

In my view, it can be confirmed that the value of the Charter is to recognise and not to set up fundamental rights. Someone referred the model of the "restatement of law" from the American experience.[3] In other words, we could say that the Charter offers a presumption of existence of the rights mentioned,[4] but European courts may, in any case, create other rights using Art. 6 TEU-Maastricht and the common constitutional traditions.

2 Six Levels of Juridical Relevance of the Charter of Fundamental Rights

If we accept this starting point, it is perhaps easier to discuss the meaning and value of the Charter in the European constitutional experience.

It is possible to establish several levels of juridical relevance of the Charter in this context[5]: some of them are typical of a non-binding document (but, not for this reason irrelevant). Further levels need binding value and so they may be appreciated only after the Lisbon Treaty has entered into force. The first two steps – juridical even though not binding – concern the visibility of the "rights question" in the European Union (EU).

It is a matter in no way of minor importance, connected with the roots of constitutionalism and the effort to create a real European public opinion in the name of the protection of rights. So the Charter gives more visibility to rights and their protection (first level of relevance),[6] with a symbolic and political effect on

---

C-341/05 *Laval un Partneri ltd* (ECJ 18 December 2007) paras 90 and 91; Case C-438/05 *International Transport Workers' Federation,Finnish Seamen's Union, v Viking Line ABP,OÜ Viking Line Eesti,* (ECJ 11 December 2007) paras 43 and 44; Case T-194/04 *Bavarian Lager v Commission* (CFI 8 November 2007) para 14; Case C-303/05 *Advocaten voor de Wereld* VZW (ECJ 3 May 2007) para 46.; Case C-432/05 *Unibet* (ECJ 13 March 2007) para 37; Case T-228/02 *Organisation des Modjahedines du peuple d'Iran v Council* (CFI 12 December 2006) para 71; Case 47/07P. *Masdar Ltd. Commission* (ECJ 16 December 2008).

[2]See Judgment No. 393/2006, para 6.2, which stresses the absence of juridical effectiveness of the Charter; Judgment No. 438/2008, para 4, which quotes the Charter among other international treaties.

[3]Barbera (2002); Silvestri (2006), p. 7 et seq.; Cartabia (2007), p. 32.

[4]I would prefer to define this presumption as *juris et de jure*. This means domestic jurisdiction cannot deny the existence of rights mentioned in the Charter (but, at least, give them a meaning connected with national rights). Some prefer to write about a *praesumptio juris tantum* (which admits contrary proof): see Pollicino and Sciarabba (2008), p. 107, fn 27. See also Azzena (2001), p. 124 et seq.

[5]See von Bogdandy (2001), p. 869, for a similar operation, even though with different features.

[6]See Cartabia (2007), pp. 54 et seqq.; Cartabia (2008), p. 98.

European people(s) and helps to create a better and deeper political awareness of the main core of European identity (founded on the protection of rights) and one of the essential goals of European action in the contemporary world (affirming and protecting fundamental rights). In other terms, rights become the object of European political action (second level of relevance).[7] In this perspective, the enhanced activism of European institutions after the Charter of 2001, which led in 2007 to the establishing of the *European Union Agency for Fundamental Rights*,[8] is not incidental.

Even a non-binding act may be used by European institutions to set self-established limits to their own action (third level of relevance). Albeit not enforceable in a trial by citizens, no one could deny any juridical relevance to this dimension of the Charter (see especially Art. 41 on the right to a "good administration"): it increases the duty of loyalty between institutions[9] and, in this sense, it is connected to Art. 10 TEU (and, in this way, it can even be used in judgments as an external element that makes loyalty duty real and concrete).[10]

It is a sort of "back to the past" path to the dawn of *Rechtsstaat*, when C.F. von Gerber theorised the *Reflexrechte*, because it was not (yet) possible to enforce advantageous positions of individuals before a judge and the only possible way to give juridical relevance to them was to establish rights as objective rules of good administrative machinery.[11]

The fourth level of relevance of the Charter is the strongest level compatible with a non-binding act: earlier we have mentioned the possible use of the Charter in judicial activity like a *Restatement of law*, like a point from which the judge can start, applying fundamental rights to the concrete case law, and this is the case. We are conscious that here the line between the non-binding and binding value of the Charter becomes fine: eminent scholars of public law of the twentieth century argued that the creation of a compilation of laws (*Testo Unico* in the Italian experience) implies creative – not only interpretative – activity[12] and the same may probably be referred to the *Restatement of laws*. So, if we are before a creation of law it is hard to deny full relevance to it: the barrier with a legislative act vanishes

[7]See Diez-Picazo (2001), p. 666; Rossi (2002), p. 280; Toniatti (2002), p. 8; Palermo (2002), p. 204; Pernice (2008), pp. 236 et seqq. and pp. 252 et seqq. A critic to the transformation of fundamental rights from a limit to competences to an object of politics in von Bogdandy (2000), pp. 831 et seqq.

[8]Council Regulation (EC) No. 168/2007 *European Union Agency for Fundamental Rights*, O.J. L 53/1 (2007).

[9]The Charter is defined as an "Interinstitutional Agreement" by Ferrari (2001), p. 42 and *ivi* other authors quoted.

[10]In this perspective, it is possible to apply the "soft-law" notion to the Charter: see Palermo (2005), p. 115; Poggi (2007), p. 370; Rossi (2002), p. 266; Rossi (2009), p. 77.

[11]Cf. von Gerber (1852).

[12]Esposito (1940). Pace (2001a), p. 195 writes that the Charter looks like something like a "Testo unico" half-interpretative, half-creative.

and the architecture (the system) of rights established in the Restatement of laws binds everyone (but especially judges).

But if we prefer (and we do prefer) a softer approach, which denies the Charter's creative features and, first of all, denies a binding of the judge to the system of rights in the Charter (for the simple reason that a system of rights is not sufficiently developed in the Charter, as we will attempt to highlight further on), the fourth level remains outside the creation of law. Only the fifth and sixth levels of juridical relevance play in the full area of a binding effectiveness of the Charter. This means, according to the *Rechtsstaat* tradition, that the real enforceability of fundamental rights is granted by an independent and impartial judge, separated from other public powers.

We face an alternative: the rights mentioned (or better, stated by the Charter) are in force only against European public powers and Member States when implementing European law and not in inter-private relationships (fifth level of relevance),[13] or these rights are characterised by the quality the German classical authors called the *Drittwirkung* of fundamental rights (sixth level of relevance).[14] We will come back to this issue later on in this essay. At present it suffices to mention both possibilities.

3 Problems Arising from the 2001 Charter

The years between 2001 and 2008 show the "rights question" as one of the most problematic in European law. It would be useful to highlight two profiles of this complexity and analyse them.

3.1 The Vertical Profile

This is the "classical" profile about the relationship between the EU and its Member States in matters involving the protection of rights. The framework of Art. 51 of the Charter is founded on the separation between *normative competences* and *protection of rights*: the idea is that the second item cannot interfere with the first one. The experience of federal countries, first of all the history of federalism in the United States, shows, however, that the basic idea of Art. 51 of the Charter is quite axiomatic.[15]

[13]See Cartabia (2001), p. 345; Marini (2004), p. 57.

[14]See Grossi (2003), p. 54. Some provisions of the Charter (especially in Chap. IV: see Arts. 27, 28, 30 31) cannot receive a meaningful interpretation, if not considered *erga omnes*.

[15]See Diez-Picazo (2001), pp. 674 et seqq.; De Siervo (2001a), p. 156; Cartabia (2001), pp. 346 et seqq; Caretti (2005), p. 378. In the opinion of Turpin (2003), p. 620 Art. 51 as amended in 2007 can establish a stronger limit to the "*rampantes*" competences of the EU.

The problem was already apparent in its complexity to G. Hamilton in the worldwide commentary No. 84 of the Federalist. What is remarkable is that the American constitutional system developed in the precise way Hamilton was afraid of[16]: if the *Bill of Rights* in 1791 was added to the Constitution in order to link it closer to the hard core of constitutionalism, the list of rights showed itself very soon as a real lever to change normative competences between the Federation and Member States: the relationship between these two entities relies upon concrete standards of protection, not upon abstract legislative competences,[17] and the upper level, introducing higher standard, changes competences.

This is not the right moment to speak about this unavoidable path.[18] It is just the case to remember the outcome of this evolution in which "only in a theoretical perspective, federal Governments establish bases, the constitutional minimum, to ensure the protection of fundamental rights, while Member States, developing this starting point, offer additional guarantees which their own citizens desire. In an institutional perspective, the logic is a bit different. The basic decisions for the protection of rights are up to the Member States (their political and judicial powers). Federal intervention compensates the omissions of the Member States. It allows the courts of the States to freely develop a doctrine of civil liberties".[19]

During this period the "incorporation doctrine"[20] goes forward and reaches relevant results in decisions like *K.B.*, *Richards*, and *Maruko*.[21] A sort of "prelimi-nary condition" linked with fundamental rights attracts competences, and thanks to fundamental rights the competences of the EU and its Member States can change.

3.2 The Horizontal Profile

The second example is even more relevant in my opinion. It refers to the effective-ness of European fundamental rights in their mutual relationship. It is remarkable

[16]For this assessment, see Pace (2001a), p. 193; Mangiameli (2008a), p. 309.

[17]See Caretti (2005), p. 379. With regard to the deep connection between competences and rights, see Azzena (1998).

[18]Regarding the evolution of federal systems concerning the protection of rights, see the classical pages of Stern (1994), for the German experience. See also Fercot (2008), for a comparison between the United States, Germany and Switzerland. For a different opinion which establishes rights as "negative competences" of European Institutions, see Pernice and Kanitz (2004), p. 17 et seq.

[19]Turr (2005), p. 56.

[20]With regard to the application of the "incorporation doctrine" to EU law, see Weiler (1985); Toniatti (2002), p. 15 et seq., referring to EUCFR. Cartabia (2007), pp. 27 et seqq. stresses the enlargement of the application of the "incorporation doctrine", after EUCFR proclamation.

[21]Case C-117/01 *K.B.V National Health Service Pensions Agency* (ECJ 7 January 2004), Case C-423/04 *Richards v Secretary of State for Work and Pensions* (ECJ 27 April 2006), Case C-267/06 *Mamko v Versorgungsanstalt der deutschen Bühnen* (ECJ 1 April 2008). With regard to this decision, see Ronchetti (2009).

that the mutual interferences between protected situations do not only refer to the articles of the Charter, but – as has been highlighted – involve rights from the EU Treaty too. And this is what Art. 6 TEU-Maastricht confirms.

The analysis of this profile, all within European law, requires a systematic approach, or, at least, some fundamentals of the architecture of constitutional doctrine of fundamental rights[22] and this makes the analysis more difficult and delicate.

The *Schmidberger*, *Omega* and *Dynamics Medien Vertriebs GmbH* cases[23] are not, in my opinion, so emblematic of this new perspective: the "general interest" clause applied in these decisions, against economic liberties, does not hide a conflict between two (or more) fundamental rights. The dialectic is between the fundamental (subjective) rights and objective limits (human dignity) to it. And this is a rather easier task for the ECJ, because there are no relevant doubts about the fact that objective limits to a subjective protected right must be restrictively applied with a severe proportionality test.[24]

The worldwide (or Europewide) *Laval*, *Viking Line* and *Rüffert* judgments[25] offer, indeed, the best recent examples of problems originating from the collision of fundamental subjective rights. There is a widespread awareness among scholars that these three decisions nullify the provision of Art. 137 TEU about the lack of relevance in European law of collective action, also considering Art. 28 EUCFR as lacking binding value: notwithstanding the refusal of the competence of the ECJ on collective bargaining and strike actions, the right to strike is here balanced with some fundamental economic liberties.

Here it is not possible to discuss the appropriateness of the Court's solution in the specific case. We have to stress, indeed, that the result of the balancing is a *new regulation* of social and trade union matters. It is impossible, in my opinion, to avoid this point. The importance of *Laval*, *Viking* and *Rüffert* is to show a clear and real conflict between social and economic liberties: both of them are fundamental, but in the absence of positive elements about prevalence (prevalence which ought to be decided by the constitution maker, in accordance with the teachings of C. Schmitt[26]) they have to be balanced by Courts, first of all the ECJ, using self-made instruments.

---

[22]The importance of the support of the academic world in order to solve problems of the overlapping of different levels of protection of fundamental rights is enhanced by Blanke (2006), p. 277.

[23]Case C-112/00 *Schmidberger v Republik Österreich* (ECJ 12 June 2003), Case C-36/02 *Omega Spielhallen v Oberbürgermeisterin der Bundesstadt Bonn* (ECJ 14 October 2004), Case C-244/06 *Dynamics Medien Vertriebs GmbH v Avides Media AG* (ECJ 14 February 2008).

[24]On these aspects, see Morijn (2006). See also, in a more systematic approach, referring to the Italian constitutional system, Mangiameli (2006), p. 513.

[25]Case C-341/05 *Laval v Svenska Byggnadsarbetareförderbundet et al.* (ECJ 18 December 2007), Case C-438/05 *International Transport Workers Federation et al. v Viking Line* (ECJ 11 December 2007), Case C-346/06 *Rüffert v Land Niedersachsen* (ECJ 3 April 2008).

[26]The reference is obviously to Schmitt (1928).

The point of focus, which I shall attempt to develop in the following pages, is the absence of clear statements of the Charter about the mutual relationship between the rights it mentions. Even if we do not want to reason about a *Wertordnung* of protected situations, we need some minimal spurs to build the European Bill of Rights systematically. Otherwise, the lack of reference points of interpreters will reflect (and it reflects) on judges and judgments, too.

4 The Charter of Fundamental Rights After the Lisbon Treaty

Could the Charter of 2007, in the perspective of its incorporation in European treaties, offer help to solve problems arising from the aforementioned situation (especially as far as para 3.1 is concerned) and give a real orientation to European judges, reducing their creative role?

4.1 The EU Treaty and the Charter: Art. 6 and Consequent Problems

Let us begin with the formal element. In the Lisbon Treaty the Charter does not become part of the treaty, that is, a part of the text itself. In other words, the Charter is not incorporated in the EU Treaty as happened in the Constitutional Treaty, but Art. 6 TEU confers to the Charter "*the same legal value as the Treaties*".[27] Will this be enough to give the provisions of the Charter the same range as other provisions of the Treaties or is there a risk of creating a "golden cage" for the Charter, reduced to a preamble with a different (reduced) juridical *status*?

In my opinion, the problem of the collocation of the Charter outside the core of the treaties may be quite easily overcome by conferring to it really the same value as the provisions of the two fundamental Treaties. The choice of a separated Bill of Rights is probably connected to the opt-out decision of United Kingdom and Poland. The opt-out solution – apart from any question of its practical relevance[28] – would be more difficult to justify and to build too, from a juridical point of view, if the Charter was a part of the EU Treaty, producing perhaps a denial of ratification of some of the articles of the international treaty from the two states just mentioned.

The explicit reservation of the United Kingdom and Poland in Protocol No. 30 annexed to reform treaties, reaffirmed in Protocol No. 53 and Declarations No. 61

[27]With regard to other possible solutions to insert the EUCFR in the binding European law, see Weber (2003), p. 220; Michetti (2006), p. 176.

[28]For a sceptical approach to the opt-out problem, see Dutheil de la Rochère (2008), pp. 127 et seqq.; Pernice (2008), p. 244 et seq.; Pollicino and Sciarabba (2008), p. 112.

and 62, may confirm, on the grounds of *argumentum a contrario*, the legal value of the Charter. The separate position of the Charter in the treaties may be ambiguous from a different point of view: the idea that between the fundamental rights of the EU and the EUCFR there exists a complete correspondence; that is, there would be no fundamental rights outside the Charter.

As Art. 6.3 TEU clarifies, the drawing up of the Charter is not exhaustive: the rights guaranteed by the ECHR[29] and the constitutional traditions common to the Member States are the other sources to identify and protect the European heritage of fundamental rights. In this sense, the separated topographic position of the European Bill of Rights may cause misunderstandings and problems of systematic interpretations, but nothing more than this. Otherwise, we would be facing a dramatic crisis in the European legal system, if it was possible to create a "constitutional apartheid", with reduced binding value for the rights enshrined in the Charter. If someone were to emphasise a separate *status* for the Charter, reducing it to a "son of a lesser god", he or she could set off the unhappy provisions of Art. 6.1 TEU which recommends the "due regard to the explanations referred to in the Charter", and the similar provision of Art. 52.7 of the Charter. Both of them refer to the explanations drawn up in 2000 and modified during the European Conventions.

Notwithstanding the reference to the explanations is an undoubted step backwards to the interpretative instruments – belonging to the tradition of international law more than to constitutional law – chosen to guarantee some of the Member States with regard to the risks of the effectiveness of the Charter, the importance of this point must not be overestimated.[30] According to the explanations themselves, they "do not have as such the status of law, [although] they are a valuable tool of interpretation intended to clarify the provisions of the Charter".[31]

In any case, the classical theory of interpretation well knows the typical *Entfremdung* of sources of law and the modest importance of subjective interpretation in this area. So it is difficult for European and national judges to remain tied down to the explanations of 2001 and 2007.

More problems stem from the above-mentioned circumstance that the Charter is not the only text in which European rights are established[32]: The provisions of EU and European Community (EC) Treaties (like the provisions on the basic four free movement liberties), the European Social Charter, the communitarian charter of 1989 and, of course, common constitutional traditions crowd the already chaotic scene of the protection of rights in Europe. This plurality of levels establishing rights[33] (some in a text, some without a text) may cause interpretative problems,

---

[29]About relationship between ECHR and EUCFR, see Stern (2006). A critical approach in Jacobs (2006).

[30]*Contra*, see Petrangeli (2004). Doubts about this technique of interpreting the Charter also in Turpin (2003), pp. 631 et seqq.; Caretti (2005), p. 377.

[31]See the Premise to the Explanations of the Charter.

[32]See Dutheil de la Rochère (2008), p. 121 and p. 129.

[33]See Lenaerts (2000).

because it is impossible to identify a hierarchy of European rights depending on their formal seat. So it will be up to the interpreter (especially the courts) to determine the borders[34] and relationship among different rights.[35]

On the contrary, the separation of the Charter from the Treaty may constitute a positive resource according to some scholars[36]: the separate position gives more visibility to the act, making the reference by European citizens easier first of all. Instead of a "son of a lesser god", the Charter would receive an enhanced evidence in the Treaty of Lisbon and its symbolic importance would increase, not decrease. In this interpretative path, it has even been possible to affirm that the Charter, in its own separate position, would represent the core of a proper constitutional text, while the (remaining) Treaties would be connected to a more traditional agreement ruled by international law.[37]

In a more technical profile, someone rightly asked whether it was necessary to ratify the Charter separately (from the Treaties) and the correct procedure in the case of the future amendment of the same.[38] The first question may be resolved thanks to the technique of cross-reference to the Charter from states ratifying the Treaties (and Art. 6 TEU). But this is necessarily a so-called *fixed* cross-reference, which maintains the problem of future modifications of the Charter open – problems that we only mention in this text: First of all, is it possible to amend the Charter, because it is not part of the treaties? If the answer is affirmative, is the same procedure required (and is it enough) for its adoption (the "Convention system") or is it necessary to ratify it as an amendment to the Treaty (that is, in the Lisbon system by majority rule), or even, by reason of its separate position, the unanimity of the states?

4.2 Substantial Problems of the Protection of Rights According to the Charter Before and After Lisbon

The answer to the question asked at the beginning of paragraph 4 cannot avoid dealing with the problems stemming from the structure of the Charter and its

[34]See Blanke (2006), p. 272 about "considerable uncertainty" in the present protection of fundamental rights in European law.

[35]It is interesting to notice how some authors move from this point to criticise *ex fundamentis*, the idea of a catalogue of rights, which would be reductive and inappropriate: in Italian literature, see Palermo (2002), p. 202; Chessa (2006), pp. 249 et seqq.

[36]A positive evaluation of the separate position of the Charter, with regard to the Charter of Nice, in Manzella (2002), pp. 242 et seqq.; Floridia (2001), p. 165. With regard to the Constitutional Treaty, see Turpin (2003), p. 631. See now, after the Lisbon Treaty, Rossi (2007), p. 1 et seq. (the author focuses lights and shadows of the Lisbon Treaty on this theme). Dutheil de la Rochère (2008), p. 121.

[37]Manzella (2002), p. 242.

[38]On this issue, see Daniele (2008).

technique of the guarantee of rights. From this point of view we must refer to the peculiarities already focused on during these years, from the adoption of the Charter in 2000, and – as is mentioned later – unchanged after the amendment in 2007 and the ratification of the Treaty of Lisbon.

First of all, some provisions of the Charter are *principles* more than *rights*, more objective proclamations of values than subjective granted situations. It is an assessment claimed, if we may say so, by the same (new) Art. 52.5 of the Charter, and in Protocol No. 53, in order to bridle the relevance of provisions like Arts. 1, 20–23, 34–38 EUCFR. Distinguishing principles from rights does not mean making their juridical relevance disappear. On the contrary, it is true that Art. 52.5, even in a rather concise way, recognises some important effects of the guaranteeing of principles in the Charter[39]: they can and must lead the interpretation of ambiguous laws, so we must prefer interpretations according to the principle and reject the others (not according to them). Furthermore, referring to principles – when ruling the legality of the acts implementing them – must lead to invalidate these acts, if it is not possible to justify them on the grounds of principles.

This immediate relevance of principles as sources of law has already been highlighted, for example, in the Italian experience, in the debate about the so-called *norme programmatiche* (programmatic provisions) of the Constitution, and it was considered a successful demonstration of the full normativity of the whole Constitution.[40]

Something similar is happening today: the distinction between principles and rights does not necessarily cause the loss of any juridical meaning in the former. It requires scholars to understand the differences between these two different kinds and levels of normativity, according to the will of the Founding Fathers of the Charter or, better, according to a systematic interpretation of its provisions.

When I refer to the problems stemming from the presence of principles in the Charter of Fundamental Rights, I do not mean the – false – problem of their inconsistency, but something different: the close inherence of any principle with the value underlying it and the consequent difficulty to apply to the interweaving of rights (sometimes opposed rights) and the limitations to these rights which every constitutional text has. In other words, it is the "absolute attitude" (tyrannical, as C. Schmitt demonstrated[41]) of the value transmitted to the principle and not translated into the relational language of rights (with its graduations, inner and

---

[39]With reference to the impossibility of making these effects disappear, see Petrangeli (2004) (who strongly criticises the Charter over the distinction between rights and principles). As far as the different status of principles in a binding Charter is concerned, see Turpin (2003), pp. 628 et seqq. On the possibility to cross the border of judicial relevance of "principles" thanks to the application of Art. 234 EC to national laws implementing principles, see Michetti (2006), p. 183 and, more recently, Pollicino and Sciarabba (2008), p. 120. For a critical approach to the fortune of social rights in European law, see Luciani (2000). Critical remarks about social rights in EUCFR in Caretti (2001), p. 944 et seq.

[40]See Crisafulli (1952).

[41]Schmitt (1967).

outer limitations, the *Wertordnung* established in the Constitution) to make the concrete usage of principles difficult by interpreters of the *Charter*. But this uncertainty affects the rights of the Charter, too. This is the second – and more relevant – substantial problem arising from a scientific examination of the Charter.

It is the scientific analysis of contemporary constitutions that shows us that fundamental rights are not monads. They often interfere with each other and the interpreter needs to control this interference: increasing the protection of a right may mean increasing its limits or reducing the area of protection of other rights.[42] The constitutional text itself often offers important guidelines to this delicate activity, establishing inner and outer limits to single rights and grading the relevance of rights.

The rights granted by the Charter are, on the contrary, "one-dimensional": they are not characterised by internal limits (i.e. public order, decency, dignity) and they are set up on a uniform landscape.[43] It often happens that rights (and the abovementioned principles) collapse among themselves (i.e. Art. 7 vs. Art. 11; Art. 10 vs. Art. 11 and 12 [I refer to satire in religious matter]; Art. 14 vs. Art. 25; Art. 16 vs. Art. 37; Art. 16 vs. Art. 38). In these cases it is unavoidable that opposed rights (or principles) have to be balanced with a wide (perhaps too wide) discretionary power by the judge.[44]

It is important to add that this structural characteristic of the Charter was not changed in 2007: the *pre-Lisbon* and *post-Lisbon* eras are not different, if we consider the particular perspective of protection of fundamental rights.

4.3 Articles 52 and 53 of the Charter: Real Barriers to Protect National Law?

The width of the general limits set down in Art. 52 of the Charter does not help in such a model. The limitation "*by law*", set out in Art. 52, may unlikely play the role we are used to seeing in national law. The meaning and role of "law" in the European experience is still too different from the usual constitutional experiences: European law will not belong to parliament as long as the co-decision method is not the rule but the exception (also if we have to admit that the Treaty of Lisbon is going to improve the model).

---

[42]See, among others, Pace (2001b), p. 9, referring to ECHR; Villani (2004), para 8; Sorrentino (2008), p. 354 et seq.

[43]See De Siervo (2001a), pp. 156 et seqq.; De Siervo (2001b); Caretti (2001), pp. 944 et seqq.; Trucco (2007), p. 330 who writes of the "apparent simplicity" arising from the Charter. A critique to this approach, based on comparative suggestions, in von Bogdandy (2001), p. 889. See also, Groppi (2001), p. 353.

[44]The importance of the "particular case" in judicial balancing operations is enhanced by Lenaerts (2000), p. 581.

Furthermore, in advanced constitutional experiences, law-limiting liberties often find substantial guidelines in the constitution itself, so the constitution does not place a mere formal regulation, but rules (elements of) contents of law-affecting liberties, depriving the discretionary power of the legislator. So this kind of guarantee is lacking in the Charter.[45]

Last but not least, what do we mean when we are reasoning about the "law" mentioned in Art. 52? It is not clear which kind of source of law Art. 52 refers to. After the failure of the Constitutional Treaty to attempt to introduce "European law",[46] probably the reference in the Charter must be interpreted in a broad way, including secondary sources of law, not only in European law but at national level, too, according to the internal source system. Nor can the guarantee of "*respect the essence of those rights and freedoms* [of the Charter]" offer a safer standard of protection for its unavoidable uncertainty.[47] In any case, even if we want to appreciate this clause, it is impossible to avoid the fact that it can be appreciated – as the "*principle of proportionality*" – only by the Courts and the Courts say what *essence* of fundamental right and *proportionality* of its limitation is (case by case).

The aforementioned problems of the vertical profile of the Charter and the real possibility to separate the European guarantee from the national guarantee of rights should make us sceptical about the success of Art. 53 of the Charter and the maintenance of a "higher national level of protection of rights" with respect to Charter provisions.

The *Viking*, *Laval* and *Rüffert* judgments are emblematic in this perspective, too. The balancing of the ECJ between the free circulation of services and collective bargaining and the right to strike impacts on quite different – and always delicate – balances inside national systems, and it is difficult to invoke a "higher national level of protection" when this level reduces the protection of another European right.

5 A Short Conclusion in the Line of Continuity Between Pre- and Post-Lisbon Treaty, for What Concerns the Protection of Fundamental Rights

It is enough, I hope, to further justify my personal scepticism about the strength of the Lisbon Treaty to radically change the system of the protection of fundamental rights in the EU.

If the problem is restraining the judicial creativity of European (and national) judges through the Charter, we probably need a different style of drafting the

---

[45]See authors quoted at fn. 43.

[46]With regard to the sources of the system in European law, see, among others, Nettesheim (2006); Wölker (2007); Baroncelli (2008).

[47]See Blanke (2006), p. 273.

Charter. Until this happens – that is, until a fundamental decision at least about *Wertordnung* of fundamental rights is taken – the European courts, including in this multi-level system national judges applying the Charter, will continue to play the central role they already have, according to the common law model and the spillover expansion of European competences, also through fundamental rights.[48]

The Charter will play and improve upon a role of political legitimacy of the EU, according to the principles of classic and contemporary constitutionalism and integration of the legal system, while judicial protection of rights will go further with light and dark areas. Since it is not yet time for those "fundamental decisions" which C. Schmitt described, the system described here is the only possible system, and probably not such a bad one.

References

Azzena L (1998) L'integrazione attraverso i diritti. Dal cittadino italiano al cittadino Europeo. Giappichelli, Torino

Azzena L (2001) Prospettive della Carta Europea dei diritti e ruolo della giurisprudenza. In: Ferrari GF (ed) I diritti fondamentali dopo la Carta di Nizza. Il costituzionalismo dei diritti. Giuffrè, Milano, pp 123–145

Barbera A (2002) La Carta Europea dei diritti e la Costituzione italiana. In: La libertà e i diritti nella prospettiva Europea. Cedam, Padova, pp 117 et seqq

Baroncelli S (2008) Le fonti del diritto nell'Ue dal Trattato di Roma al Trattato di Lisbona: verso un'accresciuta complessità del sistema. www.osservatoriosullefonti.it. Accessed on 9th October 2009

Bermann GA (2006) The "Highest Court" in Federal Systems. In: Pernice I, Kokott J, Saunders C (eds) The future of the European Judicial System in a comparative perspective. Nomos, Baden-Baden, pp 91 et seqq. www.elcn.net

Bilancia P (2004) Possibili conflittualità e sinergie nella tutela dei diritti fondamentali ai diversi livelli istituzionali. In: Bilancia P, De Marco E (eds) La tutela multilivello dei diritti. Punti di crisi, problemi aperti, momenti di stabilizzazione. Giuffrè, Milano, pp 113 et seqq.

Blanke HJ (2006) Protection of Fundamental Rights afforded by the European Court of Justice in Luxembourg. In: Blanke HJ, Mangiameli S (eds) Governing Europe under a constitution. The Hard Road from European Treaties to a European Constitutional Treaty. Springer, Berlin, pp 265–277

Caretti P (2001) I diritti fondamentali nell'ordinamento nazionale e nell'ordinamento comunitario: due modelli a confronto. Dir Pubbl, pp 939 et seqq.

Caretti P (2004) La tutela dei diritti fondamentali nella prospettiva della Costituzione Europea. In: Bilancia P, De Marco P (eds) La tutela multilivello dei diritti. Punti di crisi, problemi aperti, momenti di stabilizzazione. Giuffrè, Milano, pp 71 et seqq.

Caretti P (2005) La tutela dei diritti fondamentali nel nuovo trattato che istituisce una Costituzione per l'Europa. Dir Un Eur, pp 371 et seqq.

[48]With regard to the central role of jurisprudence in the European "system" of the protection of rights, before and after Lisbon, see Caretti (2001), p. 947; Toniatti (2001), pp. 186 et seqq.; Toniatti (2002), pp. 21 et seqq.; Dutheil de la Rochère (2008), p. 122; Rossi (2009), pp. 79 et seqq. (highlighting the values mentioned in Art. 2 TEU, which look more widely than those in Art. 6); Huber (2009), pp. 10 et seqq. *Contra*, for the efficiency of the Charter to restrict the discretionary power of Courts, see Pinelli (2002), p. 214; Pinelli (2008), p. 58 et seq.

Cartabia M (2001) Art. 51. In: Bifulco R, Cartabia M, Celotto A (eds) L'Europa dei diritti. Commento alla Carta dei diritti fondamentali dell'Unione Europea. Il Mulino, Bologna, pp 344–351
Cartabia M (2007) L'ora dei diritti fondamentali nell'Unione Europea. In: Cartabia M (ed) I diritti in azione. Universalità e pluralismo dei diritti fondamentali nelle Corti Europee. Il Mulino, Bologna, pp 13–66
Cartabia M (2008) I diritti fondamentali e la cittadinanza dell'Unione. In: Bassanini F, Tiberi G (eds) Le nuove istituzioni Europee. Commento al Trattato di Lisbona. Il Mulino, Bologna, pp 89–107
Celotto A, Pistorio G (2004) L'efficacia giuridica della Carta dei diritti fondamentali dell'Unione Europea (rassegna giurisprudenziale 2001–2004). Giur It, pp 427 et seqq.
Chessa O (2006) La tutela dei diritti oltre lo Stato. Fra "diritto internazionale dei diritti umani" e "integrazione costituzionale Europea". In: Nania R, Ridola P (eds) I diritti costituzionali, vol I, 2nd edn. Giappichelli, Torino, pp 229–276
Crisafulli V (1952) La Costituzione e le sue disposizioni di principio. Giuffrè, Milano
Daniele L (2008) Carta dei diritti fondamentali dell'Unione Europea e Trattato di Lisbona. Dir Un Eur, p. 655 et seqq.
De Siervo U (2001a) I diritti fondamentali Europei ed i diritti costituzionali italiani (a proposito della Carta dei diritti fondamentali). Dir Pubbl Comp Eur, pp 153 et seqq.
De Siervo U (2001b) L'ambigua redazione della Carta dei diritti fondamentali nel processo di costituzionalizzazione dell'Unione Europea. Dir Pubbl, pp 33 et seqq.
Diez-Picazo LM (2001) Notes sur la nouvelle Charte des droit fondamentaux de l'Union Européenne. Riv It Dir Pubbl Com, pp 665 et seqq.
Dutheil de la Rochère J (2008) The protection of fundamental rights in the EU: community of values with opt-out? In: Pernice I, Tanchev E (eds) Ceci n'est pas une Constitution- Constitutionalisation without a Constitution? Nomos, Baden-Baden, pp 119 et seqq. www.elcn.net
Esposito C (1940) Testi unici. In: Nuovo Digesto it., vol XII. UTET, Torino
Fercot C (2008) Perspective on federalism. Diversity of constitutional rights in federal systems. A comparative analysis of German, American and Swiss Law. Eur Constitut Law Rev, pp 302 et seqq
Ferrari GF (2001) I diritti tra costituzionalismi statali e discipline transnazionali. In: Ferrari GF (ed) I diritti fondamentali dopo la Carta di Nizza. Il costituzionalismo dei diritti. Milano, Giuffré, pp 1–122
Floridia GG (2001) "Nell'intenzion dell'artista, e agli occhi degli abitanti" (osservazioni sulla "Dichiarazione di diritti" di Nizza). Dir Pubbl Comp Eur, pp 163 et seqq.
Groppi T (2001) Art. 52. In: Bifulco R, Cartabia M, Celotto A (eds) L'Europa dei diritti. Commento alla Carta dei diritti fondamentali dell'Unione Europea. Il Mulino, Bologna, pp 351–360
Grossi PF (2003) Dignità umana e libertà nella Carta dei diritti fondamentali dell'Unione Europea. In: Siclari M (ed) Contributi allo studio della Carta dei diritti fondamentali dell'Unione Europea. Giappichelli, Torino, pp 41–60
Huber PM (2009) Unitarizzazione attraverso i diritti fondamentali comunitari o dell'esigenza di riesaminare al giurisprudenza ERT. Riv It Dir Pub Com, pp 1 et seqq.
Jacobs FG (2006) The European convention on human rights, the EU charter of fundamental rights and the European court of justice. In: Pernice I, Kokott J, Saunders C (eds) The future of the European judicial system in a comparative perspective. Nomos, Baden-Baden, pp 291 et seqq. www.elcn.net
Lenaerts K (2000) Fundamental rights in the European Union, E.L. Rev., pp 575 et seqq
Luciani M (2000) Diritti sociali e integrazione Europea. Pol Dir, pp 367 et seqq
Luciani M (2001) Riflessioni minime sulla Carta Europea dei diritti fondamentali. Dir Pubbl Comp Eur, pp 172 et seqq
Mangiameli S (2001) La Carta dei diritti fondamentali dell'Unione Europea. Dir Pubbl Comp Eur, pp 173 et seqq

Mangiameli S (2006) Il contributo dell'esperienza costituzionale italiana alla dommatica Europea della tutela dei diritti fondamentali. In: Pace A (ed) Corte costituzionale e processo costituzionale. Giuffrè, Milano, pp 471 et seqq
Mangiameli S (2008a) Funzioni nazionali e normativa comunitaria nella garanzia dei diritti. In: Mangiameli S (ed) L'esperienza costituzionale Europea. Aracne, Roma, pp 299–324
Mangiameli S (2008b) L'esperienza costituzionale Europea. Aracne, Roma, pp 343–354 et seqq.
Manzella A (2002) Dopo Nizza: la Carta dei diritti "proclamata". In: Rossi LS (ed) Carta dei diritti fondamentali e costituzione dell'Unione Europea. Giuffrè, Milano, pp 239–248
Marini FS (2004) I diritti fondamentali della CEDU e della Carta dell'Unione Europea come diritti pubblici soggettivi. In: D'Atena A, Grossi PF (eds) Tutela dei diritti fondamentali e costituzionalismo multilivello. Tra Europa e Stati nazionali. Giuffre, Milano, pp 51–70
Michetti M (2006) La tutela dei diritti fondamentali nell'ordinamento Europeo. In: Mangiameli S (ed) L'ordinamento Europeo * I principi dell'unione. Giuffrè, Milano, pp 147–195 et seqq
Morijn J (2006) Balancing fundamental rights and common market freedoms in union law: Schmidberger and Omega in the light of the European Constitution. Eur Law J, pp 15–40
Nettesheim M (2006) Normenhierarchien im EU-Recht. Europarecht, pp 737 et seqq
Pace A (2001a) A che serve la Carta dei diritti fondamentali dell'Unione Europea? Appunti preliminari. Giur Cost, pp 193 et seqq
Pace A (2001b) La limitata incidenza della C.E.D.U. sulle libertà politiche e civili in Italia. Dir Pubbl, pp 1 et seqq
Pagano E (2008) Dalla Carta di Nizza alla Carta di Strasburgo dei diritti fondamentali. Dir Pub Com Eur, pp 94 et seqq
Palermo F (2002) La Carta dei diritti fondamentali dell'Unione Europea tra diritto positivo e positività del diritto. In: Toniatti R (ed) Diritto, diritti, giurisdizione. La Carta dei diritti fondamentali dell'Unione Europea. Cedam, Padova, pp 195–212
Palermo F (2005) La forma di stato dell'Unione Europea. Per una teoria costituzionale dell'integrazione sopranazionale. Cedam, Padova
Pernice I (2008) The Treaty of Lisbon and fundamental rights. In: Griller S, Ziller J (eds) The Lisbon Treaty: EU constitutionalism without a constitutional treaty. Springer, New York, pp 234–256
Pernice I, Kanitz R (2004) Fundamental rights and multilevel constitutionalism in Europe, in WHI – Paper 7/04. www.whi.de
Petrangeli F (2004) I diritti fondamentali nella bozza di "Trattato costituzionale dell'Unione Europea": alcune prime osservazioni. In: Bilancia P, De Marco E (eds) La tutela multilivello dei diritti. Punti di crisi, problemi aperti, momenti di stabilizzazione. Giuffrè, Milano
Pinelli C (2002) Il momento della scrittura. Contributo al dibattito sulla Costituzione Europea. Il Mulino, Bologna
Pinelli C (2008) I diritti fondamentali in Europa fra politica e giurisprudenza. Pol Dir, pp 45 et seqq
Poggi A (2007) Soft law nell'ordinamento comunitario, in Annuario Aic 2005. L'integrazione dei sistemi costituzionali Europeo e nazionali. Cedam, Padova, pp 369–419
Pollicino O, Sciarabba V (2008) La Carta di Nizza tra "sdoganamento giurisprudenziale" e Trattato di Lisbona. Dir Pub Com Eur, pp 101 et seqq
Ronchetti L (2009) I due volti dell'Europa: il principio di non discriminazione tra libertà e uguaglianza. A proposito delle sentenze Maruko e Rüffert della Corte di Giustizia. Giur It, pp 3 et seqq
Rossi LS (2002) "Costituzionalizzazione dell'UE e dei diritti fondamentali. In: Rossi LS (ed) Carta dei diritti fondamentali e costituzione dell'Unione Europea. Giuffrè, Milano, pp 249–290
Rossi LS (2007) I diritti fondamentali nel Trattato di Lisbona. www.europeanrights.eu
Rossi LS (2009) How fundamental are fundamental principles? Primacy and fundamental rights after Lisbon. In: Eeckhout E, Tridimas T (eds) Yearbook of European Law 2008. Oxford University Press, Oxford, pp 65–87
Ruggeri A (2001) La "forza" della Carta Europea dei diritti. Dir Pubbl Comp Eur, pp 182 et seqq

Schmitt C (1928) Verfassungslehre. Duncker & Humblot, Berlin
Schmitt C (1967) Die Tyrannei der Werte. In: Säkularisation und Utopie. Erbracher Studien Ernst Forsthoff zum 65 Geburstag, Stuttgart
Silvestri G (2006) Verso uno ius commune Europeo dei diritti fondamentali. Quad Cost, pp 7 et seqq
Sorrentino F (2008) Annuario Aic 2004. Separazione dei poteri e funzione giurisdizionale. Cedam, Padova, pp 353–374
Spadaro A (2001) Sulla "giuridicità" della Carta Europea dei diritti: c'è ma (per molti) non si vede. In: Ferrari GF (ed) I diritti fondamentali dopo la Carta di Nizza. Il costituzionalismo dei diritti. Giuffrè, Milano, pp 257–269
Stern K (1994) Das Staatsrecht der Bundesrepublik Deutschland, Band III/2. Allgemine Lehren der Grundrechte (unter Mitwirkung M. Sachs). Beck, München, pp 1409 et seqq
Stern K (2006) From the European Convention on Human Rights to the European Charter of Fundamental Rights: The prospects for the protection of human rights in Europe. In: Blanke HJ, Mangiameli S (eds) Governing Europe under a constitution. The Hard Road from European Treaties to a European Constitutional Treaty. Springer, Berlin, pp 169–184
Toniatti R (2001) La via giurisdizionale per la legittimazione dell'Unione Europea. Dir Pubbl Comp Eur, pp 186 et seqq
Toniatti R (2002) Verso la definizione dei "valori superiori" dell'ordinamento comunitario: il contributo della Carta dei diritti fondamentali dell'Unione Europea. In: Toniatti R (ed) Diritto, diritti, giurisdizione. La Carta dei diritti fondamentali dell'Unione Europea. Cedam, Padova, pp 7–31
Trucco L (2007) Tecniche di normazione e tutela dei diritti fondamentali nella Carta dei diritti fondamentali dell'Unione Europea. In: Ruggeri A, D'Andrea L, Saitta A, Sorrenti G (eds) Tecniche di normazione e tutela dei diritti fondamentali. Giappichelli, Torino, pp 317–340
Turpin F (2003) L'intégration de la Charte des droits fondamentaux dans la Constitution Européenne. Projet de Traité établissant une Constitution pour l'Europe. Rev Trim Dr Eur, pp 615 et seqq
Turr GA (2005) Federalismo y la protecciòn de los derechos en los Estados Unidos. In: Aparicio M (ed) Castellá JM, Exposito E (coords) Derechos y libertades en los Estados compuestos. Atelier, Barcelona, pp 39–65
Villani U (2004) I diritti fondamentali tra Carta di Nizza, Convenzione Europea dei diritti dell'uomo e progetto di Costituzione Europea. Dir Un Eur, pp 73 et seqq
von Bogdandy A (2000) The European Union as a Human Rights Organization? Human rights and the core of the European Union. CMLRev, pp 1307 et seqq
von Bogdandy A (2001) Comunità di diritti fondamentali come meta dell'integrazione? I diritti fondamentali e la natura dell'Unione Europea. Dir Pubbl, pp 829 et seqq
von Gerber CF (1852) Über öffentliche Rechte. Tübingen, Laupp
Weber A (2003) Einheit und Vielfalt der Europäischen Grundrechtordnung(en). Zur Inkorporation der Grundrechtscharta in eine Europäischen Verfassungsvertrag. DVBl. pp 220 et seqq
Weiler JHH (1985) Il sistema comunitario Europeo. Il Mulino, Bologna
Weiler JHH (2002) Diritti umani, costituzionalismo ed integrazione: iconografia e feticismo. Quad Cost, pp 521 et seqq
Wölker U (2007) Die Normenhierarchie im Unionrecht in der Praxis. EuR, pp 2007 et seqq

The Distribution of Competences Between the Union and the Member States

Albrecht Weber

1 Introduction

The order of competency of the Lisbon Treaty largely follows the vertical division of powers between the Union and the Member States. It is based on main principles elaborated by the jurisprudence of the European Court of Justice (ECJ), but has been innovated and reformed by the Lisbon Treaty in several aspects. Both the "Declaration on the Future of the Union" and the "Declaration of Heads of Government of Laeken" underlined the question of division of competences in the post-Nice process. The mandate of the Constitutional Convention even considered the rendering of attributed competencies to the Member States as a possibility.[1] The divergent linguistic versions of the "Declaration on the Future of the Union" as well as the mandate of the European Council based on the Declaration of Laeken gave leeway to rather differing concepts in the search for a better vertical delimitation of competences between the Union and the Member States. The mandate also aimed at the re-examination of Art. 95 and 308 EC to bar the extension of the Union versus the Member States. Within Working Group I ("Subsidiarity and Additional Competences") there was consensus to reformulate the competency in order to find a clearer definition and structural division of powers.

[1]See Hermann (2008a), p. 85.

A. Weber (✉)
Fachbereich Rechtswissenschaften, Universität Osnabrück, Heger-Tor-Wall 14, 49069 Osnabrück, Germany
e-mail: aweber@uos.de

H.-J. Blanke and S. Mangiameli (eds.), *The European Union after Lisbon*, 311
DOI 10.1007/978-3-642-19507-5_12, © Springer-Verlag Berlin Heidelberg 2012

2 Structure of Competency

2.1 Basic Principles

The structure of the new competence order is composed of two fundamental elements. First of all, the principle of conferral (*compétence d'attribution*) – although indirectly recognised and continuously interpreted by the ECJ – is now expressly anchored in Art. 5.1 1st sentence TEU. Additionally, the principles of subsidiarity and proportionality (ex-Art. 5 EC) are now incorporated into Art. 5 .1 2nd sentence TEU which says: *The use of Union competences is governed by the principles of subsidiarity and proportionality.*

2.2 Systematisation of Competences

As already proposed by the Draft Constitutional Treaty (Art. I-12, I-13, I-14 TCE), the Lisbon Treaty fortunately follows the latter's systematisation and cataloguisation of the Union's competences, which reveals the innovative element compared to the still existing competence order.[2] This reformed substance of the competential order apparently lies in the *dual* attribution of competences via attribution of exclusive competences to the European Union (EU) on the one hand and the *shared* or *concurring* competences to the Member States and the Union on the other hand. This dual model has evidently been influenced by the German vertical distribution of powers between the federal state and the German Länder (as has been mentioned by the President of the Convention, Giscard d'Estaing, in his final conclusion before the Convention).[3] Primarily the systematisation of competences aims at more transparency of the existing competential order, especially with regard to the original version of the Treaty establishing a Constitution for Europe (TCE) (Part I and its specification in Part III); unfortunately the catalogue of competences has been suppressed in the wording of Art. 5 TEU, where in the second paragraph the second sentence only states simply the principle of subsidiary competences of the Member States: *Competences not conferred upon the Union in the Treaties remain with the Member States.* This may be viewed as a second (or first and general) principle of subsidiarity referring to the distribution of competences between the Union and the Member States, whereas the above-mentioned principle of subsidiarity and proportionality is limited to the exercise of competences; this will be dealt with in more detail later. The dualistic approach (apparently follows the model of the federal competence order of Germany) may be seen as a further step into a federal future, but it should not be

[2]Oppermann (2003), p. 1165.

[3]Oppermann (2003), p. 1172 (fn. 39); with a different view Götz 2004, p. 44.

forgotten that the distribution of competences in federal systems shows a variety of types of competential attribution, e.g. the dualistic model of Canada with exclusive competences of the provinces and those of the federal state, or the very complicated distribution of competences between the federacy of Belgium as such and the competences of the Belgian communautés and provinces. With regard to the modified wording of the Lisbon Treaty, where the attribution of competences and its typology are now listed in Art. 2 TFEU, no serious disadvantages flow from this, because the precise circumscription of the shared competences was not exclusively enumerated in the former wording (Art. I-14 TCE); some specific competences were not enumerated in the first Draft.[4]

3 Basic Principles

3.1 Compétence d'attribution

The principle of *compétence d'attribution* or conferral remains the basic principle of the vertical distribution of powers (Art. 5.1 TEU-Nice, Art. 3b.1 EC → Art. I-11.1, 2 TCE → Art. 5.1 TEU). Therefore the Union does not dispose of the power to decide on competences (*Kompetenz-Kompetenz*).[5] The principle of conferral binds the EU with respect to any unional action and can be understood as a presumption in favour of the competences of Member States. A number of authors [among them Blanke] have rightly remarked that a written catalogue of competences would facilitate transparency and understandability.[6] The semantic modifications of Art. 5.1 TEU more clearly refer now to the principle of conferral for the purpose of delimitation of unional competences whereas the principles of subsidiarity and proportionality are relevant for the exercise of competence which qualifies the existing practice. Furthermore, the modified wording of Art. 5.2 TEU *(Under the principle of conferral, the Union shall act only within the limits of the competences conferred upon it by the Member States in the Treaties to attain the objectives set out therein)* underscores that the Union has no *Kompetenz-Kompetenz*, but does not reflect any substantial innovation.[7] The additional second sentence of the same Article *(Competences not conferred upon the Union in the Treaties remain with the Member States*) reflects (as has been remarked by Blanke) a remembrance to the Tenth Amendment of the US Constitution[8] and does not speak in favour of a general clause. The logical reverse side of the principle of

[4]See Schwarze (2004), p. 510; Nettesheim (2004), p. 528; Dougan (2003), p. 769.

[5]Case 6/64 *Flaminio Costa v E.N.E.L.* (ECJ 15 July 1964) p. 1269.

[6]For example, Blanke (1991), p. 143 et seqq.

[7]Pache and Rösch (2008), p. 479.

[8]Blanke (2004), p. 234.

conferral, which in the terminology of federal systems might be called the referral of the attribution, should not be confused with the subsidiarity in the following sense.

3.2 *Principle of Subsidiarity*

The principle of subsidiarity signifies that the smaller and nearer unit shall act and that the next hierarchical unit shall only act in case the former is not capable of doing so itself.[9] The subsidiarity principle was first introduced in the Treaty of Maastricht (ex-Art. 3b EC) and was mainly supported by the German government, the Länder and Great Britain. The introduction of the subsidiarity principle into the Treaty of Maastricht may be viewed – as Professor D'Atena pointed out – as a preferential decision in favour of the Member States reversing the hierarchy of values having prevailed before.[10]

The subsidiarity principle does not comprise measures within the exclusive competence of the Union or, in other words, the principle is only applicable if the Union has a shared (concurring or parallel) competence or supporting, coordinating and complementary competence.[11] The further criteria of the application of the subsidiarity principle (negative criterion, positive criterion) shall not be explained in detail in so far as the wording of the subsidiarity principle has not been modified. The negative criterion has been more precisely defined in so far *as the objectives of the proposed actions cannot be sufficiently achieved, either at central level or at regional and local level* (Art. 5.3 EC). The criterion had "not sufficiently" been concretised by the guidelines of the Protocol of Amsterdam which were based on the general Concept on the Application of subsidiarity, as in the "Agreement on the Procedure for the Application of the Subsidiarity Principle" proposed by the European Council of Edinburgh.[12] These guidelines were not incorporated into the *Protocol No. 2* on the "Application of the Principles of Subsidiarity and Proportionality"; this was rightly criticised by a number of authors.[13] The more precise definition of criterion *either at central level or at regional and local level* was already proposed in the Draft Constitutional Treaty and reflects better the multilevel system of the exercise of competences within Member States. Even if this clarification could also have been achieved by way of interpretation, the clarification of the negative criterion is a positive outcome.

[9]Herzog (1963), p. 400.

[10]d'Atena (2004), p. 136.

[11]Calliess & Ruffert (2006), Art. I-11, para 24.

[12]EG Bull 12–1992, I.

[13]See e.g. Wuermeling (2004), p. 224; Calliess & Ruffert (2006), Art. I-11, para 28.

Protocol No. 2 on the Application of the Principles of Subsidiarity and Proportionality concretises the principles in a more procedural manner. Article 2 provides that the Commission shall consult – and where appropriate also take into account – the regional and local dimensions of the envisaged actions, which de facto and de jure implies the right to hearing for sub-national entities. The draft legislative acts must be forwarded by the Commission to the national parliaments as well as to the Union legislator at the same time and these acts must be justified with regard to the principles of subsidiarity and proportionality (Art. 4, 5). Any draft legislative act should contain a detailed statement, making it possible to appraise compliancy with the mentioned principles and the statement should contain an assessment of the financial impact and the implication for the rules in the case of a directive. In addition, the reasons for the positive criterion that the objective rule shall be substantiated by qualitative and, wherever possible, quantitative indicators must be given. This proceduralisation of participation of national entities is not new, but more refined.

The only minor modification of the so-called early warning system monitored by the national parliaments is a prolongation of the delay from 6 to *8* weeks in order to send to the Presidents of parliaments or chambers, the European Parliament, the Council and the Commission reasoned opinions stating why the draft does not comply with the principle of proportionality (Art. 6 Protocol No. 2). The prolongation of the delay for the reasoned opinion of national parliaments is due to the fact that many parliaments are not able to submit a reasoned opinion within a comparably short delay with respect to the increasing bulk of legislative drafts coming from the EU. One might also have considered extending the delay on the demand of a national parliament according to the qualitative or quantitative dimension of the legislative draft as an important reason (like Art. 76 II 3 GG). Apart from the taking into account of the reasoned opinions issued by national parliaments (or any of their chambers), the original protocols like Protocol No. 2 have allocated a sort of objection procedure where national parliaments by casting one third of all the votes allocated to them can demand that the draft be reviewed with regard to the non-compliance with the principle of subsidiarity (Art. 7.2). After such review, the Commission or other institutions may decide to maintain, amend or withdraw the draft by a reasoned decision. If the Commission chooses to maintain the proposal, it must by reasoned opinion justify the proposal with the principle of subsidiarity (Art. 7.3 (2)). This reasoned opinion must be submitted to the Union legislator for consideration; it will consider whether the proposal is compatible with the principle of subsidiarity, or if by a majority of 55% of the members of the Council or a majority of votes cast in the European Parliament, the legislator declares that the proposal is not compatible with the principle of subsidiarity, the proposal will not be considered further.

Apart from the ex ante control of the principle of subsidiarity, there is also an ex post control laid down in Art. 8 of Protocol No. 2. The ECJ has jurisdiction for actions on the grounds of the infringement of the principle of subsidiarity against legislative acts in accordance with the complaints procedure of Art. 263 TFEU. Moreover, the Committee of the Regions may bring actions against legislative acts for the adoption of the act where the Committee had been consulted. Actions may be submitted according to the respective internal legal order of the Member State by the national parliament, a chamber of the parliament (in Germany the Federal Diet (*Bundestag*) and the Federal Council (*Bundesrat*)). Until now there was no possibility of bringing an action of a Member State in the name of or on behalf of its national parliament or its respective chambers; this may be viewed as a sort of procedural standing in the name of national parliaments or their chambers (*Prozeßstandschaft*).[14] However, it is not quite clear whether infringements concerning the principles of conferral admonished by the national parliaments can be brought before the Court.

3.3 The Principle of Proportionality

The third basic principle is the principle of proportionality, now guaranteed in Art. 5.1, 4 TEU. The principle has been recognised as one of the unwritten principles of community law. The terms "necessary", "apt" or others reflecting the changing terminology of the ECJ circumscribe the principle, but do not lend to a general identity with the German terminology and dogmatic of the principle of proportionality.[15] The appropriateness of a measure does not play an essential role in the ECJ jurisprudence in contrast to the Federal Constitutional Court; it restricts the scrutiny if the measure does not appear manifestly inappropriate for the realisation of the targeted aim.[16] As to the criterion of necessity, it is scrutinised by the ECJ in a similar way as in German law, and the proportionality in the narrow sense is controlled similarly by balancing the means and the targeted aim in the light of the legislative or administrative goals. Interestingly the Federal Constitutional Court has partly used the argument in the *Maastricht* judgment[17] (safeguarding national identity against excessive regulation). Necessity signifies the use of the softest means especially with regard to the instrument of action and the density of regulation. Article 5.4 TEU clearly stipulates that the principle of proportionality comprises the choice of content and form of the unional action. Therefore the practice of the Union must respect the hierarchy of means regarding the types of action and the content. The reformulation of Art. 5.4 TEU as to the content and form of the action does not modify the established criteria of the principle of proportionality. The latter formulation aims at the concretisation of the regulatory density and the type of action. From this follows that the Union shall – according to the hierarchy of means – use at first the non-binding measures

[14]See Meyer and Hölscheidt (2003), p. 621; Ruffert (2004), p. 182.

[15]Nettesheim (1995), p. 107.

[16]Calliess & Ruffert (2006), Art. I-11, para 39 with further references.

[17]German Federal Constitutional Court, 2 BvR 2134, 2159/92 (12 October 1993) para 162 (in: BVerfGE 89, 155 [212]).

before binding legal acts; the regulation therefore should only be chosen if any less infringing means cannot be used vis-à-vis the envisaged aim. Regarding the concretisation of the principle of proportionality in Protocol No. 2 there are no comparable rules which could secure the principle in the legislative process or in cases before the Courts.[18] However, Art. 5 Protocol No. 2 refers to the financial charges and administrative costs which must be adequate in relation to the targeted aim. Therefore the drafts of legislative acts must contain a reasoning concerning the proportionality and must be added to the documentation of the proposed legislative act. Thus the principle of proportionality gains more precision and the information concerning the criteria must be made accessible to the respective national institutions.

4 Typology of Competences

The new codification of competences is – as I have mentioned before – the great achievement of the TCE and in a less spectacular manner now in the Reform Treaty. Whereas the Lisbon Treaty does not set out the typology of competences in the Union Treaty in the first part like in the TCE, the typology of exclusive, shared competences, supporting coordinating and supplementing measures is now laid down in Title I (Categories and Areas of Union Competences) of the Treaty on the Functioning of the European Union (TFEU). The functional connection of the competence order reveals Art. 1.1: *This Treaty organises the functioning of the Union and determines the areas of, delimitation of, and arrangements for exercising its competences.* The substantive finality of the competences is one of several primary criteria such as division of competence, allocation of competence, degree of normativity or degree of juridification of the monitoring of competence.[19]

4.1 Exclusive Competences

The notion of exclusive competence has been controversial for a long time and has not been clarified by the jurisprudence of the ECJ; however, the Court has made clear that an exclusive competence is independent of the concrete action of the Union and is complete and final.[20] The wording of the TCE and the TFEU apparently follows the concept that the exclusive competence excludes totally and definitely any respective measures notwithstanding the fact that the Union

[18]Davies (2003), p. 692.

[19]Nettesheim (2006), p. 309 et seqq.

[20]Case 804/79 *United Kingdom v Commission* (ECJ 5 May 1981), note 17.

has exercised its competence or not.[21] The exclusive competence does not commute to a retroactive exclusive competence when the legislative organs issue secondary legislation *(compétence exclusive par exercice)*. This is not identical with the so-called *pre-emption doctrine* of US American federalism or the so-called *Sperrwirkung* in the case of the exercise of concurring competences according to Art. 72 II GG. The pre-emption doctrine or the *Sperrwirkung* can only apply within the realm of shared competences which clearly stipulates now Art. 2.2 TFEU. Therefore it has been rightly assumed that the posterior exercise of a shared competence cannot alter the system of allocated exclusive competences.[22]

The exclusive competences are enumerated in Art. 3.1 TEU and comprise the customs union; the establishing of the competition rules for the functioning of the internal market; the monetary policy for the Member States which have joined the Euro; the conservation of marine biological resources under the common fishery policy and the common commercial policy. The definition of the exclusive competences follows the existing case law of the ECJ and also encompasses the conclusion of international agreements when it is provided in a legislative act of the Union or is necessary to enable the Union to exercise its internal competence or in so far as the conclusion may affect common rules or alter their scope. This is a consequence of the ECJ case law after the *Accord Européen sur les Transports Routiers (AETR)* case: The Union does not only act on the basis of a primary enabling clause but also where the envisaged measure falls within the internal competence area; this exclusive treaty making power now also extends to the second and third pillar.[23]

4.2 Shared Competences

The type of shared competence corresponds to the concurring competence known in the German Basic Law and in community law. Article 2.2 TEU clearly states: *when the Treaties confer on the Union a competence shared with the Member States in a specific area, the Union and the Member States may legislate and adopt legally bindings acts in that area. Member States shall exercise their competence to the extent that the Union has not exercised its competence. The Member States shall again exercise their competence to the extent that the Union has decided to cease exercising its competence.* This text reflects the wording of Art. 72 GG except that the additional condition of federal legislation as the establishment of equal life conditions or the safeguarding of the legal and economic unity does not appear in the wording of the Union Treaty. From a theoretical standpoint the competence

[21]CONV 375/1/02 REV1 final report WG V, p. 6; Craig (2004), p. 80.

[22]Calliess & Ruffert (2007), Art. 5, para 33.

[23]Calliess & Ruffert (2006), Art. I-14, para 16.

rests with the Member States as the Union has not exercised the respective competence or has decided to cease its competence. The peremptory effect (*Sperrwirkung*) depends on the extension of regulatory power of the Union and may be especially difficult to assess if the Union has exercised one of its concurring competences but indicates that it will not exercise the competence any more: Which organ is competent to decide upon the non-exercise of the competence?[24] The enumeration of the shared competences comprise the internal market, social policy, economic, social and territorial cohesion; agriculture and fishing, consumer protection; transport; trans-European networks; energy; area of freedom, security and justice; common safety concerns and public health matters. It has been controversial from the beginning whether the competence concerning the internal market belongs to the category of exclusive or shared competence. As the most prominent representatives of the first opinion, according to which the harmonisation of the internal market is an exclusive competence, are the Commission and Advocate-General Sennelly in the case of the prohibition of tobacco advertising. However, in this case (British American Tobacco) the ECJ falsified this viewpoint and shared the predominant opinion of the literature by stating that Art. 95 EC does not confer an exclusive competence for the regulation of economic activities in the internal market.[25]

Apart from this clarification the above-mentioned problem of delimitation of competences in so far as the Union decides upon the future non-exercise of a specific competence should have been clarified by the Declaration No. 28 of 19 October 2007 by the Heads of Governments.[26] The Declaration firstly reaffirms the principle of residual competences of the Member State in the aforementioned areas whereas §2 gives indications when the Community will not exercise a specific competence in the future. The second sentence of §2 of Declaration No. 18 particularly underlines to better safeguard the continuous respect of the principles of subsidiarity and proportionality. Furthermore the third sentence of the same paragraph enables the Council to ask the Commission to submit proposals for the repeal of a legislative act. Furthermore, Protocol No. 25 on the Exercise of Shared Competences states:

> With reference to Article 2 of the Treaty on the Functioning of the European Union on shared competence, when the Union has taken action in a certain area, the scope of this exercise of competence only covers those elements governed by the Union act in question and therefore does not cover the whole area.

It is quite evident that this attempt of clarification is difficult to assess when it comes to the constitutive elements of a legislative act or not; this concerns the

---

[24]Calliess & Ruffert (2006), Art. I-12, para 19 et seqq.

[25]Case C-491/01 *The Queen v Secretary of State for Health, ex parte: British American Tobacco* (ECJ 10 December 2002) note 1.

[26]Weber (2008), p. 12.

thorny problem of annexed competence or implied powers of federal organs which is well known to federal systems like the United States or Germany.

4.3 Supporting, Coordinating and Supplementing Measures

This type of competence as articulated in Art. 2.5 TFEU is a subcategory of the shared competency. According to Art. 6 TFEU the Union shall at the European level have additional competences concerning the protection and improvement of human health; industry; culture; tourism; education, vocational training, youth and sport; civil protection; and administrative cooperation. They correspond to the supporting and supplementary measures already existing in the actual community law.[27]

4.4 Specific Types of Competences (Coordination of Economic and Occupational Policy/CFSP)

As regards the Common Foreign and Security Policy (CFSP), the Union shall have competence to define an implemented common security and defence policy (Art. 2.4 TFEU). The competence appears to be rather autonomous besides the exclusive, shared competences and the supporting, coordinating and supplementing measures. The autonomy of the CFSP is also underscored by the further relevant provisions in the TFEU which shall not be explained here. There are a number of problems of delimitating competences.[28]

4.5 Flexibility Clause

The flexibility clause anchored until now in Art. 352 TFEU as a subsidiary enabling clause aims to enable the Council on the proposition of the Commission and after consultation of the European Parliament to issue the appropriate legislative acts. This subsidiary clause of competence was meant to fill the gap between a Union's target and the missing allocation of a specific competence. This flexibility clause was already modified in Art. I-18 TCE and now appears in Art. 352. The Commission must inform national parliaments of the proposals based on this Article and

[27]Weber (2008), p. 12.

[28]See Hermann (2008b), p. 116.

may not contain rules of harmonisation or where harmonisation Treaties or regulations in cases where the Treaties exclude such harmonisation.

The Council acting unanimously on a proposal from the Commission and after obtaining the consent of the European Parliament may adopt the appropriate measures. This also applies for specific legislative procedures. The flexibility clause cannot apply for attaining objectives set out for the CFSP in Art. 40 TEU.

5 Conclusions

The Reform Treaty has undoubtedly clarified the delimitation of competences according to the model of codified and enumerated competence of federal or pre-federal systems even if it has not brought revolutionary changes to the existing order of competency. The Principles of subsidiarity and proportionality will apply largely according to the same criteria as earlier. There will remain enough problems of detail to be interpreted by future commentaries and case law of the European Courts.

References

Blanke H-J (1991) Das Subsidiaritätsprinzip als Schranke des Europäischen Gemeinschaftsrechts? Zeitschrift für Gesetzgebung 6:133–148

Blanke H-J (2004) Die Zuständigkeiten der Union. Zeitschrift für Gesetzgebung 19:225–249

Calliess Ch, Ruffert M (eds) (2006) Verfassung der Europöischen Union. Kommentar. C. H. Beck, München

Callies C, Ruffert M (eds) (2007) EUV/EGV: Das Verfassungsrecht der Europäischen Union mit Europäischer Grundrechtecharta. Kommentar. C. H. Beck, München

Craig P (2004) Competence: clarity, containment and consideration. In: Pernice I, Maduro M (eds) A constitution for the European Union. Nomos Verlagsgesellschaft, Baden-Baden, pp 75–93

d'Atena A (2004) Subsidiarity and division of competencies between European Union, its member states and their regions. In: Miccú R, Pernice I (eds) The European Constitution in the making. Nomos Verlagsgesellschaft, Baden-Baden, pp 135–140

Davies G (2003) The post-Laeken division of competences. Eur Law Rev 28:686–698

Dougan M (2003) The Convention's Draft Constitutional treaty: bringing Europe closer to its lawyers? Eur Law Rev 28:763–793

Götz V (2004) Kompetenzverteilung und Kompetenzkontrolle in der Europäischen Union. In: Schwarze J (ed) Der Verfassungsentwurf des Europäischen Konvents. Nomos Verlagsgesellschaft, Baden-Baden, pp 43–61

Herrmann C (2008a) § 11- Kompetenzordnung der Union. In: Streinz R, Ohler C, Herrmann C (eds) Der Vertrag von Lissabon zur Reform der EU, 2nd edn. C. H. Beck, München, pp 85–90

Herrmann C (2008b) § 17 – Die Gemeinsame Außen- und Sicherheitspolitik (GASP). In: Streinz R, Ohler C, Herrmann C (eds) Der Vertrag von Lissabon zur Reform der EU, 2nd edn. C. H. Beck, München, pp 114–126

Herzog R (1963) Subsidiaritätsprinzip und Staatsverfassung. Der Staat 2:399–423

Meyer J, Hölscheidt S (2003) Die Europäische Verfassung des Europäischen Konvents. Europäische Zeitschrift für Wirtschaftsrecht 14(20):613–621

Nettesheim M (1995) Grundrechtliche Prüfdichte durch den EuGH. Europäische Zeitschrift für Wirtschaftsrecht 6(4):106–108

Nettesheim M (2004) Die Kompetenzordnung im Vertrag über eine Verfassung für Europa. Europarecht 39(4):511–546

Nettesheim M (2006) The order of competence within the Treaty establishing a Constitution of Europe. In: Blanke H-J, Mangiameli S (eds) Governing Europe under a constitution. Springer, Heidelberg, pp 309–343

Oppermann T (2003) Eine Verfassung für die Europäische Union. Deutsches Verwaltungsblatt 118(18):1165–1124

Pache E, Rösch F (2008) Der Vertrag von Lissabon. Neue Zeitschrift für Verwaltungsrecht 28(5):473–480

Ruffert M (2004) Schlüsselfragen der Europäischen Verfassung der Zukunft: Grundrechte – Institutionen – Kompetenzen – Ratifizierung. Europarecht 39(2):165–201

Schwarze J (2004) Der Verfassungsentwurf des Konvents – Struktur, Kernelemente und Verwirklichungschancen. In: Schwarze J (ed) Der Verfassungsentwurf des Europäischen Konvents. Nomos Verlagsgesellschaft, Baden-Baden, pp 489–562

Weber A (2008) Vom Verfassungsvertrag zum Vertrag von Lissabon. Europäische Zeitschrift für Wirtschaftsrecht 19(1):7–14

Wuermeling J (2004) Kalamität Kompetenz: Zur Abgrenzung der Zuständigkeiten in dem Verfassungsentwurf des EU-Konvents. Europarecht 39(2):216–229

The Revision Procedures of the Treaty

Luis Jimena Quesada

1 Introductory Issues: Do the Revision Procedures of the Lisbon Treaty Really Participate in a Constitutional Approach of the Structure of the European Union?

A review of the diverse reforms of constituent Treaties of the European Communities shows that the revision procedures have not occupied an outstanding place in the design of the constitutional structure of the European Union (EU). That is especially true if we consider two terms in connection: revision (of the Treaties) and ratification (by the States Parties).

Indeed, with the exception of some specific revision modalities (the so-called autonomous revision procedures, the bridging clauses or the implied powers clauses), the ordinary revision of the European Treaties (including the Single European Act, the Maastricht Treaty, the Amsterdam Treaty, the Nice Treaty and the Lisbon Treaty – and even the Constitutional Treaty) has been marked by a strong uncertainty as a result of the rule of ratification by all the Member States.[1] Therefore, a real risk of blockage of the process of deepening in European integration has always existed.

Thus, the original aim towards *federalisation* that was present in the 1950 Schuman Declaration or the most recent bet for the *constitutionalisation* of the EU has always had a "sword of Damocles": the potential threat of the rule of unanimity in the revision of the European Treaties and, therefore, the risk of paralysis of the constitutional structure of the Union. From this point of view, the ordinary revision procedure has actually been conceived as a taboo (the taboo of

[1]Maulis (2004), p. 299.

L.J. Quesada (✉)
Departament de Dret Constitucional i Ciència Política i de la Administració, Universitat de València, Avinguda dels Tarongers, s/n, 46071 Valencia, Spain
e-mail: Luis.Jimena@uv.es

H.-J. Blanke and S. Mangiameli (eds.), *The European Union after Lisbon*,
DOI 10.1007/978-3-642-19507-5_13, © Springer-Verlag Berlin Heidelberg 2012

"the constitutional" revision), rather than as an instrument of opening towards new horizons of integration.[2]

It could be said that, on the occasion of each new reform, the emphasis has been put on quantitative or substantial aspects (new transfers of competences to the European Communities or the extension of the qualified majority vote to new areas) instead of on qualitative or formal aspects: in this sense, we have not been conscientious of the importance of the "constitutional theory" in so far as the impact of the procedural route which has been followed in each case went unnoticed or ignored.

Furthermore, even on the occasion of the elaboration and process of ratification of the 2004 European Constitution, the revision procedures of the European Treaties were excluded from the "constitutional language" (the "constitutional concept") or, otherwise said, from the constitutional theory. In particular, the four challenges on the future of Europe (which were included in the 2001 Laeken Declaration as well as in the 2001 Nice Declaration – No. 23 – on the future of Europe) have capitalised or monopolised the reference to the process of constitutionalisation of Europe.[3] In addition, another challenge, the redesign of the "European judicial system" (formally not integrated as a challenge in these two Declarations), has been likewise considered in terms of "constitutional justice", that is to say, as a mechanism of the "European Constitution's" ordinary defence both in good constitutional theory and daily political practice.[4]

In contrast with the previous conception, the revision procedures have never been undertaken in terms of "constitutional reform" as a mechanism of defence of the European constitutional order. In fact, the cause of the rigidity of the European Treaties (including the Lisbon Treaty and the previous Constitutional Treaty) is not only its formal revision procedure (the existence – still – of unanimous ratification by the Member States), but also its substantial process of negotiation (the absence – for the moment – of a *European constitutional consensus* together with a *European constitutional feeling*).[5] If the rigidity were considered only in procedural terms it would be very difficult to understand how, in spite of the rule of unanimity concerning the ratification by the Member States, all the successive reforms of

[2]See Blanke and Mangiameli (2005), in particular paragraph I.1. ("The European Constitution and the crisis in the procedure for ratifying the Treaty establishing a Constitution for Europe"), p. xxv: "The constitutional future of Europe appears uncertain, (...). But the science of European public law is duty-bound to explain constitutional phenomena and institutional crises, not emotionally and the back of public opinion affected by such problems as unemployment, the value of the Euro and the lack of economic growth in Europe, which have wrongly been pinned onto the Constitutional Treaty, but to do so thoroughly and, if the intention is to be prescriptive, with the capacity to link the recent events to the history of the institutions in order to draw lessons for the future."

[3]Cf. Alegre Martínez and Jimena Quesada (2006), p. 298.

[4]Sáiz Arnaiz (1999), pp. 223–256. Cf. also Vidal Prado (2006), pp. 273–310.

[5]This notion is used by Jimena Quesada (2001), pp. 87–88. In effect, the absence of a "European public opinion" is surely the most important element of the weakness of the European constituent process: Pace (2002), p. 650. See also Ruipérez (2000).

European Treaties have been adopted (the frustrated Constitutional Treaty would confirm the exception to that general rule).[6]

The question, however, is not if we should maintain that inertia in order to advance in "small steps" (according to the 1950 Schuman Declaration), although this is the dynamics of the European integration process. The problem appears, in my opinion, when new dynamics emerge from "great slips" that prevent progress (the frustrated European Constitution) and that, at the same time, may constitute a dangerous pretext to back down through "intermediate obstacles" (the Treaty of Lisbon). But as will be exposed in the following section, the Lisbon Treaty not only receives the unanimity barrier from a procedural perspective, but it even introduces the possibility of recovering the substantial scope already transferred by the states to the EU.

2 The Concrete Revision Procedures of the Lisbon Treaty

2.1 Its Modalities: Comparison with the Previous Reforms of the European Treaties

The Lisbon Treaty introduces a new wording of Art. 48 TEU. Its paragraph 1 distinguishes between two procedures for revising the Treaties (both the *Treaty on European Union* (TEU) and the *Treaty establishing the European Community* (TCE), which is renamed *Treaty on the Functioning of the European Union* (TFEU)): on the one hand, the modification "in accordance with an ordinary revision procedure" and, on the other and, the amendment "in accordance with simplified revision procedures".

The present work will concentrate on the above-mentioned revision procedures, without analysing the Acts of Accession of new Member States or the flexibility clause (*implied powers clause*) established in the new Art. 308 TFEU by means of the Lisbon Treaty.[7]

2.1.1 The Ordinary Revision Procedure

With respect to the ordinary revision procedure (Art. 48.2 TEU), the *initiative* is attributed to a Member State's government, the European Parliament or the Commission. They present the proposed amendments to the Council, which submits

[6]Cf. Pace (1996).

[7]See Besné Mañero et al. (1998), in particular the section "Revisión de los Tratados" (pp. 174–179).

them to the European Council. The national parliaments are also notified on the proposal.

In the *intermediate phase*, the European Council, after consulting the European Parliament and Commission (as well as the European Central Bank in the case of institutional changes in the monetary area), carries out a *first filter* of the revision proposal. The European Council decides by simple majority whether to examine the amendments. If approved, the Presidency of the European Council will then convene a Convention (composed of representatives of the national parliaments, of the Heads of State or Government of the Member States, of the European Parliament and of the Commission – that is to say, the "legislative powers" as well as the "executive powers" at both European and national levels). In effect, the *second filter* (for "important modifications") will be carried out by this Convention (which, after examining the proposals for amendments, will adopt a recommendation to a conference of representatives of the governments of the Member States by consensus).

The European Council can decide to bypass the Convention process and proceed straight to the conference of representatives by simple majority after consulting the Commission and with the consent of the European Parliament. In this case, that second filter (for "less important modifications") will be exercised by an intergovernmental conference (IGC – "Conference of representatives of the Governments of the Member States"), which will determine the amendments that need to be made by the Treaties.

In the *final phase*, whether the second filter has been verified before the Convention or before the IGC, Art. 48.4 TEU establishes that "the amendments shall enter into force after being ratified by all the Member States in accordance with their respective constitutional requirements"; when the unanimous ratification fails, Art. 48.5 TEU foresees that "if, two years after the signing of a treaty amending the Treaties, four fifths of the Member States have ratified it and one or more Member States have encountered difficulties in proceeding with its ratification, *the matter shall be referred to the European Council*". It turns out to be a very complex problem to interpret the real impact of this last clause, which was also present in the 2004 Constitutional Treaty (*infra*). Apart from that, this interpretation is still more difficult if we keep in mind that the English version of the above-mentioned clause ("the matter shall be referred to the European Council") does not exactly coincide with other official versions.[8]

[8]For example, in the Spanish version of Article 48.5 TEU it is stated that "el Consejo examinará la cuestión"; in the French version we find "le Conseil européen se saisit de la question"; the German version presents this wording: "so befasst sich der Europäische Rat mit der Frage"; the Italian version foresees that "la questione è deferita al Consiglio europeo"; according to the Portuguese version "o Conselho Europeu analisa a questão".

2.1.2 The Simplified Revision Procedures

The text of the new Art. 48 TEU includes two simplified revision procedures. This simplification consists basically in either avoiding the filter of the Convention or the IGC when the revision affects the third part of the TFEU (paragraph 6) in the intermediate phase, or making flexible the "autonomous" procedures for the adoption of decisions and acts by the European institutions (paragraph 7).

(A) The procedure which is foreseen in Art. 48.6 TEU may be *initiated* by the "Government of any Member State, the European Parliament or the Commission", who "may submit proposals for revising all or part of the provisions of Part Three of the Treaty on the Functioning of the European Union relating to the internal policies and action of the Union to the European Council". In the *intermediate phase*, the European Council is empowered to adopt that decision (amending all or part of the provisions of Part Three of the TFEU) "by unanimity after consulting the European Parliament and the Commission, and the European Central Bank in the case of institutional changes in the monetary area". The *final phase of the revision*, with the possible entrance into force of the revision, will take place once it has been "approved by the Member States in accordance with their respective constitutional requirements". Once again, the approval is not equivalent here to a unanimous ratification.

(B) Article 48.7 TEU introduces two procedural modalities by means of which both the adoption of decisions by the Council (with a move from unanimity to qualified majority voting – except for decisions having military implications or concerning the area of defence) and the adoption of legislative acts (with a change from special legislative procedure to the ordinary legislative procedure) are made flexible. In both cases, for the adoption of those decisions and those acts, the European Council shall notify the initiative to the national parliaments: in this stage, "if a national Parliament makes its opposition known within six months of the date of such notification, the decision referred to in the first or the second subparagraph shall not be adopted. In the absence of opposition, the European Council may adopt the decision". Does the possibility of opposition by a national parliament not imply once again a unanimous ratification – a parliamentary one?

Additionally, in the last stage of the procedure, for the adoption of the above-mentioned decisions and acts (those foreseen in Art. 48.7 TEU) "the European Council shall act by unanimity after obtaining the consent of the European Parliament, which shall be given by a majority of its component members". In other words, the two procedural modalities introduced in Art. 48.7 TEU may be successful only if they fulfil a rule of double unanimity (by national parliaments as well as by national governments – those within the European Council), together with the consent of the European Parliament.

2.1.3 A First Critical View

The critique to the revision procedures of the Lisbon Treaty can be based on formal and substantial reasons.

(A) As far as the ordinary revision procedure is concerned, from a formal perspective it can be affirmed – with a certain degree of optimism – that a progress has taken place with regard to both the starting and the intermediate phases: on the one hand, the list of actors who are entitled for initiating the revision is wider (the Lisbon Treaty provides the European Parliament with the power to enact legislative acts jointly with the European Union's Council); on the other hand, the intervention of the Convention model in the elaboration of the revision is also made possible. To sum up, there is a greater legitimacy in the phase of the initiative (that is to say, this procedure strengthens the democratic nature of the EU by bringing the European Parliament into play) as well as a "stronger constitutional image" in the intermediate phase of the revision procedure.

By contrast, it can be argued – with certain pessimism – that the great Achilles' heel of the ordinary revision procedure is still in its final phase, because of the requirement of the unanimous ratification by the Member States.[9] Regarding this, the very long and winding process of ratifications goes together with the legal uncertainty which arises from the following clause: "the matter shall be referred to the European Council" (in case of non-ratification by one or more Member States).[10] This clause has been considered as an "anodyne",[11] "enigmatic"[12] or "modest"[13] provision.

From a substantial perspective, Art. 48.2 TEU introduces an incredible clause which is not in accordance with the principle of progressiveness and irreversibility in the European integration process, in so far as it explicitly foresees that the proposals for the amendments of the Treaties "may, *inter alia*, serve either to increase or *to reduce the competences conferred on the Union* in the Treaties". In particular, if we take that possible reduction of competences into consideration ("less Europe"), where is the classic doctrine of the irreversible limitation of the "sovereign rights" which has been settled by the European Court of Justice (ECJ)? From this point of view, if the constitutional approach of the revision procedure is weaker (the constitutional reform as a basic element of the constitutional theory), can we consider that the constitutional bases outlined by European justice are now being doubted (let us remember how the "constitutional visibility or appearance" of the EU is very often founded in the statements made by the ECJ – in interaction with national courts)?[14]

[9]See *mutatis mutandis* Giscard d'Estaing (2003), p. 76: "Tout en étant consciente du problème qui poserait le maintien de la procédure actuelle, la ratification unanime par tous les États membres, dans une Europe élargie, la Convention n'a pu qu'esquisser certains pistes possibles (pour la révision)".

[10]Article 48.5 TEU.

[11]Groppi (2004), p. 231.

[12]Leanerts and Gerard (2004), p. 304.

[13]Oberdorff (2005), p. 9.

[14]See Dehousse (1998), p. 28: this author talks on a system of "court-to-court dialogue" by reference to the preliminary rulings mechanism. The interaction between the ECJ and national courts produces "constitutional dialogues": Stone Sweet (1998), p. 305.

Of course, Art. 48.2 TEU likewise foresees that "these proposals shall be submitted to the European Council by the Council and the national Parliaments shall be notified". But, is it realistic to think that the European Council – which, like the Council, represents the interest of the states in the European concert – will rectify and will be against a reduction of the competences conferred on the Union in the Treaties? In the same way, is it possible to hope that the national parliaments will show a negative reaction in relation to this reduction of European competences or, on the contrary, will they applaud the possibility of recovering national legislative competition that had been previously "stolen" by the national government in the context of the ascending phase of the European construction (the process of framing EU decisions)?

(B) As for the simplified revision procedures and, particularly, its modality tending to the modification of Part Three of the TFEU, we can reiterate the positive critique already carried out in relation to the *phase of initiative* of the ordinary revision procedure, that is to say, we can put the emphasis in the inclusion of the European Parliament in the list of actors who have been entitled for initiating the revision (together with national governments and the Commission). In the *intermediate phase*, consultation to the European Parliament and the Commission, as well as to the European Central Bank in the case of institutional modifications in the monetary area, does not raise any special problem. Nevertheless, in the *final phase*, the fact of submitting the entry into force of the proposed revision to the approval "by the Member States in accordance with their respective constitutional requirements" can provoke interpretative problems. In my opinion, that approval would not have to be assimilated by means of ratification (parliamentary or, where appropriate, popular) foreseen for the ordinary revision procedure, but it must be considered as an "autonomous" procedure by virtue of which this approval could take place in each state according to the respective constitutional provisions that allowed the accession to the EU: which means that it would be possible to approve the proposed revision through the respective state representative in the European institutions (Council or European Council).

However, as in the case of the ordinary revision procedure, when dealing with the simplified revision procedures contemplated in the new Art. 48.6 TEU, the potential "attack" to the principle of progressiveness and irreversibility of the European integration progress must once again be criticised from a substantial perspective. In effect, if we follow a *sensu contrario* interpretation of the provision according to which the decision of the amendment "shall not increase the competences conferred on the Union in the Treaties", could this decision reduce them?

For its part, the simplified revision procedure which is foreseen in the new Art. 48.7 TEU presents, as a positive aspect from a formal point of view, the possibility of overcoming the rigidity of the unanimity rule (which is replaced by the qualified majority voting) in the adoption of decisions by the Council. And, with the same positive philosophy, it makes the use of the ordinary legislative procedure instead of the more complex and difficult special legislative procedure easier, thereby widening the scope for co-legislation and democratic accountability through the European Parliament.

Nonetheless, that flexibilisation of the procedure (qualified majority instead of unanimity, and ordinary legislative procedure instead of special legislative procedure) turns out to be a partial truth, since in the final phase of the procedure it is necessary in both cases to overcome the unanimity – and twice! In particular, this means that the success of the final decision depends on the fact that it is not vetoed by a national executive (within the European Council) or by a national parliament, as well as on the fact that it is not vetoed by the European Parliament (by a majority of its component members).

Finally, from a substantial perspective, there is no controversy on the fact of excluding from the procedure established in Art. 48.7 TEU those "classic" decisions with military implications or those in the area of defence (considering the direct connection with the sovereignty).

2.2 *Its Impact: A Mere Vision of European Union Law*

The 2007 Lisbon Treaty was born with a clear disadvantage: it was considered from the beginning as a kind of poor substitute of the 2004 Constitutional Treaty. In fact, the Lisbon Treaty was not allowed to emulate or at least to use the name of the Constitutional Treaty.

Indeed, from the Constitutional Treaty, the Lisbon Treaty could not, first of all and mainly, adopt the "constitutional concept". As a result, during the discussions concerning the denomination of the Lisbon Treaty there appeared terms such as "fundamental treaty" or others which, not being as ambitious as "constitutional treaty" (or, furthermore, "European Constitution"), would show a new "small step" in the European construction without generating a perception according to which all the way walked towards the constitutionalisation of Europe (the process of elaboration and ratification of the European Constitution) would have been a succession of "lost steps". In view of this, it has been stated that "a mini-treaty represents a mini-Europe".[15]

In any case, the official denomination of the Lisbon Treaty turned out to be quite aseptic, which is one more reform of the European Treaties: *Treaty of Lisbon amending the Treaty on European Union and the Treaty establishing the European Community, signed at Lisbon, 13 December 2007.* In truth, from the revision procedures' point of view, the Lisbon Treaty is conceived as a further amendment of the original or primary EU Law, with a mere International Law approach (instead of a Constitutional Law approach that could allow "constitutional shows"). Then, the background is that "the Treaty of Lisbon marks a stage in the development of

[15]Torreblanca (2007).

the EU. In spite of evolving internal decision-making rules and democratic elements in EU law beyond the scope of ordinary international organisations, the EU remains an international organization based on treaty law. The member states are still the *masters of the Treaties*, holding on to the ultimate power of Treaty change (German: *Kompetenz-Kompetenz*). Still, the Lisbon Treaty rules for amending the Treaties refine and develop the current Treaty provisions".[16]

That mere vision of EU law has entailed that the comparison between the diverse amendments of European Treaties has very often been amounted to the number of matters susceptible to be decided by the co-decision legislative procedure and qualified majority voting or, in parallel, the number competences conferred on the European Community. Lamentably, the idea of "more Europe" has not been accompanied by a safeguard system of the European political structure (of a "stronger Europe"). In practice, the successful reforms of the EU have acquired a smaller impact than the frustrated ones ("*occasions manquées*").

We could say that the "the empty chair" crisis had more of a repercussion than the Luxembourg compromise: thus, we could hold *mutatis mutandis* that the "death" of the European Constitution has had greater impact than its process of elaboration. Consequently, the Lisbon Treaty must constitute the occasion not to regret that its "death" has had a more major spread than its approval. For this purpose, we must take advantage of the process leading to its entry into force in so far as this process is a great opportunity to construct, on more solid bases, a European Constitutional order by means of new procedures of revision and ratification of European Treaties.

3 Critique to the Revision Procedures of the Lisbon Treaty

3.1 Its Weaknesses: Comparison with the 2004 Constitutional Treaty

As exposed earlier, not even the 2004 Constitutional Treaty decided to give a qualitative jump in terms of "constitutional theory" when approaching its revision procedures. The revision procedures were not conceived in the European Constitution as a challenge on the future of the EU, that is to say, as an authentic "constitutional amendment" in terms of defence of the constitutional order. This may be proven by written evidence: the less ambitious Lisbon Treaty practically reproduces *verbatim* the provisions on the revision procedures of the Constitutional Treaty.

(A) In fact, the ordinary revision procedure which is established in the Lisbon Treaty (Art. 48.2-5 TEU) constitutes an almost complete reproduction of Art. IV-443 TCE. Thus, Art. 48 TEU rescues the two main novelties introduced by

---

[16]Granh (2008).

Art. I-443 TCE: on the one hand, the first innovation is that it enables the European Parliament to submit proposals for revising the Constitution, thereby putting it on an equal footing with the Commission and the governments of the Member States who already have this right; on the other hand, the Lisbon Treaty perpetuates the model of the European Convention so that future revisions of the TEU and the TFEU will also be prepared by such a body (this model began with the Convention on the Charter of Fundamental Rights in 1999 and was also practised with the Convention on the European Constitution in 2002/2003).

Although these procedural innovations are significant in terms of greater legitimacy or democratic participation, the truth is that their real impact becomes relative. In particular, the participation of the European Parliament is placed in the initiative *phase* and the participation of the European Convention takes place in the *intermediate phase*,[17] whereas the final phase (the entry into force of the proposed modification as much in the TCE as in the Lisbon Treaty) depends on the ratification by all the Member States in accordance with their respective constitutional provision. To those formal elements which are shared by both the TCE and the Lisbon Treaty (including the barrier of the unanimity rule), the latter adds in Art. 48.2 TEU a negative substantial element which was not present in Art. IV-443 TCE: the disappointing novelty according to which it would be possible to reduce the competences conferred on the Union in the Treaties.

(B) On the other hand, the simplified revision procedures introduced by the Lisbon Treaty in Arts. 48.6 and 7 TEU coincide essentially likewise with Art. IV-445 TCE (which provided a simplified revision procedure for the provisions under Title III of Part III on the Union's internal policies and action) and Art. IV-444 TCE (according to which two general bridging clauses enabled the European Council, by a unanimous decision, to apply qualified majority voting or the ordinary legislative procedure in a field for which the Constitution still provided for unanimity or a special legislative procedure) , respectively.

Finally, between Art. 48.6 TEU and Art. IV-445 TCE as well as between Art. 48.7 TEU and Art. IV-444 TCE, substantial differences do not exist. Perhaps it is worth highlighting that the Lisbon Treaty has excluded the logical "constitutional" terminology which was present in the TCE from its text: thus, what in Art. IV-445 TCE was a denominated "European decision" has been renamed "decision" *tout court* in Art. 48.6 TEU whereas the reference in Art. IV-444 TCE to "European laws or framework laws" has become "legislative acts" in Art. 48.7 TEU.

---

[17]In addition, according to Article 48.3 TEU "the European Council may decide by a simple majority, after obtaining the consent of the European Parliament, not to convene a Convention should this not be justified by the extent of the proposed amendments".

3.2 *Its Challenges: A Necessary Approach of European Constitutional Law*

In the field of the Constitutional Law the rigidity of the procedure of constitutional amendment is very often associated with the defence of the Constitution (as Supreme Norm), as well as with the idea of safeguarding the constitutional consensus (and the political stability of the constitutional system). Paradoxically, in the framework of the EU the rigidity of the revision procedures of the Treaties (whose main characteristic is the unanimous agreement between the Member States) has not been designed as a mechanism for defending the European constitutional order, but as a sign of weakness of the constitutional structure of the Union.

Even taking the ordinary revision procedure which is established in the Lisbon Treaty as a reference (Art. 48.2-5 TEU) it can be verified that the "classic" rules of amendment of constituent Treaties essentially stay in the same situation. If in relation to the ordinary revision procedure which was contemplated in the TCE it has been affirmed that "apart from the increased role of the Parliament and the inclusion of the model of the Convention in the revision procedure, Art. IV-443 TCE does not therefore substantially change the current revision procedure",[18] such affirmation must be applied a fortiori to the 2007 Lisbon Treaty.

At least, as far as the ordinary revision procedure and the ratification of the Lisbon Treaty are concerned, the EU cannot continue maintaining its traditional dynamics based on the unanimity rule. The parallelism between what happened on the occasion of the process of ratifications concerning the TCE and the Lisbon Treaty is evident. In both cases, it was after failing their "normal" entry into force because, with the required unanimous ratification in all Member States[19] (definitive blockage and death of the TCE after the negative referenda in France and the Netherlands, and block of the Lisbon Treaty after the negative referendum in Ireland), an analogous situation was in play. The same problem arises when dealing with the ordinary revision procedure in both cases, that is to say, if the unanimity rule is not fulfilled, analogous clauses are in play: the one according to which "if, two years after the signature of a treaty amending the Treaties/(of the treaty amending this Treaty), four fifths of the Member States have ratified it and one or

---

[18]Gateway to the European Union: "A Constitution for Europe" (http://europa.eu/scadplus/constitution/final_en.htm).

[19]According to Article 6 of the Lisbon Treaty: "1. This Treaty shall be ratified by the High Contracting Parties in accordance with their respective constitutional requirements. [...] 2. This Treaty shall enter into force on 1 January 2009, provided that all the instruments of ratification have been deposited, or, failing that, on the first day of the month following the deposit of the instrument of ratification by the last signatory State to take this step." Article IV-447 TCE had a similar wording: "1. This Treaty shall be ratified by the High Contracting Parties in accordance with their respective constitutional requirements. [...] 2. This Treaty shall enter into force on 1 November 2006, provided that all the instruments of ratification have been deposited, or, that having failed, on the first day of the second month following the deposit of the instrument of ratification by the last signatory State to take this step."

more Member States have encountered difficulties in proceeding with ratification, *the matter shall be referred to the European Council*" [Art. 48.5 TEU/(Art. IV-443.4 TCE].

If we keep the parallelism between the ordinary revision procedure and the ratification (once again with reference to both the Constitutional Treaty and the Lisbon Treaty), which conclusion can we reach?

As is well known, in the case of the Constitutional Treaty, the clause included in Art. IV-443.4 (in parallel with the one included in Article IV-447) has not been useful at all. In effect, according to the European Constitution, the ratification process was expected to last for two years, and the Constitution was due to enter into force no later than 1 November 2006. Following the ratification problems encountered in certain Member States, the Heads of State and Government decided at the European Council of 16 and 17 June 2005 to launch a "period of thinking" on the future of Europe. The idea was to initiate a broad debate with European citizens. At the European Council meeting on 21 and 22 June 2007, European leaders reached a compromise and agreed to convene an IGC to finalise and adopt, not a Constitution, but a "Reform Treaty" for the EU. The final text of the treaty, drawn up by the IGC, was approved at the informal European Council in Lisbon on 18 and 19 October. The Lisbon Treaty was signed by the Member States on 13 December 2007.

After the Irish negative referendum regarding the Lisbon Treaty (with a non-surprising parallelism!) we were faced with a similar situation. On that occasion, would the above-mentioned new Art. 48.5 TEU (in parallel with Art. 6 of the Lisbon Treaty) have been good for anything? To tell the truth, could the European Council have taken any decision determining the entry into force of the Lisbon Treaty without Ireland's consent or, in other words, would it have been possible to overcome that new *impasse* of the European construction without Ireland's ratification? A positive answer does not seem possible to this question.[20] To refer the matter to the European Council (in order for it to examine or analyse this matter) is not the same as to take a decision on this matter. The adoption of a decision by the European Council in such a sense (to decide the entry into force without the unanimous ratification) would not have been considered to be exactly in accordance with the spirit of the Lisbon Treaty.

In this context, in relation to the final clause of Art. IV-443.4 TCE it has been suggested that, once the treaty had been ratified by four fifths of the Member States, the European Council could decide its entry into force even in the absence of unanimous ratification. With such a solution, the only exit for the states who hadn't ratified the Treaty would be their withdrawal from the Union, the Lisbon Treaty reproducing this possibility foreseen for the first time in the Constitutional Treaty. Nevertheless, in my opinion that proposal is not possible, neither according to the Constitutional Treaty nor according to the Lisbon Treaty: on the one hand, that

[20]See Bar Cendón (2008).

would have been a unilateral decision of the European Council without respecting the text and the purpose of the Constitutional Treaty or the Lisbon Treaty (unanimous ratification). On the other hand, it would have been a forced or non-voluntary withdrawal, which is in conformity with neither the Constitutional Treaty nor the Lisbon Treaty.[21]

Correlatively, I think that the inverse process would have been possible, that is to say: if we take the example of Ireland with regard to the Lisbon Treaty, it would have first been possible to voluntarily withdraw one's country from the Union in order not to unilaterally block the Treaty and, later, the formal verification that there would be unanimity by the Member States (at that moment, Ireland would no longer have been a Member State of the Union). However, I also consider that such a solution (including Ireland's voluntary withdrawal) would have been very drastic, since that would mean finding Ireland (or another state in the same situation) guilty of a collective failure. Indeed, the whole evolutionary process of the European construction suffers from an endemic problem (the unanimity rule) whose responsibility affects all the Member States. In addition, this solution leads to reflect on another question: why the adoption of this measure in relation to Ireland (Lisbon Treaty) and not earlier in relation to France and the Netherlands (Constitutional Treaty)?

Moreover, a unilateral decision of the European Council – not inclusion in nor withdrawal from the Union, but a less forceful sanction (for example, to suspend the right to vote within the Council in relation to Member States not having ratified the Lisbon Treaty in those areas amended by this treaty) – would not have been in accordance with the Treaty either. Were there actually any alternatives to the unanimous ratification for the Lisbon Treaty to enter into force? I do not think so. This feeling was apparently present likewise in Ireland prior to the negative referendum in June 2008; according to the collective consciousness of the Irish people, if the referendum was not successful, everything would have followed as it did in any case (with the Nice Treaty in force).

What then was the effectiveness of the final clause of Art. 48.5 TEU? The only thing the European Council was doing was what this clause foresees, that is to say, examining or analysing the matter. Thus, when the European Council met on 15 and 16 October 2008 they decided to hear the Irish prime minister's analysis of the Irish referendum on the Treaty of Lisbon and agreed to review the issue in December in order to define the elements of a solution and the approach to take for 2009 (considering the 2009 European Parliament elections and renewal of the European

[21]See Laffrangue (1999), pp. 497–502: this author emphasises that awareness of the possibility of withdrawal from the Union is necessary already at the pre-accession phase. Since no provision of the European Community law regulates the issue, the paper reflects on the question of how to interpret that legal gap, what are the reasons for the gap and what are the legal effects if a Member State declares its intention to withdraw from the EU. Finally, the author analyses the issue in the context of recognised principles of international law and comes to the conclusion that the nature of the EU makes withdrawal from the Union legally impossible. Further, the author focuses on possibilities of de facto withdrawal from the Union.

Commission). The perspective of a solution including the final entry into force of the Lisbon Treaty was rather pessimistic and, in fact, it was quite symptomatic that that same European Council had also approved the composition of the group to reflect on the future of Europe proposed by the president of the group (Felipe González).

Was it worth continuing to insist on the Lisbon Treaty entering into force? Yes, sure, in so far as in the last instance the Lisbon Treaty means a *substantial rescue* of the TCE,[22] although "the Brussels European Council (21/22 June 2007) and the Reform Treaty, elaborated from this Council, have produced a paradoxical situation: on the one hand, this new Treaty includes contents of the Constitutional Treaty; on the other hand, the word Constitution has been erased. We have moved from a Constitution *with the form of a Treaty* to a Constitution *with the name of a Treaty*. The conclusion that we can reach is not very pleasing for the European Institutions: either the Constitutional Treaty was not a Constitution and the Institutions wanted us to consider it as one, or the Reform Treaty is a Constitution and the Institutions want us to consider it as a simple Treaty".[23]

With this philosophy, it has been underlined that "the Treaty of Lisbon will be a decisive step forward in the constitutional evolution of the European Union. In historic terms it is at least as significant as the Treaty of Maastricht (1991) which introduced the single currency and established early provisions for foreign and security policy and for cooperation in police and judicial affairs. Agreement on the new Treaty will mark the end of the phase of controversial political integration which began with the Convention on the Charter of Fundamental Rights in 1999, and was later developed by the Treaty of Nice (2000), the Declaration of Laeken (2001), the Convention on the Future of Europe (2002–2003), the Treaty establishing a Constitution for Europe (2004), the referendums in France and The Netherlands (2005), and the subsequent 'period of reflection'. With the new Treaty in force, the Union will not need and will not seek the transfer of new competences from member states. Although some further rationalisation and simplification will continue to be both possible and desirable, the system of government achieved by Lisbon should, in all essentials, be strong and durable".[24]

Suppose that that is true from a substantial point of view. Could we then be satisfied with this exit? I feel that it would not be sufficient. The success of the Lisbon Treaty in such conditions would be partial, in so far as the procedural obstacle of the unanimous revision would remain in the future. We have obtained a "constitutional product" from a substantial point of view, but we have followed a procedural road based on a mere vision of EU Law (an approach to International Law as far as the revision procedure is concerned).[25] Therefore, the first and most

[22]See Aldecoa Luzarraga and Guinea Lorente (2008).

[23]Balaguer Callejón (2007), p. 40.

[24]Duff Mep (2009).

[25]For some political actors, the authors of the Lisbon Treaty would have reproduced the 2004 European Constitution with a few "cosmetic changes" dealing with the "constitutional terminology".

urgent task of the EU Reflection Group on the future of Europe would have been to approach, with constitutional profiles, the reform of the revision procedures: this means to assume the model of the existing procedures of constitutional amendments in federal states (in coherence with the federal vocation present in the 1950 Schuman Declaration), where the unanimous ratification of the Member States is not demanded (*confederal model*), but a qualified majority of these states is.

Summarising the previous reflections we may argue that, considering the important substantial impact of this Treaty, the unanimous ratification in the ordinary revision could have been maintained, but it would have been necessary to replace the unanimity rule by the qualified majority voting at least in the simplified revision procedures. We must approach that necessary vision of European Constitutional Law in a more profound way.

4 Between the Democratic Deficit and the Constitutional Deficit

If the classic and famous *democratic deficit* of the European Parliament in the decision-making process has been compensated by moving from unanimity to qualified majority voting in the Council (by extending co-decision procedure with the Council to new areas of policy), *the constitutional deficit* of the revision procedures Treaties not being corrected by means of the suppression of the unanimous ratification by all the Member States is incomprehensible.

It is worth insisting on the above-mentioned paradoxical situation: with the entry into force of the Lisbon Treaty not only has a Constitution with the name of a Treaty been approved, but also a Constitution following a procedure of International Law, which is still the "classic" revision procedure of European Treaties (based on the unanimity rule). This approach of International Law demonstrates a restricted and little dynamic vision on the amendment of international treaties according to the rules which are foreseen in the 1969 Vienna Convention on the Law of Treaties (VCLT). Indeed, it can be argued that the VCLT does not impose that the amendment of international treaties (in this case, of European Treaties) must comply with ratification by all the State Parties in these treaties. In fact, the international practice demonstrates that the constituent treaties of diverse international organisations (among others, the Statute of the Council of Europe) can be reformed by a majority of Contracting Parties. It is true, however, that in such situations, the amendment of the Treaty is only applied to the States that have given their consent.

Consequently, this rule of International Law is not satisfactory when referring to a supranational organisation sui generis as is the EU. Thus, there would have been no sense in assuming the entry into force of the Lisbon Treaty only for the Member States who had ratified it and to reject this possibility for those having refused this ratification, in so far as this solution would imply going beyond the current examples of "variable-geometry" Europe, of "multispeed Europe", of "concentric circles" or of "Europe 'à la carte'". Furthermore, without prejudice of the "enhanced co-operations" mechanism, if we analysed the use of opt-out Protocols with the intention of not blocking the reform Treaties (for instance, Annex Protocols to the Maastricht Treaty or Annex Protocols to the Lisbon Treaty), this analysis would lead to the conclusion that these Protocols are somehow reservations that are "incompatible with the object and purpose of the treaty".[26] Thus, how should we assume that several Member States are excluded from the common currency (the Euro) in the case of the Maastricht Treaty (that is to say, excluded from an element which is considered as one of the symbols of constitutional identity of the EU)? Or how should we accept that some Member States are excluded from the EUCFR in the case of the Lisbon Treaty?

If we apply the previous reflections to the revision procedures of the Lisbon Treaty, we can launch a series of critiques and proposals with regard to the real impact of this Treaty:

- The correction of the *democratic deficit* of the European Parliament when allowing its participation in the ordinary revision procedure constitutes an irrelevant element in comparison with the existence of *constitutional deficit* as a result of the rule of the unanimous ratification by all the Member States.
- The correction of the *democratic deficit* of national parliaments when allowing their participation in the simplified revision procedures does not have a great value, since the opposition of only one national parliament blocks the proposed reform.
- In both previous cases the compensation of the *democratic deficit* suffers from misunderstanding about the *democratic legitimacy* or, in other words, about the correct implementation of the *democratic principle* as *majority rule with respect to minority*. Indeed, with the possibility of veto, either by a Member State in relation to the ratification of the ordinary revision or by a national parliament in relation to a simplified revision, the democracy becomes a *minority rule without respect to majority*. The world is turned upside down!
- In congruence with the precedent idea, my proposal cannot be other than to reform the revision procedures, in order to submit to the qualified majority voting (not to the unanimity rule) the ratification of the ordinary revision as well as the rule of the majority decision of national parliaments (not of all national parliaments) for the approval of the simplified revisions.

Of course, the most interesting option to reduce the *constitutional deficit* in the framework of the revision procedures (especially, the ordinary one) would consist of assuming the constitutional amendment model which exists in federal states in the EU, so that the revision of European Treaties would enter into force for all the

[26] Article 19 VCLT (*formulation of reservations*). It must also be remembered that Article 2.d) VCLT includes the definition of "reservation" with these terms: "reservation" means "a unilateral statement, however phrased or named, made by a State, when signing, ratifying, accepting, approving or acceding to a treaty, whereby it purports to exclude or to modify the legal effect of certain provisions of the treaty in their application to that State".

Member States of the Union when it had been ratified by a qualified majority of the Member States (in addition, a significant percentage of the represented European citizenship may be required). Obviously, it would be possible to distinguish between more or less sensitive sovereign areas and, in such a case, to foresee or not the possibility of opt-out Protocols.

Together with the model of federal states, there have been interesting proposals in the EU with a constitutionalist-federal approach: thus, we can mention, among others, the 1984 Spinelli constitutional project and the 1994 Herman constitutional project. These projects had a great interest to make a *constitutional choice*. By contrast, the Convention that drafted the TCE refused to do so under the pretext that the unanimity rule was one *conditio sine qua non* for amending and ratifying the European Treaties.

5 Concluding Thoughts: Do We Need a New Procedural Impetus from the Political Elite to Secure a Solid Constitutional Structure?

If the democratic deficit, by antonomasia, of the EU was reduced thanks to a process of "atypical" amendment of the constituent Treaties consisting in introducing the universal suffrage for the election of the European Parliament (by means of a Decision of the Council introducing this new electoral procedure), it could be likewise conceived to articulate a new revision mechanism of the Treaties aiming at defending the constitutional structure of the EU with regard to each new uncertain unanimous process of ratification in all the Member States. The great challenge consists in avoiding the potential veto deriving from a negative referendum or a parliamentary rejection in a Member State (or in an insignificant number of states and population). This way, we could borrow once again the expression "multilevel constitutionalism",[27] in which the historical relevance and present-day

[27]For the original concept see Pernice (1999), p. 703; later, Pernice (2002), pp. 511–529; finally, Pernice (2009): in this last paper, the author explains what multilevel constitutionalism means as a theoretical approach to conceptualise the constitution of the European system as an interactive process of establishing, dividing, organising, and limiting powers, involving national constitutions and the supranational constitutional framework as two interdependent components of a legal system governed by constitutional pluralism instead of hierarchies. The ongoing process of trial and error in the continued reform of the Union where constitutional initiatives regularly lead to increasingly extensive debates with modest contractual results, with the entry into force of the Treaty of Lisbon still being uncertain, is taken as an example for explaining multilevel constitutionalism in action. The author seeks to show that both the process showing increased public participation and the results achieved in Lisbon are characteristic for the consolidation of a multilevel constitutional structure of a new kind, based upon functioning democratic Member States, complementary to them and binding them together in a supranational unit without it being a state or aiming at statehood.

relevance of this "constitutional national phase" of European Treaty making is uncertain.[28] In this sense, the idea of multilevel constitutionalism has been considered in connection with the structural possibilities of the subsidiarity principle (in terms of pluralistic legal culture to be incorporated into all national constitutional systems).[29] Moreover, the inclusion of "European clauses" in the constitutional text of each Member State has been suggested as a suitable instrument for the constitutionalisation of Europe.[30]

Reforming the revision procedures of European Treaties is in this case one of the European Union's – of course – "typical" revisions of European Treaties. There is no doubt that it is easier to prepare a reform on a concrete point (the revision procedures of European Treaties) than to elaborate a package of reforms. In parallel, in the countries whose constitutional requirements demand the celebration of a national referendum, it is easier to organise a consultation with a specific question rather than making a general question meaning the acceptance *in toto* of the Treaty.

In effect, in the countries whose constitutional order demands the celebration of an ad hoc referendum (as is the case of Ireland), the political actors would not have to manipulate the real impact of the consultation on the reform of the revision procedures of European Treaties. For example, it would be unfair to forge a collective feeling according to which the citizenship would approach the reform of the revision procedures (when introducing the majority rule instead of the minority rule) as an attack against the popular will of a Member State. On the contrary, the question of the celebration of the referendum being compatible with the constitutional identity would have to be explained: in particular, the constitutional requirements for the ratification of the reform Treaty would be respected with the celebration of that referendum, but the decision (perhaps a negative one) taken in such a national referendum for the ratification of the treaty could not prevail over the positive will of the other countries (the big majority) that have already ratified it.

The acceptance of such a veto would be as much as to conceive of democracy in an erroneous way: this is not a mechanism in which the voters of a country would always have to be the winners. The majority rule with respect to minority must lead to the understanding that the most important thing is not winning (each electoral process or each popular consultation), but taking part in it (participative democracy). The previous reasoning (the minority need not prevail over the majority in an unreasonable way) becomes still more reinforced if the idea that sometimes the majority will even have to accept the minority's rights when some top values are in play at the international level is remembered.

In this sense, in relation to the ratification process of the Constitutional Treaty it has been highlighted that, in spite of the failure provoked by the negative consultations in France and the Netherlands, the assessment of the countries where

[28]See de Witte (2005).

[29]Rodríguez-Izquierdo Serrano (2008), pp. 155–156.

[30]Astola Madariaga (2004), p. 234.

national referenda took place indicates that the percentage of the population that said "yes" was less than that of the voters that said "no". From this perspective, in order to avoid asymmetries between countries regarding the ratification mechanism (parliamentary or popular) the introduction of the European referendum for the ratification of reforms of European Treaties on important matters has been proposed.[31] In practice, the referendum (national or European) may be a very good opportunity to inform the citizenship on the basic elements of the European construction.

In this kind of "reform of double degree" (reform of the revision procedure) some could probably observe a procedural fraud. Nevertheless, the design of the revision procedures of European Treaties is developing more as a hand-thrown weapon than as a mechanism for defending the constitutional structure of the Union.[32] In fact, an abusive remedy (fraud) to those revision procedures could be denounced to some extent when they are approached as a potential veto to the constitutionalisation process of Europe. The rigidity of the procedure has not meant a defence of the institutional order of the EU, but its paralysis. What is needed, to sum up, is a bigger degree of flexibility in the design of the revision procedures of European Treaties, with the introduction of the qualified majority voting instead of the unanimity rule as well as the possibility of celebrating a European referendum for the most relevant revisions.[33] In any case, the Lisbon Treaty should be seen as a step in the long process of European integration rather than an end point – at least from the perspective of the Constitutional Law.[34]

References

Aldecoa Luzarraga F, Guinea Lorente M (2008) El rescate sustancial de la Constitución Europea a través del Tratado de Lisboa: la salida del laberinto. Documento de Trabajo/Working Paper n. 9/2008, Real Instituto Elcano. www.realinstitutoelcano.org

Alegre Martínez MA, Jimena Quesada L (2006) Fundamentos constitucionales de la Unión Europea. Biblioteca Nueva, Madrid

Astola Madariaga J (2004) De la legitimidad democrática de la Unión Europea y de la legitimación democrática de sus decisiones: una reflexión sobre el proyecto de Constitución Europea. Teoría y Realidad Constitucional 15

Auer A, Flauss JF (eds) (1997) Le référendum européen. Bruylant, Bruxelles

Balaguer Callejón F (2007) La Constitución europea tras el Consejo Europeo de Bruselas y el Tratado de Lisboa. Revista de Derecho Constitucional Europeo 8

Bar Cendón A (2008) Cowen got what he asked for, but it was a pyrrhic victory. The Irish Times, Wednesday, December 17, 2008. http://www.irishtimes.com/newspaper/opinion/2008/1217/1229035813202.html

---

[31]See Auer and Flauss (1997).

[32]See Ehlermann and Mény (2000).

[33]Jimena Quesada (2004), p. 661.

[34]Cf. Mangiameli (2001), p. 25.

Besné Mañero R, Canedo Arrillaga JR, Pérez de las Heras B (1998) La Unión Europea: Historia, instituciones y sistema jurídico. Universidad de Deusto, Bilbao
Blanke HJ, Mangiameli S (2005) Introduction. In: Blanke HJ, Mangiameli S (eds) Governing Europe under a constitution. The hard road from the European Treaties to a European Constitutional Treaty. Springer, Berlin
de Witte B (2005) European Treaty Revision: a case of Multilevel Constitutionalism. In: Pernice I and Zemanek J (eds) A Constitution for Europe: The IGC, the Ratification Process and Beyond. Nomos, Baden-Baden, pp 59–76
Dehousse R (1998) The European Court of Justice. Macmillan, Houndmills
Duff Mep A (2009) True guide to the Treaty of Lisbon Treaty. Portal Europe. http://www.alde.eu/fileadmin/files/Download/True-Guide-NEW.pdf
Ehlermann CD, Mény Y (coords) (2000) Réformer les procédures de révision des Traités. Institut Universitaire Européen/Robert Schuman Centre for Advanced Studies, Firenze
Giscard d'Estaing V (2003) La Constitution pour l'Europe. Albin Michel, Paris
Granh R (2008) EU Treaty of Lisbon: Treaty revision procedures, in *Grahnlaw* (Blawg about EU law and for a democratic European Union), Sunday, 3 February 2008. http://grahnlaw.blogspot.com/2008/02/eu-treaty-of-lisbon-treaty-revision.html
Groppi T (2004) La revisione della Costituzione. In: Álvarez Conde E, Garrido Mayol V (dirs) Comentarios a la Constitución Europea, vol I. Tirant lo Blanch/Consejo Jurídico Consultivo de la Comunidad Valenciana, Valencia
Jimena Quesada L (2001) Los ciudadanos como actores en el proceso de construcción europea. Hacia una Teoría del Estado Europeo. Cuadernos Europeos de Deusto 24
Jimena Quesada L (2004) Los instrumentos de democracia directa y la nueva Constitución Europea. In: Álvarez Conde E, v. Garrido Mayol (dirs) Comentarios a la Constitución Europea, vol I. Tirant lo Blanch/Consejo Jurídico Consultivo de la Comunidad Valenciana, Valencia
Laffrangue R (1999) Legal possibilities of withdrawal from the European Union. Juridica
Leanerts K, Gerard D (2004) The structure of the Union according to the Constitution for Europe: the emperor is getting dressed. Eur Law Rev 3
Mangiameli S (2001) Integrazione europea e Diritto costituzionale. In: Anuario di Diritto tedesco. Giuffrè Editore, Milano
Maulis E (2004) Révision d'un traité ou émergence d'un pouvoir constituant ? La procédure d'adoption et de révision de la constitution européenne. In: Beaud O (ed) L'Europe en voie de constitution. Bruylant, Bruxelles
Oberdorff H (2005) La ratification et la révision du traité établissant une Constitution pour l'Europe. Notre Europe – Études & Recherces 38
Pace A (1996) La causa della rigidità costituzionale. Cedam, Padova
Pace A (2002) La Dichiarazione di Laeken e il processo costituente europeo. Rivista Trimestrale di Diritto Pubblico 3:650
Pernice I (1999) Multilevel constitutionalism and the Treaty of Amsterdam: European Constitution-making Revisited? Common Market Law Rev 36
Pernice I (2002) Multilevel constitutionalism in the European Union. Eur Law Rev 5
Pernice I (2009) The Treaty of Lisbon: multilevel constitutionalism in action. Columbia J Eur Law 5(3)
Rodríguez-Izquierdo Serrano M (2008) Posibilidades constitucionales del principio de subsidiariedad. Universidad de Granada, Granada
Ruipérez J (2000) La Constitución europea y la teoría del poder constituyente. Biblioteca Nueva, Madrid
Sáiz Arnaiz A (1999) El Tribunal de Justicia de las Comunidades Europeas como Tribunal Constitucional. Revista Vasca de Administración Pública 53
Stone Sweet A (1998) Constitutional Dialogues in the European Community. In: Slaughter AM et al (eds) The European Court and National Courts. Hart Publishing, Oxford
Torreblanca JI (2007) A mini-treaty represents a mini-Europe. Eurotopics. http://www.eurotopics.net/es/magazin/politik-verteilerseite/eu-vertrag-2007-12/interview_torreblanca_20070301/
Vidal Prado C (2006) Nuevos (y viejos) recelos del Tribunal Constitucional Federal alemán frente a la eficacia del Derecho comunitario. Revista Española de Derecho Constitucional 77

Withdrawal from the Union

Anna Wyrozumska

1 General Remarks

Despite several threats of withdrawal,[1] up till now no state has actually seceded from the European Union (EU). Previous treaties governing the EU did not contain any provision on withdrawal. They instead provided in Art. 312 EC and Art. 51 TEU that these Treaties were "concluded for an unlimited period." The issue of whether the Member States still might withdraw under these clauses was discussed from time to time. Those who advocated for such a right gave as an example of its practical exercise the withdrawal of Greenland (Danish autonomous territory). This, however, may be questionable due to the particular circumstances of the case: Greenland was not a direct member of the European Community (EC), but in a sense a part of the territory of Denmark, and it was not Greenland that applied for withdrawal but Denmark seeking redefinition of the application of the Treaties to its territory after a referendum in Greenland on the continued European Economic Community (EEC) membership.[2]

The mechanism used for the "withdrawal" of Greenland was the revision procedure laid down in the Community Treaties (e.g. Art. 236 EEC). Denmark brought to the Council a proposal for the purpose of revising the Treaties so that they cease to apply to Greenland and to place Greenland under the arrangements for the association of the overseas countries and territories laid down in Part Four of the

[1]For discussion of attempts of withdrawal, e.g. French policy of the empty chair, plans for withdrawal of Great Britain, Greece, etc., see Harbo (2008), p. 139 et seq.

[2]Krämer (1983), p. 273 et seqq.; Harnhoff (1983), p. 13 et seqq.; Weiss (1985), p. 173 et seqq.; Friel (2004), p. 409 et seqq.; Harbo (2008), p. 140.

A. Wyrozumska (✉)
Faculty of Law and Adm., Uniwersytet Lódzki, Uniwersytecka 3, 90-137 Lódz, Poland
e-mail: awyrozumska@uni.lodz.pl

H.-J. Blanke and S. Mangiameli (eds.), *The European Union after Lisbon*,
DOI 10.1007/978-3-642-19507-5_14, © Springer-Verlag Berlin Heidelberg 2012

Treaty. The request was submitted then to the Commission and the Parliament for consultation. It obtained the approval of both institutions, although with some objections in the Parliament.[3] Since this operation required adjustments of important interests of the EC and Greenland with respect to fisheries, Member States asked the Commission to prepare proposals. The "withdrawal" was then regulated by the Treaty amending, with regard to Greenland, the EC Treaties of 1984 and the Protocol on special arrangements for Greenland attached to it.[4] The process had specific features: there was no unilateral withdrawal, all the Member States had agreed for it, the institutions were consulted, special adjustments and arrangements were made (e.g. Greenland obtained free trade rights, fisheries were regulated and it was afforded new status under the Treaties).

The Greenland case demonstrates that the question of withdrawal shall be perceived in the perspective of the consent of all other Member States and that it involves necessary adjustments and special arrangements.

The problem of withdrawal could be approached from different perspectives, i.e. political, economic, social or legal. This paper is focused on legal issues leaving aside, for example, political or economic undesirability of withdrawal of the Member State, social repercussions, its costs for the EU, etc. It deals first with the issue of withdrawal under the former treaties which did not contain any clause in that respect. Generally, in legal discussions on admissibility of withdrawal from the EC/EU there were two main perspectives, international law and federal law. International law arguments were used by whose who perceived the EC/EU as an international organization (or structure) based on treaties and governed by international law and federal arguments by those who viewed it in the light of the autonomous character of its legal order, a new federal polity not being, however, a state. We will address first the argument based on the right to withdraw from an international organization (or the right based on the law of treaties) and then the arguments based on special character of the EC/EU legal order. Finally, the exit clause introduced by the Lisbon Treaty will be considered.

2 Application of the Law of Treaties to Withdrawal from the EU before the Lisbon Treaty

There are several ways in which the membership of the international organisation may be terminated. This can happen according to the Vienna Convention on the Law of Treaties (VCLT) of 1969, by consent of all the members,[5] by withdrawal (a voluntary act of the Member State), by expulsion (a measure taken by the organisation against the Member State), by a loss of membership upon failure to

[3]Respectively, COM (83) 66 final, and EP Doc 1-264/83, 17.

[4]*Protocol on special arrangements for Greenland*, O.J. L 29/7 (1985).

[5]Art. 54 VCLT: "The termination of a treaty or the withdrawal of a party may take place: (*a*) in conformity with the provisions of the treaty; or (*b*) at any time by consent of all the parties after consultation with the other contracting States."

accept an amendment of the constitution of the organisation,[6] by the dissolution of the organisation or by the disappearance of a Member State.[7]

We confine ourselves rather to a voluntary, i.e. unilateral, withdrawal. It happens quite often that such a right to withdraw is expressly provided for in the constitution of an international organisation. The problem arises when such right is not expressly granted. If some constitutions purportedly do not contain a withdrawal clause, does it mean that the right is excluded? The answer to this question has to be cautiously given since certainly no conclusion should be drawn of itself from the mere absence of a withdrawal clause.[8]

Some guidance on how to proceed in such cases is given by Art. 56 VCLT.[9] It has to be noticed first that a general rule laid down in Art. 56.1 VCLT is a negative one. "A treaty which contains no provision regarding its termination and which does not provide for denunciation or withdrawal is not subject to denunciation or withdrawal." It provides, however, for two exceptions. The first one concerns the intention of the parties. The denunciation or withdrawal from such a treaty is possible if "it is established that the parties intended to admit the possibility of denunciation or withdrawal" (Art. 56.1 lit. a). The customary character of the "chapeau" of Art. 56.1 and the first exception (reference in point (a) to the intention of the parties) is not questioned. There is no customary (tacit) right to withdraw unilaterally or any general presumption in its favour.[10]

Reference to the intention of the parties may be useful in some cases only, as for example in the case of the United Nations (UN).[11] The intention of the UN Charter's parties was expressed in the special declaration of the San Francisco Conference establishing the UN adopted after extensive discussions on the right to

---

[6]See e.g. declaration of the conference establishing WHO: "A member state is not bound to remain in the Organization, if its rights and obligations as such are changed by an amendment of the constitution in which it has not concurred and which it finds itself unable to accept" (Proceedings of the International Health Conference 1946, Official Records WHO, No. 2, p 26. 74). Similarly, the declaration of the San Francisco Conference establishing the UN: "Nor would it be the purpose of the Organization to compel a member to remain in the Organization if its rights and obligations as such were changed by Charter amendment in which it has not concurred and which it finds itself unable to accept, or if an amendment duly accepted by the necessary majority in the Assembly or in a general conference fails to secure the ratification necessary to bring such amendment into effect", Goodrich et al. (1969), p. 74 et seq.

[7]Amerasinghe (1996), p. 117; Schermers and Blokker (2003), para 117.

[8]Waldock (1966), p. 250.

[9]According to its Art. 5 the VCLT "applies to any treaty which is the constituent instrument of an international organization and to any treaty adopted within an international organization without prejudice to any relevant rules of the organization." On customary character of Art. 56 see Christakis (2006), p. 1957 et seqq.; Villiger 2009, p. 705

[10]Christakis (2006), p. 1958 et seq.

[11]The UN Charter does not contain a withdrawal clause to emphasise the permanent character of the organisation. It was perceived that the clause will weaken the organisation. Klabbers noticed that the lack of the clause in the Charter "may not make withdrawal impossible, but it does create something of a political and psychological barrier. Indeed, in the more than fifty years of its existence, no state has formally withdrawn from the United Nations" [Klabbers (2002), p. 21]. There is some uncertainty as regards Indonesia's attempt to withdraw in 1965.

withdraw from the organisation. The declaration shows clearly that the right to withdraw, however, in very exceptional circumstances was conceded.[12]

Sometimes, however, the task to find out the intention of the parties could be difficult, especially for the lack of clear *travaux préparatoires*. This case raises again the issue of whether there exists an implied right to withdraw or whether this right is inherent in the nature of a treaty constituting the international organisation. It brings us back to Art. 56 VCLT and the second exception offered by it. Article 56.1 lit. b provides that "a right of denunciation or withdrawal may be implied by the nature of the treaty". Christakis holds that there are serious doubts as to the customary character of this exception in Art. 56. He, however, admits that the prevailing view is that withdrawal may be implied by the nature of the treaty constituting the international organisation.[13] Particularly interesting from the EU perspective seems to be Oppenheim's opinion. While referring to the UN Charter he emphasised that

> "although the Charter itself does not expressly mention the right to withdrawal, in the absence of an express prohibition to that effect, the members of the United Nations must be deemed to have preserved the right to sever what is, in law, a contractual relation of indefinite duration, imposing upon states far-reaching restrictions of their sovereignty."[14]

A more general concept was developed by Singh:

> "[I]n the absence of an express stipulation in a constituent instrument, it may be rightly presumed that the international organisation so created does not put any limitation on the right of the member-states to withdraw. Anything which is not conceded in favour of the international organisation is retained by the member-state, which by virtue of its sovereignty must be vested with the residuary jurisdiction."[15]

The main argument in favour of unilateral withdrawal from an international organisation is thus based on sovereignty (a right to withdraw is a sovereign prerogative of a state). On the other hand, the sovereignty argument is rejected by other authors, such as Kelsen:

> "From the right of sovereignty one has deducted the legal power of a State to withdraw by an unilateral act from an international community in spite of the fact that the treaty constituting this community does not confer upon the members such a right. But no such power can be deduced from the alleged "right" of sovereignty."[16]

---

[12]"If (. . .) a member because of exceptional circumstances feels constrained to withdraw, and leave the burden of maintaining international peace and security on the other members, it is not the purpose of the Organization to compel that member to continue its cooperation in the organization. It is obvious, however, that withdrawal or some other form of dissolution of the Organization would become inevitable if, deceiving the hopes of humanity, the Organization was revealed to be unable to maintain peace or could do so only at the expense of law and justice" Goodrich et al., pp. 74 et seq. See also the Report of the Committee 1/2 of the San Francisco Conference: UNCIO. Doc. 1178, 1/2/76(2) p. 5.

[13]Christakis (2006), p. 2006; compare Villiger 2009, p. 702 et seq.

[14]Oppenheim (1948), pp. 373–374, para 168.

[15]Singh (1958), p. 80 et seq.

[16]Kelsen (1952), p. 157.

Schermers and Blokker criticise the sovereignty approach based upon the nineteenth-century absolute concept of state sovereignty, somewhat contrary to *pacta sunt servanda*. If sovereign states decide not to include a withdrawal clause in the constitution, "it would amount to disrespect of this agreement among sovereigns if states were subsequently able to withdraw."[17] They also discuss the other arguments based on equity,[18] general principle of law[19] or expediency (pragmatic rather than legal approach: there is no sense in prohibiting withdrawal if such a prohibition cannot be enforced). They find that all these arguments are in favour of the inclusion of a withdrawal clause rather than supporting the main contention.[20] Furthermore, state practice seems not to confirm the existence of the implied right to withdraw.[21]

In a more nuanced form the idea is put by Amerashinge. He concurs that the nature of a treaty constituting the organisation raises the presumption that a state must be deemed to be free to withdraw from it, unless it has surrendered that right either expressly or impliedly and gives twelve months notice required by Art. 56.2 VCLT.[22] The presumption is therefore rebuttable and in each case the real intention of the parties has to be established.

There is thus no clear answer and it remains doubtful that constitutions of international organisations would generally be covered by the exceptions under Art. 56 VCLT.[23] Each case has to be studied separately to find out the intentions of the parties and the character of the treaty. Reuter seems right stating that "(t)he problem is essentially one of intention, but it is not an easy task to fix upon generally reliable signs of such intention".[24]

At first glance, the application of Art. 56 VCLT to the EU seems to be excluded taking into account the objectives, the character of the EU Treaties and also Articles 312 EC and 51 EU.[25] Moreover, the EU case may be viewed in the light of the

[17]Schermers and Blokker (2003), para 117.

[18]States enjoy the freedom to participate in international organisations. If non-members are not obliged to enter, there is no reason not to allow the members to leave.

[19]The argument is based on private law (membership of private organisation may be terminated unilaterally) and on the law of some federations allowing for withdrawal.

[20]Schermers and Blokker (2003), p. 87 et seqq.

[21]For example, WHO rejected the effectiveness of withdrawal of the nine members in 1949 and 1950, similarly UNESCO of three members in 1952 and 1953. Those states were treated as "inactive members" and were later reintegrated. In a consequence, in 1954 the express clause on withdrawal was introduced into the UNESCO constitution. See Christakis (2006), paras 70, 96, 98. Compare Schermers and Blokker (2003), p. 97 et seq. and p. 101; Dock (1994), p. 111 et seq.

[22]Amerasinghe (1996), p. 120.

[23]See Schermers and Blokker (2003), p. 102.

[24]Reuter (1990), p. 128, para 233.

[25]Compare Hill (1982), p. 345–347. The opposite view is, however, taken by Schmitz (2001, Chap. 2-C.VI.2.c.aa-cc) for whom Art. 56.1 (b) is fully applicable on the ground of the nature of the treaty as a treaty of integration. The goal of a treaty of integration is not the short-sighted defence at any price of the level of integration which has been achieved. Rather, the goal is sustainable, long-term integration, and voluntary participation in every phase of the integration process is an

Gabčikovo-Nagymaros Project case where the International Court of Justice (ICJ) rejected the right of Hungary to rely on Art. 56 VCLT underlining the permanent character of the regime established by the treaty in question. The Court noticed:

> The 1977 Treaty does not contain any provision regarding its termination. Nor is there any indication that the parties intended to admit the possibility of denunciation or withdrawal. On the contrary, the Treaty establishes a long-standing and durable régime of joint investment and joint operation. Consequently, the parties not having agreed otherwise, the Treaty could be terminated only on the limited grounds enumerated in the Vienna Convention.[26]

Those limited grounds enumerated in the Vienna Convention are the grounds set out in Art. 60, namely breach of the treaty by other parties; Art. 61, supervening impossibility of performance; and Art. 62, fundamental change of circumstances with respect to those existing at the time when the treaty was concluded. The *Gabčikovo-Nagymaros* case leaves no doubt that these grounds should be extremely narrowly interpreted.[27]

Not going deep into details, because of the complete and self-sufficient EU system of judicial protection (especially Art. 227 EC, Art. 292 EC) the application of the principle enshrined in Art. 60 to the EU Treaties seemed not to be possible. In cases 90/63 and 91/63 *Commission EEC v Luxembourg and Belgium* the European Court of Justice (ECJ) emphasised that "the Treaty is not limited to creating reciprocal obligations", and that the "basic concept of the Treaty requires that Member States shall not fail to carry out their obligations and shall not take the law into their own hands".[28]

If some authors allowed application of Art. 60, they did so on highly limited grounds. Schmitz, for example, suggested that the state could be allowed to invoke that provision if the other Member States and the union's organs collectively committed fundamental violations of the treaty, "then a dissenting member state might, after fruitless recourse to the prescribed remedies, make use of the right – for example, where the union's organs, with the other member states' approval, "compensated" a refusal to accede to new union competences by what was clearly a deliberately "overgenerous" interpretation of existing competence provisions".[29] In fact, Schmitz presupposed not only that the institutions' acts were *ultra vires* but also the total collapse of the value system of the EU.

The same could be said on the principle of the impossibility of performance. This ground requires that the impossibility should result from the permanent disappearance or destruction of an object indispensable for the execution of the

---

indispensable prerequisite if that goal is to be reached (English summary of Chap. 2 point 30), similarly Weiler (1985), p. 298.

[26]Gabočikovo-Nagymanos Project (Hungary v Slovakia) (Judgement of 25 September 1997) ICJ Rep. 1997, para 100.

[27]See Gabočikovo-Nagymanos Project (Hungary v Slovakia) (Judgement of 25 September 1997) ICJ Rep. 1997, para 102 et seq.

[28]Joined Cases 90/63 *Commission of the European Economic Community v Grand Duchy of Luxembourg* and 91/63 *Commission of the European Economic Community v Kingdom of Belgium* (ECJ 13 November 1964), p. 625.

[29]Schmitz (2001), Chap. 2-C.VI.2.c.aa-cc (English summary of Chap. 2, point 30).

treaty. The *Gabčikovo-Nagymaros* case implies that the term "object" could refer to "physical object" or "legal régime". Thus to invoke Art. 61 VCLT in regard to the EC/EU Treaty would naturally require the complete destruction of the whole Treaty system. In the *Gabčikovo-Nagymaros* case the ICJ observed that the legal régime in question had not definitively ceased to exist, because the treaty "actually made available to the parties the necessary means to proceed at any time, by negotiation, to the required readjustments between economic imperatives and ecological imperatives".[30] The same holds good for the EU Treaties which offered to the parties a unique and incomparable variety of means of cooperation, adjustment and revision. These mechanisms should also have completely ceased to work.

Given the presumed dynamism of the EU system, specifically apt to enable a joint response to unforeseen situations and developments like energy, economic or political crises, it seems difficult to conceive what could justify the application of Art. 62 VCLT to the EC/EU Treaty.[31] Schmitz again allowed a right of secession if the membership of the union changes unexpectedly (or if expected changes fail to occur), e.g., if a state with which a Member State has a particularly close relationship secedes, or is refused membership in defiance of prior expectations. But these situations have to be tested under the stringent conditions of Art. 62. The changed circumstances which could be relied on must have been of such gravity that their effect would radically transform the extent of the obligations still to be performed. Moreover, "a fundamental change of circumstances must have been unforeseen; the existence of the circumstances at the time of the Treaty's conclusion must have constituted an essential basis of the consent of the parties to be bound by the Treaty".[32]

As a matter of fact, in a period before the Lisbon Treaty unilateral withdrawal from the EU under normal circumstances, normally functioning institutions and the Treaty mechanisms was not admissible under the law of treaties. The withdrawal by consent of all the parties, e.g. in a form of a revision of treaties, was possible.

3 Voluntary Withdrawal and the special character of the EC/EU Treaties

The doctrine seemed divided on whether traditional international law could be applied to unilateral withdrawal from the EU Treaties. Its application was questioned mostly by submitting an autonomous (federal) character of the EC/

[30] Gabočikovo-Nagymanos Project (Hungary v Slovakia) (Judgement of 25 September 1997 ICJ Rep. 1997, para 103 et seqq.

[31] Hill (1982) p. 353-354, Schmitz (2001), Chap. 2-C.VI.2.c.aa-cc (English summary of Chap. 2 point 30).

[32] Gabočikovo-Nagymanos Project (Hungary v Slovakia) (Judgement of 25 September 1997 ICJ Rep. 1997, para 104.) Lenaerts and Van Nuffel (2005), para 8–012, exclude the possibility to rely on Arts. 60–62 VCLT of the EU Treaties, the only way to withdraw from the EU is to use the procedure under Art. 48 TEU. Bruha and Nowak (2004), p. 10 et seq. exclude Art. 61 and Art. 60. The reliance on Art. 62 is for them difficult to conceive, however, possible as *ultima ratio*; similarly Folz (2001), p. 163 et seq.

EU law (*vocation fédérale*). In fact, since the EU was not a state[33], there was no good reason to deny that international law applied to the EU. International law does not contradict the right of state parties to agree some stricter rules governing the structure established by the Treaty. Even if the EU was perceived as a federal polity, the international law applies to federations as well. International law does not recognise the right of the federated states to secede from the federation, but it also does not prohibit the secession'[34] and it does not prohibit granting a right to secession in the constitution.[35] Thus the main federal argument, that the secession from federation is in principle prohibited, is a political not a legal argument.

Independent, however, of the label given to the EU or the EU Treaties, both those who advocated application of customary international law to the EU and those who prefered to speak about the autonomous or federal character of the EC/EU refered in fact to the intention of the parties and/or the nature of the founding Treaties.

For some authors Member States may not unilaterally withdraw because the objectives of the Treaties presupposed the definitive or irreversible character of the membership in the Communities or the EU[36] or since they were no longer the sole masters of the treaty (sole subjects of the Community).[37] Those concepts were grounded in the well-known ECJ case law on autonomous, definite and constitutional character of the EC/EU law (*Van Gend en Loos*, *Costa v ENEL*, *Simmenthal*, *Internationale Handelgesellschaft*, etc.). In all these cases the Court underlined

---

[33]Engle (2006–2007), p. 49, however, maintained that the EU was a confederated state. He defined such a state as "an international legal person, constituted of states which irrevocably cede some of their sovereign power to the confederation, and which retain their own international legal personality". He further emphasized that the member states to confederacy have a right to secede.

[34]Christakis (2006), p. 2008. See also Christakis (1999), p. 73 et seqq. It could be added that the right to secession under the right to self-determination is accepted by the doctrine and practice of international law in principle only under the condition of the parent-state consent for secession. See Crawforol (1997), p. 2.

[35]The Russian Constitution of 1977 expressly provided for the right of secession in art 72 ("Each Union Republic shall retain the right freely to secede from the USSR."). In practice it appeared illusory. The right to self-determination, including the right to secession, was included in the Constitution of the former Socialist Federal Republic of Yugoslavia of 1974, now e.g. in the constitution of Ethiopia, South Africa. The Canadian constitution is silent on secession of the province. Nonetheless, the Canadian Supreme Court holds that the secession of a province is possible if in a referendum "the clear majority of people" answers "the clear question on secession", and after the negotiations on conditions of secession. The Court assumed that there is an inherent right to secede from the federation based on the democratic nature of Canada. Secession, however, cannot be unilateral and unconditional [regarding Secession of Quebec from Canada (1998) 161 DLR (4th) 385], see discussion in Friel (2004), p. 417 et seq. The United States Supreme Court found secession to be in violation of American federal law (Texas v. White, 74 U. S. 700, 724–26 (1869). On secession right in federal states see Harbo (2008), p. 135 et seq.

[36]Hill (1982) p. 339 et seq., Isaac (1998), p. 21; Simon (2001), para 31, 70.

[37]As Klabbers (2002, p. 95 fn. 62) puts it, the argument is made by Everling (1983), p. 173 et seq.

unlimited duration of the Community, limitation of sovereign rights of the Member States by creating a Community comprising not only Member States but also individuals, special and original nature of the law stemming from the Treaty, which independent of the legislation of the Member States imposes obligations and confers rights on individuals which become part of their legal heritage and cannot be overridden by domestic law.[38]

Referring to this case law, especially on the primacy of EU law, Friel, for example, came to the conclusion that according to the federal character of the EU law, particularly the rule on primacy and express abrogation by the courts of some of the Member States, those states' right to determine their relationship with the EU, including the right to unilateral withdrawal, excluded the right to secession[39]:

> "By its very nature, a State that seeks to secede from the EU would undertake actions which conflict with EU law and since EU law is superior to State law, that State law is overturned. Legally speaking therefore secession is impossible, since the cumulative effect of the lack of an express process of secession, when coupled with the doctrine of supremacy, would negate any State act to withdraw from the EU. The doctrine of supremacy however asks the courts of each Member State for divided loyalties, and in the case of a conflict to see themselves as courts for the EU, in reality a federalization of the national courts. It would seem therefore that a federal jurisdiction has come into being with clear rules on supremacy and which appear on the surface to prevent any departure, or at least unilateral departure, by a Member State from the EU."[40]

On the other hand, some authors argued that the right to withdrawal was implicit since the Treaty on European Union (TEU) guaranteed the respect of state identity. In a case of "fundamental incompatibility between the EU action and the Member State desires, withdrawal constitutes the manifestation of the maintenance of that identity".[41] This position was strengthened by the precedence of the British renegotiations of 1974 and the referendum of 6 June 1975 on British withdrawal from the Communities, which was not opposed as such,[42] and by the Greenland withdrawal.[43] Furthermore, ultimate possibility of withdrawal was anticipated by

[38]The most important passage on primacy of this law is contained in the famous Case 6/64 *Costa v ENEL* (ECJ 15 July 1964) pp. 590: "The transfer by the States from their domestic legal system to the Community legal system of the rights and obligations arising under the Treaty carries with it a permanent limitation of their sovereign rights, against which a subsequent unilateral act incompatible with the concept of the Community cannot prevail."

[39]Friel (2004), pp. 413–414, discuses British cases. For French case law see fn. 34, p. 414.

[40]Friel (2004), pp. 412–413.

[41]Manin (1999), p. 80.

[42]The United Kingdom joined the EEC in January 1973 under the Conservative party government. After the change of the government (Labour's 1974 election manifesto promised a referendum on membership of the EEC) the Treaty of 1972 was renegotiated in 1974 and in 1975 the referendum was organised on withdrawal (the question posed was: "Do you think the UK should stay in the European Community (Common Market)?").

[43]Christakis (2006), p. 2008.

the *Maastricht* judgment of the German Federal Constitutional Court,[44] and recently by the Polish Constitutional Court.[45]

Friel was therefore right in saying that there were good arguments for both contentions:

> "[T]he failure to replicate the limited duration of the ECSC Treaty, in either the EEC or Euratom Treaties could be regarded as a sign that the parties did not intend for withdrawal to be possible (...). As against this, one might argue that sovereign States would not have intended to abandon permanently and irrevocably their right to withdrawal without expressly so doing. This argument seems convincing, particularly with the passage of subsequent Treaties implementing closer and closer integration and centralized control between the Member States as the EEC has evolved into the current EU. Equally this argument can be countered by another: Member States were aware of the ever increasing trend towards closer integration and the changing nature of the European project from simply a common market to a political union. In the light of this, the failure to expressly confer a right of withdrawal demonstrates an intention that there should be no such right."[46]

4 Withdrawal from the EC/EU in the Light of the ECJ Case Law

It could be argued that the ECJ case law excluded unilateral withdrawal of a Member State under the former Treaties. In its case *San Michele* the ECJ noticed that once the instrument of ratification of the Treaty is deposited by the Member State, a new jurisdiction is assumed on a supranational level by the institutions of the Communities. Their jurisdiction is entitled to effect within the domestic law of that Member State. Neither the Member States nor the individuals may question that.[47] More explicitly in the case *Commission v French Republic* the Court

[44]German Federal Constitutional Court, 2 BvR 2134, 2159/92 (12 October 1993) para 112 (in: BVerfGE 89, 155 [190]). However, Bruha and Nowak (2004), pp. 4 et seq., hold that the judgment is not clear on that point.

[45]Polish Constitutional Court K 18 04 (11 May 2005), para 6.4. The Court did not recognise the primacy of the EU law over the Polish Constitution. In a case of irresolvable conflict between their norms withdrawal is viewed as a measure of last resort. Decision on withdrawal has to be taken by the sovereign (the People) or the state organ representing it. See also Lord Denning's view in *Bulmer v Bollinger* case (1974), cit. in House of Commons Research Paper 04/66, 6 September 2004, Treaty Establishing Constitution for Europe, Part I, http://www.parliament.uk/commons/lib/research/rp2004/rp04-066.pdf, Accessed 5 February 2009, p. 18.

[46]Friel (2004), p. 408.

[47]Order of the Court in Case 9–65 *Acciaierie San Michele SpA (in liquidation) v High Authority of the ECSC*, (ECJ 22 June 1965) p. 29 et seq.: "Whereas, however, the Court of Justice, as the institution entrusted with ensuring that in the interpretation and application of the Treaty the law is observed, can only take into consideration the instrument of ratification, which itself was deposited on behalf of Italy on 22 July 1952 and which, together with the other instruments of ratification, brought the treaty into force. Whereas it is clear from the instruments of ratification, whereby the Member States bound themselves in an identical manner, that all States have adhered to the Treaty on the same conditions, definitively and without any reservation other than those set out in the supplementary protocols, and that therefore any claim by a national of a Member State questioning such adherence would be contrary to the system of Community law."

underlined the irreversible character of the consent of the Member States to be bound by the Treaty repeating some statements contained in *Costa v ENEL*:

> "The Member States agreed to establish a Community of *unlimited duration, having permanent institutions* invested with real powers, stemming from *a limitation of authority or transfer of powers from the states to that Community*. Powers thus conferred could not, therefore, be withdrawn from the Community, nor could the objectives with which such powers are concerned be restored to the field of authority of the Member States alone, *except by virtue of an express provision of the Treaty*."[48]

In Opinion 1/91, probably following the judgment of the German Federal Constitutional Court,[49] the ECJ went further clearly emphasising the constitutional character of the Treaties:

> [T]he EEC Treaty albeit concluded in the form of an international agreement, nonetheless constitutes the constitutional charter of a Community based on the rule of law. As the Court of Justice has consistently held, the Community treaties established a new legal order for the benefit of which the States have limited their sovereign rights, in ever wider fields, and the *subjects of which comprise not only Member States but also their nationals*.[50]

In Opinion 1/92 the Court emphasised again that "(t)he powers conferred on the Court by the Treaty may be modified pursuant only to the procedure provided for in Art. 236 of the Treaty".[51]

Due to the specific features of the Community, i.e. the intention of the parties and the nature of the Treaty, the ECJ seemed to excluded unilateral withdrawal from the EC/EU,[52] allowing, however, withdrawal under the amendment procedure, provided for in Art. 48 TEU former Art, 236 EC. That would have obviously meant withdrawal by consent of all the parties to the treaty.

5 Withdrawal Clause in the Treaty Establishing a Constitution for Europe of 2003

The issue of withdrawal from the EU was taken up by the Convention established by the European Council meeting in Laecken, to investigate the future development of the EU.[53] The proposals submitted at the beginning stage of the work of the

---

[48]Case 7/71 *Commission of the European Communities v French Republic. Supply agency* (ECJ 14 December 1971) paras 19–20. Weiler (1985, p. 286) finds the ECJ *dicta* highly suggestive, it "indicates the preference of the Court for interpretation restricting rather than enlarging the options for unilateral Member State action".

[49]In 1967 this Court qualified the Treaty Establishing the European Economic Community (EEC) as a sort of constitution of the Community with a legal order of its own. (German Federal Constitutional Court, 1 BvR 248/63 and 216/6722, (18 October 1967), para 13 (in: BVerfG 22, 293 [296])).

[50]Opinion 1/91 (ECJ 14 December 1991), para 21.

[51]Opinion 1/92 (ECJ 10 April 1992), para 32.

[52]Weiler (2005), p. 18, noted that unilateral withdrawal from the EU would be illegal.

[53]On earlier attempts to include the right to withdraw see Harbo (2008), p. 140 et seq.

Convention envisaged the right to withdrawal and they seem to dominate the rationale of the Praesidium. Lamassoure,[54] for example, while presenting several options was strongly advocating for an improved community model for the EU in which constituent authority resides with the Member States and the right to withdrawal is enshrined in the constitution. However, "it is subject to strict and deterrent conditions, but every State is acknowledged to hold that right at all times".[55]

On the contrary, Professor Dashwood's proposal (submitted by UK) provided for an absolute right of withdrawal on every state following notification to the Council. Withdrawal would be exclusively a matter for the Member State, a right stemming from its sovereignty (retained sovereign right of the Member States). It would require institutional modifications of the Treaty by the Member States acting in unanimity after consulting the European Parliament.[56]

Under the draft exit clause proposed by Badinter,[57] a Member State could voluntarily withdraw. The internal decision was to be taken according to the procedure on the revision of constitutional provisions. The Member State had to notify its decision to the European Council. It is for the European Council to decide on the effective date of withdrawal. Before, the agreement had to be reached between the Union (negotiated by the Council) and the Member State on all the modalities of the exercise of the right of withdrawal and its consequences for the

[54]CONV 235/02, *The European Union: Four Possible Models*, p 6. In the federal model he excluded withdrawal: "once a State has become a member, it will be a member for ever". He then rejected the federal model for the EU as being unlikely to be acceptable to the people of Europe. The confederal model was rejected as not meeting the needs of today's Europe. It would be a retrograde step, signifying reduction in the level of integration, aggravating current difficulties of the Union, and producing new ones for an enlarged Union.

[55]CONV 235/02, *The European Union: Four Possible Models*, p 6. In the federal model he excluded withdrawal: "once a State has become a member, it will be a member for ever". He then rejected the federal model for the EU as being unlikely to be acceptable to the people of Europe. The confederal model was rejected as not meeting the needs of today's Europe. It would be a retrograde step, signifying reduction in the level of integration, aggravating current difficulties of the Union, and producing new ones for an enlarged Union, p 12.

[56]Submission by Peter Hain (UK) of draft Dashwood treaty on Union by Professor Alan Dashwood (15 October 2002), at http://register.consilium.eu.int/pdf/en/02/cv00/00345en2.pdf, Accessed 5 February 2009, p. 49.

[57]CONV 317/02 (30 September 2002), *A European Constitution* Contribution from Robert Badinter, alternate member of the Convention. Article 80: "Any Member State may denounce this Treaty and give notice of its decision to withdraw from the European Union. The decision of the Member State shall be made within that State in accordance with the procedure required for amendment of constitutional provisions of the highest level. The withdrawal of the State shall not take effect until after the end of a time-period to be decided by the European Council. During this period, the Union and the withdrawing State shall negotiate an agreement defining the withdrawal procedure and its possible consequences for the interests of the Union. The withdrawing State shall be responsible for any loss that may be suffered by the Union due to its withdrawal. In the absence of any agreement between the withdrawing State and the Council of Ministers, the Court of Justice shall be seized of the dispute. It shall also hear any actions relating to the interpretation and execution of withdrawal agreements."

Union and for the Member State, or in a case of the dispute between the Council and the Member State, the case would go to the ECJ. The Court would adjudicate as well on the interpretation and application of the agreement. The compensation would have to be paid for any loss arising to the EU.

On the basis of those proposals, the regulation providing for withdrawal from the EU was inserted into first Praesidium's drafts and the Constitutional Treaty (Art. 46, later Art. 57, 59, and finally Art. I-60 TCE). It confirmed the right to withdraw and established the procedure to be followed if a Member State were to decide to withdraw. The explanatory note attached to the draft of Art. 46 clarified that the provision draws on the procedure in the VCLT.[58] Later on the Praesidium explained:

> The Praesidium considers that the Constitution must contain a provision on voluntary withdrawal from the Union. Although many consider that it is possible to withdraw even in the absence of a specific provision to that effect, the Praesidium feels that inserting a specific provision in the Constitution on voluntary withdrawal from the Union clarifies the situation and allows the introduction of a procedure for negotiating and concluding an agreement between the Union and the Member State concerned setting the arrangements for withdrawal and the framework for future relations. Moreover, the existence of a provision to that effect is an important political signal to anyone inclined to argue that the Union is a rigid entity which it is impossible to leave.[59]

The same reasoning was applied to explain that withdrawal would not necessarily require the conclusion of an agreement between the withdrawing Member State and the EU:

> The Praesidium considers that, since many hold that the right of withdrawal exists even in the absence of an explicit provision to that effect, withdrawal of a Member State from the Union cannot be made conditional upon the conclusion of a withdrawal agreement. Hence the provision that withdrawal will take effect in any event two years after notification. However, in order to encourage a withdrawal agreement between the Union and the State which is withdrawing, Article I-57 [now I-60] provides for the possibility of extending this period by common accord between the European Council and the Member State concerned.[60]

At the outset the provision, as it was presented in the Convention, seems to be based on the wrong assumption that the right to voluntary withdrawal exists independently of the Treaties. Such an assumption does not have a good basis either in the law of the treaties or in EU law.[61] However, Member States may amend the Treaties and insert a respective provision.

---

[58] CONV 648/03, Brussels, 2 April 2003 (03.04).

[59] CONV 724/03 ANNEX 2, p. 134.

[60] CONV 724/03 Annex 2, Draft Constitution, Volume I – Revised text of Part One, p. 135.

[61] See Bruha and Nowak (2004), p. 8.

6 Article 50 TEU Under the Treaty of Lisbon

The Treaty of Lisbon is the second of the EU Treaties offering a clear exit clause – Art. 50 TEU. The clause was transferred from the Constitutional Treaty without any substantial change,[62] and only necessary technical adjustments to the provisions of the Lisbon Treaty were made, and as Art. I-60 TCE did, it "ends the mystery of how to withdraw from the EU".[63] The decision to keep the clause was contained in the IGC Mandate of December 2007. The provision was not further discussed. Discussions on the terms of Art. 50 TEU took place much earlier and they refer to Art. I-60 TCE or its predecessors.[64]

6.1 The Right to Withdrawal

Article 50 TEU makes clear that the Member States retain the right to leave the EU. In the Treaty establishing a Constitution for Europe (TCE) the provision for withdrawal was preceded by the heading "Voluntary Withdrawal". The title of the provision, additionally, made clear that withdrawal would be "voluntary" (i.e. it is not dependent on the consent of the other Contracting Parties). There are no heads to the Articles in the Lisbon Treaty; this does not change the nature of withdrawal in Art. 50. Withdrawal under Art. 50 is a purely voluntary act (does not depend on the consent of the Member States). Pursuant to Art. 50.3, the Treaties shall cease to apply to the state in question from the date of entry into force of the withdrawal agreement, which does not require unanimity in the Council or ratification by other Member States or, failing that, two years after the notification referred to in para 2, unless the European Council, in agreement with the Member State concerned, unanimously decides to extend this period.

The inclusion of the right to withdraw in the TCE was controversial.[65] The proposal was criticised on several grounds. For some members of the Convention the clause was not compatible with the nature of the Union, with the mutual obligations of solidarity and with the provisions enshrining the "irreversibility" and "irrevocability" of the third stage of Economic and Monetary Union.[66] However, no member of the Convention expressly held that the right of the Member State to withdraw does not exist.[67] Even the representatives of the Dutch

---

[62]See Decision of the Brussels European Council 21/22 JUNE 2007, Brussels, 23 June 2007, 11177/07 CONCL 2, IGC Mandate, point 16.

[63]Dougan (2003), p. 8.

[64]For criticism see eg. Snavely 2004–2005, p. 228–230, Athanassiou 2009, p. 23 et seq., Hofmeister 2010, p. 592 et seq.

[65]See Spinant (2003).

[66]Amendment by Brook, Santer, Styliandis, Szajer et al.

[67]See amendment by Joschka Fischer, who explained that at the moment there is no need for a withdrawal clause.

government strongly advocating for deletion of the provision, while stressing that "facilitating" the possibility to withdraw from the Union is contrary to the idea of European integration as set out in the preamble of the TEU – 'Resolved to continue the process of creating an ever closer union among the peoples of Europe' – seemed to anticipate such a right.[68] Similarly, German representatives emphasised that the explicit inclusion of a withdrawal clause is incompatible with a European Constitution and with the integration objective shared by all Member States of 'creating an ever closer union among the peoples of Europe". It would, moreover, contradict the idea of a Union which is based on the solidarity of citizens and states if individual Member States could decide to withdraw easily and risk potential abuse by the opponents of the EU in the Member States. However, it was admitted that according to existing law no state can be forced to remain in the Union in any case.[69] European People's Party Convention Group preferred to delete an explicit exit clause since it "could allow Member States to blackmail the Union, paralyse its decision-making processes and even endanger the stability of the Union. It would also give a wrong political signal with regard to the required mutual solidarity in the Union."[70] If the provision stays, it is necessary to create a political balance: a right of withdrawal would have to be complemented by a right of the Union to expel a Member State. "A Union which every Member is free to leave must also be free to get rid of Members which violate persistently its values or which paralyse its functioning. Such a parallel right of the Union to expel Members would also reduce the risk of political blackmailing through the means of exit threats".[71]

The other group wanted to delete the clause just because the right of a Member State to withdraw exists.[72] It was argued that the VCLT already provides a sufficient basis for termination of membership and as the Constitutional Treaty (by analogy the Lisbon Treaty) is regarded an international agreement, the Convention applies and the provision is not necessary.[73] The nature of the Union is not compatible with such an exit clause. "Besides, being the Union the result of the will of sovereign States, no one questions their right to withdraw from the Union".[74]

On the other hand, some authors thought that since the Member States' right to withdraw follows from the basic principles of international law this should therefore be referred to in the Article itself.[75]

The majority of the members of the Convention preferred to insert the right to withdraw; however, some of them thought that it should not be unilateral

[68] Amendment by de Vries and de Bruijn.

[69] Amendment by Professor Jürgen Meyer.

[70] Amendment on behalf of the EPP Convention Group by Brok, Szajer et al.

[71] Amendment on behalf of the EPP Convention Group by Brok, Szajer et al.

[72] See amendments Santer, Fayot and Schmit.

[73] See amendments by Farnleitner, Ernani Lopes and Manuel Antunes.

[74] See amendment by Ernani Lopes and Manuel Antunes.

[75] Amendment by Kimmo Kiljunen and Matti Vanhanen; similarly Tiilikainen, Peltomäki and Korhonen.

(voluntary; the withdrawal agreement is necessary)[76] and should apply in absolutely exceptional cases, e.g. fundamental change of the composition or the nature of the Union[77] or in a case of Member State's failure to ratify the amending treaty.[78] One speaker was of the opinion that, since the right of secession from the Union has a wide range of direct consequences to the internal market and the Member States it should be described in detail and should contain an exhaustive list of the conditions upon which a certain country could withdraw from the Union.[79] However, no such list was presented.

Despite the concerns expressed earlier, the right to withdraw in Art. 50 TEU is voluntary and unilateral. Probably because it seemed obvious that, in fact, taking into account all the costs of the withdrawal, especially economic and political ones, it would be applied, if at all, only in very exceptional cases (as *ultima ratio*). Partial withdrawal, however not explicitly prohibited, is not allowed.[80] However, the provision leaves open the form of the future relations between the withdrawing state and the Union. It also does not address the issue of liability for damages in case of the withdrawal without the consent of the other parties.

6.2 *Procedure of Withdrawal*

Article 50.1 TEU provides for the adoption of the decision to withdraw in accordance with constitutional requirements of the Member State. The same provision was contained in draft Art. 46, draft I-Art. 59 and Art. I-60 TCE. Its purpose seems to be to assure that the state's decision is duly taken and in accordance with the state constitution, to minimise possible abuse of the clause for political reasons.[81]

[76]For example, amendment by French government (de Villepin); amendment by Tiilikainen, Peltomäki and Korhonen., amendment by Lamassoure. See also Summary Report of the Plenary Session – Brussels, 24 and 25 April 2003, CONV 696/03, p. 10.

[77]Amendment by Lamassoure.

[78]See amendment by de Villepin. Similarly amendment by de Gucht, di Rupo et al.

[79]Amendment by Hübner.

[80]In the opinion of the EPP Group "a right of Member States to 'pick and choose' rights and duties stemming from Union Membership (single market yes, rest no)" should be explicitly excluded (see respective amendment). A kind of partial withdrawal was proposed in the Convention by Lang and Lord Maclennan. In their opinion a Member State should be permitted to choose "a looser partnership in preference to full membership. Such a category of privileged partnership would allow for the nexus of (mostly economic) relationships that had built up with the Union during the period of membership to be conserved in a functional form. The category would also be more useful for the current members of the European Economic Area."

[81]There was also a proposal in the Convention to make the decision dependent on the referendum (amendment by Migaš). On the other hand, there were proposals to delete it. For Paciotti the provision was superfluous and harmful. It would not be any problem for the Union to evaluate whether the government of the Member State respected its own constitution (see respective amendment).

The requirement specified above was criticised by Friel, for example. Since a withdrawal clause (he referred to draft Art. 59) would be justiciable by the ECJ, the Court would become the final arbiter of a significant issue of constitutional law, which is something unprecedented.[82] If the dispute arose as to the validity of the national decision, its constitutionality would ultimately fall to the ECJ. Freil's fears seem, however, unsupported by the Treaty provisions and the ECJ case law. The ECJ has no competence under the Lisbon Treaty to adjudicate upon validity of the internal law procedures in similar situations, and the Court was consequently rejecting its competence in similar cases.[83] The provision is not unprecedented, as it seems to play a similar role to the reference to "respective constitutional requirements" in the decision-making process under, for example, Art. 22, 190, 229a, 269 EC or Art. 17, 24, 34, 42 TEU-Nice.

Pursuant to Art. 50.2 TEU, a Member State which decides to withdraw shall notify the European Council of its intention. In an earlier draft of the Constitutional Treaty (draft Art. 46) the organ first addressed by the Member State was the Council. The change seems to be the consequence of the change of the status of the European Council under the Treaty decided probably at a later stage in the Convention. The European Council has to provide guidelines in which light the Union[84] shall negotiate and conclude an agreement with the withdrawing state.

The withdrawal will certainly cause not only institutional changes for the EU. There could also be the problem of damages noticed earlier by Badinter or continued fulfilment of some earlier obligations for a certain period. In the amendment submitted to the Convention it was suggested that the provision should explicitly state that full account shall be taken of the possible consequences of such a withdrawal on the rights and obligations of natural and legal persons.[85] All these issues have to be necessarily addressed by such an agreement. Furthermore, the withdrawal at a certain level of economic integration of the Member States may require maintenance of specific relations between the withdrawing state and the EU. That is why Art. 50 requires that the agreement set out the arrangements for the withdrawal, taking account of the framework for the state's future relationship with the Union.

The agreement shall be negotiated in accordance with the procedure provided for in Art. 218.3 TFEU on the conclusion of international agreements by the EU. Under this provision, the Commission has to submit the recommendations to the Council. The Council shall then authorise the opening of negotiations, adopt

---

[82] Friel (2004), p. 425.

[83] See e.g. Order of the Court in Case 9–65 *Acciaierie San Michele SpA (in liquidation) v High Authority of the ECSC* (ECJ 22 June 1965), p. 29 et seq.

[84] See amendment by Lekberg and Lennmarker. They were of the opinion that the agreement should be concluded by Member States on the grounds that the membership or non-membership of the Union is not conferred competence, and thus is an issue for an IGC and not for the Council as a Union body.

[85] Amendment by Lekberg and Lennmarker; similarly, by Tiilikainen, Peltomäki and Korhonen.

negotiating directives and nominate the head of the Union's negotiating team. Article 50 is silent on signing of the agreement (Art. 218.3 does not apply to signing). However, Art. 218.5 TFEU should be applied; the Council authorises then the signing of the agreement. In the light of Art. 218 TFEU the term "conclude" in Art. 50.2 TEU refers to the consent to be bound by the treaty. The Council makes its respective decision acting by a qualified majority, after obtaining the consent of the European Parliament. Thus the procedure laid down in Art. 50 involves all decision-making institutions, including a new one under the Lisbon Treaty, the European Council.

The qualified majority in the Council is defined in accordance with Art. 238.3 lit. b TFEU. The consent of the European Parliament is given by a majority of the votes cast (Art. 231 TFEU). At the early stages of 2003, the Praesidium offered "to adopt the voting rule corresponding to the substantive content of the agreement". The proposal was rejected because of its unclear meaning and its implications.[86] It was also suggested that a kind of *actus contrarius* should be applied. If for admission to the EU unanimity in the Council is required, it should be required also for withdrawal.[87] The present formula avoids all the complications that may arise with unanimity rule and makes the agreement easier.

According to Art. 50.4 TEU, the member of the European Council or of the Council representing the withdrawing Member State shall not participate in the discussions of the European Council or the Council or in decisions concerning it. The provision is restricted to discussions and decisions referred to in Art. 50.2 and Art. 50.3 TEU. Thus the Member State will not take part in any discussions or decisions concerning or connected with its withdrawal. The provision implies that in the period between the notification of the will of withdrawal and the entry into force of the withdrawal agreement/ or in a two-year period envisaged in para 3, the Member State still seats and decides in the European Council and in the Council on matters not connected with its withdrawal (i.e. matters not specified in Art. 50.2 and Art. 50.3 TEU).[88]

---

[86]CONV 648/03, 2 April 2003.

[87]Amendment by Demiral; see also amendments by Tiilikainen, Peltomäki and Korhonen, by Kiljunen and Vanhanen, and by Roche. The latter argued that since unanimity is required to conclude Association Agreements under Art. 310 EC, it is therefore the appropriate procedure here. Bonde, Heathcoat-Amory, Seppänen & Zahradil proposed 2/3 majority instead of the present qualified majority.

[88]The present reaction seems to be close to the clarifications proposed in the Convention that a Member State should rather take part in the discussions or decisions concerning it (amendment by Bonde, Heathcoat-Amory, Seppänen and Zahradil) and not participate in the Council's discussions or decisions concerning "these negotiations", and, further, "It may continue to benefit from its rights and privileges under this Treaty in all other matters". The authors of the latter amendment explained that the purpose is to avoid the interpretation that the withdrawing state "no longer has *any* input into the Council, including discussing unrelated issues" (amendment by David Heathcoat-Amory and Bonde).

There is no equivalent provision on participation in the other institutions, e.g. in the debate of the European Parliament. This omission was criticised on the grounds that the representatives of the withdrawing Member State may naturally feel loyal to the national interests instead of the general Union interest they were originally elected to represent. It would be therefore preferable if they were expressly excluded from any role in that area.[89] On the other hand, their participation in the debate might be useful. There is no reason why their voice could not be heard as well.

The Treaties shall cease to apply to the state in question from the date of entry into force of the withdrawal agreement (Art. 50.3 TEU). The agreement is highly desirable; however, the idea enshrined in Art. 50.3 TEU is that it should not constitute a condition for withdrawal so as not to void the concept of voluntary withdrawal of its substance. Thus, failing the agreement, the Treaties shall cease to apply to the state in question, two years after the notification made to the European Council.[90] In order to encourage a withdrawal agreement between the EU and the state which is withdrawing, Art. 50 TEU envisaged the possibility of extending this period by the unanimous decision of the European Council,[91] in agreement with the Member State concerned. It meets the concerns that the period of two years may appear too short to adequately deal with all complicated issues involved with the withdrawal.[92]

The provision is silent on legal consequences of withdrawal where there is no agreement between the Union and the withdrawing state. This kind of withdrawal will necessitate the adjustments and the amendments of the Treaties equally as the withdrawal under the agreement. For this purpose a special, expedited procedure was introduced; thus the revision procedures provided for in Art. 48 TEU apply. The procedures (ordinary or simplified) require the ratification by all other Member States.

Article 50 TEU foresees expressly the possibility to rejoin the Union, but there is no automatic right to rejoin. A state having once withdrawn must apply to rejoin. Its application is subject to the procedure laid down in Art. 49 TEU. Article 50 TEU does not provide for any waiting period as it was proposed earlier (five years) in order to avoid the use of the withdrawal right for political and short-term purposes.[93]

---

[89]See Dougan (2003), p. 8.

[90]On the one hand, a two-year period seems to be reasonable time for negotiating the agreement or terminating the relations and preparing necessary amendments to the Treaties. On the other hand, it may seem too long if withdrawal is to be applied in exceptional cases. The delayed withdrawal was criticised for various reasons, e.g. by Freil (2004), p. 427 et seq., as threatening both the withdrawing state and the stability of the EU. The Dashwood proposal was, in his opinion, logically consistent. Withdrawal should happen instantly without forced negotiation as to its terms. The present system favours larger States and provides extra leverage for them.

[91]Pursuant to Art. 50.4, the member of the European Council representing the withdrawing Member State shall not participate in the discussions of the European Council or Council or in decisions concerning it.

[92]For discussion see e.g. Herbst (2005), p. 1757 et seq.

[93]Amendment by Vastagh, similarly Lamassoure.

Article 50 TEU is silent on whether it is possible to withdraw the notification of withdrawal within a two-year period provided for in para 3.[94] There would be no problem if all the Member States consented. It seems, however, that Art. 50 TEU anticipates that such a withdrawal does not require the consent of the other parties, especially since there are no new arrangements necessary. The representatives of that Member State still seat in all the institutions of the EU and work normally, except for the Council's and the European Council's representatives who do not participate in the discussions and decisions surrounding the withdrawal.

7 Conclusions

The contention that a sovereign party may unilaterally withdraw from a treaty just because of its sovereignty is false (without any legal basis and contrary to *pacta sunt servanda* principle). Obviously, such a unilateral right and the respective procedure may be laid down in a treaty. The breach of the treaty procedure entails then international state responsibility (either based on the treaty system or general international law).

Opinions on the effects of inclusion of the withdrawal clause in the Lisbon Treaty (previously Constitutional Treaty) vary and depend upon the author's position on the character of the European integration (international law-based structure or autonomous one) and the applicable law. From a federal perspective it could be perceived as a step backwards perpetuating the intergovernmental nature of the EU, contrary to the unlimited duration clause in the same Treaty (Art. 53 TEU) or even viewed as a "bold affirmation of national sovereignty".[95] It could be regarded as well as "an example of how the EU has become an autonomous entity different from classic international organisations, not depending on international law"[96] and a proof that the EU will not become a superstate.

If the Lisbon Treaty confirms only that the TEU and the Treaty on the Functioning of the European Union (TFEU) are no more than treaties, and the rules laid down in the Vienna Convention apply, Art. 50 TEU could be viewed as having more political than legal significance.[97] In our opinion, the principles of the law treaties did not allow the unilateral withdrawal from the EU. The ECJ allowed withdrawal only by the amendment of the Treaties. Even if the grounds under Arts. 60, 61 or 62 VCLT could have been invoked, it would have been done only in extreme circumstances. In that light, Art. 50 TEU marks a significant departure

[94]Criticised e.g. by Friel (2004), p. 426.

[95]Sieberson (2007), p. 249, see also pp. 122–123; Harbo (2008), p. 143 et seq.

[96]Kielhorn (2000), pp. 48–49, who holds that public international law allows withdrawal from a treaty only by consent of all the contracting parties. Contrary to that procedure, the withdrawal would be concluded by an agreement by the Council.

[97]House of Commons S 77 Research Paper 04/66.

from the former Treaties. The right to unilateral withdrawal under Art. 50 is dependent only on procedural but not on substantive conditions.

Such an easy access to withdrawal procedures may have negative consequences. The right may be easily invoked for temporary political reasons and used as a tool of national policy to blackmail, at least for two years, the other partners to enforce the interests at stake. The Member State may withdraw at any time the notification of its withdrawal. On the other hand, Art. 50 TEU should be interpreted in the light of the principle of loyalty and Art. 53 TEU (former Art. 51) preserved by the Lisbon Treaty, confirming that the Treaty is concluded for "an unlimited period". That raises again the issue of necessary substantive requirements for unilateral withdrawal. The open question is who and if the ECJ how the ECJ will adjudicate on those issues.

Inclusion by the Lisbon Treaty of Art. 50 TEU may produce positive effects as well. Bast argues, for example, that paradoxically, it may increase the unity of the Union. He refers to the judgment of the Spanish Constitutional Court in which the Court approved the unconditional primacy of the Union law, particularly in view of the ultimate possibility of withdrawal.[98]

Finally, Art. 50 could be perceived as the provision harmonising the two types of approaches to the EU, international and federal.[99] Nevertheless, it perpetuates the hybrid character of the EU.

References

Amerasinghe CF (1996) Principles of the institutional law of international organizations, Cambridge University Press, Cambridge

Athanassiou P (2009) Withdrawal and Expulsion from the EU and EMU, European Central Bank Legal Working Papers, 10

Bast J (2005) The constitutional treaty as a reflexive constitution. German Law J 6(11)

Bruha T, Nowak C (2004) Recht auf Austritt aus der Europäischen Union? Archiv des Völkerrechts 42(1):1–25

[98]Declaración del Pleno del Tribunal Constitucional, DTC 1/2004 (13 December 2004), http://www.tribunalconstitucional.es/JC.htm. Accessed 5 February 2009; English translation in *Common Market Law Reports* (2005) 1, p. 39; see, in particular, paras 47 and 58; Bast (2005), p. 1436. It could be added that the Czech Constitutional Court used inter alia the argument based on Art. 50 to find that the Lisbon Treaty is not inconsistent with the Constitution: "However, it is important to point to the ability of a member state to withdraw from the European Union by the process set forth in Art. 50 of the Treaty on EU; the explicit articulation of this possibility in the Treaty of Lisbon indisputably confirms the principle that 'States are the Masters of the Treaty' and the continuing sovereignty of member states" Czech Constitutional Court Pl.US. 19/08 (26 November 2008) para 106.

[99]Herbst (2005, p. 1759) argues that its best expression is that the power to conclude the withdrawal agreement is vested in the Council, and not in the Member States. By exercising this power the Council "acts as a treasure and custodian of the 'legal heritage of rights' of the individuals emphasized by the ECJ in its well-established jurisprudence". It is for him the key element to understand the withdrawal provision.

Crawforol J (1997) State practice and International Law in Relation to unilateral secession, Report to government of Canada concerning unilateral secession by Quebec, http://Canada2.justice.gc.ca/en/news/nr/1997/factum/craw_pt4.html, Accessed 20 May 2011
Christakis T (1999) Le droit à l'autodétermination en dehors des situations de décolonisation, Bruylant, Bruxelles
Christakis T (2006) Article 56. In: Corten O, Klein P (eds) Les conventions de Vienne sur les droits des traités. Commentaire article par article, vol III.
Dock MC (1994) Les retraits des États members des organisations internationales de la famille des Nations Unies. Annuaire Français de Droit International XL:106–155
Dougan M (2003) The convention's draft constitutional treaty: a 'tidying-up exercise' that need some tidying-up of its own, Online Paper 27/03 The Federal Trust for Education and Research, pp 1–18
Engle E (2006-2007) Theseus's Ship of State: Confederated Europa Between the Scylla of Mere Alliance and the Charybdis of Unitary Federalism, *Florida Coastal Law Review*, 8
Everling U (1983) Sind die Mitgliedstaaten der Europäischen Gemeinschaft noch Herren der Verträge? Zum Verhältins von Europäischem Gemeinschaftsrecht und Völkerrecht. In: Bernhardt R et al (eds) Völkerrecht als Rechtsordnung, internationale Gerichtsbarkeit, Menschenrechte: Festschrift für Hermann Mosler, Springer, Berlin
Friel RJ (2004). Providing a Constitutional Framework for Withdrawal from the EU: Article 59 of the Draft European Constitution. ICLQ 53: 407–428
Folz HP (2001) Austritt und Ausschlus aus der Europäischen Union, Schriften des Österreichen Völkerrechtstages, In: Ginter K, Benedek W, Isak H, Kicher R (eds) Völker- und Europarecht. 25 Österreiches Völkerrechtstag
Goodrich LM, Hambro E, Simons AP (1969) The charter of the United Nations, Columbia. Univ. Press, New York
Harbo F (2008) Secession right – an anti-federal principle? Comparative study of federal states and the EU. J Polit Law 1(3)
Harnhoff F (1983) Greenland's withdrawal from the European Communities. CMLR 20:13–33
Herbst J (2005) Observations on the right to withdraw from the European Union: who are the "Masters of the Treaties? German Law J 6(11)
Hill JA (1982) The European Economic Community: The Right of Member State Withdrawal, *Georgia Journal of International and Comparative Law (GA. J. Int'l & Comp. L.)* 12
Hofmeister, H. (2010). 'Should I Stay or Should I Go?' – A Critical Analisis of the Right to Withdraw from the EU, *European Law Journal*, 16 (5)
Isaac G (1998) Droit communautaire general, 6th edn. Colin, Paris
Kelsen H (1952) Principles of international law, Rinehart & Company, Inc., New York
Kielhorn M (2000) The constitution for Europe, the Point of no return?, LIT, Münster
Klabbers J (2002) An introduction to international institutional law, Cambridge University Press, Cambridge
Krämer HR (1983) Greenland's European Community (EC-) referendum, background and consequences. German Yearb Int Law 25:273–289
Lenaerts K, Van Nuffel P (2005) Constitutional law of the European Union, Sweet & Maxwell Ltd., London
Manin P (1999) Les Communauté européenne, 5th edn., Pédone, Paris
Oppenheim L (1948) International law, 7th edn., Longmans, Green & Co., London
Reuter P (1990) Introduction to the law of treaties, Pinter Publ., London
Schermers HG, Blokker NM (2003) International institutional law, 4th edn., Martinus Nijhoff Publishers, Leiden
Schmitz T (2001) Integration in der Supranationalen Union. Das europäische Organisationsmodell einer prozeßhaften geo-regionalen Integration und seine rechtlichen und staatstheoretischen Implikationen
Sieberson S (2007) Dividing lines between the European Union and its member states, Asser Press, The Hague

Simon D (2001) Le système juridique communautaire, Presses universitaires de France, Paris
Singh N (1958) Termination of membership of international organisations
Snavely AC (2004–2005) Should We Leave the Backdoor Open? Does an Agreement Uniting States Need a Withdrawal Provision: The European Union Draft Constitution, *UMKC Law Review*, 73
Spinant D (2003) Giscard forum set to unveil controversial EU 'exit clause', European Voice, 3–9 April. http://www.europeanvoice.com/article/imported/giscard-forum-set-to-unveil-controversial-eu-%E2%80%98exit-clause-/47086.aspx. Accessed 5 Feb 2009
Villiger M (2009) Commentary on the 1969 vienna Convention on the Law of Treaties
Waldock H (1966) Yearbook of the international law commission, II
Weiler JHH (1985) Alternatives to withdrawal from an international organization: the case of the European Community. Israel Law Rev 20
Weiler JHH (2005) On the power of the word: Europe's constitutional iconography. In: Curtin D, Kellermann AE, Blockmans S (eds) The EU constitution: the best way forward?, Asser Press, The Hague
Weiss F (1985) Greenland's withdrawal from the European communities. ELRev 10

Part II
The Economic and Monetary Constitution of the Union

The Economic Constitution of the European Union

Hermann-Josef Blanke

1 The Internal Market as a Source of Europe's Economic Prosperity

An aphorism that is attributed to *Jacques Delors* goes: "Nobody falls in love with a single market." This, as well as *Lothar Späth*'s[1] observation on the subordination of the internal market within the primary interest in unifying Europeans by merging "cultural Europe" with "a free democratic system", stems from a much-quoted saying by *Jean Monnet*.[2] All these evaluations are taken into account by critics who complain that "an incomprehensible 'economism' is taking over the discussions, as if the 'business location Germany' would be all, as if Europe would just be the 'Euro'".[3] From an opposite point of view and with a bias towards the economic interest in integration, *Edgar Morin* pointed out that the European consciousness was "limited to an economic core".[4] At least those critics who have identified this economism of the

---

Translated by Robert Böttner, assistant at the Chair for Public Law, International Public Law and European Integration at the University of Erfurt.

[1]L. Späth, Markt der Menschlichkeit, speech given at the award ceremony for the Zukunftspreis *der Christlich-Demokratischen Arbeitnehmerschaft Deutschlands (CDA)* on 9 June 2001: "When I talk about Europe, I do not love the internal market. Who would love an internal market? I want to know if we can manage to unite the Europeans and make sure that this cultural Europe merges into a free democratic system" (our translation).

[2]"If I had to begin the project of European integration once more, I would start with culture, not with economy".

[3]Cf. Häberle (2008), p. 250 et seq. (our translation).

[4]Morin (1991) (our translation).

H.-J. Blanke (✉)
Chair for Public Law and International Public Law, University of Erfurt, Postfach 90 02 21, 99105 Erfurt, Germany
e-mail: LS_Staatsrecht@uni-erfurt.de

H.-J. Blanke and S. Mangiameli (eds.), *The European Union after Lisbon*,
DOI 10.1007/978-3-642-19507-5_15,

European integration process as its main problem[5] have to admit that "growing wealth has caused many positive developments for European unification".[6]

The European internal market is of essential significance for wealth and economic success in the Member States of the Union. It has contributed to a Europe-wide increase in wealth and number of jobs and thus promoted social progress in Europe. The latest evidence is the development in the new Member States from Central and Eastern Europe, where the increase in per capita income within the past decade has caused a clear convergence towards the economic and social status of the older Member States.[7] At the same time the Member States of the Union provide the markets that up to this day absorb most German exports. It was only in the course of globalisation that this began to shift.

The European internal market is the core project of European integration. Since 2007 it comprises nearly 500 million people and is thus the largest marketplace in the world. With a gross domestic product (GDP) of 11.81 trillion euro, which is slightly larger than that of the USA (11.37 trillion euro), the Union is still far ahead – at least in the medium term – of China (7.00 trillion euro), Japan (3.32 trillion euro) and India (2.81 trillion euro).[8] According to estimates of the European Commission, since 1993 the internal market has created about 2.75 million new jobs within the EU, causing an increase in the European GDP of 2.15% and a growth of wealth of more than 900 billion euro.[9] A significant contribution was made by the internal market for goods, which makes up 75% of intra-EU trade.[10]

2 The Ordoliberal Character of the Internal Market in Its Development

2.1 The Fundamental Decisions of the European Economic Community (EEC) Treaty

The fundamental decisions of economic policy that have been laid down in the supranational constitution[11] by the Treaties of Rome of 1957 – namely the opening

[5]Cf. Siedentop (2002); Schachtschneider (2007), p. 59 et seq.

[6]Cf. Häberle (2008), p. 536, who underlines Europe's "depth of cultural history" as one of the "last or next-to-last resources" (our translation).

[7]Cf. Bundesverband Deutscher Arbeitgeber, Binnenmarkt als Motor für Wohlstand und sozialen Fortschritt fördern – Protektionismus verhindern, February 2010, http://www.arbeitgeber.de/www/arbeitgeber.nsf/res/2PPLaval.pdf/$file/2PPLaval.pdf

[8]IMF and Eurostat, data as of 2009.

[9]Commission of the European Union, *The Internal Market – Ten Years without Frontiers*, SEC (2002) 1417; Commission of the European Union, *A Single Market for Citizens*, COM(2007) 60 final, as well as European Economy Economic Papers, No. 271, January 2007, p. 8.

[10]Commission of the European Union, *The Internal Market – Ten Years without Frontiers*, SEC (2002) 1417.

[11]Cf. for the characterisation of the Treaties as the "the constitutional charter of a Community based on the rule of law" Opinion 1/91 (ECJ 14 December 1991).

up of the national economies by means of the free market and the principle of non-discrimination as well as the increase in competition within a more open market, which is protected from distortion by rules of competition – can be interpreted as a decision to establish an economic constitution that is based on ordoliberal ideas on the general conditions of a free market economy. Its main representatives – *Walter Hallstein*,[12] *Franz Böhm*,[13] *Alfred Müller-Armack*[14] and *Walter Eucken*[15] – fought successfully for Europe at an early stage and enforced the theory of ordoliberalism. With this conception one could plausibly reason the principle construed in the rulings of the European Court of Justice (ECJ) which held that the "Community is a new legal order of international law [. . .] the subjects of which comprise not only Member States but also their nationals"[16] and which is an "independent source of law [that] because of its special and original nature [cannot] be overridden by domestic legal provisions".[17] The Court linked this to an economic policy content which at the same time limits it. With this interpretation of the economic provisions of the Treaties as an order based on law and dedicated to ensuring economic freedom the Community gained an individual legitimacy independent of the institutions of the democratic constitutional founding States, from which, however, arose restrictions for its organisation as well.[18]

The economic and legal concept of ordoliberalism had been extended, refined, and modified.[19] Its constitutional core, however, remained unchanged: The validity of the supranational economic legal provisions did not need any legitimation by constitutional institutions and political processes – and thus had to limit its control to the (competitive) organisation of the economy.[20]

2.2 The Planning Strategy of the Community Constitution

H. P. Ipsen underlined – with an understanding of the Communities as "special-purpose associations [*Zweckverbände*] for functional integration" – the "planning strategy" (*Planungscharakter*) of the Community, which is the result of the "dynamics of integration". Including this element he defined the supranational

---

[12]Hallstein (1946), p. 1 et seqq.; Hallstein (1969).

[13]Böhm (1946), p. 141 et seqq.

[14]Müller-Armack (1947).

[15]Eucken (1959).

[16]Case 26/62 *Van Gend en Loos v Administratie der Belastingen* (ECJ 5 February 1963) p. 24.

[17]Case 6/64 *Flaminio Costa v E.N.E.L.* (ECJ 10 July 1964). p. 1270

[18]Cf. Joerges (2002), with reference to Müller-Armack (1966), p. 401 et seqq.

[19]More detailed, Mussler (1998), p. 58 et seqq., 91 et seqq., 125 et seqq.

[20]Cf. Joerges (2002), p. 62 et seq.

economic constitution as the "normative general framework of the Community Treaties for the attainment of the Community's objectives, which are pursued through the customs union of the common market under the plans by the Community institutions in a legally structured competition of citizens as market participants [*Marktbürger*] who are not distinguished nationally and who are free and equal in their economic activity".[21]

At the same time, this free market orientation of the Union is opposed by some elements which are in parts highly regulating and even inspired by command economy, e.g. in the fields of the common agricultural policy – which is in principle integrated into the internal market (Art. 38 TFEU)[22] – as well as the industrial policy (Art. 173 TFEU). The character of this "mixed" or "relatively open" economic constitution is also revealed in the socio-political provisions of the Treaty, as becomes quite evident in the objectives of the improvement of living and working conditions (Art. 151 (1) TFEU) and their explicit confrontation with the competitiveness of the Union (Art. 151 (2) TFEU). All in all, however, the relationship between the functional guarantees of the economic constitution based on the principles of a free market economy on the one hand and state interventions on the other – e.g. in the area of environmental protection (Art. 191 TFEU) – remain that of rule and exception.[23]

2.3 The White Paper on the Completion of the Internal Market

It was due to the White Paper "Completing the Internal Market"[24] (1985) and its implementation by the Single European Act (1987) that the European process of economic integration gained new momentum. In accordance with the rulings of the Court of Justice in the case of *Cassis de Dijon*[25] – i.e. following the new legal principle of "mutual recognition" of the legal systems of the Member States established in that case[26] – the "immediate unrestricted recognition of different quality standards and regulations" was accepted as a "rule". Only "in a small area" was the approximation of laws considered necessary so that "businesses could

[21]Cf. Ipsen (1972), Sect. 8 para 27, Sect. 28 para 31 (our translation).

[22]Cf. Case C-280/93 *Germany v Council* (ECJ 5 October 1994) para 61; Case C-456/00 *France v Commission* (ECJ 12 December 2002) para 33; Joined Cases T-217/03 and T-245/03 *FNCBV et al. v Commission* (CFI 13 December 2006) para 199.

[23]Cf. Nowak (2009), p. 162 et seqq.

[24]Commission of the European Communities, *White Paper from the Commission to the European Council on the Completion of the Internal Market*, COM(85) 310 final.

[25]Case 120/78 *Rewe v Bundesmonopolverwaltung für Branntwein (Cassis de Dijon)* (ECJ 20 February 1978).

[26]Cf. Commission Communication *concerning the consequences of the judgment given by the Court of Justice on 20 February 1979 in case 120/78 ('Cassis de Dijon')*, O.J.C 256/2 (1980).

freely distribute their goods in all parts of the Community". For this purpose about 300 directives and regulations for the establishment of the internal market have been adopted. It was mainly the Commission that proposed directives, which generally do not become immediately binding Community law, but rather establish binding objectives for the Member States, which then have a choice as to how to implement them in accordance with their respective national legislative procedure.[27]

3 The Competition Policy Concept of the Union

3.1 Characteristics of a Market-Oriented Social Order

The European market integration assigns the principle of competition a central role for the functioning of the private sector. It is the Archimedean point of a market-oriented social order whose economic life takes place on markets and in competition. Markets are "those places where rational consumers and profit-maximising businesses get into contact"[28] – and that only due to the scarcity of the traded good.

In economic science a competition policy is related to the aim of a performance-based distribution of income and a sufficient level of technological progress,[29] thereby focusing on the innovative function of "competition as a discovery process" (*F. A. v. Hayek*). Innovations are necessary since the legal rules are fallible and the economic and social frameworks under which they are to apply are in a constant process of change. Economic scientists call this idea-generating character of competition "dynamic efficiency",[30] which implies a process of action and interaction. The dynamics of competition is expressed in that it exerts cost and pricing pressure on the participants which threatens to minimise gained profits[31] and in return forces competitors to economically rational behaviour, i.e. an optimum allocation of factors.

According to an institutional economic approach, competition of ideas triggers innovations through parallel experimenting with a different set of rules and the exchange of the results.[32] Only within institutional competition, which stimulates

[27]Moravcsik (1998), p. 314 et seqq; Joerges (1991), p. 225; Joerges (1994), p. 91 et seqq.; Rationalisierungsprozesse im Recht der Produktsicherheit: Öffentliches Recht und Haftungsrecht unter dem Einfluß der Europäischen Integration, in: Jahrbuch für Umwelt- und Technikrecht 14, p. 141 et seqq.

[28]Cf. Rittner (1998), pp. 522, 531.

[29]Cf. Kantzenbach (1966), p. 16 et seqq.

[30]Cf. Weck-Hannemann (1998), p. 96.

[31]Cf. Clark (1961), p. 11; C. Kaysen & Turner (1959), pp. 14, 48; W. Zohlnhöfer (1968), p. 7 et seq.

[32]Cf. Kerber (2000), p. 75.

the suppliers to improve their supply so that it would be chosen by as many consumers as possible, can an active search for those solutions, which are best adapted to the needs of the consumers, be expected; only in this way does the competition of ideas become "binding". This is true for Directive 2006/123/EC of 12 December 2006 on services in the internal market[33] (Services Directive), which in its Chaps. VI and VII combines the concepts of administrative simplification – with the core element being the Point of Single Contact – and cooperation of the national administrations, thereby trying to spark competition not only between providers in Europe, but also, separately from private law companies, in the public sector.[34]

But for those for whom competition is not necessarily linked to the achievement of such concrete aims, freedom of competition on the one hand and market-based efficiency, increased productivity and the pursuit of general welfare on the other mark aspects of the same competitive process, i.e. two sides of the same coin.[35] Thus, in principle, only competition can generate economic advantages for all due to the genuine characteristic of the absence of monopoly power within the market.[36] The Chicago School acknowledges as the only aim of competition policy the maximisation of consumer surplus. According to this – admittedly – controversial view, the market and its competition can create consumer surplus even without any influence from the outside.[37]

3.2 Characteristics of the Market-Oriented Leitmotif in Union Law

The European Union does not follow this theory of an unbridled competitive system, but rather installs its economic constitution under the Leitmotif of "the constant improvements of the living and working conditions of their peoples" (recital 3 of the preamble of the TFEU), especially by establishing an internal market and a "system ensuring that competition in the internal market is not distorted" (former Art. 3.1 lit. g EC) and the commitment to "the principle of an open market economy with free competition" (Art. 119.1 and 2, 120, 127.1 TFEU) or respectively to a "system of open and competitive markets" (Art. 173.1 (2) TFEU).

[33]Cf. European Parliament/Council Directive 2006/123/EC *on services in the internal market*, O.J.L 376/36 (2006).

[34]Cf. Blanke (2010), p. 359 et seqq.

[35]Cf. Mehde (2005), p. 34 et seq., according to whom competition under the condition of scarcity is "exclusively a vehicle to achieve other specially defined aims (efficiency, enhanced productivity)".

[36]Cf. Stigler (1957), p. 14.

[37]Schmidt (2005), p. 21.

The Treaties of Rome and their successors convey the idea of competition, according to which macroeconomic efficiency arises from the allocation of scarce resources with respective innovations in a system of free movement of goods and services within the "Common Market". In a model this leads to freedom of choice for the market participants and to a socio-politically legitimised potential to control and take power from private economic governance.[38] In order to protect this system, regulation of the cost advantages of businesses for which the state is responsible is inevitable. This explains the Treaty provisions to ensure equal pay for male and female workers (Art. 157 TFEU) and also the provisions on social policy (Art. 151–161 TFEU) which try to prevent cost advantages due to low social standards. The same objective also explains the provisions to prevent restrictions of competition and to control the merging and concentration of businesses and companies (Art. 101–109 TFEU), the prohibition for the Member States on distorting competition by means of aids granted by them (Art. 107–109 TFEU), and lastly the establishment of an Economic and Monetary Union (EMU), which is to preclude competition through exchange rate losses and to ensure compliance with the convergence criteria, and thus price and currency stability, by setting the general conditions for economic policy (Art. 120–126 TFEU).

This orientation of the Union corresponds to the stated will of the Member States "to guarantee steady expansion, balanced trade and fair competition" (recital 4 of the preamble of the TFEU). In this respect the Court of Justice has ruled that the application of the principle of an open market economy with free competition calls for complex economic assessments which are a matter for the legislature or the national administration.[39] This includes consideration of the numerous competences of the Union for interventionist measures.[40] According to this ruling the market-oriented objectives of the Treaty do not impose on the Member States clear and unconditional obligations on which individuals could rely before national courts.[41]

In the Charter of Fundamental Rights the European Union acknowledges the freedom to choose an occupation, the freedom to conduct a business and the right to property (Art. 15–17 EUCFR), which are core elements of a market-based order (*infra* Sect. 5). But this does not complete the picture of a farther-reaching coherent system of economic policy, whose preservation the individual could not judicially enforce beyond protecting himself from specific infringements of individual fundamental rights.[42] There is no special fundamental right in Union law to a general and

---

[38]Cf. Böhm (1933).

[39]Case C-9/99 *Échirolles Distribution v Association du Dauphiné et al.* (ECJ 3 October 2000) para 25 – with regard to the imposition of book prices by law in France.

[40]Critical Mestmäcker (2001).

[41]Case C-9/99 *Échirolles Distribution v Association du Dauphiné et al.* (ECJ 3 October 2000) para 25.

[42]Cf. Nicolaysen (2003), p. 741; for economic and competitive freedom in German constitutional law cf. Nicolaysen (1981).

overall "economic freedom" or the "freedom of competition", which as an objective principle would make economic models legally binding for the Union and judicially enforceable.[43]

3.3 Competition as an Element of the National and Supranational Economic Constitution

At the same time, competition is often understood as an attribute of the national and supranational "economic constitution". Nevertheless, this term is also "unclear, ambiguous and controversial".[44] From an economic perspective it describes the part of the legal order which functionally separates the political and the economic sphere from each other but also makes them compatible according to justiciable criteria.[45] The legal discussion is, however, conditioned by the question of the relationship of legal norms to these economic policy models. The economic constitution in this diction can be understood as the "sum of constitutional architectural elements of the economic order",[46] but which do not claim to form partial economic constitutional law. On the other hand, it has become evident that it is not possible to attempt to draw conclusions from legal norms of a national or supranational constitution to a consistent model of economic policy.

Undoubtedly the existence of the private law society in the sense of binding individuals to legal norms can only be guaranteed if the subjects of private law in exercising their economic planning rights are confronted with mutual control through competition.[47] This shows the "constitutive connection" (*P. Behrens*) between the autonomy of the economy and the legal enclosure of the competitive system. This in turn is a consequence of the functional differentiation between economy and politics, between market and intervention.[48]

---

[43]Controversial: in the same sense Everling (1996), p. 375; Pernice and Mayer, in Grabitz and Hilf (2002), nach Art. 6 EUV para 141; differently Scorl (2007), p. 355 et seq.; the principle of an "open market economy with free competition" is partly seen as "systemic decision" which offers a "sufficiently precise standard for control through the ECJ and national courts. [. . .] The normative content of the economic constitution of the EU results from the guarantees of a market-based economy on the one hand and economic policy competences of Union and state actors on the other" (our translation): cf. Hatje (2009), p. 809; Sodan (2000), p. 367; even further as regards the burden for justification and explanation in case of differing Union and Member State action see Müller-Graff (2002b), p. 22.

[44]Cf. Nicolaysen (2003), p. 740, our translation; Hatje (2009), p. 803 et seqq.; Ruffert (2004), p. 3 et seqq.; Semmelmann (2009), p. 230 et seqq.

[45]Cf. Behrens (1994), p. 76 et seq.

[46]Cf. Schmidt (1986), Sect. 83 para 17 et seq. (our translation).

[47]Cf. Behrens (1994), p. 76 et seq.

[48]Cf. Behrens (1994), p. 77 et seqq., 84 (our translation).

3.4 The Leitmotif of the Union's Competitiveness After the Treaty of Lisbon – A Paradigm Change?

The Lisbon Treaty mentions the "well-being of its peoples", a "balanced economic growth" as well as a "highly competitive social market economy" (Art. 3.1 and 3 TEU) among the aims of the EU. Within the ranking of aims the achievement of the internal market as an area for the development of the economic and socio-political concept of the Union appears to be subordinate to the area of freedom, security and justice (Art. 3.2 TEU).[49] While Art. I-3.2 TCE offered the "citizens an area of freedom, security and justice without internal frontiers, and an internal market where competition is free and undistorted", the expression of free and undistorted competition has been excised in the Treaty of Lisbon due to pressure from France and with German acquiescence. In Protocol (No. 27) on the Internal Market and Competition, adopted on a British initiative, the Contracting States acknowledge that "the internal market as set out in Art. 3 of the Treaty on European Union includes a system ensuring that competition is not distorted" and have agreed that "[t]o this end, the Union shall, if necessary, take action under the provisions of the Treaties, including under Art. 352 of the Treaty on the Functioning of the European Union [scil.: the so-called lacuna-filling competence]". This indirectly confirms the implementation of the competition rules (Art. 101 et seqq. TFEU) and state aid policy (Art. 107 et seqq. TFEU) as fields of activity of the Union. However, through this shamefaced expression "if necessary" the vision on the function of European competition law as guarantor and driving force of the private autonomy concept of European economic integration is somewhat blurred.[50]

According to critical voices competitiveness has become a mere attribute of the social market economy, which has been regarded as a shift in emphasis[51] or even "downgrading" (*B. Heitzer*). It is argued that – regardless of the status of the Protocol on the Internal Market and Competition as an integral part of the Treaties – a weaker orientation on competition runs the risk of favouring a centralised economy and protectionist tendencies.[52] Undoubtedly the aim for a "competitive social market economy" has been shaped by a number of other goals of economic and social policy, which illustrates the transformation of the Union from a mere economic community to a political union with "more comprehensive" aims.[53] In this sense, the ninth recital of the preamble of the Union Treaty proclaims the

[49]Müller-Graff (2009), p. 179 refers to a "textual gradation of market integration".

[50]Cf. Müller-Graff (2009), p. 179 et seq.

[51]Cf. Wernicke (2008); Behrens (2008), p. 193, notices that the "the internal market of Art. 2 TEU is more than ever surrounded by other aims of the Treaties that may be a potential basis for regulations restricting competition".

[52]Cf. Kotzur (2008), p. 198.

[53]Even further Müller-Graff (2009), p. 184, who speaks of the transition into an early stage of statehood.

Contracting States' determination "within the context of the accomplishment of the internal market [. . .] to implement policies ensuring that advances in economic integration are accompanied by parallel progress in other fields" while cohesion, environmental protection, economic and social progress as well as sustainable development are stressed in this context. Nevertheless, one should not ignore the continuing connection of the Union's orientation towards an *open* market economy with the principle of "free competition" as laid down in Art. 119.1 and 2, 120 and 127.1 TFEU.[54]

4 The Post-Lisbon Concept of the Internal Market of the Union

4.1 The Replacing of the "Common Market" by the "Internal Market"

The Lisbon Treaty overcomes the parallel use of the terms "Common Market" and "Internal Market", which could be found since the adoption of the Single European Act, by generally using the term "Internal Market". This can be interpreted as a confirmation of the "synonym theory", which has never drawn any substantial distinction between the content of the two terms.[55] In the sense of the definition of the ECJ in the case of *Gaston Schul*, which was before the Single European Act, it is by the Treaties (Arts. 3.2 and 3 TEU, Art. 26 TFEU) directed towards "the elimination of all obstacles to intra-community trade in order to merge the national markets into a single market bringing about conditions as close as possible to those of a genuine internal market".[56]

The definition in Art. 26.2 TFEU refers explicitly, as did the preceding provision, only to the fundamental freedoms, i.e. the free movement of goods (Art. 28 et seqq. TFEU), the freedom of movement for workers (Art. 45 et seqq. TFEU) and the right of establishment (Art. 49 et seqq. TFEU) as well as the free movement of capital and payments (Art. 63 et seqq. TFEU). According to the ruling of the ECJ this also comprises "a system ensuring that competition is not distorted" (Protocol on the Internal Market and Competition) and/or its components in the form of the

---

[54]With the same result Nowak (2009), pp. 182 et seqq.; Drexl (2009), p. 918, regards the "transfer of the systemic guarantee of an open market economy with free competition (into a Protocol) as hindering the correct judicial understanding" (our translation); similar Müller-Graff (2009), p. 185, who talks about "normative camouflage of role and content of the economic constitution of the Union"; however, the "normative clockwork for application of laws and legal policies remains unchanged" (our translation).

[55]Cf. Barents (1993), p. 105; Frenz (2004), para 36; Nowak (2009), p. 139.

[56]Cf. Case 15/81 *Gaston Schul Douane Expediteur BV v Inspector of Customs and Excise* (ECJ 5 May 1982) para 33; inter alia confirmed in Case C-41/93 *France v Commission* (ECJ 17 May 1994) para 19.

rules of competition as constitutive elements of the internal market.[57] According to the Treaty, the upgrade of trans-European networks in the areas of transport, telecommunications and energy infrastructure is another contribution "[t]o help achieve the objectives referred to in Articles 26 and 174 [the internal market]" (first sentence of Art. 170.1 TFEU). The term "Internal Market" is thus characterised by a fundamental freedoms dimension, a competition law dimension and a trans-European ("supergrid"[58]) dimension. It is all the more surprising that the Lisbon Treaty has not included it in the principles of the TFEU, but only assigns it to Part Three on "Union Policies and Internal Actions".

In its Communication of 3 March 2010 "Europe 2020 – A strategy for smart, sustainable and inclusive growth" the Commission once more underlines the importance of a "stronger, deeper, extended single market" for the twenty-first century. It considers growth and job creation to be hindered by the reality of fragmented markets, a situation which – in competition with China, the USA and Japan – could only be overcome by the creation of an open single market (i.e. the internal market) for services, the improvement of infrastructure access for small and medium enterprises and consumers to the internal market (European networks), simplification of company law and the free "flow of on-line content".[59]

4.2 The Position of the Market Freedoms

The fundamental freedoms (market freedoms) have been adopted by the TFEU – except for some editorial modifications – without further change (Art. 28 et seqq. TFEU). The free movement of goods remains at the beginning and is not – as has been the case in the Constitutional Treaty – pushed aside by the freedom of movement for workers. This continuity in the order and significance as well as their content clearly shows that the Contracting States abstained from making any new and especially express instructions to the ECJ with regard to the future application and interpretation of these subjective rights. In the case law of the Luxembourg Court all these freedoms have been interpreted, beyond their meaning as special non-discrimination rules, as a *comprehensive* prohibition of restrictions.[60] Particularly the implementation of the horizontal clauses, namely

[57]Cf. Case C-300/89 *Commission v Council (titanium dioxide)* (ECJ 11 June 1991) para 14 et seq.

[58]Cf. the term used in the Commission Communication *Europe 2020 – A strategy for smart, sustainable and inclusive growth*, COM(2010) 2020 final, p. 16.

[59]Cf. Commission Communication *Europe 2020 – A strategy for smart, sustainable and inclusive growth*, COM(2010) 2020 final, p. 20 et seq.

[60]See the famous formula in ECJ 8/74, *Procureur du Roi v Benoît and Gustave Dassonville* (ECJ 11 July 1974) para 5: "All trading rules enacted by Member States which are capable of hindering, directly or indirectly, actually or potentially, intra-Community trade are to be considered as measures having an effect equivalent to quantitative restrictions"; Case C-415/93, *Union royale*

the fight against discrimination (Art. 8 and 10 TFEU) as well as the policy-overlapping observance of duties of environmental, consumer and animal protection (Art. 11–13 TFEU) – which also affect the fundamental freedoms – is left to the EU institutions which implement primary law.

4.3 The Competence for the Approximation of Laws Related to the Internal Market

The Union Treaty contains no substantial changes in the area of approximation of laws related to the internal market (Art. 114 et seqq. TFEU). Approximation of laws is directed towards a harmonised Union standard for all Member States in order to *a limine* avoid conflicts which could result from restrictions to the market freedoms due to a justified interest of a Member State in protection of its legal assets. This integrative approach is expressed by the authorisation of Art. 114.1 TFEU for the European Parliament and the Council to "adopt the measures for the approximation of the provisions laid down by law, regulation or administrative action in Member States which have as their object the establishment and functioning of the internal market". The EU institutions – partly under protection of ECJ rulings – have not always developed convincing solutions or concepts.[61]

Requirements for the approximation of laws according to the consistent case law of the ECJ[62] are:

(a) Disparities or potential disparities between national rules "which are such as to obstruct the fundamental freedoms or to create distortions of competition"[63] and "thus have a direct effect on the functioning of the internal market".[64]

---

belge des societiés de football association ASBL et al. v Jean-Marc Bosman (ECJ 15 December 1995) para 96; Case 427/85, *Commission v Germany* (ECJ 25 February 1988) para 39 et seqq.; Case 107/83, *Ordre des avocats au barreau de Paris v Onno Klopp* (ECJ 12 July 1984) para 20; Case 203/80, *Criminal proceedings against Guerrino Casati* (ECJ 11 November 1981) para 8 et seqq.

[61]Cf. Case C-376/98 *Germany v Parliament and Council (ban on tobacco advertising I)* (ECJ 5 October 2000); Case C-380/03 *Germany v Parliament and Council (ban on tobacco advertising II)* (ECJ 12 December 2006); also Case C-58/08 *Vodafone et al. v Secretary of State for Business Enterprise and Regulatory Reform* (ECJ 8 June 2010) on the Roaming Regulation (Parliament/Council Regulation (EC) No 717/2007 *on roaming on public mobile telephone networks within the Community and amending Directive 2002/21/EC*, O.J. L 171/32 (2007)) and furthermore Parliament/Council Regulation (EC) No 2560/2001 *on cross-border payments in euro*, O.J. L 344/13 (2001).

[62]See Case C-58/08, *Vodafone et al. v Secretary of State for Business, Enterprise and Regulatory Reform*, Opinion of Advocate-General Poiares Maduro, para 7 et seq.

[63]Case C-301/06 *Ireland v Parliament and Council* (ECJ 10 February 2009) para 63 et seq. ("Retention of Data").

[64]See Case C-58/08, *Vodafone et al. v Secretary of State for Business, Enterprise and Regulatory Reform* (ECJ 8 June 2010) para 32.

(b) Measures enacted on this basis will be upheld "only where it is actually and objectively apparent from the legal act that its purpose is to improve the conditions for the establishment and functioning of the internal market"[65]; therefore, Art. 114 TFEU does not provide the basis for a general power to regulate the internal market.[66]
(c) Moreover, legislation based on Art. 114 TFEU must not merely seek to regulate the internal market in ways which are considered desirable by the Union legislator.
(d) However, recourse to Art. 114 TFEU is possible "if the aim is to prevent the emergence of obstacles to trade resulting from the divergent development of national laws; [. . .] the emergence of such obstacles must be likely and the measure in question must be designed to prevent them".[67]
(e) The exercise of the competence of Art. 114 TFEU must not come into conflict with the existence of other legal bases in the Treaty which specifically grant powers to the Union to regulate particular aspects of the market.
(f) Provided that the conditions for recourse to Art. 114 TFEU as a legal basis are fulfilled, the Union legislature "cannot be prevented from relying on" that legal basis on the grounds that the implementation of other Union policies (e.g. public health protection, security or consumer protection) "is a decisive factor in the choices to be made".[68]
(g) By using the expression "measures for the approximation" in Art. 114 TFEU "the authors of the Treaty intended to confer on the (Union) legislature a discretion, depending on the general context and the specific circumstances of the matter to be harmonised, as regards the method of approximation most appropriate for achieving the desired result, in particular in fields with complex technical features"[69]; i.e. Art. 114 TFEU must be interpreted "as allowing the (Union) legislator to pursue and balance a variety of regulatory goals once its competence is triggered by the need to harmonise a particular field".[70]

---

[65]Case C-217/04 *United Kingdom v Parliament and Council* (ECJ 2 May 2006) para 42.

[66]Case C-376/98 *Germany v Parliament and Council* (ECJ 3 April 2000) para 83.

[67]Case C-376/98 *Germany v Parliament and Council* (ECJ 3 April 2000) para 38; Case C-301/06 *Ireland v Parliament and Council* (ECJ 10 February 2009) para 64; see also Case C-217/04 *United Kingdom v Parliament and Council* (ECJ 2 May 2006) para 60–64.

[68]See, regarding public health protection, Case C-380/03 *Germany v Parliament and Council (ban on tobacco advertising II)* (ECJ 12 December 2006) para 39; C-491/01, Case C-491/01 *British American Tobacco (Investments) and Imperial Tobacco* (ECJ 10 December 2002) para 62; Joined Cases C-154/04 and C-155/04 *Alliance for Natural Health et al. v Secretary of State for Health et al.* (ECJ 12 July 2005) para 30; regarding consumer protection see Case C-58/08, *Vodafone et al. v Secretary of State for Business, Enterprise and Regulatory Reform* (ECJ 8 June 2010) para 36.

[69]Case C-217/04 *United Kingdom v Parliament and Council* (ECJ 2 May 2006) para 43; Case C-58/08, *Vodafone et al. v Secretary of State for Business, Enterprise and Regulatory Reform* (ECJ 8 June 2010) para 35.

[70]See Case C-58/08, *Vodafone et al. v Secretary of State for Business, Enterprise and Regulatory Reform*, Opinion of Advocate-General Poiares Maduro, para 8.

The Treaty of Lisbon confers upon the Union the competence to "establish measures for the creation of European intellectual property rights to provide uniform protection of intellectual property rights throughout the Union and for the setting up of centralised Union-wide authorisation, coordination and supervision arrangements".[71] Thus, recourse to the flexibility clause – now Art. 352 TFEU – will no longer be necessary. This reflects the compromise between the Member States, according to which rights can be created at Union level to which enterprises can refer back in addition or as an alternative to national regulation.

Apart from that – except for some editorial changes – the achievements of the Single European Act in the field of approximation of laws remain unaffected. Thus, it is left to the right of initiative of the Commission (Art. 17.1 (2) sentence 1 TEU) and the decisions of the Council and the Parliament as to how the aim of the internal market (Art. 26 TFEU) is to be achieved through approximation of laws. In its Communication "Europe 2020" the Commission announced to "press ahead with the Smart Regulation agenda, including considering the wider use of regulations rather than directives".[72] This seems to be a move away from the philosophy of the White Paper on the Completion of the Internal Market for the purpose of simplification of company law, but also marked by a "stronger economic governance"[73] and the establishment of a real internal market for online content and services as well as trans-European networks, in particular an internal market for energy. To guarantee the unity of the European legal area the Commission prefers the directly applicable regulation instead of the previously favoured directive, which needs to be implemented by the Member States. But the Commission also knows that Europe neither follows the uniform discipline of "negative integration" in terms of competition among systems[74] nor submits to a centralised regime.

4.4 *Services of General Economic Interest: Art. 14 TFEU and Protocol (No. 26)*

4.4.1 Creating a Union Competence

The former regulation of the services of general economic interest (Art. 16 EC) is altered in Art. 14 TFEU by adopting the relevant provisions of the

[71]Cf. Parliament/Council Directive (EC) No 2004/48/EC *on the enforcement of intellectual property rights*, O.J. L 195/16 (2004).

[72]Commission Communication *Europe 2020 – A strategy for smart, sustainable and inclusive growth*, COM(2010) 2020 final, No. 3.1.

[73]Commission Communication *Europe 2020 – A strategy for smart, sustainable and inclusive growth*, COM(2010) 2020 final, p. 6.

[74]Cf. to federalism of law and competition of regulation Blanke and Thumfart (2010), p. 24 et seqq.

Constitutional Treaty[75] and is supplemented by "Protocol (No. 26) on Services of General Interest" (see Sect. 4.4.4). Services of general interest are not defined by the Lisbon Treaty either and thus remain – as was the case with the EC Treaty – a "fountainhead of uncertainties and debates".[76] Moreover, a new competence is conferred upon the Union in the field on services of general interest – again on French initiative. According to this, the European Parliament and the Council could in the future establish principles and set conditions, especially those of economic and financial nature, on a European basis for the functioning of services of general economic interest, acting by means of "regulations" in accordance with the ordinary legislative procedure (sentence 2 of Art. 14 TFEU). The European Parliament together with the Council is authorised to set the framework for the providing of services of general economic interest with direct application and binding in all respects – without the need for national implementation. Due to this authorisation, basing such regulation on competition law or the internal market is no longer necessary.[77]

This creates a Union competence [*Verbandskompetenz*], limited however due to the efforts of the German Federal Government as it is "without prejudice to the competence of Member States, in compliance with the Treaties, to provide, to commission and to fund such services" (second clause of sentence 2 of Art. 14 TFEU). Also, it has been expressly underlined that the Union and the Member States may act only within their respective competences. Furthermore, Art. 2 of the Protocol states that the "provisions of the Treaties do not affect in any way the competence of Member States to provide, commission and organise non-economic services of general interest". According to case law, the economic character of an action is only negated if it is carried out by government authorities, i.e. if the respective action is to serve a task of general interest which is part of essential state functions.[78]

Regarding the organisation of services of general interest the Lisbon Treaty retains the shared competence between the Union and the Member States according to the principle of subsidiarity (Art. 4.1 lit. c TFEU).[79] However, the reduction of potential instruments of Union actions to that of the "regulation" – and excluding directives and decisions[80] – as was the case in the Constitutional Treaty (sentence

[75]Article III-122, sentence 2 TCE. Welti (2005), p. 550 under recourse to SEC(2004) 326, p. 11 calls it one of the most controversial provisions of the Constitutional Treaty.

[76]Müller-Graff, in: Vedder and Heintschel von Heinegg (2007), Art. III-122 para 4 (our translation).

[77]Also Schweitzer (2004), p. 2297; von Danwitz (2009), p. 106.

[78]See Case C-364/92 *SAT-Fluggesellschaft v Eurocontrol* (ECJ 19 January 1994) para 30; Case C-343/95 *Cali`& Figli v Servizi Ecologici Porto di Genova* (ECJ 18 March 1997) para 22 et seq.

[79]Cf. Scotti, in Mangiameli (2008), p. 29 et seqq. (40).

[80]As a new category of legal acts – adopted from the Constitutional Treaty (Art. I-33.1 (5) TCE) – the decision cannot only address a natural and legal person, but also an individual Member State in the field of state aid law. It is non-legislative and can be adopted by the Commission as an administrative authority.

2 of Art. III-122 TCE)[81] reveals the problem of specific Member State regulations in favour of those services for the realisation of the economic constitutional aims of an internal market with undistorted competition. From the perspective of the creators of the Lisbon Treaty, the services of general economic interest require a Union-wide setting of the framework which is binding for all Member States and which ensures "that such services operate" according to the tasks. This power of legal regulation refers to the "principles and conditions" of the providing of such services, especially if economic and financial aspects are concerned.

This amounts to a specification of the undefined and vague legal terms of Art. 106.2 TFEU – such as "general economic interest" or "obstruct the performance, in law or in fact" – and the central provision of state aid law, Art. 107.1 TFEU, in the field of services of general interest. Sentence 1 of Art. 14 TFEU expressly states that it is without prejudice to those regulations.[82]

4.4.2 Rule and Exception

According to the opt-out clause of competition law (Art. 106.2 TFEU, ex-Art. 86.2 EC), the Treaty provisions apply to "[u]ndertakings entrusted with the operation of services of general economic interest or having the character of a revenue-producing monopoly" only in so far "as the application of such rules does not obstruct the performance, in law or in fact, of the particular tasks assigned to them", while at the same time the development of trade must not be affected to such an extent as would be contrary to the interests of the Union. The Court of Justice has considered the purpose of sentence 1 of Art. 86.2 EC "to reconcile the Member States' interest in using certain undertakings, in particular in the public sector, as an instrument of economic or fiscal policy with the Community's interest in ensuring compliance with the rules on competition and the preservation of the unity of the Common Market".[83] Thus, in the area of services of general economic interest the establishment of concordance between the guarantee of the provision of services of general interest and the enforcement and implementation of European rules on competition is deemed to be required.[84] It is especially necessary that services of general

[81]The Constitutional Treaty provided in Art. III-122, sentence 2, TCE for the instrument of the "European law". According to Art. I-33.1 (2) TCE this was supposed to be the new name given to the "regulation", thereby differentiating it from the "European regulation".

[82]Cf. the (recent as well as former) opening of Art. 14, sentence 1, TFEU: "Without prejudice to Article [...] 106 and 107 of this Treaty [...]".

[83]Case 202/88 *France c Commission (telecommunications terminals equipment)* (ECJ 19 March 1991) para 12; continued in Case C-157/94 *Commission v Netherlands* (ECJ 23 October 1997) para 40 et seqq. and Case C-159/94 *Commission v France* (ECJ 23 October 1997) para 56 et seqq. – monopolies for electricity of a commercial character; Nowak (2009), pp. 175 et seq. calls this a "rather generous" ruling which regards the preventive character [Verhinderungsmaßstab] of Art. 86.2, sentence 1, EC more in the sense of a scale for threat [Gefährdungsmaßstab].

[84]Cf. von Danwitz (2009), p. 124.

economic interest are embedded by European policies into a concept of *regulated* competition: so far, the regulatory criteria condition competition in accordance with public interest obligations and cohesion, i.e. in the sense of social, ecological, economic, technical and territorial needs. From an academic point of view, this task is to be accompanied by the development of principles for balancing different interests for the design of markets that are obliged to act in the public interest.[85]

Article 106.2 TFEU, which on the one hand restricts the application of the rules on competition in the field of services of general economic interest but on the other hand limits this restriction to the viability of trade, shows the relation of rule and exception between market integration of services of general interest on the one hand and the need for justification for Member States' preserving exclusive rights and monopolies on the other hand.[86] It is problematic in this respect to predict if the abolition of such exclusive right or monopoly impedes the realisation of a public purpose.[87] Therefore, the ECJ deems it sufficient that the public purpose is jeopardised.[88]

While up until the Treaty of Amsterdam services of general economic interest had only been an exception for Member States' action in the competition law of the Community, being subject to justification, Art. 86.2 EC-Amsterdam (= Art. 106.2 TFEU) even defined the interest in the functionality of those services as general interest. Thus, ever since the Treaty of Amsterdam the internal market and social cohesion – as purposes of the services of general economic interest – are equivalent aims of the Union.[89] In this regard the Union's legislative competence under the second sentence of Art. 14 TFEU is of particular importance.

4.4.3 Legislative Replacement of Former Communications and "Packages of Measures"

On the basis of Art. 14 TFEU the Union can now – taking into account the exceptions of Art. 106.2 TFEU, especially with regard to European state aid law – establish a consistent legal framework to regulate the financing of services of general economic interest by public authorities regarding the financial dimension ("equalisation payments for public interest obligations" and "notification requirement"), set criteria for the selection of enterprises for the providing of services of

[85]Cf. for both aspects Kersten (2010), pp. 320 et seqq., 328 with regard to competition as an administrative task.

[86]Cf. Mann (2002), p. 823; Kämmerer (2001), p. 121; Welti (2005), p. 536 et seqq. (with further reference in FN 5); Nowak (2009), p. 175; Schink (2005), p. 866 et seq., who as well has a narrow interpretation of this exception and who only considers restrictions of competition legal "if they provide the condition for carrying out of tasks that is related to the public welfare" (our translation).

[87]Welti (2005), p. 539, 544.

[88]See Case C-157/94 *Commission v Netherlands* (ECJ 23 October 1997) para 58.

[89]Kämmerer (2002), p. 1042; Storr (2002), p. 361; Welti (2005), p. 544 et seq.

general interest and secure the implementation of public procurement law[90] – also for Public Private Partnerships.[91]

Until now the Commission has been restricted to Communications and "packages of measures". This includes the "Monti Kroes Package" of 2005 which outlines the conditions justifying state aid according to Art. 86.2 EC (Art. 106.2 TFEU).[92] This guarantees that undertakings can be subject to subsidies for executing public remits without causing an overcompensation that might restrict competition. The transformation and consistent development of such rules to sectoral regulations provides the Member States – with regard to their heterogeneous national organisation of services of general economic interest[93] – with a common "tool kit" in order to

---

[90]Cf. Parliament/Council Directive 2004/17/EC *coordinating the procurement procedures of entities operating in the water, energy, transport and postal services sectors* (utilities/sector-based directive), O.J.L 134/1 (2004), as well as Parliament/Council Directive 2004/18/EC *on the coordination of procedures for the award of public works contracts, public supply contracts and public service contracts* (classical directive), O.J.L 134/114 (2004). With Commission Regulation (EC) 1177/2009, O.J.L 314/64 (2009) the Commission changed the threshold values of the EU Public Procurement Directives 2004/17/EC, 2004/18/EC and 2009/81/EC; Cf. also Commission Decision No. 2005/15/EC *on the detailed rules for the application of the procedure provided for in Article 30 of Directive 2004/17/EC of the European Parliament and of the Council coordinating the procurement procedures of entities operating in the water, energy, transport and postal services sectors*, O.J.L 7/7 (2005).

[91]The hopes of Welti (2005), p. 552, according to whom the European regulation is restricted to "a clear differentiation of controversial features when applying market or competition law, e.g. in the specification of the principles of the Altmark Trans ruling" or to "a specification of the difficult differentiation between economic and non-economic activities as well as the relevance of local services of general interest for the internal market" or by that could create "an effective differentiation to the scope of the Services Directive" as exclusive regulatory content appears to not correspond to the political aim of this regulatory authority (our translation).

[92]This package includes: (1) an opt-out decision explaining the conditions under which generally and without further examination by the EU Commission (i.e. without notification) state aid that is compatible with EU law can be adopted (Commission Decision 2005/842/EC *on the application of Article 86(2) of the EC Treaty to State aid in the form of public service compensation granted to certain undertakings entrusted with the operation of services of general economic interest*, O.J.L 312/67(2005)); (2) a Community framework explaining the conditions under which payments or the like which do not meet the criteria as established by the ECJ in its *Altmark-Trans* decision and which fall neither under the *De minimis* regulation nor under the opt-out decision can be declared compatible with the EC Treaty according to the exceptions of Art. 86.2 EC (Art. 106.2 TFEU), O.J. C 297/4 (2005); and (3) a directive amending the transparency directive (Commission Directive 2005/81/EC *amending Directive 80/723/EEC on the transparency of financial relations between Member States and public undertakings as well as on financial transparency within certain undertakings*, O.J.L 318/17 (2006); see now the Commission's Communication on the Reform of the EU State Aid Rules on Services of General Economic Interest, 23.3.2011, COM(2011) 146 final, and the Commission staff working paper on "The Application of EU State Aid rules on Services of General Economic Interest since 2005 and the Outcome of the Public Consultation" – http://ec.europa.eu/competition/state_aid/legislation/sgei.html.

[93]To Italy cf. the contributions by W. Giulietti (pp. 83 et seqq.), S. D'Antonio (p. 109 et seqq.) and P. Lazzara (p. 271 et seqq.), in: Mangiameli (2008); for the situation in Sweden, Italy, Poland and Austria cf. Lippert, Donati/Grasse, Knopp and Pürgy, in: Krautscheid (2009).

prevent individual strategies of deviation from the integration of the internal market and to create legal certainty.[94] The tension-filled wording of Art. 14 TFEU which on the one hand leaves unaffected the economic constitutional principle of the Union set out in Art. 106 TFEU and on the other hand underlines the importance of (national) services of general economic interest[95] requires – with regard to the exceptions of Art. 106.2 TFEU – resolution in Union law through binding norms. The discussion that has been triggered by the ambition of France, Belgium and the Fraction of the Party of European Socialists (PSE) in the European Parliament to use a "framework directive" by the Union for public services[96] has been ended by the use of the more precise instrument of a "regulation".

As a result, the Lisbon Treaty confirms the views of those European Law scholars who, regarding the predecessor Art. 16 EC, refused to see it as "a fundamental re-orientation of the economic constitution" of the Union.[97] Article 14 TFEU – as did the fundamental provision of the economic constitution of Art. 16 EC – accepts alternative economic systems than that of the competitive market-based economy, recognising the provision of services of general interest in an independent meaning.[98] However, it does not exclude the validity of rules on competition in the area of services of general interest.[99] Thus, the Union's right to use regulations under Art. 14 TFEU will form the more binding and more transparent limits of services of general interest as far as competition law is concerned ("competification" or "*Verwettbewerblichung*") without forcing a complete privatising of the providing of services of general interest.[100]

---

[94]See already for the Constitutional Treaty Müller-Graff, in Vedder and Heintschel von Heinegg (2007), Art. III-122 para 6; for reasons of legal security even the Committee of the Regions (Opinion "Single Market, Social Vision and Services of General Interest", 12/13 February 2009, ECOS-IV-020, No. 28) welcomes the introduction of a "new legal basis for services of general economic interest. This [. . .] will [. . .] put an end to the legal insecurity which has been created by the case by case legislative (sector-based directives) and litigious approach adopted hitherto by the Commission".

[95]Jung, in Calliess and Ruffert (2011), Art. 106 para 52, calls it an "ambivalent", Müller-Graff, in Vedder and Heintschel von Heinegg (2007), Art. III-122 para 2, a "highly convoluted" formulation.

[96]Cf. European Parliament resolution of 22 February 2005 *on State aid in the form of public service compensation* (2004/2186(INI)), recital H; Schink (2005), p. 865 et seq., 870; Waiz (2009).

[97]Cf. Nettesheim (2002), p. 50 et seq. (our translation).

[98]Cf. as well Jung, in Calliess and Ruffert (2011), Art. 14 AEUV para 21; Jung in Calliess and Ruffert (2011), Art. 106 para 44.

[99]Cf. Schwarze (2001a), p. 336; Schwarze (2001b), p. 13 et seqq.; Jung in Calliess and Ruffert (2011), Art. 14 AEUV para 24.

[100]Schink (2005), p. 866, recognises in the regulatory power of the Union both "threats and chances for ensuring services of general interest" (our translation).

4.4.4 The Protocol on Services of General Interest

The expansion of competences in Art. 14 TFEU must be taken together with the Protocol (No. 26) on Services of General Interest. It replaces Declaration No. 13 annexed to the Final Act of the Treaty of Amsterdam, referring to public services. For the local level it is significant that for the first time in the primary law of the Union the importance of the role and the wide discretion of the national, regional and local authorities for the organisation of those services have been recorded. In the Protocol it says (Art. 1, first indent): "The shared values of the Union [...] include in particular the essential role and the wide discretion of national, regional and local authorities in providing, commissioning and organising services of general economic interest as closely as possible to the needs of the users."

With regard to this guideline, those services – even according to the interpretation of the Commission – are to be provided to meet the demands and as closely as possible to the citizen or the enterprise. In its actions the EU has to observe the principles of subsidiarity and proportionality.[101] However, the Protocol only repeats what the TFEU itself (clause 2 of sentence 2 of Art. 14 TFEU) grants to the Member States, i.e. their competence "to provide, commission and organise non-economic services of general interest".

The acknowledgement of the Member States' right to organise is confirmed by the other substantive principles[102] of the Protocol, namely:

1. The requirement for differentiation among services of general economic interest: According to this, the different needs and preferences of citizens, users and consumers have to be taken into account with regard to the respective economic, social, geographic, cultural or personal background, including the variety of services, the background of the provisions, the special characteristics of the providers of such services and the flexibility that is necessary for adaptation of the services to meet the demands.
2. The enabling of practical (transnational) access to services: A substantial aim of the Union's actions is the promotion of high-quality, assured and affordable services of general economic interest. This includes the possibility of equal access to services across borders, a reasonable price/quality ratio, and the affordability of services including special regulations for low-income groups and people with special needs, especially in the field of social welfare services, security, reliability and continuity of benefits, high quality and variety in supply

[101] In that sense the interpretation of the Commission in: Commission Communication *accompanying the Communication on "A single market for 21st century Europe". Services of general interest, including social services of general interest: a new European commitment of the European Communities* (accompanying communication), COM(2007) 725 final, No. 3.

[102] Cf. Commission of the European Communities, accompanying communication, COM(2007) 725 final, No. 3.

as well as transparency and information by the providers and the regulating authorities.[103]

3. The principle of non-discrimination: Gender equality and the prohibition of discrimination in access to services of general interest. Any exclusion of citizens of other Member States from the provision of national services of general interest is thus prohibited by Union law. As far as national services of general interest are concerned, Union law attributes to all Union citizens a *status positivus* (i.e. an identical status).[104]
4. Transparency and protection of users: the rights of citizens, users and customers have to be clearly defined, published and, if necessary, protected by establishing an independent regulatory authority.[105] According to the Commission, this requires "provisions for the representation and active participation of consumers and users in the definition and evaluation of services".[106]

As a result, the Protocol does not change the inherent "programmatic message" of Art. 14 TFEU that the functionality of services of general economic interest must not fail due to practical and legal irregularities in the principles of the market-based economy of the European economic constitution[107] and that thus – according to the view of the Contracting Parties – a regulatory competence of the Union is indispensable.

5 "Economic Fundamental Rights" and "Fundamental Rights with Reference to Social and Labour Law" in the Charter of Fundamental Rights of the European Union

5.1 Principles

5.1.1 Economic Rights and Freedoms

The freedom to choose an occupation, the freedom to conduct a business and the right to property constitute the triad of fundamental rights on which the economic

---

[103]However, this confession of primary law had already been mapped out by the remarks of the Commission in its Green Paper, cf. Commission of the European Communities, *Green Paper on Services of General Interest*, COM(2003) 270 final, para 83.

[104]See also Welti (2005), p. 555 et seqq., who is, however, referring to the fundamental right of Art. 36 EUCFR.

[105]In that sense the interpretation of the Commission in: Commission of the European Communities, accompanying communication, COM(2007) 725 final, No. 3.

[106]Commission of the European Communities, accompanying communication, COM(2007) 725 final, No. 3.

[107]Cf. Müller-Graff, in Vedder and Heintschel von Heinegg (2007), Art. I-122 para 4; Nowak (2009), p. 176 et seq., who excludes "spillover effects of this Protocol".

constitution and competition within the Union are based. They are part of the Charter of Fundamental Rights (Art. 15–17 EUCFR) whose "rights, freedoms and principles" the Union recognises in Art. 6.1, first clause, TEU. The Charter has the same legal value as the TEU and the TFEU (Art. 6.1, second clause, TEU). Following the case law of the ECJ regarding fundamental rights and the property-related rulings of the European Court of Human Rights (ECtHR), the economic fundamental rights of the Charter's title "Freedoms" have another direction and dimension in contrast to the fundamental freedoms. Fundamental rights secure the freedoms of the individual in cross-border economic activities by regulating in particular the modalities of these activities and providing for the exercise of subjective rights under private autonomy ("individual effects of the fundamental freedoms"[108]). This protection is guaranteed by the fundamental freedoms prohibiting discrimination as well as imposing restrictions.[109] On the other hand, the supranational fundamental rights, including the economic fundamental rights, protect the individual within the jurisdiction of the Union in a comprehensive way.[110] In that respect the fundamental rights of the Union as negative rights are more extensive and provide more stable a shield against infringements by the Union or the Member States (Art. 51.1 EUCFR).

5.1.2 Equality and the Principle of Non-discrimination

Ever since the beginnings of the economic and social constitution of the Union (Art. 119 EEC = Art. 157 TFEU),[111] the core of economic fundamental rights has been supplemented under the title "Equality" by the principle of gender equality (Art. 23 EUCFR). In addition to the *individual right* of mere formal equal treatment the Charter develops an overall and *substantive* concept of gender equality in Union law. As a *collective right* it extends to every section of social life ("in all areas").[112] In order to promote equal opportunities, it is about application of the same set of rules to men and women. This requires equality in the initial situation (subjective individual component) to compensate inequalities in social reality and if necessary

[108]For the immediate individual effects of the fundamental freedoms and a right to sovereign protection deduced from them cf. Kingreeen (2009), p. 743.

[109]Cf. Case 8/74 *Procureur du Roi v Benoît and Gustave Dassonville* (ECJ 11 July 1974) para 5.

[110]Cf. Frenz (2004), para 61, 74; Müller-Graff (2002a), p. 1281; Blanke, in Tettinger and Stern (2006), Art. 15 para 6; for the more selective distinction between fundamental freedoms as phenomenon of transnational integration (in the meaning of a need for protection of cross-border transactions) and fundamental freedoms as elements of supranational legitimation (in the meaning of an "overall liberalisation") cf. Kingreeen (2009), p. 725 et seqq.

[111]Cf. Case 43/75 *Defrenne v SABENA (Defrenne II)* (ECJ 8 April 1976) para 8 et seqq., in which for the first time the double character of Art. 119 EEC (Art. 157 TFEU) with an economic and a social objective has been emphasised.

[112]Cf. Nußberger, in Tettinger and Stern (2006), Art. 23 para 57 et seqq.

equality in the results.[113] Realisation of this collective (not individual) right to compensation is only possible within the political process of changing working and social conditions and implies specific action measures ("positive discrimination").[114] It is about a "right to fulfil" that goes beyond the "right to protect" as the first level of formal gender equality in Art. 23 EUCFR.[115] The introduction of this *general* entitlement to equal treatment in working life into primary law of the Union enables the European Parliament and the Council to "adopt measures to ensure the application of the principle of equal opportunities and equal treatment of men and women in matters of employment and occupation" according to Art. 157.3 TFEU.[116] The principle of non-discrimination in Art. 21 EUCFR, with a non-enumerative listing of seventeen criteria, and in a reduced version in Art. 10 TFEU (eight forbidden criteria), besides the other prohibited distinguishing criteria (Art. 21.1 EUCFR) including nationality (Art. 21.2 EUCFR),[117] is aimed primarily at *factual* gender equality, which prohibits unequal treatment "based on any ground such as sex". It is also based on a mere formal approach and overlaps as an individual right with the first component of Art. 23 EUCFR (equality in the initial situations). In both cases it resembles the negative right to the prohibition of unequal treatment,[118] so that unequal treatment has to be justified by objective reasons which might be found in the provisions on solidarity of the Charter (Art. 27 et seqq. EUCFR).[119] In the form of a prohibition of discrimination based on nationality (Art. 18.2 TFEU and 21.2 EUCFR) the principle of non-discrimination is the matrix of all market freedoms (e.g. Art. 45.2, 49.1, 56.1 TFEU).

5.1.3 The Fundamental Rights with Reference to Labour and the Principle of Solidarity

The labour-related fundamental rights of the title "Solidarity" (Art. 27–32 EUCFR) contain subjective negative rights ("right to respect": Art. 28 EUCFR, free collective bargaining), as well as positive rights such as Art. 29 EUCFR (right of access to placement services), and rights having a protective character (Art. 27 EUCFR, workers' right to information and consultation within the undertaking;

---

[113]Cf. Nußberger, in Tettinger and Stern (2006), Art. 23 para 70, with reference to Case C-450/93 *Kalanke v Freie Hansestadt Bremen* (ECJ 17 October 1995) para 23 on the one hand and Case C-409/95 *Marschall v Land Nordrhein-Westfalen* (ECJ 11 November 1997) para 31 on the other.

[114]Rodriguez Iglesias (2003), p. 144.

[115]Cf. Nußberger, in Tettinger and Stern (2006), Art. 23 para 75.

[116]See Council Directive 2000/78/EC of 27 November 2000 *establishing a general framework for equal treatment in employment and occupation*, O.J. L 303/16 (2000).

[117]See with regard to the prohibition of discrimination on grounds of age Case C-447/09 *Airline pilots v Deutsche Lufthansa AG* (ECJ 13 September 2011) para 37 et seqq.

[118]In this respect Nußberger, in Tettinger and Stern (2006), Art. 23 para 66, 74.

[119]Cf. Iliopoulos-Strangas (2010), p. 937.

Art. 30 EUCFR, protection in the event of unjustified dismissal; Art. 31 EUCFR, fair and just working conditions). The concept of protection on which the Charter is based ("right to protect") contains the imperative requirement for the Union (and the Member States in accordance with Art. 51.1 EUCFR) to take measures to safeguard effective exercise of the fundamental rights while ensuring equal access to certain services. The prohibition of child labour in Art. 32 EUCFR deals with two levels of protection through fundamental rights: It contains a negative right ("right to respect": specific prohibition of employment of school-age children) as well as a positive right ("right to protect": entitlement to appropriate working conditions) in the sense of an obligation of the Union or the Member States to apply effective protective measures and to ensure that the right is observed.[120] However, the possibility of judicial enforcement of these rights vis-à-vis the Union and the Member States only exists for the negative right.

The protective character of one of these fundamental rights *can* correspond to the term "principles" in Art. 6.1 TEU. This distinction between "rights" and "freedoms" on the one hand and "principles" on the other is another confusing and unsatisfactory peculiarity of the Charter that is made permanent by its adoption in Art. 51.1 and 52.5 EUCFR. It was to take into account the peculiarities of some provisions of the Charter, especially the specific character of some (not all) "social fundamental rights". The differentiation seems to be based on the assumption that "principles" are only justiciable in so far as institutions, bodies, offices and agencies of the Union or the Member States have adopted "acts" (i.e. laws or administrative actions) while "implementing" Union law – in accordance with their respective powers (Art. 52.5 EUCFR).[121] Subjectively enforceable fundamental rights are different from the fundamental principles intended to be implemented through legislation.[122] A determining factor would be, whether the relevant provision (also) contains substantive *protection of rights of individuals* or if this is expressly excluded.[123] So the character of "principle" is assumed in the Charter for fundamental rights such as the right to information and consultation (Art. 27 EUCFR: "in the cases and under the conditions provided for by Union law and national laws"),

[120]Cf. Riedel, in Meyer (2006), Art. 32 para 10.

[121]Cf. G. Hogan, Der Einfluß der Europäischen Grundrechte-Charta auf die irische Verfassung, in: Tettinger and Stern (2006), A VI para 41; the French Constitutional Council, 2004–505 DC (19 November 2004), consideration 15 – *Treaty establishing a Constitution for Europe*, has ruled that principles "qui constituent des objectifs ne (peuvent) être invoqués qu'à l'encontre des actes de portée générale relatifs à leur mise en oeuvre [. . .]". For the British position see Herm.-J. Blanke, The Protection of Fundamental Rights in Europe (sub. 3), in this volume.

[122]Cf. the *Declaration concerning the explanations relating to the Charter of Fundamental Rights (Declaration 12)* annexed to the Treaty establishing a Constitution for Europe, O.J. C 310/424 (2004), updated once more in O.J. C 303/17 (2007). These explanations "do not as such have the status of law, they are a valuable tool of interpretation intended to clarify the provisions of the Charter" (cf. Introduction to the explanations, O.J. C 303/17 (2007)).

[123]Cf. Ladenburger, in Tettinger and Stern (2006), Art. 52 para 98 et seqq.; Borowsky, in Meyer (2006), Art. 51 para 33 et seq., Art. 52 para 45 et seqq.

but not, however, for Art. 31 and 32 EUCFR.[124] Therefore, some social and economic rights will not be mere principles but may constitute justiciable rights. Even if this is not the case, all social rights guarantees of the Charter constitute binding law and as such impose obligations on the institutions and bodies of the Union and on the Member States (in accordance with Art. 51.1 sentence 1 EUCFR). These provisions of the Charter are therefore guidelines for the interpretation of other legal acts of the Union and its Member States and serve as legal benchmarks for the (judicial) review of the legality of acts and omissions of the institutions and bodies of the Union and of the Member States within their respective sphere of competences.[125] "They shall therefore respect the rights, observe the principles and promote the application thereof in accordance with their respective powers" (Art. 51.1 sentence 2 EUCFR).

5.2 The Triad of Economic Fundamental Rights in the Union

5.2.1 The Freedom to Choose an Occupation (Art. 15 EUCFR)

A central human rights guarantee is Art. 15.1 EUCFR, which confers on "everyone" the freedom to choose an occupation, including its temporal and local reference, and the right to seek and to engage in work in any Member State. This fundamental right is to be understood in the legal order of the Union as a comprehensive guarantee for the freedom of economic activity. The distinguishing characteristic for the activities to be included in this guarantee is the purpose of profit-making. As far as duration is concerned, the Charter uses the term occupation (*Beruf/ profession/profesión*), which requires more than just a single action.[126]

As to the comprehensiveness of the freedom to choose an occupation, one may also point to the individual guarantees spelled out by the ECJ. Freedom of trade in particular is considered by the ECJ to be a fundamental right.[127] The work-related freedom of contract in the form of the freedom to choose with whom to do business

---

[124] The explanations of the Praesidium of the Convention (updated under the responsibility of the Praesidium of the European Convention, in the light of the drafting adjustments made to the text of the Charter by that Convention – notably to Art. 51 and 52 EUCFR) classify individual articles of the Charter of Fundamental Rights as principle (e.g. Art. 25, 26 and 27, but also Art. 34.1 and 3, 35, 36, 38); see also the explanations relating to the Charter of Fundamental Rights (footnote 121); critical Iliopoulos-Strangas (2010), p. 934.

[125] Cf. Iliopoulos-Strangas (2010), p. 936 et seqq.

[126] Cf. Ruffert (2009), para 11.

[127] Cf. Case 4/73 *Nold KG v Commission* (ECJ 14 May 1974) para 14; Case 240/83 *Procureur de la République v ADBHU* (ECJ 7 February 1985) para 9.

is also regarded by the ECJ as part of occupational freedom.[128] Freedom of competition is also part of the freedom to choose an occupation.[129]

The subjective right to provide employment cannot be deduced from this guarantee. In the economic systems of the Member States, public authorities do not have a monopoly for the creation and provision of jobs. An entitlement would collide with the occupational freedom, the freedom to conduct a business and the right to property by which the Member States are bound. Thus, the authors of the Charter of Fundamental Rights have consciously abandoned the idea of a "right to work".[130]

Article 15.2 EUCFR regarding the freedom of the citizens of the Union "to seek employment, to work, to exercise the right of establishment and to provide services in any Member State" cannot be accepted as containing a substantive right to work. This provision can only be understood as a clarification that the market freedoms exclusively apply to Union citizens in so far that this is not already evident from the wording of the provisions to which Art. 52.2 EUCFR refers. This is the case for the free movement of workers.

5.2.2 The Freedom to Conduct a Business (Art. 16 EUCFR)

In accordance with the case law of the ECJ since its decision in the case of *Nold*,[131] the freedom to conduct a business as laid down in Art. 16 EUCFR has to be considered as an aspect of the freedom to choose an occupation. The Court of Justice pointed out the close connection of the freedom of action, the freedom of contract and the freedom of competition as manifestations of occupational freedom. The wording of Art. 16 EUCFR implies an independent economic activity. The freedom to conduct a business in its core covers the freedom to economic or business activity, i.e. the founding of a business. In terms of this provision, a business is any profit-making entity, regardless of its legal form of financing.

Uncertainties remain in the interpretation of Art. 16 EUCFR and its reserve competence as regards national laws and practices, which could weaken the Union's fundamental right of the freedom to conduct a business and thus the European economic constitution in general.[132] It remains to be seen whether the ECJ in its future case law will recognise this vertical limitation clause as an (additional) limitation that would go beyond Art. 52.1 EUCFR[133] or whether it will

[128]Case C-90/90 *Neu et al. v Secrétaire d'État à l'Agriculture and à la Viticulture* (ECJ 10 July 1991) para 13.

[129]Case 133/85 *Rau v BALM* (ECJ 21 May 1987) para 15; Case C-200/96 *Metronome Musik v Music Point Hokamp* (ECJ 28 April 1998) para 28.

[130]Cf. Blanke, in Tettinger and Stern (2006), Art. 15 para 21.

[131]With this tendency Case 230/78 *Eridania* (ECJ 27 September 1979) para 20.

[132]Cf. Nowak (2009), p. 178 et seqq.

[133]With an expressly different view Blanke, in Tettinger and Stern (2006), Art. 16 para 12.

refuse to regard the national laws and the practices of the Member States as independent limitations[134] that cannot circumvent the legal reserve competence in Art. 52.1 EUCFR regarding the "practices" either.[135]

5.2.3 The Right to Property (Art. 17 EUCFR)

The idea of competition is closely related to the system of property ownership, for it determines the legitimacy of "owning and acquiring".[136] The definition of ownership in the Charter – as in German constitutional law – is characterised by the normative scope of protection.[137] The object of protection has to be defined by the legislator (Art. 345 TFEU) – within the limits of private benefit (*Privatnützigkeit*) and the guarantee for the establishment of this institution (*Einrichtungsgarantie*). In addition to the traditional ownership of movable and immovable things all acquired rights are protected. Initially the ECJ left unanswered the question whether legal positions of a public law nature (e.g. social security benefits) are covered by the scope of the protection of property.[138] In its more recent case law, however, the Court has answered it in the affirmative, where these positions are at least partly based on personal contributions of the person entitled.[139] This factor is absent in cases of commercial benefits resulting from measures of market control, e.g. the allocation of reference quantities in the context of common organisation of the markets.[140]

According to its wording, Art. 17 EUCFR only protects "lawfully acquired possessions". Assets as such, e.g. entitlements to financial contributions, are not covered by this interpretation of property.[141] Nor are mere chances covered, such as commercial interests or expectancies, whose uncertainty is part of the nature of economic activity.[142] This includes the expectation to achieve a certain market share.[143] Thus, one cannot deduce from Art. 17.1, sentence 1 EUCFR, a right to

[134]See Bernsdorff, in Meyer (2006), Art. 16 para 15.

[135]So Rengeling (2004), 453 (459).

[136]Fikentscher (1993), p. 132 (our translation).

[137]Cf. Calliess (2009), para 14.

[138]Cf. Joined Cases 41/79, 121/79 and 796/79 *Vittorio Testa, Salvino Maggio and Carmine Vitale v Bundesanstalt für Arbeit (Testa)* (ECJ 19 June 1980) para 22.

[139]Case C-44/89 *Von Deetzen v Hauptzollamt Oldenburg* (ECJ 22 October 1991) para 27.

[140]Case C-416/01 *Sociedad Cooperativa General Agropecuaria (ACOR) v Administración General del Estado* (ECJ 20 November 2003) para 50.

[141]Case 143/88 *Zuckerfabrik Süderdithmarschen and Zuckerfabrik Soest v Hauptzollamt Itzehoe and Hauptzollamt Paderborn* (ECJ 21 February 1991) para 74; Calliess (2009) para 19; Depenheuer, in Tettinger and Stern (2006), Art. 17 para 37 et seq.

[142]Cf. Case 4/73 *Nold KG v Commission* (ECJ 14 May 1974) para 14; Joined Cases 154, 205, 206, 226 to 228, 263 and 264/78, 39, 31, 83 and 85/79 *SpA Ferriera Valsabbia et al. v Commission* (ECJ 18 March 1980) para 89.

[143]Case C-280/93 *Germany v Council (Bananas)* (ECJ 5 October 1994) para 79.

acquisition of property. Intellectual Property is also covered by the protection of the Charter (Art. 17.2 EUCFR). The question of whether the furnished and established business undertaking is covered by the guarantee for property has so far remained unanswered by the case law of the ECJ.[144]

Regulations that demand or prohibit a certain use of property are permitted in so far as this is necessary for the general interest (third sentence of Art. 17.1 EUCFR). The general interest orientation reflects a traditional limitation of ownership which is specific to Union law.[145] However, there have to be legitimate aims of European general interest, to which the ECJ has assigned a "remarkably great importance"[146] and the regulations on the use have to be proportionate.[147] According to Art. 17.1, second sentence, EUCFR deprivation of property is only lawful "in the public which is spelled out in the case law as the "objectives of general interest".[148] Any measure pursuing a legitimate political aim – be it of social, economic or any other nature – can be in the public and thus be viewed in relation to the social function of property.[149] Expropriation for the benefit of private *interests* is impermissible, not however for private *individuals*. As with regulations on its use, the deprivation of property has to observe the principal of proportionality; there has to be "a reasonable relationship of proportionality between the means employed and the aim thought to be realised".[150]

6 The Future of the Economic and Monetary Union

The Lisbon Treaty has not led to dramatic changes in the provisions on economic and monetary policy (Art. 119 et seqq. TFEU).[151] The special constitutional structure of EMU in which the legal framework of the Economic Union totally differs from that of the Monetary Union is not altered by the Lisbon Treaty. While within the Monetary Union the relevant competences are assigned to the EU as a field of exclusive authority, the Economic Union continues to be based on the EU's decentralised structure as a confederation. Only the establishment of a so-called dominant budget

[144] This is affirmed by Rengeling (2004), p. 460.

[145] Case 4/73 *Nold KG v Commission* (ECJ 14 May 1974) para 14; Case 44/79 *Hauer v Land Rheinland-Pfalz* (ECJ 13 December 1979) para 23; Case 265/87 *Schräder v Hauptzollamt Gronau* (ECJ 11 July 1989) para 15.

[146] Bernsdorff, in Meyer (2006), Art. 17 para 22 (our translation).

[147] Cf. Case 44/79 *Hauer v Land Rheinland-Pfalz* (ECJ 13 December 1979) para 23; Case 265/87 *Schräder v Hauptzollamt Gronau* (ECJ 11 July 1989) para 15.

[148] Case C-491/01 *British American Tobacco* (ECJ 10 December 2002) para 149.

[149] Case 8793/79 *James et al. v United Kingdom* (ECtHR 21 February 1986) para 45; Depenheuer, in Tettinger and Stern (2006), Art. 17 para 65.

[150] This is the consistent case law of the ECtHR: Case 8225/78 *Ashingdane v United Kingdom* (ECtHR 28 May 1985), para 57.

[151] Cf. the contribution by U. Häde in this Volume.

at the level of the Union in the sense of a comprehensive shaping of revenues and expenditures could change the design of the EMU in principle. This would require the Member States to surrender to the EU their responsibilities and competences for infrastructure, social, educational scientific, research and – which matters most – defence policies. In the absence of the necessary political will, and this is also the case with regard to national tax and fiscal policies, the Member States remain the masters of the Treaties. The call for greater centralisation of national economic and fiscal policy within the EU, a question raised also by the International Monetory Fund (IMF), has to go, therefore, beyond a constitutional reorganisation of the EMU. The European Economic Government in this way takes its first step (Sects. 6.4 and 6.4.5).

Nevertheless, some modifications show that – even before the crisis of the euro area, caused by the imminent sovereign default of Greece,[152] Ireland[153] and Portugal,[154] all averted by collective bail-outs, and the critical budgetary situation of Spain and Italy which have jeopardised stability[155] – the Member States were aware of the need for stronger coordination of their economic policies as well as a more effective excessive deficit procedure for Member States not meeting the convergence criteria. With the Lisbon Treaty, the European Central Bank becomes an EU institution (Art. 13.1 TEU). This does not, however, change its specific function of ensuring price stability.

6.1 New provisions for Member States whose currency is the euro (Art. 136–138 TFEU)

The Treaty of Lisbon has introduced into the TFEU provisions "specific to Member States whose currency is the euro". Article 136.1 TFEU authorises the Council to adopt measures to "ensure the proper functioning of the [EMU]". These include measures "to strengthen the coordination and surveillance of [the] budgetary

---

[152]Cf. the "Loan Facility Agreement" between the states of the euro area and the Hellenic Republic (Greece); also the "Intercreditor Agreement" concluded between the members of the euro in which rights and duties among those states are laid down and lastly the "Memorandum of Understanding on Specific Economic Policy Conditionality" of 2 May 2010, which sets the conditions for the granting of credits and especially ties the payments of financial assistance to strict requirements regarding budgetary consolidation. In its Communication, *Reinforcing economic policy coordination*, COM(2010) 250 final, the Commission accuses Greece of "data misreporting in the past" and "mainly ... inappropriate fiscal policy".

[153]The excessive granting of credits by Irish banks led to a real estate bubble that bursted due to negative economic developments. The interventions by the Irish government resulted in nationalisation of large parts of the financial sector. The resulting desastrous budgetary situation led to Ireland to call for international help of a total of 85 billion euro. Cf. Statement by the Eurogroup and ECOFIN Ministers, 28th December 2010.

[154]Cf. Statement by the Eurogroup and ECOFIN Ministers, 16th May 2011.

[155]Cf. the Council Decision 9609/10 ECOFIN 264 UEM 178 of 9 May 2010 based on Art. 122.2 TFEU on a "European stabilisation mechanism" and Council Regulation (EU) No 407/2010 of 11 May 2010 *establishing a European financial stabilisation mechanism*, O.J. L 118/1 (2010) which is the basis for the mechanism.

discipline" of the Member States (lit. a) as well as the setting out and surveillance of economic policy guidelines for members of the euro area (lit. b). Thus, specific policy guidelines regarding economic policy of Member States, whose currency is the euro, will be permitted as long as they are compatible with measures adopted for the Union as a whole. According to Art. 136.2 TFEU, Member States with a derogation will not be eligible to vote in that respect.

Furthermore, the Euro Group has been promoted to a formal body within the primary law of the Union (Art. 137 TFEU in conjunction with the Protocol No. 14 on the Euro Group). Additionally, there are provisions on the external representation of the euro currency area in the sense of concerted positioning as well as a uniform representation (including common positions) within the competent international financial institutions and conferences (Art. 138 in conjunction with Art. 219.3 TFEU). The promotion of the Euro Group, however, is essentially no more than the formal recognition in the Treaties of a body that has already been responsible for economic policy coordination within the scope of the ECB. Article 1 of Protocol No. 14 provides that the Ministers of the Member States whose currency is the euro shall meet informally. Thus, measures for which the Council is competent according to the Treaties can be prepared but not adopted by the Euro Group. Although the independence of the ECB is not challenged by establishing this body, the existence of the Euro Group nonetheless shows that the struggle for power between the ECB, whose primary aim is to ensure price stability, and politics, which tends to be focused on economic growth and full employment, will continue.[156] In this context, the ECB's right to attendance of Euro Group meetings will be of particular importance.

6.2 *The Commission's Right to Early Warning (Art. 121.4 TFEU)*

Article 121.4 TFEU has introduced for *all* Member States an early warning right for the Commission within the framework of its multilateral surveillance of the economic policies of the Member States. The Commission may address a warning to a Member State if under the procedure of Art. 121.3 TFEU it is established that the economic policies of that Member State are inconsistent with "the broad guidelines of the economic policies" referred to in paragraph 2 or "risk jeopardising the proper functioning of Economic and Monetary Union". The competence for recommendations to the Member State concerned nevertheless remains with the Council acting on a recommendation from the Commission. The respective Member State can no longer take part in the vote (Art. 121.4 TFEU).

Thus, in the field of the economic policies of the Member States, being "a matter of common concern" that needs coordination (Art. 121.1 in conjunction with Art. 120 TFEU), a new element of economic governance to the economic

[156] Cf. Häde, in Calliess and Ruffert (2011), Art. 138 para 9.

multilevel governance system of the Union has been introduced. In order to effectively exercise its new competences the Commission needs reliable statistical budgetary data from the Member States. This is to be achieved by amended Regulation No. 479/2009 of 26 July 2010 (*infra* Sect. 6.4.2) which revises the Protocol on the excessive deficit procedure.[157]

6.3 The Stability and Growth Pact

In Declaration No. 30 (on Art. 104 TFEU) the Contracting States underline the significance of the Stability and Growth Pact (SGP). This is aimed at "strengthening and clarifying" the obligation of the Member States to comply with the Pact, after years during which large Member States, such as France, Germany and Italy, have disregarded its fiscal thresholds.

6.3.1 The Resurgence of a Politically Weakened Pact

At the same time, the reaffirmation of the SGP by the Contracting States appears like an act of contradiction and doublespeak and lacks credibility when considered against the background of prior undermining.[158] After the Council (Economic and Financial Affairs – ECOFIN) in its meeting of 25 November 2003 had suspended the deficit procedure under Art. 126 TFEU (ex-Art. 104 EC) against Germany (with an expected deficit for 2003 of 4%) and France (with an expected deficit for 2003 of 3.6%), making obvious the infringement of the Pact by these two main engines of integration,[159] the next step was to "update and amend" the Pact – as they say in Eurospeak – by the European Council at its spring meeting in 2005. This so-called flexibilisation of the Pact, however, led to its severe weakening by Regulations 1055/2005 and 1056/2005.[160] In recital 5 of Regulation 1055/2005 it says: "In the light of the economic and budgetary heterogeneity in the Union, the medium-term budgetary objective should be differentiated for individual Member States, to take into account the diversity of economic and budgetary positions and developments

---

[157]Council Regulation (EU) No. 679/2010 *amending Regulation (EC) No. 479/2009 as regards the quality of statistical data in the context of the excessive deficit procedure*, O.J. L 198/1 (2010).

[158]For an analysis of the first nine years of the implementation period of the SGP cf. Heipertz and Verdun (2010), p. 113 et seqq.

[159]Cf. Palm (2004); Case C-27/04 *Commission v Council* (ECJ 13 July 2004).

[160]Council Regulation (EC) No. 1055/2005 *amending Regulation (EC) No. 1466/97 on the strengthening of the surveillance of budgetary positions and the surveillance and coordination of economic policies*, O.J. L 174/1 (2005) and Council Regulation (EC) No. 1056/2005 *amending Regulation (EC) No. 1467/97 on speeding up and clarifying the implementation of the excessive deficit procedure*, O.J. L 174/5 (2005).

as well as of fiscal risk to the sustainability of public finances, also in the face of prospective demographic changes".

Hence, compliance by the Member States with the fiscal reference values ("convergence criteria") is interpreted and monitored in the light of political priorities of the Member States ("major structural reforms" according to Art. 1 (1) of amended Regulation 1466/97). This had to be regarded by Member States without developed stability discipline – especially in times of economic and financial crisis – as an invitation to increase public debt. As a result, government budgets in the EU have gone from close to balance (−0.8% of GDP in EU and −0.6% in the euro area) in 2007 to an expected deficit of close to 7% of GDP in 2010. Public debt continues to rise: it will reach 84% of GDP in the EU as a whole in 2011 (88% in the euro area).[161]

6.3.2 The Excessive Deficit Procedure (Art. 126 TFEU)

According to Art. 126.6 TFEU the Council decides whether an excessive deficit exists, acting "on a proposal" from the Commission, rather than, as before, "on a recommendation". This means that the Council can only amend the Commission proposal by a unanimous vote (Art. 293.1 TFEU). A Council decision still requires a qualified majority. The Member State concerned is now excluded from voting for the decision on the existence of an excessive deficit (Art. 126.13 (2) TFEU) whereas before Lisbon the Member State was excluded only after this had been established.

Another change refers to the procedure for Council recommendations for the reduction of the excessive deficit (Art. 126.7 TFEU). In the future the Council will act by a qualified majority vote without taking into account the vote of the Member State concerned (Art. 126.13 (2) TFEU) while previously a two thirds majority was required, again not counting the vote of this Member State. At this stage, however, the position remains where the Commission has only a right to make recommendations, so that amendments by the Council do not require unanimity.

6.4 An Economic Government for the Union

6.4.1 Commission Communication "Reinforcing Economic Policy Coordination"

On 12 May 2010 the Commission presented a Communication on the reinforcement of economic policy coordination[162] in which it spells out certain matters that were

[161]Cf. Commission Communication *Reinforcing economic policy coordination*, COM(2010) 250 final of 12 May 2010, p. 3, with reference to services' forecasts by Eurostat.

[162]Cf. Commission Communication *Reinforcing economic policy coordination*, COM(2010) 250 final.

already covered by its Communication "Europe 2020" with the aim of "stronger economic governance".[163] The Commission proposes specific measures to be taken in the short term to improve the functioning of current mechanisms of economic policy coordination in the EU. It admits, moreover, that "the functioning of the Economic and Monetary Union has been under particular stress, due to earlier failures to comply with the underlying rules and principles".[164]

As centrepiece of an improvement of "the economic governance of the EU" the Commission recommends to the Member States to "reinforce the preventive dimension of budgetary surveillance" (ex ante coordination within a "European Semester", a six-month cycle of economic policy coordination which has started at the beginning of 2011 for the first time – *infra* Sect. 6.4.3a).[165] For this purpose, emphasis has to be put on the preparation and the constant surveillance of the implementation of the Stability and Growth Programmes in the form of a peer review.[166]

The most far-reaching element of governance must be regarded as the proposal of the Commission, already mentioned in Communication "Europe 2020", to (politically) regulate both the revenue and the expenditure side of national budgets by "coordination at EU".[167] Depending on the specific challenges of the economy concerned, policy recommendations could address both the revenue and expenditure sides of fiscal policy (in the context of the SGP).[168] In the view of the Commission, programmes for budget consolidation are to give priority to growth-stimulating measures in the fields of education, research and development, innovation and investments in network infrastructures such as high-speed Internet infrastructure as well as the interconnection of transport and energy networks, i.e. in the core areas of the "Europe 2020" strategy.[169]

Such Europeanisation of the Member States' budgetary policies is the crucial point of a European Economic Government for this would include interventions into the budgetary autonomy of the Member States which even in times of

---

[163]Cf. Commission Communication *Europe 2020 – A strategy for smart, sustainable and inclusive growth*, COM(2010) 2020 final, p. 6, 27 et seq.

[164]Cf. Commission Communication *Reinforcing economic policy coordination*, COM(2010) 250 final, p. 2.

[165]Cf. Council Decision of 7 September 2010 *amending Decision 2010/320/EU addressed to Greece with a view to reinforcing and deepening fiscal surveillance and giving notice to Greece to take measures for the deficit reduction judged necessary to remedy the situation of excessive deficit*, O.J. L 241/12.

[166]Cf. Commission Communication *Reinforcing economic policy coordination*, COM(2010) 250 final, p. 3, 6, 8.

[167]Commission Communication *Europe 2020 – A strategy for smart, sustainable and inclusive growth*, COM(2010) 2020 final, p. 30.

[168]Cf. Commission Communication *Reinforcing economic policy coordination*, COM(2010) 250 final, p. 7.

[169]Cf. Commission Communication *Reinforcing economic policy coordination*, COM(2010) 250 final, p. 7.

economic and financial crisis they have constantly defended as "the core of a State's sovereignty" (*G. Westerwelle*). By this exertion of influence on the national revenue and expenditure policies the Commission seeks to avoid future deficit spending, which was characteristic of the Greek debt crisis and of the budgetary situation of other Member States. In the debate on a European Economic Government, European Central Bank (ECB) President *J.-C. Trichet* has expressed the view that this would be "equivalent to a fiscal Union" that "allows for observation and surveillance of the national budgetary policies".[170]

At the same time the Commission recommends that Member States include the objective of "sound public finances" in their national legal orders. The provisions on the excessive deficit procedure (EDP), a milestone in the corrective part of the EMU, have to be implemented more quickly in case of a Member State's breach of its obligations in order to encourage at an early stage to seek to overcome fiscal problems – especially those Member States that have repeatedly exceeded the reference values (*infra* Sect. 6.4.3).[171]

Member States with debt ratios in excess of 60% of GDP[172] should become subject to the EDP if the decline of debt in a given preceding period falls short of an appropriate benchmark. The Commission recommends taking better account of the interplay between debt and deficit (*infra* Sect. 6.4.3). Cohesion policy should have a clearer role to play in supporting Member States' actions to address structural weaknesses and competitiveness challenges.[173] That way the Structural and Cohesion Funds will also become instruments of control of budgetary policies in the beneficiary countries.

6.4.2 Strengthening the Rules Concerning Statistical Data

Council Regulation 2223/96 of 25 June 1996[174] has introduced a European system of accounts for the purposes of EMU which has been used for the establishment of national and regional accounts required by legal acts of the Community. According to Regulation 479/2009 on the application of the Protocol on the excessive deficit procedure the "Commission (Eurostat) shall regularly assess the quality both of actual data reported by Member States and of the underlying government sector accounts compiled according to ESA 95 [scil.: System of Integrated Economic Accounts]" (Art. 8.1 of Regulation 479/2009). With the amendments to Regulation

[170]Cf. *J.-C. Trichet*, Le Monde, 31.5.2010 (our translation).

[171]Cf. Commission Communication *Reinforcing economic policy coordination*, COM(2010) 250 final, p. 5.

[172]Only Finland, Slovenia, Slovakia and Luxembourg meet the 60% threshold in 2010.

[173]Cf. Commission Communication *Reinforcing economic policy coordination*, COM(2010) 250 final, p. 5.

[174]Council Regulation (EC) No. 2223/96 *on the European system of national and regional accounts in the Community*, O.J. L 310/1 (1996).

3605/93 to improve transparency of the statistics on government debt having been less severe than intended by the Commission,[175] a fundamental reform was inevitable due to the experience of the Union with the budgetary situation in Greece, Spain and Portugal. Budgetary autonomy of the Member States has become subject to a more intense surveillance by the European Commission in that the instrument of "methodological visits" according to Art. 11.1 of Regulation 479/2009 has been strengthened.[176] These "visits" are designed to "monitor the processes and verify the accounts which justify the reported data and to draw detailed conclusions as to the quality of reported data" (Art. 2a, Art. 11b.1 of Regulation 479/2009). Despite a proposal of the ECB[177] which suggested that the Member States should be obliged to "as promptly as possible provide the Commission (Eurostat) with access to *all the statistical and budgetary information* requested for the needs of the data quality assessment" the regulation has been restricted to "the relevant statistical information requested for the needs of the data quality assessment" and "limited to the information strictly necessary to check the compliance with ESA rules" (Art. 8.2 of Regulation 479/2009). At the same time Eurostat has been provided access to the "accounts of government entities at central, state, local and social security levels, including the provision of underlying detailed accounting information" such as transactions and balance sheets, relevant statistical surveys and questionnaires and further related information, respecting the legislation on data protection as well as statistical confidentiality (Art. 12.2 of Regulation 479/2009).[178]

6.4.3 Necessity for and Key Elements of a Reform of the Stability and Growth Pact

The European Commission and the Member States have realised that the existing construction of the SGP "has apparently not sufficed as an instrument to prevent undesirable fiscal developments".[179] A reform of the SGP should re-strengthen the exception clauses which had been relaxed and apply more pressure in the preventive part of the Pact in case it is not complied with. In general, there needs to be faster reaction to undesirable developments and thus an acceleration of the existing procedure. It is central to improve the rules which

[175]Council Regulation (EC) No. 2103/2005 *amending Regulation (EC) No. 3605/93 as regards the quality of statistical data in the context of the excessive deficit procedure*, O.J. L 337/1 (2005).

[176]Change in the System of Integrated Economic Accounts by Council Regulation (EU) No. 679/2010 *amending Regulation (EC) No. 479/2009 as regards the quality of statistical data in the context of the excessive deficit procedure*, O.J. L 198/1 (2010).

[177]See Opinion of the European Central Bank of 31 March 2010, O.J. C 103/1,3 (2010).

[178]Cf. Council Regulation (EU) No. 679/2010 *amending Regulation (EC) No. 479/2009 as regards the quality of statistical data in the context of the excessive deficit procedure*, O.J. L 198/1 (2010).

[179]Cf. for the perspective of Germany: Bundesministerium der Finanzen (2010).

until now have been insufficiently implemented, e.g. by preventing the exertion of influence during the political negotiations for the imposing of sanctions and making the process more rule-based. In case of apparently and severely improper developments it is necessary to have intensified macroeconomic surveillance on a European level.[180]

On the occasion of the crisis management for the Hellenic Republic the German Federal Government formulated nine cornerstones for a reform of the Pact:[181]

(a) Budgetary surveillance within the EU is to be intensified, maybe by consulting with the ECB or a commission of independent research institutes
(b) Enhanced integration of national parliaments into European fiscal policy
(c) Stronger integration of the principles of the SGP into national budgetary planning including a "debt brake" according to the model of the German Basic Law (Art. 109.3 in connection with Art. 143 d)
(d) Earlier and more effective sanctions through the deficit procedure including the cutting of structural funds of Member States with an excessive deficit
(e) Subjugation of states with high government debt to an accelerated deficit procedure
(f) Suspension of votes in the Council of those Member States that "grossly" violate the Pact
(g) Consistent implementation of the systems of early warning and specific recommended corrections ("blue letters")
(h) Enhanced coordination of economic policies "of the euro area with greater recognition and concentration on uncompetitive Member States"
(i) Introduction of a procedure for an orderly restructuring solution within a "robust framework of "crisis management" in the case of a financial collapse

A study of 2006 proves "that a large majority of economists implicitly or explicitly view fiscal rules" with regard to the reform of the SGP "as desirable" and consider "common supranational fiscal rules [. . .] necessary to address the risk of externalities (spillovers) from domestic fiscal policies". The exact functions of such a common fiscal policy within the SGP are nevertheless highly controversial. Economists are not in agreement about the proper goals, instruments and institutional framework for fiscal policy-making. This state of affairs reflects a lack of a commonly accepted theory for fiscal policy. "After the demise of the Keynesian majority view on fiscal policy of the 1950s and 1960s, several rival theories for stabilization policies have competed in the market for ideas. In short, there is no ruling paradigm for fiscal policy-making and there are no signs of a new consensus view emerging."[182]

In order to increase fiscal discipline, broaden economic surveillance and deepen coordination the Council and the European Parliament adopted a legislative "six pack"

[180]Deutsche Bundesbank, Monthly Report May (2010), p. 6 (13).

[181]Bundesministerium der Finanzen (2010) (our translation).

[182]Fischer, Jonung & Larch (2006), p. 25, 31 et seq.

on the reform of the SGP and other related measures[183] which, however, only unsatisfactorily translate the reform proposals of the German Federal Government with regard to the SGP. Along these lines is the report "Strengthening Economic Governance in the EU",[184] which originates from the Member States within the framework of the Task Force on Economic Governance. In coordination with the Commission proposals this is to bring "deficit and debt onto a more sustainable path".[185]

(a) The Reform of the Regulation on the Strengthening of Surveillance and Coordination of Economic Policies (Preventive Part of the SGP) from the Standpoint of the European Commission

The procedure for surveillance and coordination of Regulation 1466/97 of 7 July 1997, aiming towards "prudent fiscal policies" of the Member States, is the so-called preventive part of the SGP. According to the Commission[186] this is to be strengthened as in the future Member States are required to present stability[187] and convergence[188] programmes, outlining – within a multi-annual fiscal perspective – their plans to achieve medium-term budgetary objectives which are defined as a percentage of GDP in structural terms (individual "adjustment path") and are differentiated across countries around a close-to-balance position to reflect the level of public debt and liabilities related to ageing.[189] The submission of such medium-term budgetary strategies by each Member State within its stability and

[183]See the following six proposals: (1) the proposal for a Parliament/Council Regulation *amending Regulation (EC) No. 1466/97 on the strengthening of budgetary positions and the surveillance and coordination of economic policies*; COM(2010) 526 final; (2) the proposal for a Council Regulation *amending Regulation (EC) No. 1467/97 on speeding up and clarifying the implementation of the excessive deficit procedure*, COM(2010) 522 final; (3) the proposal for a Council Directive *on requirements for budgetary frameworks of the Member States*, COM(2010) 523 final; (4) the proposal for a Parliament/Council Regulation *on the effective enforcement of budgetary surveillance in the euro area*, COM(2010) 524 final; (5) the proposal for a Parliament/Council Regulation *on enforcement measures to correct excessive macroeconomic imbalances in the euro area*, COM (2010) 525 final; (6) the proposal for a Parliament/Council Regulation *on the prevention and correction of macroeconomic imbalances*, COM(2010) 527 final.

[184]http://www.consilium.europa.eu/uedocs/cms_data/docs/pressdata/en/ec/117236.pdf

[185]Cf. also the aim outlined by the President of the European Council in the Conclusions of the summit of 28/29 October 2010 sub I. 3, available online at http://www.consilium.europa.eu/uedocs/cms_data/docs/pressdata/en/ec/117496.pdf

[186]Commission proposal for a Parliament/Council Regulation *amending Regulation (EC) No. 1466/97 on the strengthening of budgetary positions and the surveillance and coordination of economic policies*, COM(2010) 526 final.

[187]"Participating member states" are requested to present stability programmes (Art. 3.1 of the proposed Regulation).

[188]"Member States with a derogation" are requested to present convergence programmes (Art. 7.1 of the proposed Regulation).

[189]Article 3.2 lit. a and Art. 7.2 lit. a, respectively, of the proposed Regulation in conjunction with Arts. 8 and 9 of the proposed Council Directive on requirements for budgetary frameworks.

convergence programmes in the month of April[190] constitutes another stage within the "European Semester", which in June and July is followed by policy advice before the Member States finalise their budgets for the following year.[191] The essential aim is to ensure that revenue windfalls are not spent but are instead allocated to debt reduction.[192] Member States not having reached their medium-term budgetary objectives are expected to converge towards it at an annual pace of 0.5% of GDP in structural terms.[193] Failure to keep to the agreed rate of growth of expenditure, in conjunction with the stipulated revenue measures, will make the Member State concerned liable to a warning from the Commission and, if persistent and/or particularly serious, a Council recommendation to take corrective action.[194] Such a recommendation, while being issued in the context of the preventive part, in accordance with the proposed "Regulation of effective enforcement of budgetary surveillance in the euro area" (Art. 3)[195] will be backed, for the first time and for euro area countries only, by an enforcement mechanism under Art. 136 TFEU, in the form of an interest-bearing deposit, amounting to 0.2% of GDP. A "reverse voting" mechanism will be introduced for imposing the interest-bearing deposit.[196] On the issue of a recommendation for corrective action by the Council, the deposit would become due on a proposal by the Commission, unless the Council decides to the contrary by qualified majority within ten days. The Council could reduce the amount of the deposit only unanimously or on the basis of a Commission proposal and a reasoned request from the Member State concerned. The deposit is returned with the accrued interest once the Council is satisfied that the situation giving rise to it has come to an end.

(b) The Reform of the Regulation on the Excessive Deficit Procedure (Corrective Part of the SGP) from the Standpoint of the European Commission

With the proposal of the Commission[197] amending Regulation 1467/97 (corrective part in order to avoid gross errors in budgetary policies), the SGP shall be relieved of its one-sided orientation in the 3% of GDP threshold in giving the debt threshold "a more prominent role" compared to the deficit (Art. 1.1) together with the criterion of an "overall sustainability". Meanwhile, the debt criterion of the

[190]Article 4 and Art. 8, respectively, of the proposed Regulation.

[191]Article 5.2 and Art. 9.2, respectively, of the proposed Regulation.

[192]Article 5.1 (4) of the proposed Regulation.

[193]Article 5.1 (2) and Art. 10.2 (2), respectively, of the proposed Regulation.

[194]Articles 6.2, 6.3 and 10.3, respectively, of the proposed Regulation.

[195]Cf. Commission proposal for a Parliament/Council Regulation *on the effective enforcement of budgetary surveillance in the euro area*, COM(2010) 524 final.

[196]Article 3.1 of the proposed Regulation on the effective enforcement.

[197]Cf. Commission proposal for a Council Regulation *amending Regulation (EC) No. 1467/97 on speeding up and clarifying the implementation of the excessive deficit procedure*, COM(2010) 522 final.

European deficit procedure is to be made operational, namely by the adoption of a "numerical benchmark", to gauge whether the debt ratio is sufficiently diminishing towards the 60% of GDP threshold.[198] A debt-to-GDP ratio above 60% of GDP reference value diminishes to a sufficient extent if the ratio with respect to the 60% of GDP reference value has reduced over the previous three years at a rate on the order of one twentieth per year.[199] Non-compliance with this numerical benchmark is not, however, necessarily expected to result in the country concerned being placed in excessive deficit, as this decision would need to take into account all relevant factors, in particular for the assessment of debt developments, debt structure, private sector indebtedness and implicit liabilities related to ageing ("flexible approach").[200]

Enforcement[201] is strengthened in accordance with the proposed Regulation on effective enforcement by introducing a new set of financial sanctions for euro area Member States, which would apply earlier in the process according to a graduated approach. Specifically, a non-interest-bearing deposit amounting to 0.2% of GDP[202] would apply upon a decision to place a country in excessive deficit, which would be converted into a fine of up to 0.5% in the event of non-compliance with the initial recommendation to correct the deficit.[203] Further non-compliance would result in the sanction being stepped up, in line with the already existing provisions in the SGP. To reduce discretion in enforcement, the "reverse voting" mechanism is envisaged for imposing the new sanctions in connection with the successive steps of the deficit procedure.[204] Specifically, at each step of the deficit procedure, the Commission will make a proposal for the relevant sanction, and this will be considered adopted, unless the Council decides to the contrary by qualified majority within ten days.[205] The size of the non-interest-bearing deposit of the fine could only be reduced or cancelled by the Council unanimously or based on a specific proposal from the Commission on grounds of exceptional economic circumstances or following a reasoned request by the Member State concerned.[206]

To ensure the effectiveness of the excessive deficit procedure, the Commission proposal on requirements for budgetary frameworks of the Member States requires provision for public accounting systems, macroeconomic and budgetary forecasts, numerical fiscal rules as well as observance of the principles of transparency of general government finances and a comprehensive scope of budgetary frameworks.[207] It can

[198]Article 126.2 TFEU in conjunction with the Protocol on the excessive deficit procedure.

[199]Article 2.1 (1) and Art. 2.1a of the proposed Regulation.

[200]Articles 2.3 and 2.4 of the proposed Regulation.

[201]Article 11 of the proposed Regulation in conjunction with Art. 104.11 TFEU.

[202]Article 4 of the proposed enforcement Regulation.

[203]Article 5 of the proposed enforcement Regulation.

[204]Article 4.1, second sentence, and Art. 5.1, second sentence, of the proposed enforcement Regulation.

[205]Article 4.1 of the proposed enforcement Regulation.

[206]Article 5.4 of the proposed enforcement Regulation.

[207]Cf. Art. 3, 4, 5, 6 and 10 of the proposed Directive on requirements for budgetary frameworks.

be expected that making operational the deficit criterion will put euro area Member States under further pressure to consolidate their public finances.[208]

(c) The Standpoint of the Member States: The Report of the Task Force on "Economic Governance"

On 18/19 October 2010[209] the Eurogroup and the Economic and Finance Ministers Council, joined in a "Task Force on Economic Governance", came to a compromise on stricter budget rules[210] which was endorsed by the Heads of State or Government of the Member States at the European Council meeting on 28/29 October 2010. The compromise worked out in the Task Force was possible due to the agreement reached between France and Germany in Deauville according to which the Federal Government within the context of reform of the Pact gave up its insistence on the automatic imposition of sanctions on the Member States which do not comply with the so-called Maastricht criteria and the relevant decisions of the Council based on the SGP (in the excessive deficit procedure).[211] Instead, France and Germany agreed to seek an amendment of the Treaties which would embed this mechanism in the TFEU. The Conclusions of the European Council of 28/29 October 2010 state that "the issue of the right of euro area members to participate in decision making in EMU-related procedures in the case of a permanent threat to the stability of the euro area as a whole" will be "subsequently examined in consultation with the Member States" by the President of the European Council.[212]

(d) Comparing Both Proposals

Neither of the two proposals – the comprehensive package of legislative measures of the Commission and the Final Report of the Task Force – required any revision of the Lisbon Treaty. Both aim at a closer interaction between the guidelines for

[208]According to the plans of the European Commission, necessary consolidation for 2011 will amount in Germany and France to 26 bill. €, in Italy to 45.7 bill. €, in Greece to 8.6 bill. €, in Belgium to 7 bill. €, in Spain to 6.6 bill. € and in Portugal to 2.7 bill €, cf. DB Research (30 September 2010), Ambitioniert? Ja. Wirksam? Vielleicht. Die Vorschläge der Kommission zum Stabilitätspakt, p. 2.

[209]http://www.euractiv.de/finanzplatz-europa/artikel/merkel-und-sarkozy-einig-bei-stabilitatspakt-reform-003799

[210]Cf. "Strengthening Economic Governance in the EU" – Report of the Task Force to the European Council, 21 October 2010.

[211]Germany, the Netherlands, Nordic Member States and Slovakia wanted sanctions imposed almost automatically on countries that do not abide by the EU's 3% of GDP limit on budget deficits and public debt limit of 60 percent of GDP.

[212]European Council, Conclusions of the President of 28/29 October 2010, para 2 in fine.

common fiscal policies and the attempts to solve macroeconomic imbalances. One central element is the provision of more severe sanctions. The report of the Task Force, however, concedes to the Member States' greater political influence on the decisions on sanctions than does the Commission proposal. Although both proposals provide that imposition of sanctions by the Commission on non-complying Member States can only be averted by a qualified majority vote in the Council ("reverse majority rule"),[213] the Task Force proposal provides that before a decision on the imposition of sanctions the Council must (more than once) decide by reverse majority that the Member State concerned is in breach.[214] Therefore, the European Council has to take a political decision each time when countries do not abide by the EU's 3% of GDP limit on budget deficits and public debt limit of 60% of GDP; this might make it more difficult to impose sanctions. At the same time and unlike the Commission, the Member States do not want sanctions to be imposed before a delay of at least six months.[215] Nonetheless, one innovation is supported by both proposals: Sanctions will also be possible in the case that a Member State, without exceeding the reference values for public deficit (3% of the GDP), does not provide for measures adequate to reduce public debt.[216] With regard to the SGP, conflicts are no longer found between individual Member States but rather between the Member States and the Commission.

Thus, due to the reform of the SGP, sanctions can gradually be intensified – beginning with increased reporting obligations to interest-bearing or non-interest bearing deposits up to penalty payments. The European Commission will assume a more important role in the decision-making of the Council in the context of the Pact since the voting modalities of the Council are modified in parts. Nonetheless, the decisive momentum will remain the Council's decision, i.e. no rigid automatism has been installed. Moreover, the debt criterion has been specified. However, due to numerous exceptions it can be doubted that the binding effect has been increased. It seems furthermore problematic that the deficit criterion can be relaxed in the event that the debt ratio is beneath the reference value. Thus, the overall reform of the SGP is too cautious. The effectiveness of the rules remains dependent on the political will of the Member States with euro currency. Euro area members with budgets that are not in conformity with the Pact will use these weaknesses to evade the rules of the SGP.[217]

---

[213] "Strengthening Economic Governance in the EU" – Report of the Task Force to the European Council, paras 24 and 25.

[214] "Strengthening Economic Governance in the EU" – Report of the Task Force to the European Council, para 22.

[215] "Strengthening Economic Governance in the EU" – Report of the Task Force to the European Council, para 21.

[216] "Strengthening Economic Governance in the EU" – Report of the Task Force to the European Council, paras 6–8.

[217] Cf. Deutsche Bank, Monthly Report April 2011, p. 53 et seqq.

(e) The Compromise from June / September 2011

During the discussions on the reform package on "Economic Governance" in June 2011 the Council has conceded to the European Parliament that (1) the EP will be involved in the European Semester through the whole economic cycle;[218] (2) the "economic dialogue" among European institutions, including the EP and the Council and individual Member States will be institutionalised;[219] (3) the EP will be involved in the establishment and functioning of the scoreboard to forecast macroeconomic imbalances;[220] (4) the independence of statistical authorities will be enhanced and a fine will be introduced for Member States who falsify their fiscal statistics;[221] (5) the application of reverse qualified majority voting will be expanded, reinforcing the already existing "comply or explain" procedure by making it public;[222] (6) additional sanctions will be introduced for Member States in the the excessive imbalance procedure (EIP);[223] (7) the Commission is invited to regularly review the effective function of the regulation and the progress in ensuring closer coordination of economic policies, and to report on the issue of Euro-securities.[224]

In September 2011 European Parliament, Council and Commission have reached an agreement on some further issues that include (1) strengthening the decision-making process in the preventive arm of the SGP, (2) improving the dialogue between European institutions on macroeconomic issues, (3) surveillance of the EIP of both, countries with a deficit as well as those with a surplus in the current account, according to a differentiated assessment of the two cases.[225]

---

[218] Art. 2a number 4 of the Draft European Parliament legislative resolution on the proposal for a *regulation of the European Parliament and of the Council amending Regulation (EC) No 1466/97*.

[219] Art. 2a and 2b of the Draft European Parliament legislative resolution on the proposal for a *regulation of the European Parliament and of the Council amending Regulation (EC) No 1466/97*.

[220] Art. 3.1, 4.4, 6.1 and 6.2, 9.1 of the Draft European Parliament legislative resolution on the proposal for a *regulation of the European Parliament and of the Council on the prevention and correction of macroeconomic imbalances*.

[221] Art. 3.1c and 6a.2 of the Draft European Parliament legislative resolution on the proposal for a Council Directive on *requirements for budgetary frameworks of the Member States*.

[222] Art. 10 of the Draft European Parliament legislative resolution on the proposal for a *regulation of the European Parliament and of the Council amending Regulation (EC) No 1466/97*.

[223] Report of the Hungarian Council Presidency of 21 June 2011, http://www.eu2011.hu/news/package-six-proposals-council-offers-compromise-parliament

[224] Report of the Hungarian Council Presidency of 21 June 2011, http://www.eu2011.hu/de/sechserpaket-der-rat-schlaegt-dem-parlament-einen-kompromiss-vor

[225] Report of the Hungarian Council Presidency of 16 September 2011, http://www.consilium.europa.eu/uedocs/cms_data/docs/pressdata/en/ecofin/124640.pdf

6.4.4 Robust Framework for Crisis Management ("European Stability Mechanism")

In order to ensure balanced and sustainable growth, the Heads of State or Government agreed at their meeting on 28/29 October on "the need for Member States to establish a permanent crisis mechanism to safeguard the financial stability of the euro area as a whole".[226] The aim is the implementation of a European Stability Mechanism (ESM) to replace the European Financial Stability Facility (EFSF) and the European Financial Stability Mechanism (EFSM) after June 2013. The function of the ESM – in the form of a general authorisation contained in Art. 136.3 TFEU – is "to safeguard stability of the euro area as a whole".[227] The ESM will have a total subscribed capital of € 700 billion. Financial assistance from the ESM – which will be provided through loans[228] – will in all cases be activated on a request from a Member State to the other euro area members. The Eurogroup will inform the Council that such a request has been made. Financial assistance will be subject to a rigorous analysis of the sustainability of the public debt and a strict economic and financial adjustment programme that will be elaborated by the Commission, together with the IMF and in liaison with the ECB, on a mandate by the Board of Governors of the ESM.[229]

The Commission will propose to the Council a decision endorsing the macro-economic adjustment programme. The Board of Governors will decide on the granting of financial assistance and the terms and conditions under which assistance is provided. On adoption of the programme by the Council, the Commission will sign a Memorandum of Understanding on behalf of the euro area Member States subject to prior mutual agreement by the Board of Governors.[230] Depending on the budgetary situation of the requesting State, measures for restructuring of the public debt will be introduced. A differentiation will be made on a case-by-case basis between sustainable debt (temporary liquidity crisis) and an actual sovereign default: In a temporary liquidity crisis the national measures for debt restructuring would merely be accompanied by the request to the private sector to maintain their exposures in accordance with

[226]This reform is indispensable since on European level there is no procedural framework or feasible instruments to counteract sovereign default of Member States. Cf. von Lewinski 2011, p. 454 et seq.

[227]The following paragraph 3 shall be added to Art. 136 TFEU: "The Member States whose currency is the euro may establish a stability mechanism to be activated if indispensable to safeguard the stability of the euro area as a whole. The granting of any required financial assistance under the mechanism will be made subject to strict conditionality". Cf. European Council 24/25 March 2011, Conclusions, Annex II, p. 21.

[228]However, the ESM may intervene, as an exception, in debt primary markets on the basis of a macro-economic adjustment programme with strict conditionality and if agreed by the Board of Governors by mutual agreement.

[229]The Board of Governors will be composed of the Ministers of Finance of the euro-area Member States (as voting members), with the European Commissioner for Economic and Monetary Affairs and the President of the ECB as observers.

[230]European Council 24/25 March 2011, Conclusions, Annex II, p. 27.

international rules and in line with IMF practice while in case of an actual insolvency private-sector creditors would be committed to (adequate and proportionate) involvement in the restructuring process.[231] This procedure will ensure that in order to restore debt sustainability the beneficiary State will first of all have to rely on itself, then on the private creditors and as ultima ratio on the international community.[232]

With the preferred creditor status of the ESM the tax-payers of the contributing Member States are somewhat protected from losses. From June 2013, in order to facilitate the restructuring process all new euro area government securities will include standardised and identical collective action clauses in their terms and conditions. This would enable the creditors, in case of insolvency of the debtor, to agree with the qualified majority on a binding amendment of the payment terms.[233] The interest rate of ESM financial assistance will exceed the ESM funding cost by 200 basic points (bps) (with a surcharge of 100 bps for loan amounts outstanding after three years), thus in effect 100 bps below the charges in the framework of the EFSF. This, however, lowers the threshold (and thus the inhibition) for seeking external support, hence reducing incentives to return to financing on the capital market.

As a result, the introduction of the ESM, at least in form of the provision of loans below market interest rates, a "soft restructuring" or even a "haircut" of the debts of the States concerned will contradict the no bail-out clause of Art. 125 TFEU, if this provision is interpreted as a strict and absolute prohibition addressed to the Union and the Member States to assume liabilities of other Member States. At the same time, the reform of financial market regulation appears at least as urgent as the creation of a permanent crisis management mechanism. Critics regard this new international organisation ESM not only as a safeguard mechanism but also as a rescue "of banks at the citizens' expense" (*M. Otte, H.-O. Henkel*).

6.4.5 Settlement of the Dispute on the Introduction of a European Economic Government

The assistance for indebted states as well as the reform of the EMU have led to the emergence of a European Economic Government whose role and competence in coordinating national economic policies, however, have not yet clearly manifested. Also as a partner in a common dialogue with the ECB, its functions still lie in the dark, especially when it gets to enforce a supposed primacy of politics in the field of monetary and fiscal policy.

At a speech given before the European Parliament on 21 October 2008, French President *N. Sarkozy* made a further plea for a "European Economic Government". "The euro area", he said, "cannot be sustained without a clearly defined economic government". Its task would be "to hold discussions with the European Central Bank" without threatening its independence: "Dialogue, democracy and mutual

[231]European Council 24/25 March 2011, Conclusions, Annex II, p. 29 et seq.

[232]Sinn and Carstensen 2010, p. 9.

[233]European Council 24/25 March 2011, Conclusions, Annex II, p. 31.

independence resemble the spirit of the Treaty". As regards the structure of the European Economic Government, he explained that it would have to be "a euro group at the level of Heads of State and Government. With a crisis like the one we have now, a meeting of the Finance Ministers on their own is not sufficient".[234]

In those words he reasserted an old French proposition which had been formulated by the *Delors* Committee during the preparations for the far-reaching reform project which led to the Maastricht Treaty (1992). That Committee said that the process of integration demands "more intensive and effective policy coordination [...] not only in the monetary field but also in areas of national economic management affecting aggregate demand, prices and costs of production". In particular, an EMU that goes substantially beyond the project of an internal market "will require further major steps in all areas of economic policy-making [...]. For this reason it would not be possible simply to follow the example of existing federal States; it would be necessary to develop an innovative and unique approach."[235]

Other Member States have opposed such an economic government, in particular the small States that are afraid of being patronised by the large Member States. For that reason Luxembourg Prime Minister *J.C. Juncker* rejects a European Economic Government that would include the entire Union and instead wants to strengthen the instruments of coordination between the States within the euro area. The coordination that he suggests would be far more comprehensive than what is proposed by the European Commission for he also wants to include wage policy[236] in this process. The place for such coordination should be the euro group whose current president is *Juncker*. In the light of "stronger economic growth in the European Union", Protocol (No. 14) on the Euro Group annexed to the Lisbon Treaty confers upon the Group the task of initiating "enhanced dialogue between the Member States whose currency is the euro". Nevertheless, the Protocol only provides for a rather weak means of action for that purpose, according to which the "Member States whose currency is the euro shall meet informally [...] when necessary". The Commission shall take part in, and the ECB shall be invited to, such meetings. These are the first institutional approaches for economic governance in the euro area and its development is largely dependent upon the political consensus of the States whose currency is the euro.

In its opposition to an economic government that would comprise the entire Union the representatives of the small States were at first supported by one of the larger Member States. Germany, represented by *A. Merkel*, had repeatedly stated that it was not in favour of the proposal of the French President.[237] The German Chancellor voiced her opposition against the idea put forward in the Commission

[234] http://library.fes.de/pdf-files/bueros/paris/06060.pdf

[235] Cf. Committee for the Study of Economic and Monetary Union 1989, p. 15 et seqq.; see also Baum-Ceisig (2002), p. 34 et seqq.; Wendt (2002), p. 112 et seqq.

[236] Cf. Baum-Ceisig (2002).

[237] Differently former Foreign Minister J. Fischer in an article in *Die Zeit* of 20 October 2008 titled "Europa braucht eine Wirtschaftsregierung [Europe needs an Economic Government]".

Communication "Europe 2020" to link the Union's control regarding the growth targets stated in the "strategy" to the surveillance of the SGP. For her, the Heads of State and Government of the Union's Member States *are* the European Economic Government,[238] for according to the opinion of the German Federal Government a European Economic Government can threaten the independence of the ECB's monetary policy and at the same time constitute an intervention into collective bargaining policies between the respective social partners. Budget consolidation could be at stake if within a European Economic Government Germany would be obliged to provide for economic stimulation.

The German Federal Government prevailed with these ideas at the informal meeting of Heads of State and Government of the European Council on 11 June 2010. At this meeting German Chancellor *Merkel* declared that "the Heads of State and Government regard themselves as an economic government of the 27 Member States. This means that we coordinate better and can act better in public". By that she accepted the French concept of an "economic government", although not as a new institution of the States of the euro area but rather as a requirement for coordination and cooperation between all Member States of the Union. The European Economic Government is the European Council of the 27 Heads of State and Government.[239] In such a "budgetary Union" (*J.-C. Trichet*) the "key figures of the national budgets of the Member States" are to be governed for the sake of a new transparency in order to be able to proceed more quickly against those Member States that do not comply with the SGP by means of "monitoring" or the imposition of sanctions.[240] Such enhanced cooperation between the Member States in connection with the obligation to provide data on their fiscal policies to the Statistical Office of the EU is covered by the Treaties in Art. 119.1 and 121 TFEU.

The coordination of the economic policies of the Member States could be achieved more effectively outside the institutional setting of the Union, e.g. by establishing a "European Council of Experts". As a committee of economic policy advisors, European "Economic Experts" could be entrusted with the task of examining the macroeconomic development of the European Union. This could help facilitate the forming of opinions and decision-making with the Heads of State and Government and the Economic and Finance Ministers of the Member States as well as with the European public sphere. At the same time this would create an element of institutional rivalry (*J. Zweynert*) that could enter into competition with the often weak institutional design of economic and fiscal policy of the peripheral States about the best ideas of national competitiveness.

---

[238] Cf. the statement attributed to A. Merkel towards French President Sarkozy "We are the Economic Government". Differently the opinion of the SPD-near Friedrich Ebert Stiftung; cf. Busch (2010), p. 2, 6 et seqq.: "The euro area needs an Economic Government with a Europeanisation of budgetary competences in order to conduct effective fiscal policy and generally be able to prevent excessive debts of the Member States" (our translation).

[239] Cf. statement by Chancellor A. Merkel to President Sarkozy at a press conference on 11 June 2010 (transcript).

[240] Cf. Busch (2010), p. 3 et seqq., who favours a "mix of monetary and fiscal policy" (our translation).

6.4.6 The Effects of the Euro Crisis on Public Opinion in Germany Regarding European Integration

According to the results of current surveys,[241] Germans have lost part of their confidence in the European currency, even though its acceptance slowly but surely rose between 2002 (when it started from a low value of 21%) and the crisis within the euro area due to the Greek national debt. This on the whole rather sceptical attitude of the Germans towards the Union currency is, however, to be contrasted with the appreciation in the other 16 Member States within the euro area. Before the economic and financial crisis, in September 2008, 71% of respondents in the euro area stated that the euro has had a positive influence on Europe. Only 16% regarded it as a negative phenomenon.[242] For a minority of the persons questioned (22%), the euro was a catalyst for a European identity.[243] Nonetheless it is significant that a majority of the respondents (59%) in the Member States for which the Council has not (yet) determined that they meet the criteria necessary for the introduction of the euro – the so-called "Pre-ins" according to Art. 139 TFEU – felt that they were not properly informed.[244] This finding could probably be replicated for the citizens of the Member States with euro currency.

The results of the survey amongst the German citizens show that there is a link between the approval rate of the euro and the benefits of European integration for Germany: The lower the approval rate, the more sceptical people are towards the membership of the EU. For 42% of the German respondents there are no advantages of EU membership that outweigh the disadvantages; rather there is equilibrium. One fifth of the population is convinced that Germany would experience disadvantages if it left the Union. For 26% there are more disadvantages, and 52% of them do not have confidence in the euro. The solid pro-European core within Germany is apparently not unshakable. However, given the global political importance of the United States and the rise of China and India, the majority is convinced that for European States there is no way other than close cooperation and a common political course to be able to assert their interest in this new global balance of power.[245]

In this respect, the findings of the survey resulting from the correlation between confidence in the euro and advantages of an EU membership are somewhat relative. In public opinion the Union is still an important factor as an economic community

[241]Cf. for the survey Köcher (2010), p. 5 and table 4, in parts published in FAZ of 28 April 2010, p. 5.

[242]Cf. European Commission, Flash Eurobarometer no. 251, Public attitudes and perceptions in the euro area, Analytical report, 2008, p. 5.

[243]Cf. European Commission, Flash Eurobarometer no. 251, Public attitudes and perceptions in the euro area, Analytical report, 2008, p. 5.

[244]CF. European Commission, Flash Eurobarometer no. 280, Introduction of the euro in the new Member States, 2009, p. 5. Only in the Czech Republic a majority of respondents felt well informed (52%), compared to 45% of citizens who felt they had a low level of knowledge.

[245]Cf. Köcher (2010), p. 10 et seq. and table A 10.

for the facilitation and promotion of trade between European States (64%). In public awareness it is also a force for political stability (57%) and for peace and security in Europe (54%).[246] Its central contribution to global politics seems to have replaced its role as a simple economic union in the minds of the Germans.

References

Barents R (1993) The Internal Market Unlimited: Some Observations on the Legal Basis of Community Legislation. CMLR 30, pp 85 et seqq
Baum-Ceisig A (2002) Lohnpolitik unter den Bedingungen der Europäischen Wirtschafts- und Währungsunion, Dissertation Osnabrück
Behrens P (1994) Die Wirtschaftsverfassung der Europäischen Gemeinschaft. In: Brüggemeier G (ed) Verfassungen für ein ziviles Europa. Nomos, Baden-Baden, pp 73 et seqq
Behrens P (2008) Der Wettbewerb im Vertrag von Lissabon. EuZW, 193 et seqq
Blanke H-J (2010) Die Dienstleistungsfreiheit. In: Blanke H-J, Scherzberg A, Wegner G (eds) Dimensionen des Wettbewerbs. Mohr Siebeck, Tübingen, pp 345 et seqq
Blanke H-J, Thumfart A (2010) Generalbericht. In: Blanke H-J, Scherzberg A, Wegner G (eds) Dimensionen des Wettbewerbs. Mohr Siebeck, Tübingen, pp 1 et seqq
Böhm F (1933) Wettbewerb und Monopolkampf. Berlin: Heymann
Böhm F (1946) Die Bedeutung der Wirtschaftsordnung für die politische Verfassung, Süddeutsche Juristen-Zeitung, pp 141 et seqq
Bundesministerium der Finanzen (2010) Neue europäische Task Force, Eckpunkte der Bundesregierung zur Stärkung der Eurozone (http://www.bundesfinanzministerium.de/nn_97140/DE/Wirtschaft__und__Verwaltung/Europa/Der__Euro/20100520-Task-Force.html) accessed 15 January 2011
Busch K (2010) Europäische Wirtschaftsregierung und Koordinierung der Lohnpolitik. http://library.fes.de/pdf-files/id/ipa/07108.pdf
Calliess Ch (2009) Eigentumsgrundrecht. In: Ehlers D (ed) Europäische Grundrechte und Grundfreiheiten, 3rd edn. de Gruyter, Berlin, pp 593 et seqq
Calliess Ch, Ruffert M (2011) EUV/AEUV, Das Verfassungsrecht der Europäischen Union mit Europäischer Grundrechtecharta, Kommentar, 4th edn. Beck, München
Clark JM (1961) Competition as a dynamic process, Brookings Institution, Washington
Deutsche Bundesbank (2010) European monetary union facing crucial challenges. Monthly Report, May 2010
Drexl J (2009) Wettbewerbsverfassung. In: von Bogdandy A, Bast J (eds) Europäisches Verfassungsrecht. Theoretische und dogmatische Grundzüge, 2nd edn. Springer, Berlin, pp 905 et seqq
Eucken W (1959) Grundsätze der Wirtschaftspolitik, Ausgabe für Rowohlts Deutsche Enzyklopädie
Everling U (1996) Wirtschaftsverfassung und Richterrecht in der EG, Fs. J. Mestmäcker, pp 365 et seqq
Fikentscher W (1993) Recht und wirtschaftliche Freiheit, Mohr, Tübingen
Fischer J. Jonung L. Larch M (2006) 101 Proposals to reform the Stability and Growtj Pact. Why so many? A Survey (http://ec.europa.eu/economy_finance/publications/publication833_en.pdf) accessed 15 January 2011
Frenz F (2004) Handbuch Europarecht, Bd. 1: Europäische Grundfreiheiten. Springer, Berlin
Grabitz E, Hilf M (2002) Das Recht der Europäischen Union, Kommentar. Beck, München

[246]Köcher (2010), p. 9 et seq. and table A 9.

Häberle P (2008) Europäische Verfassungslehre, 5th edn. Nomos, Baden-Baden
Hallstein W (1946) Wiederherstellung des Privatrechts, Süddeutsche Juristen-Zeitung, pp 1 et seqq
Hallstein W (1969) Der unvollendete Bundesstaat. Düsseldorf: Econ-Verlag
Hatje A (2009) Wirtschaftsverfassung im Binnenmarkt. In: von Bogdandy A, Bast J (eds) Europäisches Verfassungsrecht. Theoretische und dogmatische Grundzüge, 2nd edn. Springer, Berlin, pp 801 et seqq
Heipertz M, Verdun A (2010) Ruling Europe. The Politics oft he Stability and Growth Pact. Cambridge University Press, Cambridge
Iliopoulos-Strangas J (2010) Klassifizierung – Aufstellung und Rechtsnatur der sozialen Grundrechte. In: Iliopoulos-Strangas J (ed) Soziale Grundrechte in Europa nach Lissabon. Nomos, Baden-Baden, pp 865 et seqq
Ipsen HP (1972) Europäisches Gemeinschaftsrecht. Mohr, Tübingen
Joerges Ch (1991) Markt ohne Staat? Die Wirtschaftsverfassung der Gemeinschaft und die regulative Politik. In: Wildenmann R (ed) Staatswerdung Europas? Optionen für eine politische Union. Nomos, Baden-Baden
Joerges Ch (1994) Legitimationsprobleme des europäischen Wirtschaftsrechts und der Vertrag von Maastricht. In: Brüggemeier G (ed) Verfassungen für ein ziviles Europa. Nomos, Baden-Baden, pp 91 et seqq
Joerges Ch (2002) Das Recht im Prozess der Konstitutionalisierung Europas. In: Kohler-Koch B, Jachtenfuchs M (eds) Verfassungspolitik in der Europäischen Union, pp 53 et seqq. Mannheim. http://www.mzes.uni-mannheim.de/publications/books/verfassungspolitik_EU.pdf
Kämmerer JA (2001) Privatisierung: Typologie - Determinanten - Rechtspraxis - Folgen, Mohr Siebeck, Tübingen
Kämmerer JA (2002) Daseinsvorsorge als Gemeinschaftsziel oder: Europas soziales Gewissen, NVwZ, pp 1041 et seqq
Kantzenbach E (1966) Die Funktionsfähigkeit des Wettbewerbs. Vandenhoeck & Ruprecht, Göttingen
Kaysen C, Turner DF (1959) Antitrust Policy: An Economic and Legal Analysis, Oxford University Press, London
Kerber W (2000) Rechtseinheitlichkeit und Rechtsvielfalt aus ökonomischer Sicht. In: Grundmann St (ed) Systembildung und Systemlücken in Kerngebieten des Europäischen Privatrechts. Mohr Siebeck, Tübingen, pp 67 et seqq
Kersten, J (2010) Die Herstellung von Wettbewerb als Verwaltungsaufgabe. VVDStRL 69, pp 288 et seqq
Kingreeen Th (2009) Grundfreiheiten. In: von Bogdandy A, Bast J (eds) Europäisches Verfassungsrecht: Theoretische und dogmatische Grundzüge, 2nd edn. Springer, Berlin, pp 705 et seqq
Köcher R (2010) Vertrauensverlust für die europäische Währung. Institut für Demoskopie Allensbach, Allensbach
Kotzur M (2008) Die soziale Marktwirtschaft nach dem Reformvertrag. In: Pernice I (ed) Der Vertrag von Lissabon: Reform der EU ohne Verfassung? Nomos, Baden-Baden, pp 197 et seqq
Krautscheid A (ed) (2009) Die Daseinsvorsorge im Spannungsfeld von europäischem Wettbewerb und Gemeinwohl – Eine sektorspezifische Betrachtung. VS, Wiesbaden
Krueger AO (2002) A new approach to sovereign debt restructuring. International Monetary Fund. http://www.imf.org/external/pubs/ft/exrp/sdrm/eng/sdrm.pdf
Mann Th (2002) Öffentliche Unternehmen im Spannungsfeld von öffentlichem Auftrag und Wettbewerb, JZ, pp 819 et seqq
Mangiameli St (ed) (2008) I servizi pubblici locali. Giappichelli, Torino
Mehde V (2005) Wettbewerb zwischen Staaten, Nomos, Baden-Baden
Mestmäcker E-J (2001) Die Wirtschaftsverfassung der EG zwischen Wettbewerb und Intervention. In: Bruha Th et al (eds) Welche Verfassung für Europa? Nomos, Baden-Baden, pp 163 et seqq

Meyer J (2006) Charta der Grundrechte der Europäischen Union, Kommentar, 2nd edn. Nomos, Baden-Baden
Moec G (2010a) Discussing "orderly restructuring". Deutsche Bank, Focus Europe, 5 November 2010, p 8
Moec G (2010b) Beyond emergency, a tentative road-map for EMU. Deutsche Bank, Focus Europe, 22 October 2010, p 3
Moravcsik A (1998) The Choice for Europe: Social Purpose and State Power from Messina to Maastricht. Cornell University Press, Ithaca
Morin E (1991) Europa denken. Campus-Verlag, Frankfurt/Main, New York
Müller-Armack A (1947) Wirtschaftslenkung und Marktwirtschaft. Hamburg : Verlag für Wirtschaft und Sozialpolitik
Müller-Armack A (1966) Die Wirtschaftsordnung des Gemeinsamen Marktes. In: Müller-Armack A (ed) Wirtschaftsordnung und Wirtschaftspolitik, pp 401 et seqq
Müller-Graff P-Ch (2002a) Grundfreiheiten und Gemeinschaftsgrundrechte. In: Cremer H-J, Giegerich Th, Richter D, Zimmermann A (eds) Tradition und Weltoffenheit des Rechts, Festschrift für Helmut Steinberger: Beiträge zum ausländischen öffentlichen Recht und Völkerrecht Band 152. Springer, Heidelberg, pp 1281 et seqq
Müller-Graff P-Ch (2002b) Die Verdichtung des Binnenmarktes zwischen Handlungsfreiheiten und Sozialgestaltung. EuR-Beiheft 1, pp 7 et seqq
Müller-Graff P-Ch (2009) Das wirtschaftsverfassungsrechtliche Profil der EU nach Lissabon. In: Fastenrath U, Nowak C (eds) Der Lissabonner Reformvertrag: Änderungsimpulse in einzelnen Rechts- und Politikbereichen. Duncker & Humblot, Berlin, pp 173 et seqq
Mussler W (1998) Die Wirtschaftsverfassung der Europäischen Gemeinschaft im Wandel. Von Rom nach Maastricht. Nomos, Baden-Baden
Nettesheim M (2002) Mitgliedstaatliche Daseinsvorsorge im Spannungsfeld zwischen Wettbewerbskonformität und Gemeinwohlverantwortung. In: Hrbek R, Nettesheim M (eds) Europäische Union und mitgliedstaatliche Daseinsvorsorge. Nomos, Baden-Baden, pp 39 et seqq
Nicolaysen G (1981) Wirtschaftsfreiheit. In: R Bieber et al. (eds) Das Europa der zweiten Generation. Gedächtnisschrift für Christoph Sasse, Volume 2, Nomos, Straßbourg, pp 651 et seqq
Nicolaysen G (2003) Die gemeinschaftsrechtliche Begründung von Grundrechten. EuR, pp 719 et seqq
Nowak C (2009) Binnenmarktziel und Wirtschaftsverfassung der Europäischen Union vor und nach dem Reformvertrag von Lissabon. EuR Beiheft 1, pp 129 et seqq
Palm U (2004) Der Bruch des Stabilitäts- und Wachstumspaktes. EuZW, pp 71 et seqq
Rengeling H-W (2004) Die wirtschaftsbezogenen Grundrechte in der Grundrechtecharta. DVBl, pp 453 et seqq
Rittner F (1998) Drei Grundfragen des Wettbewerbs. In: Hörn G et al (eds) Festschrift für Alfons Kraft zum 70. Geburtstag. Luchterhand, Neuwied, pp 519 et seqq
Rodriguez Iglesias GC (2003) Die Rechtsprechung des Europäischen Gerichtshofs zu Art. 141 EG-Vertrag und ihre Auswirkungen auf die Gleichberechtigung von Frauen und Männern in den Rechtsordnungen der Mitgliedstaaten. In: Wolfrum R (ed) Gleichheit und Nichtdiskriminierung im nationalen und internationalen Menschenrechtsschutz. Springer, Heidelberg, pp 135 et seqq
Ruffert M (2004) Die Wirtschaftsverfassung im Vertrag über eine Verfassung für Europa, Zentrum für Europäisches Wirtschaftsrecht (ed), Nr. 144
Ruffert M (2009) Grundrecht der Berufsfreiheit. In: Ehlers D (ed) Europäische Grundrechte und Grundfreiheiten. De Gruyter, Berlin, pp 574 et seqq
Schachtschneider KA (2007) Quo vadis Europa? Ad finem Democraticae. In: Lachmann W, Haupt R, Farmer K (eds) Zur Zukunft Europas: Wirtschaftsethische Probleme der Europäischen Union. Lit, Berlin, pp 16 et seqq
Schink A (2005) Kommunale Daseinsvorsorge in Europa. DVBl, pp 861 et seqq

Schmidt R (1986) Staatliche Verantwortung für die Wirtschaft. In: Isensee J, Kirchhof P (eds) Handbuch des Staatsrechts der Bundesrepublik Deutschland, Bd. III, 2nd edn. Müller, Heidelberg et al
Schmidt I (2005) Wettbewerbspolitik und Kartellrecht: Eine interdisziplinäre Einführung, 8th edn. Lucius & Lucius, Stuttgart
Schwarze J (2001a) Daseinsvorsorge im Lichte des europäischen Wettbewerbsrechts. EuZW, pp 334 et seqq
Schwarze J (2001b) Einführung. In: Schwarze J (ed) Daseinsvorsorge im Lichte des Wettbewerbsrechts. Nomos, Baden-Baden, pp 9 et seqq
Schweitzer H (2004) In: Schwarze J (ed) Der Verfassungsentwurf des Europäischen Konvents: verfassungsrechtliche Grundstrukturen und wirtschaftsverfassungsrechtliches Konzept. Nomos, Baden-Baden, pp 269 et seqq
Scorl K (2007) Begriff, System und Grenzen deutscher und europäischer Wirtschaftsverfassung. In: Gornig GH, Kramer U, Volkmann U (eds) Staat – Wirtschaft – Gemeinde, Festschrift W. Frotscher, Berlin: Duncker and Humblot, pp 335 et seqq
Semmelmann C (2009) Die Wirtschaftsverfassung der EG zwischen Markt und Recht – Eine institutionelle und prozedurale Persepektive. In: Towfigh EV et al (eds) Recht und Markt. Nomos, Baden-Baden, pp 227 et seqq
Siedentop L (2002) Demokratie in Europa. Klett-Cotta, Stuttgart
Sinn H-W, Carstensen K (2010) Ein Krisenmechanismus für die Eurozone. *ifo Schnelldienst*, Sonderausgabe
Sodan H (2000) Vorrang der Privatheit als Prinzip der Wirtschaftsverfassung. DÖV, pp 361 et seqq
Stigler GJ (1957) Perfect Competition. Historically Contemplated, The Journal of Political Economy 65, pp 1 et seqq
Storr St (2002) Zwischen überkommener Daseinsvorsorge und Diensten von allgemeinem wirtschaftlichen Interesse, DÖV, pp 357 et seqq
Tettinger PJ, Stern K (2006) Kölner Gemeinschaftskommentar zur Europäischen Grundrechte-Charta, Kommentar. Beck, München
Vedder Ch, Heintschel von Heinegg W (2007) Europäischer Verfassungsvertrag, Handkommentar. Nomos, Baden-Baden
von Danwitz Th (2009) Dienste von allgemeinem wirtschaftlichen Interesse in der europäischen Wettbewerbsordnung. In: Krautscheid A (ed) Die Daseinsvorsorge im Spannungsfeld von europäischem Wettbewerb und Gemeinwohl – Eine sektorspezifische Betrachtung. VS, Wiesbaden, pp 103 et seqq
von Lewinski K (2011) Öffentlichrechtliche Insolvenz und Staatsbankrott. Tübingen: Mohr Siebeck
Waiz E (2009) Daseinsvorsorge in der Europäischen Union – Etappen einer Debatte. In: Krautscheid A (ed) Die Daseinsvorsorge im Spannungsfeld von europäischem Wettbewerb und Gemeinwohl – Eine sektorspezifische Betrachtung. VS, Wiesbaden, pp 41 et seqq
Weck-Hannemann H (1998) Globalisierung: Herausforderung oder Anwendungsfall der Neuen Politischen Ökonomie? In: Streit M et al (eds) Globalisierung, Systemwettbewerb und nationalstaatliche Politik. Jahrbuch für Neue Politische Ökonomie 17. Mohr Siebeck, Tübingen, pp 84 et seqq
Welti F (2005) Die kommunale Daseinsvorsorge und der Vertrag über eine Verfassung für Europa, Archiv des öffentlichen Rechts. AöR 130, pp 529 et seqq
Wendt V (2002) Die Schaffung der Europäischen Wirtschafts- und Währungsunion: Spill-over und internationale Entscheidung? Eine Analyse für Deutschland und Frankreich, Dissertation Passau
Wernicke S (2008) Der Vertrag von Lissabon und das Wettbewerbsprinzip – Status quo ante, Neugewichtung oder Unwucht? In: Pernice I (ed) Der Vertrag von Lissabon: Reform der EU ohne Verfassung? Nomos, Baden-Baden, pp 190 et seqq
Zohlnhöfer W (1968) Wettbewerbspolitik im Oligopol, Kyklos-Verlag, Basel

The Treaty of Lisbon and the Economic and Monetary Union

Ulrich Häde

After a long wait, the Treaty of Lisbon entered into force on 1 December 2009. The Treaty provides for changes in the area of the Economic and Monetary Union (EMU). Especially, the European Central Bank (ECB) becomes a European Union (EU) institution. This essay will outline the most important innovations and will especially deal with the future position of the ECB in the institutional framework of the EU.

1 From Maastricht to Lisbon

Until the end of November 2009, the *Treaty establishing the European Community* (EC) had been in force in the form it was given by the Treaty of Maastricht, the Treaty of Amsterdam and the Treaty of Nice. Actually, the EC Treaty and the *Treaty on European Union* (TEU) were to be succeeded by the *Treaty establishing a Constitution for Europe* (TCE). However, the ratification of the Constitutional Treaty failed. After the positive outcome of the referendum in Ireland, the 2007 Reform Treaty of Lisbon[1] now forms a new primary legal basis for the Union.

This contribution is based on an article that has been published in German in the journal "Europarecht" (2009, p. 200 et seqq.); The author would like to thank Nomos Verlagsgesellschaft for permission to publish this article; translated by Robert Böttner, assistant at the Chair for Public Law, International Public Law and European Integration at the University of Erfurt.

[1] *Treaty of Lisbon amending the Treaty on European Union and the Treaty establishing the European Community, signed at Lisbon, 13 December 2007* O.J. C 306/1. For general overview on development and content of the Reform Treaty, see Hatje and Kindt (2008); Oppermann (2008); Raepenbusch (2007); Weber (2008).

U. Häde (✉)
Lehrstuhl für Öffentliches Recht, insbesondere Verwaltungsrecht, Finanzrecht und Währungsrecht, Europa-Universität Viadrina, Postfach 1786, 15207 Frankfurt (Oder), Germany
e-mail: Haede@europa-uni.de

H.-J. Blanke and S. Mangiameli (eds.), *The European Union after Lisbon*, 421
DOI 10.1007/978-3-642-19507-5_16, © Springer-Verlag Berlin Heidelberg 2012

One of the substantial changes is that the EU has replaced and succeeded the EC. Consequently, the Union is equipped with legal personality (Art. 47 TEU). The form of the EU Treaty will remain while the EC Treaty is renamed *Treaty on the Functioning of the European Union* (TFEU). The Treaties shall have the same legal value and shall form the future primary legal basis of the Union (Art. 1(3) TEU). One important innovation of the Lisbon Treaty is that Art. 13.1 (2) TEU lists the former EC institutions (European Parliament, Council, Commission, Court of Justice and Court of Auditors) as well as the European Council and the ECB as EU institutions. Moreover, further modifications have been made regarding the monetary policy.

2 Contents of the Economic and Monetary Union

2.1 Status Quo

The provisions of the EC Treaty as of 1 November 1993 (amended by the EU Treaty) regarding the EMU led to the introduction of the euro currency on 1 January 1999.[2] By now, the euro is the common currency of 16 Member States.[3] Most recently, Slovakia has introduced the euro effective 1 January 2009 in spite of strong concerns of the ECB regarding the sustainability of the reached price stability.[4, 5] The Member States with euro currency have substantially conferred their competences for tasks of monetary policy to the EC. These functions are performed on the European level by the *European System of Central Banks* (ESCB), composed of the ECB and the national central banks (Art. 282.1 TFEU). The legal basis for this is the provisions of the Treaties and the annexed ESCB Statute, which is an integral part of the Treaties (Art. 51 TEU; annexed Protocol No. 4).

---

[2]Article 2 of Council Regulation (EC) 974/98 *on the introduction of the euro*, O.J. L 139/1 (1998).

[3]As soon as 15 Member States have introduced the euro, the rotation principle for the voting right in the Governing Council of the ECB as provided for in Art. 10.2 ESCB Statute applies, regardless of the Treaty of Lisbon. Cf. Gaitanides (2005a), p. 92 et seqq.; Wagner and Grum (2005), p. 78 et seqq. The Governing Council has used, however, the possibility to "decide to postpone the start of the rotation system until the date on which the number of governors exceeds 18", as provided for in Art. 10.2 ESCB Statute; cf. http://www.ecb.int/press/pr/date/2008/html/pr081218.en.html

[4]ECB, Convergence Report May 2008, p. 89.

[5]Cf. The positive evaluation by the Commission in: European Commission, Convergence Report 2008 (http://ec.europa.eu/economy_finance/publications/publication12574_en.pdf), p. 27 et seqq.

2.2 *Economic Union*

2.2.1 Asymmetry of the EMU

The European EMU is characterised by a clear asymmetry. The monetary policy, which is almost completely conferred to the Union, is opposed by the general economic policy which still resides with the Member States. The best that could be agreed to in the Treaty of Maastricht was the coordination of economic policies and Community supervision over national debt policies. Future changes to the Treaty were nothing more than cosmetic ones.[6] Nevertheless, the Constitutional Treaty was going to adopt these provisions without any further adjustments. The provisions on coordination of economic policies (Art. 98 et seqq. EC) were almost literally adopted by Art. III-178 TCE, of course adapted to the new terminology. The Lisbon Treaty follows along those lines; however, there are minor changes towards applicable law that can make quite a difference in individual cases.

There is no substantial modification in the almost continuous omission of the reference that the Council makes certain decisions with a qualified majority. This is now provided for in Art. 16.3 TEU, which makes qualified majority votes the usual case. This majority is, however, to be calculated by the new standards of the Lisbon Treaty.

2.2.2 Strengthening of the Commission

The competences of the Commission are new.[7] Both within the so-called multilateral surveillance of national economic policies and in the procedure for the identification of an excessive deficit, the Commission can now autonomously take actions against Member States. According to the first sentence of Art. 121.4 TFEU it can address a warning to a Member State whose economic policy is inconsistent with agreed guidelines or which risks jeopardising the proper functioning of the EMU.[8] Also, Art. 126.5 TFEU authorises the Commission to address an opinion to a Member State if an excessive deficit exists or may occur. So far, respective authorisation was not provided for by Art. 99.4 and Art. 104.5 EC. The Commission could only consult the Council and recommend measures. As experience teaches, however, the larger Member States, especially Germany and France, often tried to block such warnings.[9]

[6]To the most important changes, see Häde (2001).

[7]Cf. Gloggnitzer (2008), p. 87 et seq.; Walter and Becker (2007), p. 8.

[8]Cf. Fischer (2008), p. 263; Rodi, in Vedder and Heintschel von Heinegg (2007), Art. III-179 para 11.

[9]On Germany's resistance to an early warning 2002 see Bark (2004), p. 200 et seq.; Selmayr (2003). France refused to accept a decision in spring 2008; cf. Proissl (2008), p. 14.

Another new aspect is that the Council decides on the existence of an excessive deficit in one of the Member States not on a recommendation (as provided for by Art. 104.6 EC), but on a proposal from the Commission (Art. 126.6 TEU). This inconspicuous change means that the Council may now deviate from the Commission proposal only by a unanimous vote. This is due to the fact that while it principally acts by a qualified majority vote (Art. 16.3 TEU), the amendment of a proposal of the Commission according to Art. 293.1 TFEU (former Art. 250.1 EC) requires unanimity. This modification also strengthens the position of the Commission towards the Council in excessive deficit procedures. However, this is only a subarea, because on further actions (notices, imposition of sanctions) the Council continues to decide only on recommendation of the Commission (first sentence of Art. 126.13 TFEU).

2.2.3 Suspension of Voting Rights

The budgetary discipline is sharpened up a little in that the Member State whose debt policy is under consideration cannot take part in the Council vote. So far this has already applied to any further actions taken after the identification of an excessive deficit (Art. 104.13 EC). Article 126.13 (2) TFEU, however, now also excludes the vote of the representative of the Member State concerned from the decision according to paragraph 6. Thus, the Council decision on whether an excessive deficit exists in one of the Member States is now made without the involvement (in form of a vote) of that Member State. This reduces the possibility of blocking that vote, even though it must be assumed that Member States with an excessive deficit could come to each other's defence.

2.2.4 Differentiation Between States with and Without Euro Currency

The differences between those Member States with and those without euro currency are more strongly emphasised. The latter, called "Member States with a derogation" (Art. 139.1 TFEU),[10] are already ineligible to vote in the Council in certain decisions regarding euro-zone countries. However, as far as the excessive deficit procedures are concerned, this only applied to Art. 104.9 and 11 EC, and thus to decisions on giving notice to a Member State and the imposition of sanctions. However, proposals of the Council according to paragraphs 6, 7, 8 and 12 were not mentioned by the relevant Art. 122 EC in its paragraphs 3 and 5. This meant that Member States with a derogation had the right to vote on Council proposals according to Art. 104.6, 7 and 8 EC. The same applied to the abrogation of proposals they were involved in (Art. 104.12 EC). Nevertheless, the existing law

[10]Denmark and Great Britain have a special status. However, the same rules apply for the areas referred to in this text. Thus, they are not discussed separately.

should have prevented, pursuant to correct interpretation, the Member States with a derogation from participating in the vote on Council decisions on the abrogation of measures according to Art. 104.9 and 11 EC.[11] Since 1 December 2009, Art. 139.4(1) lit. b TFEU provides for the suspension of the voting rights of members of the Council representing Member States with a derogation for all measures against Member States with euro currency as laid down in Art. 126.6, 7, 8, 12 and 13 TFEU and clarifies the cases addressed above. By mentioning paragraph 13, however, the Member States have gone well beyond the target, since it does not even provide for actions to be taken by the Council.

According to Art. 139.4 (1) lit. a TFEU the voting rights of Member States with a derogation are also suspended when the Council addresses recommendations to Member States with euro currency within the framework of the multilateral surveillance of national economic policies based on Art. 121.4 TFEU (former Art. 99.4 EC). These provisions of Art. 139.4 TFEU are linked to the tendency of a clear distinction between Member States with and without euro currency, as is expressed in the heading of the new chapter on "provisions specific to Member States whose currency is the euro". The relevant Art. 136-138 TFEU have already been in the Constitutional Treaty as Art. III-194-196 TCE. In the context of the Economic Union, Art. 136 TFEU is of special relevance. According to this provision, the Council adopts measures that only apply to those Member States whose currency is the euro. In the Council, only the representatives of those Member States have the right to vote. The provisions provide for the proper functioning of the EMU. Article 136 TFEU lists two areas to which these provisions can apply: on the one hand the strengthening of the coordination and surveillance of the budgetary discipline of the euro-zone countries and on the other hand the setting out of economic policy guidelines for those states.

In the euro area there is a central monetary policy, but economic policies with decentralised accountability. This requires coordination of the general economic and budgetary policies of the Member States of the euro-zone that needs to be more intense than that of the Member States with a derogation. Article 136 TFEU takes this into account, while at the same time it limits the possible decoupling of the states with euro currency from the rest of the Union.

Although it may seem as if this regulation authorised further actions, its paragraph 1 notes that these measures are adopted "in accordance with the relevant provisions of the Treaties [and] with the relevant procedure from among those referred to in Arts. 121 and 126". This regulatory system is unlikely to improve comprehensibility. One can also interpret Art. 136.1 TFEU as meaning that all measures must be in accordance with Art. 121 and 126 TFEU. Thus, this provision does not provide for further actions. More likely its function is to expressly allow differentiations between Member States with and without euro currency that in

[11]Cf. Häde, in Calliess and Ruffert (2007), Art. 104 para 85. Different Bandilla, in Grabitz and Hilf (2007), Art. 104 para 50.

reality, and based on the formulated guidelines under Art. 99 EC, already exist anyway.[12]

On the one hand, Art. 136.1 TFEU establishes limits through the clause that the guidelines of the economic policies of the Member States with euro currency must (of course) be compatible with those adopted for the entire Union. A more important and also legally significant restriction is the exclusion of a procedure according to Art. 126.14 TFEU. This provision refers to Protocol No. 12 on the excessive deficit procedure and its amendment or replacement. The practically rather important deficit criteria that limit the maximum permissible value of the budgetary deficit in relation to the gross domestic product (GDP) to 3% and that of the government debt to 60% are not found in the Treaties, but in this Protocol. Since Art. 136.1 TFEU does not permit a proceeding according to Art. 126.14 TFEU, there cannot be any changes of the reference values or other regulations in the deficit Protocol that could privilege the Member States with euro currency.[13] This restriction can be understood more easily by recalling that the Union's objective is to eventually introduce the euro in all Member States.[14] A tightening of the deficit criteria would undermine this objective because the deficit criteria are a significant concern of the convergence criteria required for the introduction of the euro. Thus, different reference values would be problematic.

2.2.5 Declaration on Art. 126 TFEU

There are a number of Declarations attached to the Final Act of the Intergovernmental Conference that has adopted the Treaty of Lisbon, whose No. 30 is the Declaration to Art. 126 TFEU.[15] In it the Conference confirms that raising growth potential and securing sound budgetary positions are the two pillars of the economic and fiscal policy of the Union and the Member States. It calls the Stability and Growth Pact[16] an important tool to achieve these goals. This Declaration appears as if there had been a power struggle between those Member States for which price stability is most important and those which would like to put more emphasis on economic growth; however, it does not become apparent who has won. On the one hand, budgetary discipline is affirmed; on the other hand, the word "price stability" appears just once and in the list only after economic growth. That the Declaration

[12]See Rodi, in Vedder and Heintschel von Heinegg (2007), Art. III-194 para 4.

[13]Also Rodi, in Vedder and Heintschel von Heinegg (2007), Art. III-194 para 3.

[14]Cf. Häde, in Calliess and Ruffert (2007), Art. 4 EC para 13.

[15]*Declarations annexed to the Final Act of the Intergovernmental Conference which adopted the Treaty of Lisbon*, O.J. C115/347 (2008).

[16]For additional details, see Hentschelmann, Der Stabilitäts- und Wachstumspakt, 2009; Konow, Der Stabilitäts- und Wachstumspakt, 2002; Sutter, Der Stabilitäts- und Wachstumspakt in der Europäischen Währungsunion, 2000; Häde, in: Calliess and Ruffert (2007), Art. 104 para 112 et seqq. with further reference of most recent literature.

otherwise does not mention the relationship between budgetary policy and the monetary policy orientated towards price stability[17] is of no legal significance, for such declarations do not become an integral part of the Treaties and are thus not legally binding. However, they can be important for the interpretation of the law of the Treaties.[18] It remains to be seen if this Declaration might set a political signal for a detrimental interpretation or development of the provisions on budgetary policies.

2.3 Monetary Union

2.3.1 Implementation of the Euro into Primary Law

While the EC Treaty had referred to the European Currency Unit (ECU) basket (Art. 118, 121, 123, 124 EC), the Treaty of Lisbon consistently implements the euro currency into the primary law of the Union. Article 3.4 TEU already mentions the establishment of "an economic and monetary union whose currency is the euro" as one of the aims of the Union. Moreover, Art. 3.1 lit. c TFEU lists the "monetary policy for the Member States whose currency is the euro" as part of the exclusive competences of the Union. In addition, Art. 133 TFEU contains an express authorisation to "lay down the measures necessary for the use of the euro as the single currency". The legislative competence for monetary law was so far provided for by an expanding interpretation of sentence 3 of Art. 123.4 EC.[19]

While the European Parliament had not been heard by the Council before the enactment of measures concerning monetary policy, the Parliament and Council are now both competent for legal acts based on Art. 133 TFEU, for these measures are decided on by the ordinary legislative procedure, in which the Council and European Parliament act jointly on a proposal from the Commission (Art. 289 TFEU). The rules of procedure are provided for in Art. 294 TFEU. While for measures based on Art. 133 TFEU only the members of the Council representing Member States whose currency is the euro are eligible to vote (Art. 139.2 lit. f TFEU), no such regulation applies for the Parliament. There, the Members of Parliament from Member States with a derogation can also take part in the vote.

[17]See Häde, in Calliess and Ruffert (2007), Art. 104 para 6 et seq.; Ongena, in von der Groeben and Schwarze (2003), Art. 104 EG para 2.

[18]Cf. Kokott, in Streinz (2003), Art. 311 para 7; Schmalenbach, in Calliess and Ruffert (2007), Art. 311 para 4.

[19]Cf. Häde, in Calliess and Ruffert (2007), Art. 123 para 21; Kempen, in Streinz (2003), Art. 123 para 21.

2.3.2 Monetary Policy

Articles 105 et seqq. EC are used to describe the tasks and powers of the ESCB concerning monetary policy. They were adopted by Art. III-185 TCE and can now be found in Art. 127 et seqq. TFEU without any significant changes as regards the content. Details regarding monetary policy instruments and the internal division of competences in the ESCB are laid down in the Statute of the ESCB and the ECB (ESCB Statute) that was until now annexed to the EC Treaty as Protocol No. 18.[20] The terminologically adjusted Statute, which contains no transitional agreements, is now annexed to the TFEU as Protocol No. 4.[21] Changes in content have so far not been made to date. The Lisbon Treaty preserves continuity in monetary policy and monetary law.

2.3.3 Introduction of the Euro

At this point in time, not all the Member States have introduced the euro so there is a need for a procedure to integrate the euro into those Member States with other currencies. Corresponding regulations and those on the position of the Member States with a derogation had been provided for in the Constitutional Treaty in Art. III-197 et seqq. TCE. They had updated the former provisions of Art. 121-124 EC but contained no substantial changes in content. The Lisbon Treaty adopted these provisions in Art. 139 et seqq. TFEU. The Contracting Parties thus continue to follow the principle that the same conditions apply to the introduction of the common currency for all Member States.[22] The economic and legal convergence criteria, which so far were laid down in Art. 121.1 EC, are now found in Art. 140.1 TFEU with identical content.

However, some changes have been made regarding the procedure. According to the law previously in force (Art. 122.2 EC), the Council, after consulting the European Parliament and after discussion in the Council, meeting in the composition of the Heads of State or Government, decided on the abrogation of the derogations and the introduction of the euro. This provision, however, appears to be the result of insufficient editorial coordination, for it seemed rather odd that the Council in the composition of the Economics and Finance Ministers took the decision, while the same institution only contributed in an advisory way in a superior composition.[23] Article 140.2 TFEU revised this so that now the

---

[20]*Consolidated Versions of the Treaty on European Union and of the Treaty establishing the European Community*, O.J. C 321E/256 (2006).

[21]*Consolidated versions of the Treaty on European Union and the Treaty on the Functioning of the European Union*, O.J. C 115/230 (2007).

[22]See already Madrid European Council, Presidency Conclusions, Bull.EC 12/1995, p. 9 (11, point I.6); Häde, in Calliess and Ruffert (2007), Art. 122 para 8 et seqq.

[23]Cf. Häde, in Calliess and Ruffert (2007), Art. 122 para 5.

aforementioned discussion takes place in the European Council. This is equivalent to Art. 121.2 TFEU (former Art. 99.2 EC), according to which the Council decides after a discussion in the European Council.

Another innovation is that the Council, whose members representing the Member States are still all eligible to vote, decides upon recommendation of the representatives of the euro-zone countries.[24] So far the Council takes action, not the Euro Group (on this difference see infra 4).[25] The recommendation must be made no later than 6 months upon receiving the still necessary proposal of the Commission (Art. 140.2 (2) TFEU). This may cause an increased influence of the Member States with euro currency on the selection process. However, legally the Council may deviate from this recommendation.

2.3.4 External Relations

Previously, Art. 111 EC, whose provisions have been basically adopted by Art. 219 TFEU, provided for the exchange rate policies as well as the external relations of the euro currency area. Furthermore, the chapter on provisions specific to Member States whose currency is the euro includes a new regulation that concerns the establishment of common positions, which the respective bodies shall take within the competent international institutions and conferences in the financial area to issues of special concern to the EMU (Art. 138.1 TFEU). Additionally, Art. 138.2 TFEU authorises the Council to adopt measures to ensure a unified representation within the international financial institutions and conferences while only the Council members representing Member States with euro currency can participate in the vote (Art. 138.3 TFEU). With these measures the Contracting Parties try to ensure the position of the euro in the international monetary system. "Ensure" in this context does not only mean to preserve the status quo, but also to strengthen the position of the euro-zone in international politics.[26] A single representation and speaking with one voice should be suitable contributions.

3 Changes to the Status of the European Central Bank

3.1 The ECB in the EC Treaty

In accordance with the procedures laid down in the EC Treaty, Art. 8 EC provided for the establishment of an ESCB and an ECB which should act within the limits of

[24] Cf. ECB, Monthly Bulletin December 2007, p. 81 et seq.

[25] Cf. also Walter and Becker (2007), p. 9.

[26] Cf. Walter and Becker (2007), p. 10.

the powers conferred upon them by the EC Treaty and the ESCB Statute. Based on this provision the ECB was founded on 1 June 1998. Together with the national central banks of the Member States it forms the ESCB. The ESCB is governed by the decision-making bodies of the ECB (Art. 8 ESCB-Statute). In Art. 107.2 EC Community law assigned legal personality only to the ECB but not to the ESCB.[27] This is rather reasonable, for the ESCB was merely a collective name for the ECB and the national central banks, not an independent actor of monetary policy. As far as Community law conferred competences to the ESCB it did so basically to its bodies.

One of the basic tasks of the ESCB, according to Art. 105 EC, is the definition and implementation of the monetary policy of the Community that is focused on the primary objective of price stability. Due to the hierarchic structure, decision-making powers are concentrated at the ECB. Its decision-making bodies, the Governing Council and the Executive Board, govern the ESCB. While the former defines the monetary policy of the Union, the latter principally implements it. In this context it relies on the national central banks. Therefore, their (only) task is to implement the monetary policy of the Community in accordance with the guidelines and instructions of the ECB (Art. 14.3 ESCB Statute). However, we are not dealing with a centralized institution, for the governors of the national central banks, as members of the Governing Council, hold seats and vote in the most important decision-making body of the ECB. This can be understood as a kind of compensation for the loss of authority in monetary policy on the national level. However, the ECB holds a unique status so that one could call it the central bank of the EC.[28]

As a function, the ECB carried out Community tasks in the monetary policy that were not attributed to any institution of the Community itself. It was not subordinate to, but on the same level as, these institutions. Thus, it could be referred to as a *quasi*-institution or an institution-like body of the Community.[29] However, Art. 7.1 EC, which listed the institutions, did not name the ECB. Neither did Part Five Title I Chapter 1 on the provisions governing the institutions. Thus, as far as its legal status was concerned, the ECB was no EC institution.

3.2 *The European Central Bank in the Constitutional Treaty*

The Constitutional Treaty was to provide for some innovations. While Art. I-19.1 (2) TCE still did not list the ECB as an institution, the first sentence of Art. I-30.3 TCE stated that the "European Central Bank is an institution". This would have meant a

[27]Cf. earlier Hahn (1992), p. 69.

[28]Cf. Häde (2006), p. 1612; Smits (2005), p. 445.

[29]In this sense Beutel (2006), p. 39; Decker (1995), p. 884; Hatje, in Schwarze (2000), Art. 8 EC, para 2; Häde (1996), p. 338; Schütz (2001), p. 292; Weiß (2002), p. 169.

change in the status of the ECB[30] even though the ECB itself denied this and defended the view that it would keep its position as an institution sui generis.[31]

However, one could infer from the heading of Title IV Chapter II of the Constitutional Treaty that the ECB was only to hold the position of an "other Union institution". This means that this Treaty wanted to make the ECB an institution while still differentiating it from the actual EU institutions as listed in Chapter I. Other than the ECB, only the Court of Auditors, which is, under applicable law, an actual institution, was to hold the position of "other Union institution". The establishment of this separate institutional category could be understood in that it tried to underline their independence from the actual EU institutions and the division between them.[32]

3.3 *The ECB in the Treaty of Lisbon*

3.3.1 The ECB as Regular Institution

The Lisbon Treaty goes further than the Constitutional Treaty and assigns to the ECB the unrestricted status as an EU institution.[33] Article 13.1 (2) sixth dash TEU lists the ECB among the other institutions of the Union and in Art. 282 et seqq. TFEU the institutional provisions of the ECB receive equal treatment as Section 6 of Part Six Chapter 1 on the institutions. Thus, since 1 December 2009 the ECB is one of the seven regular institutions of the Union. While the ECB has already carried out the task of an institution, the express assignment of this status means at least officially a substantial change.

However, this status has only been assigned to the ECB, not the ESCB. The inclusion of the ESCB in the circle of institutions would not do justice to the position of the national central banks. Union law decoupled them more widely from the national context than other authorities of the Member States that execute EU law. According to Art. 14.3 ESCB Statute they are an integral part of the ESCB and are bound by ECB instructions. Moreover, if they fail to comply with their obligations in the framework of the ESCB, these violations are not ascribed to the Member States. Thus, in those cases an infringement proceeding (Art. 258 and 259 TFEU, former Art. 226 and 227 EC) is not permissible.[34] Instead it remains

---

[30] Cf. Gaitanides (2005b), FS Zuleeg, p. 556.

[31] ECB (2004), p. 55 (66). Cf also Lindner and Schmidt (2004), p. 61.

[32] Cf. Häde, in Calliess and Ruffert (2006), Art. I-30 para 9.

[33] See Gloggnitzer (2008), p. 84.

[34] Cf. Gaiser (2002), p. 523; Karpenstein, in Grabitz and Hilf (2007), Art. 237 (editing July 2000) paras 26, 28; Wegener, in Calliess and Ruffert (2007), Art. 237 para 6. Partly different Schwarze, in Schwarze (2000), Art. 227 EC para 9, who considers a proceeding according to Art. 227 EC (Art. 259 TFEU) possible. However, the independence of the national central banks may stand in the way.

that the ECB can take legal steps against unlawfully acting national central banks in the way of a special proceeding according to Art. 271 lit. d TFEU (former Art. 237 EC). The national central banks are and will remain authorities of the Member States as their name suggests. Thus, only the ECB can be an EU institution.

3.3.2 Special Status of the ECB

In spite of the far-reaching equalisation of the ECB with the other EU institutions, its status remains special as the only institution of the Union which has legal personality. This fact was sporadically used to argue against the classification of the ECB as an institution of the EC.[35] However, as the provisions of Art. 13 TEU prove, it is not impossible for a legal body that has institutions itself to be an institution of another legal body.[36]

It seems to have been rather difficult to equalise the ECB and the other Union institutions without providing for changes of any other kind. The outcome in the TFEU was somewhat awkward since Art. 282 TFEU appears to be a kind of puzzle, composed of formulations of the former Art. 105-108 EC. Thus, this article repeats some passages of Art. 127-130 TFEU or briefly refers to the more detailed regulations therein. Only a few regulations of Art. 282 TFEU go beyond what has already been stated in the chapter on monetary policy. This is especially true for Art. 282.1 TFEU, which in its first sentence defines the ESCB. Its second sentence introduces the Eurosystem as a new legal term, which is defined as the ECB, together with the national central banks of the Member States whose currency is the euro, thereby differentiating it from the ESC, whose members are also the Member States with a derogation. This term, however, is no real practical innovation. The Governing Council of the ECB has been using it since 1998/1999[37] and suggested this terminology for the Constitutional Treaty.[38]

Only the legal personality of the ECB is exclusively mentioned in Art. 282 TFEU (first sentence of paragraph 3). Furthermore, sentence 3 of Art. 282.3 TFEU, by indicating that the ECB is independent in the management of its finances, underlines an aspect of central bank autonomy[39] that had already been covered by previous law in Art. 108 EC[40] and which is now included in Art. 130 TFEU. As a consequence of this financial independence on the one hand and the new institutional position on the other, Art. 314.1 TFEU excludes the ECB from the regulation, otherwise applying to all institutions, that in the context of the establishment of

[35]In this sense Streinz (2008), para 402. Streinz et al. (2005), p. 40, call the intended institutional position of the ECB in the TCE a "unique legal specimen".

[36]Cf. already Häde (2006), p. 1612.

[37]Cf. ECB (1999).

[38]Cf. ECB (1999), p. 51 (62).

[39]Cf. Gloggnitzer (2008), p. 85.

[40]Cf. Galahn, (1996), p. 142; Weinbörner (1998), p. 450 et seq.

the Union's budget they are required to draw up an estimate for the following financial year. Another result of the financial independence and the special status in budget law is regulated by Art. 340 (3) TFEU, which clarifies that in the case of non-contractual liability, the ECB itself has to make good any damage caused by it or by its servants in the performance of their duties. While this could have been equally inferred by interpreting the law previously in force,[41] Art. 288 (3) EC was worded as if the EC would have to take responsibility for the ECB.[42]

All other provisions repeat regulations provided for elsewhere. Difficulties with interpretations could arise, where the wording of Art. 282 TFEU differs from that of parallel provisions. This is especially true for Art. 282.5 TFEU, which provides that "[w]ithin the areas falling within its responsibilities", the ECB has to be consulted on all proposed Union acts as well as proposals for regulations of the Member States. This provision adopts the formulation of the Constitutional Treaty whose Art. III-185.4 TCE also applied the right to consultation to legislative provisions "in areas within its powers". Thus, both regulations differ from the wording of the previously relevant Art. 105.4 EC that talked about Community acts and legislative provisions of the Member States "in its fields of competence". While Art. 127.4 TFEU has adopted this very formulation, Art. 282.5 TFEU follows the example of the Constitutional Treaty. This might be an editorial mistake but could, however, become significant, for it cannot be excluded that the differing wording of the Constitutional Treaty ("powers") intended to limit the ECB's right to consultation compared to the existing legal position ("fields of competence").[43]

3.3.3 Concerns Regarding the Institutional Position

In the literature there have been concerns that the position of the ECB as "other institution" as assigned by the Constitutional Treaty would bind it tighter to the aims of the Union which might distract it from concentrating on the task of preserving price stability.[44] The present positioning of the ECB as a regular EU institution could reinforce these concerns, because the second sentence of Art. 13.2 TEU calls for mutual sincere cooperation among all institutions of the Union. If the ECB was obliged to focus more on the Union's aims, this could in fact mean a

---

[41] Cf. Baur (2000), p. 225 et seqq.; Gaiser (2002), p. 531; Hahn and Häde (2001), p. 58 et seq.; Zilioli and Selmayr (2007), p. 397.

[42] Cf. Capelli and Nehls (1997), p. 140 fn. 35.

[43] More details on the right to consultation, see Häde (2008), p. 1027 et seqq. See also Hafke (2003), p. 199 et seqq.

[44] Belke et al. (2004), p. 75 (76); Bergmann (2005), p. 122; Gramlich and Manger-Nestler (2005a, b), p. 480; Starbatty (2003), p. 549 et seqq.; Thiel (2003), p. 528 et seq. See also Statement by the Executive Board of the Deutsche Bundesbank on the draft EU Constitution and the Stability and Growth Pact (10 December 2003), in: http://www.bundesbank.de/download/presse/pressenotizen/2003/20031210bbk2_en.pdf, p. 3.; Deutsche Bundesbank (2003), p. 65 (67).

change of direction. The second sentence of Art. 3.3 TEU requires the Union to "work for the sustainable development of Europe based on balanced economic growth and price stability, a highly competitive social market economy, aiming at full employment and social progress, and a high level of protection and improvement of the quality of the environment". It is pleasing that price stability is even mentioned in this conglomerate of aims. An early draft of the Constitutional Treaty got along without this reference.[45] However, it becomes quite apparent that price stability in this context does not play a leading role, but is merely one among many.

Nevertheless, under the Lisbon Treaty it remains that the ESCB and thus with it the ECB are obliged to ensure price stability as their primary objective. The provisions of Art. 105.1 EC are also adopted by Art. 127.1 TFEU in so far that the ESCB may (and in that case perhaps even must) only support the general economic policies in the Union in accordance with the objectives of Art. 3 TEU as long as this is "[w]ithout prejudice to the objective of price stability". The Constitutional Treaty made provisions for the same, which in return means that even under the TCE the ECB would have had to pay price stability the same attention as under the law currently in force.[46] The Lisbon Treaty and its provision for a new institutional position of the ECB have not changed this.

The concerns expressed in the literature also referred to the issue of whether the status of an "other institution" would have affected or even questioned the independence of the ECB. This is said to follow from the wording of the third sentence of Art. 282.3 TFEU (fourth sentence of Art. I-30.3 TCE) which determines that the ECB "shall be independent in the exercise of its powers and in the management of its finances".[47] That a limitation of independence follows from the wording of this provision appears rather doubtful, for this guarantee of autonomy does not stand by itself, but is rather added to the one already existing. With the usual terminological adjustments, Art. 130 TFEU has adopted the content of Art. 108 EC. The Lisbon Treaty does not contain any explicit limitation of this independence. From the obligation to sincere mutual cooperation and the competence of the European Council to "define the general political directions and priorities" it could only be concluded that the ECB has to comply with this at the expense of price stability and its independence[48] if these definitions had priority. However, this is opposed by Art. 127.1, first sentence, and Art. 130 TFEU, which as specific provisions derogate the general obligations of the institutions. Thus, the independence of both the ECB and the national central banks has not been affected.[49]

---

[45]Cf. Manger-Nestler (2008), p. 321 et seq.; Müller-Graff (2004).

[46]Cf. Gaitanides (2005b), FS Zuleeg, p. 556; Oppermann (2003), p. 1236; Seidel (2004), p. 6.

[47]Cf. Gramlich and Manger-Nestler (2005a), p. 193.

[48]As feared by Manger-Nestler (2008), p. 323 et seq.

[49]With the same conclusion ECB, Monthly Report December 2007, p. 91; Gloggnitzer (2008), p. 85; Oppermann (2008), p. 479; Pache and Rösch (2008), p. 478; Rodi, in: Vedder and Heintschel von Heinegg (2007), Art. I-30 para 11; Siekmann (2005), p. 53; Weber (2008), p. 9; Zilioli and Selmayr (2007), p. 390 et seqq.

In this context it should also be noted that the provisions of Part Three TFEU and thus the regulations regarding the EMU including Art. 127 and 130 TFEU are subject to a simplified revision procedure (Art. 48.6 TEU), which some consider a weakening of the ESCB.[50] Indeed, one should not underestimate the effects of procedural rules. The amendments decided on in accordance with both the ordinary and the simplified revision procedures have ultimately to be ratified by the Member States according to their respective requirements provided for by their constitutions (Art. 48.4 (2) and Art. 48.6 (2), third sentence, TEU). At least the *Grundgesetz* (German Basic Law) opposes, in its Art. 88, second sentence, GG, any change that would affect or even nullify the independence of the ESCB or its commitment to the overriding goal of assuring price stability.[51] The consent of German constitutional bodies regarding any such plan would not be possible or at least not without a simultaneous amendment to the *Grundgesetz*. Thus, the simplified revision procedure also is unlikely to affect the independence of the ESCB.[52]

3.3.4 Changes in the Appointment of Members of the Executive Board

The Lisbon Treaty also provides for a change in the appointment procedure for vacant seats in the Executive Board of the ECB. Previously, the members of the Executive Board were appointed by common accord of the governments of the Member States at the level of Heads of State or Government (Art. 112.2 lit. b EC). Now the European Council is competent and decides by a qualified majority. Individual Member States thus lose the possibility of blocking the appointment of the President or any other member of the Executive Board of the ECB. A situation like in 1998, when France withdrew its candidate only after the Dutch candidate, who had been preferred by all the other Member States, promised not to serve the full term[53] is thus improbable to reoccur.[54]

3.3.5 The General Council

The central banks of Member States with a derogation are members of the ESCB but not, however, of the Eurosystem. Their governors are thus not members of the Governing Council of the ECB. Especially with regard to the objective to introduce the euro in all states of the EU, there is a need for cooperation between the central

[50]Cf. Gaitanides (2005b), FS Zuleeg, p. 557; Manger-Nestler (2008), p. 326 et seq.

[51]Cf. Hahn/Häde, in Dolzer et al. (1999), Art. 88 para 314.

[52]Cf. already Häde, in Calliess and Ruffert (2006), Art. I-30 para 13.

[53]For a legal evaluation of this occurrence cf. Häde (1998), p. 1092 et seq.

[54]In this sense Walter and Becker (2007), p. 4. See also Caesar and Kösters (2004), p. 300; Gramlich and Manger-Nestler (2005b), p. 481 et seq., who consider this alteration a weakening of the independence, without, however, giving reasons for this.

banks within and outside the euro-zone. Therefore, Art. 123.3 EC constituted the General Council as the third decision-making body of the ECB. In accordance with Art. 44.2 ESCB Statute (former Art. 45.2) it comprises all governors of the national central banks and the President and Vice-President of the ECB. The tasks of the General Council are substantially provided for in the ESCB Statute. Additionally, Art. 46 ESCB Statute (former Art. 47.1) confers upon it the responsibility to perform the transitional tasks that in accordance with Art. 43 ESCB Statute (former Art. 44) the ECB has taken over from the European Monetary Institute (EMI). Which tasks these are only results from the list in Art. 4.1 EMI Statute. However, Art. 1 No. 9 lit. c of Protocol No. 1[55] annexed to the Lisbon Treaty provided to repeal the EMI Statute. That is why there was a need for action.[56] The Contracting Parties solved this minor problem by having Art. 141.2 TFEU expressly name the relevant tasks.

4 The Euro Group

The new chapter on provisions specific to Member States whose currency is the euro also includes some institutional regulations while other articles of this chapter intensify the coordination of economic policies (Art. 136 TFEU) and ensure a better coordination in an international context (Art. 138 TFEU), thereby taking into account the particular need for coordination of the euro-zone countries. In this context Art. 137 TFEU anchors the Euro Group, which is already existing for a longer period of time, in primary law and, regarding the details, refers to the respective Protocol on the Euro Group[57] that is also part of primary law.

According to Art. 1 of the Protocol, the Euro Group is composed of the Ministers of the Member States whose currency is the euro; typically these will be the Economics and Finance Ministers (ECOFIN Council). They have already been meeting informally without their colleagues of those Member States without euro currency prior to the meetings of the Council. Under present law, these meetings of the Euro Group remain informal (first sentence of Art. 1 of the Protocol). Consequently, the Euro Group cannot make binding decisions in the Council's stead but rather deliberate. But even in ECOFIN Council cases in which only the members of the Euro Group can take part in the vote, it is the Council, not

[55] *Protocol No. 1 amending the Protocols annexed to the Treaty on European Union, to the Treaty establishing the European Community and/or to the Treaty establishing the European Atomic Energy Community*, O.J. C 306/165 (2007).

[56] See earlier Opinion of the European Central Bank of 5 July 2007, O.J. C 160/ 2 (2007) at p. 4 No. 5.

[57] *Consolidated versions of the Treaty on European Union and the Treaty on the Functioning of the European Union, Protocol (No. 14) on the Euro Group*, O.J. C 115/283 (2007).

the Euro Group, which makes decisions.[58] This also applies to measures under Art. 136 and 138 TFEU. This is important because the meetings of the Euro Group take place without participation of those members representing Member States with a derogation. In the Council, those Member States are only excluded from the vote, but not, however, from the attendance of the meeting itself and the opinion-forming.

The members of the Euro Group elect a President for a two-and-a-half-year term (Art. 2 of the Protocol). Thus, the Protocol formalises something the Euro Group has been practising since 2005 in anticipation of the respective provision of the Constitutional Treaty[59]; however, this implementation into primary law increases its emphasis. But in spite of this fact, the Euro Group remains an informal committee. The regulations of the Protocol now also officially lead to its institutional independence.

There is no doubt on the need for particular coordination between the euro-zone countries. This has become unmistakeably clear through the recent global financial crisis. Thus, there is basically no complaint that Art. 137 TFEU and the Protocol on the Euro Group annexed to the Treaties anchors this committee in primary law. This process, however, becomes more explosive due to the French call, never abandoned and recently reappeared, for the establishment of a kind of economic government as counterpart to the ECB.[60] Article 137 TFEU and the Protocol thus codify what has already been achieved but in the view of the supporters of such an economic government of the euro-zone is merely an intermediate stop. Therefore, the struggle for power between the ECB, which is dedicated to price stability, and politics, tending to be focused more strongly on economic growth and full employment, will continue.

In this context there are calls for an increased dialogue between the Euro Group and the ECB.[61] At least some actors might hope that the ECB can be induced to provide a stronger support for economic policies of the Member States. In the context of the objective of price stability important to the ECB this can be problematic. The provision of the fourth sentence of Art. 1 on the Euro Group to invite the ECB to the Euro Group meetings may thus be ambivalent for the ECB. It is, however, not obliged to attend. The ECB can therefore use the opportunity for a dialogue. However, it needs and may not let this influence it in a way that would affect its independence (Art. 108 EC; Art. 130 TFEU) and the maintenance of price stability. Nonetheless, it is striking that the Protocol does not name the addressee of the invitation. While Art. 283.2 TFEU (former Art. 113.2 EC) states that the

---

[58] Thus unclear Gloggnitzer (2008), p. 86, where it is stated that the areas of autonomous decision-making would be extended by the Euro Group.

[59] Cf. Walter and Becker (2007), p. 6 et seq.; Gloggnitzer (2008), p. 86. By now the President of the Euro Group is Luxembourg's Prime and Finance Minister Jean-Claude Juncker.

[60] Cf. Caesar and Kösters (2004), p. 298 et seq.; Gramlich and Manger-Nestler (2005b), p. 483. See also Walter and Becker (2007), p. 3; Proissl (2008), p. 14; Zilioli and Selmayr (2007), p. 356.

[61] Cf. Walter and Becker (2007), p. 7.

President of the ECB shall be invited to Council meetings dealing with matters relating to objectives and tasks of the ESCB, the fourth sentence of Art. 1 of the Protocol on the Euro Group only mentions the ECB as a whole, which leaves the ECB more room to manoeuvre. For example, it can indicate the importance it attaches to this informal committee by the choice of its participants.

5 Conclusion and Prospects

Regarding the EMU the Lisbon Treaty, in spite of changing some regulations, preserves much continuity. It redefines the status of the ECB by making it an institution of the Union while keeping its independence and the pursuance of the primary objective of price stability legally unaffected. This redefinition also does away with doubts brought up in the literature regarding the status of the ECB within the Community.[62] Attempts to assign to the ECB the position of a supranational organisation in addition to the EC[63] were turned down by the European Court of Justice (ECJ) for law previously in force in the judgment of the *OLAF* case.[64] Under present law there can be no doubt that the ECB as an institution of the Union is embedded in the EU's legal framework.[65]

The political debate on the relationship between politics and the Central Bank that partly focuses on a limitation of the ECB's independence and its primary maintenance of price stability may give rise to critical reflections of legally harmless changes. Every single provision of the Treaties that includes a deviation from applicable law can be interpreted in a way that preserves the independence of the ESCB. In a general view one might, however, be sceptic and suspect a political intent to weaken the position of the Central Bank.[66] This already applied to the provisions of the Constitutional Treaty. The ECB had already pronounced some changes and clarification in its opinion on the draft Treaty,[67] but did not, however, manage to get through. Neither did it succeed with its request for the status of a regular institution of the Union in the Lisbon Treaty – as provided for in the

[62]Cf. Streinz et al. (2005), p. 40; Weber (2008), p. 9.

[63]So Zilioli and Selmayr (2001), p. 29 et seqq. similar Seidel (2004), p. 7: ESCB as "multilateral organisation".

[64]Case C-11/00 *Commission v ECB*, (ECJ 10 July 2003) para 135 et seq. See also Gaitanides (2005a), p. 52 et seqq.; Häde (2002), p. 921; Kempen, in: Streinz (2003), Art. 107 para 4; Louis (2004), p. 599 et seqq. with further reference; Zilioli and Selmayr (2007), p. 365 et seqq., with a different view on the ECJ judgment.

[65]Cf. regarding the TCE Louis (2004), p. 603; Smits (2005), p. 444 et seq.; Streinz et al. (2005), p. 40.

[66]Cf. also Thiel (2003), p. 528 et seq.

[67]*Opinion of the European Central Bank of 19 September 2003 at the request of the Council of the European Union on the draft Treaty establishing a Constitution for Europe*, O.J. C 229/7 et seq. (2003).

Constitutional Treaty.[68] The implementation of the Euro Group into primary law can also be understood as a kind of mosaic. However, that the supporters of an independent Central Bank that is dedicated to maintain price stability were able to prevent the opposite course is more than symbolically reflected in the Treaties. Due to its legal personality and functional independence, the ECB still holds a special position within the framework of the Union that exists only because ensuring price stability has been, and will be, its primary objective.

References

Bark F (2004) Das gemeinschaftsrechtliche Defizitverfahren. Reformansätze und ihre rechtlichen Umsetzungsmöglichkeiten. Lang, Frankfurt/Main et al

Baur I (2000) Die Haftung der Europäischen Zentralbank, Dissertation, Würzburg

Belke A, Baumgärtner F, Kösters W (2004) Zur Aushöhlung der europäischen Währungsordnung im Entwurf eines EU-Verfassungsvertrags, Kreditwesen

Bergmann (2005) Staatswerdung durch Konstitutionalisierung? - Zur neuen EU-Verfassung, VBlBW, p 121

Beutel J (2006) Differenzierte Integration in der Europäischen Wirtschafts- und Währungsunion. de Gruyter, Berlin

Caesar R, Kösters W (2004) Europäische Wirtschafts- und Währungsunion - Europäische Verfassung versus Maastrichter Vertrag, Integration, p 288

Calliess Chr, Ruffert M (2006) Verfassung der Europäischen Union. Kommentar der Grundlagenbestimmungen (Teil I). Kommentar. Beck, München

Calliess Chr., Ruffert M (2007) EUV/EGV, das Verfassungsrecht der Europäischen Union mit Europäischer Grundrechtecharta. Kommentar, 3rd edn. Beck, München

Capelli F, Nehls A (1997) Die außervertragliche Haftung der Europäischen Gemeinschaft und Rechtsbehelfe zur Erlangung von Schadensersatz gemäß Art.215 EGV, EuR, p 132

Decker A (1995) Die Organe der Europäischen Gemeinschaften und der Europäischen Union. JuS, p 883

Deutsche Bundesbank (2003) Zur Währungsverfassung nach dem Entwurf einer Verfassung für die Europäische Union. Monthly Report November, p 65

Dolzer R, Kahl W, Waldhoff Chr, Grasshof K (1999) Bonner Kommentar zum Grundgesetz. Müller, Heidelberg

ECB (1999) The institutional framework of the European System of Central Banks. Monthly Bulletin July, p 55

ECB (2004) The European Constitution and the ECB. Monthly Bulletin August, p 51

Fischer K (2008) Der Vertrag von Lissabon. Nomos, Baden-Baden

Gaiser (2002) Gerichtliche Kontrolle im Europäischen System der Zentralbanken, EuR, p 517

Gaitanides Ch (2005a) Das Recht der Europäischen Zentralbank. Mohr Siebeck, Tübingen

[68]Cf. the letter of ECB President Trichet to the then Council President Manuel Lobo Antunes of 2 February 2007, http://www.ecb.int/pub/pdf/other/jct1080en.pdf. See as well the mention in EZB, Annual Report 2007, 2008, p. 135, while there is, however, no reference to the failing of the initiative. See earlier *Opinion of the European Central Bank of 5 July 2007 at the request of the Council of the European Union on the opening of an Intergovernmental Conference to draw up a Treaty amending the existing Treaties*, O.J. C 160/2 (4).

Gaitanides Ch (2005b) Die Verfassung für Europa und das Europäische System der Zentralbanken. In: Gaitanides Ch et al (eds) Europa und seine Verfassung. Festschrift für Manfred Zuleeg zum siebzigsten Geburtstag. Nomos, Baden-Baden, p 550
Galahn G (1996) Die Deutsche Bundesbank im Prozeß der europäischen Währungsintegration. de Gruyter, Berlin
Gloggnitzer (2008) Der Vertrag von Lissabon. In: Oesterreichische Nationalbank, Geldpolitik & Wirtschaft Q1/08, p 74
Grabitz E, Hilf M (2007) Das Recht der Europäischen Union, Kommentar. Beck, München
Gramlich L, Manger-Nestler C (2005a) Währungsrechtliche Defizite der Verfassung für Europa, EuZW, p 193
Gramlich L, Manger-Nestler C (2005b) Währungsrechtliche Aspekte des Reformprojekts "Europäische Verfassung", Kreditwesen, p 478
Häde U (1996) Finanzausgleich. Mohr, Tübingen
Häde U (1998) Zur Rechtmäßigkeit der Entscheidungen über die Europäische Wirtschafts- und Währungsunion, JZ, p 1088
Häde U (2001) Der Vertrag von Nizza und die Wirtschafts- und Währungsunion, EWS, p 97
Häde U (2002) The Law of the European Central Bank. EuR, p 920
Häde U (2006) Zur rechtlichen Stellung der Europäischen Zentralbank, WM, p 1605
Häde U (2008) Die Pflicht zur Anhörung der Europäischen Zentralbank nach Art. 105 Abs. 4 EGV. In: Gornig GH, Schöbener B, Bausback W, Irmscher T (eds) Iustitia et Pax, Gedächtnisschrift für Dieter Blumenwitz. Duncker & Humblot, Berlin, pp 1027 et seq
Hafke HC (2003) Einige rechtliche Anmerkungen zur Praxis der Autonomie im Europäischen System der Zentralbanken (ESZB). In: Ekkenga J et al (eds) Bankrecht und Kapitalmarkt in der Entwicklung, FS Kümpel. Erich Schmidt, Berlin, p 185
Hahn H (1992) Der Vertrag von Maastricht als völkerrechtliche Übereinkunft und Verfassung. Nomos, Baden-Baden
Hahn H, Häde U (2001) Die Zentralbank vor Gericht. ZHR 165:30
Hatje A, Kindt A (2008) Der Vertrag von Lissabon - Europa endlich in guter Verfassung? NJW, p 1761
Lindner I, Schmidt P (2004) Der Vertrag über eine Verfassung für Europa: Institutionelle Aspekte für die Währungsunion. In: Oesterreichische Nationalbank, Geldpolitik & Wirtschaft Q3/04, p 57
Louis J-V (2004) The economic and monetary union: law and institutions, CMLRev 41:575
Manger-Nestler C (2008) Par(s) inter pares - Die Bundesbank als nationale Zentralbank im Europäischen System der Zentralbanken. Duncker & Humblot, Berlin
Müller-Graff P-Chr (2004) Wandel des Europäischen Wirtschaftsverfassungsrechts. ZHR 168:1
Oppermann Th (2003) Eine Verfassung für die Europäische Union, DVBl, p 1234
Oppermann Th (2008) Die Europäische Union von Lissabon, DVBl, p 473
Pache E, Rösch F (2008) Der Vertrag von Lissabon, NVwZ, p 473
Proissl (2008) Sarkozy blitzt in Brüssel mit Euro-Plan ab, FTD vom 28.4.2008, p 14
Raepenbusch (2007) La réforme institutionelle du Traité de Lisbonne: L'émergence juridique de l'Union Européene, Cahiers de droit européen, p 573
Schütz Ch (2001) Die Legitimation der Europäischen Zentralbank zur Rechtsetzung. EuR, p 291
Schwarze J (2000) EU-Kommentar. Nomos, Baden-Baden
Seidel M (2004) Die Stellung der Europäischen Zentralbank nach dem Verfassungsvertrag, Policy Paper B 19/2004. Zentrum für Europäische Integrationsforschung, Bonn
Selmayr M (2003) Ende der Stabilitätskultur? Europablätter, p 131
Siekmann H (2005) Die Unabhängigkeit von EZB und Bundesbank nach geltendem Recht und dem Vertrag über eine Verfassung für Europa, Institute for Law and Finance. Working Paper Series No. 35, 01/2005, Universität Frankfurt/Main
Smits R (2005) The European Constitution and EMU, CMLRev 42:425

Starbatty J (2003) Regeln für das Club-Gut Euro - die Währungsunion nach dem Konvent. In: Hankel W, Schachtschneider KA, Starbatty J (eds) Der Ökonom als Politiker - Europa, Geld und die soziale Frage, FS Nölling. Lucius und Lucius, Stuttgart, p 535
Streinz R (2003) EUV/EGV. Kommentar. Beck, München
Streinz R (2008) Europarecht, 8th edn. Müller, Heidelberg
Streinz R, Ohler Chr, Herrmann Chr (2005) Die neue Verfassung für Europa. Beck, München
Thiel E (2003) Die Wirtschaftspolitik im Europäischen Verfassungsentwurf, Integration, p 527
Vedder Chr, Heintschel von Heinegg W (2007) Europäischer Verfassungsvertrag, Handkommentar. Nomos, Baden-Baden
von der Groeben H, Schwarze J (2003) Kommentar zum Vertrag über die Europäische Union und zur Gründung der Europäischen Gemeinschaft, 6th edn. Nomos, Baden-Baden
Wagner Th, Grum G (2005) Adjusting ECB decision-making to an enlarged Union, In ECB (ed) Legal aspects of the European system of Central banks, p 73
Walter N, Becker W (2007) EU-Vertragsreform: Folgen für die Geldpolitik. In: Deutsche Bank Research, EU-Monitor 50 (23.10.2007)
Weber A (2008) Vom Verfassungsvertrag zum Vertrag von Lissabon, EuZW, p 7
Weinbörner S (1998) Die Stellung der Europäischen Zentralbank (EZB) und der nationalen Zentralbanken in der Wirtschafts- und Währungsunion nach dem Vertrag von Maastricht. Lang, Frankfurt/Main et al
Weiß W (2002) Kompetenzverteilung in der Währungspolitik und Außenvertretung des Euro. EuR, p 165
Zilioli Ch, Selmayr M (2001) The law of the European Central Bank. Hart Publishing, Oxford
Zilioli Ch, Selmayr M (2007) The constitutional status of the European Central Bank. CMLRev 44:355

Public and Private Enforcement of EU State Aid Law

Legal Issues of Dual Vigilance by the Commission and National Courts

Paul Adriaanse

1 Introduction

European Union (EU) competition policy is considered to be one of the basic elements of the European economic constitution, originally established by the Treaty on the European Economic Community and now transferred into the Treaty on the Functioning of the European Union (TFEU). The EU competition rules should guarantee fair and undistorted competition, which according to Art. 3.1 (b) TFEU is necessary for the functioning of the internal market. These rules apply to undertakings (Arts. 101–106 TFEU) as well as to Member States (Arts. 107–109 TFEU).

The financial and economic crisis from the last few years has put high pressure on EU competition policy, in particular on the application of the State aid rules. Voices were raised to relax competition rules in order to tackle problems encountered by business. Nevertheless, former Commissioner for Competition policy Neelie Kroes held on several occasions that State aid rules should be seen as part of the solution, not part of the problem.[1] The Commission therefore continued to apply competition rules in accordance with the basic principles, notwithstanding several initiatives to adapt its policy to the circumstances and urgent needs during the crisis.[2]

Associate Professor of Constitutional and Administrative Law at Leiden University.

[1]See e.g. Kroes (2008).

[2]See e.g. the Communication from the Commission – Temporary framework for State aid measures to support access to finance in the current financial and economic crisis, O.J. C 83/1 (2009).

P. Adriaanse (✉)
Leiden University, Institute for Public Law, Department of Constitutional and Administrative Law, Steenschuur 25, 2311 ES Leiden, The Netherlands
e-mail: p.c.adriaanse@law.leidenuniv.nl

H.-J. Blanke and S. Mangiameli (eds.), *The European Union after Lisbon*, 443
DOI 10.1007/978-3-642-19507-5_17, © Springer-Verlag Berlin Heidelberg 2012

The approach chosen by the Commission is understandable, given the various calls on the Commission and the Member States by the European Council in earlier years, each in accordance with their respective powers, to further their efforts to promote fair and uniform application of and compliance with the State aid rules. Member States have also been asked to reduce the general level of State aid, shifting the emphasis from supporting individual companies or sectors towards tackling horizontal objectives of EU interest, such as employment, regional development, environment and training and research.[3] Given these calls, the Commission has thoroughly reformed the State aid rules in recent years, based on four guiding principles: (1) less and better targeted State aid; (2) a refined economic approach; (3) more effective procedures, better enforcement, higher predictability and enhanced transparency; and (4) a shared responsibility between the Commission and Member States.[4]

As far as the aim of better enforcement is concerned, it should be noted that the Commission itself plays an important role in the 'public enforcement' of EU State aid law. However, the Commission is not the only actor involved. Member State authorities, as well as private parties and national courts, have important roles to play, both in public enforcement and so-called private enforcement. Overall, effective enforcement of the applicable rules in situations where they have been breached is essential for the effectiveness and credibility of the whole system.[5] Recent studies show that there has been a reasonably large increase in the number of court cases at national level in this field over the last few years in a wide variety of legal proceedings.[6]

This contribution therefore endeavours to shed more light on different legal issues of the various ways of public and private enforcement of EU State aid law, taking into account the fact that the EU's legal order and the national legal orders of the Member States are strongly interwoven, as well as the fact that several actors with conflicting interests could be involved in State aid cases. First, a brief overview of EU State aid control in general will be given (Sect. 2). Then, various breaches will be distinguished in which any action of enforcement of EU State aid law could be required (Sect. 3), followed by a discussion of the general legal framework in which such enforcement of EU law will have to be carried out (Sect. 4). The different

---

[3]See e.g. the Conclusions of the European Council, Brussels, March 2006, para 33; Conclusions of the European Council, Brussels, March 2005, para 23.

[4]The guiding principles for this reform were first laid down in the State Aid Action Plan. 'Less and better targeted state aid; a roadmap for state aid reform 2005–2009' (COM(2005) 107 final) (hereinafter referred to as the State aid Action Plan), and referred to in later documents, e.g. in the State Aid Scoreboard, Autumn 2009 update (COM(2009) 661), p. 11.

[5]See also the State Aid Action Plan, p. 13, and various Reports on Competition Policy by the Commission (e.g. 2004, Volume I, pp. 4, 5 and 115; 2006, p. 18; State Aid Scoreboard spring 2006, COM(2006) 130 final, p. 33. See also Anestis et al. (2005).

[6]See the 2009 Update of the 2006 Study on the enforcement of State aid rules at national level, directed by J. Derenne, Lovells 2009 (http://ec.europa.eu/competition/state_aid/studies_reports/enforcement_study_2009.pdf)

enforcement possibilities, both for the Commission and for national courts, in relation to the distinguished breaches will be discussed in Sects. 5 and 6. This contribution will be concluded with some final remarks in Sect. 7.

2 EU State Aid Control

EU State aid control, based on Arts. 107–109 TFEU, consists of constant reviewing of all existing aid in the Member States, combined with a system of preventive control exercised by the Commission of any new plans to grant or alter aid measures. In this respect, State aid is defined as any aid granted by a Member State or through State resources in any form whatsoever which distorts or threatens to distort competition by favouring certain undertakings or the production of certain goods, in so far as it affects trade between Member States. The concept of State aid, as defined in Art. 107.1 TFEU, is according to the Court of Justice a legal concept which must be interpreted on the basis of objective factors.[7] In order to qualify a measure as State aid in the sense of Art. 107.1 TFEU, only the effects of the measure will be relevant, not the name, its causes or its aims.[8]

State aid in the sense of Art. 107.1 TFEU is in principle prohibited, since it is concerned to be incompatible with the internal market. However, it is recognised that in some circumstances, government interventions are necessary for a well-functioning and equitable economy. Therefore, the second and third paragraph of Art. 107 TFEU provide for several grounds to consider State aid measures compatible with the internal market. As the Commission remarked in the State Aid Action Plan 'appreciating the compatibility of state aid is fundamentally about balancing the negative effects of aid on competition with its positive effects in terms of common interest'.[9]

It is the exclusive task of the Commission to examine the compatibility of State aid measures on the basis of the provisions of Art. 107 TFEU.[10] Neither Member State authorities nor national courts are allowed to perform this task. According to Art. 108.2 TFEU, however, the Council also may in exceptional circumstances decide that aid which a State is granting or intends to grant shall be considered to be compatible with the internal market, in derogation from the provisions of Art. 107 TFEU or from the regulations provided for in Art. 109 TFEU.

In order to make it possible for the Commission to fulfil its supervisory task within EU State aid control, several obligations rest upon the Member States. They shall, according to Art. 108.1 TFEU, constantly inform the Commission of relevant

[7]See e.g. Case C-83/98 P *France v Ladbroke Racing and Commission* (ECJ 16 May 2000) para 25.

[8]See e.g. Case 173/73 *Italy v Commission* (ECJ 2 July 1974) para 13; Case C-159/01 *Netherlands v Commission* (ECJ 29 April 2004) para 51.

[9]State Aid Action Plan, p. 4.

[10]See Case C-39/94 *SFEI et al.* (ECJ 11 July 1996) para 42.

developments or changes in existing aid measures. They shall also inform the Commission, in sufficient time to enable it to submit its comments, of any plans to grant new aid or alter existing aid. This notification obligation is laid down in Art. 108.3, first sentence, TFEU. According to the last sentence of this provision, the Member States shall not put proposed measures into effect until the investigation procedure of the Commission has resulted in a final decision authorising the aid concerned, which is called the standstill obligation.

Based on these basic Treaty provisions, over the years many acts of secondary legislation have been adopted, both by the Council and the Commission. Besides, the Commission has issued various communications and other soft law documents in which it has explained its State aid policy to the main actors concerned. This complex framework of State aid law has given rise to many preliminary questions by national courts and, as a consequence, many judgments from the European Courts, resulting in a comprehensive body of case law concerning various subjects related to State aid.

It appears that EU State aid control applies to a broad range of measures in many sectors of society. In order to keep this far-reaching control mechanism manageable in a growing EU, the Commission has adopted two important regulations and a Simplification Package regarding State aid proceedings. The first regulation concerns so-called *de minimis* measures. Except for certain sensitive sectors, *de minimis* aid is considered not to affect trade between Member States and/or not to distort or threaten to distort competition, and therefore not to fall under Art. 107.1 TFEU, as long as it does not exceed a fixed ceiling of €200,000 over any period of 3 years. Aid granted to a particular enterprise by any State authority or organ should be taken into account for this purpose even when financed entirely or partly from Union resources.[11] The second regulation adopted by the Commission in order to simplify State aid control concerns the General block exemption Regulation.[12] The Member States are allowed to grant aid measures that fulfil the criteria of this regulation without prior notification to the Commission. National courts will be able to review these decisions *ex post*, since the provisions of this regulation are considered to be directly effective within the national legal orders (see also Sect. 6). Further initiatives by the Commission as part of the Simplification Package regarding State aid proceedings concern the adoption of a Notice on a simplified procedure[13] and a Best Practices Code.[14]

---

[11]Commission Regulation (EC) No. 1998/2006 *on the application of Articles 87 and 88 of the Treaty to de minimis aid*, O.J. L 379/5 (2006).

[12]Commission Regulation (EC) No. 800/2008 *declaring certain categories of aid compatible with the common market in application of Article 87 and 88 of the Treaty* (General block exemption Regulation), O.J. L 214/3 (2008).

[13]Commission Notice on a simplified procedure for the treatment of certain types of State aid, O.J. C 136/3 (2009).

[14]Commission Notice on a Best Practices Code on the conduct of State aid control proceedings, O.J. C 136/13 (2009).

3 Breaches of EU State Aid Law

The large numbers of State aid judgments of the European Courts, secondary legislation and soft law documents on top of the basic Treaty provisions on State aid have resulted in a complicated and opaque regime of State aid rules. It is not surprising that these State aid rules, either male or bone fide, are not always complied with correctly in practice.[15] Several kinds of breaches of EU State aid law could therefore be distinguished: unlawful aid, misuse of aid and failure to implement a Commission recovery decision.

Unlawful aid concerns, according to Art. 1(f) of Council Regulation (EC) No. 659/1999,[16] new aid (including alteration of existing aid) put into effect in breach of the procedural requirements of Art. 108 TFEU. In other words, an aid measure will be unlawful when it is implemented wrongly without being notified to the Commission, but also when, although notified to the Commission, it is implemented in breach of the standstill obligation as laid down in the last sentence of Art. 108.3 TFEU, i.e. before the Commission has given its approval. As has been noted in Sect. 2, aid measures that fulfil the criteria of the *de minimis* Regulation or the General block exemption Regulation can be implemented without prior notification to the Commission. However, if after implementation it appears that those criteria were not applied correctly, the aid concerned will be qualified as unlawful State aid.

Since the procedural requirements, as laid down in Art. 108.3 TFEU, only impose specific obligations on the Member States, unlawful State aid will be considered as a breach of EU State aid rules by the Member State concerned, irrespective of which authority may have breached these rules. In the *SFEI* case the Court of Justice concluded that Community law does not provide a sufficient basis for the recipient of unlawful State aid to incur liability where he/she has failed to verify that the aid received was duly notified to the Commission. According to the Court of Justice, that does not, however, prejudice the possible application of national law concerning non-contractual liability.[17]

Misuse of aid concerns, according to Art. 1(g) of Regulation (EC) No. 659/1999, aid used by the beneficiary in contravention of decisions taken by the Commission. The decisions referred to here, concern positive Commission decisions in which given aid is considered not to raise objections as to the compatibility with the internal market either after a preliminary examination (Art. 4.3) or after closure of the formal investigation procedure (Arts. 7.3 and 7.4 of Regulation (EC) No. 659/1999). According to the fourth paragraph of Art. 7, the Commission may attach to such a positive decision conditions subject to which an aid may be considered

[15] See the State Aid Scoreboard, Autumn 2009 update (COM(2009) 661), p. 12.

[16] Council Regulation (EC) No. 659/1999 *laying down detailed rules for the application of Article 93* [now Art. 108 TFEU] *of the EC Treaty*, O.J. L 83/1 (1999).

[17] Case C-39/94 *SFEI et al.* (ECJ 11 July 1996) paras 74 and 75.

compatible with the internal market and may lay down obligations to enable compliance with the decision to be monitored, referred to in the Regulation as a 'conditional decision'. It follows from this description that the concept of misuse of State aid, unlike unlawful State aid, explicitly refers to a breach of the State aid rules by private parties, i.e. recipients of State aid, and therefore not by public authorities. According to the Court of First Instance in its judgment in the Joined Cases *Saxonia Edelmetalle and ZEMAG v Commission*, however, aid can only be regarded as being misused if the recipient could be blamed for this practice.[18]

Failure to implement a Commission recovery decision adopted under Art. 14 of Regulation (EC) No. 659/1999 occurs when the authorities of the Member State to which the decision is addressed do not fully recover the aid from the beneficiary within the prescribed time, or in case of an insolvent beneficiary, when the company is not liquidated under market conditions.[19] The power of the Commission to adopt such recovery decisions will be discussed further in Sect. 5.

4 General Aspects of Enforcement of EU State Aid Law

Enforcement of EU State aid law will normally be a process in which several actors could be involved. To be mentioned in particular are the State aid granting authority, the central authorities of the Member State, being the body responsible for the interaction with the Commission, the recipient(s) of State aid, the Commission as the monitoring actor at EU level, competitors of the State aid recipient(s), national courts and the European courts, as well as other interested parties, like taxpayers or interested associations. All these actors could play different roles in the process of enforcement of EU State aid law, depending on the rights, obligations and/or competences that they can derive from either EU law or national law of the Member State concerned. In this respect it should be noted that the chance that the State aid rules will be enforced in practice will strongly depend on the possibilities for the Commission at EU level and private parties like competitors of State aid recipients at national level to learn, or at least to suspect, that the State aid rules have been breached in a particular case. This can be complicated when State aid is granted in a veiled or hidden way, which is often the case, for example, in the fiscal field.

It should further be noted that the effectiveness of the enforcement of EU law depends to a large extent on the availability of applicable and effective procedures in the Member States. The Union's legal order does not in general provide for EU

[18]Joined Cases T-111/01 and T-133/01 *Saxonia Edelmetalle and ZEMAG v Commission*, (CFI 11 May 2005) para 96.

[19]See also the Notice from the Commission 'Towards an effective implementation of Commission decisions ordering Member States to recover unlawful and incompatible State aid', O.J. C 272/4 (2007), para 69.

law procedures.[20] Also in State aid cases, as a rule, therefore the actual enforcement will have to be carried out at national level, depending on the applicable procedures of the Member State concerned. This will be dealt with further in Sects. 5 and 6.

For the space which is left to the Member States in such an integrated legal order, often the concept of 'institutional and procedural autonomy' of the Member States is used.[21] That concept supposes that Member States are free to choose which institutions will be responsible for the actual enforcement at national level and which procedures should be applied. However, procedural impediments in national law could be a real risk for the proper realisation of the goals of the Union. To solve these kinds of problems (also referred to as 'indirect collisions') it will not suffice to simply rely on the general principle of supremacy of EU law, since no rule of EU law exists by which the national provision could be replaced.[22] In order to avoid all Member States applying different procedural rules, which could lead to different outcomes in similar cases or which could make enforcement of Union law impossible, the Court of Justice has applied the principles of 'effectiveness' and 'non-discrimination'. These principles, based on Art. 4.3 TEU in which the loyalty between the Union and Member States has been expressed, serve as minimal requirements for the application of national procedural law in cases dealing with EU law. They should guarantee that substantial Union law be enforced effectively within the legal orders of the Member States, according to the so-called principle of *effet utile*.

The next two sections will discuss the way in which these general principles for the enforcement of EU law apply in State aid cases, both in relation to public enforcement and private enforcement measures.

5 Public Enforcement of EU State Aid Law

5.1 Investigation Powers of the Commission in Cases of Alleged Unlawful Aid or Alleged Misuse of Aid

One of the general tasks of the Commission is to ensure the application of the provisions of the Treaties and the measures taken by the institutions pursuant to them.[23] This task also applies to the field of EU State aid law which, as described in Sect. 2, is based on the Arts. 107–109 TFEU. Therefore, the Commission shall, in accordance with its powers and under the supervision of the European Courts, ensure compliance with the State aid rules by Member States and private parties

[20]See also Adriaanse et al. (2008).

[21]See Jans et al. (2007), pp. 3–32. See also e.g. Kilpatrick et al. (2000), pp. 3–4.

[22]See Lonbay and Biondi (1997), p. 26.

[23]Article 17.1 TEU.

and, if necessary, take care of enforcement of these rules in cases where they are not complied with correctly.

According to Art. 10 in conjunction with Art. 16 of Regulation (EC) No. 659/1999, the Commission shall examine without delay any information from whatever source regarding alleged unlawful aid or alleged misuse of aid. If necessary, it shall request information from the Member State concerned. It follows from Art. 20 of the same procedural regulation that any interested party may inform the Commission of any alleged unlawful aid and any alleged misuse of aid.

Article 11 of Regulation (EC) No. 659/1999 provides for several measures to be taken by the Commission while it carries out its investigation. In case of alleged unlawful aid, as well as alleged misuse of aid, the Commission can give injunctions to suspend the aid concerned until it has taken a decision on the compatibility of the aid with the common market. Before the enactment of Regulation (EC) No. 659/1999 it was still accepted that once the Commission had established that aid had been granted or altered without notification, the Commission had the power, after giving the Member State in question an opportunity to submit its comments on the matter, to issue an interim decision requiring it to suspend immediately the payment of such aid pending the outcome of the examination of the aid. In order to be effective, the State aid control system presupposes, according to the Court of Justice, that measures may be taken to counteract any infringement of the rules laid down in Art. 108.3 TFEU.[24] Besides the power to give a suspension injunction, Art. 11.2 provides for another injunction which only applies to unlawful aid. According to this provision, the Commission may, after giving the Member State concerned the opportunity to submit its comments and only on certain conditions, adopt a decision requiring the Member State provisionally to recover any unlawful aid until the Commission has taken a decision on the compatibility of the aid with the internal market.[25]

Article 22 of Regulation (EC) No. 659/1999 provides further that where the Commission has serious doubts as to whether decisions not to raise objections, positive decisions or conditional decisions with regard to individual aid are being complied with, the Member State concerned, after having been given the opportunity to submit its comments, shall allow the Commission to undertake on-site monitoring visits.[26]

---

[24]See Case C-301/87 *France v Commission (Boussac)* (ECJ 14 February 1990) paras 18 and 19.

[25]The conditions laid down in Art. 11.3 are: according to an established practice there are no doubts about the aid character of the measure concerned, there is an urgency to act and there is a serious risk of substantial and irreparable damage to a competitor. This competence was not yet accepted in case law before Regulation 659/1999 entered into force.

[26]No examples of such on-site monitoring visits have been found.

5.2 *Public Enforcement Measures in Cases of Unlawful Aid and Misuse of Aid*

If the Commission, after closure of a formal investigation procedure, comes to a negative decision in case of unlawful aid, it shall according to Art. 14 of Regulation (EC) No. 659/1999, decide that the Member State concerned shall take all necessary measures to recover the aid from the beneficiary. In fact, Art. 14 codifies consistent case law of the Court of Justice and a consistent practice of the Commission, in which it was recognised yet that the only way to restore the competition positions and to guarantee to all Member States an equal application of the State aid rules in situations of unlawful State aid is to require recovery *ex tunc* from the Member State concerned.[27] It has subsequently been confirmed that recovery could be considered as the logical consequence of the unlawful character of State aid.[28] Only through recovery, which means that the aid will be reimbursed, will the recipient forfeit the advantage that it enjoyed over its competitors on the market and will the situation as it existed prior to the grant of State aid be restored.[29] According to Art. 16 of the procedural regulation, Art. 14 equally applies in case of misuse of aid.

Art. 14 provides that the Commission shall not require recovery of the aid if this would be contrary to a general principle of Community law. For that reason, the question could arise as to how much discretion has been left to the Commission. The clause 'a general principle of Community [i.e. Union] law' has been formulated rather openly. Which principles could fall under this clause? One could think of the principle of proportionality. In its jurisprudence, however, the Court of Justice has made clear that, in general, recovery cannot be considered to be disproportionate in comparison with the objectives of the Treaty provisions related to State aid (Arts. 107–109 TFEU).[30] The clause seems to refer rather to the principle of legal certainty.[31] Regulation (EC) No. 659/1999 does not explain in which situations a beneficiary could invoke this principle in order to avoid recovery. From the case law of the European Courts, however, it follows that undertakings to which an aid has been granted may not, in principle, entertain a legitimate expectation that the aid is lawful unless it has been granted in compliance with the procedure laid down in Art. 108 TFEU. According to the Court of Justice, a diligent businessman should normally be able to determine whether that procedure

---

[27]Case C-70/72 *Commission v Germany* (*Kohlegesetz*) (ECJ 12 July 1973) para 13.

[28]See e.g. Case 310/85 *Deufil GmbH & Co. KG v Commission* (*Deufil*) (ECJ 24 February 1987) para 24; Case C-142/87 *Belgium v Commission* (*Tubemeuse*) (ECJ 21 March 1990) para 66; Case C-305/89 *Italy v Commission* (ECJ 21 March 1991) para 41.

[29]See Case C-382/99 *Netherlands v Commission* (ECJ 13 June 2002) para 89; Case C-298/00 P *Italy v Commission* (ECJ 29 April 2004) para 76.

[30]See e.g. Case C-142/87 *Belgium v Commission* (*Tubemeuse*) (ECJ 21 March 1990) para 66.

[31]See also Keppenne (1999), p. 294.

has been followed. Only in exceptional circumstances it is accepted that recipients of State aid could legitimately rely on expectations based on statements from the Commission in prior, comparable cases.[32] Member States cannot themselves invoke the protection of legitimate expectations against a recovery decision of the Commission, since according to the Court, the effectiveness of Arts. 107 and 108 TFEU would be nullified where the Member State concerned could rely on its own unlawful conduct to escape from the compliance with the Treaty provisions.[33]

Although general principles of Union law play an important role in the examination of whether recovery should be required, the consequences of recovery do not have to be taken into account. Potential liquidation of the beneficiary could therefore not be a reason to repeal a recovery decision.[34] In general it can be said that only in exceptional circumstances will the Commission decide not to recover the unlawful aid. When it comes to a recovery decision, it will be obliged to require not only recovery of the State aid itself, but also interest to be paid from the date on which the unlawful aid was at the disposal of the beneficiary until the moment of recovery.[35] According to Art. 15 of Regulation 659/1999 the powers of the Commission to require recovery of aid shall be subject to a limitation period of 10 years.

5.3 Implementation of Recovery Decisions at Member State Level

As far as the Member State is concerned, a recovery decision lays down an obligation which will, according to Art. 288 TFEU, be binding in its entirety upon those to whom it is addressed. The decision is addressed to the Member State concerned, but the obligation to recover is applicable to all public entities, in particular towards the entity that has granted the aid unlawfully. Moreover, national courts are, on the basis of Art. 4.3 TEU, in principle obliged to give full effect to the Commission decision (see further paragraph 6).

The obligation to comply with the Commission decision implies that the Member State concerned will have to take all necessary measures to make recovery possible. The question as to whether any discretion will be left to the national authorities is generally answered in the negative. In the *Land Rheinland-Pfalz* case the Court of Justice explicitly ruled thus: 'It must be noted that where State aid is

[32] See Case C-5/89 *Commission v Germany* (ECJ 20 September 1990) paras 14–16; Case C-24/95 *Land Rheinland-Pfalz v Alcan Deutschland* (ECJ 20 March 1997) para 25.

[33] See Case C-303/88 *Italy v Commission* (ECJ 21 March 1991) para 43; Case C-75/97 *Belgium v Commission* (ECJ 17 June 1999) paras 71 and 72.

[34] See Case C-404/97 *Portugal v Commission* (ECJ 27 June 2000) para 53.

[35] Before the enactment of Regulation (EC) No. 659/1999, the Commission still seemed to have a discretionary power regarding whether it could require interest. See Hancher et al. (1999), p. 390. See also Sinnaeve (1997), p. 49 et seq.

found to be incompatible with the internal market, the role of national authorities is (...) merely to give effect to the Commission's decision. The authorities do not, therefore, have any discretion as regards revocation of a decision granting aid. Thus, where the Commission, in a decision which has not been the subject of legal proceedings, orders the recovery of unduly paid sums, the national authorities are not entitled to reach any other finding.'[36] The Commission is supposed to have taken into account all relevant interests of the actors at stake. It is for this reason that Art. 14 of Regulation (EC) No. 659/1999 requires Member States to take all necessary measures to recover the aid from the beneficiary according to the procedures under the national law of the Member States (including provisional measures, without prejudice to Union law), but provided that they allow the immediate and effective execution of the Commission's decision. This formulation seems to exclude every discretionary power of the Member States.

From several studies on the enforcement of State aid law at national level it follows that while recovery of unlawful and incompatible State aid has improved over the last few years, recovery of such aid by Member States still faces a number of obstacles.[37] The authors of the 2006 study mentioned a lack of clarity as to the identity of the national body responsible for issuing a recovery decision, of the beneficiary required to repay the aid and as to the exact amount of the aid to be repaid, absence of a clear predetermined procedure to recover aid in some Member States, no availability or no use of interim relief to recover aid, stay of the recovery proceedings while an appeal is pending and difficulties experienced by the governmental authorities of a Member State when recovering aid at local level.[38] However, positive examples can also be mentioned, like decisions of national courts contributing to the effective enforcement of recovery decisions at national level. The German Federal Court of Justice, for example, held that public authorities, who are required to recover unlawful aid following a decision by the Commission, do have to be qualified as first-class creditors even though, absent the State aid issue, they would have qualified as subordinated creditors.[39] Legislative initiatives for effective recovery procedures in the Member States, like the State aid recovery bill which is currently pending in the Netherlands, will also help to ensure the effectiveness of enforcement of EU State aid law at national level.[40]

[36]Case C-24/95 *Land Rheinland-Pfalz v Alcan Deutschland* (ECJ 20 March 1997) para 34.

[37]See the 2006 Study on the Enforcement of State Aid Law at National Level, coordinated by Th. Jestaedt, J. Derenne and T. Ottervanger, March 2006; 2009 Update of the 2006 Study on the enforcement of State aid rules at national level, directed by J. Derenne, Lovells 2009. See also Nemitz (2007).

[38]See the results of the 2006 Study on the Enforcement of State Aid Law at National Level, coordinated by Th. Jestaedt, J. Derenne and T. Ottervanger, March 2006, p. 34.

[39]Federal Court of Justice (FCJ) (Bundesgerichtshof (BGH)), IX ZR 221/05 (5 July 2007).

[40]See Adriaanse and den Ouden (2009).

5.4 Public Enforcement Measures in Case of Failure to Implement Commission Recovery Decisions

In case of non-compliance with recovery decisions of the Commission, Art. 23.1 of Regulation (EC) No. 659/1999 provides that the Commission may refer the matter to the Court of Justice directly in accordance with Art. 93.2 EC [now 108.2 TFEU]. In addition, as explained in the Notice of the Commission on the implementation of recovery decisions,[41] if certain conditions are met, the Commission may require the Member State to suspend the payment of a new compatible aid to the beneficiary or beneficiaries concerned in application of the Deggendorf principle.[42]

From the case law of the Court of Justice, it can be ascertained that only in exceptional circumstances can Member States rely on difficulties in order to avoid recovery. The only argument that could be accepted is that recovery will be absolutely impossible.[43] Union law seems to determine to a large extent the interpretation of these words. It appears from the case law of the Court of Justice that a provision of domestic law, national practices or circumstances cannot impede the reimbursement of aid.[44] Financial problems of the recipient, which could be the result of recovery, are not considered as problems that make recovery absolutely impossible. The fear of invincible problems of recovery alone cannot justify the fact that the recovery obligation will not be carried out correctly. As long as the Member State has not made any attempt to recover the unlawful aid, it will not be accepted that recovery will be absolutely impossible. The Commission and the Member State concerned must respect the principle underlying Art. 4.3 TEU, which imposes a duty of genuine cooperation on the Member States and the EU institutions, and must work together in good faith with a view to overcoming difficulties whilst fully observing the Treaty provisions, and in particular the provisions of State aid.[45]

If the Court of Justice finds that a Member State has failed to fulfil its obligation, the State shall, according to Art. 260 TFEU, be required to take the necessary measures to comply with the judgment of the Court. If the Commission then considers that the Member State concerned has not taken the necessary measures to comply with the judgment of the Court, it may bring the case before the Court after giving that State the opportunity to submit its observations. If the Court finds that the Member State concerned has not complied with its judgment, it may ultimately impose a lump sum or penalty payment on it.

---

[41]O.J. C 272/4 (2007) para 71.

[42]Case C-355/95 P *Textilwerke Deggendorf GmbH (TWD) v Commission* (ECJ 15 May 1997).

[43]See e.g. Case 94/87 *Commission v Germany (Alcan)* (ECJ 2 February 1989) para 8-9; Case C-415/03 *Commission v Greece* (ECJ 12 May 2005) para 35; Case C-214/07 *Commission v France* (ECJ 13 November 2008) para 44.

[44]See Case C-369/07, *Commission v Greece* (ECJ 7 July 2009) para 45.

[45]Case C-214/07 *Commission v France* (ECJ 13 November 2008) paras 45 and 46.

5.5 *Conclusions*

As it follows from the current State aid rules and the interpretation of these rules by the European courts, the Commission can only act against breaches of EU State aid rules within the context of an investigation into the compatibility of State aid measures with the internal market,[46] for which the Commission has exclusive competence subject to review by the European Courts. It also emerges from these rules, that the Commission can only take enforcement measures addressed to the Member State concerned. Recipients of unlawful State aid or misused (conditionally) approved aid cannot be addressed directly, since the State aid rules themselves do not impose any specific obligations on the recipients of State aid, as has been made clear in the *SFEI* case.[47] The fact that recovery decisions have to be carried out in accordance with the procedures under the national law of the Member State concerned appears to be a further limitation for the effectiveness of public enforcement of EU State aid rules. Given these remarks, the following section will deal with the possibilities for private parties, in particular competitors of State aid recipients, to help enforce EU State aid law by relying on directly effective provisions of EU law in procedures before national courts, in addition or as an alternative to public enforcement by the Commission.

6 Private Enforcement of EU State Aid Law

6.1 *General Remarks*

When an undertaking finds out that aid to one or more of its competitors has been granted in breach of the EU State aid rules, several reasons could be mentioned as to why it would prove very helpful for this undertaking to be able to act against that breach at national level independently of the Commission. One thinks of the situation where the Commission does not start the formal investigation procedure that could result in a recovery decision. Or one thinks ‘simply’ of the competition disadvantages suffered by the competitor during the investigation period as a result of the recipient’s gains. Moreover, as appears from Sect. 5 of this contribution, the Commission can only require recovery of unlawful State aid in cases where the aid turns out to be incompatible with the internal market. From a State aid policy perspective, the Commission therefore considers that private enforcement actions before national courts could offer considerable benefits.[48]

---

[46]See Case C-301/87 *France v Commission (Boussac)* (ECJ 14 February 1990) paras 9–22.

[47]See Case C-39/94 *SFEI et al.* (ECJ 11 July 1996) para 73.

[48]Commission Notice on the enforcement of State aid law by national courts (hereinafter Enforcement Notice), O.J. C 85/1 (2009) para 5.

The assumption of private enforcement of EU law is that private parties could go to their national court whenever rights acknowledged to them by Union law are in issue. Already in 1962 the Court of Justice emphasised in the *Van Gend & Loos* case: 'The vigilance of individuals concerned to protect their rights amounts to an effective supervision in addition to the supervision entrusted by articles 169 and 170 to the diligence of the commission and of the member states.'[49] National courts have to guarantee to private parties the full protection of these rights and if necessary, they will have to repair or to compensate them. Although these private enforcement actions will be primarily focused on getting judicial review by national courts, at the same time they could have a deterrent effect on the behaviour of the actor that breached the rules. According to Roach and Trebilcock, private plaintiffs could so be considered as 'private attorneys-general'.[50]

The question thus is whether EU law offers the competing undertaking (hereinafter 'competitor'), or other interested private parties in the playing field of State aid policy, sufficient legal bases to start actions before national courts against unlawful aid or other breaches of EU State aid law. Should this question be answered in the negative, these private parties will have to 'wait and see' whether and when the Commission will act against the aid. They might be thought to be at a disadvantage in these circumstances, since they could suffer damages in the period between the grant of the aid and the examination by the Commission.

6.2 Grounds for Private Enforcement

The main condition for private enforcement actions, as indicated in Sect. 6.1, is that the rights that EU law confers upon private parties are directly effective, since not all Union law is meant to be applied directly by national courts. It follows from the case law of the Court of Justice that, within the legal framework of EU State aid rules, direct effect could be given to several kinds of provisions.

In the first place, Art. 108.3, last sentence TFEU, should be mentioned, in which the standstill obligation, directed to Member States, has been laid down.[51] The question as to whether this provision has direct effect was first raised in the *Costa v Enel* case,[52] at that time concerning Art. 93 of the Treaty of Rome. The Court, however, could not give a proper decision with regard to the question in that case. Later, in the *Lorenz* case the Court explicitly recognised the direct effect of now Art. 108.3 TFEU, last sentence, concerning the so-called standstill obligation. The Court explained that the immediately applicable nature of this prohibition extends to the whole of the period to which it applied. Thus, according to the Court, the

[49]Case 26/62 *Van Gend & Loos* (ECJ 5 February 1963).

[50]Roach and Trebilcock (1997), p. 471 et seq. See also Naysnerski and Tietenberg (1992), p. 46.

[51]The same clause is laid down in Art. 3 of Regulation (EC) No. 659/1999.

[52]Case 6/64 *Costa v E.N.E.L.* (ECJ 3 June 1964).

direct effect 'extends to all aid which has been implemented without being notified and, in the event of notification, operates during the preliminary period and, if the Commission sets in motion the contentious procedure, until the final decision'.[53] Since the enactment of Regulation (EC) No. 659/1999 it is clear that 'final decision' has to be read as 'a decision authorising such aid'.[54] Competitors and other interested parties can invoke the direct effect of Art. 108.3, last sentence TFEU, in cases before national courts, as soon as Member State authorities grant aid in breach of the standstill clause.

From the judgment of the Court of Justice in the *Van Calster and Cleeren* case it follows that private enforcement actions based on Art. 108.3 TFEU can be directed not only against unlawful State aid itself, but also against contributions (like taxes) specifically levied for the purpose of financing that aid, not being notified to the Commission.[55] The Member State concerned is required to notify not only planned aid in the narrow sense, but also the method of financing the aid inasmuch as that method is an integral part of the planned measure. According to consistent case law, the method by which an aid is financed may render the entire aid scheme incompatible with the internal market. If this requirement of notification is not satisfied, it is possible that the Commission may declare that an aid measure is compatible, when, if the Commission had been aware of its method of financing, it could not have been so declared.[56]

In the second place, the provisions of the *de minimis* Regulation and the General block exemption Regulation could be mentioned as possible grounds for private enforcement actions in the field of EU State aid law. As has been remarked in Sect. 2, the Member States are allowed to grant aid measures that fulfil the criteria of these regulations without prior notification to the Commission. Given their direct applicability, according to Art. 288 TFEU, the provisions of these regulations can be subject to direct effect within the national legal orders. It will be the task of national courts to check whether the Member States correctly apply the criteria of these regulations in practice. Should a national court conclude that the criteria of these Regulations have not been applied correctly, the granted aid will have to be considered as unlawful.

In the third place, the provisions of Commission decisions taken after a formal investigation procedure have to be mentioned as possible grounds for private enforcement actions, since the provisions of these decisions could have direct effect in the national legal orders. In the *Capolongo* case the Court of Justice ruled that 'whilst, for projects introducing new aids or altering existing ones, the last sentence of Art. 93(3) [now 108.3 TFEU] establishes procedural criteria which the national

---

[53]Case 120/73 *Lorenz GmbH v Germany et al.* (ECJ 11 December 1973) para 8.

[54]See also Struys (1999), p. 290.

[55]Joined Cases 261/01 and C-262/01 *Van Calster and Cleeren* (ECJ 21 October 2003) para 52 (confirmed in later judgments).

[56]Joined Cases 261/01 and C-262/01 *Van Calster and Cleeren* (ECJ 21 October 2003) paras 49–51.

court can appraise, the same does not hold true for existing systems of aid referred to in Art. 93(1) [now 108.1 TFEU]. With regard to such aids, the provisions of Art. 92(1) [now 107.1 TFEU] are intended to take effect in the legal systems of member states, so that they may be invoked before national courts, where they have been put in concrete form by acts having general application provided for by Art. 94 [now 109 TFEU] or by decisions in particular cases envisaged by Art. 93 (2) [now 108.2 TFEU].'[57] Given this last phrase, one could think of recovery decisions that have not been put into effect within the prescribed time or incorrectly. One could also think of actions related to misuse of aid, in case of breach of provisions of (conditional) positive decisions.

So, in theory the possibilities for private enforcement actions in procedures before national courts based on directly effective EU State aid provisions seem rather comprehensive. One should be aware of the fact, however, that the State aid rules themselves do not impose any specific obligations on the recipients of State aid, as has been explained in Sect. 3.[58] For that reason the aid recipients cannot be summoned by competitors or other interested private parties in national procedures based directly on the EU State aid rules. In other words, a horizontal direct effect of the State aid provisions has not been accepted so far.[59] The legal grounds for private enforcement actions, as mentioned above, could therefore only be used towards the authorities of the Member State concerned. However, as the Commission states in its Enforcement Notice, this does not in any way prejudice the possibility of a successful action against the beneficiary on the basis of substantive national law.[60]

6.3 Private Enforcement Actions in Cases of Unlawful State Aid

Once private enforcement actions will be based on the grounds as mentioned above, national courts must, in accordance with their national law, draw the necessary consequences of the unlawfulness of State aid, in order to protect the rights that private parties (e.g. competitors of the aid recipients) can derive from EU law.[61] Measures taken in disregard of the prohibition laid down by Art. 108.3 TFEU will be invalid.[62] The Court of Justice has further held that the national court must in

[57]Case 77/72 *Capolongo v Azienda Agricola Maya* (ECJ 19 June 1973) para 6.

[58]See Case C-39/94 *SFEI et al.* (ECJ 11 July 1996) para 73.

[59]See also Sasserath (2001), pp. 224–227.

[60]Enforcement Notice, O.J. C 85/1 (2009) para 55.

[61]Case C-354/90 *FNCE v France ('Salmon')* (ECJ 21 November 1991) para 12; Case C-39/94 *SFEI* (ECJ 11 July 1996) para 40; Case C-368/04 *Transalpine Ölleitung* (ECJ 5 October 2006) para 47.

[62]Case C-354/90 *FNCE v France ('Salmon')* (ECJ 21 November 1991) para 12. See also Joined Cases C-261/01 and C-262/01 *Van Calster and Cleeren* (ECJ 21 October 2003) para 52; Joined Cases C-34/01-C-38/01 *Enirisorce* (ECJ 27 November 2003) para 46; Case C-174/02 *Streekgewest Westelijk Noord-Brabant* (ECJ 13 January 2005) para 16.

principle allow an application for repayment of aid paid in breach of Art. 108.3.[63] Other remedies include preventing the payment of unlawful aid, recovery of illegality interest, interim measures against unlawful aid and damages for competitors and other interested parties.[64]

In the *Van Calster and Cleeren* case the Court of Justice ruled that since the obligation to notify aid also covers the method of financing the aid, the consequences of a failure by the national authorities to comply with the last sentence of Art. 108.3 TFEU must also apply to that aspect of the aid measure. The Court therefore confirmed that where an aid measure of which the method of financing is an integral part has been implemented in breach of the obligation to notify, national courts must in principle order reimbursement of charges or contributions levied specifically for the purpose of financing that aid.[65]

As far as recovery of unlawful State aid is concerned, the Court of Justice has left a margin of appreciation to the national courts. The Court ruled that in exceptional circumstances recovery could be inappropriate.[66] It will be the task of national courts to determine and to interpret these circumstances under close cooperation with the Commission and the possibility of preliminary questions to the Court.[67] No clear positive indications on exceptional circumstances could be derived yet from the case law of the Court. Given the severe approach of the Court towards recipients of unlawful State aid, however, exceptional circumstances may be supposed only when a diligent businessman could have got legitimate expectations on the basis of acts or statements of the Commission.

Moreover, in the *CELF* case the Court of Justice held that the national court is not bound to order the recovery of aid implemented contrary to the last sentence of Art. 108.3 TFEU, where the Commission has adopted a final decision declaring that aid be compatible. In such a situation the national court must order the aid recipient to pay interest in respect of the period of unlawfulness.[68]

In the *CELF* case the Court of Justice also confirmed that interested parties that suffer a loss from the unlawfulness of State aid may claim for compensation for damage.[69] Such a claim may be combined with a request to the national court to order recovery of the unlawful State aid. When competitors are able to prove that they have suffered loss caused by unlawful implementation of aid, the Member

[63]Case C-199/06 *CELF/SIDE* (ECJ 12 February 2008) para 39. See also Joined Cases C-261/01 and C-262/01 *Van Calster and Cleeren* [(ECJ 21 October 2003) paras 53 and 54.

[64]See Enforcement Notice, O.J. C 85/1 (2009) para 26.

[65]See Joined Cases C-261/01 and C-262/01 *Van Calster and Cleeren* (ECJ 21 October 2003) paras 53 and 54; Joined Cases C-34/01-C-38/01 *Enirisorce* (ECJ 27 November 2003) para 45; Case C-174/02 *Streekgewest Westelijk Noord-Brabant* (ECJ 13 January 2005) paras 16 and 17.

[66]Case C-39/94 *SFEI et al.* (ECJ 11 July 1996) paras 68–71.

[67]See Case C-39/94 *SFEI* (ECJ 11 July 1996) para 70.

[68]Case C-199/06 *CELF/SIDE* (ECJ 12 February 2008) paras 52 and 53. See on this judgment Adriaanse (2009); Jaeger (2008); Slot (2009).

[69]Case C-199/06 *CELF/SIDE* (ECJ 12 February 2008) paras 52 and 53.

State might be obliged, according to the general principle of State liability for breach of Union law, based on cases like *Francovich* and *Brasserie du Pêcheur*,[70] to award damages against these competitors.[71] Since the Court of Justice has ruled in the *SFEI* case that the State aid rules do not impose any specific obligation on the recipients of aid, claims for damages directly against the beneficiary of the aid, arguing that the beneficiary has not verified whether the aid has been notified to the Commission in accordance with Art. 108.3 TFEU, will not be possible.[72] EU law, according to the Court, does not provide a sufficient basis for the recipient to incur liability where he has failed to verify that the aid received was duly notified to the Commission.[73] In its judgment in the *SFEI* case the Court, however, it added that this decision does not prejudice the possible application of national law concerning non-contractual liability.[74]

All these remedies with regard to unlawful State aid shall be granted in accordance with the applicable provisions and procedures of the national law of the Member State concerned, according to its so-called institutional and procedural autonomy. However, the provisions of national law can only be applied as long as the EU principles of effectiveness and equivalence will be respected, as has been explained in Sect. 4 of this contribution.

6.4 Private Enforcement Actions Based on the Provisions of Commission Decisions Taken After a Formal Investigation Procedure

As has been stated in Sect. 6.2, provisions of Commission decisions taken after a formal investigation procedure could be relied on directly by private parties as a basis for private enforcement actions before national courts. One may then think of actions against alleged misuse of aid after a (conditional) positive decision has been taken, but also of actions related to negative decisions ordering recovery. In its Notice on the implementation of recovery decisions the Commission recalls that a Commission decision addressed to a Member State is binding on all organs of that State, including the courts of that State.[75] By relying on the provisions of these decisions in procedures before national courts private parties could help to enforce

[70]Case C-6/90 and C-9/90 *Andrea Francovich et al. v Italy* ECJ 11 November 1991); Case C-46/93 and C-48/93 *Brasserie du Pêcheur SA v Germany* (ECJ 5 March 1996).

[71]See also the Enforcement Notice, O.J. C 85/1 (2009), paras 43–52; Flynn (2003), p. 333; Bacon (2003), p. 354; Soltész (2001); Sasserath (2001), p. 169.

[72]Case C-39/94 *SFEI et al* (ECJ 11 July 1996) para 73.

[73]Case C-39/94 *SFEI et al* (ECJ 11 July 1996) para 74.

[74]Case C-39/94 *SFEI et al* (ECJ 11 July 1996) para 75.

[75]O.J. C 272/4 (2007) para 45. Reference is made to Case 249/85 *Albako Margarinefabrik Maria von der Linde GmbH & Co v. Bundesanstalt für landwirtschaftliche Marktordnung* (ECJ 21 May 1987).

the decisions, possibly in addition to public measures taken by the Commission, like infringement procedures in the sense of Art. 108.2 TFEU, as discussed in Sect. 5 of this contribution. In its Enforcement Notice the Commission deals in particular with damages claims under the above-mentioned *Francovich* and *Brasserie du Pêcheur* jurisprudence for failure by the Member State authorities to comply with a Commission recovery decision under Art. 14 of Regulation (EC) No. 659/1999. Acccording to the Commission, 'the treatment of such damages claims mirrors the principles as regards violations of the standstill obligation'.[76]

6.5 The Role of National Courts

As regards the supervision of Member States' compliance with their obligations under Arts. 107 and 108 TFEU, the Court of Justice has explained in the *SFEI* case that the national courts and the Commission fulfil complementary and separate roles.[77] National courts cannot rule on the compatibility of aid with the internal market, in drawing the appropriate conclusions from an infringement of the last sentence of Art. 108.3 TFEU. That determination is an exclusive matter for the Commission, subject to review by the European courts.[78] According to the Court in the *FNCE ('Salmon')* case, the role of national courts is to safeguard rights which individuals enjoy as a result of the direct effect of the prohibition laid down in the last sentence of Art. 108.3 TFEU. As just mentioned above, national courts also play a role in the enforcement of Commission decisions taken after a formal investigation procedure, in particular negative decisions ordering recovery.

However, a national court asked to safeguard the rights of private parties in the context of EU State aid control could face several difficult questions, varying from the concept of State aid to procedural issues of national law, like time limits and aspects of evidence. When a national court will have to decide whether a measure in question falls under the scope of EU State aid control, Art. 107.1 TFEU will be the guiding provision in this respect. The national court will have to examine whether all the criteria in this provision are met. Having established this, the national court might also have to examine whether that measure has been notified either individually or under a scheme and, if so, whether the Commission has had sufficient time to come to a decision.[79] Moreover, for difficulties with regard to that part of the decision, the national courts can be guided, in interpreting EU law, by the case law of the European Courts, as well as by decisions and other documents issued by the Commission.

---

[76]O.J. C 85/1 (2009) para 69.

[77]Case C-39/94 *SFEI et al.* (ECJ 11 July 1996) para 41.

[78]Case C-39/94 *SFEI et al.* (ECJ 11 July 1996) para 42. See also Case C-354/90 *FNCE v France ('Salmon')* (ECJ 21 November 1991) para 14. See also the Enforcement Notice, O.J. C 85/1 (2009) para 19 *et seq.*

[79]See Case 120/73 *Lorenz v Germany* (ECJ 11 December 1973) para 6.

For questions on the interpretation of Union law national courts may request the Court of Justice for a preliminary ruling on the interpretation of Art. 107 TFEU.[80] It should be noted, however, that State aid questions will often concern factual questions for which reference to the European Courts will not be possible.[81] Therefore, national courts may also request assistance from the Commission by asking it to transmit to them relevant information in its possession. One could think of information concerning a pending Commission procedure, but also of other information, like copies of existing Commission decisions, factual data, statistics, market studies and economic analysis. Moreover, national courts can ask the Commission for an opinion concerning the application of the State aid rules.[82]

Since the Commission and national courts might have to decide on identical issues, like the characterisation of aid and whether the aid should have been notified, they have, according to Art. 4.3 TEU, a mutual duty of loyal cooperation in order to avoid conflicting decisions on the same issue.[83] This means that national courts will be bound by Commission decisions concerning new aid, the compatibility of aid or the (un)lawfulness of aid.[84] However, the Court of Justice confirmed in the *SFEI* case that a (preliminary) examination by the Commission cannot release the national courts from their duty to safeguard the rights of individuals in the event of a breach of the requirement to give prior notification.[85] In this case the Court also held that a national court, seized of a request that it should draw the appropriate conclusions from an infringement of the last sentence of Art. 108.3 TFEU, is not required to declare it lacks jurisdiction or to stay proceedings until such time that the Commission has adopted a position on how the measures in question are to be qualified, where the matter has also been referred to the Commission.[86]

6.6 *Private Enforcement in Practice*

Several studies on the enforcement of State aid law at national level show that there has been a significant increase in the number of State aid cases before national courts over the last few years.[87] From the latest study, carried out in 2009, it appears that the increase of cases is not yet equally shared between Member States. Most of

---

[80] See Case C-39/94 *SFEI et al.* (ECJ 11 July 1996) para 51.

[81] See Keppenne (1999), p. 313. See also Ross (2000).

[82] Enforcement Notice, O.J. C 85/1 (2009) para 77 *et seq.*

[83] Enforcement Notice, O.J. C 85/1 (2009) paras 77 and 78.

[84] See Case C-312/90 *Spain v Commission* (ECJ 30 June 1992) para 23. See also Keppenne (1999), p. 305.

[85] Case C-39/94 *SFEI et al.* (ECJ 11 July 1996) para 44.

[86] Case C-39/94 *SFEI et al.* (ECJ 11 July 1996) para 53.

[87] See the 2006 Study on the Enforcement of State Aid Law at National Level, coordinated by Th. Jestaedt, J. Derenne and T. Ottervanger, March 2006 and the 2009 Update of the 2006 Study on the

the cases before national courts deal with tax measures. In genuine private enforcement cases, initiated by competitors of recipients of unlawful State aid, a number of competitors have been successful in their claims, in particular where they were seeking the suspension or the recovery of unlawful aid. No examples of successful claims for damages have been reported so far.[88] The way in which national courts deal with State aid cases varies.[89] The 2009 update Study on the enforcement of the State aid rules at national level shows several positive examples, as well as negative examples. We mention, first, a few positive examples.

The Swedish administrative court in Blekinge was confronted with an appeal of local residents to a decision of the municipal council in Karlskrona to sell a piece of land to an enterprise.[90] The applicants argued that the land had been sold at an amount below market price, which would be contrary not only to domestic law, but also to EU State aid law. The administrative court did what it is supposed to do in such a situation. It first assessed whether the sale of land could be qualified as State aid under Art. 107.1 TFEU. Having confirmed this, the court then came to the conclusion that the authorities, by not notifying the aid measure to the Commission, had infringed Art. 108.3 TFEU. Consequently, the disputed decision was annulled.

Another good example of State aid private enforcement offers a judgment of the Finnish Supreme Administrative Court.[91] A company active in the construction, sale and letting of business premises in the province of Aland applied for an interim measure claiming that several decisions, among which one on the grant of a guarantee of the Province Government to a competitor, involved State aid incompatible with the internal market. Since the Commission initiated a formal investigation procedure on the issues relating to the measures of the Province Government, the Supreme Administrative Court suspended the handling of the appeal until the Commission took its final decision. Referring to Art. 108.3 TFEU, the national court offered effective judicial protection to the applicant in the meanwhile, as it is required to do according to the settled case law of the Court of Justice. The Finnish Supreme Administrative Court ordered the suspension of the granting of the provincial guarantee until the issue was finally resolved.

As a positive example of loyal cooperation between a national court and the Commission in the State aid field, a judgment of the Dutch Council of State could be mentioned. The Dutch State had granted more than €18 million to Airport Eelde in the Netherlands. The Dutch Council of State, confronted with questions

---

enforcement of State aid rules at national level, directed by J. Derenne, Lovells 2009. See also Nemitz (2007).

[88]2009 Update of the 2006 Study on the enforcement of State aid rules at national level, Final Report, directed by J. Derenne, Lovells 2009, p. 2 (http://ec.europa.eu/competition/court/state_aid_info.html)

[89]See the website of DG Competition with selected summaries of judgments from national courts: http://ec.europa.eu/competition/court/state_aid_judgments.html

[90]Administrative Court in Blekinge ("Länsrätten i Blekinge"), 316-08 (21 October 2008).

[91]Supreme Administrative Court ("Korkein hallinto-oikeus"), Dno. 3170/2/06 (29 December 2006).

on the interpretation of the concept of State aid and the application of the relevant State aid rules, referred several questions to the Commission and delivered its final judgement, based on the answers of the Commission, only 4 months later.[92]

The 2009 update Study on the enforcement of the State aid rules at national level, however, also revealed several examples of judgments of especially German courts which seem, as the authors of the study rightly put it, 'at odds with the fundamental principles enshrined in the *Costa v Enel*, *SFEI*, and *Streekgewest* cases'.[93] The German Higher Regional Court Schleswig-Holstein had to deal with the appeal against an earlier decision of the Kiel Regional Court about allegedly unlawful State aid to Ryanair following from an agreement between the latter and an undertaking managing the airport of Lübeck.[94] According to the Kiel Regional Court the agreement would amount to State aid. In accordance with consistent case law of the Court of Justice, therefore, the Kiel Regional reasoned that Art. 108.3 TFEU (at the time 88.3 EC) would give a competitor of the beneficiary, like Air Berlin, the right to request recovery of the unlawful State aid and to file an action for damages. The Higher Regional Court Schleswig-Holstein, however, quashed the earlier decision and rejected Air Berlin's claims on grounds of inadmissibility and on the merits. As far as the EU State aid rules are concerned, the Higher Court found that these rules cannot be considered to be rules, aimed at the protection of individuals. In the view of this Court it is not obvious that the European State aid rules were developed in order to give a competitor the possibility either to oblige the beneficiary to repay the received State aid to the granting authority or to oblige the authority that granted the aid to recover such aid from the beneficiary. As far as the Court of Justice ruled in 1996 that the national courts are in principle obliged to order the recovery of unlawful State aid in reaction to a claim by a competitor, according to the Higher Regional Court, this can only hold true as long as there is a respective legal basis in the national law. Third parties such as competitors are in the view of this Court sufficiently protected as they can make their views known to the Commission during the formal procedure. In case the Commission fails to take a decision and violates its obligations, third parties can bring an action for injunction before the European Courts. Another German court, the Bad Kreuznach Regional Court, ruled in a similar way on claims of Lufthansa about allegedly unlawful State aid to Ryanair granted by an undertaking that operates the Frankfurt Hahn airport.[95] Denying its own task under the State aid rules, as it follows from settled case law of the Court of Justice, the Bad Kreuznach Regional Court found that it was not relevant to decide on the State aid issues, as long as the Commission had not taken any (negative) decision. It further found that it was not relevant for the case that the underlying agreements between the

[92]Council of State ("Afdeling bestuursrechtspraak Raad van State"), *AB* 2008, 371 (11 June 2008).

[93]Oberlandesgericht Koblenz 25 February 2009. Since several of these cases are currently under appeal before the German Supreme Court, the final outcome may be different.

[94]Higher Regional Court Schleswig-Holstein (Court of Appeal), 6 U 54/06 (20 May 2008).

[95]Bad Kreuznach Regional Court (Landgericht Bad Kreuznach), 2 O 441/06 (16 May 2007).

defendant and Ryanair could be null and void due to a potential violation of Art. 108.3 TFEU. And even the question of prescription was found not to be decisive in this case. Following the same erroneous line of reasoning as the Higher Regional Court Schleswig-Holstein did, the Bad Kreuznach Regional Court ruled that the claims were unfounded as there was no legal basis under national law for this competitor to claim recovery of unlawful State aid. This judgment has been confirmed by the Coblence Higher Regional Court.[96]

Besides these rather clear examples (both positive and negative) of State aid private enforcement, one could also find examples somewhere in the middle. Before the Portugese Supreme Administrative Court several companies providing passenger transport by bus in the area of Lisbon complained about distortion of competition by State aid allegedly granted to two public undertakings holding public service concessions.[97] The Supreme Administrative Court decided to stay the proceedings and to refer to the Court of Justice for a preliminary ruling. Among other questions, it asked the Court of Justice whether the intervention by the Commission provided for in EU law would be the only way of enforcing the State aid rules. Apparently not aware of consistent case law of the Court of Justice on private enforcement of EC State aid law, the Portugese Supreme Court asked in particular whether the effectiveness of Community law additionally requires the possibility of direct application of those rules by the national courts at the request of those private parties who consider themselves to be adversely affected by the grant of a subsidy or aid contrary to the competition rules. As expected, this question was answered in the affirmative by the Court of Justice.[98]

6.7 Conclusions

Private enforcement of EU State aid law could, at least theoretically, be considered as a valuable contribution to public enforcement measures which could be taken by the Commission. Several situations could be distinguished: when the Commission, after a preliminary investigation into a complaint, decides not to investigate that complaint any further; during a formal investigation procedure of the Commission; when the Commission, after a formal investigation procedure, decides that unlawful State aid is compatible with the internal market; when the Commission has issued a recovery decision, but the Member State concerned fails to carry it out correctly; when private parties act against unlawful contributions levied specifically for the

[96]Coblence Higher Regional Court (Oberlandesgericht Koblenz), 4 U 759/07 (25 February 2009).

[97]Supreme Administrative Court (Supremo Tribunal Administrativo), 01050/03 (23 October 2007).

[98]Case C-504/07 *Associação Nacional de Transportadores Rodoviários de Pesados de Passageiros (Antrop) a.o. v Conselho de Ministros, Companhia Carris de Ferro de Lisboa SA (Carris) and Sociedade de Transportes Colectivos do Porto SA (STCP)* (ECJ 7 May 2009).

purpose of financing that aid; when private parties want to sue the authority that has granted the unlawful State aid, not being the central Member State. However, in practice private enforcement still faces several difficulties. Moreover, the effectiveness of private enforcement actions strongly depends on the willingness of interested private parties, like competitors of recipients of State aid, to start procedures at national level, and the willingness of national courts to rule in accordance with consistent case law of the Court of Justice.

7 Concluding Remarks

In this contribution several ways of enforcement of EU State aid law have been discussed, focusing on legal issues of dual vigilance by the Commission and national courts on the basis of the current regime for EU State aid control in an integrated legal order. In 2005 the Commission issued the State Aid Action Plan, meant as an indicative roadmap for state aid reform during the period 2005–2009. Meanwhile, several initiatives have been realised, like improvement of the internal practice and administration of the Commission, increase of efficiency, enforcement and monitoring, best practices guidelines, more predictable timelines and more information on the Internet. Both public and private enforcement measures have been the subject of growing attention over the last few years. However, the enforcement of EU State aid rules still faces a number of obstacles. In order to remedy these obstacles, it will be important to continue initiatives to raise awareness and understanding of the State aid rules at all levels, given the fact that the EU legal order and the national legal orders of the Member States strongly interact with respect to State aid control. Further advocacy by the Commission on both public and private enforcement measures should be welcomed. Member States should make an effort to improve their efficiency, transparency and implementation of State aid policy, and as far as necessary, adapt their national laws to the requirements of EU law. Granting authorities should be helped in designing measures that are compatible with the treaty rules, whereas national courts and other actors should be further informed about their tasks, rights, competences and/or obligations under the State aid regime.

References

Adriaanse PC (2009) Appropriate measures to remedy the consequences of unlawful state aid. An analysis of the ECJ Judgment of 12 February 2008 in Case C-199/06 (*CELF/SIDE*). Review of European Administrative Law 2009:73–86

Adriaanse PC, den Ouden W (2009) Legislative initiative for effective recovery procedures in Dutch law. EStAL:15–26

Adriaanse PC et al (2008) Implementation of EU enforcement provisions: between European control and national practice. REALaw:83–97

Anestis P, Mavroghenis S, Drakakakis S (2005) Recent developments in EC state aid policy. Eur Antitrust Rev:68–72

Bacon K (2003) State aids in the English Courts: definition and other problems. In: Biondi A, Eeckhout P, Flynn J (eds) The law of state aid in the European Union. Oxford University Press, Oxford

Flynn J (2003) The role of national courts. In: Biondi A, Eeckhout P, Flynn J (eds) The law of state aid in the European Union. Oxford University Press, Oxford

Hancher L, Ottervanger T, Slot PJ (1999) EC state aids. Sweet & Maxwell, London

Jaeger Th (2008) The CELF-judgment: a precarious conception of the standstill obligation. EStAL:279–289

Jans JH et al (2007) Europeanisation of public law. Europa Law Publishing, Groningen

Keppenne JP (1999) Guide des aides d'État en droit communautaire; Réglementation, jurisprudence et pratique de la Commission. Bruylant, Brussels

Kilpatrick C, Novitz T, Skidmore P (eds) (2000) The future of remedies in Europe. Hart, Oxford

Kroes N (2008) EU State aid rules – part of the solution. EStALI Conference Luxembourg 5 December 2008 (SPEECH/08/679)

Lonbay J, Biondi A (eds) (1997) Remedies for breach of EC law. Wiley, Chichester

Naysnerski W, Tietenberg T (1992) Private enforcement of federal environmental law. Land Economics 68(1):28–48

Nemitz PF (ed) (2007) The effective application of EU state aid procedures. The role of national law and practice. Kluwer Law International, Alphen a/d Rijn

Roach K, Trebilcock MJ (1997) Private enforcement of competition laws. Osgood Hall Law Journal 34(3):461–508

Ross M (2000) State aid and national courts: definitions and other problems – a case of premature emancipation? CMLRev 37(2):401–423

Sasserath N (2001) Schadenersatzansprüche von Konkurrenten zur Effektivierung der Beihilfenkontrolle? Duncker & Humblot, Berlin

Sinnaeve A (1997) Die Rückforderung gemeinschaftsrechtswidriger nationaler Beihilfen, Kollisionen im Spannungsverhältnis zwischen Gemeinschafts- und nationalem Recht. Duncker & Humblot, Berlin

Slot PJ (2009) Case C-166/06, Centre d'exportation du livre Français (CELF) v. Société internationale de diffusion et d'édition (SIDE), judgment of the Court (Grand Chamber) of 12 February 2008, [2008] ECR I-469. CMLRev:623–639

Soltész U (2001) Der Rechtsschutz des Konkurrenten gegen gemeinschaftsrechtswidrige Beihilfen vor nationalen Gerichten. EuZW 7:202–207

Struys ML (1999) Le rôle des juridictions nationales. In: Les aides d'etat en droit communautaire et en droit national. Bruylant, Brussels

Part III
The Common Foreign and Security Policy

The Role and the Interactions of the European Council and the Council in the Common Foreign and Security Policy*

Piergiorgio Cherubini

1 Added Value of a CFSP

The rather recent entry into force of the Lisbon Treaty makes it very difficult, at this stage, to clearly detect what has changed in the interaction and the respective role of the Council and the European Council in defining and implementing the European Common Foreign and Security Policy (CFSP). We are in a moment of transition, where many of the previous rules and habits are no more helpful, while the new ones are still developing.

There are, in fact, three levels at which novelties introduced by the Treaty of Lisbon affect a smooth transition: the level of the new provisions in the Treaty regarding the two bodies, the level of new actors called to fill new tasks and the level of procedures and interactions among the different institutions.

But first of all one should take into account the spirit that breathes through the Treaty of Lisbon as far as the CFSP is concerned. After the enlargement of the Union and following a trend that originates from the beginning of the CFSP, Member States have become more and more convinced of the added value of a "Common foreign and security policy".

It is evident nowadays that a national, i.e. individual, foreign policy is bound not to be influential at all in the international arena, unless it is embodied in a concerted multinational effort. The dilemma between national and common foreign policy turns into a real challenge for the European Union (EU) now that it has grown in number with the admission of 12 new Member States, and at a time when in the

*This contribution deals with the practice of the relationship between the European Council and the Council. Revised and updated by Robert Böttner, assistant at the Chair for Public Law, International Public Law and European Integration at the University of Erfurt.

P. Cherubini (✉)
Ministero Affari Esteri, DGAP Unità PESC/PSDC, Piazzale Della Farnesina, attn. Dott.ssa Silvia Chiave, 00100 Roma, Italy
e-mail: piergiorgio.cherubini@esteri.it

H.-J. Blanke and S. Mangiameli (eds.), *The European Union after Lisbon*,
DOI 10.1007/978-3-642-19507-5_18, © Springer-Verlag Berlin Heidelberg 2012

international context no position of power is given for granted and competitiveness is more acute. Nevertheless, the foreign policies of both the Union and the Member States will continue to complement each other. Taking into account the principle of subsidiarity, the Member States are still competent when an agreement on a European level is neither feasible nor necessary.

Facing that new situation the Union is under pressure to strengthen all the institutional tools that may reinforce cohesion and coherence of its external action and, in order to do that, sets out for a path of increased integration, of supranational decision making, of "communitarisation" of the CFSP.

Therefore, the novelties introduced by the Treaty need to be examined, also regarding expectations of further integration, and evaluated in terms of their efficacy to this end. To do so it is appropriate to develop the reflection along these preliminary remarks.

2 The New Provisions of the Treaty

In examining the wording of the new provisions of the Treaty on the CFSP, a comparison with the previous version of the Treaty on European Union (TEU) on an "article by article" basis would be very difficult due to the completely different architecture of the two texts. For this reason it will be easier to discover the differences while reviewing the new provisions of the Treaty as referred to the different actors of the CFSP. It therefore seems to be a proper way to start with a comparison between the two bodies, the European Council and the Council.

2.1 The European Council

The first time the European Council is mentioned in the Treaty, a vague reference is made to its competences as far as the CFSP is concerned (Art. 15.1 TEU):

> The European Council shall provide the Union with the necessary impetus for its development and shall define *the general political directions* and priorities thereof. [. . .]

In the same article CFSP is mentioned again when talking about the duties of the President of the European Council, when, at the end of para 5, it is said:

> The President of the European Council shall, at his level and in that capacity, *ensure the external representation of the Union on issues concerning its common foreign and security policy*, without prejudice to the powers of the High Representative of the Union for Foreign Affairs and Security Policy.

Then, the European Council is referred to once again, in conjunction with the CFSP, in Art. 18.1 TEU when its power of appointing the High Representative (as well as of ending his mandate!) is quoted:

> The European Council, acting by a qualified majority, with the agreement of the President of the Commission, *shall appoint the High Representative of the Union for Foreign Affairs and Security Policy*. The European Council may end his term of office by the same procedure.

As is well known, Title V of the Treaty deals with the "General provisions on the Union's external action and specific provisions on the CFSP". Article 22.1 TEU therein outlines the tasks of the European Council in the domain of external action and CFSP:

> On the basis of the principles and objectives set out in Article 21, the European Council shall identify the strategic interests and objectives of the Union.
>
> *Decisions of the European Council on the strategic interests and objectives of the Union shall relate to the common foreign and security policy and to the areas of external action* of the Union. Such decisions may concern the relations of the Union with a specific country or region or may be thematic in approach. They shall define their duration, and the means to be made available by the Union and the Member States.

Moreover, those tasks are defined in Art. 26.1 TEU:

> The European Council shall identify the Union's strategic interests, determine the objectives of and *define general guidelines for the common foreign and security policy*, including for matters with defence implications. It shall adopt the necessary decisions.
>
> If international developments so require, the President of the European Council shall convene an extraordinary meeting of the European Council in order to define the strategic lines of the Union's policy in the face of such developments.

Finally, Art. 31 TEU refers to "Decisions" in matters related to CFSP and explains how they are taken within the European Council and within the Council, whether unanimously or by a qualified majority vote.

2.2 The Council

As for the Council, we need first of all to clarify that, of all the different Council configurations (Art. 16.6 TEU), the *Foreign Affairs Council* is the one we are interested in the most, which

> [...] shall elaborate the Union's external action on the basis of strategic guidelines laid down by the European Council and ensure that the Union's action is consistent.

The above-mentioned Art. 26 TEU, in parallel with what prescribes for the European Council in its first paragraph, defines in the second one the tasks for the Council (Foreign Affairs Council):

> The Council *shall frame the common foreign and security policy and take the decisions necessary for defining and implementing it* on the basis of the general guidelines and strategic lines defined by the European Council.
>
> The Council and the High Representative of the Union for Foreign Affairs and security Policy shall ensure the unity, consistency and effectiveness of action by the Union.

From this first overview of the provisions of the Treaty it seems obvious that little has changed in so far as the relationship between the Council and the European Council is concerned, in matters related to the CFSP.

Article 26 TEU, in fact, spells out the following quite clearly:

- While the European Council *identifies* the Union *strategic interests* and *defines general guidelines* for the CFSP
- The Council *frames* the CFSP and *takes the decisions* necessary for *defining and implementing* it
- In addition, it is worthy considering that the scope of activity of the Council (the FAC) is somehow enlarged when in Art. 16.6 TEU it is said that it "[. . .] shall *elaborate* the Union's *external action* on the basis of strategic guidelines laid down by the European Council and *ensure* that the Union's action is *consistent*."

3 The New Actors

If there is no big difference in the relationship between the European Council and the Council in comparison with the former version of the Treaty, much of the difference comes from the new actors called to promote, guide, interpret and implement the CFSP: the *President* of the European Council and the *High Representative* of the Union for Foreign Affairs and Security Policy. They constitute the real innovation of the Lisbon Treaty.

With these two innovations the Union definitely sets aside the concept (and therefore the responsibilities) of the "rotating presidency" by substituting it with two actors that, being appointed on a personal basis, and for a longer period, are expected to be really independent from the individual Member States they come from.

3.1 The President of the European Council

The duties of the President, listed in Art. 15.6 TEU, are indeed mostly linked to the need for a smooth and coherent *internal* activity of the European Council and a balanced relationship of it with the other EU institutions, for

> [H]e shall [. . .] *chair* and *drive forward* its work, *ensure* the preparation and continuity of the work [. . .], *endeavour to facilitate* cohesion and consensus within the European Council, present a report to the European Parliament after each of the meetings.

In this framework it appears almost "residual", among his tasks, that the President should also "*ensure* the external representation of the Union on issues concerning its common foreign and security policy." But it is not so, because such external representation, though exercised "*without prejudice* to the powers of the High Representative of the Union for Foreign Affairs and Security Policy", is linked to the President's function of leadership of the European Council, when the latter identifies the strategic interests of the Union, determines the objectives and defines the general guidelines for the CSFP. Thus its function is narrower than that of the High Representative, who also performs external competences of the Union (Arts. 18.2, 18.4, sentence 2, TEU).

Furthermore, the external representation is also important per se, although, besides the High Representative, the Commission as well maintains a role of external representation. One should not forget, for instance, that an important part of the CFSP (and of the external action) of the EU is represented by Summits with third countries. From now on those meetings will be headed, on the European side, by the President of the European Council alongside with the President of the Commission and the High Representative. The rotating presidency will disappear, its place being taken by the President of the European Council.

Should this imply in some way that the EC President's presence in that format represents somehow the "intergovernmental" component of the external action of the EU? The latter is a compromise ("without prejudice") that leaves open an exact differentiation between the competences of the High Representative and those of the President of the European Council. It is difficult to say at this early stage. No doubt his task will be associated with his paramount duty of *reinforcing the cohesion* of the Union.

But in the end practice, which is dependent on the person holding the respective office, rather than doctrine, will clarify that.

3.2 The High Representative of the Union for Foreign Affairs and Security Policy

As for the High Representative, the innovation introduced by the Lisbon Treaty is enormous compared to the functions of the High Representative for the CFSP (Arts. 26, 18.3 TEU-Amsterdam). The High Representative, who is also on of the Vice-Presidents of the European Commission, has to unite the CFSP and what used to be the external relations of the European Community. Ideally, he will resemble a personal union of the former Secretary-General of the Council and the Commissioner for Foreign Affairs. This double function for CFSP and the Commission ("double hatting")[1] might bear both great potential and also tension between the institutions; the High Representative will have to take the role of an arbitrator.

The responsibilities of the High Representative, who is now an independent organ, are well defined in Art. 27 TEU:

[1]See also the contributions of Wessel and Denza in this volume.

> The High Representative [...], who *shall chair* the Foreign Affairs Council, *shall contribute* towards the preparation of CFSP and *shall ensure implementation* of the decisions adopted by the European Council and the Council.
>
> The High Representative *shall represent* the Union for matters relating to the CFSP [...] *shall conduct political dialogue* with third parties on the Union's behalf and *shall express the Union's position* in international organisations and at international conferences.

He also enjoys a power of initiative on negotiation of new agreements, as specified by Art. 218.2 TFEU:

> the High Representative [...] where the agreement relates exclusively or principally to the common foreign and security policy, *shall submit recommendations* to the Council, which shall adopt a decision authorising the opening of negotiations and, depending on the subject of the agreement envisaged, nominating the Union negotiator or the Head of the Union's negotiating team.

Many of these powers and responsibilities were entrusted earlier to the *rotating presidency*. Deprived of the rotating presidency, the Council remains almost fully "at the mercy" of the High Representative, who decides on the agenda of its meetings. It is true that Member States keep maintaining the right of referring any question relating to the CFSP to the Council, and of submitting to it initiatives and proposals as appropriate (Art. 30 TEU), but the role of the presidency has considerably changed.

In this context, even the responsibilities attributed to the Political and Security Committee (the high-level body that monitors on behalf of the Member State the international situation and contributes to the definition of policies) are bound to inevitably change and adapt to the new reality; within that body also the rotating presidency disappears and its role is taken over by the High Representative.

4 Establishment of the European External Action Service[2]

In order to allow both the High Representative and, in some respects, the President of the European Council, to fully exercise their duties and responsibilities in foreign policy, the Treaty, as did already the Constitutional Treaty (Art. III-296 TCE), provides for the establishment of a European External Action Service (EEAS) (Art. 27.3 TEU). On 26 July 2010 the Council adopted a decision establishing this EEAS,[3] which is to be set up by December 2010 for the first anniversary of the entry into force of the Treaty of Lisbon. Current High Representative *Catherine Ashton* explained that "Europe needs to shape up to defend better our interests and values in a world of growing complexity and fundamental power shifts".[4]

---

[2]Cf. the website of the EEAS at http://www.eeas.europa.eu/

[3]Council Decision 2010/427/EU *establishing the organisation and functioning of the European External Action Service*, O.J. L 201/30 (2010).

[4]See Council Press Release 12589/10 of 26 July 2010.

The headquarter of the EEAS will be located in Brussels, the "European capital", and it will be staffed with the contribution of personnel coming from the Commission, the General Secretariat of the Council and the Diplomatic services of the Member States (Art. 6). However, Union personnel will make up about two thirds of the entire staff, making the European component the predominant one in order to guarantee a Union identity of the service, thereby reflecting the "Community method" also in this field of action. At the same time, the EEAS is to work in close cooperation with these organs (Art. 3.1 of the Council Decision). Nevertheless, the Commission will not fully give up its external actions in favour of the new External Action Service of the EU. Although 136 former delegations of the Commission will be incorporated into the diplomatic service (due to the entry into force of the Lisbon Treaty itself), the management of the Union's external cooperation programmes will remain under the responsibility of the Commission (Art. 9.1). Moreover, in the areas in which the Commission is competent pursuant to Treaty provisions and in accordance with Art. 221.2 TFEU, "the Commission may [. . .] also issue instructions to delegations, which shall be executed under the overall responsibility of the Head of Delegation" (Art. 5.3 (2) of the Decision).

The EU now has the right to establish and staff diplomatic missions in third countries and at international organisations (Art. 221 TFEU). This was an innovation made by the Constitutional Treaty (Art. III-328 TCE) in order to enable the Union to gain an own profile in external policy and make the EU a truly global actor. These delegations are placed under the authority of the High Representative (Art. 221.2 TFEU), who decides, in agreement with both Council and Commission, to open or close a delegation (Art. 5.1). As Art. 5.6 of the Decision spells out, the staff and property of the Union delegations will enjoy the same privileges and immunities equivalent to those of nation state diplomatic missions as laid down in the Vienna Convention on Diplomatic Relations of 18 April 1961.

The EEAS is to be "a functionally autonomous body of the European Union [. . .] under the authority of the High Representative" with the necessary legal capacity to perform its tasks (Arts. 1.2, 3). It shall both "support the High Representative" and "assist the President of the European Council, the President of the Commission, and the Commission" in the exercise of their respective mandates and functions (Art. 2). However, the Service will be accountable to the Parliament, both politically and regarding its budget.

For the purpose of this paper it is worth saying that outlining the organisational scheme, deciding which existing units of the Commission and the General Secretariat of the Council will have to move to the new structure, and defining the lines of "command and control" of it – all these delicate aspects will have great repercussions on the ability of the High Representative to perform his new responsibilities. It is, however, worth making a few remarks on the structure of the EEAS (especially as laid down in Art. 4 of the Decision). The EEAS is managed by an Executive Secretary-General, placed under the authority of the High Representative, who is responsible for both administrative and budgetary affairs. The central administration of the EEAS shall be organised in directorates-general, including both geographical desks and departments for administrative, staffing, budgetary, security and communication and information system matters. This structure in combination with the Union delegations abroad will make the EEAS a true diplomatic service of the Union comprehensive of a central as well as an "external" component.

The Member States' interests are also at stake. And they are not homogeneous. Just to cite an example, while small Member States look at the EEAS as a surrogate for a diplomatic service of their own, which would be terribly expensive for them to set up worldwide, bigger countries look at the Service as an opportunity to strategically position themselves in critical junctures, where decisions are taken on matters of CFSP. The former are more inclined to entrust the future EEAS as their own diplomatic service (some of them would like it to include even consular affairs), while the latter aim to influence its activities.

As for the "culture" of the future EU diplomatic service, two only apparently opposed sets of minds are present among Member States. On one side, the need is stressed to grow a really coherent and cohesive European service (common training of all the agents, regardless of their origin, is essential). On the other side, the necessity that agents bring with themselves their national mindset, and reflect somehow priorities and sensitivities proper of their home country (richness and variety are special assets in European integration) is also underlined. Nonetheless, for a true "European" External Action Service to develop it will be necessary that the civil servants at EU level and in the national foreign ministries work together, not only in Europe, but also in third countries with EU and national diplomatic representations.

As for now, the EU foreign policy is managed by the High Representative, and by the President of the European Council, with the support of the units of both the Commission and the General Secretariat of the Council, and with a substantial help from the present rotating presidency, Spain.

The following two examples, which are very indicative of the present situation, will shed light on the issue:

- A recently distributed COREU (the ordinary message circulating among Member States on CFSP issues) began with the following sentence: "In coordination with the *Services* of the High Representative, the *rotating presidency* is pleased to hereby circulate the following draft HR Declaration on behalf of the EU on [. . .]".
- An internal document was recently circulated which was introduced by the following sentence: "Delegations will find attached a note issued under the responsibility of the *Cabinet* of the *President of the European Council*, in close cooperation with *the six-monthly Presidency*, the *Commission* services and the General Secretariat of the Council services put at the disposal of the *High Representative*". This was a document related to the organization of the next EU-Japan summit, and it is interesting to note how many different EU institutions are involved in it. Besides, it shows that not only does the HR await as a matter of urgency the setting up of the EEAS (to replace the *"services put at her disposal by the Commission and the GSC"*.), but also the President of the European Council (in order to replace his *Cabinet*, which does not have institutional foundation).

5 Conclusions

An assessment of the present situation is somehow ambivalent. On the one hand, the institutions of the EU – old and new ones alike – are doing their utmost to fill the gap of the absence of any experience in the new procedures and modalities which need to be established around the new responsibilities. There is, apparently, a genuine and generous effort to work all together in the same direction of achieving quickly the "full operational capacity" (to use a term borrowed from the Common Security and Defence Policy (CSDP) missions and operations).

On the other hand, every new decision, especially as far as the organisation of the EEAS is concerned, reflects different possible balances between the *old* actors of the external action of the EU, namely the Commission and the Council.

The moment is therefore not only a moment of implementation, but also a creative one, on which the future of the CFSP will depend.

Perhaps, through the disappointing vicissitudes which in the last seven or more years have accompanied the making, the signing and eventually the entry into force of the Lisbon Treaty, the initial burst of enthusiasm towards the creation of more effective institutions in charge of the implementation of the CFSP has been lost.

We must today recover that spirit and that philosophy, adapting them to the renewed international circumstances and encouraging all the actors to combine their efforts towards the most advanced solutions.

We must keep in mind that either we will have an effective HR, supported by a properly functioning EEAS, or any prospect of a CFSP really worthy of such a name will be definitely lost and national foreign policies will re-emerge (as we have already occasionally and unfortunately seen in the past), as much pretentious as ineffective, and disruptive of any effort for a true European integration.

But in order to succeed in the new construction that the Treaty of Lisbon proposes us, we need to be realistic and have to give the States the proper role that the end of the rotating presidency has taken away from them.

Without a close connection with Member States' foreign affairs interlocutors any new mechanism of creation and implementation of an EU foreign policy is bound to remain a theoretical and abstract exercise and to be an inevitable failure.

Beyond any complex well-designed construction, the real challenge is how much the new institutions will, on their own, facilitate the creation of a European CFSP, or how far will the abandoned "rotating presidency", and the consequent loss of the contribution of real, actual approach, that only a State can offer, be the cause of the failure of an ambitious project?

The answer will be clearer in the next months and it will show whether the Member States, still having a say and an influence on the upcoming institutional developments, want to embark upon an ambitious project of construction of a CFSP, or feel satisfied with just a more enhanced coordination of their foreign policies, as very often appears to be the case with the CFSP of the Union today.

The Role of the High Representative of the Union for Foreign Affairs and Security Policy

Eileen Denza

1 Background

When the Treaty on European Union (TEU) signed at Maastricht in 1991 established the common foreign and security policy (CFSP) on a formal and legally binding basis, it retained the primary responsibility of the presidency for its formulation, for its implementation and for the external representation of the European Union (EU) on the international plane. It was, however, soon apparent that there were two disadvantages in this method – a lack of continuity resulting from the six-monthly rotation of Presidencies having different foreign affairs experience and objectives, and a low level of recognition internationally for the Union's representative and by extension for its foreign policy.

The Reflection Group, established as mandated by the Maastricht Treaty to review its provisions, concluded in 1995 that efforts to improve continuity through assistance from previous and succeeding presidencies (the Troika system) had not achieved the desired result and also that a higher representational profile was required for successful conduct of international actions. Any changes recommended to the Treaty provisions on foreign policy making "must reconcile respect for the sovereignty of States with the need for diplomatic and financial solidarity".

But the Group was divided on whether a new independent post should be created in order to discharge these enhanced responsibilities or whether they should be assigned to the Secretary-General of the Council, with increased support from the Council Secretariat.[1] The eventual wording in the 1997 Treaty of Amsterdam

[1]Report of the Reflection Group, SN 520/95 (REFLEX 21), First Part II; Denza (1992) pp. 125, 157–158.

E. Denza (✉)
e-mail: eileen.denza@btinternet.com

H.-J. Blanke and S. Mangiameli (eds.), *The European Union after Lisbon*,
DOI 10.1007/978-3-642-19507-5_19, © Springer-Verlag Berlin Heidelberg 2012

leaned towards the second of these options. Article 18.3 TEU-Amsterdam provided that

> The Presidency shall be assisted by the Secretary-General of the Council who shall exercise the function of High Representative for the common foreign and security policy.

This wording established the status of the post as subservient to the Council and to the Presidency. On the other hand, the first person appointed to the post was a high-profile political figure – *Javier Solana Madariaga* – who had been foreign minister of Spain and later Secretary-General of the North Atlantic Treaty Organization (NATO). The choice of such an experienced statesman did indeed provide a higher profile for European foreign policy and his energetic contribution to consistent policy formation was highly rated.

He was, however, not encouraged to explore publicly, far less to advance independent positions not formally endorsed by the Council. In 1999, for example, he was reported as publicly supporting the idea that the EU should be given a permanent seat on the United Nations Security Council in addition to those of the United Kingdom and France, and Ministers in those countries were quick to clarify that his remarks did not reflect agreed EU policy.[2]

At first it was difficult for *Solana* and for the newly established Policy Planning and Early Warning Unit – set up in order to assist him and to assist the Council as a whole – to contribute effectively to Presidency proposals. *Solana* himself was frequently abroad on representative or negotiating duties, the Policy Planning and Early Warning Unit could not operate without his approval and successive Presidencies allowed little time for and gave little weight to input from the High Representative into their proposals. The establishment of authority by *Solana* was incremental.[3]

2 Objectives of Treaty Changes

When the role of the High Representative for the CFSP was reviewed by the Convention on the Future of Europe and later during the negotiation of the Treaty of Lisbon, it was generally agreed that it should be strengthened. There were three principal objectives of an enhanced role for the High Representative: first, greater independence from the Council and from the Presidency in formation of policy proposals; second, a higher international profile for the post and its occupant; and third, unitary representation of the Union – to replace the complex rules under

[2] *The Times*, 18 November 1999.

[3] Sir Brian Crowe, former Director-General for External and Politico-Military Affairs, EU Council of Ministers, at paras 177–183 of 1993 interview in *British Diplomatic Oral History*, transcript available in Churchill College, Cambridge and online at http://www.chu.cam.ac.uk/archives/collections/BDOHP/Crowe:pdf

which the European Commission represented the Union in some areas of competence and the Presidency or High Representative in others. The changes contained in the Treaty of Lisbon reflect all of these three ambitions.

2.1 *Greater Independence in Policy Formation*

Article I-27 TCE would – had it entered into force – have created a post of Union Minister for Foreign Affairs, and under paragraph 1 the Minister would have been given power "to conduct the Union's common foreign and security policy". This responsibility – even though it was to be carried out within the mandate of the Council of Ministers – would have been a novel concept for an individual working within and representing an international organization, and given that only States currently appoint ministers for foreign affairs, the title was perceived as implying aspirations of statehood for the European Union.[4]

Both the proposed title and the proposed power to "conduct" European foreign policy were among aspects of the Constitutional Treaty which on grounds of presentation as well as substance were dropped or modified when the Treaty of Lisbon was signed in 2007 and Art. 27.1 TEU is more modest, though it still goes some way towards the ambition of greater independence for the new post of High Representative of the EU for Foreign Affairs and Security Policy.

Article 27.1 TEU provides that

> The High Representative of the Union for Foreign Affairs and Security Policy, who shall chair the Foreign Affairs Council, shall contribute through his proposals towards the preparation of the common foreign and security policy and shall ensure implementation of the decisions adopted by the European Council and the Council.

This enabling provision must be read together with Art. 24 TEU, which prescribes in paragraph 1 that the CFSP "shall be defined and implemented by the European Council and by the Council, acting unanimously, except where the Treaties provide otherwise" and "shall be put into effect by the High Representative of the European Union for Foreign Affairs and Security Policy and by Member States, in accordance with the Treaties". Taken together the provisions clearly emphasize the European Council and the Council as the authors of European foreign policy and suggest a subordinate role for the High Representative.

Enhanced independence for the High Representative, however, flows from the new separation of the post from that of the Secretary-General of the Council, from the express powers under other Articles of the Treaty for the High Representative to make proposals to the Council, from the specific responsibility given under Art. 26.2 TEU to "ensure the unity, consistency and effectiveness of action by the

[4] Denza (2004), at p. 270.

Union",[5] from the permanent chairing by the High Representative of the Foreign Affairs Council (which should confer a greater degree of freedom from rotating presidency ambitions) and from the enhanced support which will be available from the European External Action Service (EEAS) to be established under Art. 27.3 TEU. Concurrent appointment as a Vice-President of the European Commission – which is further discussed later – is also intended to provide a greater degree of independence for the post since proposals of the High Representative will reflect the views of the College of Commissioners and so carry a source of authority external to that of the Council of Ministers and the individual holding the post.[6]

2.2 *Higher International Profile for the Post*

Article 18 of the TEU as revised by the Treaty of Amsterdam gave primary responsibility for representation of the Union to the Presidency. The Presidency was to "be assisted" by the High Representative, and "if need be" by the next Member State to hold the Presidency. The role of the Member State who had last held the Presidency – the third member of the Troika as originally constituted – had already disappeared from the treaty language if not entirely from practice.[7]

The Council might also appoint Special Representatives with a mandate for particular policy issues. In contrast to these provisions, Art. 27.2 TEU gives sole power to represent the Union to the High Representative. The representative power of the Presidency and of any other Member State has totally disappeared from the Treaty. The representative function is further elaborated by specifying that "He shall conduct political dialogue with third parties on the Union's behalf and shall express the Union's position in international organisations and at international conferences."

Since the High Representative clearly cannot carry out alone negotiating and representational functions in all the non-Member States and in all the numerous international organizations in whose work the EU has an interest, Art. 27.3 TEU provides the following:

> In fulfilling his mandate, the High Representative shall be assisted by a European External Action Service. This service shall work in cooperation with the diplomatic services of the Member States and shall comprise officials from relevant departments of the General Secretariat of the Council and of the Commission as well as staff seconded from national diplomatic services of the Member States. The organisations and functioning of the European External Action Service shall be established by a decision of the Council.

[5]On this aspect see Hillion (2008) at pp. 33–34.

[6]Declaration 14 to the Treaty of Lisbon *concerning the common foreign and security policy*, O.J.C 115/343 (2008), however, emphasises that the provisions on the CFSP 'do not give new powers to the Commission to initiate decisions'.

[7]For an account of practice, see Wessels (1999) at pp. 274–282.

> The Council shall act on a proposal from the High Representative after consulting the European Parliament and after obtaining the consent of the Commission.

This provision will go some way towards giving the High Representative the equivalent of the support in terms of political, legal and technical advice available to a national minister of foreign affairs from his own diplomatic and consular service. The members of the Service are, however, clearly servants of the High Representative and although it is to be expected that senior members will themselves become high-profile figures they are not intended to replace the central representational role of the High Representative.

2.3 *Unitary Representation of the Union*

The provision in the Constitutional Treaty for the European Union, repeated in the Treaty of Lisbon, which makes the High Representative a Vice-President of the European Commission as well as giving extensive powers to implement and to represent policies determined by the Council of Ministers has been the most widely questioned and criticised of the changes designed to enhance the status and powers of the post.

It is a bold and risky attempt to respond to the question supposedly asked by *Henry Kissinger* (though he is said to deny ever having posed it): "When I want to call Europe what number do I ring?" In any event it was widely believed that outsiders were confused by the legal complexities whereby the Commission represented the European Community in matters where the Community had exclusive competence – in particular trade and in areas where the Community had adopted common rules – while the Presidency or sometimes the High Representative represented the Union on other matters and in particular on pure foreign policy issues.[8]

In practice the rules on representation also caused within the EU confusion, uncertainty and sometimes litigation before the European Court of Justice. This was due in part to the fact that the rules were evolutionary in nature and sometimes required modification to international circumstances (such as the practices of particular international organisations). Although by most accounts the complex and complementary relationship worked well between *Christopher Patten* as Commissioner for External Affairs and *Javier Solana*,[9] it was argued that a single point of external representation would limit disputes over competence and lead to greater consistency and cooperation between the institutions of the Union.

[8]For a detailed account of practice, see Hoffmeister (2008) at p. 52.

[9]Examples of their close cooperation include the joint launch of the European Neighbourhood Policy in 2003 and their Joint Report to the Council of Ministers in 2003 *Strengthening the EU's partnership with the Arab World,* Council doc. 15945/03.

The creation of this fused post is not, however, reflected by any Treaty change in the differing and complementary powers and functions of the European Commission and the Council. There is in the Treaty of Lisbon no indication of where the loyalties of the High Commissioner are expected to lie in the event of conflict, and even litigation between Commission and Council. It appears that *Christopher Patten*, *Javier Solana* and *Sir Brian Crowe* – all with wide experience of the relationship between Commission and Council on external affairs – were initially sceptical of the wisdom of trying in this way to bridge the divided responsibilities of the Commission and the Council on foreign policy.[10]

3 Implementation of the Role of the High Representative Under the Lisbon Treaty

As soon as it was apparent that the Treaty of Lisbon would come into force and even before its actual entry into force on 1 December 2009, European leaders selected the new High Representative. In contrast to what occurred after the entry into force of the Treaty of Amsterdam – when limited powers for the new post were counter-balanced by the choice of a high-profile figure to fill it – the much extended powers under the Treaty of Lisbon were to some extent counter-balanced by the choice of a candidate much less well known internationally.

Baroness *Ashton of Upholland* had been, as Leader of the House of Lords, a member of the British Cabinet and had steered the legislation necessary for the UK ratification of the Treaty of Lisbon through the Upper House. She was then appointed as a European Commissioner responsible for trade and so had experience of European institutions, though for only a short time. The choice was influenced by her political position on the centre left rather than by her direct experience of international relations.

The challenges in taking over such a potentially influential post and in ensuring that an acceptable and workable structure for the new EEAS is agreed by the Council and Commission are formidable. On the basis of a short period of time it may, however, be useful to hazard some opinions as to how the objectives of the changes made by the Lisbon Treaty are likely to work out.

---

[10]Sir Brian Crowe, former Director-General for External and Politico-Military Affairs, EU Council of Ministers, at para 184 of 1993 interview in *British Diplomatic Oral History*, transcript available in Churchill College, Cambridge and online at http://www.chu.cam.ac.uk/archives/collections/BDOHP/Crowe:pdf

3.1 Independent Policy Formation

Only a few months after the entry into force of the Treaty of Lisbon, it is too early even for insiders to assess the extent to which this objective is being met and it is always difficult to evaluate the quality of policy proposals in external affairs. There are two problems in evaluating success of foreign policy initiatives whether emanating from a State, an individual or an organization.

The first is that unforeseeable "events" may thwart or torpedo even an imaginatively planned and energetically implemented policy. A change of government in the target country whether through election or through revolution may completely invalidate the assumptions on which policy objectives, incentives and threats have been based. In the case of Iran, for example, a sustained initiative on the part of the EU to persuade Iran to forgo its apparent efforts to enrich uranium to the point of capability of producing nuclear weapons, which was carefully designed by the Council of Ministers and implemented at the level of the foreign ministers of France, Germany and the United Kingdom and which seemed to have a good chance of success, stalled abruptly following the election of President *Ahmedinejad.*

The second difficulty in evaluation is that for the most part, publicity for foreign visits and initiatives is readily provided only if they are seen to fail, whereas success is silent. A coup averted, a failing State saved through intervention from collapse, a potential international quarrel skilfully defused or a mediation between warring factions leading to quiet reconciliation – all of these attract little public attention or praise. Only much later may the wisdom of a policy initiative be shown in diplomatic memoirs or through the analysis of historians.

The EEAS has not yet been formally established by the Council and it will take some time for it to establish effective working practices and to acquire the kind of cohesion and experience developed over generations by a national diplomatic service. It is only to be expected that the habits of national competition for influence through the securing of top posts will die hard – and this is shown by early reports of resentment on the part of France and Germany that Baroness *Ashton*'s first appointments have been excessively weighted in favour of British candidates.[11]

The outsider can only comment that, in the long run, with the support offered to the High Representative both from the EEAS and from Union delegations, the escape from the succession of rotating Presidencies with their emphasis on securing short-term "Presidency successes" will be likely to lead to more consistent and better informed policies designed for longer-term viability.

[11]A leaked document from the German Ministry of Foreign Affairs was cited in The Guardian – see http://www.guardian.co.uk/world/2010/feb/28/germany-france-dispute-ashton-europe

3.2 Higher International Profile for the Post

The risk in creating a single figure and a single telephone number to represent the Union is that it raises excessive expectations in the context of international meetings, events and public ceremonies. The High Representative cannot be everywhere at once. Difficult choices have to be made between events, and between emphasis on the policy formation role in Brussels and the representational role abroad.

Soon after her installation, Baroness *Ashton* was criticized in a number of Member States for her decision to attend the inauguration of President *Yanukovich* in the Ukraine rather than a meeting of European defence ministers with the Secretary-General of NATO.[12] She was also criticized for failing to visit Haiti to demonstrate solidarity in the immediate aftermath of the earthquake there – even though she reasonably maintained that such a visit, given the early difficulties in transporting essential aid into Haiti for reconstruction, would not have been a productive use of limited facilities and was more appropriate some weeks later when she did visit.[13] The problem of selecting the appropriate level of representation at a conference or ceremony abroad is of course a familiar one for States in the conduct of their foreign relations. A decision to offer a visiting dignitary less than top-level reception at the airport may lead to a frosty official visit, a failure to make progress on significant negotiations or a treaty left unsigned.

At conferences and international organisations (and in particular the United Nations), the High Representative must work within existing procedural rules. A change of title from "European Commission delegations" or "European Community delegations" to "Union delegations" is straightforward, but a request for enhanced substantive status for the Union or for the High Representative may have to await treaty or at least procedural rules revision. An enhanced profile for the High Representative will depend on diplomacy, alliances and effective policy formation.

There is so far little indication that others with some claim to be "representatives" of the Union (the new President of the European Council, the President of the Commission, even Ambassadors of the rotating Presidency) are willing to stand back in the shadows in favour of the new High Representative. Within days of the entry into force of the Lisbon Treaty, the Swedish Presidency sought against determined opposition to ban Foreign Ministers from joining their Heads of State or Government at the European Council.[14] For the official launch of the Spanish Presidency in the following month, however, the new President of the European Council, *Herman van Rompuy*, assembled along with the Commission President *Jose Manuel Barroso* and Spain's Prime Minister *Zapatero* – a gathering quite

---

[12] *The Times*, 26 February 2010.

[13] *The Times*, 5 March 2010.

[14] *The Times*, 11 December 2009.

similar to what would have been expected before the entry into force of the Lisbon Treaty. There is therefore some risk that the changes made by the Lisbon Treaty – intended to establish a single representative for the Union on the world stage – may instead make confusion worse confounded.

3.3 Unitary Representation of the Union

The tensions which were forecast as a result of the dual loyalty and responsibility of the High Representative to the Council of Ministers and to the Commission offer a challenge to the first appointee. As emphasised by *Dashwood*:

> It is vital that the first holder of this post should establish an authority across the whole field of the Union's external action, and an independence from sclerotic interests within the institutions, that will enable borderline issues of competence to be resolved in a pragmatic fashion.[15]

The strains have become apparent soon after the entry into force of the Lisbon Treaty in the context of the negotiation of the basic structure of the EEAS under Art. 27.3 TEU. Article 27 TEU provides for the High Representative to make a formal proposal for the EEAS "after consulting the European Parliament and with the consent of the Commission" and for the Council to take a decision on the organisation and functioning of the Service. The Treaty does not, however, prescribe whether the EEAS should be a part of the Council Secretariat, of the Commission or a separate Agency. Although the centre of gravity of the functions of the Service in Brussels appears to lie with the Council, the great majority of EU staff currently engaged in external activities work for the Commission. Nor does the Treaty prescribe which of the external and foreign activities of the Union should be placed directly under the control of the High Representative rather than under that of the European Commission.

Preparatory work on the EEAS was carried out in advance of the entry into force of the Treaty by the Member States, the Commission and the Council Secretariat in the hope that the High Representative would on the basis of agreed guidelines be able to make formal proposals to the Council at an early stage and that the Council would endorse these. The results of this work were reflected in a Report by the Swedish Presidency to the European Council drawn up in October 2009.[16] The Report illustrates the difficulties involved in the choice of a structure and of the functions to be assigned to the EEAS. It recommends that the EEAS should have

> an organisational status reflecting and supporting its unique role and functions in the EU system. The EEAS should be a service of a *sui generis* nature separate from the Commission and the Council Secretariat. It should have autonomy in terms of administrative budget and management of staff.

---

[15] In 'Article 47 TEU and the relationship between first and second pillar competences', chapter 3 in Dashwood and Maresceau (2008), at p. 103.

[16] Council doc. 14930/09, 23 October 2009.

Setting up an independent agency would, however, require extensive changes to the Financial Regulation and to Staff Regulations within the Union. Such a course – which is not required by the Lisbon Treaty – not only entails major structural changes but also risks disengaging EEAS from the existing power bases with which it must work in close cooperation and on which it depends.

Foreign policy is not a self-contained function which can be carried out in isolation but is integrated into many other functions carried out by the Union. A newly established agency which, to be effective, must recruit from the cream of Commission and Council officials and from the diplomatic services of Member States should not have to build up its own prestige from scratch. A separate agency would moreover inevitably require a greater duplication of functional staff such as legal advisers, translators and financial and accounting experts.

There are strong arguments for placing the EEAS within the Council as an enhanced form of the Policy Planning and Early Warning Unit established under the Treaty of Amsterdam. Such a course would at least keep the power base of the Service within the institution, which has the overwhelming responsibility for the formation and the conduct of the Union's foreign and security policy. It would also reduce the possibility of new distances and rivalries emerging between the EEAS and the Council Secretariat and would be less complex in terms of revisions to financial and staffing regulations.

On functions, the Report argues that trade and development as well as enlargement should remain within the responsibility of the Commission. It appears to be generally accepted that trade policy – until recently the responsibility of Baroness Ashton as European Trade Commissioner – should remain entirely within the Commission, and given the continuing and extensive responsibilities of the Commission for trade under the Lisbon Treaty, this seems inescapable. During the negotiations for the Constitutional Treaty and later for the Lisbon Treaty, concern had been expressed at adverse consequences for the long-established and successful common commercial policy resulting from its inclusion within the overall scheme of external relations.[17]

While it is apparent that the Commission is reluctant to lose these central external functions on which a high proportion of its staff are currently engaged and on which coherent structures and practices are now in place, such a substantial retention within the Commission of central tools of a modern foreign policy will greatly limit the capacities of the EEAS. Consistency and coherence in the conduct of an enlightened foreign policy does not depend simply on a single individual at the top of the command chain but on integration of the supporting staff providing advice on policy. The "thematic desks" advocated in the Report for the EEAS would be narrow in their scope if trade, development and enlargement were all to be left entirely within the remit of the Commission. It may well be necessary in order to minimise disruption for functions to be transferred from the Commission on an incremental basis as staff are newly recruited or transferred.[18]

---

[17]See Müller-Graff (2008).

[18]For analysis of the options for the EEAS in the light of existing practice, see Vanhoonacker and Reslow (2010), pp. 1–18.

4 Continuing Powers of the Member States to Conduct Foreign Policy

In assessing the role of the High Representative and of the EEAS under the Treaty of Lisbon it is also important to recall that the Member States have expressed their determination regarding their own powers to conduct independent foreign policy and to maintain separate representation in other States and in international organisations. Declaration 13 concerning the CFSP,[19] attached to the Lisbon Treaty, provides in part:

> The Conference underlines that the provisions in the Treaty on European Union covering the Common Foreign and Security Policy, including the creation of the office of High Representative of the Union for Foreign Affairs and Security Policy and the establishment of an External Action Service, do not affect the responsibilities of the Member States, as they currently exist, for the formulation and conduct of their foreign policy nor of their national representation in third countries and international organisations.

Declaration 14 concerning the CFSP[20] also provides in part (with some overlap with Declaration 13) that the new treaty provisions on CFSP and the EEAS "will not affect the existing legal basis, responsibilities, and powers of each Member State in relation to the formulation and conduct of its foreign policy, its national diplomatic service, relations with third countries and participation in international organisations, including a Member State's membership of the Security Council of the United Nations".

These Declarations compensate for the inadequacy of the provisions in the Treaty of Lisbon regarding the nature of the competence of the Union for the formulation and implementation of foreign and security policy. The Treaty on the Functioning of the European Union establishes at the outset clear categories of Union competence – exclusive competence, shared competence, competence to carry out actions to support, coordinate or supplement the actions of the Member States – but makes no attempt to define or describe the nature of its competence to formulate and implement the CFSP.

Declarations 13 and 14 appear to be designed to leave no room for any argument that the new powers, functions and bodies set up by or under the Treaty might "occupy the field" and thereby diminish the independent powers of the Member States for the conduct of their foreign relations. There is no sign that the Member States are preparing to relinquish ultimate control of their foreign relations – and indeed the bargaining among Member States which took place before the decision to appoint Baroness Ashton and the resentment publicly expressed over her alleged preference for British appointments to key posts in Brussels and in other capitals

[19]Declaration 13 *concerning the common foreign and security policy*, O.J. C 115/343 (2008).

[20]Declaration 14 *concerning the common foreign and security policy*, O.J. C 115/343 (2008).

underlines that the familiar national rivalries still flourish with undiminished vigour. It cannot be expected that diplomats seconded to the EEAS will replace their national loyalties and national career aspirations with a purely European outlook. What should be the primary hope is that the secondment is perceived as a valuable career move so that those selected ensure through their quality and enthusiasm that the EEAS gives real added value to European foreign and security policy.

It must also be recalled that although the Foreign Affairs Council is now chaired by the High Representative, the Committee of Permanent Representatives (COREPER) and the supporting Working Groups within the Council will continue to be chaired by the rotating Presidencies – so that before an item reaches the level of the Council essential decisions and compromises may already have been forged under national influence.

5 Resources

Finally, an important restraint on the establishment of the EEAS is that of budgetary resources. In the current climate of tight financial controls Member States are closing or cutting back permanent embassies and consulates and exploring cost-saving options provided by the Vienna Conventions on Diplomatic and Consular Relations such as multiple accreditation and protection of the interests of another State (normally a fellow Member State) where a permanent mission cannot be justified. They are increasingly sharing mission facilities such as accommodation and communications networks among themselves in foreign capitals as well as carrying out functions such as reporting on a joint basis. Against this background, the general public will insist that new facilities and new appointments made on behalf of the EU reflect "added value" for the Member States or new functions to be performed.

Such an approach can more easily be carried out with the Union delegations abroad. In most capitals there have already been successfully established practices of cooperation among the embassies of Member States and the European Commission delegations. There are regular meetings devoted to sharing of information and analysis, to the implementation of common positions and joint actions formulated under the CFSP and to effective methods of carrying out diplomatic and consular protection of citizens of the Union. These can be further developed on a case-by-case basis in each capital. As cooperation among Member States on visas, immigration and border controls intensifies, closer coordination among embassies and consulates on visas would illustrate this approach – driven by an attempt to perform new functions more efficiently rather than by any attempt to centralize for its own sake, or to "enhance" the public profile of the Union delegations.

References

Dashwood A, Maresceau M (eds) (2008) Law and practice of EU external relations. Cambridge University Press, Cambridge, p 103

Denza E (1992) The intergovernmental pillars of the European Union. Oxford University Press, Oxford, pp 125, 157–158

Denza E (2004) Lines in the sand: between common foreign policy and single foreign policy, Chap. 15. In: Tridimas P, Nebbia P (eds) European law for the 21st century. Kluwer, New York, p 270

Hillion Ch (2008) Tous pour un, un pour tous? Coherence in the external relations of the European Union, Chap. 2. In: Cremona M (ed) Developments in EU external relations law. Oxford University Press, Oxford, pp 33–34

Hoffmeister F (2008) The contribution of EU Practice to international law, Chap. 3. In: Cremona M (ed) Developments in EU external relations law. Oxford University Press, Oxford, p 52

Müller-Graff P-Ch (2008) The common commercial policy enhanced by the reform treaty of Lisbon, Chap. 7. In: Dashwood A, Maresceau M (eds) Law and practice of EU external relations. Cambridge University Press, Cambridge

Vanhoonacker S, Reslow N (2010) The European external action service: living forwards by understanding backwards. Eur Foreign Aff Rev 15:1–18

Wessel RA (1999) The European Union's foreign and security policy. Kluwer, New York, pp 274–282

Initiative and Voting in Common Foreign and Security Policy: The New Lisbon Rules in Historical Perspective

Ramses A. Wessel

1 Introduction

The entry into force of the Lisbon Treaty on 1 December 2009 is generally believed not to have had a large impact on the Union's Common Foreign and Security Policy. In fact, most commentators would argue that the 'second pillar' remained in place.[1] The place of the common foreign and security policy (CFSP) as the only policy area in a separate treaty (the Treaty on European Union (TEU)), even distinct from all other rules on external relations (in the Treaty on the Functioning of the European Union (TFEU)), indeed supports this view. In addition, the treaty itself makes quite clear that "The common foreign and security policy is subject to specific rules and procedures" (Art. 24.1 TEU). Hence, at first sight, the CFSP maintained the 'intergovernmental' nature that it, allegedly, had when it was established in 1992.[2]

However, over the past years research revealed that these days CFSP is clearly different from the policy that was created 20 years ago.[3] The legal order of the European Union proved to have its own dynamics, which resulted in an increasing number of similarities between CFSP and the policies of the European

[1]Cf. Cremona (2006), as well as Cremona (2003).

[2]At the time of the formation of the European Union it was quite common to view the non-Community parts of the Union as "a legal framework based on international law". See Denza (2002), p. 5.

[3]Obviously, the development of Europe's foreign and security policy goes back to the years of the European Political Cooperation before the CFSP, which meant that CFSP did not have to start from scratch. See for instance Smith (2004).

R.A. Wessel (✉)
Department of Legal and Economic Governance Studies, University of Twente, PO Box 217 7500 AE Enschede, The Netherlands
e-mail: r.a.wessel@utwente.nl

H.-J. Blanke and S. Mangiameli (eds.), *The European Union after Lisbon*,
DOI 10.1007/978-3-642-19507-5_20, © Springer-Verlag Berlin Heidelberg 2012

Community.[4] Step by step the subsequent treaty modifications introduced sometimes rather technical innovations, which in turn led to a new legal and political situation. In addition and apart from formal treaty changes, the CFSP legal order was affected by the case law of the European Court of Justice, which further defined its relation to the external relations of the Community as well as the effect of its instruments.[5] This development was even labelled 'progressive supranationalism' by one (close) observer.[6]

The purpose of the present paper is to take a closer look at two elements in the CFSP decision-making procedure: the right of initiative and the voting rules. These two elements are generally believed to define the distinct nature of CFSP when compared to other Union policies. After all, both the exclusive right of initiative of the Commission and the turn to (evermore) qualified majority voting (QMV) belong to the 'Community method', which over 50 years has characterised European cooperation.[7] By comparing the current (post-Lisbon) treaty provisions on the right of initiative and the voting rules with the ones in previous texts, we hope to be able to point to a progressive development in this area. Based on earlier research on the development of the CFSP legal order,[8] our hypothesis is that the new Lisbon rules on the right of initiative and the voting rules shows a move towards a less intergovernmental CFSP, or perhaps even a 'progressive supranationalism'.[9]

Section 2 will first of all deal with the right of initiative to submit initiatives and proposals under the CFSP rules. This will be followed by a related issue: the right to convene an extraordinary Council meeting (Sect. 3). Section 4 will deal with the basic rule of unanimity and the introduction of the so-called constructive abstention. The core of this issue is to be found in the exceptions to the unanimity rule; do we see a shift towards more QMV in CFSP? (Sect. 5). Section 6, finally, will be used to draw some conclusions on the development of the CFSP legal regime regulating the right of initiative and the voting rules.

---

[4]See more extensively Wessel (2007, 2009). Compare for a political science perspective also Stetter (2007).

[5]More extensively: Hillion and Wessel (2009). See further van Ooik (2008).

[6]See (Director of the Legal Service of the Council) Gosalbo Bono (2006), p. 349.

[7]This is not to deny that other elements may be of equal importance, in particular the role of the European Court of Justice and the involvement of the European Parliament in the decision-making process.

[8]See references in *supra*, note 4.

[9]It goes beyond the scope of this paper to further define 'intergovernmentalism' and 'supranationalism'. The bottom line, however, is that we hope to reveal a move from a 'Member States driven' policy to a policy that is defined and implemented at EU level.

2 The Right to Submit Initiatives or Proposals Under CFSP

2.1 From Maastricht to Nice

The importance of the right of initiative is to be found in the fact that it defines the *source* of CFSP decisions. Ever since the Maastricht Treaty the right of initiative was above all used by the Presidency to initiate new CFSP decisions. Although the Presidency was not mentioned in the original treaty, it could base its actions on the fact that it was a Member State. The original Art. J.8 TEU-Maastricht listed the same provision in its paragraph 3 in the following wordings:

> Any Member State or the Commission may refer to the Council any question relating to the common foreign and security policy and may submit proposals to the Council.

The absence of an exclusive right of initiative for the Commission was one of the characteristics that distinguished CFSP from the Community policies. Although from the outset the Commission had a shared right of initiative under CFSP it has barely used it. The reason is that the Commission held that the CFSP belonged to the Council. To quote former Commissioner Chris Patten: "Some of my staff [. . .] would have preferred me to have a grab for foreign policy, trying to bring as much of it as possible into the orbit of the Commission. This always seemed to me to be wrong in principle and likely to be counterproductive in practice. Foreign policy should not in my view [. . .] be treated on a par with the single market. It is inherently different."[10]

The original text was maintained by the 1997 Amsterdam Treaty (Art. 22 TEU-Amsterdam) as well as by the 2001 Nice Treaty (Art. 22 TEU-Nice).

2.2 From the Constitutional Treaty to the Treaty of Lisbon

The first modifications could be found in the 2005 Treaty establishing a Constitution for Europe, which – as is well known – never entered into force, due to negative referenda outcomes in France and the Netherlands. Article III-299.1 TCE provided the following text:

> Any Member State, the Union Minister for Foreign Affairs, or that Minister with the Commission's support, may refer any question relating to the common foreign and security policy to the Council and may submit to it initiatives or proposals as appropriate.

First of all, this provision allows for initiatives or proposals to be submitted by "the Union Minister for Foreign Affairs", either individually or "with the Commission's support". The Constitutional Treaty introduced the "Union Minister

[10] See Spence (2006), p. 360.

for Foreign Affairs" as the successor of the "High Representative for Common Foreign and Security Policy", introduced by the Amsterdam Treaty. It thus introduced a new, more supranational, element into the CFSP by allowing initiatives in this area to be taken by an 'agent' of the Union, rather than just by Member States. By 2005 the High Representative (the Spanish politician and diplomat Javier Solana) had developed into a key player in CFSP, while making sure that he had the support of the Member States for his actions. Providing him with a formal role in the decision-making process could certainly be seen as an important breakthrough in the character of the Union's foreign and security policy. It is interesting to note that by using the term 'Union Minister' the Constitutional Treaty went beyond the recommendations of the Convention on the Future of Europe. In its Final Report, Working Group VII on External Action had proposed the term "European External Representative". As the report notes with obvious premonition: "Other titles have also been put forward in the course of discussion, notably 'EU Minister of Foreign Affairs' and 'EU Foreign Secretary'. The prevailing view was that the title of 'European External Representative' had the advantage of not corresponding to a title used at national level."[11]

The other 'supranational' element in this phase of the decision-making process could be found in the competence of the Commission. On the other hand, as we have seen, from the outset the Commission decided not to make use of its formal right of initiative. This is not to say that the Commission was not involved in CFSP. The Commission was, and still is, represented at all levels in the CFSP structures. Within the negotiating process in the Council, the Commission is a full negotiating partner as in any working party or Committee (including the Political and Security Committee). The President of the Commission attends European Council and other ad hoc meetings. The Commission is in fact the 'twenty-eighth' Member State at the table. Practice thus showed an involvement of the Commission, both in the formulation and the implementation of CFSP decisions, not in the least because Community measures were in some cases essential for an effective implementation of CFSP policy decisions.

The Constitutional Treaty deleted the individual competence of the Commission to submit CFSP proposals and replaced it by a possibility to submit initiatives together with the new Union Minister for Foreign Affairs. It thus introduced three sources for CFSP proposals and initiatives: the Member States, the Union Minister and the Union Minister together with the Commission. We will come back to some implications of this division later.

The version in the TEU is similar to the one included in the Constitutional Treaty. Article 30.1 TEU now provides:

> Any Member State, the High Representative of the Union for Foreign Affairs and Security Policy, or the High Representative with the Commission' support, may refer any question relating to the common foreign and security policy to the Council and may submit to it initiatives or proposals as appropriate.

[11]Final report of Working Group VII on External Action, CONV 459/02 (16.12.2002), footnote 1.

The only difference is the replacement of the term 'Union Minister for Foreign Affairs' with 'High Representative of the Union for Foreign Affairs and Security Policy'. This replacement was caused by the changes discussed during the Lisbon Intergovernmental Conference (IGC) with the more general purpose of removing 'state-like' terms. At first sight, the scope of the High Representative's competences seems broader because of the extension to 'security policy', but in fact the reason was to only marginally change the already existing name of the function, introduced by the TEU-Amsterdam ("High Representative for the Common Foreign and Security Policy"). Although not explicitly mentioned in Art. 30 TEU, proposals of the High Representative may cover the Common Security and Defence Policy (CSDP). Article 18.2 TEU explicitly provides:

> The High Representative shall conduct the Union's common foreign and security policy. He shall contribute by his proposals to the development of that policy, which he shall carry out as mandated by the Council. The same shall apply to the common security and defence policy.

In the Lisbon version, the Member States retained their right of initiative. Proposals to limit this right of Member States – for instance by allowing proposals from there or more Member States or to allow the European Parliament to submit proposals – were unacceptable to a number of Member States.

A proposal by the Presidium of the Convention to allow for joint proposals by the Commission and the High Representative was not accepted, because this would mean that the High Representative would need approval from the Commission for his/her proposal.[12] A number of Member States were against any role of the Commission in this area.[13] The result is that an active initiating role of the Commission is now formally excluded. Thus, in the current provision, and in line with the text of the Constitutional Treaty, the individual right of initiative of the Commission disappeared. However, the possibility of a mandate from the Commission to the High Representative to submit a proposal may not be excluded.[14]

The position of the High Representative was clearly updated by the Lisbon Treaty.[15] The modification from 'High Representative' to 'High Representative of the Union' further underlined his role as Union actor, rather than as representative of the Member States.

Following the text of the Constitutional Treaty, the Lisbon Treaty added the High Representative to the actors with a right to submit proposals. The High Representative may use this initiative individually or "with the Commission's support". Given the position of the High Representative in the Commission and

[12]Draft sections of Part Three with comments, CONV 727/03 (28.05.2003), p. 51.

[13]Amendments No. 2 (de Villepin) and No. 6 (Hain), Summary sheet of proposals for amendments concerning external action, including defence policy: Draft Articles for Part One, Title V (Arts. 29, 30 and X), Part Two, Title B (Arts. 1–36) and Chapter X (Art. X) of the Constitution, CONV 707/03 (09.05.2003), p. 56.

[14]As argued by the Presidium of the convention; CONV 727/03 (27.05.2003), p. 51.

[15]More extensively: Kaddous (2008), p. 206.

the clear links between the different aspects of EU external relations, it is difficult to see how he could initiate new CFSP in the absence of support by the Commission. On the other hand, the position of the High Representative is independent. Within the broad area of EU external relations different or even conflicting proposals by the Commission and the High Representative are not excluded.

Until the European External Action Service (EEAS) is fully operational,[16] it is assumed that preparation of CFSP decisions takes place by the Council secretariat rather than by the Commission's DG Relex. In practice the difference between an autonomous High Representative initiative and one supported by the Commission will primarily have consequences for the way in which the proposal is prepared. Also, assumedly, it will have consequences for the subsequent decision-making procedure as the Commission's involvement may point to a legal basis in the TFEU.

Article 30 TEU mentions that apart from proposals 'initiatives' may be submitted to the Council. The term already appeared in the text of the Constitutional Treaty. The difference between the two is not clarified by the Treaty itself. In other areas of the Union only 'proposals' may be submitted (by the Commission; compare Arts. 293 and 294 TFEU). The reason may be that not all CFSP actions take the form of formal decisions. On the basis of Art. 25 TEU the Union shall conduct its CFSP not only by adopting decisions, but also by defining the general guidelines and by strengthening systematic cooperation between the Member States in the conduct of policy. The use of the term 'initiative' in Art. 30 TEU is striking as one could argue that an 'initiative' by, for instance, the High Representative in most cases is not a prerequisite for the Council to adopt a decision. It may adopt decisions in the absence of a formal initiative being taken by the High Representative and it may also deviate from a proposal submitted by a Member State. Only in a limited number of cases the Treaty seems to have foreseen a true procedural function of initiatives by the High Representative, in the sense that an initiative is needed for the Council to be able to act. On the basis of Art. 31.2 TEU the Council may act by qualified majority "on a proposal which the High Representative of the Union for Foreign Affairs and Security Policy has presented following a specific request from the European Council" and Art. 33 TEU provides that "the Council may, on a proposal from the High Representative of the Union for Foreign Affairs and Security Policy, appoint a special representative with a mandate in relation to particular policy issues."

In addition, the Treaty refers to a number of other specific institutional issues in which a proposal by the High Representative seems to have a more formal role. Thus, Art. 27.3 TEU states that "The Council shall act on a proposal from the High Representative after consulting the European Parliament and after obtaining the consent of the Commission" when deciding on the organization and functioning of the EEAS; Art. 42.3 TEU states that "The Council shall adopt by a qualified majority, on a proposal from the High Representative of the Union for Foreign

[16]See on the EEAS see, for instance, Crowe (2008); Vanhoonacker and Reslow (2010); Duke (2009); Duke and Blockmans (2010); see also the contribution of Cherubini in this volume.

Affairs and Security Policy" decisions related to the start-up fund for expenditure arising from operations having military or defence implications; Art. 218.3 TFEU states that "the Commission, or the High Representative of the Union for Foreign Affairs and Security Policy [. . .] shall submit recommendations to the Council" in relation to the negotiation of international agreements; and Art. 329.2 TFEU states that "the High Representative of the Union for Foreign Affairs and Security Policy [. . .] shall give an opinion on whether the enhanced cooperation proposed is consistent with the Union's common foreign and security policy."

3 The Right to Convene an Extraordinary Council Meeting

3.1 From Maastricht to Nice

The possibility to convene an extraordinary Council meeting when it is not possible or not preferred to await the next regular Council meeting is closely linked to the right of initiative and has been part of the CFSP institutional machinery from the outset. The original Art. J.8.4 TEU-Maastricht listed the possibility as follows:

> In cases requiring a rapid decision, the Presidency, of its own motion, or at the request of the Commission or a Member State, shall convene an extraordinary Council meeting within forty-eight hours or, in an emergency, within a shorter period.

The initiative was thus laid in the hands of the Presidency, albeit that the Commission and Member States could request the Presidency to convene an extra meeting. The provision returned in the TEU-Amsterdam in the same wordings (Art. 22.2) as well as in the TEU- Nice (Art. 22.2), with one minor modification ('48 hours' instead of 'forty-eight hours').

3.2 From the Constitutional Treaty to the Treaty of Lisbon

The Constitutional Treaty moved the competence to convene an extraordinary meeting from the Presidency to the 'Union Minister for Foreign Affairs' (Art. III-299 TCE), in line with the foreseen role of the Union Minister as president of the Foreign Affairs Council. Although there are good reasons to argue that the Presidency operates as a 'Union actor' rather than as a Member State, the importance of this shift should not be underestimated. For the first time the Council could be convened on the initiative of the EU itself.

Following the text of the Constitutional Treaty, Art. 30.2 TEU moved the competence to convene an extraordinary Council meeting from the Presidency to the High Representative. Article 30.2 TEU now states:

> In cases requiring a rapid decision, the High Representative, of his own motion, or at the request of a Member State, shall convene an extraordinary Council meeting within 48 hours or, in an emergency, within a shorter period.

It is interesting to note that the possibility for the Commission to request an extraordinary meeting was deleted. Taken together with the removal of the individual right of initiative of the Commission under CFSP (*supra*) this underlines the upgraded position of the High Representative, but at the cost of the Commission. Member States still have a possibility to request the High Representative to convene an extraordinary emergency meeting.

4 Unanimity and Constructive Abstention

4.1 From Maastricht to Nice

The unanimity rule is at the heart of the 'intergovernmental' image of CFSP. Indeed, it is safe to assume that the inclusion of CFSP in the Maastricht Treaty was possible only because of the absence of majority voting, or more generally, the inapplicability of the 'Community method'. The original Art. J.8.2 TEU-Maastricht stated:

> [. . .] The Council shall act unanimously, except for procedural questions and in the case referred to in Article J.3(2).

This is not to say that majority voting has not been debated. The Rome II European Council meeting in 1990 decided on the wish to include a provision which would make decision-making possible, despite the non-participation or abstention of some Member States.[17] However, this idea did not lead to a reference to the provision on QMV in the EC Treaty, but to a Declaration (No. 27) adopted by the IGC, providing that "with regard to Council decisions requiring unanimity, Member States will, to the extent possible, avoid preventing a unanimous decision where a qualified majority exists in favour of that decision".[18] Member States under the Maastricht provisions indeed seemed to have an obligation to explain why the use of a qualified majority would not be possible in a certain case, but the Declaration could never be used to overrule the provision in Art. J.8 TEU-Maastricht. Nevertheless, it is generally assumed that the possibility of QMV has never been used in practice and that unanimity was at the basis of the cooperation.

The slow progress of CFSP in the early days was partly blamed on the fact that because of the unanimity rule the entire decision-making process could be hijacked

[17]See European Council, Presidency Conclusions, Rome, 1990.

[18]A similar provision was already included in the Single European Act, Art. 30, paragraph 3(c). It is striking that this provision was 'reduced' to a Declaration.

by one individual Member State. The 1997 Amsterdam Treaty therefore introduced the possibility of abstentions. Article 23.1 TEU-Amsterdam stated:

> Decisions under this Title shall be taken by the Council acting unanimously. Abstentions by members present in person or represented shall not prevent the adoption of such decisions.

This was the general rule: decisions could (and can) be adopted when there are no 'No' votes. Article 23 TEU-Amsterdam also introduced a different possibility to prevent Member States from being bound by the decision:

> When abstaining in a vote, any member of the Council may qualify its abstention by making a formal declaration under the present subparagraph. In that case, it shall not be obliged to apply the decision, but shall accept that the decision commits the Union. In a spirit of mutual solidarity, the Member State concerned shall refrain from any action likely to conflict with or impede Union action based on that decision and the other Member States shall respect its position. If the members of the Council qualifying their abstention in this way represent more than one third of the votes weighted in accordance with Article 148 (2) of the Treaty establishing the European Community, the decision shall not be adopted.

At first sight this opened the possibility of so-called coalitions of the able and willing; CFSP actions no longer depended on the approval and implementation of all Member States, and the more flexible approach allowed for smaller groups of states to engage in a certain action or to adopt a position. On closer inspection, however, non-participation through the issuing of a formal declaration did not at all deprive the abstaining Council member from obligations based on the adopted decision. After all, the decision taken by the Council remains a 'Union decision'. While the abstaining state may not be asked to actively implement this decision, it has to accept that 'the decision commits the Union'.

This is underlined by the rule that "in a spirit of mutual solidarity, the member state concerned shall refrain from any action likely to conflict with or impede Union action based on that decision". The wording of this provision closely resembles that in the general loyalty clause, which at the time could be found in Art. 11.2 TEU-Amsterdam: "[the Member States] shall refrain from any action which is contrary to the interests of the Union or likely to impair its effectiveness as a cohesive force in international relations" (the loyalty obligation can currently be found in Art. 24.3 TEU-Lisbon in a slightly different wording). Indeed, both provisions seriously limited the freedom of Member States, even in the case where a formal declaration of abstention has been issued. No national action that *could possibly* conflict with or impede Union action was allowed. From the outset this limited the advantage of the option of abstention to cases in which the Member State had little or no interest and indeed no plans for an individual national policy. Moreover, the declarations of dissent could even seriously undermine the effectiveness of CFSP decisions in relation to third states. This is the reason why the option of 'constructive abstention' in Art. 23 TEU-Amsterdam was sometimes referred to as 'destructive abstention'. It is acknowledged that this, indeed, took away much of the *rationale* of the declaration of abstention.

Nevertheless, the possibility of *constructive abstention* returned in the 2001 Nice Treaty. In addition, Art. 23 TEU-Nice brought an end to all possible speculations as to whether abstentions can or cannot block a decision by stipulating that "Abstentions by members present in person or represented shall not prevent the adoption of such decisions". This implied that in that case a decision could be taken. However, there seemed to be no legally relevant advantage in using this opportunity, since it followed from the text of this provision that the abstaining Member State(s) would nonetheless be bound by the adopted decision.

4.2 From the Constitutional Treaty to the Treaty of Lisbon

The 2005 Constitutional Treaty maintained both the unanimity and the abstention rules in Art. III-300.3 TCE with minor changes in terminology only. The general rule that "[a]bstentions by members present in person or represented shall not prevent the adoption by the Council of acts which require unanimity" was no longer referred to in the CFSP provisions, but returned in Art. III-343.3 TCE. In turn, the Lisbon Treaty adopted the text of the Constitutional Treaty in its Art. 31.1 TEU:

> Decisions under this Chapter shall be taken by the European Council and the Council acting unanimously, except where this Chapter provides otherwise. The adoption of legislative acts shall be excluded.
>
> When abstaining in a vote, any member of the Council may qualify its abstention by making a formal declaration under the present subparagraph. In that case, it shall not be obliged to apply the decision, but shall accept that the decision commits the Union. In a spirit of mutual solidarity, the Member State concerned shall refrain from any action likely to conflict with or impede Union action based on that decision and the other Member States shall respect its position. If the members of the Council qualifying their abstention in this way represent at least one third of the Member States comprising at least one third of the population of the Union, the decision shall not be adopted.

Thus unanimity is still the rule, which stands in stark contrast to the other EU policies where QMV has been established as the default voting rule. German and French proposals to make QMV the default option did not make it.[19]

A novel element in this provision is the explicit exclusion of the adoption of 'legislative acts'. If anything, this element clearly distinguishes CFSP from the other Union policy areas. The Constitutional Treaty already excluded "European laws and framework laws" from the instruments to be used for CFSP, which could only be shaped on the basis of "European decisions" (Art. I-40.6 TCE). The exclusion of 'legislative acts' in Art. 31.1 TEU is confirmed by Art. 24.1 TEU:

> [...]The common foreign and security policy is subject to specific rules and procedures. It shall be defined and implemented by the European Council and the Council acting unanimously, except where the Treaties provide otherwise. The adoption of legislative acts shall be excluded.[...]

[19]Amendments No. 6 (de Villepin) and No. 10 (Fischer), CONV 707/03 (09.05.2003), p. 60.

The CFSP instrument is therefore the 'Decision' (compare Art. 25.1 TEU), which should not be confused with the 'Decision' used in other policy areas. This latter type of 'Decision' is still one of the key legal acts of the Union and is described in Art. 288 TFEU ("A decision shall be binding in its entirety. A decision which specifies those to whom it is addressed shall be binding only on them"). The exclusion of the adoption of legislative acts does not deprive the CFSP Decisions of their legal nature. Their binding nature is confirmed by Art. 28.2 TEU ("Decisions referred to in paragraph 1 shall commit the Member States in the positions they adopt and in the conduct of their activity"). In fact, the exclusion of legislative acts primarily has to do with the exclusion of the legislative *procedure* and hence with the inapplicability of the role of the Commission and the European Parliament in this procedure.

As in the pre-Lisbon TEU, abstentions do not prevent the adoption of decisions, unless the number of Member States qualifying their abstention by issuing a formal declaration represent *at least one third* of the Member States *comprising at least one third of the population of the Union*. The phrasing of these criteria deviates somewhat from the pre-Lisbon text, which referred to *more than one third of the votes* weighted according to the QMV rules. The new rule can be explained on the basis of the changed QMV rules, although there does not seem to be an exception for the period until 2014. The general *rationale* of this rule is clear: it is difficult to maintain a CFSP Decision once it is not supported by the vast majority of the Member States (including the larger ones).

Article 31.1 TEU does, however, introduce a novelty in relation to the actors involved in decision-making. The explicit competence of the European Council to adopt CFSP decisions is new, although the pre-Lisbon TEU already allowed for the European Council to adopt 'Common Strategies'. The new competences in Art. 31 TEU should be seen in the context of Art. 22 TEU, which allows for the European Council to "identify the strategic interests and objectives of the Union." That article furthermore provides:

> Decisions of the European Council on the strategic interests and objectives of the Union shall relate to the common foreign and security policy and to other areas of the external action of the Union. Such decisions may concern the relations of the Union with a specific country or region or may be thematic in approach. They shall define their duration, and the means to be made available by the Union and the Member States.

In addition Art. 26.1 TEU provides:

> The European Council shall identify the Union's strategic interests, determine the objectives of and define general guidelines for the common foreign and security policy, including for matters with defence implications. It shall adopt the necessary decisions.

The last sentence in the Article seems to imply that the 'general guidelines' are not to be seen as 'decisions'. The practical relevance of that distinction is not clear, apart from the obvious fact that guidelines may not be adopted on the basis of QMV (see Sect. 5). They do seem to be binding on the Member States as the loyalty obligation in Art. 24.3 TEU is not limited to 'Decisions'. On the other hand, they do not seem to be able to function as a source of QMV in the Council, as Art. 31.2 TEU only refers to 'a *decision* of the European Council'.

5 Towards Qualified Majority Voting in CFSP?

5.1 From Maastricht to Nice

The debate on majority voting has been present in CFSP negotiations from the outset. An early compromise was found in Declaration No. 27, adopted by the Maastricht IGC, providing that "with regard to Council decisions requiring unanimity, Member States will, to the extent possible, avoid preventing a unanimous decision where a qualified majority exists in favour of that decision" (see *supra*). At the same time QMV was never completely ruled out. An explicit possibility was already included in the 1992 Maastricht Treaty. "The case referred to in Article J.3(2)" was mentioned in Art. J.8 TEU-Maastricht as one of the exceptions to the general rule that "the Council shall act unanimously". Article J.3.2 TEU-Maastricht indeed ordered the Council to define the matters on which decisions were to be taken by qualified majority when it adopted a Joint Action and during the further development of the Joint Action. Nevertheless, the decision to adopt a Joint Action remained subject to the rule of unanimity. When the Council would make use of this possibility, the votes of its members would have to be weighted in accordance with the Community procedures on QMV. However, the rare attempts to introduce majority voting in particular decision-making procedures were supposedly blocked by the British, which made others reluctant to make further proposals to that end.[20]

An important step was taken in the 1997 Amsterdam Treaty. Whereas the 1992 Treaty limited QMV to the implementation of Joint Actions (and only after a unanimous decision to that end had been taken), the new Art. 23.2 TEU-Amsterdam called for QMV by the Council when it adopts Joint Actions, Common Positions or other Decisions on the basis of a European Council Common Strategy, or when it adopts a decision *implementing* a previously adopted Joint Action or Common Position. Art. 23.2 TEU-Amsterdam thus read:

> By derogation from the provisions of paragraph 1, the Council shall act by qualified majority:
> – when adopting joint actions, common positions or taking any other decision on the basis of a common strategy;
> – when adopting any decision implementing a joint action or a common position.

In addition, a Council member could still declare that, for *important and stated reasons of national policy*, it intended to oppose the adoption of a decision to be taken by qualified majority, in which case a vote would not be taken (Art. 23.2, part 2 TEU-Amsterdam). Since 'important' was not defined by the Treaty, this provision provided opportunities for Member States to block Council decision-making. A way out of this was offered by the provision that in that event, the Council

[20] Keukeleire (1998), p. 291.

may, acting by a qualified majority, request that the matter be referred to the European Council for decision by unanimity. While the Heads of State and Government may indeed be able to settle the issue in connection with other agenda items, it is obvious that this provision put the possibility of QMV into perspective.

The Amsterdam TEU provided that the votes of the members of the Council shall be weighted in accordance with the Community rules and that "[f]or their adoption, decisions shall require at least 62 votes in favour, cast by at least 10 members." At the same time, it made clear that QMV could never be used for the adoption of "decisions having military or defence implications" (para 2; see further).

Irrespective of the fact that the Council continued to strive for consensus, the 2001 Nice Treaty maintained the possibility of QMV. In Art. 23.2 TEU-Nice it even added a third possibility to the two introduced by the Amsterdam TEU. Apart from decisions based on a European Council Common Strategy and implementing decisions, QMV could also be used "when appointing a special representative in accordance with Article 18(5)."

QMV continued to be based on the Community rules, but the Nice Treaty somewhat tightened the rules with a view to ensuring that adopted CFSP decisions would enjoy sufficient support by the (larger) Member States:

> For their adoption, decisions shall require at least 232 votes in favour cast by at least two thirds of the members. When a decision is to be adopted by the Council by a qualified majority, a member of the Council may request verification that the Member States constituting the qualified majority represent at least 62% of the total population of the Union. If that condition is shown not to have been met, the decision in question shall not be adopted.

A completely different opportunity for the Council to escape unanimity is when the question is 'procedural', in which case the Council shall act by a majority of its members. Article J.8.2 TEU-Maastricht already included this exception:

> [. . .] The Council shall act unanimously, except for procedural questions [. . .].

Nowhere in Art. J.8 TEU-Maastricht, or in any other part of the Treaty, were these 'procedural questions' further defined or was the procedure for their adoption provided. The only possible conclusion on the basis of Art. J.8 TEU-Maastricht was that they need not be adopted unanimously. Hence, one could argue that a simple majority would be sufficient. However, the conclusion that the adoption of procedural questions was subject to the rules governing QMV was more in line with the context of the CFSP Title in the Maastricht TEU, in which the only other exception to the unanimity rule was dealt with by QMV as well.

The 1997 Amsterdam Treaty settled the question on what kind of majority should be used to decide on procedural questions in its Art. 23.3 TEU-Amsterdam:

> For procedural questions, the Council shall act by a majority of its members.

This text returned in the 2001 Nice version with exactly the same wording (Art. 23.3 TEU-Nice).

Finally, one issue still managed to escape from QMV: decisions having military or defence implications continue to be taken on the basis of unanimity. The Maastricht Treaty allowed for the possibility that the Council decide on an ad hoc basis that implementation of a particular decision could take place on the basis of QMV (see earlier). Ironically, this option was used for a decision which obviously had defence implications (a Joint Action on anti-personnel mines).[21] Since the Treaty of Amsterdam, in which the structural possibility of QMV was introduced, the treaties have excluded "decisions having military or defence implications" from decision-making by QMV (see Art. 23.2 TEU-Amsterdam and TEU-Nice: "This paragraph shall not apply to decisions having military or defence implications").

5.2 *From the Constitutional Treaty to the Treaty of Lisbon*

At the time of the Convention for Europe which was to prepare the IGC on the 2005 Constitutional Treaty, it became clear that a 'communautarisation' of CFSP would meet strong resistance from some larger Member States (led by the United Kingdom). It became obvious that CFSP would maintain a somewhat distinct position in the Treaty, despite the fact that a preference for more QMV was expressed by Working Group VII on External Action. In its final report this Working Group argued the following in relation to decision-making in CFSP[22]:

– The Working Group underlines that, in order to avoid CFSP inertia and encourage a pro-active CFSP, maximum use should be made of existing provisions for the use of QMV, and of provisions allowing for some form of flexibility, such as constructive abstention.

– In addition, the Working Group recommends that a new provision be inserted in the Treaty, which would provide for the possibility of the European Council agreeing by unanimity to extend the use of QMV in the field of CFSP.

– Several members consider that 'joint initiatives' should be approved by QMV.

Article III-300.1 TCE nevertheless maintained the 'unanimity rule ("The European decisions referred to in this Chapter shall be adopted by the Council acting unanimously").

Article III-300.2 TCE listed four exceptions to the unanimity rule. Three situations in which QMV could be used were already part of the Amsterdam regime (albeit perhaps in a somewhat modified language):

(a) when adopting European decisions defining a Union action or position on the basis of a European decision of the European Council relating to the Union's strategic interests and objectives, as referred to in Article III-293(1);

---

[21]Council Decision 95/170/CFSP *concerning the joint action adopted by the Council on the basis of Article J.3 of the Treaty on European Union on anti-personnel mines*, O.J. L 115/1 (1995) Art. 6, paragraph 3.

[22]CONV 459/02 (16.12.2002), point 8.

In line with the overall use of the term 'European decisions' for all CFSP legal acts, in this provision the Common Strategies of the European Council were replaced by 'European decisions of the European Council relating to the Union's strategic interests and objectives'.

> (c) when adopting a European decision implementing a European decision defining a Union action or position;
> (d) when adopting a European decision concerning the appointment of a special representative in accordance with Article III-302.

One situation was new:

> (b) when adopting a European decision defining a Union action or position, on a proposal which the Union Minister for Foreign Affairs has presented following a specific request to him or her from the European Council, made on its own initiative or that of the Minister;

This could certainly be seen as a major step. The Constitutional Treaty thus allowed for the Council to adopt CFSP decisions by QMV once these decisions were based on a proposal by the Union Minister for Foreign Affairs. At the same time the compromise is clearly visible in this provision: at the level of the European Council all Member States would have the possibility to block a request to the Union Minister to submit a proposal.

In a different part of the Constitutional Treaty one comes across an additional exception to the unanimity rule. Article III-313.3 TCE regulated the setting up and financing of a start-up fund for expenditure arising from operations having military or defence implications. Article III-311.2 TCE allows for QMV to be used in relation to the establishment of the European Defence Agency; and Art. III-312 TCE mentions QMV in relation to some decisions taken with regard to the Permanent Structured Cooperation in the CSDP (see later).

All in all, the Constitutional Treaty thus substantively extended the possibilities for QMV in the CFSP area. At the same time, however, the possibility introduced by the Amsterdam Treaty to allow Member States to block the possibility of QMV returned in Art. III-300.2 TCE:

> If a member of the Council declares that, for vital and stated reasons of national policy, it intends to oppose the adoption of a European decision to be adopted by a qualified majority, a vote shall not be taken. The Union Minister for Foreign Affairs will, in close consultation with the Member State involved, search for a solution acceptable to it. If he or she does not succeed, the Council may, acting by a qualified majority, request that the matter be referred to the European Council for a European decision by unanimity.

Note that the 'important and stated reasons' were replaced by '*vital* and stated reasons', by which – at least on paper – the possibility to oppose QMV was further restricted. At the same time, the Constitutional Treaty introduced the possibility of the Union Minister for Foreign Affairs to act as a broker and to try and solve the issue at the level of the Council.

The 2007 Lisbon Treaty largely followed the text of the Constitutional Treaty, albeit that the terminology has been adapted to the new 'Lisbon language' ('Decision' instead of 'European decision', 'High Representative' instead of 'Union Minister'). Article 31.2 TEU thus lists the possibilities for QMV in the area of CFSP, and can hence be seen as providing the exceptions to the general rule of unanimity:

> – when adopting a decision defining a Union action or position on the basis of a decision of the European Council relating to the Union's strategic interests and objectives, as referred to in Article 22(1),
> – when adopting a decision defining a Union action or position, on a proposal which the High Representative of the Union for Foreign Affairs and Security Policy has presented following a specific request from the European Council, made on its own initiative or that of the High Representative,
> – when adopting any decision implementing a decision defining a Union action or position,
> – when appointing a special representative in accordance with Article 33.

In addition the use of QMV is possible in a limited number of other cases, which are to be found in other parts of the Treaty. First of all, the use of QMV for the establishment and financing of a start-up fund for military and defence operations was taken over from the Constitutional Treaty. This possibility is now mentioned in Art. 41.3 TEU:

> The Council shall adopt by a qualified majority, on a proposal from the High Representative of the Union for Foreign Affairs and Security Policy, decisions establishing:
> (a) the procedures for setting up and financing the start-up fund, in particular the amounts allocated to the fund;
> (b) the procedures for administering the start-up fund;
> (c) the financial control procedures.

Second, one comes across QMV in Art. 45.2 TEU in relation to the establishment of the European Defence Agency:

> The European Defence Agency shall be open to all Member States wishing to be part of it. The Council, acting by a qualified majority, shall adopt a decision defining the Agency's statute, seat and operational rules.

Finally, some decisions in relation to the Permanent Structured Cooperation in the CSDP may be taken by QMV. With regard to notification by Member States that wish to participate in the Permanent Structured Cooperation, Art. 46.2 TEU states:

> Within three months following the notification [...] the Council shall adopt a decision establishing permanent structured cooperation and determining the list of participating Member States. The Council shall act by a qualified majority after consulting the High Representative.

Later accession to the Permanent Structured Cooperation is also decided on by QMV (Art. 46.3 TEU):

> Any Member State which, at a later stage, wishes to participate in the permanent structured cooperation shall notify its intention to the Council and to the High Representative.
> [...] The Council shall act by a qualified majority after consulting the High Representative. Only members of the Council representing the participating Member States shall take part in the vote.

Similarly, suspension of a Member State from the Permanent Structured Cooperation may be decided upon by the Council on the basis of QMV (Art. 46.4 TEU):

> If a participating Member State no longer fulfils the criteria or is no longer able to meet the commitments [...], the Council may adopt a decision suspending the participation of the Member State concerned.
>
> The Council shall act by a qualified majority. Only members of the Council representing the participating Member States, with the exception of the Member State in question, shall take part in the vote.

As a counter-weight to all these new exceptions to the unanimity rule, the Treaty maintained the 'emergency brake' for situations in which a member of the Council declares that, for *vital* (the term was already introduced by the Constitutional Treaty) and stated reasons of national policy, it intends to oppose the adoption of a decision to be taken by QMV. In that case the High Representative will first search for a solution, before the Council may, acting by a qualified majority, request that the matter be referred to the European Council for a decision by unanimity. In line with the text of the Constitutional Treaty, the High Representative may thus act as a broker to reach a compromise at the level of the Council. The opposing Member State is just been given a choice: either accept decision-making by QMV (which will only be realistic once the draft decision takes the objections raised by the Member State into account), or move the issue to the level of the European Council (where the Member State would have the possibility to block the decision, or to link it to other strategic issues).

With regard to the question of using QMV for procedural questions, it is interesting to note that the specific CFSP provision had disappeared in the 2005 Constitutional Treaty. A reference to the procedural question could only be found in the general title on the Council of Ministers, in Art. III-344.3 TCE:

> The Council shall act by a simple majority regarding procedural matters and for the adoption of its Rules of Procedure.

Post Lisbon not only does this provision return (in Art. 240.3 TFEU), but also the old Nice provision in relation to the specific CFSP voting rules: "For procedural questions, the Council shall act by a majority of its members."

At the same time this is the only situation in CFSP where neither unanimity nor QMV is used, but where decisions are being taken by a simple majority. The fact that the adjective 'simple' is left out does not seem to cause problems of interpretation. After all, in any other case the text of the Treaty refers to *qualified* majority voting. A question that has been left open concerns the definition of 'procedural questions'. They are not defined in the Treaties or in the Council's Rules of Procedure.[23] This also leaves open the question whether the decision to establish that a question is procedural should itself be treated as a procedural or a non-procedural question. In other words, the Council's decision to turn an issue into a procedural question may only be taken by a majority vote once this decision is itself considered procedural. It is doubtful whether the Treaty negotiators had this

---

[23]Council Decision 2009/937/EU *adopting the Council's Rules of Procedure*, O.J. L 325/35 (2009).

last possibility in mind. After all, acceptance of this issue being procedural would potentially open a large number of issues to be decided by a simple majority.

Perhaps the most important innovation in this regard was taken by the Constitutional Treaty in the sense that it introduced a 'dynamic' move to more QMV (sometimes referred to as a *passarelle* clause[24]). Article III-300.3 TCE allowed the European Council to unanimously adopt a European decision stipulating that the Council shall act by a qualified majority. This opened the way to more QMV in CFSP without a formal treaty amendment. The provision was taken over by Art. 31.3 TEU:

> The European Council may unanimously adopt a decision stipulating that the Council shall act by a qualified majority in cases other than those referred to in paragraph 2.

Irrespective of the fact that unanimity is still the rule in the CFSP, the exceptions to the rule have increased over time. In addition to the specific exceptions that were introduced since the Treaty of Amsterdam, the Lisbon Treaty took over the more general rule from the Constitutional Treaty that the European Council may unanimously adopt a decision stipulating that the Council shall act by a qualified majority. Potentially this new QMV possibility allows for a more speedy process in the Council, once the European Council has agreed on it. However, the question remains as to what the actual impact will be. It may be assumed that this situation relates to more structural issues as the possibility to use QMV once a Council decision is based on a decision by the European Council is mentioned separately. This would mean that the European Council has been given the competence to extend the list of (currently) four exceptions to the unanimity rule, which would indeed resemble a true *passarelle*. Nevertheless, in some Member States (e.g. the United Kingdom and Germany), the government will not be able to agree to the use of this *passarelle* without prior approval by its parliament.[25]

Finally, also in the post-Lisbon period, QMV is excluded at all times in relation to 'decisions having military or defence implications' (Art. 31.4 TEU). This provision was again taken over from the Constitutional Treaty (Art. III-300.4 TCE), which also made sure to exclude the possibility that the European Council would decide on a future possibility for QMV in this area. The original draft of the provision did not exclude this possibility and the version in the Constitutional Treaty (as well as in the TEU-Lisbon) is the result of a British amendment to the text.[26]

Still, the distinction between 'military' and 'defence' is not made clear. At the same time it remains striking that paragraph 4 does not simply refer to 'decisions taken in the framework of the Common Security and Defence Policy (CSDP)', but to 'decisions having military or defence implications'. This could imply that general CFSP (non-CSDP) decisions having military or defence implications also

[24]See also the contribution by Hrbek in this volume.

[25]Piris (2010), p. 262.

[26]Amendment No. 11 (Hain), CONV 707/03 (09.05.2003).

require unanimous support. This is underlined by the fact that this rule is mentioned under the CFSP voting modalities, rather than merely in the CSDP Title. In practice this would imply that general CFSP (non-CSDP) decisions (for instance on humanitarian assistance) would require unanimity in all phases when they would have military or defence implications. How to decide on the nature of the decisions (and hence on the applicable voting procedure) is not regulated by the Treaty, but one may assume that in these cases Member States may fall back on the general possibility to block QMV in cases of "vital and stated reasons of national policy" (see earlier).

6 Concluding Observations

The purpose of this paper was to establish whether – and to what extent – the Lisbon Treaty could be seen as another step in the development of the CFSP with a view to two main elements: the right of initiative and the voting rules. Based on earlier research on the development of the CFSP legal order, the hypothesis was that the new Lisbon rules would show a move towards a less intergovernmental CFSP.

From a historical perspective a development is indeed undeniable, but the finally emerging picture is, at best, mixed. Indeed the inclusion of CFSP, together with all other Union policies in one 'Constitutional Treaty' in 2005, seemed to bring an end to the specific nature of the CFSP. In addition, the Constitutional Treaty introduced the "Union Minister for Foreign Affairs" – modified by the Lisbon Treaty to 'High Representative of the Union' – as the successor to the "High Representative for Common Foreign and Security Policy". Thus a new, more supranational, element entered into the CFSP by allowing initiatives in this area to be taken by an 'agent' of the Union, rather than just by Member States. Similarly, the competence to convene an extraordinary meeting was moved from the Presidency to the High Representative, which implied that for the first time the Council could be convened on the initiative of the EU itself.

Also with regard to the voting rules, some major steps have been taken over time. The introduction of 'constructive abstention' by the Amsterdam Treaty was maintained by later treaty modifications. Together with the fact that non-participation by a Member State through the issuing of a formal declaration did not at all deprive this abstaining Council member from obligations based on the adopted decision, the procedure in practice comes closes to QMV. After all, the decision taken by the Council remains a 'Union decision'. While the abstaining state may not be asked to actively implement this decision, it has to accept that 'the decision commits the Union'. In addition both the Constitutional Treaty and the Treaty of Lisbon extended the possibilities for QMV. The most important innovation in this regard may very well be the introduction of the *passarelle* clause, which allows the European Council to unanimously adopt a decision stipulating that the Council shall act by a qualified majority. This opened the way to more QMV in the CFSP without a formal treaty amendment. Finally, it is worth noting that the 'important and stated reasons' which could be invoked by Member States wishing to block QMV were replaced by '*vital* and stated reasons', by which – at least on paper – the possibility to oppose QMV was further restricted.

At the same time, during the Convention for Europe which was to prepare the IGC on the 2005 Constitutional Treaty it became clear that a 'communautarisation' of CFSP would be met by strong resistance from some larger Member States. The final text of the Constitutional Treaty, which largely returned in the Treaty of Lisbon, therefore even maintained many of the specific characteristic of the CFSP and also introduced a few new ones. First of all, the individual competence of the Commission to submit proposals (one of the crown jewels of the 'Community method') has been deleted and replaced by a possibility to submit initiatives together with the new Union Minister for Foreign Affairs. Even a proposal by the Presidium of the Convention to allow for joint proposals by the Commission and the High Representative was not accepted, because this would mean that the High Representative would need approval from the Commission for his proposal. In addition the term 'Union Minister for Foreign Affairs' in the Constitutional Treaty was replaced with 'High Representative of the Union for Foreign Affairs and Security Policy'. This replacement was caused by the changes discussed during the Lisbon IGC with the more general purpose of removing 'state-like' terms. Moreover, proposals to limit the right of initiative of individual Member States were unacceptable to a number of them.

Thus unanimity is still the rule, which stands in stark contrast to the other EU policies where since 'Lisbon' QMV has been established as the default voting rule. German and French proposals to make QMV the default option for CFSP did not make it. Still, as a counter-weight to the new exceptions to the unanimity rule that did make it to the final text, the Treaty maintained the 'emergency brake' for situations in which a member of the Council declares that, for vital and stated reasons of national policy, it intends to oppose the adoption of a decision to be taken by QMV. Finally, the explicit exclusion of the adoption of 'legislative acts' reveals that, despite the binding nature of its decisions, the CFSP remains the odd one out in terms of the role of the European Parliament and the Court of Justice.

Even on balance, it is difficult to assess the impact of the Lisbon Treaty on the rules on the right of initiative and voting in the CFSP. The new rules have come a long way since Maastricht and a development is clearly visible. However, the Treaty introduced both a number of 'intergovernmental' elements and some innovations that may potentially change the nature of CFSP. It seems to be up to the dynamics of the process itself to use the latter to make full use of the innovations in practice.

References

Cremona M (2003) The draft constitutional treaty: external relations and external action. CMLRev 40(6):1347–1366

Cremona M (2006) A constitutional basis for effective external action? An assessment of the provisions on EU external action in the constitutional treaty. EUI Working Paper, LAW No. 2006/30

Crowe B (2008) The Chatham House Report, The European External Action Service: roadmap for success. http://www.chathamhouse.org.uk/files/11583_0508eas_report.pdf. Accessed date 20 May 2011
Denza E (2002) The intergovernmental pillars of the European Union. Oxford University Press, Oxford
Duke S (2009). Providing for European-level diplomacy after Lisbon: the case of the European external action service. Hague J Diplom:211–233
Duke S, Blockmans S (2010) The Lisbon Treaty stipulations on development cooperation and the council decision of 25 March 2010 (Draft) establishing the organisation and functioning of the European External Action Service. CLEER Legal Brief, 4 May 2010. www.cleer.eu
Gosalbo Bono R (2006) Some reflections on the CFSP legal order. CMLRev 43(2):337–394
Hillion C, Wessel RA (2009) Competence distribution in EU external relations after *Ecowas*. Clarification or continued fuzziness? CMLRev 46(2):551–586
Kaddous C (2008) Role and position of the high representative of the Union for Foreign Affairs and Security Policy under the Lisbon Treaty. In: Griller S, Ziller J (eds) The Lisbon Treaty: constitutionalism without a Constitutional Treaty? Springer, Vienna, pp 205–221
Keukeleire S (1998) Het buitenlands beleid van de Europese Unie. Kluwer, Deventer
Piris J-C (2010) The Lisbon Treaty: a legal and political analysis. Cambridge University Press, Cambridge
Smith ME (2004) Europe's Foreign and Security Policy: the institutionalization of cooperation. Cambridge University Press, Cambridge
Spence D (2006) The commission and the common foreign and security policy. In: Spence D (ed) The European Commission, 3rd edn. John Harper Publishing, London
Stetter S (2007) EU foreign and interior policies: cross-pillar politics and the social construction of sovereignty. Taylor & Francis, London
van Ooik RH (2008) Cross-pillar litigation before the ECJ: demarcation of community and union competences. Eur Constitut Law Rev 4:399–419
Vanhoonacker S, Reslow N (2010) The European external action service: living forwards by understanding backwards. EFA Rev:1–18
Wessel RA (2007) The EU's foreign, security and defense policy fifteen years after Maastricht: a constitutional momentum? In: Ehrhart H-G, Jaberg S, Rinke B, Waldmann J (eds) Die Europäische Union im 21. Jahrhundert. Theorie und Praxis europäischer Außen-, Sicherheits- und Friedenspolitik. VS Verlag für Sozialwissenschaften, Wiesbaden, pp 302–316
Wessel RA (2009) The dynamics of the European Union legal order: an increasingly coherent framework of action and interpretation. Eur Constitut Law Rev 1:117–142

The Intergovernmental Branch of the EU's Foreign Affairs Executive

Reflections on the Political and Security Committee

Daniel Thym

1 Introduction

Among the Lisbon Treaty's reform steps the reconfiguration of the Union's external representation assumes a central role. It is often referred to as one of the Treaty's most prominent achievements which allows Europe to move beyond institutional introspection and concentrate on 'reinforcing the European identity and its independence in order to promote peace, security and progress in Europe and in the world'.[1] It remains to be tested whether the new institutional architecture permits the Union to translate the Treaty's grand declaration into specific policy actions. Definite answers may so far not yet have been given. Our legal analysis may, however, shed light on the role of the political and security committee, thereby identifying both the executive character of the Union's foreign policy powers and their continued intergovernmentalism.

In order to evaluate the Lisbon Treaty's reform steps we need to understand their inherent pragmatism, which on the one hand abolishes the pillar structure by extending the powers of the High Representative and creating the European External Action Service, while at the same time ascertaining that they 'will not affect the existing legal basis, responsibilities, and powers of each Member State in relation to the formulation and conduct of its foreign policy'.[2] In short, the Treaty of Lisbon does not revolutionise the former second pillar but rather continues the tradition of incremental changes which have characterised the evolution of the Common Foreign and Security Policy (CFSP) and the Common Security and Defence Policy

[1]Indent 11 of the Preamble to the EU Treaty, O.J. C115/13 (2008).

[2]Declaration (No. 14) concerning the Common Foreign and Security Policy O.J. C 306/255 (2008) describing in how far the CFSP 'is subject to specific rules and procedures' (Art. 24.1 (2) TEU).

D. Thym (✉)
Chair of Public, European & International Law, Universität Konstanz, Fach D116, 78457 Konstanz, Germany
e-mail: thym@uni-konstanz.de

H.-J. Blanke and S. Mangiameli (eds.), *The European Union after Lisbon*,
DOI 10.1007/978-3-642-19507-5_21, © Springer-Verlag Berlin Heidelberg 2012

(CSDP) during the past two decades. The new rules build upon past reform steps without undoing the underlying dichotomy between the intergovernmental and supranational branches of the Union's foreign affairs constitution.

The continued particularity of the CFSP may be demonstrated by the specific role of the Political and Security Committee (PSC), which has become the political 'mind' of CFSP decision-making and serves as the 'linchpin' between the national foreign ministers and the Council's administrative infrastructure (Sect. 2). Both these functions allow us to recognize the executive character of foreign and security policy (Sect. 3) and its continued intergovernmentalism behind the façade of uniform external representation (Sect. 4). On this basis, we may identify the constitutional challenges raised by the new Treaty regime. Instead of associating the new rules with legislative functions we should explore the existing achievements and pitfalls of the attempts to hold the Union's intergovernmental foreign affairs executive, including the PSC, to account.

2 Evolution of the 'Linchpin' PSC Within the CFSP

After the failure of the supranational European Defence Community (EDC) in the 1950s, foreign policy cooperation followed an intergovernmental path. The regular meetings of the political directors served as a focal point of intergovernmental policy coordination within the informal framework of European Political Cooperation (EPC).[3] In 1986, the Single European Act reinforced this tradition by officially requesting the political directors to 'meet regularly in the Political Committee in order to give the necessary impetus, maintain the continuity of [EPC] and prepare Ministers' discussions'.[4] In 1992, the Maastricht Treaty integrated this existing function into the European Union's (EU's) single institutional framework: henceforth the Council was responsible for the coordination of national policies within the framework of the CFSP. In order to prepare the Council meetings the 'Political Committee consisting of Political Directors'[5] was entrusted with the monitoring of the international situation and the definition of common policies.

As the Political Committee was composed of political directors residing in national capitals it remained a non-permanent institution. However, Member States argued for more continuity in the 1990s with a view to the increase of the CFSP workload; for this reason Art. 25 TEU-Amsterdam allowed for the Political Committee's flexible composition.[6] On this basis, the extraordinary evolution of the

[3] Like ministers the political directors met in national capitals to underline the intergovernmental character of cooperation; for the emerging practice see Smith (2004), pp. 78–82.

[4] Article 30.10(c) SEA; for meetings at short notice see Art. 30.10(d) SEA.

[5] Article J-8.5 TEU-Maastricht corresponds, *mutatis mutandi*, to Art. 38(1) TEU.

[6] Article 25 TEU-Amsterdam deleted the reference to the Committee's composition of political directors without there being a consensus whether an alternative formation should be established;

defence policy after 1999 transformed the Committee without any further Treaty change into a quasi-permanent structure which would serve as the '*linchpin* of the European Security and Defence Policy (ESDP)'.[7] In 2000, the Council established a Committee formation composed of national representatives at senior or ambassadorial level residing in Brussels.[8] From now on, CFSP would have a quasi-permanent decision-making body which could perform political control and strategic direction of the Union's civil and military crisis management operations – mirroring the corresponding functions of North Atlantic Treaty Organization's (NATO's) North Atlantic Council.

Its quasi-permanent ESDP oversight function explains the Committee's remarkable success during the past decade.[9] The revamped Political Committee would serve as the motor of security and defence integration, whose operative character required stable institutional structures, which the monthly Council meetings could not provide. One step further, the Treaty of Nice not only rebranded the committee as the Political *and Security* Committee, which is also known by its French acronym COPS (*Comité politique et de sécurité*), but also formalised its ESDP oversight function by establishing an autonomous decision-making power for ongoing ESDP operations in between the monthly Council meetings.[10] These changes survived the constitutional reform process with only minor adaptations concerning the role of the High Representative.[11] In the age of the Lisbon Treaty, the PSC therefore maintains its role as a central forum for CFSP decision-making and the supervision of the Common Security and Defence Policy (CSDP). A closer inspection of its functions and working methods demonstrates both the CFSP's executive character and its continued intergovernmentalism.

3 Executive Character of the CFSP Institution

Reading the Treaty articles governing CFSP the path dependency of European integration stands out. While the Intergovernmental Conferences drafting the Treaties of Maastricht, Amsterdam, Nice and Lisbon certainly rejected the CFSP's

cf. Declaration No. 5 on Art. 25 TEU attached to the Amsterdam Treaty, Regelsberger (2004), pp. 35–38 and Howorth (2007), pp. 72–73.

[7]This formulation is taken from the Presidency Report on the ESDP, Council doc. 14056/2/00 of 4 Dec 2000, Annex III (emphasis added), which was approved by the Nice European Council of 7–9 Dec 2000, Presidency Conclusions, para 11.

[8]See Art. 1 Council Decision 2000/143/CFSP *setting up the Interim PSC*, O.J. L 49/1 (2000).

[9]See Duke (2005), pp. 14–16.

[10]See Art. 25(2), (3) TEU-Nice which codify earlier political agreement on how the ESDP institutions should evolve; it should be noted that the PSC functioned on the basis of Art. 25 TEU-Amsterdam until the Nice Treaty entered into force in October 2003.

[11]Art. 38 TEU corresponds to Art. III-307 TCE, which both foresee the HR assuming the earlier function of the Commission and the Council in Art. 25(1), (2) TEU-Nice.

supranationalisation, they followed the Community method in so far as they conceptualised CFSP as a quasi-legislative undertaking: The foreign affairs provisions in the EU Treaty assume that the CFSP is being realised through the adoption of legal instruments (Arts. 25, 26, 28, 29 TEU) on the basis of formalised decision-making procedures, which in specific circumstances provide for qualified majority voting and for the association of the European Parliament (Arts. 31, 36 TEU).[12] Against this background, it seemed a foregone conclusion that the CFSP would follow the example of other policy fields and be communitarised sooner or later – with the extension of quality majority voting in the Council and co-decision powers of the European Parliament.[13]

The narrative of gradual communitarisation is of intuitive appeal to European lawyers who have experienced Europe's epic constitutional reform process stretching over a quarter century from the Single European Act to the Lisbon Treaty.[14] But arguably the plausibility of the Community method as a blueprint and model for CFSP blurs our understanding of the constitutional specificities of foreign, security and defence policies. European foreign policy is much less about rule-making than the realisation of the single market. I therefore suggest an alternative, counterintuitive reading of the Treaty articles, which does not follow the supranational Community method. Both CFSP and CSDP require the identification of strategic goals and the constant adjustment of methods for their realisation. This specificity of foreign affairs explains why an extensive administrative institutional infrastructure has been established under the auspices of the PSC in recent years (Sect. 3.1), whose effective operation and collaboration with national foreign services and armed forces requires regular communication and mutual understanding (Sect. 3.2). On this basis, we may recognise the executive, non-legislative character of CFSP and CSDP and the corresponding oversight function of the PSC (Sect. 3.3).

3.1 *Administrative Institutional Infrastructure*

In order to understand the constitutional specificity of CFSP we need to expand our analysis beyond the Treaty articles and their quasi-legislative design. More specifically, we need to acknowledge that during the past 15 years the Council has set up a significant administrative infrastructure for CFSP and CSDP whose powers

---

[12]In particular the Treaty of Amsterdam followed this path with the reform of legal instruments, qualified majority voting and the specific mechanism of 'constructive abstention' foreseen in Art 23.1(2) TEU-Amsterdam; one step further, enhanced cooperation was extended to the CFSP by Art. 27a TEU-Nice.

[13]See Ginsburg (1997), pp. 297–318 and for the debate in the European Convention drafting the Constitutional Treaty Thym (2004), pp. 9–17.

[14]For the regular calls for parliamentary and judicial CFSP oversight see, e.g., Bieber (2002), pp. 107–109 and Eeckhout (2005), p. 4.

rival the supranational prerogative of the Commission in other policy fields. This genuine intergovernmental bureaucracy consists of different components which concentrate on the CFSP and CSDP staff in the Council Secretariat. A crucial first measure was the formation of the 'Policy Unit' of seconded national diplomatic personnel which served as the nucleus for the expansion of strategic foreign policy thinking within the Council Secretariat.[15] The creation of the Policy Unit under the responsibility of the first High Representative, Javier Solana, underlined that the Council Secretariat's role was changing substantially: It was no longer a mere supporting body which facilitated the Council decisions and the deliberations in the preparatory working groups, COREPER and the PSC. Rather, it would perform original administrative functions similar to national foreign and defence ministries.[16]

One step further, substantial military expertise was integrated into the Council Secretariat after the 1999 decision to launch the ESDP. Within a few years, the decidedly civil bureaucratic culture of the Council Secretariat was complemented with strategic-military orientation through the integration of the EU Military Staff (EUMS) and the EU Military Committee (EUMC). The EUMC in particular assumes a crucial role by linking the Council bodies to national armed forces; it is composed of national military experts and shall be 'responsible for providing the PSC with military advice and recommendations on all military matters within the EU'.[17] The EUMC's expertise is crucial for the successful planning and deployment of military operations. For civil crisis management operations similar bodies have been set up which are more independently supervised by the Council Secretariat and its rudimentary operational headquarters for civil missions.[18] Also, the EU Satellite Centre, the European Defence Agency and the European Defence College are meant to support the improvement of national military capabilities; as CSDP agencies they complement the Council activities as institutional satellites in orbit.[19] With the establishment of the European External Action Service all these bodies have been transformed into EEAS departments.[19a]

[15]See the Declaration (No. 6) attached to the Treaty of Amsterdam on the Establishment of a Policy Planning and Early Warning Unit; see also Duke (2008), p. 81.

[16]For a more detailed analysis see Christiansen (2002), pp. 80–97, Duke and Vanhoonacker (2006), p. 363 and Dijkstra (2008), pp. 155–164.

[17]Council Decision 2001/79/CFSP *setting up the Military Committee of the EU*, O.J. L 27/1 (2001), annex, point 2; for the EUMS see Council Decision 2005/395/CFSP *on the establishment of the Military Staff of the EU*, O.J. L 132/17 (2005).

[18]For the Civilian Planning and Conduct Capability (CPCC), which as an integral part of the Council Secretariat (now the EEAS) did not require a Council decision for its establishment, see Thym (2010), Sect. 17 paras 29, 45.

[19]See Council Joint Action 2001/555/CFSP *on the establishment of a EU SatCen*, O.J. L 200/5 (2001), Joint Action 2004/551/CFSP *on the establishment of the EDA*, O.J. L 245/17 (2004) and Council Joint Action 2005/575/CFSP *establishing a ESDC*, O.J. L 194/15 (2005); for details, Dijkstra (2008), pp. 155–164.

[19a]See Council Decision 2010/427/EU establishing the European External Action Service, O.J. L 201/30 (2010), Annex.

The EU Treaty does not explicitly sanction the considerable extension of the Council Secretariat's administrative infrastructure during the past decade. It rather presupposes its existence when Art. 38 TEU explicitly tasks the PSC to 'monitor the implementation of agreed policies' and exercise 'the political control and strategic direction of the crisis management operations'.[20] Also in the future, its reorganisation will be governed by Art. 240.2 TFEU and the Council's Rules of Procedure.[21] For our purposes it should be emphasised that the executive responsibilities of the Council Secretariat and the PSC transcend the preparation of legislative deliberations which define the Council's regular activities. Instead, the Council Secretariat and the PSC assume executive functions, including extended operative responsibilities relating to the oversight and control of civil and military CSDP missions.[22] Such executive functions are within the single market regularly entrusted upon the Commission.[23] So far, the parallel formation of the extensive intergovernmental executive powers of the Council Secretariat is the most prominent expression of the EU's dual executive encompassing the supranational Commission and the intergovernmental Council.

3.2 *'Brusselisation' Under the Living Constitution*

The extensive executive powers of the Council Secretariat and the corresponding oversight function of the PSC do not only concern the legal analysis. Political science explains that the institutionalisation of the CFSP and the CSDP has – even without supranationalisation – resulted in the de facto 'Brusselisation'[24] of European foreign policy-making. Regular contacts between national and European policy actors, the reorganisation of national foreign ministries and the formation of dedicated staff facilitate support the gradual alignment of national foreign policy preferences as the bedrock for the formulation and realisation of joint European approaches.[25] The formation of administrative CFSP and CSDP infrastructure led to a collegial impulse supporting the convergence of policy preferences.[26] As the 'mind' and 'brain cells' of foreign policy decision-making the PSC and the

---

[20]Article 38(1) second sentence TEU (first reference) and Art. 38(2) TEU (second reference).

[21]See, in particular, Arts. 19 and 23 Council Rules of Procedure, annexed to Council Decision 2009/937/EU, O.J. L 325/35 (2009); additionally Art. 27.3 and 28 TEU may be referred to.

[22]On the extension of the Council's executive functions in other policy fields see Curtin (2009), pp. 85–90 and Curtin (2004).

[23]Its executive function is generally described in Art. 17.1 TEU.

[24]Allen (1998), p. 48.

[25]See, on the basis of constructivist and neo-institutionalist theories of international relations, in particular Glarbo (2001) and Tonra (2003).

[26]For more details see Howorth (2007), pp. 175–183, Juncos and Reynolds (2007), pp. 129–146 and Duke and Vanhoonacker (2006), pp. 380–382.

administrative bodies it oversees play a crucial role in identifying common positions and methods for their realisation.

As mentioned earlier the administrative CFSP bodies were set up by means of Treaty implementation.[27] Their relevance stems from the regular contacts between national and European officials in the day-to-day management of European foreign policy. For this reason, the legal analysis of the Council's executive powers cannot limit itself to the primary law dimension but should consider the practical functioning of CFSP and CSDP. Such consideration of the 'living constitution'[28] is crucial when we evaluate the institutional practice in the light of the normative Treaty framework and its wider constitutional aspirations of legality, legitimacy and accountability.[29] For all these purposes, the 'linchpin' PSC takes centre stage: First, its quasi-permanent status substantiates the finding of de facto Brusselisation of CFSP decision-making. Second, it assumes an institutional bridging function between political actors in the Council, national foreign and defence ministries and CFSP bureaucracy in the Council Secretariat.

During the past 10 years the PSC has effectively established itself as the quasi-permanent 'executive board' for the CSDP and the CFSP. All Member States have in the meantime appointed national 'PSC ambassadors' residing in Brussels as their permanent PSC representatives.[30] The PSC's 'Brussels formation' has become the default setting with two meetings per week in the Council's Justus Lipsius building in regular circumstances.[31] Its practical working arrangements may be adapted any time, since neither Art. 25 TEU nor secondary legislation lay down specific constraints.[32] In real terms, the PSC meetings have become extensive gatherings of PSC ambassadors with supporting personnel for the different agenda items, which usually stretch from civil and military ESDP operations to recent international developments and the standard business of the CFSP. More than a hundred people usually attend these meetings which often continue into the evening.

As a newcomer the PSC had to establish its presence in Brussels vis-à-vis the pre-existing institutions. Relations with COREPER proved particularly difficult given their overlapping responsibilities for the preparation of Council meetings. After initial struggles in the 1990s, a realistic working relationship was established. The PSC concentrates on the agreement of substantive foreign policy issues relating

[27]See notes 20–22 and accompanying text.

[28]See Curtin (2009), pp. 8–11 and, specifically for CFSP, Wessel (1999), pp. 22–32.

[29]On the accountability of the CFSP executive see Sect. 3.3.

[30]The precise standing of the PSC representatives differs from Member State to Member State; usually they receive instructions and report back to the political directors in the capital; see Regelsberger (2004), p. 68 and Howorth (2007), p. 68.

[31]For details see Kaufmann-Bühler and Meyer-Landruth (2004), Art. 25 TEU para. 6 and Dehousse (2005), pp. 466–468.

[32]Cf. Council Decision 2001/78/CFSP *setting up the Political and Security Committee*, O.J. L 27/1 (2001), which lists the PSC's function in the annex but does specify neither the PSC's format nor its internal working arrangements.

to CFSP, while COREPER deals with overarching institutional, financial and legal matters.[33] Although COREPER remains the hierarchically supreme body which must consider all items on the Foreign Affairs Council's agenda,[34] the PSC usually endeavours to reach agreement at its level on all substantive dossiers. In practical terms that may require the PSC to hold special sessions, possibly in the early hours of the morning, in order to present a viable compromise to COREPER just in time for the Council deliberations later in the day.[35] It should be noted, however, that the latent rivalry between the PSC and COREPER does not extend to areas where the PSC holds an autonomous supervision and decision-making capacity.[36]

When agreed policies are being implemented by CFSP institutions the PSC possesses a strong supervision authority; its oversight powers vis-à-vis the subordinate executive bodies of the intergovernmental EU executive facilitate the effective performance of this supervisory function. In the case of CSDP operations, the PSC's supervision authority is most pronounced: military commanders report back to the PSC, which politically controls and strategically directs the course of the ongoing operation.[37] Occasionally, the PSC even implements European foreign policy by its own activities, especially when it conducts political dialogue with third-country representatives or with international organisations. On these occasions, the third-country representatives, usually of sub-ministerial standing, appear directly in the PSC or meet the PSC representatives outside the Council's Justus Lipsius building – as in the case of the regular meetings between the PSC and NATO's North Atlantic Council.[38]

One step further, the PSC may officially decide the Union standpoint whenever it formally adopts implementing decisions under Art. 38(3) TEU. While the Council retains the power (and obligation) to initiate any civil or military CSDP operation, the respective Council decision regularly authorises the PSC to take decisions concerning the political control and strategic direction of the operation within the preset framework. In practice, this delegation of decision-making authority comprises the power to amend the operational instructions (including the Operation Plan, the Chain of Command and the Rules of Engagement), to appoint the EU Operation Commander and/or EU Force Commander and to coordinate third-country contributions – while any modification of the objectives and the

---

[33]Wessel (1999), pp. 79–83 traces the initial quarrels.

[34]See Art. 19.2 Council Rules of Procedure, annexed to Council Decision 2009/937/EU, O.J. L 325/35 (2009).

[35]See Duke and Vanhoonacker (2006), p. 376 and Juncos and Reynolds (2007), p. 135.

[36]In accordance with Art. 38(3) TEU the Council may authorise the PSC to take implementing decisions which do not require COREPER involvement.

[37]For the institutional practice see Sect. 2 of the annex to Council Decision 2001/78/CFSP *setting up the Political and Security Committee*, O.J. L 27/1 (2001), and Dietrich (2006), pp. 341–345.

[38]See Duke and Vanhoonacker (2006), p. 375 and Duke (2008), p. 81.

termination of the operation remains the Council's prerogative.[39] Given the operative character of these implementing decisions, which domestically are usually subject to executive decisions within the military chain of command, we should not confuse the delegation under Art. 38(3) TEU with the delegation of legislative powers in accordance with Art. 290 TFEU. This operative character of the delegated decision-making authority entails in particular that the requirements for the specificity of the delegation in CSDP matters do not mirror the corresponding rules for delegated legislation.[40]

3.3 Accountability of CFSP Diplomacy and CSDP Operations

From the Treaty perspective, every CFSP decision must at least in principle be taken by the Council, while the PSC remains a preparatory body (with the exception of delegated decision-making powers[41]). In practice, however, European foreign policy evolves differently. The Council's daily practice illustrates that legal instruments are only adopted whenever the projection of personnel or the dispersal of funds require a formal legal basis in a Council Decision; for other foreign policy questions the Council prefers the informal vehicle of Council Conclusions to the adoption of formal legal acts under Art. 25 TEU.[42] Moreover, the everyday foreign policy business is usually being dealt with in Declarations of the High Representative, internal strategy papers or through direct contacts with third-country representatives. Hence, some questions are neither discussed in the Council nor subject to a formal Council Decision under Art. 25 TEU.

The informal character of CFSP and CSDP explains the central relevance of the PSC in the day-to-day management of European foreign policy. The informal alignment and projection of national positions in situations which do not require a sound legal basis does not command Council involvement. Instead, many foreign policy questions are discussed in the PSC and/or its preparatory bodies only, especially when the urgency or minor relevance of the topic does not lend itself

---

[39]See, e.g., Arts. 6 and 10 Council Joint Action 2008/851/CFSP *on a EU military operation to contribute to the deterrence, prevention and repression of acts of piracy and armed robbery off the Somali coast*, O.J. L 301/33 (2008); in practice the modification of the OPLAN in particular may result in important changes of direction.

[40]Cremer (2007), Art. 25 TEU para 6 however supports more detailed instructions by the Council, loosely mirroring the present rules in Art. 290.1(2) TFEU.

[41]See Art. 38(3) TEU and my earlier comments.

[42]During my traineeship (*Referendariat*) with the German Permanent Representation with the EU (Political Department) in 2004 I learned that Council Conclusions in particular are being drafted most carefully similar to a legal instrument; in addition, the European Security Strategy was deliberately not adopted as a Common Strategy, which would have allowed for implementing decisions by qualified majority under the present Arts. 22.1(2), 31.2 TEU; it was instead politically approved by the European Council on 12 December 2003 (see Council Doc 15895/03).

to the overcrowded agenda of the monthly Council meetings.[43] This autonomy of subordinate Council bodies extends to the control and guidance of civil and military CSDP operations with their decidedly operative character.[44] In short, the PSC and its preparatory bodies retain an extended autonomy in the day-to-day management of the CFSP and the ESDP.[45] Of course, the Council may at any time assume its residual decision-making power. But in the institutional practice many decisions are nonetheless being taken at sub-Council level (with national governments controlling the everyday activities of the PSC through the hierarchical control of its representative[46]).

One may rationalise the limited practical relevance of the formal decision-making procedures and legal instruments in CFSP with substantive differences between domestic law-making on the one hand and international diplomacy and military operations on the other hand.[47] Supranational law-making characterises the Community method; this model can, however, not be projected without modification to the international sphere and relations with third states. Even when all Member States unreservedly comply with a CFSP position as if it was a directly applicable supranational legal act, the Union's foreign policy would not necessarily be successful: Iran will not give up its nuclear weapons, only because the EU says so in its Official Journal. Successful foreign policy and effective military operations rather require the identification of strategic goals and the constant adjustment of methods for their realisation. The success of CFSP primarily depends on the persuasiveness and credibility of its policies, the support of the Member States and its strategic perception in third states – less on the binding force of internal decisions.

Against this background, we understand why our perspective on the CFSP requires a counterintuitive reading of the Treaty articles, which distinguishes the CFSP from the Community method with its orientation at supranational law-making. Successful CFSP diplomacy and effective CSDP operations do not primarily depend on the legal characteristics of legal acts. Instead, we should recognise their executive, non-legislative character. Within the framework of CFSP the adoption of legal acts is the exception, not the rule – even if the Treaty articles suggest otherwise. CFSP diplomacy and CSDP operations are primarily executive in nature; the corresponding functions of the PSC, the Council working groups and the administrative CFSP and CSDP infrastructure must similarly be qualified

[43]Whenever CFSP decisions do not require legal force, these issues do not even reach the Council as 'A points' for adoption without discussion (mirroring the practice of formal Council involvement in legislative questions).

[44]See Art. 38(3) TEU and Sect. 3.1.

[45]Article 38(1) TEU clarifies that the PSC does not require an explicit Council mandate before it deals with a foreign policy issue, since it shall independently 'monitor the international situation . . . and contribute to the definition of policies'.

[46]On national instructions see Sect. 4.

[47]The following ideas are based upon my contribution Thym (2009), pp. 333–334.

as executive.[48] Accordingly, the PSC and executive bodies in its orbit do not only fulfil a mere support function for the preparation of the Council's legislative activities. Instead, they gain a momentum of their own as Brussels-based executive institutions.

As a result, the public lawyers' perspective must change: if the intergovernmental CFSP and CSDP bodies exercise executive powers in their own right, public lawyers should consider institutional mechanisms to hold this intergovernmental branch of the Union's foreign affairs executive to account; controlling the national representative in the Council alone will no longer suffice.[49] We should rather shed light on the executive responsibilities of the Council Secretariat, which has been portrayed to govern 'in the shadow'.[50] We need to identify mechanisms to hold the executive to account vis-à-vis national and European oversight bodies and through channels of financial, legal and political accountability.[51] So far, the PSC has played a crucial institutional role. Although it is itself an executive body composed of unelected national officials, the Treaty explicitly sanctions its oversight function.[52] It serves as the institutional link between the political responsibilities of the Council and the administrative bodies within its sphere of responsibility and, as a quasi-permanent institution, holds the capacity to effectively oversee, direct and control their activities.[53]

4 Persistence of CFSP Intergovernmentalism

The Lisbon Treaty stipulates in welcome clarity that the realisation of CFSP differs from the harmonisation of national laws under the Community method: 'The common foreign and security policy is subject to specific rules and procedures. It shall be defined and implemented by the European Council and the Council acting unanimously, except where the Treaties provide otherwise. The adoption of legislative acts shall be excluded. The common foreign and security policy shall be put into effect by the High Representative of the Union for Foreign Affairs and Security

[48]I use the term 'executive' as an overarching category comprising both the political Council responsibilities and the administrative support it receives, mirroring the categorisation by Curtin (2009), Chaps. 4 and 5. Like in other policy fields, the internal distinction between the 'political' and the 'administrative' executive cannot always be neatly drawn for the CFSP and the CSDP, e.g. in the case of the PSC.

[49]Read Curtin (2009), pp. 246–276 and, more generally, on the normative framework of EU constitutional principles von Bogdandy (2010).

[50]Christiansen (2002), pp. 80–97.

[51]For further considerations see Harlow (2002), Chaps. 1 and 7, Oliver (2009), pp. 14–32 and, again, Curtin (2009), Chap. 9.

[52]Read again the second sentence of Art. 38(1) TEU and Art. 38(2) TEU.

[53]For the Parliament's role and the Court of Justice see Thym (2010), Sect. 17 paras 54–63.

Policy and by Member States, in accordance with the Treaties. The specific role of the European Parliament and of the Commission in this area is defined by the Treaties. The Court of Justice of the European Union shall not have jurisdiction with respect to these provisions'.[54]

While the Treaty expressly underlines the institutional intergovernmentalism of CFSP decision-making, our legal analysis may conclude that the constitutional characteristics similarly differ from the supranational blueprint which applies to other areas of European foreign policy, such as external trade, development cooperation and the external dimension of environmental policy. The latter areas are subject to a transfer of sovereign powers, whose exercise at European level commands direct and supreme in national legal orders, entails the exclusivity of external representation and is subject to European Court of Justice (ECJ) adjudication.[55] By contrast, the intergovernmental characteristics of intergovernmental Union law are based on the absence of transferred national competences which are capable of having direct and supreme effect and pre-empt the exercise of national powers.[56] Or, in the words of the German constitutional court: 'Also after the entry into force of the Treaty of Lisbon, the [CFSP], including the [CSDP], will not fall under supranational law'.[57]

How far does the continued intergovernmentalism of the CFSD and the CSDP affect our analysis? It implies in particular that we need to distinguish between the intergovernmental branch of the CFSP and its supranational counterpart in fields such as external trade within the EU's overall foreign affairs power. This dichotomy extends to the identification of existing and/or desirable accountability mechanisms. As a pragmatic merger of the pillars, both the 'double-hatted' High Representative/Vice-President (HR/VP), currently Catherine Ashton, and the European External Action Service (EEAS) continue the dualism between the supranationalism and intergovernmentalism behind the surface of external unity.[58] Their accountability must consider this hybrid character.

In practical terms, the intergovernmental executive function of the PSC, the Council working groups and the Council Secretariat have been integrated into the EEAS. In line with the EEAS' overall institutional design the military and foreign policy experts within the Council Secretariat will however maintain their

---

[54]Article 21.1(2) TEU.

[55]For these features of supranational external relations law see Cremona (1999) and Thym (2009), pp. 316–330.

[56]For details see Thym (2009), pp. 330–338 and Cremona (2003), pp. 1352–1361.

[57]German (Federal) Constitutional Court 2 BvE 2/08 'Lisbon Judgment' (30 June 2009) para 390 under reference to Art. 24.1, 40 TEU, Art. 2.4 TFEU and Declaration (No. 14) attached to the Lisbon Treaty.

[58]As far as the High Representative is concerned he/she is fully integrated into the decision-making procedures of supranational external relations as a Vice-President of the Commission under Art. 18.4 TEU, while he/she is bound by intergovernmental decisions within the CFSP framework; see also Thym (2009), pp. 341–342.

institutional responsibilities. As intergovernmental bodies within the EEAS they will continue to receive their instructions from and report back to the PSC, the HR/VP and the Council; the internal chains of command and reporting within the intergovernmental foreign affairs executive need to be distinguished from the corresponding oversight and control channels which exist in supranational policy fields.[59] As the intergovernmental branch of the EEAS both the CFSP and the CSDP personnel will continue to be directed by the PSC and Council under the overall responsibility of the High Representative. While the collaboration between the intergovernmental and the supranational branches of the EEAS may ease the underlying dichotomy between intergovernmentalism and supranationalism,[60] we nonetheless need to distinguish the different channels of responsibility, also for purposes of accountability.

More specifically, the PSC will not only retain its crucial oversight and control function as the 'management board' of the CFSP and the CSDP and its administrative infrastructure. It also remains – like the Council and COREPER – a standing formation of Member State representatives, which coordinate national foreign policies and which are, unlike the Commission, not independent in the exercise of their function. PSC representatives may develop an *esprit de corps* which facilitates their collaboration, but remain integrated into the bureaucratic hierarchy of national foreign ministries which frequently issue policy instructions and to which the PSC members report back. While the PSC regularly decides by consensus, any formal vote would be subject to the majority requirements of Art. 31 TEU, which foresees unanimity for all major decisions.

While the continued dominance of national representatives in the PSC certainly reflects the political choice not to entrust a supranational body such as the Commission with the independent exercise of foreign, security and defence policy, we should be aware of the tangible benefits of this construction. Arguably, the effective realisation of the CFSP benefits decisively from the political expertise, personal networks, international clout and logistical support of the Member States.[61] This benefit of the intergovernmental method is particularly pronounced in the CSDP given the national responsibility for the improvement and deployment of military capabilities.[62] The intergovernmental structure of the CFSP and CSDP executive guarantees that it is not detached from national capitals and ministries upon whose support it crucially depends. Without the continued Member State support CFSP and CSDP would soon become lame policies; the intergovernmental structure of the

---

[59]See the EEAS Decision, above notes 1940.

[60]From a constructivist or neo-institutional standpoint, the integration into the EEAS may ease earlier tensions, mirroring the 'Brusselisation' effect after the formation of intergovernmental CFSP staff mentioned in notes 24 and 25 above.

[61]For the crucial role of the Member States in implementing the CFSP see Art. 26.3 TEU as well as Duke and Vanhoonacker (2006), pp. 369–376.

[62]See Art. 42.3 TEU.

CFSP executive supports that decisions in Brussels are effectively being implemented by the Member States.

As an institution composed of Member State representatives the PSC and the administrative bodies within its orbit maintain an ambiguous relationship with the HR/VP. While an agent of the HR/VP will in future chair the PSC meetings (instead of the Member State holding the rotating Council Presidency),[63] its decisions are taken by the Member States. The HR/VP representative may steer the PSC towards agreement, but does not possess the power to impose his/her view in the absence of consensus.[64] The HR/VP and the EEAS may thus exercise considerable influence in practice, but are nonetheless bound by the substantive policy decisions upon which the Member States agree in the PSC or the Council. The HR/VP is no foreign minister who independently 'conducts'[65] the Union's foreign policy, but continues to be integrated into the Union's sophisticated decision-making procedures, which moreover differ between the intergovernmental and supranational branches of European foreign affairs. It remains to be seen how the institutional practice evolves in this respect and which channels are developed in practice to guide and control the Union's foreign policy decisions. On this basis future contribution will be able to conclude how the intergovernmental branch of the Union's foreign affairs executive governs post Lisbon.

5 Conclusion

Our analysis of the Political and Security Committee illustrates both the continued intergovernmentalism of CFSP and the executive character of most decisions. Both these conclusions help us to embed the changes brought forward by the Lisbon Treaty into the wider institutional and constitutional context of European foreign affairs. More specifically we need to acknowledge that the Council has set up a significant administrative infrastructure for the realisation of foreign, security and defence policies, whose powers rival the supranational prerogatives of the Commission in other policy fields. This genuine intergovernmental bureaucracy consists of different components which concentrate on the CFSP and CSDP staff in the Council Secretariat and the EEAS, the PSC, the Council working groups and

---

[63]See Art. 2.2 European Council Decision 2009/881/EU *on the exercise of the Presidency of the Council, and on the chairmanship of preparatory bodies of the Council*, O.J. L 315/50 (2009); moreover, annex II to the implementing Council Decision 2009/908/EU, O.J. L 322/28 (2009) specifies the modalities for appointment 'on the basis of competence, while ensuring adequate geographical balance and transparency.'

[64]Both the HR and the EEAS are – as the 'voice' of the CFSP – bound to respect the position of the Member States; cf. Arts. 18, 26 and 27 TEU as well as Thym (2009), p. 342 and Kaufmann-Bühler and Meyer-Landruth (2004), Art. 24 para 14.

[65]Article 18.2 TEU remains overambitious with its formulation.

several agencies. Their formation supports a collegial impulse of the intergovernmental, Brussels-based institutions which facilitates the convergence of policy preferences. As the 'mind' and 'brain cells' of foreign policy decision-making the CFSP executive plays a crucial role in identifying common positions and methods for their realisation.

The non-legislative character of CFSP diplomacy and CSDP operations explains the limited practical relevance of the Treaty's formal decision-making procedures. In the day-to-day management of European foreign policy, the PSC and the various bodies it oversees enjoy an extended autonomy – reflecting the difference between domestic law-making and foreign and defence policy, whose success crucially depends on the persuasiveness and credibility of its policies, the operative capabilities and the support of the Member States. Public lawyers should recognise this executive character of CFSP diplomacy or CSDP operations and examine institutional mechanisms for the control of the Union's foreign affairs executive. Within this context the CFSP's and CSDP's continued intergovernmentalism in the age of the Lisbon Treaty supports the identification of a suitable mechanism to hold the executive to account vis-à-vis national and European oversight bodies. Again, the PSC plays a prominent role. Although it is itself an executive body composed of unelected national officials, the Treaty explicitly sanctions its oversight function within the Council's intergovernmental executive.

References

Allen D (1998) Who speaks for Europe? The search for an effective and coherent external policy. In: Peterson J, Sjursen H (eds) A common foreign policy for Europe? Competing visions of the CFSP. Routledge, Abingdon, pp 41–58

Bieber R (2002) Democratic control of international relations of the European Union. In: Cannizzaro E (ed) The European Union as an actor in international relations. Kluwer, The Hague, pp 105–116

Christiansen T (2002) Out of the shadows: the general secretariat of the council of ministers. J Legis Stud 8:80–97

Cremer H-J (2007) Artikel 25 EUV. In: Calliess C, Ruffert M (eds) Das Verfassungsrecht der Europäischen Union mit Europäischer Grundrechtecharta. Kommentar, 3rd edn. C.H. Beck, München

Cremona M (1999) External relations and external competence: the emergence of an integrated policy. In: Craig P, de Búrca G (eds) The evolution of EU law. OUP, Oxford, pp 137–176

Cremona M (2003) The draft constitutional treaty: external relations and external action. CML Rev 40:1347–1366

Curtin D (2004) European Union executives: out of the shade, into the sunshine? In: de Zwaan J, Jans J, Nelissen F (eds) The EU: an ongoing process of integration. Liber Amicorum Alfred E. Kellermann. T.M.C. Asser, The Hague, pp 97–110

Curtin D (2009) Executive power of the European Union. Law, practices, and the living constitution. OUP, Oxford

Dehousse F (2005) La Politique étrangère et de sécurité commune. In: Dony M, Louis J-V (eds) Commentaire J. Mégret 12 – relations extérieures, 2nd edn. Université libre de Bruxelles, pp 439–588

Denza E (2002) The intergovernmental pillars of the European Union. OUP, Oxford

Dietrich S (2006) Europäische Sicherheits- und Verteidigungspolitik ESVP. Nomos, Baden-Baden
Dijkstra H (2008) The council secretariat's role in the common foreign and security policy. EFA Rev 18:149–166
Duke S (2005) The Linchpin COPS: assessing the workings and institutional relations of the Political and Security Committee, EIPA Working Paper 2005/W/05
Duke S (2008) Peculiarities in the institutionalisation of CFSP and ESDP. In: Blockmans S (ed) The European Union and international crisis management. Legal and policy aspects. T.M.C. Asser, The Hague, pp 75–106
Duke S, Vanhoonacker S (2006) Administrative governance and CFSP. In: Hofmann H, Türk A (eds) EU administrative governance. Elgar, Cheltenham, pp 361–387
Eeckhout P (2005) Does Europe's constitution stop at the water's edge? Law and policy in the EU's external relations. Europa Law Publishing, Groningen
Ginsburg R (1997) The EU's CFSP: The politics of procedure. In: Holland M (ed) Common foreign and security policy: the record and reforms. Pinter, London, pp 297–318
Glarbo K (2001) Reconstructing a common foreign and security policy. In: Christiansen T et al (eds) The social construction of Europe. Sage, Thousand Oaks, pp 140–157
Harlow C (2002) Accountability in the European Union. OUP, Oxford
Howorth J (2007) Security and defence policy in the European Union. Palgrave, New York
Juncos A, Reynolds C (2007) The political and security committee: governing in the shadow. EFA Rev 12:127–147
Kaufmann-Bühler W, Meyer-Landruth N (2004) Art. 18-28 EUV (Nizza-Fassung). In: Grabitz E, Hilf M (eds) Das Recht der Europäischen Union 24. EL. C.H. Beck, München
Oliver D (2009) Executive accountability: a key concept. In: Verhey L, Kiiver P, Loeffen S (eds) Political accountability and European integration. Europa Law Publishing, Groningen, pp 9–32
Regelsberger E (2004) Die Gemeinsame Außen- und Sicherheitspolitik der EU. Nomos, Baden-Baden
Smith M (2004) Europe's common foreign and security policy. CUP, Cambridge
Thym D (2004) Reforming Europe's common foreign and security policy. Eur Law J 10:5–22
Thym D (2009) Foreign affairs. In: von Bogdandy A, Bast J (eds) Principles of European constitutional law, 2nd edn. Hart, Oxford, pp 309–343
Thym D (2010) Europäisches Wehrverwaltungsrecht. In: Terhechte J (ed) Verwaltungsrecht der Europäischen Union: Zur Ausdifferenzierung und Globalisierung der europäischen Verwaltungsrechtsordnung (Sect. 17). Nomos, Baden-Baden
Tonra B (2003) Constructing the CFSP: the utility of a cognitive approach. JCMSt 41:731–756
von Bogdandy A (2010) Founding principles of EU law: a theoretical and doctrinal sketch. Eur Law J 16:95–111
Wessel R (1999) The European Union's foreign and security policy. A legal institutional perspective. Kluwer, The Hague

Decisions on Operational Action and Union Positions: Back to the Future?

Aurel Sari

1 Introduction

The Treaty of Lisbon,[1] which was signed on 13 December 2007 and entered into force on 1 December 2009, has made extensive changes to the legal framework governing the Common Foreign and Security Policy (CFSP).[2] In fact, not a single provision of Title V of the Treaty on European Union (TEU) dealing with the CFSP has remained unaffected by the most recent round of treaty revision. In addition to making numerous substantive and institutional amendments, the Lisbon Treaty has also recast the legal instruments available for the conduct of the CFSP. In the past, the Union could rely on three specific instruments in this area: common positions, joint actions and common strategies.[3] In an attempt to simplify this line-up, the Lisbon Treaty has now replaced these three instruments with a single legal act: Union decisions.

The simplification of the Union's instruments was a key objective of the reform process launched by the Laeken European Council in December 2001.[4] This chapter suggests that the manner in which the Treaty of Lisbon gave effect to this objective in the context of the CFSP signals a return, in essence, to a state of

[1]Treaty of Lisbon Amending the Treaty on European Union and the Treaty Establishing the European Community, 13 December 2007, O.J. C 306/1 (2007).

[2]A consolidated version of the TEU can be found at O.J. C 83/13 (2010).

[3]However, as is evident from Art. 12 TEU-Nice, these were not the only instruments available under the CFSP. See Denza (2002), pp. 134–135; Eeckhout (2005), pp. 407–408.

[4]Laeken Declaration on the Future of the European Union, Annex I to Presidency Conclusions, European Council Meeting in Laeken, 14 and 15 December 2001.

A. Sari (✉)
School of Law, University of Exeter, Cornwall Campus, Penryn, Cornwall TR10 9EZ, UK
e-mail: A.Sari@exeter.ac.uk

H.-J. Blanke and S. Mangiameli (eds.), *The European Union after Lisbon*,

DOI 10.1007/978-3-642-19507-5_22,

affairs that existed under the Maastricht Treaty. While not exactly regressive in its effects, this return to an earlier set of arrangements cannot be described as a truly progressive development either, since the Lisbon Treaty dealt with the simplification of the CFSP's instruments in a rather superficial manner. Indeed, it seems fair to say that the Lisbon Treaty has merely rearranged what was already lying around in the CFSP's toolbox without taking the trouble to sharpen those tools for the job at hand. The present chapter falls into two main parts. Section 2 charts the historical evolution of common positions and joint actions from mere policy objectives of European foreign policy cooperation to formal legal instruments of the CFSP. Section 3 examines how the simplification of the Union's acts was implemented in the CFSP and highlights some of the shortcomings of the Lisbon Treaty in this area.

2 Common Positions and Joint Action: From Policy Objectives to Legal Instruments

Western European integration in the post-war era developed at different speeds along separate economic, political and military strands. The demise of the European Defence Community and the European Political Community during the first half of the 1950s illustrated not only the unsuitability of the Monnet method in the field of foreign policy and defence, but it also meant that European cooperation in these areas would commence subject to a considerable delay and develop in an incremental fashion.[5] When the Member States of the European Economic Community (EEC) finally decided to extend the scope of European integration to foreign policy matters in 1970, their ambitions were decidedly modest. Instead of pursuing grand institutional designs, the Member States focused their efforts on promoting cooperation between themselves on an intergovernmental level in areas of mutual interest. Over the next three decades, European foreign policy cooperation became increasingly more formalised, developing its own dedicated instruments and decision-making procedures.[6] Since the simplification of the legal instruments of the CFSP by the Treaty of Lisbon may be understood as a partial reversal of this gradual process of specialisation, it is useful to briefly revisit the key stages of its evolution.

[5]Among the considerable body of literature on the European Defence Community, see in particular Fursdon (1980); Ruane (2000); Legaret and Martin-Dumesnil (1953). On the European Political Community, see Griffiths (2000); Berthold (2003). Generally, see Duke (2000).

[6]See Smith (2001).

2.1 European Political Cooperation

In 1970, the Member States of the EEC launched the European Political Cooperation (EPC) to serve as a framework for the regular exchange of information and consultation among themselves on matters of foreign policy.[7] The EPC consisted of a set of broadly worded arrangements and understandings designed to enable the Member States to adopt a common attitude on the international scene and to take joint action where they considered this feasible and desirable.[8] To safeguard its informal and intergovernmental nature, the Member States pursued the EPC outside the framework of the Community legal order, setting out the principles governing its operation in a series of reports prepared by their Foreign Ministers.[9] As a process aimed at coordinating national policies, the EPC's output was precisely that: increased consultation and coordination between the Member States leading to the adoption of common positions and joint action whenever possible.[10] Such common positions and joint action mainly took the form of diplomatic declarations and *démarches* and, once the Member States learnt to utilise the Community for this purpose, the imposition of economic sanctions on third countries.[11] Unsurprisingly, the EPC did not develop its own dedicated legal instruments to give effect to these measures,[12] but instead relied on decisions made collectively by the Member States on the intergovernmental level.[13]

[7]On the EPC generally, see Nuttall (1992).

[8]First Report of the Foreign Ministers to the Heads of State or Government of the Member States of the European Community (Luxembourg Report), 27 October 1970, in Hill and Smith (2000), p. 77.

[9]In addition to the Luxembourg Report of 1970, see in particular the Second Report of the Foreign Ministers to the Heads of State or Government of the Member States of the European Community (Copenhagen Report), 23 July 1973 and the Report Issued by the Foreign Ministers of the Ten on European Political Co-operation (London Report), 13 October 1981, both in Hill and Smith (2000), p. 84 and p. 115. See Allen and Wallace (1982).

[10]For instance, when the European Council resolved in 1983 'to strengthen and develop European Political Cooperation through the elaboration and adoption of joint positions and joint actions', what it had in mind was to increase collective action by the Member States. See Solemn Declaration on European Union by the European Council (Stuttgart Declaration), 19 June 1983, in Hill and Smith (2000), p. 131.

[11]On sanctions and the relationship between EPC and the EC, see Nuttall (1987); Holland (1991a, b); Koutrakos (2001), pp. 49–66. On the diverse output of the EPC more generally, see Rummel (1988).

[12]Stein (1990), p. 184.

[13]Gröne (1993), pp. 60–62. For a detailed discussion of the legal nature of these decisions, see Jürgens (1994), pp. 128–181.

While the EPC's institutional structure strengthened over time, its basic purpose and character remained unchanged even after the Single European Act (SEA) provided it with a treaty basis.[14] In Art. 30 SEA, the High Contracting Parties undertook to inform and consult each other 'to ensure that their combined influence is exercised as effectively as possible through co-ordination, the convergence of their positions and the implementation of joint action.'[15] In terms of output, the SEA thus envisaged a clearly defined three-stage process whereby the EPC progressed from consultation to policy formulation and implementation.[16] The Member States would exchange information and consult one another on a regular basis on any foreign policy question of general interest. Such consultations would enable them to formulate common positions on specific matters. Finally, by gradually defining common principles and objectives, the Member States would increase their capacity for joint action.

2.2 The Maastricht Treaty

The Maastricht Treaty turned a new chapter in the development of European foreign policy cooperation when it replaced the EPC with the CFSP in 1993.[17] However, the newly created CFSP did not herald a radical departure from the basic features of the EPC.[18] The Maastricht Treaty retained the three-stage character of European foreign policy cooperation, albeit the wording of the relevant provisions now differentiated between these distinct stages less clearly than Art. 30.2.a SEA did. According to Art. J.1.3 TEU-Maastricht, the Union was to pursue the objectives of the CFSP

- By establishing systematic cooperation between Member States in the conduct of policy, in accordance with Art. J.2
- By gradually implementing, in accordance with Art. J.3, joint action in the areas in which the Member States have important interests in common.

Reading Art. J.1.3 together with Art. J.2 reveals that systematic cooperation between the Member States in the conduct of policy was founded on their mutual

[14]On Art. 30 SEA, see Nuttall (1985); Perrakis (1988); Murphy (1989).

[15]Art. 30.2(a) SEA.

[16]See Art. 30.2 SEA.

[17]For a useful overview of the negotiating history, see Laursen and Vanhoonacker (1992); de Schoutheete de Tervarent (1997). For a comparison of the CFSP with the EPC, see Edwards and Nuttall (1994).

[18]Rather than endow the European Community with legal competences in the field of foreign and security policy, the Member States decided to maintain the separation between the Community legal order and their cooperation in foreign policy and security matters in the form of the EU's pillar structure. See Curtin (1993).

duty to 'inform and consult one another within the Council on any matter of foreign and security policy of general interest.'[19] As in the case of the EPC, the purpose of this duty of mutual information and consultation was to allow the adoption of common positions as defined in Art. J.2.2 and the implementation of joint action as foreseen in Art. J.1.3.

Like the EPC before it, the CFSP was still essentially conceived as a process of systematic cooperation progressing from regular consultation among the Member States to the formulation of common positions and the gradual implementation of joint action.[20] Nevertheless, the Maastricht Treaty put this process of systematic cooperation on a more formal footing in two important respects. First, it embedded the CFSP within the institutional framework of the EU.[21] Whereas previously the Member States were the sole actors of the EPC, driving it forward in their capacity as sovereign States,[22] the Maastricht Treaty now entrusted the Council with various responsibilities in relation to the CFSP. Amongst other things, the Council was tasked to ensure that the Member States comply with the principle of loyal cooperation,[23] to define common positions whenever it deemed necessary to do so[24] and to decide, on the basis of general guidelines from the European Council, that a matter should be the subject of joint action.[25] The Council thus assumed an independent role in the formulation and implementation of the CFSP alongside the Member States and did not just serve as a convenient institutional backdrop for their intergovernmental cooperation and collective action.[26] Second, Art. J.3 TEU-Maastricht set out in considerable detail the procedure governing the adoption of joint action and the rights and duties that arose for the Member States in this context. These detailed procedural rules reflected the overall turn of the Maastricht Treaty towards employing more precise legal language in the sphere of foreign and security policy and thus imposing tighter obligations on the Member States than Art. 30 SEA did.[27]

---

[19] Article J.2.1 TEU-Maastricht.

[20] Cf. Jürgens (1994), p. 341.

[21] Notably, Art. J.1 TEU-Maastricht declared that the CFSP should be defined and implemented by the newly created 'Union and its Member States'. However, this formulation was apparently intended to stress the intergovernmental nature of the second pillar. See Fink-Hooijer (1994), p. 177.

[22] Thus, in Art. 30.1 SEA they undertook to 'endeavour jointly to formulate and implement a European foreign policy' in their capacity as 'High Contracting Parties', rather than as Member States of the EEC.

[23] Article J.1.4 TEU-Maastricht.

[24] Article J.2.2 TEU-Maastricht.

[25] Article J.3.1 TEU-Maastricht.

[26] See also Jürgens (1994), p. 353.

[27] Denza (2002), p. 55.

2.3 Subsequent Reconceptualisation

Despite the increased institutional and legal density of the CFSP compared to the EPC, the Maastricht Treaty did not treat common positions or joint action as legal instruments of the CFSP analogous to, for instance, Community law directives or regulations. Instead, they continued to represent the specific outcome to which European foreign policy cooperation aspired: the harmonisation of national positions and the implementation of collective action by the Member States and the Union on the international scene. This point is reflected in the wording of the relevant provisions of Title V, which clearly differentiated between Council decisions as legal instruments on the one hand, and common positions and joint action as their subject matter on the other hand.[28] Decision-making in the area of the CFSP was governed by Art. J.8, which set out the Council's competence in the following terms: the 'Council shall take the decisions necessary for defining and implementing the common foreign and security policy on the basis of the general guidelines adopted by the European Council'.[29] Article J.2.2 TEU-Maastricht directed the Council to define common positions to which the national policies of the Member States had to conform, while Art. J.3.1 provided that the 'Council shall decide ... that a matter should be the subject of joint action'.[30] Under the scheme of the Maastricht Treaty, the Council would therefore define and implement the CFSP primarily by taking decisions on common positions and joint action.

The early practice of the Council confirms this reading. Following the entry into force of the Maastricht Treaty on 1 November 1993, the Council gave effect to common positions and joint action agreed to by the Member States in the form of Council decisions. Thus, on 8 November 1993, the Council adopted a decision 'concerning the joint action decided on by the Council on the basis of Art. J.3 of the Treaty on European Union on support for the convoying of humanitarian aid in Bosnia and Herzegovina',[31] while on 22 November 1993, it adopted a decision 93/614/CFSP 'on the common position defined on the basis of Art. J.2 of the Treaty on European Union with regard to the reduction of economic relations with Libya'.[32] Their respective wording indicates that these decisions constituted the formal legal instruments adopted by the Council on the basis of Arts. J.2 and J.3 TEU-Maastricht, whereas the common position and joint action they defined merely represented their envisaged outcome.

---

[28]See also MacLeod et al. (1996), p. 418.

[29]Article J.8.2 TEU-Maastricht.

[30]Emphasis added.

[31]Council Decision 93/603/CFSP *concerning the joint action on support for the convoying of humanitarian aid in Bosnia and Herzegovina*, O.J. L 286/1 (1993).

[32]Council Decision 93/614/CFSP *on the common position with regard to the reduction of economic relations with Libya*, O.J. L 295/7 (1993).

This initial practice soon changed, however. From November 1994 onwards, the Council began to adopt common positions in their own right, rather than in the guise of Council decisions. The first such instrument appears to be the Common Position of 28 November 1994 adopted on the basis of Art. J.2 TEU-Maastricht on the objectives and priorities of the EU towards Ukraine.[33] In late 1995, this new practice was also extended to joint actions; the first such instrument seems to be the Joint Action of 11 December 1995 on the basis of Art. J.3 TEU-Maastricht concerning the participation of the EU in the implementing structures of the peace plan for Bosnia-Herzegovina.[34] It is unclear what prompted this change of course and why it affected common positions and joint actions at different points in time. One clue may lie in a report prepared by the Council at the request of the European Council on the likely development of the CFSP, which described joint action 'as a means for the definition and implementation by the Union of a policy in the framework of the CFSP in specific issues'.[35] The report plainly takes a functional view of common positions and joint action as means or instruments for the definition and implementation of the CFSP by the Union, rather than seeing them as policy processes or outcomes of European foreign policy cooperation between the Member States. It is likely that the independent institutional role assumed by the Council in the CFSP has played a significant role in the emergence of this new functional understanding of common positions and joint action and their subsequent reconceputalisation as formal legal instruments of the CFSP.

2.4 The Amsterdam Treaty

The Amsterdam Treaty confirmed and consolidated this change in the Council's practice relating to Arts. J.2 and J.3 TEU-Maastricht. According to a report prepared by the Italian Presidency in June 1996, a 'fairly general desire' prevailed among the representatives of the Member States at the intergovernmental conference convened pursuant to Art. N TEU-Maastricht in favour of clarifying the scope of the CFSP's instruments.[36] A number of amendments were proposed to this end

[33]Council Common Position 94/779/CFSP *on the objectives and priorities of the European Union towards Ukraine*, O.J. L 313/1 (1994).

[34]Council Joint Action 95/545/CFSP *with regard to the participation of the Union in the implementing structures of the peace plan for Bosnia-Herzegovina*, O.J. L 309/2 (1995).

[35]Report to the European Council in Lisbon on the likely development of the Common Foreign and Security Policy (CFSP) with a view to identifying areas open to joint action vis-à-vis particular countries or groups of countries, Annex I to Lisbon European Council Conclusions, 26 and 27 June 1992, SN 3321/1/92, p. 29.

[36]Strengthened External Action Capability, 24 May 1996, CONF 3850/96, p. 5. Indeed, the need to distinguish more carefully between common positions and joint actions in order to strengthen the consistency of the Union's external action was already noted by members of the Reflection Group established in preparation of the intergovernmental conference and by commentators. See

in a draft prepared by the Irish Presidency.[37] The draft text would have transformed Art. J.1.3 TEU-Maastricht into a separate provision stating that the Union should pursue the objectives of the CFSP by three means: by establishing systematic cooperation between Member States in the conduct of policy and by adopting common positions and joint actions.[38] The next three articles would have defined the key features of these measures in turn.[39] In addition, a separate provision was drafted to regulate the voting procedures governing the adoption of joint actions and other decisions taken under Title V of the TEU.[40] The obvious appeal of this scheme was that it identified the three traditional stages of European foreign policy cooperation in much clearer terms than the Maastricht Treaty, but at the same time managed to consolidate the function of common positions and joint actions as formal legal instruments of the CFSP.

The actual amendments introduced by the Amsterdam Treaty were in some respects less attractive. The Amsterdam Treaty followed the Irish draft by converting what used to be Art. J.1.3 into a separate provision. This new provision, Art. 12 TEU-Amsterdam, provided that the Union should pursue the CFSP by

- Defining the principles of and general guidelines for the common foreign and security policy
- Deciding on common strategies
- Adopting joint actions
- Adopting common positions
- Strengthening systematic cooperation between Member States in the conduct of policy.

The purpose of Art. 12 is not clear and its wording is confusing. It is neither an exhaustive catalogue of the legal instruments of the CFSP nor a reliable guide to the process of policy formulation in this area. While Art. 12 lists three legal instruments of the CFSP, including the newly created common strategies, it fails to mention others, such as international agreements concluded by the Council in accordance with Art. 24 TEU-Amsterdam.[41] Nor does Art. 12 respect the progressive character of the three traditional stages of European foreign policy cooperation, given that

Reflection Group's Report, 5 December 1995, SN 520/95 (Reflex 21), para 150; Regelsberger (1997), pp. 79–80.

[37]Adapting the European Union for the Benefit of Its Peoples and Preparing it for the Future: A General Outline for a Draft Revision of the Treaties (Dublin II), 5 December 1996, CONF 2500/96.

[38]Dublin II, 5 December 1996, CONF 2500/96, p. 82.

[39]Dublin II, 5 December 1996, CONF 2500/96, pp. 82–84.

[40]Dublin II, 5 December 1996, CONF 2500/96, pp. 85–86.

[41]Given the uncertainty surrounding the international legal personality of the EU, a lively debate has ensued in the literature as to whether international agreements concluded by the Council under Art. 24 TEU-Amsterdam were instruments of the Member States acting collectively or instruments of the Union. For an overview of this issue and the relevant literature, see Sari (2008), pp. 69–82.

it relegates systematic cooperation to the very end of the list. In fact, Title V of the TEU-Amsterdam stands the three traditional stages of cooperation on their head, reversing their logical order: it regulates joint actions in Art. 14, common positions in Art. 15 and the duty of mutual consultation and information sharing in Art. 16.

By contrast, the Amsterdam Treaty fared better when it came to distinguishing between common positions and joint actions more clearly.[42] For the first time, it identified the purpose of these two instruments. According to Art. 14 TEU-Amsterdam, joint actions 'shall address specific situations where operational action by the Union is deemed to be required', while Art. 15 specified that common positions 'shall define the approach of the Union to a particular matter of a geographical or thematic nature.' Moreover, the Amsterdam Treaty evidently treated joint actions and common positions not as policy outcomes or intergovernmental forms of cooperation, but as formal legal instruments of the CFSP in line with the Council's practice. This is reflected above all in the fact that Arts. 14 and 15 directed the Council to *adopt* joint actions and common positions, rather than to decide on their subject matter or to define them.[43] This wording not only indicates the formal nature of the procedure, but also suggests that the instruments thus adopted are legal acts of the Council as an institution.[44]

3 The Treaty of Lisbon: Back Again at Maastricht?

In 2003, the Treaty of Nice introduced a number of amendments to Title V of the TEU, mostly to reflect the launch of the European Security and Defence Policy.[45] Except for Art. 24 TEU concerning international agreements, the provisions dealing with the instruments of the CFSP remained unaffected by these amendments. Far more extensive changes to the CFSP as a whole were proposed in the Draft Treaty Establishing a Constitution for Europe (TCE) drawn up by the European Convention and submitted to the European Council in Rome on 18 July 2003.[46] This document served as the basis for the TCE, which was signed by the representatives of the Member States on 29 October 2004.[47] Following the failure of the Constitutional Treaty, most of the amendments it envisaged for the CFSP, including those relating to its instruments, found their way into the Lisbon Treaty.

---

[42] Monar (1997), pp. 425–426; Mahncke (2001), pp. 236–240.

[43] Wessel (1999), p. 156; Denza (2002), p. 147.

[44] Dashwood (1998), p. 1032.

[45] For an assessment of these changes, see Duke (2001); Österdahl (2001); Wessel (2003).

[46] Draft Treaty establishing a Constitution for Europe, 18 July 2003, CONV 850/03. See Cremona (2003), pp. 1352–1361; Howorth (2004); Thym (2004).

[47] Treaty Establishing a Constitution for Europe, 29 October 2004, O.J. C 310/1 (2004). See Naert (2005); Trybus (2006); Koutrakos (2006), pp. 481–506.

3.1 The Need to Simplify

Less than 1 year following the signing of the Treaty of Nice, the European Council launched an ambitious treaty reform process aimed at making the EU more democratic, more transparent and more efficient. One of the objectives of this process was the simplification of the Union's instruments and decision-making processes. In its Laeken Declaration of December 2001, the European Council observed that

> [s]uccessive amendments to the Treaty have on each occasion resulted in a proliferation of instruments, and directives have gradually evolved towards more and more detailed legislation. The key question is therefore whether the Union's various instruments should not be better defined and whether their number should not be reduced.[48]

These issues were examined in detailed by the Working Group on Simplification established by the European Convention, which was convened by the Laeken European Council to pave the way for an intergovernmental conference. A broad consensus prevailed among the members of the Working Group 'on the need to reduce the excessive number of instruments available to the Union and the Community for exercising their competences.'[49] This consensus was fuelled by the widely held view that the multiplication of the instruments across the EU's three pillars and the lack of clarity concerning their exact functions and distinguishing features has over the years led to unnecessary complexity and even legal uncertainty.[50]

This general perception certainly seemed to fit the CFSP.[51] On the one hand, Title V of the TEU made provision for what to the casual observer must have seemed like a bewildering array of legal acts and forms of action, including systematic cooperation between Member States in the conduct of policy,[52] the principles of and general guidelines for the CFSP adopted by the European Council,[53] common strategies,[54] joint actions,[55] common positions,[56] mutual consultation and information,[57] sui generis decisions of the Council and international

---

[48]Laeken Declaration on the Future of the European Union, Annex I to Presidency Conclusions, European Council Meeting in Laeken, 14 and 15 December 2001, p. 5.

[49]Mandate of Working Group IX on the Simplification of Legislative Procedures and Instruments, 17 September 2002, CONV 271/02, p. 6.

[50]See e.g. Simplifying Legislative Procedures and Instruments – Paper by Mr. M. Michel Petite, 31 October 2002, WG IX – WD 08; How to simplify the instruments of the Union? – Paper by Prof. Koen Lenaerts, 6 November 2002, WG IX – WD 07.

[51]See The Legal Instruments: Present System, 13 June 2002, CONV 162/02, pp. 7–8; EU External Action, 3 July 2002, CONV 161/02, pp. 6–10.

[52]Article 12 TEU-Nice.

[53]Article 13.1 TEU-Nice.

[54]Article 13.2 TEU-Nice.

[55]Article 14 TEU-Nice.

[56]Article 15 TEU-Nice.

[57]Article 16 TEU-Nice.

agreements.[58] In addition, a range of informal instruments not expressly mentioned in the TEU, such as declarations, statements, codes of conduct and conclusions adopted by the Council and the Presidency, continued to play an important role in the CFSP.[59] On the other hand, certain ambiguities continued to surround joint actions and common positions, despite the attempts of the Amsterdam Treaty to differentiate between these two instruments more sharply. In principle, joint actions were meant to address operational questions, while common positions were reserved for defining the Union's overall approach to a matter. However, in practice, common positions frequently expressed detailed and significant operational objectives, making the distinction between these two types of instruments appear less certain.[60]

3.2 Drafting the Constitutional Treaty

One solution to these problems was proposed to the Working Group on Simplification by Jean-Claude Piris, the Director-General of the Council Legal Service.[61] In order to drastically reduce the number of legal instruments available to the institutions, Piris suggested that the diverse concepts of 'decision' employed in the Treaties should be replaced by a single generic definition applicable in all areas of the Union's activities, including the CFSP. This standardised definition was to be modelled on the notion of a decision found in Art. 14.2 of the former Treaty establishing the European Coal and Steel Community, which simply provided that decisions 'shall be binding in their entirety.' According to Piris, such standardisation would not have had any appreciable legal effects in the sphere of the CFSP.[62] Indeed, reducing the concept of a decision to the notion of a legal act that is binding in its entirety is almost tautological in its simplicity. It certainly encapsulates the essence of joint actions and common positions as legal instruments of the CFSP, which is precisely to be binding in their entirety. Piris thus concluded that joint actions and common positions could be renamed 'decisions' while

---

[58] Article 24 TEU-Nice.

[59] For example, European Union Code of Conduct on Arms Exports, 5 June 1998, 8675/2/98 REV2.

[60] For example, Common Position 2003/805/CFSP *on the universalisation and reinforcement of multilateral agreements in the field of non-proliferation of weapons of mass destruction and means of delivery*, O.J. L 302/34 (2003).

[61] Simplification of legislative procedures and instruments – Paper by Mr Jean-Claude Piris, 6 November 2002, WG IX – WD 06.

[62] Simplification of legislative procedures and instruments – Paper by Mr Jean-Claude Piris, 6 November 2002, WG IX – WD 06, pp. 9–11.

retaining their specialised functions.[63] He further suggested that 'principles and general guidelines' referred to in Art. 12 TEU should be removed from that provision, considering that they are not a legal instrument.[64] Finally, Piris recommended abolishing common strategies altogether, as this instrument had not lived up to the expectations of the drafters of the Amsterdam Treaty and offered no added value to the CFSP.[65]

Some of these recommendations have proved more influential than others. The Convention decided to adopt a single provision, Art. 32 of the Draft TCE, setting out the legal instruments available to the institutions under all policy areas of the Union. This included 'European decisions', which the first paragraph of Art. 32 defined in reliance on the former Treaty establishing the European Coal and Steel Community as 'a non-legislative act, binding in its entirety'. As one of the preparatory documents to the Draft Treaty explained, this broader definition was chosen partly so as to 'make decisions the legal instrument in the CFSP area, in place of "the joint action" and the "common position".'[66] Accordingly, Art. III-198 of the Draft Treaty replaced joint actions with European decisions on actions of the Union, while Art. III-199 replaced common positions with European decisions on positions of the Union. Contrary to the recommendations of the Director-General of the Council Legal Service, the European Convention decided to retain common strategies on the advice of its Working Group on External Relations,[67] which seemed prepared to give this instrument a second chance.[68] However, common strategies too were renamed, becoming European decisions of the European Council on the strategic interests and objectives of the Union under Art. III-194.[69] Nor did the European Convention follow the Director-General's proposal to remove the reference to the 'principles and general guidelines' of the CFSP from Art. III-195.3 of the Draft Treaty, the successor of Art. 12 TEU-Nice. However, it did delete the reference to common strategies, or European decisions of the European Council on the strategic interests and objectives of the Union as they

[63]Simplification of legislative procedures and instruments – Paper by Mr Jean-Claude Piris, 6 November 2002, WG IX – WD 06, pp. 12.

[64]Simplification of legislative procedures and instruments – Paper by Mr Jean-Claude Piris, 6 November 2002, WG IX – WD 06, pp. 13.

[65]Simplification of legislative procedures and instruments – Paper by Mr Jean-Claude Piris, 6 November 2002, WG IX – WD 06, pp. 13.

[66]Draft of Arts. 24–33 of the Constitutional Treaty, 26 February 2003, CONV 571/03, p. 10.

[67]Draft Articles on External Action in the Constitutional Treaty, 23 April 2003, CONV 685/03, pp. 26–27.

[68]Final report of Working Group VII on External Action, 16 December 2002, CONV 459/02, pp. 3–4.

[69]In addition, Art. III-194 expressly directed the European Council to adopt such European decisions across all areas of the external action of the Union, not just in the context of the CFSP.

now became, from that provision. This is surprising, given that such European decisions were clearly conceived as one of the legal instruments of the CFSP.

The relevant provisions of the Draft Treaty were subsequently incorporated into the TCE. European decisions accordingly became one of the instruments of the EU under Art. I-33 TCE, which in the context of the CFSP would be available to the institutions in the form of European decisions on the strategic interests and objectives of the Union (Art. III-293.1), European decisions on actions to be undertaken by the Union (Art. III-297) and European decisions on positions to be taken by the Union (Art. III-298).

3.3 The Lisbon Treaty: A Sense of Déjà Vu

Despite the failure of the Constitutional Treaty, most of the changes introduced by that text to the CFSP were carried over into the Lisbon Treaty. Decisions (rather than 'European decisions') have become one of the legal acts of the Union under Art. 288 TFEU. Decisions have also become the standard legal instrument of the CFSP: joint actions have been replaced by 'decisions on actions to be undertaken by the Union' adopted by the Council under Art. 28 TEU, while 'decisions on positions to be taken by the Union' adopted pursuant to Art. 29 TEU have now taken the place of common positions. As in previous texts, common strategies live on in Art. 22 TEU, which directs the European Council to adopt decisions on the strategic interests and objectives of the Union.

Seen from an evolutionary perspective, this development can be understood as a return to the state of play under the Maastricht Treaty, where decisions constituted the basic form of legal action under the CFSP. The Council's general competence to adopt decisions is currently set out in Art. 26 TEU, which in almost identical terms to Art. J.8 TEU-Maastricht declares that the 'Council shall frame the common foreign and security policy and take the decisions necessary for defining and implementing it on the basis of the general guidelines and strategic lines defined by the European Council.' The decisions adopted on the basis of Arts. 28 and 29 TEU concerning Union actions and positions are therefore simply manifestations of the same legal act employed for different practical ends, rather than distinct legal instruments. This corresponds exactly to the arrangements put into place by the Maastricht Treaty, whereby decisions represented the formal legal instrument adopted by the Council and common positions and joint action merely formed their respective subject matter. The Director-General of the Council Legal Service was therefore right to suggest that joint actions, common positions and common strategies could be replaced by Council decisions without too much difficulty, whilst retaining their separate functions: we have been here before.

3.4 A Conservative Approach?

Nevertheless, this levelling of the CFSP's instruments does raise certain questions. First, are CFSP decisions identical with the 'decisions' mentioned in Art. 288 TFEU, the provision setting out the legal acts of the Union? The question is of more than just theoretical interest. Even though the Court of Justice of the European Union does not have jurisdiction over the provisions of the CFSP,[70] its future jurisprudence on the decisions referred to in Art. 288 TFEU could affect the practice of CFSP decisions if the two instruments were found to be identical. Should this be the case, does it mean, for instance, that CFSP decisions are also capable of having direct effect?[71] At first sight, it may not seem obvious that CFSP decisions and those mentioned in Art. 288 TFEU are one and the same instrument. Under the Constitutional Treaty, the provision on the legal acts of the Union, Art. I-33 TCE, not only preceded the detailed rules governing the adoption of decisions in the area of the CFSP, but these articles all employed the term 'European decisions', thereby making it plain that they were referring to the same type of legal act. By contrast, following the Lisbon Treaty, the detailed provisions on the CFSP are set out in the TEU, whereas Art. 288 on the instruments of the EU is found in the Treaty on the Functioning of the European Union (TFEU). Since all of these provisions use the generic term 'decision', it is not evident whether or not they refer to the same legal instrument.

The better view is that the TEU and the TFEU do in fact employ the same concept of a decision. This is borne out not only by the drafting history of the Draft TCE adopted by the European Convention and, more importantly, by the TCE signed by the representatives of the Member States, but a different interpretation would conflict with the clear intention of the Laeken European Council to simplify the Union's legal instruments. The fact that the rules governing the adoption of CFSP decisions are found in the TEU, while the definition of a decision is governed by Art. 288 TFEU makes little difference, given that the two Treaties have the same legal value.[72] The fact that the EU has replaced the European Community is far more relevant, since one would expect a single legal person to use a single set of legal instruments. However, none of this means that decisions adopted in the field of the CFSP must necessarily have the same legal effects as decisions adopted in other areas of the Union's activities. Whereas decisions adopted by the institutions of the Union are capable, in principle, of having direct effect and to be directly applicable, there are ample signs in the Treaties and related acts that the Member States did not intend to clothe the CFSP and the legal instruments adopted within its framework with these qualities.[73]

---

[70]Article 24.1 TEU.

[71]de Witte (2008), p. 90.

[72]Article 1 TEU.

[73]Article 24.1 TEU thus declares that the CFSP is 'subject to specific rules and procedures'.

A second major question that the standardisation of the CFSP's legal instruments raises is why the Member States did not consolidate the separate provisions dealing with CFSP decisions into a single article. As the Working Group on Simplification noted, the reduction in the number of the EU's legal instruments 'serves no purpose unless accompanied by a genuine effort to rationalise instruments by redefining them'.[74] The Lisbon Treaty falls woefully short when measured against this yardstick.[75] While the Lisbon Treaty has succeeded in reducing the number of formal legal instruments in the CFSP, this was not accompanied by a rationalisation of their functions. The traditional three stages of European foreign policy cooperation thus live on in the division between Council decisions on action undertaken by the Union on the one hand and Council decisions on positions taken by the Union on the other hand. There is no reason to maintain that distinction in the form of separate treaty provisions: it would be more economical to use a single article to direct the Council to adopt a decision on operational action and Union positions. Beyond reasons of economy, maintaining separate treaty articles also fosters legal uncertainty. Whereas Art. 28 TEU lays down detailed procedural rules governing decisions on Union actions, none of these rules are repeated in Art. 29 TEU dealing with decisions on Union positions. Given that both provisions are concerned with the same legal instrument, namely Council decisions, it would be reasonable to expect Arts. 28 and 29 TEU to contain identical procedural rules and give rise to the same rights and duties on part of the Member States. It is regrettable that the Member States missed this opportunity to clarify these matters and to consolidate the relevant articles into a single provision.

4 Conclusion

The simplification of the legal acts available to the institutions of the Union is to be welcomed. However, the extent to which it succeeds in making the EU more democratic, more transparent and more efficient yet remains to be seen. The present chapter has argued that the replacement of common positions, joint actions and common strategies with a single legal instrument, Council decisions, heralds a return to the days of the Maastricht Treaty. This is not to suggest that simplification in the field of the CFSP is a step in the wrong direction: much can be said in favour of reducing the number and complexity of the legal acts employed in this area. However, mechanically replacing one set of instruments with a generic legal act smacks of a public relations exercise: it has certainly reduced the overall number of instruments, yet it has done nothing to rationalise their functions and usage. Perhaps this is something that another round of treaty revision might tackle one day.

References

Allen D, Wallace W (1982) European political cooperation: the historical and contemporary background. In: Allen D, Rummel R, Wessels W (eds) European Political Cooperation: towards a foreign policy for Western Europe. Butterworth Scientific, London, pp 21–32

Berthold C (2003) Die Europäische Politische Gemeinschaft (EPG) 1953 und die Europäische Union (EU) 2001: Eine rechtsvergleichende Betrachtung. Frankfurt am Main, New York

Cremona M (2003) The Draft Constitutional Treaty: external relations and external action. Common Market Law Rev 40:1347–1366

Curtin D (1993) The Constitutional Structure of the Union: A Europe of bits and pieces. Common Market Law Rev 30:17–69

Dashwood A (1998) External relations provisions of the Amsterdam Treaty. Common Market Law Rev 35:1019–1045

de Schoutheete de Tervarent P (1997). The creation of the common foreign and security policy. In: Regelsberger E, de Schoutheete de Tervarent P, Wessels W (eds) Foreign policy of the European Union: from EPC to CFSP and beyond. L. Rienner, Boulder, pp 41–63

de Witte B (2008) Legal instruments and law-making in the Lisbon Treaty. In: Griller S, Ziller J (eds) The Lisbon Treaty: EU constitutionalism without a constitutional treaty? Springer, Wien, pp 79–108

Denza E (2002) The intergovernmental pillars of the European Union. Oxford University Press, Oxford

Duke S (2000) The elusive quest for European Security: from EDC to CFSP. Palgrave, Basingstoke

Duke S (2001) CESDP: Nice's overtrumped success? Eur Foreign Aff Rev 6:155–175

Edwards G, Nuttall S (1994) Common foreign and security policy. In: Duff A, Pinder J, Pryce R (eds) Maastricht and beyond: building the European Union. Routledge, London, pp 84–103

Eeckhout P (2005) External relations of the European Union: legal and constitutional foundations. Oxford University Press, Oxford

Fink-Hooijer F (1994) The common foreign and security policy of the European Union. Eur J Int Law 5:173–198

Fursdon E (1980) The European Defence Community: a history. Macmillan, London

Griffiths RT (2000) Europe's first constitution: the European Political Community, 1952–1954. Federal Trust, London

Gröne D (1993) Die Europäische Politische Zusammenarbeit (1970–1991): Entwicklung, Struktur und Rechtswirkung. Schäuble Verlag, Rheinfelden

Hill C, Smith KE (2000) European foreign policy: key documents. Routledge, London; New York

Holland M (1991a) Sanctions as an EPC instrument. In: Holland M (ed) The future of European political cooperation: essays on theory and practice. St. Martin's Press, New York, pp 180–198

Holland M (1991b) The European Community and South Africa: European political cooperation under strain. Pinter, London

Howorth J (2004) The European Draft Constitutional Treaty and the future of the European defence initiative: a question of flexibility. Eur Foreign Aff Rev 9:483–508

Jürgens T (1994) Die gemeinsame europäische Aussen- und Sicherheitspolitik. Heymann, Köln

Koutrakos P (2001) Trade, foreign policy and defence in EU Constitutional Law: the legal regulation of sanctions, exports of dual-use goods and armaments. Hart, Portland

Koutrakos P (2006) EU international relations law. Hart, Oxford

Laursen F, Vanhoonacker S (1992) The intergovernmental conference on political union: institutional reforms, new policies and international identity of the European Community. M. Nijhoff, Dordrecht, Sold and distributed in the U.S.A. and Canada by Kluwer Academic Publishers

Legaret J, Martin-Dumesnil E (1953) La Communauté Européenne de Défense: Étude Analytique du Traité du 27 Mai 1952. Librairie J. Vrin, Paris

MacLeod I, Hendry ID, Hyett S (1996) The external relations of the European Communities: a manual of law and practice. Oxford University Press, Oxford

Mahncke D (2001) Reform of the CFSP: from Maastricht to Amsterdam. In: Monar J, Wessels W (eds) The European Union after the Treaty of Amsterdam. Continuum, New York, pp 227–248
Monar J (1997) The European Union's foreign affairs system after the Treaty of Amsterdam: a "strengthened capacity for external action"? Eur Foreign Aff Rev 2:413–436
Murphy DT (1989) european political cooperation after the Single European Act: the future of foreign affairs in the European Communities. Boston Coll Int Comp Law Rev 12:335–355
Naert F (2005) European security and defence in the EU Constitutional Treaty. J Confl Secur Law 10:187–207
Nuttall S (1985) European political co-operation and the Single European Act. Yearb Eur Law 5:203
Nuttall S (1987) Interaction between European political co-operation and the European Community. Yearb Eur Law 7:211–249
Nuttall SJ (1992) European political co-operation. Oxford University Press, Oxford
Österdahl I (2001) The EU and its member states, other states, and international organizations – the common European security and defence policy after Nice. Nord J Int Law 70:341–372
Perrakis S (1988) L'incidence de l'Acte européen sur la coopération des douze en matière de politique étrangère. Annuaire Fr Droit Int 34:807–822
Regelsberger E (1997) The institutional setup and functioning of EPC/CFSP. In: Regelsberger E, de Schoutheete de Tervarent P, Wessels W (eds) Foreign policy of the European Union: from EPC to CFSP and beyond. L. Rienner, Boulder, pp 67–84
Ruane K (2000) The rise and fall of the European Defence Community: Anglo-American relations and the crisis of European Defence, 1950–55. Macmillan, Basingstoke
Rummel R (1988) Speaking with one voice – and beyond. In: Pijpers AE, Regelsberger E, Wessels W (eds) European political cooperation in the 1980s: a common foreign policy for Western Europe? Nijhoff, Dordrecht, pp 118–142
Sari A (2008) The conclusion of international agreements by the European Union in the context of the ESDP. Int Comp Law Q 56:53–86
Smith ME (2001) Diplomacy by decree: the legalization of EU Foreign Policy. J Common Market Stud 39:79–104
Stein E (1990) External relations of the European Community: structure and process. Coll Courses Acad Eur Law 1:115–188
Thym D (2004) Reforming Europe's common foreign and security policy. Eur Law J 10:5–22
Trybus M (2006) With or without the EU Constitutional Treaty: towards a common security and defence policy. Eur Law Rev 31:145–166
Wessel RA (1999) The European Union's Foreign and Security Policy: a legal institutional perspective. Kluwer Law International, The Hague
Wessel RA (2003) The state of affairs in EU security and defence policy: the breakthrough in the Treaty of Nice. J Confl Secur Law 8:265–288

Permanent Structured Cooperation: A New Mechanism of Flexibility

Sebastian Graf von Kielmansegg

Within the new legal architecture of the European Security and Defence Policy (ESDP) created by the Treaty of Lisbon permanent structured cooperation is one of the rare genuine novelties. It constitutes a new and additional mechanism of flexibility designed for the specific needs generated by the ESDP: military capability improvement. It is closely related to the more general concept of enhanced cooperation. But there are a number of remarkable differences which indicate a specific European interest in permanent structured cooperation. Therefore it can be regarded as a privileged relative of the mechanism of enhanced cooperation.

There are two ways of looking at this set of rules: as a policy or as a mechanism. In the first sense, it is a new policy field added to the Treaty. Permanent structured cooperation deals with aspects of defence policy which have not been mentioned in the TEU so far. Here lies its importance from the point of view of defence policy. In the second sense, permanent structured cooperation constitutes a mechanism of flexibility. It is an arrangement that does not – or does not necessarily – include all Member States. This is the interesting matter from the perspective of European integration. The following contribution will focus on this second aspect because it is of a somewhat more general relevance and, moreover, it is here that the actual innovation has taken place.

S. Graf von Kielmansegg (✉)
Fakultät für Rechtswissenschaft und Volkswirtschaftslehre, Universität Mannheim, Schloß Westflügel, 68161 Mannheim, Germany
e-mail: kielmansegg@uni-mannheim.de

H.-J. Blanke and S. Mangiameli (eds.), *The European Union after Lisbon*,
DOI 10.1007/978-3-642-19507-5_23,

1 Flexible Cooperation in Defence Policy Before Lisbon

The term "flexibility" refers to the idea that not all Member States of the European Union (EU) have to join in all steps of European integration. This idea has attracted a great deal of fascination and it has inspired the academic and political debate to produce a considerable variety of concepts – each of them having its own specific label and connotation: Europe à la carte, variable geometry, multi-speed Europe, core Europe, Europe of concentric circles, differentiated integration, etc. For the present purposes it is not necessary to delve into the subtleties of this discussion. The terms "flexible cooperation" and "flexibility" may serve as a non-technical expression for the principle that the group of participants is allowed to vary in different policy fields of European integration.

Permanent structured cooperation realises this concept in the field of defence policy. That does not mean that flexibility is altogether new to the ESDP. The contrary is true: From its very beginning, the ESDP has been one of the EU policy fields which heavily rely on flexibility.[1] In fact, the whole ESDP – or at least its military dimension – is an example of flexibility. Already in 1992 Denmark had chosen not to take part in the defence-related activities of the EU.[2] Consequently, it is only 26 of the 27 EU Member States which take part in the military aspects of the ESDP.

Besides the Danish opt-out there are more examples of flexibility in the ESDP. These options might be called *case-by-case flexibility* because they allow Member States to decide on a case-by-case basis how they want to contribute to the ESDP. The so-called Irish clause, the force generation for EU operations, the Defence Agency and the involvement of third states all belong to this category. Under the Irish clause in Art. 42.2 (2) TEU (formerly Art. 17.1 (2) TEU) Member States – in particular the neutral Member States – have the right to retreat from the ESDP on a case-by-case basis where it is incompatible with the specific character of their national security and defence policy. More generally, the contribution of Member States to ESDP operations is voluntary. For each single operation it has to be negotiated on a force generation conference and remains ultimately subject to a sovereign national decision. Equally, participation in the work of the European Defence Agency and in individual armaments projects is voluntary. Finally, there is also an external dimension of flexibility with regard to the involvement of third states in ESDP operations.

Thus, the concept of flexibility is well established in the ESDP. But it has been a flexibility of a very limited range so far. The Danish opt-out was not based on any particular concept – it served as a political compromise in order to save the Danish

[1]Kielmansegg (2005), p. 387 et seq.

[2]European Council of 11 December 1992 in Edinburgh, Presidency Conclusions, Part B, Annex 1. See also Art. 6 of the Protocol (No. 5) *on the Position of Denmark*, attached to the Treaty of Amsterdam.

ratification of the Treaty of Maastricht. Case-by-case flexibility, in turn, is a useful method to run the daily business of ESDP but it is not designed to explore new fields of activities.

There is one mechanism in European law which provides for flexibility in a more general and ambitious sense – the so-called "enhanced cooperation". However, when enhanced cooperation was originally introduced by the Treaty of Amsterdam in 1997 the whole Common Foreign and Security Policy remained outside its scope of application. In 2001, the Treaty of Nice closed this gap but it did so under such restrictive terms that enhanced cooperation became no more than a purely theoretical option in the field of the CFSP. Moreover, matters having military or defence implications continued to be excluded even from this minimal solution.[3] As a result, defence policy remained the blind spot of enhanced cooperation.

This restrictive position did not stem from any principle objections against flexible cooperation in defence policy. In fact, flexibility was and is a common feature of this policy field. The Western European Union (WEU) which had been the main European forum for defence policy in the 1980s and 1990s made a subtle distinction between Full Members, Observers, Associated Members and Associated Partners. It was almost an ideal example of a Europe of concentric circles. But this model has not been transferred to the EU and the ESDP. The ultimate reason for this reluctance was the controversy about the very role that the EU should play in defence policy. In particular, the United Kingdom has traditionally taken a more Atlanticist than European stance on this issue, giving priority to the North Atlantic Treaty Organization (NATO) rather than to a defence cooperation within the EU. From this perspective it made some sense to exempt defence policy from the potential scope of enhanced cooperation. Too great seemed the danger that a group of continental and EU-focused Member States might press ahead and destabilise the ever-delicate European–Atlantic balance.

2 The Origins of Permanent Structured Cooperation

In the Treaty of Lisbon, the limitations of enhanced cooperation have been lifted. Under the new legal regime the option of enhanced cooperation is available for the CFSP, including defence policy, under the same conditions as for any other policy field.[4] One should think that, with this step, defence policy has been equipped with all the flexibility it needs. Yet permanent structured cooperation was set on top as an additional mechanism of a similar kind. This remarkable duplication of flexibility mechanisms provides the background for the analysis of the new rules.

Permanent structured cooperation has no predecessor in the former EU Treaty, but it appeared at a very early stage in the preparation of the Constitutional Treaty.

[3] Art. 27b TEU-Nice.

[4] Art. 20 TEU and Art. 326 et seq. TFEU.

Working Group VIII (Defence) of the European Convention recommended in its final report that "the new treaty should [...] provide for a form of closer cooperation between Member States, open to all Member States wishing to carry out the most demanding tasks and fulfilling the requirements for such a commitment to be credible. One of the conditions for taking part in this 'defence Euro-zone' would have to be a form of presumption that pre-identified forces and command and control capabilities would be available. Another condition might be participation in multinational forces with integrated command and control capabilities. Other factors are also important, such as force preparedness, interoperability and deployment capabilities."[5]

Similar input came from the so-called chocolate summit in April 2003, a summit meeting between Belgium, France, Germany and Luxemburg which proposed a European Security and Defence Union (ESDU) within the framework of the EU.[6] Very clearly these concepts were inspired by the Currency Union. Permanent structured cooperation as it has been realised in the Treaty of Lisbon is the small remainder of these more ambitious and far-reaching ESDU proposals.

While originally the ESDU had been conceived as a comprehensive model, the European Convention decided to leave the issue of collective self-defence to a separate legal regime – today Art. 42.7 TEU. From the remaining aspects a new mechanism was forged which, under the designation of "structured cooperation", entered the draft proposal for a Constitutional Treaty submitted by the European Convention in July 2003. However, the draft provisions on structured cooperation were received by the Member States with scepticism and opposition. This had several reasons, not least the political row over the Iraq war. On the whole the scope, design and very desirability of the new mechanism were all highly controversial. The most important objection resulted from the impression that structured cooperation might turn as an exclusive and self-electing club in which the participants determine the rules, control the access and follow their own agenda of defence policy.[7]

Indeed, the proposals of the European Convention gave rise to some concerns of this kind. Therefore, structured cooperation was one of the major challenges for the IGC which followed the work of the Convention. In the end, the Convention proposal was picked to pieces and replaced by a completely new version of what is now Art. 46 TEU.[8] This new version carefully avoids anything which could give structured cooperation an exclusive touch. Inclusiveness, openness and transparency are the guidelines which govern Art. 46 TEU. The Protocol on Permanent Structured Cooperation is also a result of this shift. According to the proposal of the European Convention it would have been left to the would-be participants to draw

---

[5]CONV 461/02 of 16 December 2002, para 54.

[6]Summit communiqué of 29 April 2003, reproduced in Missiroli (2003), p. 76 et seq.

[7]Cf. Howorth (2004), p. 486 et seq.; Biscop (2008), p. 2 et seq.

[8]Proposal of the Italian Presidency, CIG 52/03 ADD 1, Annex 17, of 25 November 2003, Art. III-213.

up their own document on the rules and standards of structured cooperation. Instead, the Intergovernmental Conference (IGC) opted to undertake itself the drafting of the Protocol, thereby involving all EU Members in this process.

As a result of these changes, on 9 December 2003 the Italian Presidency could present a text proposal which was accepted by the IGC.[9] With this agreement *permanent* structured cooperation, as it was now called, had essentially assumed its current shape. In this form it became part of the Constitutional Treaty (Art. I-41.6 and III-312 TCE) and finally made its way – unharmed by the various hiccups of the ratification procedure – into the Treaty of Lisbon.

3 The Scope and Purpose of Permanent Structured Cooperation

3.1 Permanent Structured Cooperation as an Integral Part of the ESDP

The short flashback on the origins of permanent structured cooperation has shown that the introduction of this mechanism had been on the agenda since the very beginning of the post-Nice reform process. Apparently, it was not an incidental result of political bargaining but the reaction to a widely acknowledged need for more flexibility in defence policy. This leads to the question as to why the opening up of enhanced cooperation – which is, after all, the standard mechanism of flexibility in EU law – was not regarded as a sufficient response to that need.

The reason behind this duplication of flexibility mechanisms is that permanent structured cooperation is designed to deal with a very specific problem: Europe's so-called military capability gap. Undisputedly, the European armed forces suffer from severe deficiencies, most of all with regard to key capabilities required for expeditionary operations. It is equally clear that no Member State is in a position to overcome these deficiencies on its own. The only chance for the Europeans to achieve their own capability goals is to efficiently merge their resources, in particular by coordinating their defence planning and procurement policy.[10]

Traditionally, this cooperation has been located outside the framework of the EU. Defence planning is coordinated within NATO. Armaments cooperation is pursued on the basis of the OCCAR Convention[11] or the Letter of Intent Group,[12]

[9]CIG 60/03 ADD 1, Annex 22, of 9 December 2003.

[10]See Biscop (2004), p. 514 et seq.; Biscop (2008); Lindley-French (2004), p. 203 et seq.

[11]Organisation Conjointe de Coopération en matière d'Armement. The members of this organisation are France, Germany, Italy, the United Kingdom, Belgium and Spain. For the text of the convention see Schmitt 2003, p. 45 et seq.

[12]The LoI-Framework Agreement between France, Germany, Italy, the United Kingdom, Spain and Sweden is reproduced in Schmitt (2003), p. 68 et seq.

until recently also in the Western European Armaments Group of the WEU. Equally, the zoological garden of multinational headquarters and forces is based on bilateral or multilateral agreements. With the evolution of the ESDP, the EU has arrived on the spot, too. Since 2001, the Capability Development Mechanism (CDM) has been in place as an EU-based defence planning process.[13] Moreover, in 2004 the European Defence Agency has been established with the task to coordinate and promote joint armament projects.[14] But on the whole, the European efforts on coordinated capability improvement have not been an overwhelming success story. Already the number of actors and frameworks involved suggests that there is still a long way to go for a coherent overall approach. Besides, it also indicates that the role of the EU in this field has remained rather limited so far.

The logic of the ESDP requires both to improve the results and to shift the core elements of this process into the framework of the EU. In fact, the stimulation of capability improvement has been one of the motives behind the turnaround which led to the ESDP in 1998/99. On the other hand, EU Member States differ greatly in their military potential as much as in their willingness to undertake greater efforts. It is reasonable to expect that substantial progress in this cooperation is significantly easier to achieve, if not necessarily all 27 EU Members have to be involved. Therefore it is in the interest both of capability improvement and of the EU to allow these "able and willing" Member States to go ahead with a strengthened and more ambitious cooperation in defence planning and procurement policy – that is: cooperation *within* the framework of the EU.

It is the kind and degree of this interest which distinguish permanent structured cooperation from enhanced cooperation. The option of enhanced cooperation is a concession to Member States willing to go ahead. In theory it is also regarded as a tool to stimulate further progress in European integration, but certainly it is an ambiguous tool to a highly abstract end. In the case of permanent structured cooperation, by contrast, the perspective is a different one. Here, the avant-garde group of Member States and their activities directly and specifically serve the interests of the EU or – more generally speaking – of the European cause. The EU as a policy actor needs operational resources for the conduct of its security and defence policy. These resources have to be made available by the Member States. The Member States, in turn, cannot make available assets and capabilities which they do not possess. The capability gap on the national level necessarily produces a capability gap on the European level which undermines the operational potential of the ESDP. Because of this dependency on the availability of national (or multinational) resources the EU depends on a successful cooperation in this field. Therefore, the EU has a very specific self-interest in the establishment of permanent structured cooperation. Indeed permanent structured cooperation must

[13]European Council of 15/16 June 2001 in Göteborg, Presidency Conclusions on the ESDP, para 12, printed in: Rutten (2002), p. 32 et seq.

[14]Joint Action 2004/551/CFSP *establishment of the European Defence Agency*, O.J. L 245/17 (2004). Now also Art. 45 TEU.

be regarded as an integral part of the very concept of the ESDP. Here, the advantages of flexibility for Member States and for the European cause outweigh its risks much more clearly than in other policy fields. It is for this reason that, instead of merely opening enhanced cooperation, an additional mechanism has been introduced – a mechanism specifically designed to respond to the needs generated by the ESDP, and, moreover, designed not only as an additional but as a privileged mechanism.

3.2 *No Operational Dimension*

The other side of the coin is that permanent structured cooperation is strictly limited to the issue of capability improvement. This restriction had not been part of the original proposals. Following the concept of the European Convention, permanent structured cooperation would have included the conduct of crisis management operations. It would have served as a platform for the participants to carry out military operations, be it on their own behalf or on behalf of the Union.[15] Not surprisingly, this aspect was another reason for opposition among Member States against the Convention proposal. There was little enthusiasm for handing over the operational and political control over military operations to an inner circle of interested states. Therefore, the respective paragraph was deleted by the IGC as part of the overall compromise. Moreover, this shift in the concept of permanent structured cooperation was underlined by adding a new sentence to Art. 42 TEU in the very last minute of negotiations.[16] According to this reference permanent structured cooperation does not affect the provisions of Art. 43 TEU. Article 43 TEU lists the catalogue of Petersberg tasks and allocates the decision making on ESDP operations and their implementation to the Council, the High Representative and the Political and Security Committee. These rules being unaffected, permanent structured cooperation neither authorises the participants to go beyond the Petersberg tasks nor does it remove the control of EU institutions over the conduct of ESDP operations. In short, permanent structured cooperation has no operational dimension.

The limited scope of the mechanism is also reflected in Art. 2 of the Protocol. This article lists the various activities to be undertaken by participating Member States – the "programme" of permanent structured cooperation. The list relates without exception to the issue of military capabilities. Participating Member States commit themselves to cooperate on the expenditure on military investment (Art. 2 lit. a). They aim at a more holistic and European approach on military capabilities,

[15]CONV 850/03 of 18 July 2003, Art. III-213.4. See also the comments of the Convention Praesidium on the corresponding Articles in the very first draft version, CONV 685/03 of 23 April 2003, pp. 20 and 46.

[16]CIG 60/03 ADD 1, Annex 22, of 9 December 2003. Now Art. 42.6 sentence 3 TEU.

in particular by harmonising, pooling and specialising their military capabilities (Art. 2 lit. b). And they undertake to improve their military capabilities by various other steps like enhancing a number of key capabilities, addressing the shortfalls identified in the Capability Development Mechanism, and taking part in joint equipment programmes in the framework of the European Defence Agency (Art. 2 lit. c-e). Not all participants will have to take part in each of these activities. As Sven Biscop has put it, permanent structured cooperation will have to serve as a marriage agency: as a forum to bring together the potential partners for specific projects of cooperation.[17] From this perspective, permanent structured cooperation does not merely constitute a mechanism of flexibility in itself but also an umbrella for smaller packages of flexible cooperation.

4 Enhanced Cooperation and Permanent Structured Cooperation: A Comparison

In summary, two characteristic features of permanent structured cooperation have been identified: first, it is a specific mechanism with a very limited scope – the improvement of military capabilities; and second, it is a mechanism in which the EU has a very specific self-interest. That explains why it has been introduced in addition to enhanced cooperation and why it is privileged by the Treaty. The more detailed comparison between enhanced and permanent structured cooperation has to be seen against this background.

4.1 Differences Between Enhanced and Permanent Structured Cooperation

4.1.1 The Role of Primary Law

Four major differences between the two mechanisms deserve attention. First of all, permanent structured cooperation is to a much greater extent determined by primary law. The treaty rules on enhanced cooperation essentially prescribe the procedure and conditions for the establishment of the cooperation but they do not deal with its substance. Like an empty frame it serves as a general mechanism open to all subject matters. In the case of permanent structured cooperation, by contrast, the frame comes with the picture. The subject matter of the cooperation is fixed in Art. 42.6 TEU and the Protocol. Even the "programme" of permanent structured cooperation, its aim and the various aspects which have to be addressed are

[17]Biscop (2008), p. 9.

pre-identified in some detail by primary law.[18] In this respect, permanent structured cooperation resembles the Currency Union.

4.1.2 Entry Conditions

A second peculiarity of permanent structured cooperation is the fact that Art. 1 of the Protocol establishes entry conditions – again clearly inspired by the example of the Currency Union. Conditions for participation as such are not ruled out for enhanced cooperation either, but in that case they have to be laid down by the authorising Council decision.[19] For permanent structured cooperation, by contrast, they have already been determined on the level of primary law.

The actual definition of the entry conditions in Art. 1 of the Protocol is the result of a compromise. On the one hand, the whole agreement on permanent structured cooperation was based on the understanding that it had to be as inclusive as possible. On the other hand, this had to be achieved without completely watering down the mechanism. Consequently, the entry conditions in Art. 1 linger somewhere between permitting openness and upholding ambitions. Under these circumstances, precise and meaningful convergence criteria in the style of the Currency Union were not feasible and perhaps not even desirable. Instead, the entry conditions have remained sufficiently vague and moderate to be accomplishable for any seriously interested Member State. Their purpose is not to keep Member States outside but to stimulate greater efforts on their part.[20] Interestingly, in the academic debate much thought is devoted to the development of more specific minimum criteria for participation.[21] Legally, Art. 1 of the Protocol leaves no room for such considerations. There are no additional or more specific entry conditions for permanent structured cooperation beyond those listed in Art. 1.

The Protocol distinguishes between two cumulative entry conditions. The first one is a commitment: Any participating Member State must undertake "to proceed more intensively to develop its defence capacities through the development of its national contributions and participation, where appropriate, in multinational forces, in the main European equipment programmes, and in the activity of the [...] European Defence Agency".[22] This commitment does not entail a strict obligation to take specific measures or to achieve a specific goal. Participating Member States are required to do *something* in order to improve their defence capabilities, in particular to enhance their involvement in joint European forces and programmes. It is telling that Art. 42.6 TEU does not refer to more demanding but merely to more

[18]Art. 2 of Protocol No. 10.

[19]Art. 328.1 TFEU.

[20]Cf. Biscop (2008), p. 2 et seq.

[21]See e.g. Biscop and Coelmont (2010), p. 2 et seq.; Wouters (2008), pp. 7 and 13.

[22]Art. 1 lit. a of Protocol No. 10.

binding commitments, whatever that means. Moreover, from a legal perspective it remains somewhat mysterious how a commitment can work as an entry condition. Usually a commitment follows from an agreement and does not have to precede it.

The second entry condition laid down in Art. 1 of the Protocol is a capability: Any participant must be able to supply one of the so-called EU battle groups[23] or at least a component of such a battle group.[24] Again this is a fairly moderate requirement. No minimum strength or capability of the necessary component is indicated. Consequently, very small contributions, in particular of niche capabilities, have to be regarded as a sufficient contribution. Except Malta and Denmark all EU Member States have already supplied or pledged such components to one or more battle groups, including states with very small armed forces like Luxemburg and Cyprus.[25] This underlines once more the conclusion that the entry conditions in Art. 1 of the Protocol are not meant to exclude but to encourage. Moreover, it has to be kept in mind that the entry condition is not the actual contribution to a battle group but merely the *capacity* to supply such a component.

4.1.3 Legal Obligations

Besides the programme of permanent structured cooperation and the entry conditions for the mechanism, primary law also determines substantive legal obligations of the participants. Already the so-called entry conditions in Art. 1 constitute such legal obligations. But more relevant in this respect is Art. 2 of the Protocol. This provision does not merely spell out the scope and programme of permanent structured cooperation. The wording makes quite clear that the list of activities is not of an optional but of an obligatory nature. Certainly none of these obligations hurt. They do not prescribe any specific measures to be taken or targets to be achieved. Rather, Art. 2 establishes duties to undertake certain efforts, in particular by way of cooperation. But nevertheless these duties constitute legal obligations fixed on the level of primary law, and they are more specific than the rather flowery Art. 1.

Interestingly, the IGC which otherwise was so focused on securing inclusiveness has taken one step to give teeth to these obligations. It introduced the option of suspending the participation of a Member State which no longer fulfils the criteria

---

[23]For more detailed information about the battle group concept see Lindstrom (2007).

[24]Art. 1 lit. b of Protocol No. 10: Permanent structured cooperation shall be open to any Member State which undertakes to "have the capacity to supply by 2010 at the latest, either at national level or as a component of multinational force groups, targeted combat units for the missions planned, structured at a tactical level as a battle group, with support elements including transport and logistics, capable of carrying out the tasks referred to in Article 43 of the Treaty on European Union, within a period of five to 30 days, in particular in response to requests from the United Nations Organization, and which can be sustained for an initial period of 30 days and be extended up to at least 120 days."

[25]Lindstrom (2007), p. 15; Council document 14755/09 of 21 October 2009.

or is no longer able to meet the commitments referred to in Arts. 1 and 2 of the Protocol.[26] This is a remarkable sanction which has no equivalent in enhanced cooperation or the Monetary Union. Given the vagueness of the obligations laid down in the Protocol and the likely situation that most of the participating states would have to throw stones in a glasshouse the threat of suspension is probably a rather theoretical one. If at all, it may become relevant with a view to the more detailed commitments adopted *in implementation* of permanent structured cooperation. At any rate this counterpoint makes clear that permanent structured cooperation is intended to be taken seriously. Its inclusiveness has limits.

4.1.4 Establishment

Finally, and perhaps most importantly: In comparison to enhanced cooperation the procedure for the establishment of permanent structured cooperation has been facilitated, the hurdles to be taken are significantly lower. At this point it becomes apparent that, compared to enhanced cooperation, permanent structured cooperation is a *privileged* mechanism.[27]

Under the original proposal of the European Convention, structured cooperation would have been automatically established with the entry into force of the Constitutional Treaty.[28] For the sake of inclusiveness and transparency the IGC has opted for a different solution. As in the case of enhanced cooperation, Art. 46.1 and 2 TEU provide that a Council decision is required in order to establish the cooperation. However, a closer look reveals that the respective establishment procedures are not identical. In the case of enhanced cooperation, the establishment has to be requested.[29] The Council is free whether or not to follow the request. In the case of permanent structured cooperation, by contrast, the interested Member States merely *notify* their intention. Moreover, according to Art. 46.2 TEU, the Council shall not just adopt a decision on the establishment of permanent structured cooperation but a decision *establishing* the mechanism. This language suggests that the establishment procedure in the Council has a rather limited function. Its purpose is, once again, to prevent any kind of exclusiveness, in particular to avoid that access to permanent structured cooperation is controlled by an inner circle of influential Member States. Instead, control over the access has been shifted to the full forum of the Council. Accordingly, the purpose of the procedure is not to reopen the debate on the very establishment of structured cooperation – *that* basic decision has already been taken on the level of the Treaty and the Protocol itself. Its purpose is to guarantee a transparent decision on the admission of participants, making sure that no interested

---

[26]Art. 46.4 TEU.

[27]Dietrich (2006), p. 495.

[28]CONV 850/03 of 18 July 2003, Art. III-213.1

[29]Art. 329 TEU.

and qualified Member State is rejected. If this view is correct, the Council's task is to examine whether the applicants fulfil the minimum requirements laid down in Art. 1 of the Protocol and to decide on their participation. But the Council does not have legal authority to deny the establishment of permanent structured cooperation altogether.

Besides this rather subtle peculiarity other formal requirements of the establishment procedure have been relaxed as well. Thus, the majority requirement for the Council decision has been reduced. The authorisation for an enhanced cooperation in the field of CFSP has to be decided unanimously.[30] By contrast, the establishment of permanent structured cooperation merely requires a qualified majority.[31] The same tendency can be observed with regard to the minimum number of participants. Enhanced cooperation requires the participation of at least nine Member States.[32] No such quorum has been established for permanent structured cooperation. Moreover, for permanent structured cooperation a time frame has been introduced. While there is no deadline for the authorisation of an enhanced cooperation, in the case of permanent structured cooperation the Council has to decide within 3 months.[33] And finally, while enhanced cooperation is admitted by the TEU only "as a last resort, when [the Council] has established that the objectives of such cooperation cannot be attained within a reasonable period by the Union as a whole"[34] there exists no equivalent reservation with regard to permanent structured cooperation. All these facilitations show that permanent structured cooperation is a mechanism not only permitted but intended by the Treaty. The procedural rules in Art. 46.1 and 2 TEU are clearly designed to promote its establishment.

4.2 Commonalities Between Enhanced and Permanent Structured Cooperation

The analysis has shown, so far, that the distinction between permanent structured cooperation and enhanced cooperation is not only a matter of terminology. Their legal designs are different in several respects. On the other hand, it is fairly obvious that they also share important commonalities. That begins with the overall character of the two mechanisms. In both cases a group of Member States unite in a particular policy field in order to go beyond what can be attained on the Union level. Moreover, both mechanisms do not merely constitute the option of a case-by-case

[30] Art. 329.2(2) TFEU.

[31] Art. 46.2 TEU.

[32] Art. 20.2 TEU.

[33] Art. 46.2 TEU.

[34] Art. 20.2 TEU.

flexibility but a systematic and long-term regime of cooperation covering a whole policy field. It is this quality which is highlighted by the peculiar designation *permanent structured* cooperation. But in fact, enhanced cooperation is no different in this respect.

Second, the legal and political level on which the decision on the establishment of the cooperation has to be adopted is the same in both cases. Enhanced cooperation as well as permanent structured cooperation requires a formal Council decision as a starting shot. The cooperation is permitted by primary law but it has to be established by an act of secondary law.

Third, both enhanced and permanent structured cooperation are, in principle, open to all Member States. That includes in either case the possibility to join at a later stage.[35]

Moreover, enhanced and permanent structured cooperation both are instances of *internal* flexibility. Their purpose is not simply to permit closer cooperation among Member States but to allocate this cooperation within the framework of the EU. Consequently, participating Member States use the EU institutions, EU decision-making procedures and also the legal forms of action available under EU law. Technically, the cooperation works like a small EU.

Finally, both mechanisms do not touch the principle of unanimity which still governs defence policy. Neither permanent structured cooperation nor enhanced cooperation provide or permit the introduction of majority voting in this field.[36] To put it more generally: Neither of the two mechanisms allows escaping from the intergovernmental character of the ESDP.

On the whole, the conclusion is that in most of the essential aspects permanent structured cooperation parallels enhanced cooperation. They are not identical twins, but twins they remain. Thus, permanent structured cooperation must be regarded not as an altogether new concept but as a specialised and privileged derivation from enhanced cooperation. This close relationship is not only of theoretical interest. It also has a practical consequence. The rules about permanent structured cooperation have a rather fragmentary character. Given the sweeping similarity between the two mechanisms it is possible to fall back on the general rules on enhanced cooperation in order to fill the gaps left by Art. 46 TEU and Protocol No. 10.[37]

[35]For permanent structured cooperation see Art. 46.3 TEU; for enhanced cooperation Art. 328.1 and 331 TFEU.

[36]For permanent structured cooperation see Art. 46.6 TEU; for enhanced cooperation see Art. 333.3 TFEU which exempts defence policy from the passerelle in para 1.

[37]See also Kaufmann-Bühler (2006), Art. 17 TEU para 50. Potential candidates for an analogous application are Art. 331.2 (accession procedure) or Art. 332 TFEU (financing). Opposite view: Dietrich (2006), p. 495, apparently based on the (not very convincing) assumption that Art. 46 TEU leaves no gap to fill.

5 Perspectives

Permanent structured cooperation has made its way into the Treaty but it has yet to be established. And even when that is accomplished it remains to be seen how productive the new mechanism will be. Ultimately it is a policy framework, albeit one bolstered up with a number of legal obligations and the guidance given by Protocol No. 10. In the end, it is for the participants to give substance to it. They have to adopt the necessary decisions on the achievement of expenditure goals, on the harmonisation or pooling of their forces, on the improvement of key capabilities and on armaments projects. It is not the establishment but only the implementation of permanent structured cooperation that matters for the success of European defence policy.

Yet even its establishment cannot be taken for granted. Since the first months of 2010, preparatory discussions have been held but so far there has been no hurry in Brussels to activate the mechanism. Not surprisingly, much political energy is being absorbed by digesting other changes which the Treaty of Lisbon has brought to the CFSP. Moreover, the enthusiasm of the early days appears to have faded. In the light of the progress made since 2003 permanent structured cooperation might seem redundant or at least less vital than before.[38] Since 2004, the European Defence Agency has unfolded its activities in the coordination of European defence planning and armaments projects. It must also be kept in mind that capability improvement as such is not a new policy field introduced by the Treaty of Lisbon. Although not explicitly mentioned in the old TEU it has already been embraced by the common defence policy under Art. 17 TEU-Nice. Consequently, all the activities listed in Protocol No. 10 fall within the scope of Art. 42 TEU anyway and can be pursued on this legal basis even if the Protocol is not activated.[39] Many of them have actually been dealt with by the series of capability improvement conferences held by the EU since 2001. This conference system allows a similar degree of flexibility as it would be offered by permanent structured cooperation. And the European Defence Agency is coordinating these efforts with or without permanent structured cooperation. Indeed, in many respects, permanent structured cooperation resembles an institutionalised capability improvement conference.[40]

Nevertheless, permanent structured cooperation offers more than the old system. It is institutionalised. It is stimulated by the entry conditions and the legal obligations laid down by the Protocol, even if they are vague and moderate. It is more than a wedding agency because it allows setting up a framework of general

---

[38] See the statement of the Chief Executive of the European Defence Agency, Alexander Weis, on permanent structured cooperation: "I wouldn't say it was outdated, but it has maybe been overtaken by the creation of the European Defence Agency." Quoted on http://www.europolitics.info, 10 February 2010.

[39] Kielmansegg (2005), p. 171 et seq.

[40] Biscop and Coelmont (2010), p. 3.

rules like convergence criteria. And, finally, it is not restricted to informal commitments. The toolbox of permanent structured cooperation is equipped with the set of legal instruments available for the CFSP, including the adoption of binding decisions. Thus, on the whole there is a certain added value of permanent structured cooperation in comparison to the current system. It is – or would be – Europe's most comprehensive, most flexible and legally best equipped forum for military capability improvement. But, to use a word of Sven Biscop, it is no more than a window of opportunity.[41] One might add that the capability world outside this window remains full of challenges. It is not primarily a legal problem that Europe has in this respect and so the law cannot be expected to provide miracles.

References

Biscop S (2004) Able and willing? Assessing the EU's capacity for military action. Eur Foreign Aff Rev 9:509–527
Biscop S (2008) From ESDP to CSDP: the search for added value through permanent structured cooperation. Egmont – Royal Institute for International Relations, Brussels
Biscop S, Coelmont J (2010) Permanent structured cooperation for effective European armed forces. Egmont – Royal Institute for International Relations, Brussels
Dietrich S (2006) Europäische Sicherheits- und Verteidigungspolitik. Nomos, Baden-Baden
Howorth J (2004) The European draft constitutional treaty and the future of the European defence initiative: a question of flexibility. Eur Foreign Aff Rev 9:483–508
Kaufmann-Bühler W (2006) Article 17. In: Grabitz E, Hilf M (eds) Das Recht der Europäischen Union. Beck, München
Kielmansegg S (2005) Die Verteidigungspolitik der Europäischen Union. Boorberg, Stuttgart
Lindley-French J (2004) Plugging the expanded Petersberg Tasks gap? Europe's capabilities and the European capabilities action plan (ECAP). In: Ehrhart HG, Schmitt B (eds) Die Sicherheitspolitik der EU im Werden. Bedrohungen, Aktivitäten, Fähigkeiten. Nomos, Baden-Baden, pp 201–213
Lindstrom G (2007) Enter the EU battlegroups. ISS Chaillot Paper 97, Paris
Missiroli A (2003) From Copenhagen to Brussels. European defence: core documents, vol 4. ISS Chaillot Papers 67, Paris
Rutten M (2002) From Nice to Laeken. European defence: core documents, vol 2. ISS Chaillot Papers 51, Paris
Schmitt B (2003) European armaments cooperation. Core documents. ISS Chaillot Paper 59, Paris
Wouters P (2008) Balancing defence and security efforts with a permanently structured scorecard. Egmont – Royal Institute for International Relations, Brussels

[41] Biscop (2008), p. 16.

The Financing of Common Foreign and Security Policy – on Continuity and Change

Günter Sautter

1 Introduction

The entry into force of the Lisbon Treaty on 1 December 2009 is not likely to revolutionise the financing of the European Union's (EU's) Common Foreign and Security Policy (CFSP). Article 41 TEU takes over the general principles on financing the CFSP enshrined in Arts. 28.2 and 28.3 TEU-Nice without significant amendments. Accordingly, as a rule, administrative expenditure and operational expenditure without military and defence implications continue to be financed out of the CFSP budget as a part of the EU's budget. In contrast, expenditure with military and defence implications continue to be financed from other sources. Consequently, established practice in the financing of the CFSP will continue to a large extent under the new Treaty.[1]

However, the Lisbon Treaty introduces some elements of change related to financing the rapid deployment of military and civilian missions in the framework of the EU's Common Security and Defence Policy (CSDP). Article 41.3 TEU tasks the Council to adopt a decision establishing procedures for guaranteeing rapid access to appropriations in the Union budget. It also stipulates the setting up of a start-up fund for the financing of certain activities that are necessary to prepare the deployment of CSDP missions. It is too early to judge whether or when these new mechanisms will come into being, and what they could look like. However, the recent development of the CFSP financing justifies the educated guess that they will at best bring about limited change.

[1]This general judgement is shared by several practitioners and scholars, cf. Major (2010), p. 2, Whitman and Juncos (2009), p. 45, von Ondarza (2008), p. 21.

G. Sautter (✉)
Permanent Representation of the Federal Republic of Germany to the EU
e-mail: guenter.sautter@diplo.de

H.-J. Blanke and S. Mangiameli (eds.), *The European Union after Lisbon*,
DOI 10.1007/978-3-642-19507-5_24, © Springer-Verlag Berlin Heidelberg 2012

Ironically, the most significant alteration in the financing of the CFSP may ensue from provisions outside Art. 41 TEU: More than any other innovation in the Lisbon Treaty, the creation of the office of the High Representative of the Union for Foreign Affairs and Security Policy and the European External Action Service (EEAS) will alter the institutional framework in which the CFSP budget will be managed in the future. Here, too, it is too early to predict to what extent the new institutional landscape will change the financing of the CFSP. This will to a large extent depend on the outcome of the ongoing inter-institutional debate on how to implement the Lisbon Treaty. However, the Treaty itself is a sound basis for the assumption that for the time being, even the altered institutional set-up will not radically change the financing of the CFSP.

In developing the above hypotheses, this overview seeks to answer two basic questions: How does the financing of the EU's CFSP function? And how does the Lisbon Treaty change the underlying rules of the game?

2 On Continuity in the Financing of the CFSP

Under this heading, this article will make the case that the Lisbon Treaty retains all key elements related to the financing of the CFSP enshrined in the Nice Treaty. This does not only go for the general principles on the financing of administrative and operational expenditure in the framework of the CFSP. Implicitly, the new Treaty also continues to embed the financing of the CFSP in the institutional and procedural framework established by the Treaties beyond Title V of the Treaty on European Union (TEU). With the exception of the creation of the office of the High Representative and the EEAS, this institutional framework has not undergone fundamental changes. In particular, the budgetary procedures laid down in the Treaty on the Functioning of the European Union (TFEU) remain broadly the same as under the Nice Treaty. Lastly, it goes without saying that the entry into force of the Lisbon Treaty does not have an effect on the volume of the CFSP budget. In this sense, continuity prevails in the financing of the CFSP. However, it will become evident from the following that there are exceptions to this continuity.

2.1 The General Principles

The "general principles" governing the financing of the CFSP laid down in the new Art. 41 TEU remain practically unchanged. Article 41.1 TEU establishes that administrative expenditure shall continue to be charged to the Union budget, as was the case under the Nice Treaty. In this context, the Treaty does not make a distinction between administrative costs with military and defence implications and other administrative costs in the realm of the CFSP. Accordingly, both types of administrative expenditure are to be charged to the EU's budget. Under the new

Treaty, this "old" provision gains additional importance, as it constitutes a legal basis for financing the EEAS from the EU's budget.[2]

According to Art. 41.2 TEU, operating expenditure is also charged to the Union budget as a rule. Thus, expenditure related to civilian missions and other activities without military and defence implications will continue to be financed out of the CFSP budget foreseen in Chapter 19.03 under Heading Four of the EU's budget. Article 41.2 TEU stipulates that this rule does not apply to expenditure arising from operations having military or defence implications and to cases where the Council decides so. In these cases, costs shall – as a rule – be borne by Member States in accordance with the gross national product scale.

As was the case in the past, this paragraph contains two flexibility clauses. It allows for the Council to finance CFSP-related expenditure without military or defence implications from sources other than the Union budget. In practice, this clause has played an important role to date. There are numerous cases in which CSDP activities have been partly financed from outside the CFSP budget. In the so-called preparatory phase, i.e. before the adoption of legal acts, several civilian missions have had to be "pre-financed" through Member States' contributions. The reason for this is that there was no adequate mechanism for the rapid financing related to this preparatory phase from the CFSP budget. The deployment of the EU Monitoring Mission (EUMM) in Georgia in 2008 has been the latest example of this practice. There is at least one example for the financing of a running mission's activities from alternative sources: The 2009 Joint Action on the EUSEC Congo mission set up a so-called project cell to which Member States can contribute financially. In the framework of this cell, the Head of Mission can take recourse to Member States' funds to implement projects complementing the mission's work.[3]

So far, the second flexibility clause, which opens the possibility to share burdens without taking recourse to the gross national product scale, has been more relevant in the Council's practice. One might almost say that the exception is the rule when it comes to the financing of CFSP activities with military or defence implications. It is established practice in the EU's military missions since the June 2002 General Affairs Council that *costs lie where they fall.* That is to say that each Member State participating in a given military operation covers the expenses related to the deployment of its personnel and equipment.[4]

This practice has been modified by the creation of the so-called Athena mechanism, which the Council first established in 2004. This mechanism, which has repeatedly been reviewed in recent years, follows an intergovernmental logic. Its main function

[2]Cf. Avery (2008), p. 40.

[3]Council Joint Action No. 709/2009/CFSP *on the European Union mission to provide advice and assistance for security sector reform in the Democratic Republic of the Congo (EUSEC RD Congo),* O.J. L 246/33 (2009).

[4]The CONCORDIA operation in the Former Yugoslav Republic of Macedonia launched in 2003 was one exception to this rule. In this case, the Council agreed on an ad hoc basis to define certain expenses as common costs.

is to distribute common costs related to military missions, for example for headquarters and operation headquarters, amongst Member States. Such burden sharing – and this could be viewed as the exception to the exception – is conducted in accordance with the gross national product scale. It is worth noting, however, that these common costs are not necessarily borne by all 27 Member States of the EU. Under Athena, they are split amongst participating Member States in accordance with the gross national product scale. A recent example both of the *costs lie where they fall* principle and the application of the Athena mechanism is the EU's first military training mission, EUTM Somalia, which was also the first military mission to be launched after the entry into force of the Treaty of Lisbon. In this case, each participating Member State bears the expenses related to the deployment of its instructors, while costs related to training, infrastructure and lodging are treated as common costs.[5]

It is occasionally argued that Art. 41.2 TEU also opens up the possibility to charge to the Union budget expenditure related to activities with military or defence implications. Legally, this is a plausible argument. It could base itself on provisions such as Art. 24.1 TEU, which assigns to the EU the competence to progressively frame a common defence policy that might lead to a common defence. In practice, however, such ideas are not being discussed in the Council. Given that many Member States continue to feel strongly about military and defence competences as key elements constituting their national sovereignty, this is likely to remain a politically sensitive issue for the time being.

It is in this context that Art. 41.2 TEU continues to exempt Member States from bearing costs having military or defence implications if they have constructively abstained from the relevant Council decision according to Art. 31.1 (2) TEU. The same kind of exemption routinely applies to Denmark on the basis of Protocol 20 to the TEU of 1997,[6] which is also known as the Danish *opt-out* concerning the elaboration and implementation of decisions and actions of the Union which have defence implications.

2.2 The Institutional Framework

The general provisions on the financing of the CFSP as established in Arts. 41.1 and 2 TEU are not situated in an institutional and procedural vacuum. To express this

[5]The Athena mechanism was last revised under the French Presidency in 2008. Cf. Council Decision No. 975/2008/CFSP *establishing a mechanism to administer the financing of the common costs of European Union operations having military or defence implications (ATHENA)*, O.J. L 345/96 (2008). Concerning the application of the Athena mechanism, cf. e.g. Council Decision No. 96/2010/CFSP *on a European Union military mission to contribute to the training of Somali security forces (EUTM Somalia)*, O.J. L 44/16 (2010). On the functioning of the Athena mechanism, cf. Scannell (2004), p. 534 et seqq.

[6]Protocol on the position of Denmark annexed to the Treaty on European Union and to the Treaty establishing the European Communities, O.J. C 340/101 (1997).

notion, Art. 28 TEU-Nice literally created a framework for the financing of the CFSP. Its first paragraph established which institutions of the EU had a role to play in the financing of the CFSP. The last paragraph stipulated that the European Community's (EC's) budgetary procedure applies to the CFSP budget. Thus, the structure of the article made it clear that the financing of the CFSP takes place within the institutional and procedural set-up established by the TFEU.

Article 28.1 TEU-Nice spelt out that several provisions in the EC Treaty were applicable to the CFSP. In essence, these provisions established that the European Parliament, the Council of the EU and the European Commission were part of the institutional framework in which the EU conducted the CFSP. However, these references were limited to organisational and procedural questions. They did not constitute institutional competences related to the CFSP going beyond those established under Title V of the TEU-Nice: Article 13 TEU-Nice established the European Council and the Council as key CFSP actors. With regard to the Commission, Art. 27 TEU-Nice stipulated that the Commission be fully associated with the work carried out in the CFSP field. Article 21 TEU-Nice obliged the Presidency to consult the European Parliament on the main aspects and basic choices of the CFSP and to ensure that the views of the European Parliament be duly taken into consideration. Article 28.1 TEU-Nice made no mention of the Court of Justice of the European Union, thus implying that the Court has no competences in the field of CSFP.[7]

In Art. 41 TEU, this "institutional paragraph" has disappeared. It is plausible to argue that this is rather a systematic change than a change in the substance: With the Lisbon Treaty breaking the pillar structure and abolishing the formal distinction between the EU and the European Community, it has become redundant to spell out in detail that the organisational and procedural provisions laid down in the TFEU apply to the CFSP. It is now sufficient for Art. 24.1 (2) TEU to explicitly lay down that the specific roles of the European Parliament and of the European Commission in this area are defined by the Treaties.

However, the TEU is more explicit on the role of the Court of Justice of the European Union than the former Art. 28.1 TEU-Nice used to be. Article 24.1 TEU now stipulates that the Court shall not have jurisdiction with regard to the CFSP. At the same time, it establishes as an exception to the rule that the Court does have jurisdiction to monitor compliance with Art. 40 TEU and Art. 275 (2) TFEU. These exceptions touch upon two important questions concerning the institutional competences laid down in the Treaties and the judicial protection of individuals, on which the Court has already ruled in recent years in the important cases of Kadi/al Barakaat and ECOWAS.[8]

Another provision that has disappeared is that of the old Art. 28.4 TEU-Nice, which established that the budgetary procedure laid down in the Treaty should

---

[7]Cf. Schwarze (2009), pp. 155–158.

[8]Cases C-402/05 P and C-415/05 P *Kadi and al Barakaat v Council and Commission* (ECJ 3 September 2008), Case C-91/05 *Commission v Council* (ECJ 20 May 2008).

apply to the expenditure charged to the budget of the European Communities. Here, too, the formal abolition of the pillar construction makes it dispensable to state the obvious: The procedures laid down in what is now the TFEU continue to apply to the CFSP budget – just as the institutional provisions enshrined in the TFEU continue to apply. In this sense, even if Art. 41 TEU does no longer make the institutional and procedural framework for the financing of the CFSP explicit, there can be no doubt that this framework continues to exist – even if it has undergone moderate changes under the Lisbon Treaty.

2.3 The Budgetary Procedure

The establishment and administration of the CFSP budget continue to be governed by the provisions related to the EU's general budget. With the entry into force of the Lisbon Treaty, these provisions have undergone some changes affecting both the establishment and the implementation of the EU's multiannual financial framework and its annual budget.

In principle, however, the four key steps of the budgetary procedure remain unchanged. Until the entry into force of the Lisbon Treaty, they functioned as follows: In a first step, the Council establishes the multiannual financial framework after obtaining the consent of the European Parliament. This is laid down in the so-called inter-institutional agreement. This central planning document lays down which funds the EU will allocate for what purpose in the years to come. Concerning the CFSP budget, it contains ceilings on annual commitment and payment appropriation, thus anticipating the medium-term development of the CFSP budget as a whole. In a second step, this multiannual planning is transposed and substantiated into the EU's annual budget. In this process, a draft budget is prepared by the Commission. The budgetary authority – consisting of the Council and the European Parliament – must then agree on this annual budget on the basis of this Commission's proposal. In a third step, the Commission implements the budget in cooperation with Member States, including the CFSP budget. In the fourth and last step, the European Parliament, acting on a recommendation of the Council, gives discharge to the Commission after the annual budget has been implemented.

Even if these crucial steps of the budgetary procedure continue to be enshrined under Title III of the TFEU, the Lisbon Treaty has introduced several minor changes. With regard to the multiannual financial framework, the most substantial innovation under the new Treaty is that Art. 312.2 (1) TFEU now stipulates that the Council shall adopt a regulation laying down the multiannual financial framework. In doing so, the Council shall act unanimously after obtaining the consent of the European Parliament, which shall be given by a majority of its component members. Article 312.3 TFEU adds that the Council regulation shall not only determine the amounts of the annual ceilings on commitment and payment appropriations. It shall also lay down any other provision required for the annual budgetary procedure to run smoothly. Article 312.1 (2) TFEU provides that the financial framework be established for a period of at least 5 years. In practice, this means, that in the future, all substantive aspects that have to date been formulated in the so-called inter-institutional agreement between the European Parliament, the Council and the Commission must be translated into a Council regulation.

As far as content is concerned, the inter-institutional discussion about how to transpose the dispositions of the current 2006 inter-institutional agreement is ongoing. This debate focuses on questions related to the overall financial envelope, the annual ceilings and the time span that the regulation shall cover. However, once the transposition is achieved, the new TFEU will allow for much of the established practice regarding the establishment of the multiannual framework to continue.

Concerning the establishment of the annual budget, the TFEU introduces changes which only seemingly strengthen the role of the European Parliament. In fact, the institutional balance of power within the budgetary authority remains essentially unaltered under the new Treaty. It is safe to argue that the Lisbon Treaty much rather codifies the established practice of setting up the annual budget, which has not been in outright accordance with the provisions of the EC Treaty. The most important amendment is that the Lisbon Treaty formally does away with the traditional distinction between obligatory and non-obligatory expenditure that Art. 272 EC used to establish. As a consequence, the Council and the European Parliament are now formally on an equal footing in the decision on the EU's annual budget in its entirety, including with regard to the CFSP budget.

The other key amendment is that the Lisbon Treaty considerably tightens the procedure of setting up the annual budget. Article 314 TFEU only foresees one reading on the draft budget within the European Parliament. If this reading does not bring about an agreement, the Conciliation Committee shall broker a compromise between the Council and the European Parliament. This provision is likely to shift the centre of decision-making within the budgetary authority towards this Conciliation Committee. It is sound to assume that agreements will be found here in the future. Article 314.7 (d) TFEU does establish that the European Parliament can overrule the Council if it approves a joint text elaborated by the conciliation committee which the Council rejects. In practice, however, this case is very difficult to imagine. It is much more probable that the delegates of the 27 Member States will only accept compromises in the Conciliation Committee that they can live with.

Concerning the CSFP budget in particular, the 2006 inter-institutional agreement foresees consultation mechanisms such as regular Council reports and meetings between representatives of both Council and European Parliament in order to facilitate the process of joint decision-making within the budgetary authority.[9] This practice will have to be amended in order to account for the role of the High Representative who takes over the role of the rotating Presidency in matters related to the CFSP in accordance with Art. 18.3 TEU. In principle, however, the established consultation mechanisms will remain in force.

---

[9]Cf. Inter-Institutional Agreement between the European Parliament, the Council and the Commission *on budgetary discipline and sound financial management*, O.J. C 139/1 (2006), para 43.

With regard to the implementation of the EU's annual budget, Art. 317 (1) TFEU continues to assign this task to the Commission in cooperation with Member States, thus maintaining in principle the provision of Art. 274 (1) EC. This provision continues to grant the Commission what could be called a monopoly within the EU's institutions to technically implement the Union's budget. It does not explicitly provide for the High Representative or the EEAS to administer the CFSP budget.

2.4 *The Volume of the CFSP Budget*

It is not only the institutional framework and the budgetary procedure related to the CFSP budget that remain broadly unchanged. Continuity also prevails regarding the budget's volume. To be more precise, the entry into force of the Lisbon Treaty does not entail any changes to the volume of the CFSP budget, to which operational expenditure related to CSFP activities without military and defence implications are charged. In comparison with the EU's overall budget, the CFSP budget continues to be very moderate, as the following numbers suggest. At the same time, it keeps growing at more dynamic rates than the EU's overall budget.

The EU's current overall financial framework for 2007–2013 laid down in the 2006 Inter-institutional Agreement foresees total commitment appropriations amounting to €864 billion. Under its Heading Four, this budget allocates €49 billion to the EU's external action.[10] The bulk of these funds is allocated to the various thematic and regional instruments that the Commission administers in order to shape the EU's external relations with the exception of the CFSP. The most significant of these instruments in financial terms are the Development Cooperation Instrument (€17 billion for 2007–2013), the Instrument for Pre-accession Assistance (€11 billion for 2007–2013) and the European Neighbourhood and Partnership Instrument (€11 billion for 2007–2013).

Another instrument with particular relevance to the CFSP is the Instrument for Stability (€2 billion for 2007–2013), which was established in 2006. Its objectives are to contribute to stability in situations of crisis and to help build capacity both to address specific global and transregional threats having destabilising effects and to address pre- and post-crisis situations. The instrument thus aims at being complementary to and consistent with measures taken by the EU in the context of the CFSP.[11]

In comparison with these instruments, the financial envelope for the CFSP, which is administered under Chapter 19.03 of Heading Four, is rather limited.

[10]Cf. Inter-Institutional Agreement between the European Parliament, the Council and the Commission *on budgetary discipline and sound financial management*, O.J. C 139/1 (2006), para 43.

[11]Cf. Decision of the European Parliament and of the Council No. 1717/2006 *establishing an Instrument for Stability*, O.J. L 327/1 (2006).

Table 1 CFSP budget 2007–2013 in million EUR

Year	2007	2008	2009	2010	2011	2012	2013
CFSP budget	159	285	243	281	327	363	406

It amounts to at least €1.7 billion for 2007–2013. However, the CFSP budget continues to grow dynamically. This becomes evident if one compares the 2010 budget amounting to €281 million with that of 2002, which comprised a mere €30 million. Accordingly, the budget has multiplied by nine in 8 years. Table 1 outlines this evolution of commitment appropriations in the field of the CFSP between 2007 and 2013.[12]

Within the CFSP budget, civilian CSDP missions and EU Special Representatives have traditionally been the dominant cost factors. In the 2009 budget, which amounts to €243 million, some €220 million were committed to the EU's ten ongoing civilian missions. Another €17 million were committed to the EU's 12 Special Representatives. It is too early to tell whether the CSFP budget will continue to grow at the dynamic rates of recent years. This will be up to the budgetary authority to decide.

3 On Change in the Financing of the CFSP

As shown, the apparent continuity in the financing of the CFSP under the Lisbon Treaty is not complete. By the same token, the seemingly incisive changes that the Treaty introduces in this domain turn out to be limited. This goes for the most obvious innovation concerning the financing of the CFSP, the introduction of new mechanisms to facilitate the financing of preparatory activities related to the rapid deployment of both civilian and military CSDP missions in Art. 41.3 TEU. Similarly, changes to the implementation of the CFSP budget ensuing from the creation of the office of the High Representative and the EEAS may be less far-reaching than one might imagine. Still, they have the biggest potential to alter the way in which the EU finances the CFSP.

3.1 The Rapid Deployment Provisions

Article 41.3 (1) TEU tasks the Council to adopt a decision establishing specific procedures for guaranteeing rapid access to appropriations in the Union budget for urgent financing of initiatives in the framework of the CSFP, namely for

[12]For further reading on the evolution of the CFSP budget, cf. Grevi et al. (2009), p. 92 ff. The exceptionally high amount in 2008 is related to the launching of the EU's biggest civilian CSDP mission to date, EULEX Kosovo.

preparatory activities for CSDP tasks referred to in Arts. 42.1 and 43 TEU. In addition, Art. 41.3 (2) TEU commissions the Council to create a start-up fund made up of Member States' contributions for the financing of preparatory activities for CSDP tasks referred to in Arts. 42.1 and 43 TEU which are not charged to the CFSP budget.[13]

In other words, the Lisbon Treaty does not create mechanisms for the financing of preparatory activities in the field of the CFSP. It calls upon the Council to establish such mechanisms – without setting a date or defining scope or procedures. However, the Treaty makes it clear that two separate mechanisms for the financing of preparatory activities for CSDP tasks are to be set up. One shall facilitate swift access to the CSFP budget, whereas the other shall permit financing from Member States' contributions. Following the logic of Art. 41.2 TEU, the first mechanism could serve to facilitate the financing of CFSP-related activities without military or defence implications. Accordingly, the objective of the second mechanism could be to allow for the rapid financing of activities with military or defence implications or other activities whose costs the Council decides not to charge to the CFSP budget. However, one could also make the case that the start-up fund must not be limited to activities without military or defence implications, but could also be used to finance the preparatory phase of civilian CSDP activites.

The relevance of these new provisions may not catch the eye immediately. It becomes more evident if one takes into account the EU's first 10 years of experience with civilian missions and military operations in the framework of what is now called CSDP. During this first decade, the EU has continuously struggled with the challenge of rapid deployment. EUMM Georgia is a good example showing how crucial this capacity can be for the success of a mission: The six-point agreement to stabilise the situation in Georgia was reached on 12 August 2008. On 1 September the European Council expressed the readiness of the EU to support every effort to secure a peaceful and lasting solution to the conflict. Two weeks later, on 15 September, the Council adopted the Joint Action establishing EUMM Georgia.[14] The mission's first patrol to monitor compliance with the six-point agreement was conducted on 1 October. It is evident that EUMM Georgia's setting up a speed record in terms of the EU's mission deployment strongly contributed to the political success of the mission.

One factor for this success was that in the run-up to the launching of EUMM, the EU was able to take recourse to so-called preparatory measures, a mechanism that exists since 2006. This mechanism opens up the possibility to finance pre-deployment activities before the Council Decision and financial impact statement related to a specific CSDP mission are adopted. In practice, it thus allows for exploratory and preparatory work to be conducted several weeks before a Council Decision establishes a legal and financial basis for a mission. The conditions and procedures

[13]Cf. Wessels and Bopp (2008), p. 11.

[14]Cf. Council Joint Action No 736/2008/*CFSP on the European Union Monitoring Mission in Georgia (EUMM Georgia)*, O.J. L 248/26 (2008).

under which preparatory measures may be financed in the field of CSFP are defined in Art. 49.6 (c) of the Financial Regulation. It establishes that preparatory measures shall be agreed by the Council in full association with the Commission, who shall take all necessary measures to ensure a rapid disbursement of the funds. The financing of preparatory measures is executed through a framework decision of the Commission under the Financial Regulation.[15] Currently, Chapter 19.03.05 of the CFSP budget reserves some €5 million per year for preparatory measures. This is ten times the amount needed for the preparation of EUMM Georgia in 2008.

The Council has also developed a tool to finance the preparation of EU operations having military and defence implications in the framework of the Athena mechanism. As soon as the Crisis Management Concept, the initial military planning document for an operation, has been agreed by the Council, the so-called early financing phase begins.[16] During this phase, Athena covers common costs related to transport, lodging, communications and civilian staff that are necessary to conduct exploratory and preparatory work. Furthermore, the mechanism creates the possibility of so-called payments in advance related to this early phase. It thus very much anticipates the idea of the start-up fund.

The Athena mechanism has been existing since 2004. The recourse to preparatory measures has been possible since 2006. In this context, it may seem astonishing that the Lisbon Treaty tasks the Council to create mechanisms for the financing of preparatory activities both with and without military and defence implications. The question arises: Why does the Treaty call upon Member States to build up something that already exists? A plausible answer could point to the history of the Lisbon Treaty and of Art. 41 TEU in particular. In the negotiations on the Lisbon Treaty, the article was taken over from Art. III-313 in the draft Treaty establishing a Constitution for Europe without significant amendments. The Constitutional Treaty was adopted by the European Convention in the summer of 2003, at a time in which neither Athena nor the preparatory measures mechanism existed. This makes it plausible to view Art. 41.3 TEU as an outdated provision that was simply forgotten to be taken out of the draft. Accordingly, the provision would have been overtaken by developments even before its entry into force.

---

[15]Cf. Council Regulation (EC, EURATOM) No. 1605/2002 *on the Financial Regulation applicable to the general budget of the European Communities*, as last amended by Regulation (EC, EURATOM) No. 1525/2007, O.J. L 343 (2007). Cf. also Commission Regulation (EC, EURATOM) No. 2342/2002 as amended by Commission Regulation (EC, EURATOM) No. 1261/2005, O.J. L 201 (2005), Commission Regulation (EC, EURATOM) No. 1248/2006, O.J. L 227 (2006) and Commission Regulation (EC, EURATOM) No. 478/2007, O.J. L 111 (2007).

[16]For an overview of the key procedural steps in the establishment of a CSDP mission, cf. Heise (2009), p. 12. Cf. also Council Decision No. 975/2008/CFSP *establishing a mechanism to administer the financing of the common costs of European Union operations having military or defence implications (ATHENA)*, O.J. L 345/96 (2008). For an introduction to the Athena mechanism, cf. Terpan (2008).

The Council and the High Representative have not yet started a discussion on how to fulfil the obligations formulated in Art. 41.3 TEU. As the provision does not set a time limit, it is unclear when this discussion will take place. There seem to be three possible options. One is that Member States use the opportunity to revise and "lisbonise" the existing legal acts on Athena and preparatory measures in order to formally comply with the tasking of the Treaty. Another option may be that Member States simply defer the decisions Art. 41.3 TEU tasks them to pass – even *ad calendas graecas*.

With reference to the start-up fund, the third and most creative option would be to complement Athena as a mechanism for coordinating national budgets with a fund in the true sense of the word made up of Member States' contributions. This could indeed herald an incisive change in the financing of CSFP: Once such a fund was established, the Council could authorise the High Representative to use it and report to the Council on the implementation of this remit in accordance with Art. 41.3 TEU. Politically, this could contribute to strengthening the High Representative's role within the institutional landscape of the CFSP. It would open up the possibility for the High Representative to implement certain funds independently from the Commission's control. This would create a second source of financing CSDP activities in parallel to the CFSP budget, for whose implementation the Commission remains ultimately responsible under Art. 317.1 TFEU (even though this implementation will happen under the authority of the High Representative as Vice-President of the Commission). Thus, the start-up fund could open up a margin of financial independence vis-à-vis the Commission to the High Representative. By the same token, it could create financial leeway beyond the European Parliament's budgetary control.

It could be argued that this fund would not necessarily have to be limited to the financing of operations having military and defence implications. The Treaty only speaks of CSDP activities which are not charged to the Union budget. Accordingly, the fund could serve to finance the preparation of any activity related to the CSDP, be it of a civilian or military nature. In this context, it is important to note that the Treaty leaves open the scope of the term preparatory activities. Neither does it give guidance on the dimension of the start-up fund. Thus, a start-up fund could be established in a manner that goes well beyond the limits of the existing Athena mechanism. It could provide the High Representative with a source of financing in the area of CSDP that he/she could use without the Commission's or Parliament's supervision.

In the discussions on the Constitutional Treaty, some Member States have indeed championed such a construction, taking a similar fund in the framework of the Western European Union as a model. Still, a political agreement on such an extensive interpretation of the start-up fund is unlikely to emerge. In any event, in financial terms, delegations had a modest mechanism in mind when they first drafted the provision now enshrined in Art. 41 TEU in the context of the Constitutional Treaty. The final report of the defence working group reads: "It is (...) envisaged that a relatively modest fund be set up, based on Member States' contributions, from which the preparatory stages of (a military operation) could be financed, avoiding overlap with existing instruments."[17] In other words, when drafting the provision, Member States intended to create a mechanism comparable to the Athena mechanism in its objectives and dimensions and rather different from a real parallel budget to the CFSP budget. There is little evidence that this attitude has substantially changed in the meantime.

3.2 *The Implementation of the CFSP Budget*

It is too early to judge to which extent the creation of the office of the High Representative of the Union for Foreign Affairs and Security Policy and namely the creation of the EEAS will change the way in which the CFSP budget is implemented. This depended to a large extent on the Decision establishing the External Action Service, which the Council adopted in accordance with Art. 27.3 TEU, acting on a proposal of the High Representative after consulting the European Parliament and after obtaining the consent of the Commission.[17a]

With regard to the implementation of the CFSP budget, the starting point of the inter-institutional discussion or the EEAS decision was that Art. 317 (1) TFEU stipulates that it is the Commission that implements the EU's budget. In accordance with this provision, it is legally possible to continue the established implementation practice. In the case of civilian CSDP missions, which account for the bulk of the CFSP budget, this practice works as follows: After the Political and Security Committee (PSC) appoints a Head of Mission on the basis of Art. 38 TEU, the Commission concludes a so-called Special Adviser contract with the Head of Mission in accordance with the relevant Commission Communication for the purpose of entrusting him/her with the management of appropriations from the CFSP budget and to meet the expenditure needs arising from the implementation of the Council legal act establishing the Mission. The inevitability of this contract between the Head of Mission and the Commission arises from the fact that the Commission practically holds a "monopoly" regarding the implementation of the Union's budget and that CSDP Missions currently do not dispose of a legal personality. The contract clearly limits the responsibilities of the Head of Mission to the technical implementation of the CFSP budget. It does not establish a new command and control-thread undermining the political control and strategic guidance that the PSC exercises in accordance with Art. 38 TEU.

Once a Special Adviser contract is concluded, the Commission delegates the implementation of the Mission's budget to the Head of Mission in accordance with Art. 54.2.d of the Financial Regulation in conjunction with Art. 39(a) of the relevant

[17]Cf. European Convention CONV 461/02 *Final Report of Working Group VIII – Defence*, p. 18.

[17a]Cf. Council Decision No 427/2010/ CSFP establishing the organisation and functioning of the EEAS, O.J. L 201/30 (2010).

implementing rules.[18] Where the Commission entrusts a Head of Mission with implementation tasks, it is obliged to conduct regular checks to ensure correct implementation in accordance with Art. 54.3 of the Financial Regulation. Thus the Commission continues to be ultimately responsible for the sound management of the Mission's budget.

Every time the Council launches or extends a Mission, the High Representative proposes a Council Decision on the basis of Arts. 28 and 43.2 TEU, which usually determines the financial reference amount on the foreseen expenditure related to the Mission during its mandate. This decision is accompanied by a financial impact statement prepared by the Commission, which lays down in detail the expected costs. This proposal is based on preparatory work conducted by the Head of Mission and its staff. Within the Council, it is discussed and, if necessary, amended by the Relex Counsellors Group before it is adopted by the Council. This procedure ensures that in spite of the Commission's legal responsibility for the implementation of the CFSP budget, it is the Council that has the last word on how much money is spent on what.

In contrast, the role of the European Parliament in the implementation of the CFSP budget is marginal. Article 185 of the Financial Regulation, which attributes to the European Parliament the right of discharge for the implementation of budgets entrusted by the Commission to bodies having legal personality, does not apply. Thus, Parliament cannot exercise a specific right of discharge in the field of CFSP.

The entry into force of the Lisbon Treaty raised the question whether the central role of the Commission in the implementation of the CFSP budget was still adequate given that the EU now disposes of the High Representative, who shall be assisted by the EEAS. This kindled an inter-institutional exchange of views on how the High Representative could be entrusted with executing the CFSP budget while respecting the Commission's exclusive competence in accordance with Art. 317 (1) TFEU. In these discussions, two proposals were put forward to square the circle.

The first proposal was to amend Art. 54.2 of the Financial Regulation to the effect that the Commission would entrust the High Representative with the implementation of the CFSP budget. Under this scenario, the Commission would have delegated the responsibility for the CFSP budget as a whole under the mechanism that is currently enabling Heads of Missions to manage parts of the budget. Consequently, the High Representative would have been subject to regular

[18]Cf. Council Regulation (EC, EURATOM) No. 1605/2002 *on the Financial Regulation applicable to the general budget of the European Communities*, as last amended by Regulation (EC, EURATOM) No. 1525/2007, O.J. L 343 (2007). Cf. also Commission Regulation (EC, EURATOM) No. 2342/2002 as amended by Commission Regulation (EC, EURATOM) No. 1261/2005, O.J. L 201 (2005), Commission Regulation (EC, EURATOM) No. 1248/2006, O.J. L 227 (2006) and Commission Regulation (EC, EURATOM) No. 478/2007, O.J. L 111 (2007). The future of the Special Adviser construction is currently being discussed in Brussels; in this debate, some argue that it would be preferable to endow civilian CSDP missions with a "limited legal personality".

checks conducted by the Commission to ensure correct budget implementation. Thus, the squaring of the circle would have been imperfect. Although the High Representative would implement the CFSP budget, she would inevitably be liable to the Commission's control. Another implication of this proposal would have been that the European Parliament would have been granted the right to give discharge for the implementation of the CFSP budget under Art. 185.2 of the Financial Regulation. This would have substantially broadened the scope of the Parliament's influence on decision-making in the framework of the CFSP.

A second proposal to bring together the Commission's responsibility for implementing the Union's budget and the specific role of the High Representative based itself on Art. 18.3 TEU, which establishes that the High Representative is one of the Vice-Presidents of the Commission. Here, the central idea is that the Commission shall be responsible for the technical implementation of the CFSP budget under the authority of the High Representative in her capacity as Vice-President of the Commission. This proposal assigns a role to the High Representative in the execution of the CFSP budget. At the same time, it maintains the Commission's "implementation monopoly". In contrast to the first proposal, it manages to square the circle without necessarily strengthening the role of the European Parliament. However, there is a striking parallel between the two proposals: In case of conflicting views between the High Representative and the Commission as a whole, it is the Commission that has the last word. As Art. 17.6 TEU stipulates, the Commission decides as a collegiate body. This principle delimits the authority of the High Representative regarding budget implementation under the second scenario. This delimitation has the organisational implication that the staff assisting the High Representative in executing the budget cannot formally belong to the EEAS. It continues to be part of a "residual RELEX Directorate General" inside the Commission, acting under instruction of the Commission.

Following complex negotiations between the institutions, this second proposal was enshrined in Art. 9.1 of the EEAS decision. As a consequence, the Commission ultimately remains responsible for the implementation of the CFSP budget – albeit under the authority of the High Representative in his/her capacity as Vice-President of the Commission. In terms or organisation, the newly created Service for Foreign Policy Instruments (FPI) of the Commission assists the High Representative in exercising this authority. Thus, both institutionally and organisationally, the High Representative as Vice-President has become a key figure in terms of budget implementation.

Such change in the institutional landscape may trigger the most significant innovation in the management of the CFSP budget under the Lisbon Treaty. After all, it is for the first time since the creation of the CFSP that both the political responsibility for the implementation of the Council's political decisions and the competence to execute the corresponding CFSP budget will be in the same hands. This bundling of responsibilities has the potential to yield significant practical improvements in the day-to-day business of implementing CSFP and to avoid institutional frictions between the Commission and the EEAS. Politically, the involvement of the High Representative in the implementation of the CFSP budget can increase the coherence between the CFSP and the Union's external action as a whole. Even though the overall picture remains such that the established practice in the financing of the CFSP will continue to a large extent under the Lisbon Treaty, this increased coherence can contribute to achieving one of the Treaty's foremost objectives – a more unified approach of the EU on the international stage.[19]

References

Avery G (2008) Europe's future foreign service. Int Spectator 43(1):29–41

Drent M, Zandee D (2010) Breaking pillars. Towards a civil-military security approach for the European Union. Clingendael, The Hague

Grevi G, Helly D, Keohane D (2009) European Security and Defence Policy. The first 10 Years. European Union Institute for Security Studies, Paris

Heise V (2009) Zehn Jahre Europäische Sicherheits- und Verteidigungspolitik. Entwicklung, Stand und Probleme. SWP Studie 25:1–39

Major C (2010) Außen-, Sicherheits- und Verteidigungspolitik der EU nach Lissabon. SWP Aktuell 7:1–4

Scannell D (2004) Financing ESDP military operations. Eur Foreign Aff Rev 9:529–549

Schwarze J (2009) EU-Kommentar. Nomos, Baden-Baden

Terpan F (2008) Les bases de financement des opérations militaires de l'Union européenne. ARES 60:71–78

von Ondarza N (2008) Die EU-Sicherheits- und Verteidigungspolitik im Schatten der Ungewissheit. SWP Studie 27:1–29

Wessels W, Bopp F (2008). The institutional architecture of CFSP after the Lisbon Treaty – constitutional breakthrough or challenges ahead? Challenge – The Changing Landscape of European Liberty and Security 10, pp 1–31

Whitman R, Juncos A (2009) The Lisbon Treaty and the foreign, security and defence policy: reforms, implementation and the consequences of (non-)ratification. Eur Foreign Aff Rev 14:25–46

[19] Cf. Drent and Zandee (2010).

Lightning Source UK Ltd.
Milton Keynes UK
UKOW030900140513

210604UK00008B/117/P

9 783642 195068